BOLLINGEN SERIES LXXX

The Divine Comedy

Purgatorio

2. Commentary

DANTE ALIGHIERI

The Divine Comedy

TRANSLATED, WITH A COMMENTARY, BY

CHARLES S. SINGLETON

Purgatorio

2. Commentary

BOLLINGEN SERIES LXXX

PRINCETON UNIVERSITY PRESS

THIS IS VOLUME II OF
THE DIVINE COMEDY OF DANTE ALIGHIERI
CONSTITUTING NUMBER LXXX IN BOLLINGEN SERIES
SPONSORED BY BOLLINGEN FOUNDATION.
THIS VOLUME, PURGATORIO,
IS IN TWO PARTS: ITALIAN TEXT AND TRANSLATION,
AND COMMENTARY.

Library of Congress Catalogue card no. 68-57090
ISBN 0-691-09887-5
Printed in the United States of America
by Princeton University Press, Princeton, New Jersey

CONTENTS

ILLUSTRATIONS

PLATES

FIGURES

MAP

ACKNOWLEDGMENTS

The sources for published material that has been quoted in the present commentary will be found in the List of Works Cited. The translations most frequently used include those of the Latin classics taken from the Loeb Classical Library, the translations of the works of Dante provided by the Temple Classics, the Confraternity-Douay translation of the Vulgate, and the translation of Aquinas' *Summa theologica* by the Fathers of the English Dominican Province. Translations for which no published source was used have been provided in most cases by Professor Mario Domandi of Vassar College (Italian and Latin) and Father Edwin A. Quain, S.J., of Fordham University Press (Latin).

References to the Bible are to the Vulgate; if the corresponding citation to the King James Bible differs, it is given in brackets following the Vulgate citation.

The Latin version of Aristotle that both Dante and Thomas Aquinas are assumed to have known has been quoted from the Parma edition of the *Opera omnia* of Thomas Aquinas; this "Antiqua Translatio" is the only Aristotle text quoted in the present work. Marietti editions of the Aquinas commentaries on Aristotle, which also contain the text of Aristotle in Latin, are suggested in the notes and included in the List of Works Cited for the general convenience of the reader. Bekker numbers are used in citations to the works of Aristotle to facilitate reference to any edition of Aristotle the reader may have, since Bekker numbers are not provided in the Aquinas *Opera omnia* itself; chapter numbers are those of the Loeb Classical Library.

Map 1 and Figures 3 and 4 are based on drawings by Pauline Manning Batchelder. Figure 1 was prepared after an illustration in M. A. Orr, *Dante and the Early Astronomers*, rev. edn. (London, 1956); Figure 2 was prepared after an illustration in *La Divina Commedia di Dante Alighieri*, vol. II: *Purgatorio*, edited and annotated by Manfredi Porena (Bologna, 1947); and Figure 4 was prepared after an illustration in Paget Toynbee, *A Dictionary of Proper Names and Notable Matters in the Works of Dante*, revised by Charles S. Singleton (Oxford, 1968).

Commentaries on the *Divine Comedy*, both early and modern, are usually cited by the commentator's name alone, with no specific reference to page or verse number, because commentaries ordinarily follow the canto and verse number of the *Comedy*. For modern authors other than commentators, the author's name and date of publication serve as citation.

To Joan Knoch, expert and dedicated converter of scribbled copy into perfected copy, my cordial thanks shall here be recorded. Joan has *lived* with this Bollingen edition from its inception to the present (more years, perhaps, than either of us should like to think possible!), and, as I write this, she is putting the finishing touches on the *Paradiso*, thus completing her work on the six volumes of this edition, staying with her job, long though it was, until it was finished: faithful, indispensable helper, she has seen it through to the end. Her constant and cheerful assistance, as she called attention to some error or oversight on my part, will not be forgotten. And if any errors remain (*absit!*), they are certainly mine, not Joan's.

I remain grateful to Bollingen Foundation (of happy memory) for their original support of such expert assistance; and to the Johns Hopkins University go my warm thanks as well for its generous extension of such support.

December 31, 1972

CHARLES S. SINGLETON

Purgatorio

Commentary

CANTO I

1–3. *Per correr miglior . . . crudele*: The figure of the poet
as navigator, coursing over better waters in the ship of his
"genius," now represents the positive forward movement of
this journey, which for Dante character was *then* and
for Dante poet is *now*, and by this figure Hell becomes the
"cruel sea" that is now left behind. This same figure of the
poet as navigator will again appear at the beginning of the
Paradiso (Canto II). The metaphor is a familiar one. See
Virgil, *Georg.* IV, 116-19:

> Atque equidem, extremo ni iam sub fine laborum
> vela traham et terris festinem advertere proram,
> forsitan et, pinguis hortos quae cura colendi
> ornaret, canerem, biferique rosaria Paesti . . .

And in truth, were I not now hard on the very close of
my toils, furling my sails, and hastening to turn my prow
to land, perchance, too, I might be singing what careful
tillage decks rich gardens, singing of the rose-beds of
twice-blooming Paestum.

Also see *Georg.* II, 39-41. For many other examples of the
figure in poetry, before Dante, see E. R. Curtius (1953),
pp. 128-30.

3

1. *alza le vele*: As Porena comments, Dante compares his poetic imagination to a little ship that has crossed the tempestuous waters of Hell and now starts to sail in the more gentle waters of Purgatory. Accordingly he "hoists sail," the sails that seamen lower during a storm so that the force of the wind will not overturn the ship. "Hoist sail," then, is an image taken from seamanship, but one cannot avoid feeling in it also an allegorical meaning of joy and excitement.

2. *omai*: Now, at last, after so long a stretch of "cruel" sea.

7-12. *Ma qui . . . perdono*: This is the invocation, corresponding to that made in the second canto of the *Inferno* (since *Inf.* I is a prologue canto). Similarly, invocation will be made again in the first canto of the *Paradiso*. On such invocations, see Dante's *Letter to Can Grande* (*Epist.* XIII, 46-47):

> Sed poete non solum hoc faciunt, quin ymo post hec invocationem quandam emittunt. Et hoc est eis conveniens, quia multa invocatione opus est eis, cum aliquid contra comunem modum hominum a superioribus substantiis petendum est, quasi divinum, quoddam munus.

> Whereas poets not only do this, but also utter some certain invocation after this. And this is to their purpose, for they have need of ample invocation, since they have to implore something above the common scope of man from the higher beings, as in some sort a divine gift.

7. *la morta poesì resurga*: Let the poetry which thus far has dealt with Hell and with the second death of the damned rise up now ("resurga" being the first of several touches which, on this Easter Sunday morning just before dawn, bring to mind the Resurrection of Christ). *morta*: For the use of this adjective in such a sense, cf. "la scritta morta" in *Inf.* VIII, 127. *poesì = poesia*.

8. *poi che vostro sono*: See *Purg.* XXIX, 37-39.

9-12. *e qui Caliopè . . . perdono*: The verses allude to the contest between the Muses and the nine daughters of Pierus,

4

a king of Macedonia, to whom Pierus had given the names of the nine Muses. They presumptuously challenged the Muses to a singing contest and, being defeated, were transformed into magpies (*piche*). The story is told by Ovid (*Metam.* V, 294-678) and, as an allusion coming at the beginning of the *Purgatorio*, is fitting here where humility is the keynote (see the "humble" rush at the end of this canto, vss. 100-105, 133-36), for Pierus' daughters, the Pierides, sang a song of pride, telling how the giants did battle with the gods (see *Inf.* XIV, 43-72; XXXI, 44-45, 91-96), and claimed that the giants were victorious over the gods, who took fright and fled, with Typhoeus in hot pursuit. But the Muses' song was of Ceres and Proserpina, of planting, of birth and rebirth (Proserpina being annually resurrected from Hades).

It should be noted that in Ovid's account it is precisely Calliope who is chosen by the other Muses to sing for them in this contest; and Dante's "surga" here seems to echo Ovid's "surgit," said of her as she rises to the occasion. See *Metam.* V, 337-40:

> . . . dedimus summam certaminis uni;
> surgit et inmissos hedera collecta capillos
> Calliope querulas praetemptat pollice chordas
> atque haec percussis subiungit carmina nervis . . .

We gave the conduct of our strife to one, Calliope; who rose and, with her flowing tresses bound in an ivy wreath, tried the plaintive chords with her thumb, and then, with sweeping chords, she sang this song.

Then, at the end of Ovid's account (vs. 662), Calliope is referred to as "maxima" among the immortal nine. She is the Muse of Epic Poetry and as such is invoked by Virgil in *Aen.* IX, 525: "Vos, o Calliope, precor, adspirate canenti." ("Do thou, O Calliope, thou and thy sisters, I pray, inspire me while I sing.") But the fact that she has the principal role in the contest with the Pierides is doubtless what causes Dante to invoke her here especially. For the spelling *Caliopè*, with a single *l,* see Petrocchi's note on vs. 9; for the accent on Greek proper names in Dante's usage, see n. to *Inf.* V, 4.

10. *con quel suono*: In the n. to vss. 9-12, see the verses quoted from Ovid, which refer to the instrumental accompaniment Calliope gave to her own song. "Suono" means such accompaniment, as indicated by Dante in *De vulg. eloqu.* II, viii, 5:

> Nunquam modulatio dicitur cantio, sed sonus, vel tonus, vel nota, vel melos. Nullus enim tibicen, vel organista, vel citharedus, melodiam suam cantionem vocat nisi in quantum nupta est alicui cantioni; sed armonizantes verba opera sua cantiones vocant.

> No music [alone] is ever called a canzone, but a sound, or tone, or note, or melody. For no trumpeter, or organist, or lute-player calls his melody a canzone, except in so far as it has been wedded to some canzone; but those who write the words for music call their words canzoni.

11. *sentiro = sentirono.*

12. *disperar = disperarono.* By Ovid's account, when Calliope ended her song, the nymphs appointed as judges of the contest ruled that the Pierides had lost. Whereupon they fell to reviling the Muses, which, as Torraca points out, is the sure sign of their despairing of pardon. See *Metam.* V, 662-65.

13. *Dolce color d'oriental zaffiro*: Buti comments:

> È una pietra preziosa di colore biadetto, ovvero celeste et azzurro, molto dilettevile a vedere . . . e sono due specie di zaffiri; l'una si chiama l'orientale perchè si trova in Media ch'è nell'oriente, e questa è melliore che l'altra e non traluce; l'altra si chiama per diversi nomi com'è di diversi luoghi.

> It is a precious stone of a light bluish color—sky-blue, or azure—delightful to behold . . . and there are two kinds of sapphire: one is called Oriental, because it is found in Media, which is in the East. This is the better kind, and it is not translucent. The other kind has various names, because it is found in various places.

Torraca cites Ristoro d'Arezzo, *Della comp.* VIII, 16

(p. 284): "Pare all'occhio più nobile e dilettevole a vedere che nullo altro colore" ("It is more noble and more beautiful to behold than any other color") and *Il libro di Sidrach* CDLVIII: "Quello è gentile zaffiro che somiglia al puro cielo." ("That is noble sapphire, which resembles the pure sky.")

13–18. *Dolce color . . . petto*: When Dante came forth from Hell, he looked up to see the stars (*Inf.* XXXIV, 137-39). He now continues to gaze upward at the beautiful sky and stars, noting Venus especially, the morning star, the star of love.

14–15. *nel sereno aspetto del mezzo*: Some commentators take "mezzo" to mean "center" or "zenith." More probably it means the "air," or "atmosphere," which is said to be serene and pure. See *Conv.* III, ix, 12, where Dante uses the term in this sense:

> Però puote parere così per lo mezzo che continuamente si transmuta. Transmutasi questo mezzo di molta luce in poca luce, sì come a la presenza del sole e a la sua assenza; e a la presenza lo mezzo, che è diafano, è tanto pieno di lume che è vincente de la stella, e però [non] pare più lucente. Transmutasi anche questo mezzo di sottile in grosso, di secco in umido, per li vapori de la terra che continuamente salgono.

> [Therefore,] it may so appear because of the medium which is continually changing. This medium changes from abundance to paucity of light, as at the presence or absence of the sun; and in his presence the medium, which is diaphanous, is so full of light that it overcomes the star and so seems to be brighter than it. This medium also changes from subtle to gross, and from dry to moist, by reason of the vapours of earth which are continually rising.

15. *puro infino al primo giro*: Some interpreters take "primo giro" to mean the heaven of the moon, others the heaven of the fixed stars. Given the context, however, horizon

seems the more probable meaning. Thus the sky is said to be completely clear, with no cloud or mist visible, even on the horizon.

17. *aura = aria.*

19. *Lo bel pianeto*: Venus. On the form "pianeto," instead of the more usual form *pianeta*, see Petrocchi's vol. I, *Introduzione*, p. 436. *che d'amar conforta*: In *Conv.* II, v, 13-14, on the heaven of Venus and its movement, Dante writes: "Prende la forma del detto cielo uno ardore virtuoso, per lo quale le anime di qua giuso s'accendono ad amore, secondo la loro disposizione. E perchè li antichi s'accorsero che quello cielo era qua giù cagione d'amore, dissero Amore essere figlio di Venere." ("The form of the said heaven conceiveth an ardour of virtue to kindle souls down here to love, according to their disposition. And because the ancients perceived that this heaven was the cause of love down here, they said that Love was the son of Venus.") Thus, allusively, the *Purgatorio* has its beginning under the sign of Venus or love, and so will it have its end (see *Purg.* XXVII, 95-96). Torraca cites Ristoro d'Arezzo, *Della comp.* III, 5 (pp. 110, 116), who says that Venus comes "per rallegrare, e per innamorare" ("to gladden us and make us fall in love") and is called *"lucifer, cioè stella diana e d'amore sempre benevola e chiara"* (*"lucifer*, that is to say, the morning star and the star of love, always benevolent and clear"). Later, in *Par.* VIII, 2, the love inspired by Venus can be called a "folle amore" (as invoked by the ancients), but no such meaning is implied here.

20. *faceva tutto rider l'oriente*: It is now an hour or more before sunrise on Easter morning. See M. A. Orr (1956), p. 249. E. Moore (1887, pp. 64-65) observes:

> The only point calling for notice here is the curious piece of hypercriticism on the part of some ingenious persons who have discovered by computation that "Lo bel pianeta che ad amar conforta," *i.e.* of course, Venus, was not actually a morning star in April 1300, but rose after the Sun. But it is evident that Dante wishes to de-

scribe the hour before sunrise under its most familiar, and so to speak its typical, aspect in the popular mind, and with that hour the brilliant Morning Star is generally associated. We may add too that if it *were* actually visible at that season, it would of course be associated (as Dante has with a realistic touch indicated) with the constellation Pisces, the Sun being in the next following sign of Aries.

See also E. Moore (1903), pp. 372-73, for his remarks on the discovery by G. Boffito of an ecclesiastical calendar for the year 1300 (the Almanac of Profacio), contained in a Laurentian MS contemporary with Dante, in which Venus is entered as the morning star and as being in the constellation of Pisces, in March-April of that year. See *Studi danteschi* IV (1921): 153, for further confirmation of the matter as found by G. Boffito in two Vatican MSS.

22. *I' mi volsi a man destra*: To observe Venus Dante must be facing east. Therefore, in turning now to the right, he faces south.

23. *a l'altro polo*: The South Pole is the "other" pole for those of us who inhabit the northern hemisphere of land.

23-24. *e vidi quattro stelle . . . la prima gente*: The allegorical significance of these stars will be disclosed in the course of the journey up the mountain. See C. S. Singleton (1958), pp. 159-83. "The first people" must mean Adam and Eve, but how and why this can be the meaning has yet to be revealed to the reader. On the manner in which "prima gente" represents a fusion of the account in Genesis and the classical myth of Astraea, see C. S. Singleton (1958), pp. 184-203. It has been argued that Dante here refers to the stars of the Southern Cross; but, as Porena observes, this cannot be (even were we to assume that Dante knew of such a constellation). In his commentary (pp. 15-16) Porena points out to those who do not consider the four stars an invention of Dante, and who argue that by inventing them he would have shown little respect for science, that by using them Dante is violating scientific truth in quite a different way. Dante knew that there were inhabitants at the equator; he says so in *De mon.* I, xiv, 6, where he calls them "Garamantes," and he alludes to them again in the *Questio de aqua et terra* (LV). And he knew that from the equator it was possible to see all the stars of the southern hemisphere. But, Porena remarks, Dante decided to forget all this and describe the four stars as never having been seen by anyone but the first people. Why? Because the statement has a symbolic value.

24. *a la prima gente* = *da la prima gente.*

26. *oh settentrional vedovo sito*: Only Adam and Eve, in their brief time in Eden before the Fall, were privileged to see these stars. Then, having sinned, Adam and Eve were (somehow) removed to the "northern clime," with the sad result that they and all their descendants were deprived of the sight of these four stars. Hence the northern region is said to be "widowed" of these stars. The full import of this lament can become clear only when the allegorical significance of the four stars is revealed. On the whole matter, see C. S. Singleton (1958), especially pp. 141-58. For "vedovo," cf. the verb *viduare* as used, for example, by Tertullian in his *De anima* XIX, 1: "Sed ne illi quidem praetereundi qui vel modico temporis viduant animam intellectu." ("Mention must be made of those philosophers who would deprive the soul of the intellect for even a short period of time.") For other examples, see the edition of the *De anima* of J. H. Waszink (1947), p. 270.

29. *a l'altro polo*: Dante now turns round to the left, facing toward the North Pole ("altro" with respect to the South Pole, toward which he has been looking).

30. *là onde 'l Carro già era sparito*: The Wain, or Ursa Major, is now below the northern horizon, a notable fact since in "our" northern hemisphere it never sinks out of sight (see *Par.* XIII, 7-9).

31. *un veglio*: Marcus Porcius Cato Uticensis (Cato the Younger), great-grandson of Cato the Censor, was born in 95 B.C. Brought up as a devoted adherent of the Stoic school,

he became conspicuous for his rigid morality. In 62 B.C. he was tribune of the plebs, and he supported Cicero in his proposal that the Catilinarian conspirators should be put to death. He was one of the chief leaders of the aristocratic party and vehemently opposed the measures of Caesar, Pompey, and Crassus. On the outbreak of the civil war in 49 B.C. he sided with Pompey. After the battle of Pharsalia he joined Metellus Scipio in Africa, but when the latter was defeated at Thapsus, and all of Africa, with the exception of Utica, submitted to Caesar, he resolved to die rather than fall into his hands. In 46 B.C. he therefore put an end to his own life, after spending the greater part of the night reading Plato's *Phaedo* on the immortality of the soul.

We should expect to find Cato, as a suicide and a pagan and as the bitter opponent of Caesar, founder of the Roman Empire, in Hell with Pier della Vigna, or with Brutus and Cassius, instead of here in Purgatory, destined eventually to a place in Paradise (*Purg.* I, 75). Dante, however, regards Cato not in his relation to the Roman Empire, but as the devoted lover of liberty, and consequently as the appropriate guardian of those who by purgation are freeing themselves from the last traces of sin before rising to the final beatitude of Heaven. In his treatment of Cato, Dante appears to have followed Virgil, who, instead of placing him among the suicides in Tartarus (*Aen.* VI, 434-39), represents him as a lawgiver among the righteous dead in Elysium. See *Aen.* VIII, 670: "secretosque pios, his dantem iura Catonem" ("far apart, the good, and Cato giving them laws"), a line which may well have suggested to Dante the employment of Cato as warder of Purgatory. Dante's estimate of Cato was doubtless also derived in part from Cicero (*De officiis* I, xxxi, 112) and from Lucan, who pictures him as the personification of godlike virtue (*Phars.* II, 380-91; IX, 554-55, 601-604). Dante expresses his great reverence for Cato in *De mon.* II, v, 15, and in *Conv.* IV, v, 16; vi, 9-10; xxvii, 3. In speaking of Cato's wife Marcia, whom he gave to Hortensius, and who after the death of the latter came back to him, Dante says her return to Cato symbolizes the noble soul returning to God in old age (*Conv.* IV, xxviii, 15-19).

Although Dante refers to Cato as "un veglio," Cato was only forty-eight or forty-nine years old when he took his own life, but it should be remembered that for Dante *la senettute* begins at forty-six (*Conv.* IV, xxiv, 4), by which reckoning Cato can be called a "veglio." Such an appellation clearly adds dignity to the figure, as does the long beard. Lucan's account deals with Cato in his last years.

34–36. *Lunga la barba . . . lista*: Lucan tells that from the outbreak of the civil war Cato ceased to shave or trim his beard or to cut his hair. See *Phars.* II, 372-76:

> Ille nec horrificam sancto dimovit ab ore
> Caesariem duroque admisit gaudia voltu,—
> Ut primum tolli feralia viderat arma,
> Intonsos rigidam in frontem descendere canos
> Passus erat maestamque genis increscere barbam . . .

The husband refused to remove the shaggy growth from his reverend face; nor did his stern features grant access to joy. (Ever since he saw the weapons of ill-omened war raised up, he had suffered the grey hair to grow long over his stern brow and the beard of the mourner to spread over his face.)

It should be noted that Dante has Cato's beard and hair only graying, not entirely white.

37-39. *Li raggi . . . davante*: Only later, when the allegorical significance of the four stars is disclosed, will the reader understand what is symbolized by this touch, which has Cato's face shine with the rays of the four stars as if the sun were shining upon his face.

39. *come = come se.*

40. *contro al cieco fiume*: The stream referred to in *Inf.* XXXIV, 130-32. Dante and Virgil climbed in a direction opposite to the downward flow of the stream, and the passageway made by it was very dark ("cieco").

41. *fuggita avete la pregione etterna*: Cato takes Dante and Virgil to be souls who have escaped from Hell. He will now

be told by Virgil what he apparently does not see, that Dante is a living man.

42. *quelle oneste piume*: His beard. See Horace, *Odes* IV, x, 2-3: "insperata tuae cum veniet pluma superbiae / et, quae nunc umeris involitant, deciderint comae" ("when unexpected down shall come upon thy pride and the locks have fallen that now wave upon thy shoulders").

46. *le leggi d'abisso*: "Laws" which require that Hell be an *eternal* prison for the damned.   *così rotte*: "Thus broken"—by you, now.

47. *o è mutato in ciel novo consiglio*: "Mutato" anticipates "novo."

48. *a le mie grotte*: "To my banks." See "grotta" in this sense in *Inf.* XXI, 110. Quite literally, as will be clear later, there are cliffs on this mountain, but the term may well refer to the seven terraces and their cliff-like walls (see vs. 82: "li tuoi sette regni").

49. *mi diè di piglio*: See *Inf.* XXIV, 24.   *diè = diede*.

51. *reverenti mi fé le gambe e 'l ciglio*: He had me kneel down and bow my head before Cato.   *fé = fece*.

52. *lui = a lui*.

52-54. *Da me non venni . . . sovvenni*: See Dante's words to Cavalcante in *Inf.* X, 61-62, and his reference there to Virgil as his guide. In like manner, Virgil here speaks of Beatrice, referring to Beatrice's coming to him in Limbo and to her entreaties to him there. See also Virgil's reference to Beatrice in *Inf.* XII, 88-89, and Beatrice's words in *Purg.* XXX, 139-41.

56. *vera = veramente*.

57. *esser non puote il mio che a te si nieghi*: "Il mio" (namely, *volere*) can be taken as the subject of "si nieghi" or may be construed as being the subject of "puote," some

noun such as *spiegazione* being understood as the unex-
pressed object of "si nieghi."   *puote = può.*

59. *per la sua follia*: His folly in straying from the true way
and losing himself in the dark wood of sin; see *Inf.* I, 2-3, and
nn. to vss. 2 and 3. The "folle volo" of Ulysses (*Inf.* XXVI,
125) will also be remembered in this connection.   *le fu
sì presso*: I.e., to his "ultima sera," or death.

60. *che molto poco tempo a volger era*: Dante came very
near to spiritual if not physical death (see *Inf.* I, 61; II,
107-8). But now that he is guided on the right way and
lives in grace, he can expect to have many more years of life
"if Grace does not call him to itself before the time" (see
Inf. XXXI, 128-29).

61. *Sì com' io dissi*: Virgil refers to his words in vss.
52-54.

62. *per lui campare*: Compare the similar expression in *Inf.*
II, 68.   *li = vi.* Petrocchi has "lì," but this more emphatic
form of the adverb seems out of place here.

64. *lui = a lui.*   *tutta la gente ria*: All the sinners of
Hell.

66. *sotto la tua balìa*: Cato is thus said to be the custodian
or guardian of all seven circles of Purgatory (see vs. 82).
Actually, after his return in the following canto, Cato does
not appear again in the action of the poem, nor is he men-
tioned again thereafter; but as one who renounced life for the
sake of liberty, he symbolizes the attainment of freedom
(from the stains of sin) to which souls win in this second
realm. See vss. 71-75.

67. *tratto*: "Brought." Cf. *Inf.* I, 114.   *saria = sarebbe.*

68. *de l'alto scende virtù*: A power descends from on high
(*desursum descendens*), making possible this most extraor-
dinary journey. See *Inf.* XXVI, 22, where the poet is said to
pray for guidance by such "virtù," a power that was not given
to Ulysses.

14

69. *conducer = condurre.   a vederti e a udirti*: These words are obviously a calculated part of Virgil's *captatio benevolentiae*. See Beatrice's words in *Inf.* II, 58-60.

71. *libertà va cercando*: Liberty, freedom, is thus declared to be the goal of the purgatorial journey, liberation from the slavery of sin, both original and actual. Dante mentions Cato as the symbol of liberty in *De mon.* II, v, 15. For the goal of such liberty as finally attained, see *Purg.* XXVII, 140-42. Also see Ps. 30:2[31:1]: "In iustitia tua libera me" ("in your justice rescue me") and Rom. 7:23-24: "Video autem aliam legem in membris meis repugnantem legi mentis meae, et captivantem me in lege peccati, quae est in membris meis. Infelix ego homo! Quis me liberabit de corpore mortis huius?" ("But I see another law in my members, warring against the law of my mind and making me prisoner to the law of sin that is in my members. Unhappy man that I am! Who will deliver me from the body of this death?")

73-74. *ché non ti fu . . . la morte*: See *Inf.* I, 7.

74. *Utica*: Utica, the most important city after Carthage in ancient North Africa, was a Phoenician colony more ancient than Carthage herself. It was a coastal city situated near the mouth of the river Bagradas (modern Medjerda) and about thirty miles northwest of Carthage and modern Tunis. During the third Punic War Utica sided with Rome against Carthage and was rewarded with a large part of the Carthaginian territory. It was afterwards famous as the scene of the last stand made by the Pompeian party against Caesar and of the suicide of Cato, who hence got his surname of Uticensis.

75. *la vesta ch'al gran dì sarà sì chiara*: Virgil's words leave no doubt about the ultimate salvation of Cato, which makes for a special problem since he was both a pagan and a suicide. Apparently he is appointed to serve as custodian of Purgatory until Judgment Day, after which there will no longer be a Purgatory. At that time apparently he will be admitted to Heaven as one of the blessed, who all pass then to eternal

bliss in their glorified bodies, the raiment of their flesh. See *Inf.* VI, 94-99; *Par.* XIV, 13-60; and Thomas Aquinas, *Summa theol.* III, Suppl., q. 85. *vesta = veste.* Cf. "spoglie," *Inf.* XIII, 103.

76. *per noi = da noi.* *guasti:* Cf. "rotte" in vs. 46.

77. *Minòs me non lega:* As one who is relegated to Limbo (the "cerchio" referred to in the next verse), Virgil is outside the jurisdiction of Minos. See *Inf.* V, 4-12, and n. to *Inf.* V, 11. The form "me" (rather than "mi") is emphatic here.

79. *Marzia:* Marcia, daughter of Lucius Marcius Philippus and second wife of Cato of Utica. Lucan (*Phars.* II, 326-49) relates that Cato, after the birth of their third child, ceded her to his friend Hortensius. After the death of Hortensius, Marcia persuaded Cato to remarry her (see *Phars.* II, 341-44). *che 'n vista ancor ti priega:* See Lucan's version of Marcia's former prayer to Cato (*Phars.* II, 338-44):

> Dum sanguis inerat, dum vis materna, peregi
> Iussa, Cato, et geminos excepi feta maritos;
> Visceribus lassis partuque exhausta revertor
> Iam nulli tradenda viro. Da foedera prisci
> Inlibata tori, da tantum nomen inane
> Conubii; liceat tumulo scripsisse: "Catonis
> Marcia." . . .

While there was warm blood in these veins and I had power to be a mother, I did your bidding, Cato: I took two husbands and bore them children. Now I return wearied and worn-out with child-bearing, and I must not again be surrendered to any other husband. Grant me to renew the faithful compact of my first marriage; grant me only the name of wife; suffer men to write on my tomb, "Marcia, wife of Cato."

80. *o santo petto:* See Dante, *Conv.* IV, v, 16: "O sacratissimo petto di Catone, chi presummerà di te parlare?" ("O most hallowed bosom of Cato, who shall presume to speak of thee?") See also Lucan, *Phars.* IX, 561-62: "Tua pectora sacra / Voce reple." ("Fill your breast with the god's utter-

ance.")   *che per tua la tegni*: See n. to vs. 79.   *tegni*
= *tegna*.

81. *per lo suo amore*: "For her love [of you]."   *a noi ti*
piega = *piègati a noi*.

82. *Lasciane* = *làsciaci*.   *sette regni*: The seven circles
or terraces of Purgatory.

83. *grazie riporterò di te a lei*: See *Inf*. II, 73-74. When Vir-
gil returns to Limbo and sees Marcia there, he will thank her
for the favor he now asks of Cato. In *Inf*. IV, 128, Marcia
was named among the souls who are in Limbo.

84. *mentovato* = *menzionato*.

86. *di là*: In the world of the living, beyond the ocean.

87. *volse* = *volle*.   *fei* = *feci*.

88. *di là dal mal fiume*: In Limbo, beyond Acheron, the evil
river (described in *Inf*. III and IV).

89. *più muover non mi può*: By Lucan's account (*Phars*.
II, 350), Cato is moved by Marcia's entreaties: "Hae flexere
virum voces." ("Her words moved her husband.") Thus
"muover" here and "ti piega" in vs. 81 appear to echo
Lucan's "flexere."   *per quella legge*: Even now Cato is
as one of the blessed, like Beatrice. See her words to Virgil
in Limbo (*Inf*. II, 92) and the note on *Inf*. II, 91-93. See also
Luc. 16:26, Abraham's words to the rich man in Hell: "Et
in his omnibus inter nos et vos chaos magnum firmatum est."
("And besides all that, between us and you a great gulf is
fixed.") On this "chaos," see Peter Lombard, *Sent*. IV, 1, 6:

Quid est illud chaos inter bonos et malos, nisi hinc
iustitia, inde iniquitas, quae nullatenus sociari valent?
Adeo enim sancti Dei iustitiae addicti sunt, ut nulla
compassione ad reprobos transire valeant, nulla pro eis
inter sanctos fiat intercessio. Quomodo ergo inde volunt
aliqui transire ad illos, sed non possunt? Quia si Dei
iustitia admitteret, non fieret eis molesta liberatio
eorum. Vel ita dicuntur velle et non posse, non quia

velint et non possint, sed quia etsi vellent, non possent eos iuvare. De hoc ita Gregor[ius] ait, super Lucam: Sicut reprobi a poenis ad gloriam sanctorum transire volunt, et non possunt, et ita iusti per misericordiam mente ire volunt ad positos in tormentis, ut eos liberent, sed non possunt; quia iustorum animae etsi in naturae suae bonitate misericordiam habent, iam nunc auctoris sui iustitiae coniunctae tanta rectitudine constringuntur, ut nulla ad reprobos compassione moveantur.

What else is this gulf between the good and the bad unless it be, on the one side, justice and, on the other, wickedness, which never can be joined together? The saints are so united to the justice of God that no matter how compassionate they might feel, they could not cross over to those who are damned, and the saints never make intercession for them. How is it that, though some might wish to cross over, they cannot do so? Because, if God's justice would permit it, there would be no harm in their [the damned] being freed. They are said to wish to [cross over], but they are not able; not simply that they wish to and cannot but even if [the saints] should wish to, they cannot help the damned. On this Gregory says on Luke: "Just as the damned desire to pass from their punishment to the glory of the saints and cannot do so, so also the just, because of their merciful attitude, wish to go to those who are placed in torment so as to free them, yet they are unable to do so; for although the souls of the just, in the goodness of their nature, are merciful, still they are bound to the justice of their creator with such straitness that they simply are not moved at all by compassion for the damned."

For Gregory's comment on Luke, see his *Homil.* XL, 7. The passage from Peter Lombard is quoted by E. G. Parodi (1912, p. 225).

90. *che fatta fu*: E. G. Parodi (1912, p. 226) continues on this phrase:

Aggiungo solo che "fatta fu" è probabilmente un pretto latinismo: "facta est" o "fuit," avvenne, ebbe luogo;

non il passato passivo dell'ital. verbo *fare*; e così traduce
in qualche modo più da vicino l'evangelico *firmatum est*,
in quanto ha, come questo, senso continuativo, anzichè
momentaneo, aoristico: "la legge che, da quel momento
in poi, ebbe ed ha luogo per me (come per tutti i beati);
la legge dell'impassibilità, che è il nostro necessario ac-
consentimento alla giustizia divina."

I will only add that "fatta fu" is probably a pure Latin-
ism: *facta est*, or *fuit*, which means "happened," "took
place." It is not the passive past of the Italian verb *fare*.
And therefore, in some way, it resembles the evangelical
firmatum est, inasmuch as it has, like this expression,
a continuous rather than a momentary, aoristic sense:
"The law which, from that moment on, happened and
is still happening for me (as for all the blessed); the law
of impassiveness, which is our necessary compliance
with Divine Justice."

See also C. H. Grandgent (1926).   *quando me n'uscì*
fora: Cato took his own life in 46 B.C or some eighty years
before the Crucifixion and harrowing of Hell. Hence he must
have descended to Limbo to await there the coming of Christ
(since before Christ no souls were saved, as Virgil explains
to Dante in *Inf*. IV, 62-63); and he must then have been
transferred to his present office as guardian of Purgatory.
          uscì' = uscii.

92. *di' = dici*.   *non c'è mestier lusinghe*: Cato is well
aware that Virgil's *captatio benevolentiae* has been quite full
of "flatteries."

93. *bastisi = si basti*, "let it suffice."   *richegge = richieg-*
ga, richieda. Cf. "richeggio," *Inf*. I, 130.

94. *ricinghe = ricinga*. In the *ri-* one may sense an allusion
to the cord wherewith Dante was girt, but which he put off
before entering into the third and lowest area of Hell (*Inf*.
XVI, 106-11).

95. *d'un giunco*: The rush is clearly the symbol of humility
and, as a girdle, a kind of *cingulum humilitatis*, replacing the

girdle of self-confidence which the cord represents. See "umile pianta," vs. 135.   *schietto*: Straight, without knots. By contrast, the cord was knotted and coiled before being thrown as bait to Geryon (*Inf.* XVI, 111).   *li = gli*.

96. *sucidume = sudiciume*, i.e., the grime of Hell, left by the "aere grasso" (*Inf.* IX, 82) and the smoke.   *stinghe = stinga*. Torraca considers the verb intransitive, from *stingere*, "to lose its color," and interprets this verse to mean "get all the grime to disappear from his face." He points out that people will say "a color that discolors" or "that does not discolor."

97. *converria = converrebbe*.

97–98. *l'occhio sorpriso d'alcuna nebbia*: A construction modeled on an ablative absolute.   *sorpriso = sorpreso*, "veiled," "overcast."

99. *ministro*: Angel, the first of the angels to be met in Purgatory.

100. *ad imo ad imo*: At the water's very edge.

103–5. *null' altra pianta . . . seconda*: These verses point clearly to the symbolic meaning of the rush as humility.

104. *puote = può*.

106. *reddita*: From *reddire*. Cf. *ritornata*, from *ritornare*.

107. *lo sol vi mosterrà, che surge omai*: Note the correspondence here with the "pianeta" of the initial prologue scene (see *Inf.* I, 17-18). See also *Purg.* XIII, 13-21. The importance of the sun as such a guide in Purgatory is better realized when we learn that once the sun has set there is no climbing up the mountain until a new day dawns (*Purg.* VII, 53-60).   *mosterrà = mostrerà*.

109. *Così sparì*: Cato vanishes as suddenly and mysteriously as he appeared.   *sù mi levai*: Dante has been kneeling all the while, as Virgil had bidden (vs. 51).

111. *e li occhi a lui drizzai*: Benvenuto comments: "Quasi dicerem: ecce me paratum facere obedienter omnia imperata." ("As if to say: here I am, ready to fulfill all commands, with complete obedience.")

113. *volgianci = volgiamoci.   volgianci   in   dietro*: Evidently Dante and Virgil had come forth from Hell to see the stars again at a point some distance up the slope from the shore, and Dante first stood facing east (vss. 19-20), that is, facing away from the mountain. He then turns to the right, that is, to the south (vss. 22-23), and sees the four stars in the south, following which he turns round to face the North Pole (vss. 29-30), noting that the Wain has disappeared from that quarter of the sky. Whereupon Cato mysteriously appears beside him, and he sees the light of the four southern stars shining upon Cato's face (vss. 37-38), which means that Cato is facing south. To turn back from that direction, that is, from facing north ("di qua" implies a gesture on Virgil's part), as Virgil here proposes, means that they would now turn to the south and proceed in a somewhat southerly direction, walking around the island as they seek the shore. This actually amounts to a kind of clockwise circling of the mountain at this point, whereas, in their climb afterwards, they will normally turn counterclockwise. Thus the brief descent here turns in the same direction as the descent through Hell and is a token descent to humility.

114. *questa pianura*: A "slope" (which is also a "shore"), corresponding to the "piaggia" of *Inf.* I, 29, and II, 62. See n. to *Inf.* I, 29.

115. *L'alba vinceva l'ora mattutina*: Buti comments: "La bianchezza che appare nell'oriente, quando incomincia a venire lo di' [dì], *vinceva l'ora mattutina*; cioè l'ora del mattino, ch'è l'ultima parte de la notte, *Che fuggia inanzi*; cioè a l'alba." ("The whiteness that appears in the east, when day dawns, conquers the morning hour, Matins, i.e., the hour of morning that is the last part of the night and that flees before the dawn.") Thus *ora mattutina* or *il mattutino* (Matins) stands for the last darkness of the night.

Other commentators take "ora" here to be "aura," or a morning breeze, but this, in the context, seems less acceptable since the darkness is dispelled, conquered by the dawn, so that the trembling sea becomes visible in the distance.

116. *fuggia* = *fuggiva*.

117. *il tremolar de la marina*: See Virgil, *Aen.* VII, 9: "Splendet tremulo sub lumine pontus." ("The sea glitters beneath her dancing beams.")

118. *lo solingo piano*: See the corresponding "piaggia diserta" of the prologue scene (*Inf.* I, 29; II, 62), also called a "gran diserto" in *Inf.* I, 64.

119. *com' om che torna a la perduta strada*: The climb up the mountain was impossible before, and the reason now becomes clear: Dante was not then girt with the necessary humility. Now he goes down to that humility. The notion of a return to a "lost way" suggests this.

120. *li* = *gli*.

121–22. *là 've la rugiada pugna col sole*: The dew will contend with the sun later, when it is higher than it is at the moment.

123. *ad orezza*: On this much-debated reading, see Petrocchi's note. I have accepted his reading here, in the sense which my translation declares. "Orezza" meaning "breeze" is clearly supported by "l'orezza" of *Purg.* XXIV, 150, and would here refer to a moist sea breeze that helps defend the dew against the evaporation by the sun. Dew is an established symbol of God's grace, and it is doubtless intended to bear something of that connotation here. Clearly, Virgil's movements (his "arte," vs. 126) have something distinctly ritualistic about them. See Virgil, *Aen.* VI, 635-36, where Aeneas washes himself upon leaving black Tartarus and entering the Elysian fields: "Occupat Aeneas aditum corpusque recenti / spargit aqua ramumque adverso in limine figit." ("Aeneas wins the entrance, sprinkles his body with fresh water, and plants the bough full on the threshold.")

127. *ver'* = *verso*.   *le guance lagrimose*: Cheeks stained with tears in the journey through Hell.

130-32. *Venimmo poi . . . esperto*: The verse clearly indicates that Dante now stands looking out over such "dangerous waters"; for the correspondence of this with the prologue scene, see *Inf.* I, 22-24.

130. *lito diserto*: Again, as in vss. 114 and 118, the feature that corresponds with the "piaggia diserta" (*Inf.* I, 29) of the prologue scene.

132. *omo, che di tornar sia poscia esperto*: See Virgil, *Aen.* VI, 424-25: "Occupat Aeneas aditum custode sepulto / evaditque celer ripam inremeabilis undae." ("The warder buried in sleep, Aeneas wins the entrance, and swiftly leaves the bank of that stream whence none return.") For "sia esperto," cf. the Latin *expertus sit*. "Sia" (instead of "fosse") makes this a general statement in the present and hence one that is true generally.

We the readers know of no one except Ulysses who did attempt to sail these waters, and we are thus invited to realize, through transparent allusions, that the mountain which Ulysses finally saw loom in the distance "higher than any he had ever seen," and from which the whirlwind came to sink his ship, was precisely the mountain-island of Purgatory. This aspect of the meaning is glimpsed by Benvenuto, who comments: "Hoc dicit pro Ulyxe, qui tentavit illuc accedere secundum fictionem poetae, sed cito ipsum poenituit." ("Here he means Ulysses, who according to the story of the poet sought to approach that place but soon regretted it.")

133. *sì com' altrui piacque*: "As it pleased another," Cato, who had so commanded. Or perhaps, since Cato is doing God's will, "altrui" might here be understood as God. In any event, the echo of Ulysses' own words in *Inf.* XXVI, 141 (where in its veiled way it can only mean God's will) is another obvious pointer to the hero's shipwreck and death in these very waters which the wayfaring Dante looks out upon.   *altrui*: Dative, "to another."

134-36. *oh maraviglia!* . . . *l'avelse*: The marvel is a clear allusion to Virgil, *Aen*. VI, 136-44, Aeneas' plucking of the golden bough:

> . . . latet arbore opaca
> aureus et foliis et lento vimine ramus,
> Iunoni infernae dictus sacer; hunc tegit omnis
> lucus et obscuris claudunt convallibus umbrae.
> sed non ante datur telluris operta subire,
> auricomos quam qui decerpserit arbore fetus.
> hoc sibi pulchra suum ferri Proserpina munus
> instituit; primo avolso non deficit alter
> aureus, et simili frondescit virga metallo.

There lurks in a shady tree a bough, golden in leaf and pliant stem, held consecrate to nether Juno; this all the grove hides, and shadows veil in the dim valleys. But 'tis not given to pass beneath earth's hidden places, save to him who hath plucked from the tree the golden-tressed fruitage. This hath beautiful Proserpine ordained to be borne to her as her own gift. When the first is torn away, a second fails not, golden too, and the spray bears leaf of the selfsame ore.

This suggests that the *cingulum humilitatis* is indeed Dante's "golden bough" to this new realm of Purgatory, the necessary talisman that he has gained by his descent to humility and with which he may now ascend the mountain: humility, that virtue which Ulysses did not have.

On the spiritual significance of the instantaneous springing up of the humble plant, Torraca quotes Iacopo Passavanti's "Trattato dell'umiltà" (see *Lo specchio*, p. 246): "L'umiltà non può essere vinta; però che delle ferite rinvigorisce, della infermità rinforza, della povertà arricchisce, del danno cresce, della morte rivivisce." ("Humility cannot be conquered, because it is reinvigorated by its wounds, strengthened by its infirmities, enriched by poverty; it flourishes on violence [done to it] and revives through death.")

CANTO II

1–3. *Già era 'l sole . . . punto*: As throughout the *Inferno*, the point of reference for telling the time continues for the moment to be that of an observer ideally located in Jerusalem, the center of the northern hemisphere of land; the sun is now said to have reached the horizon, as seen from Jerusalem, and there it is sunset.

4–5. *e la notte . . . fuor*: Here night, as that point which revolves opposite to the sun, means midnight. Since it is sunset at Jerusalem, it is midnight on the Ganges. The following general statement by Grandgent (pp. 336-37 of his commentary) may prove to be of help regarding these and the other time references that will follow:

> It must be understood that the *meridian* of any place on earth is a great circle in the sky, passing directly over that spot and crossing the two heavenly poles. The *horizon* of a given place is a great circle in the sky, running around the globe 90° from its meridian. The planes of the meridian and the horizon are therefore always at right angles to each other; the horizon of the north pole, for instance, is the celestial equator—which is also the horizon of the south pole, because the two poles are 180° apart. Inasmuch as Jerusalem and Purgatory are

on opposite sides of the earth, 180° from each other, they have a common horizon: when Jerusalem sees the sun rise, Purgatory sees it set, and *vice versa.* The difference in time between the two places is just twelve hours, so that Jerusalem's noon is Purgatory's midnight, six A.M. in Jerusalem is six P.M. in Purgatory, etc. The first three lines of the canto mean, then, that the sun, in its daily revolution, has descended to the horizon of Jerusalem—"that horizon, the highest point of whose meridian is over Jerusalem." But this is also the horizon of Purgatory: the sun, which is setting for Jerusalem, is rising for Purgatory.

5. *uscia = usciva.*

5–6. *con le Bilance . . . soverchia*: E. Moore (1887, p. 70) comments:

> The Sun being in Aries, the night, revolving exactly opposite to him (l. 4), is considered to be in Libra (*le bilance*), and the Scales are said to fall from the hand of night when night overcomes the day (*soverchia*), *i.e.* becomes longer than the day. This of course it does after the autumnal Equinox, and since the Sun then enters Libra, that constellation ceases to be within the range of night, and so the Scales are poetically said to fall from the hand of night.

6. *caggion = cadono.*

7–9. *sì che . . . rance*: The cheeks of Aurora, the rosy dawn (i.e., the eastern sky), are said to be gradually growing orange as the sun rises and Aurora grows older.

8. *là dov' i' era*: This touch now transfers the post of observation from Jerusalem to Purgatory mountain, where Dante is.

11–12. *come gente che pensa . . . dimora*: This is the proper spiritual condition of the Christian pilgrim, this the "unquiet heart" he should have. The verses connect with the theme of "pilgrims all" declared in Virgil's words in vss. 61-63. See Heb. 11:13-16:

Iuxta fidem defuncti sunt omnes isti, non acceptis re-
promissionibus, sed a longe eas aspicientes et salutantes,
et confitentes quia peregrini et hospites sunt super ter-
ram. Qui enim haec dicunt significant se patriam in-
quirere, et si quidem ipsius meminissent de qua exierunt,
habebant utique tempus revertendi; nunc autem melio-
rem appetunt, id est caelestem.

In the way of faith all these died without receiving the
promises, but beholding them afar off, and saluting them
and acknowledging that they were pilgrims and stran-
gers on earth. For they who say these things show plainly
that they seek a country of their own. And indeed if
they were thinking of the country from which they went
out, they certainly would have had opportunity to re-
turn; but as it is they seek after a better, that is, a heav-
enly country.

13–15. *Ed ecco, qual . . . marino*: Mars was thought to be
accompanied by vapors, which were sometimes dense and
sometimes rare and which at times became ignited of them-
selves and burned with the color of fire. See *Conv.* II, xiii, 21:

Esso Marte dissecca e arde le cose, perché lo suo calore
è simile a quello del fuoco; e questo è quello per che esso
pare affocato di colore, quando più e quando meno, se-
condo la spessezza e raritade de li vapori che 'l seguono:
li quali per lor medesimi molte volte s'accendono, sì
come nel primo de la Metaura è diterminato.

This same Mars drieth and burneth things, because his
heat is like to the heat of fire; and this is why he ap-
peareth enkindled in colour, sometimes more and some-
times less, according to the thickness and rarity of the
vapours which follow him; which vapours often blaze
up of themselves, as is established in the first of
the *Meteorics*.

(On Dante's probable use of Albertus Magnus rather than
Aristotle here, see P. Toynbee, 1902, pp. 39-40.) Dante is
actually facing east when he perceives this light coming over
the waters, but he specifically has it that Mars is "down in the

west" at dawn. Porena observes that from the Tuscan seashore the poet was accustomed to looking westward, not eastward, toward the sea.

15. *suol marino*: Cf. *Inf.* XXVI, 129.

16. *s'io ancor lo veggia*: The phrase corresponds (in its use of the subjunctive) to the formula of adjuration, but here it is one of asseveration and at the same time an expression of hope, to wit, that the poet, after his death, may be conveyed to Purgatory by such a "light," i.e., angel. In *Inf.* III, 93, Dante has Charon predict such a happy end for him. Meanwhile, coming at this particular point, when as yet the reader does not know what this light is, the phrase serves to increase the suspense and heighten the excitement of the gradual revelation. The light proves to be the angel's face, so that we know in retrospect what the wish expressed is: that he may see this angel-boatman's face again—in which case, of course, he would be with the angel and would not be standing on this shore to see him come.

18. *nessun volar pareggia*: Actually, the angel, as will become clear, follows much the same course as that taken by Ulysses, whose journey was termed a "volo" (*Inf.* XXVI, 125).

21. *rividil = lo rividi.*

22–24. *Poi d'ogne . . . uscìo*: The first whiteness proves to be the angel's wings, as vs. 26 then declares, and the other whiteness, below, its robe.

22. *appario = apparì* (as *uscìo,* in rhyme, is used for *uscì*).

23. *sapeva = sapevo.*

24. *a lui*: Connects with "di sotto" in the preceding verse: "di sotto . . . a lui."

27. *allor che ben conobbe il galeotto*: If Virgil, in this place that is strange to him, can no longer qualify as the "savio gentil, che tutto seppe" (*Inf.* VII, 3), he is at least able to

28

recognize at once that the white wings are those of an angel-boatman.   *galeotto*: Phlegyas, the boatman of Styx, is termed "galeoto" in *Inf.* VIII, 17 (in rhyme). In his gloss on that verse, Boccaccio comments: " 'Galeotti' son chiamati que' marinari li quali servono alle galee; ma qui, *licentia poëtica*, nomina 'galeotto' il governatore d'una piccola barchetta." ("*Galeotti* is the name for seamen who serve on galleys. But here, by poetic license, he uses the term for the person in charge of a small bark.") Up to this point, the focus has remained exclusively on the light and the whiteness that are gradually being disclosed to be the face and figure of an angel, and nothing has thus far been said about there being any boat here. Now "galeotto" clearly implies the presence of the boat itself.

28. *Fa, fa*: Virgil's excitement, when he finally makes out the angel, is evident enough in this urgent repetition of the verb in the imperative continued in "vedi . . . vedi" (vss. 31, 34).   *che le ginocchia cali*: Literally, "that you lower your knees." Similarly, at the appearance of the angel in Hell, Virgil ordered Dante to kneel (*Inf.* IX, 86-87).

29. *piega le mani*: Virgil is instructing Dante to fold his hands, as in prayer.

30. *omai*: "Henceforward" (the meaning in its future sense being indicated in this case by the verb "vedrai").   *sì fatti officiali*: Guardians of Purgatory, all white-robed, just as, by contrast, the guardian devils of Hell were black.

31. *argomenti umani*: "Human means," such as sails or oars. Cf. the verb *argomentarsi* used in *Inf.* XXII, 21.

33. *tra liti sì lontani*: As distant as is the shore at Ostia (as will be made clear) from Mount Purgatory, which is directly opposite Jerusalem on the earth's globe. Ulysses took over five months to make the same journey, once he had reached the open sea (*Inf.* XXVI, 130-32), for he had merely "argomenti umani" at his disposal.

34. *Vedi come l'ha dritte verso 'l cielo*: This means seeing

the angel at the moment when he has his wings "alzate e ferme" (*Inf.* V, 83), pointing heavenward to the source of the power whereof he is the instrument; but he is also seen as moving his wings, as the following verse makes clear.

36. *che non si mutan*: *Mutare*, when said of birds, means specifically "to molt" or "to mew" (cf. "muda" in *Inf.* XXXIII, 22 and the n. to that vs.).

38. *l'uccel divino*: The black angels of Hell were also called *uccelli*. See *Inf.* XXII, 96; XXXIV, 47.

39. *nol = non lo.*

40. *chinail = lo chinai.   sen = se ne.*

41. *vasello = vascello.* Only now is the boat that was first implied by "galeotto" (vs. 27), then by "remo" and "velo" (vs. 32), actually seen, and seen in a moment when Dante has his eyes down and can scarcely be looking at it. In connection with this vessel, said to be "snelletto" and "leggero" and to draw no water, see Charon's prediction in *Inf.* III, 93.

42. *tanto che l'acqua nulla ne 'nghiottiva*: Literally, "so much so that the water swallowed no part of it." The vessel draws no water, having no cargo of any weight, but only spirits. So had it been with the boat of Phlegyas until Dante, the living man, stepped into it (*Inf.* VIII, 28-30).

43. *Da poppa*: The stern is where the helmsman would stand.   *il celestial nocchiero*: The term "nocchiero" may remind the reader of Charon, who is termed the "nocchier de la livida palude" in *Inf.* III, 98, and who, as a ferryman, presents the greatest contrast to this heavenly helmsman. It should be recalled that in the *Aeneid* Charon serves as boatman for all souls going to Hades, hence for those as well whose destination is Elysium, who thus correspond, in a sense, to these who cross to Purgatory.

44. *tal che parea beato per iscripto*: He is such that he seems to have "blessed," or "blessedness," written on him ("iscripto," as "scripto" in vs. 48, to rhyme with the Latin

"Aegypto" of vs. 46). Perhaps the curious phrase was suggested by the custom, in early paintings, of inscribing labels on, or beside, certain figures to identify them.

Petrocchi (see his vol. I, *Introduzione*, pp. 189-90) has adopted the reading "tal che faria beato pur descripto," which he understands to mean "would make blessed not only anyone who should see him, but anyone who should even hear him described"; but he admits that the more traditional reading, which I have followed, is equally allowed by the MSS. It seems more probable.

45. *sediero*: Pronounced *sedièro*. E. G. Parodi (1957, p. 255) argues that the form is an archaic imperfect (for *sedieno* = *sedevano*). This is possible, but since Dante has elsewhere used in rhyme a past absolute form where the past descriptive might be expected (e.g., *Inf*. XX, 72; XXXII, 128; *Purg*. XXIX, 106), it could well be a modified form of *sederono*.

46. *In exitu Israel de Aegypto*: The initial verse of Ps. 113[114]. As vs. 48 clearly implies, this single verse is supposed to bring the rest of the psalm to mind. The song is appropriate to the time of the journey, since this is Easter Sunday morning, and Exodus signifies, of course, Passover and Easter. Presumably all souls as they reach this shore would sing this psalm, a hymn of thanksgiving for liberation from "Egypt" and the bondage (of sin), as the closing verses of the psalm make clear (Ps. 113[115]:17-18): "Non mortui laudabunt te, Domine, neque omnes qui descendunt in infernum. Sed nos qui vivimus benedicimus Domino, ex hoc nunc et usque in saeculum." ("It is not the dead who praise Thee, Lord, nor those who go down into silence [Inferno]; but we bless the Lord, both now and forever.") Buti notes this: "Questo finge l'autore che cantasseno quelle anime . . . a significare che ringraziavano Dio che erano uscite . . . de la servitù del dimonio e del peccato, e venute in terra di promissione." ("The author depicts those souls singing . . . to signify that they were thanking God because they had left behind . . . their bondage to the devil and sin and had arrived in a promised land.")

47. *cantavan tutti insieme ad una voce*: The concord of these souls in the boat contrasts greatly with the condition of the damned in Hell. No doubt the souls would be singing in the style of *cantus firmus*. See A. Bonaventura (1904), pp. 77-121.

49. *Poi fece il segno lor di santa croce*: Signing them, both as a benediction and as a signal that they should disembark, as the following verse indicates.

50. *ond' ei si gittar tutti in su la piaggia*: Again the reader may recall how differently the souls of the damned left the evil shore to enter Charon's boat (*Inf.* III, 116), yet the verb used to describe that is also *gittarsi*.   *gittar = gittarono*.

51. *ed el sen gì, come venne, veloce*: Swift to return, like the angel in Hell (*Inf.* IX, 100-103) or indeed like the devil of *Inf.* XXI, 43-45, who was also returning for more.

52. *selvaggia*: "Selvaggia" ("strange") is the opposite of "esperti" ("familiar"), Virgil's word in vs. 62.

55-56. *Da tutte parti . . . lo sol*: The sun is now entirely above the horizon and accordingly is said to be darting his rays everywhere. The figure of Apollo as archer and god of the Sun is implicit in the turn of phrase.

56. *conte*: "Well-aimed." From the Latin *cognitae*. Cf. (also in a hunting trope) the term applied to hounds in pursuit of the quarry in *Inf.* XXXIII, 31.

57. *di mezzo 'l ciel cacciato Capricorno*: Since Capricorn is on the meridian of Purgatory, it is directly overhead and is 90° from Aries, when Aries rises on the eastern horizon. It is now somewhat later, and the sun is said to have driven Capricorn from mid-sky, i.e., beyond the meridian.

59. *ver' = verso*.

60. *mostratene = mostrateci.   la via di gire al monte*: "The way to go to the mountain" must mean "the way to go up the mountain." See Cato's cry in vs. 122.

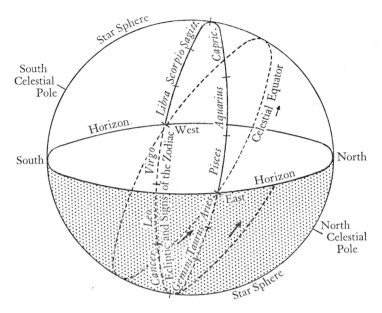

Figure 1. Signs of the Zodiac as seen at sunrise from the mountain of Purgatory at the autumnal equinox there (vernal equinox in the northern hemisphere)

62. *esto loco*: Cf. *Inf.* I, 93.

63. *noi siam peregrin come voi siete*: The notion of pilgrim and thus of pilgrimage here appears in the poem for the first time. Strikingly enough, it was never applied to the journey through Hell. Clearly it implies an exodus, a newness of life, a forward movement toward a promised land, and serves to make Virgil and Dante and these souls one group engaged in pilgrimage. Virgil thus represents himself as one who does not know his way in this new land, which is a most peculiar condition for one who is to serve here as guide to Dante, the living man.

65. *per altra via*: The way through Hell, but especially the

dark and difficult passageway made by the "cieco fiume" (*Purg.* I, 40). *aspra e forte*: This was also said of the "selva selvaggia" (*Inf.* I, 5).

66. *ne = ci.*

67. *fuor = furono.*

68. *per lo spirare*: Here it is Dante's breathing that reveals the fact; a little later it will be his shadow, but as yet the sun is not high enough for that.

69. *diventaro = diventarono.   smorte*: These souls, so recently separated from the world of the living and from their own flesh, grow pale in the presence of one who still belongs to that world and is here in his mortal body.

70. *E come a messagger che porta ulivo*: In ancient times a messenger bore an olive branch as a sign of peace and commonly in Dante's time as a sign of good news, and hence he was called an *ulivo*. See Torraca, who quotes from a *Diario di anonimo fiorentino*: "Oggi, a' dì 10 di gennaio 1370 venne in Firenze un ulivo, come, presso a Bolsena, della gente del Papa furono rotti e sconfitti." ("Today, the tenth of January, 1370, the *ulivo* [good news] came to Florence that the pope's forces had been defeated and routed, near Bolsena.") See Villani, XII, 105: "Mandonne lettere e messi con olivo al nostro comune significando la sua vittoria, e a quello di Perugia." ("He sent letters and messengers with *olivo* [olive branches] to our commune with the news of his victory and to that of Perugia.") Also see Agnolo di Tura, *Cronaca senese* for the year 1351: "Sanesi si fermoro a Querciagrossa . . . e poi introro in Siena cogli ulivi con grande onore." ("The Sienese stopped at Quercia Grossa . . . then they entered Siena with *ulivi* [olive branches], with great honor.") And note the following quotation from the *Corpus chronicorum Bononiensium* for the year 1361 (p. 137, ll. 21-26): "Adì 7 del mese de setenbre, venne uno messo da Fiorenza con llo olivo in mano, et disse che Volterra era data al comun de Fiorenza; di che fu vestito onorevolmente et fu messo l'ulivo alle fenestre dello palaxio." ("On the seventh of Sep-

tember, a messenger came from Florence with an *olivo* [olive branch] in hand and said that Volterra was now in the hands of the commune of Florence, for which he was honorably rewarded and the *ulivo* [olive branch] was put at the windows of the palace.")

71. *tragge = si trae*. Cf. vs. 76.

72. *calcar*: "To press about."

73. *s'affisar = s'affissarono*. This does not exactly serve to keep the simile, but by adding a touch to the "calcar" of the first term proves all the more effective.

74. *fortunate*: They are "fortunate," of course, because they shall one day be among the blessed of Paradise and are not among the damned, who descend to Acheron.

75. *a farsi belle*: "To make themselves beautiful," i.e., by shedding the slough (vs. 122), by cleansing themselves.

76. *una di lor*: This proves to be the soul of Casella, musician of Florence (or, according to some, of Pistoia) and friend of Dante, who finds him here in Antepurgatory among those who disembark on the shore of Purgatory. Casella is said to have set to music some of Dante's verses. In Vatican MS 3214 (see M. Pelaez, 1895, p. 113) at c. 149ᵃ is the inscription: "Lemmo da pistoia. Et Casella diede il suono," i.e., composed by Lemmo and set to music by Casella (Lemmo da Pistoia lived toward the end of the thirteenth century). The *Anonimo fiorentino* says of Casella:

> Questi . . . fue Casella da Pistoja grandissimo musico, et massimamente nell'arte dello 'ntonare; et fu molto dimestico dell'Auttore, però che in sua giovinezza fece Dante molte canzone et ballate, che questi intonò; et a Dante dilettò forte l'udirle da lui, et massimamente al tempo ch'era innamorato di Beatrice, o di Pargoletta, o di quella altra di Casentino.

> This . . . was Casella da Pistoia, a great musician, especially in the art of setting words to music. He was very well acquainted with the author, who in his youth wrote

many songs and ballads, which Casella set to music.
Dante took great delight in hearing him sing them—
especially at the time he was in love with Beatrice, or
with Pargoletta, or with that other girl of the Casentino.

Benvenuto comments:

> Iste spiritus cum quo autor tam amicabiliter loquitur fuit
> quidam suus florentinus nomine Casella, qui fuit
> famosus cantor tempore suo, vir quidem curialis,
> affabilis, ad quem Dantes saepe solebat accedere in vita
> ad recreandum spiritum cantu illius, quando erat fatiga-
> tus studio, vel stimulatus passione amoris.

> This spirit with whom the author was chatting so amica-
> bly was a fellow-citizen of Florence named Casella, who,
> in his day, was famous as a singer; he was a man of rank
> and very friendly, and Dante used to visit him to refresh
> his mind with his songs when he was weary from his
> studies or excited by love.

A record exists, among the documents preserved at Siena, of
a fine against Casella for wandering the streets at night; it is
dated July 13, 1282, so that Casella's death, the year
of which is unknown, must have occurred sometime between
that date and the year 1300.   *trarresi = trarsi.*

79. *Ohi ombre vane, fuor che ne l'aspetto*: The reader will
recall that not many hours before, in Hell, shades were most
substantial, enough so indeed that Dante's living hands could
pull hair from the head of one of them. Yet in upper Hell
they were said to be a "vanità che par persona" (*Inf*. VI,
36). The fact that souls in the afterlife have an aerial body
will be expounded in *Purg*. XXV, 79-108, but the solidity of
such bodies is everywhere made to suit the convenience and
dramatic purposes of the poet.

80-81. *tre volte . . . petto*: See Virgil, *Aen*. VI, 700-702,
where Aeneas meets with his father in the nether world:

> ter conatus ibi collo dare bracchia circum,
> ter frustra comprensa manus effugit imago,
> par levibus ventis volucrique simillima somno.

Thrice there he strove to throw his arms about his neck;
thrice the form, vainly clasped, fled from his hands, even
as light winds, and most like a winged dream.

This episode in turn derives from Homer, *Odyssey* XI,
206-8.

83. *per che l'ombra sorrise*: The soul smiles at Dante's mar-
vel. Before long Virgil will do the same (*Purg.* XII, 136), in
which smiles the contrast with Hell and its *tristizia* continues
to be most striking.

84. *mi pinsi = mi spinsi*. Cf. *Inf.* VIII, 13, and *passim*.

85. *posasse = posassi*.

86. *allor conobbi chi era*: Dante recognizes Casella, the
singer, by his voice.

88. *Rispuosemi = mi rispuose*.

89. *sciolta*: Feminine form because an "anima" is speaking.

90. *però = per ciò*.

91-92. *per tornar . . . son*: Dante's most extraordinary jour-
ney is made for his own salvation, and his present going is a
guaranty thereof. Thus, here again, the poet predicts that
after death he will pass to Purgatory, not to Hell. See *Inf.*
III, 91-93.

93. *ma a te com' è tanta ora tolta?* As mentioned in the n.
to vs. 76, the exact year of Casella's death is not known, but
the question clearly implies that he died some time before
1300, since Dante is expressing amazement that his friend is
arriving only now in Purgatory. Even so, Casella's reply,
which follows, does not entirely clear up the mystery of his
delay, a delay no doubt suggested by Virgil, *Aen.* III, 201-
206; VI, 315-30.

94. *Nessun m'è fatto oltraggio = nessun oltraggio m'è
fatto*.

95–96. *se quei che leva . . . passaggio*: In the *Aeneid* Charon is privileged to refuse to take some of the souls who want to pass to the other world. See Virgil, *Aen.* VI, 313-16.

95. *quei che leva*: The angel.   *cui = chi*.   *li = gli*.

97. *ché di giusto voler lo suo si face*: The angel acts in accordance with God's will, and this shrouds the matter in even greater mystery.   *face = fa*.

98–99. *da tre mesi . . . pace*: Souls passing to Purgatory thus appear to participate in the plenary indulgence of the year 1300 which was granted by Pope Boniface VIII (actually extending from Christmas, 1299) to pilgrims going to the great Jubilee in Rome (referred to by Dante in *Inf.* XVIII, 28-33). The bull does not mention such indulgences for the dead, but Dante is here following a common belief rather than any settled doctrine in the matter. See A. Camilli (1951) for a discussion of this point and the text of the bull issued by Boniface.

99. *con tutta pace*: Without protest.

101. *dove l'acqua di Tevero s'insala*: At or near Ostia, where the Tiber flows into the sea. The location of the entrance to Hell was left vague; not so the place of departure for Purgatory, which thus is from the "port" of Rome, "the holy place where the successor of great Peter has his seat" (*Inf.* II, 23-24).

102. *ricolto*: "Taken up," i.e., taken aboard.

103. *dritta = diretta (indirizzata)*.

104–5. *però che sempre . . . cala*: Only now do we understand Charon's words to Dante in *Inf.* III, 91-93, and the clear correspondence in function between Charon and this angel, both termed *nocchiero*.

105. *qual*: "Whosoever."

106. *nuova legge*: Some law of this new place.

107. *amoroso canto*: Lyrics in the tradition of the Provençal and early Italian poets. On the music, see J.-B. Beck (1908).

108. *che mi solea quetar tutte mie voglie*: See *Conv.* II, xiii, 23-24:

> E queste due proprietadi sono ne la Musica, la quale è tutta relativa, sì come si vede ne le parole armonizzate e ne li canti, de' quali tanto più dolce armonia resulta, quanto più la relazione è bella: la quale in essa scienza massimamente è bella, perchè massimamente in essa s'intende. Ancora, la Musica trae a sè li spiriti umani, che quasi sono principalmente vapori del cuore, sì che quasi cessano da ogni operazione: sì è l'anima intera, quando l'ode, e la virtù di tutti quasi corre a lo spirito sensibile che riceve lo suono.

> And these two properties are found in music, which all consists in relations, as we perceive in harmonised words and in tunes; wherefrom the resulting harmony is the sweeter in proportion as the relation is more beauteous; which relation is the chiefest beauty in that science, because this is what it chiefly aims at. Moreover, music so draweth to itself the spirits of men (which are in principle as though vapours of the heart) that they well-nigh cease from all operation; so united is the soul when it hears it, and so does the virtue of all of them, as it were, run to the spirit of sense which receiveth the sound.

See also Thomas Aquinas, *Exp. Eth. Nicom.* X, lect. 7, nn. 2045-46:

> Videmus enim quod illi qui sunt amatores sonitus fistularum, non possunt attendere sermonibus qui eis dicuntur, quando audiunt aliquem fistulantem, ex eo quod magis gaudent in operatione fistulativae artis, quam in praesenti operatione, scilicet in auditione sermonum sibi dictorum. . . . Manifestum est enim quod delectabilior operatio excludit aliam, intantum, quod si sit magna differentia in excessu delectationis, homo totaliter omittit operari secundum operationem minus sibi

delectabilem. Et inde est, quod quando vehementer delectamur in aliquo quocumque, nihil aliud possumus operari.

For we see that flute-favorers simply cannot hear people talking to them when listening to flute-playing because they take more pleasure in the music of the flute than in their present activity, i.e., hearing talk intended for them. . . . For it is obvious that the more pleasant activity drives out the other, to the extent that if there is a great difference in the amount of pleasure, a person entirely neglects the activity less pleasurable to him. Consequently when we take vehement pleasure in something we are incapable of doing anything else.

It should be noted that Petrocchi prefers the reading "doglie" ("anguish," "disquietude") to the more commonly accepted "voglie," but his reasons (given in his vol. I, *Introduzione,* p. 191) are not convincing, and it is clear that the evidence of the MSS which he examines will allow "voglie" quite as well as "doglie."

109. *di ciò* = *con ciò.*

110. *persona*: Cf. *Inf.* V, 101.

112. *Amor che ne la mente mi ragiona*: In this way the initial verse of one of Dante's *canzoni—canzone* II, 1 (*Conv.* III)—becomes a verse of the *Comedy*. In the *Convivio* this *canzone*, like the other two there given, is interpreted allegorically as being in praise of Lady Philosophy. But such allegorical meaning is not to be conceived as belonging to the song here. This is simply a love song, set to such sweet music that it can quiet the longings of both the living and the dead.

114. *che la dolcezza ancor dentro mi suona*: Cf. *Par.* XXIII, 128-29.

115–17. *Lo mio maestro . . . mente*: See n. to vs. 108.

117. *come a nessun* = *come se a nessun. toccasse altro la mente*: "Altro" is the subject, "mente" the object of the verb.

119. *il veglio onesto*: Cato.

122. *Correte al monte*: See n. to vs. 60.   *lo scoglio*: Literally, "slough," the skin that the snake sheds in the spring; here metaphorically the "old man," or garment of sin, which must be put off in Purgatory. See H. de Lubac (1946, p. 378), who cites passages in Johannes Scotus, Gregory of Nyssa, and Origen, which refer to this "slough" as a "leprosy," a "slime," a "sordid vestment." In *De doct. Chris.* II, xvi, 24, Augustine speaks of the snake shedding its skin:

> Nam et de serpente . . . notum est . . . per cavernae angustia coarctatus, deposita veteri tunica vires novas accipere dicitur, quantum concinit ad imitandam ipsam serpentis astutiam, exuendumque ipsum veterem hominem, sicut Apostolus dicit, ut induamur novo (Ephes. IV, 22, 24; Colos. III, 9, 10).

> It is well known that a serpent . . . having forced itself through a small opening in disposing of its old skin is said to gain new vigor. How well this agrees with imitating the wisdom of the serpent and stripping off the "old man" that we may put on the new, as the Apostle expresses it [Eph. 4:22, 24; Col. 3:9, 10].

On this word, also see H. D. Austin (1932), pp. 136-37.

126. *l'usato orgoglio*: The characteristic strutting and pouting of the pigeon.

127. *ond' elli*: I.e., *di cui essi*.

128. *esca*: Torraca cites the early Italian Aesop (fable I): "Cavando lo Gallo in alcuna parte per potere trovare alcuna esca." ("The rooster was scratching around, trying to find some *esca* [food].")

130. *masnada*: No pejorative sense attaches to the word here. Cf. *Inf.* XV, 41.   *fresca*: Cf. "nova gente" in vs. 58 and "l'arsura fresca" in *Inf.* XIV, 42.

131. *ver' = verso*.

CANTO III

1. *la subitana fuga*: See the description of this in *Purg.* II, 124-33.

3. *al monte ove ragion ne fruga*: Compare *Inf.* XXX, 70. *Frugare* can mean "to goad" (cf. *Purg.* XIV, 39; XV, 137), but here it is best understood in the sense of "probe."
   ragion: God's justice.

4. *la fida compagna*: See "compagna" for *compagnia* in *Inf.* XXVI, 101. See also *Inf.* XII, 100, where Virgil is called "la scorta fida."

6. *avria = avrebbe*.

7. *parea = pareva*.   *da sé stesso rimorso*: Virgil appears to be stung by his own conscience rather than by Cato's rebuke (which does not apply to him directly, since he is not a soul undergoing purgation); Virgil, who through Hell more than once urged Dante to hasten his steps and reprimanded him for tarrying, now recognizes that he himself is guilty of lingering and of allowing his charge to do so. For "rimorso" (*rimordere*) as a verb, see Thomas Aquinas, *Summa theol.* I, q. 79, a. 13, resp.: "Tertio modo applicatur secundum quod per conscientiam iudicamus quod aliquid quod est factum, sit bene factum, vel non bene factum; et secundum hoc con-

scientia dicitur excusare, vel accusare, seu remordere." ("In the third way, so far as by conscience we judge that something done is well done or ill done, and in this sense conscience is said to excuse, accuse, or torment.") Cf. vs. 9: "morso." Buti, commenting on vs. 9, notes: "La rimorsione del peccato è riprender sè medesmo del peccato fatto, e dolersi d'averlo fatto." ("Remorse for sin is self-reproach for the sin committed and regret for having committed it.")

10. *lasciar = lasciarono*.

10–11. *la fretta . . . dismaga*: One recalls the dignified souls of Limbo, "con occhi tardi e gravi" (*Inf.* IV, 112), and, by contrast, the undignified running of a man as old as Brunetto Latini (*Inf.* XV, 121-24) and the "fretta" of the three Florentines of that same circle. When those three souls came running, Virgil said to Dante that, were it not that fire was falling on the plain and he would be burned if he went to meet them, "i' dicerei / che meglio stesse a te che a lor la fretta" (*Inf.* XVI, 17-18). Dante could read in Aristotle (*Eth. Nicom.* IV, 3, 1125ᵃ) that "motus gravis magnanimi videtur esse, et vox gravis, et locutio stabilis." ("The movements of the magnanimous man seem deliberate, his voice solemn and his speech measured.") For the Latin translation of this passage from Aristotle's *Nicomachean Ethics* that Dante probably knew, see Thomas Aquinas, *Opera omnia*, vol. XXI, p. 136 or R. M. Spiazzi, 1964, p. 212. Benvenuto, in his gloss on vs. 7, comments: "Festinantia cursus . . . disconvenit viro gravi." ("A hasty step . . . is unbefitting to a dignified man.")

11. *dismaga*: The verb *dismagare* (OFr *esmaier*) means "to reduce," "to deprive of." In a different context it can have the meaning of "turn aside," "distract," or "dismay," its English cognate (cf. *Inf.* XXV, 146).

12. *la mente mia, che prima era ristretta*: Dante's mind has recently been restricted to one thought only, Cato's rebuke and the ensuing flight. For the same expression, see *Purg.* XVII, 22.

14. *e diedi 'l viso mio incontr' al poggio*: Compare the corresponding "diede le spalle" in *Inf*. XXXI, 117.

15. *che 'nverso 'l ciel più alto si dislaga*: *Dislagare* ("to unlake") is a verb coined by Dante; see E. G. Parodi (1957), pp. 215, 266. Porena notes that the old Italian *lago*, like the Latin *lacus*, could be used to signify any body of water. Otherwise, here it might be more exact to say "si disoceana." The reason for the great height of the mountain will become clear when the reader learns what lies at its summit. Meanwhile, it will be recalled that this, to Ulysses, was a mountain "alta tanto / quanto veduta non avea alcuna" (*Inf*. XXVI, 134-35).

16. *Lo sol, che dietro fiammeggiava roggio*: Having turned to the mountain Virgil and Dante are now facing west. Accordingly the sun, still low enough to be ruddy but high enough now to cast a shadow, shines on their backs.

17-18. *rotto m'era dinanzi . . . l'appoggio*: It is possible to understand "figura" here in the sense of "body," a common meaning of the term, and "ch'avea" as "chè aveva" (in support of which see M. Barbi, 1934b, pp. 277-78), i.e., "the sun was broken before my person, for it had the stoppage of its rays in me." But this seems awkward, because it would be redundant or too obvious. If "dinanzi" is construed as an adverb, however, and "a la figura . . . l'appoggio" as descriptive of the shape of the shadow cast before Dante, the statement becomes less obvious and more meaningful.

19. *Io mi volsi dallato con paura*: Through sunless Hell and up to this moment in Purgatory, Dante has had no occasion to observe that spirits do not cast a shadow.

22. *'l mio conforto*: Virgil, Dante's "fida compagna" (vs. 4).   *Perché pur diffidi?* "Pur," in the meaning "still," "yet" ("Why do you continue to mistrust?"), perhaps alludes to such moments in the journey as that described in *Inf*. VIII, 94-96.

23. *tutto rivolto*: Cf. *Inf*. XXIX, 100: "Lo buon maestro

a me tutto s'accolse." Virgil turns to Dante with great concern.

25–26. *Vespero è già colà . . . ombra*: In Dante's geography, Italy is halfway between Jerusalem and Gibraltar and is thus three hours, or 45°, west of Jerusalem, and its time is three hours earlier than that of Jerusalem. By now it is well after sunset in Jerusalem, and in Italy it is some time between 3:00 and 6:00 P.M.

27. *Napoli l'ha, e da Brandizio è tolto*: Virgil died at Brundusium (or Brundisium), modern Brindisi, a town on the Adriatic, in Apulia, on his return from Greece, September 21, 19 B.C. The reference here is to the transference of his body from Brindisi to Naples by order of Augustus, and perhaps to the epitaph (written probably by one of his friends) quoted by Suetonius (*Vita Virgili* XXXVI): "Mantua me genuit, Calabri rapuere, tenet nunc Parthenope; cecini pascua rura duces." ("Mantua gave me the light, Calabria slew me; Parthenope now holds me. I have sung shepherds, the countryside, and wars.") See *Purg.* VII, 6. On the form *Brandizio*, E. G. Parodi (1957, p. 367) observes that it is a French form, *Brandis*, slightly Latinized with this final *-zio*, and he points to the form in Villani and others.

28. *Ora, se*: A more normal position for "ora" would probably be after the "se" in this case, as the verse seems to imply "now that I am a spirit."   *nulla s'aombra*: "Nothing casts a shadow."

28–30. *Ora, se innanzi . . . ingombra*: See *Conv.* II, vi, 9, where Dante writes:

> Dico anche che questo spirito viene per li raggi de la stella: per che sapere si vuole che li raggi di ciascuno cielo sono la via per la quale discende la loro vertude in queste cose di qua giù. E però che li raggi non sono altro che uno lume che viene dal principio de la luce per l'aere infino a la cosa illuminata, e luce non sia se non ne la parte de la stella, però che l'altro cielo è diafano, cioè transparente, non dico che vegna questo spirito,

cioè questo pensiero, dal loro cielo in tutto, ma da la loro stella.

I say then that this spirit comes upon the "rays of the star," because you are to know that the rays of each heaven are the path whereby their virtue descends upon things that are here below. And inasmuch as rays are no other than the shining which cometh from the source of the light through the air even to the thing enlightened, and the light is only in that part where the star is, because the rest of the heaven is diaphanous (that is transparent), I say not that this "spirit," to wit this thought, cometh from their heaven in its totality but from their star.

Thus, the "cieli" here referred to are the diaphanous or transparent spheres, which do not intercept the light of the sun or of any "other" planet or star. The *ombra* or shade, the "vanità che par persona" (*Inf.* VI, 36), the mere semblance of a body which souls have and will have until the resurrection of the flesh, is thus said to be diaphanous. But the reader will not forget that whenever it suits the poet to have it otherwise, as so often in Hell, he proceeds to have it so.

31. *A sofferir tormenti, caldi e geli*: Cf. *Inf.* III, 87: "ne le tenebre etterne, in caldo e 'n gelo." What is said here applies to souls in Hell and Purgatory.

32. *la Virtù*: The power of God.

33. *come fa, non vuol ch'a noi si sveli*: To be sure, some of this mystery is explained later and "naturally," in *Purg.* XXV. Up to now, the "how" of the matter has not been questioned; here the question is brought in simply to stress the inscrutability of God's ways. See *Purg.* VIII, 67-69.

34. *nostra ragione*: Our human reason ("noi," in the preceding verse, began the generalization regarding mankind and the limits of our knowledge).

35. *possa trascorrer la infinita via*: "Via" (the "come fa" of vs. 33) echoes the scriptural "viae" of such verses as Isa.

55:8-9: "Non enim cogitationes meae cogitationes vestrae, neque viae vestrae viae meae, dicit Dominus. Quia sicut exaltantur caeli a terra, sic exaltatae sunt viae meae a viis vestris." ("For my thoughts are not your thoughts: nor your ways my ways, saith the Lord. For as the heavens are exalted above the earth, so are my ways exalted above your ways.") Also see Rom. 11:33: "O altitudo divitiarum sapientiae et scientiae Dei! Quam incomprehensibilia sunt iudicia eius, et investigabiles viae eius!" ("Oh, the depth of the riches of the wisdom and of the knowledge of God! How incomprehensible are his judgments and how unsearchable his ways!")

36. *che tiene una sustanza in tre persone*: "Che," of which "via" is the antecedent, is the object of the verb "tiene": *tener una via* means "to pursue a course." Thus "trascorrer" of the preceding verse comes, in such a context, to mean "to trace," "to go back over," proceeding from effect to God's cause and *modus operandi*, hence, "to understand." In referring to the Godhead as the Trinity, Virgil brings in another inscrutable mystery. See Thomas Aquinas, *Summa theol.* I, q. 32, a. 1, resp.:

> Impossibile est per rationem naturalem ad cognitionem Trinitatis divinarum personarum pervenire. Ostensum est enim supra, qu. 12, art. 4, et 12, quod homo per rationem naturalem in cognitionem Dei pervenire non potest nisi ex creaturis. Creaturae autem ducunt in Dei cognitionem sicut effectus in causam.

> It is impossible to attain to the knowledge of the Trinity by natural reason. For, as above explained (q. 12, aa. 4, 12), man cannot obtain knowledge of God by natural reason except from creatures. Now creatures lead us to the knowledge of God, as effects do to their cause.

And Virgil speaks of the limits of natural reason, the only light that was available to him and other pagans in this life. This line of thought connects with the "quia" of the following verse.

37. *State contenti, umana gente, al quia*: Of God, and here of God's ways, Johannes Scotus (*De div. nat.* V, 26 [col.

47

919C]) observes that we cannot know "quid est, sed quia so-
lummodo est" (". . . what He is but only the fact that He
is"). The *quia est*, as applied to God's effects in this world,
which He created and which He perpetually governs, means
the fact that such things exist. Similarly, the *demonstratio
quia*, in scholastic reasoning, begins with the effect and seeks
to arrive at the cause. See Thomas Aquinas, *Summa theol.*
I, q. 2, a. 2, resp.:

> Duplex est demonstratio. Una quae est per causam, et
> dicitur *propter quid*, et haec est per priora simpliciter;
> *alia* est per effectum, et dicitur demonstratio *quia*, et
> haec est per ea quae sunt priora quoad nos. Cum enim
> effectus aliquis nobis est manifestior quam sua causa,
> per effectum procedimus ad cognitionem causae.

> Demonstration can be made in two ways: One is
> through the cause, and is called *a priori*, and this is to
> argue from what is prior absolutely. The other is
> through the effect, and is called a demonstration *a pos-
> teriori*; this is to argue from what is prior relatively only
> to us. When an effect is better known to us than its
> cause, from the effect we proceed to the knowledge of
> the cause.

Also see Aquinas, *Summa contra Gentiles* I, 3: "Ducitur
tamen ex sensibilibus intellectus noster in divinam cogni-
tionem, ut cognoscat de Deo *quia est*, et alia huiusmodi, quae
oportet attribui primo principio." ("Yet, beginning with sen-
sible things, our intellect is led to the point of knowing about
God that He exists, and other such characteristics that must
be attributed to the First Principle.")

As for Virgil's injunction, see the similar admonition to
mankind in Dante's *Questio de aqua et terra* LXXVII-
LXXVIII:

> Desinant ergo, desinant homines querere que supra eos
> sunt, et querant usque quo possunt, ut trahant se ad
> inmortalia et divina pro posse, ac maiora se relinquant.
> Audiant amicum Iob dicentem: "Nunquid vestigia Dei
> comprehendes, et Omnipotentem usque ad perfectionem
> reperies?" Audiant Psalmistam dicentem: "Mirabilis

facta est scientia tua ex me: confortata est, et non
potero ad eam." Audiant Ysaiam dicentem: "Quam dis-
tant celi a terra, tantum distant vie mee a viis vestris";
loquebatur equidem in persona Dei ad hominem. Audi-
ant vocem Apostoli ad Romanos: "O altitudo divitia-
rum scientie et sapientie Dei, quam incomprehensibilia
iudicia eius et investigabiles vie eius!" Et denique audi-
ant propriam Creatoris vocem dicentis: "Quo ego vado,
vos non potestis venire." Et hec sufficiant ad inquisi-
tionem intente veritatis.

Let men desist therefore, let them desist, from searching
out things that are above them, and let them seek up to
such point as they may, that they may draw themselves
to immortal and divine things to their utmost power, and
may abandon things too great for them. Let them listen
to the friend of Job, when he says: "Wilt thou under-
stand the footprints of God, and search out the Al-
mighty to perfection?" Let them listen to the Psalmist,
when he says: "Thy knowledge is wonderful, and has
comforted me, and I may not attain to it." Let them lis-
ten to Isaiah, when he says: "As far as the heavens are
above the earth, so far are my ways above your ways";
for he was speaking in the person of God to man. Let
them hearken to the voice of the apostle *Ad Romanos*:
"Oh the height of the wealth, of the knowledge, and
wisdom of God! how incomprehensible are his judg-
ments and his ways are past finding out." And finally let
them hearken to the proper voice of the Creator, when
he says: "Whither I go, ye cannot come." And let this
suffice for the inquiry into the truth we set before us.

39–44. *mestier non era parturir Maria . . . altri*: Virgil
speaks of pagans such as Aristotle, Plato, and others, includ-
ing himself, who desired to know God, who is the Truth, fol-
lowing the natural desire for such knowledge that is innate
in us. Their desire was in vain, however, because they lived
and died before the Advent of Christ ("parturir Maria"). If
they could have known Christ as He was revealed in His Ad-
vent and could have believed in Him, they would have been

taken from Limbo by Christ in the harrowing of Hell and would now be among the elect who have their every desire quieted in the beatific vision. Instead they are confined to Limbo, where their only torment is to live in desire (*Inf.* IV, 41-42: "e sol di tanto offesi / che sanza speme vivemo in disio"). As was noted in the n. to *Inf.* IV, 69, their condition in Limbo matches the condition in which they lived. Some commentators consider Adam and the sin of our first parents to be part of Virgil's thought here, but this seems inappropriate. Virgil speaks primarily in terms of "knowing," and the satisfaction of our natural desire to know, of epiphany or revelation, not of sin and atonement.

40. *vedeste*: "You [human kind] saw."

41. *sarebbe*: This tense suggests that their desire would now be stilled, i.e., that they would be among the elect now. Of their desire it is not said that it would have been quieted through knowledge of Christ *while they still lived*: this would require the tense "sarebbe stato."

44-45. *e di molt' altri . . . turbato*: Clearly Virgil recognizes that he himself is among these "many others" and so bows his head in sad meditation on his own fate as a virtuous pagan who desired, but in vain, to see the Truth.

46. *Noi divenimmo*: "We arrived." Cf. *Inf.* XIV, 76.   *a piè del monte*: Virgil and Dante have thus crossed the plain, or "campagna," as it has been termed in vs. 2. Here cliffs rise abruptly, forming what is then called a "wall" (vs. 99).

48. *sarien = sarebbero*.

49. *Lerice*: Lerici, a seaport in Liguria on the eastern shore of the Gulf of La Spezia, was in Dante's day a fortified town (*castello*).   *Turbìa*: La Turbie, a village near the coast in the present department of Alpes-Maritimes in southeastern France, above Monaco. The country indicated as lying between the two places (which in Dante's day, before the construction of roads along the coast, was almost impassable) corresponds almost exactly to the coastline of the prov-

ince of Liguria, Lerici being at the eastern extremity, and La
Turbie just beyond the western boundary. All along this
coast the mountains descend very steeply to the sea. Ben-
venuto, who apparently speaks from personal experience, tes-
tifies to the aptness of Dante's comparison: "Vere qui fecit
ista itinera alpestria riperiae Januae potest imaginari, quod
poeta non poterat melius exprimere asperitatem locorum per
quae habebant modo ire." ("Anyone who has ever made the
journey through the Alps and along the Genoese coast can
well imagine that the poet could not have better expressed the
harshness of the terrain through which they now had to
travel.")

51. *verso di*: Cf. "verso," *Inf.* XXXIV, 59.   *quella*:
The "roccia" of vs. 47.

52. *cala*: Cf. *giacere* in vs. 76 below and in *Inf.* XIX, 35;
XXIII, 31.

54. *sì che possa salir chi va sanz' ala*: Cf. *Inf.* XII, 96: "ché
non è spirto che per l'aera vada."

56. *essaminava del cammin la mente*: Virgil is questioning
himself respecting the way.   *del cammin*: Cf. the Latin
de itinere.

57. *e io mirava suso intorno al sasso*: While Virgil bows his
head, trying to think of a way, Dante looks up at the wall of
the cliff to see if he can discern one.

58. *da man sinistra*: The detail will take on significance
when it is made clear that the proper direction in which to go
round Mount Purgatory is to the right, or counterclockwise.
It will be recalled that in the descent through Hell Virgil and
Dante turned, almost without exception, to the left, or clock-
wise.

58–59. *una gente d'anime*: "Gente" suggests a grouping of
the souls because of something they have in common (as, in
fact, will now prove to be the case).

59. *movieno = movevano.   ver' = verso.*

60. *e non pareva*: That is, "non pareva che movessero i piedi." A moment later, as he draws nearer, Dante sees that these souls are moving toward him, but at this moment they do not seem to advance.

62. *ecco di qua*: The words imply a gesture toward the left. The souls are on Dante's left, and Virgil is on his right. *ne = ci.*

63. *nol = non lo.*

64. *con libero piglio*: With a reassured air. Cf. *Inf.* XXIV, 20-21: "con quel piglio / dolce"; also *Inf.* XXII, 75.

65. *ch'ei vegnon piano*: They are now near enough that this can be seen. Cf. vs. 60.

66. *ferma la spene*: "Make firm your hope," "be of good cheer." Cf. *Inf.* VIII, 106-7.

69. *quanto un buon gittator trarria con mano*: "As far as a good thrower could hurl a stone" (with his hand, not with a sling).

70-72. *quando si strinser tutti . . . stassi*: The souls, perceiving that Virgil and Dante are coming toward them, are astounded, since the two now move in the wrong direction on Mount Purgatory as they go toward these souls, who are of course proceeding in the right direction. All movement here ought to be counterclockwise.

72. *com' a guardar, chi va dubbiando, stassi*: The syntax of this verse has given rise to considerable discussion. See F. D'Ovidio (1920, pp. 93-100), who lists the several possible meanings. The souls halt abruptly and huddle close together, but it is their halting in order to *look* that is the basis for the simile or pseudo-simile expressed by the verse. Most probably "va dubbiando" is simply the familiar progressive tense, while "stassi" (*si sta*) is an instance of the "distancing" or "fixing" reflexive (the so-called pleonastic reflexive, on which see the n. to *Inf.* VII, 94, and *passim*), matching the "stetter fermi" of the preceding verse. As D'Ovidio (1920, p. 100)

paraphrases it, "stetter fermi, come fa chi colto da un dubbio si sofferma a guardare." ("They stood still, just the way someone who is struck by a doubt will stop and gaze.")

73. *O ben finiti, o già spiriti eletti*: Virgil's first words to these souls are, in any case, a clear instance of *captatio benevolentiae*; but as words spoken by him, they take on a special poignancy, he having but now bowed his head in sad meditation on the fact that he would never be numbered among such "elect" souls (vss. 44-45).

74. *per quella pace*: The great contrast with Hell continues most strikingly. In Hell adjuration of this sort appealed to fame in the world and the renewal or perpetuation of it there. Here the appeal is to peace, the peace that awaits these souls in Heaven one day, since they are "già spiriti eletti." We now look forward and heavenward, not back to fame on earth.

75. *per voi = da voi*. Cf. *Inf.* I, 126: "per me si vegna."

76. *ditene = diteci.*   *dove la montagna giace*: See vs. 52.

78. *ché perder tempo a chi più sa più spiace*: Porena comments that this is a construction with two superlatives, in the Latin form: *sapientissimo cuique, maxime displicet*, "the more one knows, the more one regrets." Virgil's words seem to hark back to his recent sense of shame at having tarried over Casella's song. He knows more now.

79-87. *Come le pecorelle . . . onesta*: The suffix *-elle* of "pecorelle," along with the *-ette* of "timidette" (vs. 81), brings in the modification of a particular sentiment that prevails throughout this famous simile. The sheep are here seen not as stupid beasts, but as gentle and simple creatures, trusting yet timid, moving as a group, in concord and humility. The keynote of the whole is precisely a movement by faith, rather than by knowledge; whence the stress, by repetition, upon the *not knowing why* (vss. 84, 93). The reader will come to see that, in the broader pattern of meaning here, the figure of the Exodus is given extension by just such a group

53

movement as this, and that the image of a flock of sheep is not unrelated to a deeper symbolism in this regard. See vss. 51-53 of Ps. 77[78], which commemorates the Exodus:

> Et percussit omne primogenitum in terra Aegypti, primitias omnis laboris eorum in tabernaculis Cham. Et abstulit sicut oves populum suum, et perduxit eos tamquam gregem in deserto; et deduxit eos in spe et non timuerunt, et inimicos eorum operuit mare.

> He smote every first-born in Egypt, the first fruits of manhood in the tents of Ham; but his people he led forth like sheep and guided them like a herd in the desert. He led them on secure and unafraid, while he covered their enemies with the sea.

The whole notion of a "mandra" or *gregge*, in such a context, is reminiscent of the scriptural flock of the Lord, the "grex Domini" ("flock of the Lord") of Ier. 13:17, of the quest for the promised land, for the kingdom of God, for His justice. See Luc. 12:31-32: "Verumtamen quaerite primum regnum Dei et iustitiam eius, et haec omnia adiicientur vobis. Nolite timere, pusillus grex, quia complacuit Patri vestro dare vobis regnum." ("But seek the kingdom of God and His justice, and all these things shall be given you besides. Do not be afraid, little flock, for it has pleased your Father to give you the kingdom.") Also see Ioan. 10:1-18; Actus 20:28.

In *Conv.* I, xi, 10, Dante writes of a scene he witnessed, in which sheep were seen to follow one another; but except for this familiar point, the passage has little to do with the purpose of these verses.

84. *lo 'mperché = lo imperché (il perché)*.

85. *muovere a venir = muovere per avanzarsi*.

86. *fortunata*: Cf. *Purg.* II, 74: "anime fortunate." *allotta = allora*. Cf. *Inf.* V, 53 and "otta" in *Inf.* XXI, 112.

88. *color dinanzi*: "Those in front," i.e., "la testa" of vs. 85.

88-89. *vider rotta . . . canto*: Dante and his guide first faced the mountain in their climb, then turned to the left to go toward this band of souls; hence Dante now has the sun on his left side and the wall of the mountain ("la grotta"), against which his shadow falls, on his right.

90. *grotta*: Cf. *Purg.* I, 48.

91. *restaro = restarono. e trasser sé in dietro alquanto*: The souls halt more in amazement than in fear. Cf. *Purg.* II, 69.

92. *venieno = venivano*.

93. *non sappiendo 'l perché*: Again the keynote of the whole simile, which extends as far as this verse. *fenno = fecero*.

94. *vi confesso*: "I declare to you." Cf. *Inf.* XXIV, 106.

96. *fesso*: Literally, "cloven," "divided."

98. *non sanza virtù che da ciel vegna*: Cf. *Purg.* I, 68.

101. *intrate innanzi*: "Go on ahead of us."

102. *insegna = segno*.

104. *così andando*: Virgil and Dante have already turned back and now are proceeding ahead of the band of souls, as they were bidden. Thus the soul who now speaks does not ask Dante to stop, but only requests that he turn round to look at him as he continues on his way.

105. *di là*: In the world of the living. Following this pointer, one notes the "distancing" past absolute form "vedesti."
   unque: From the Latin *unquam*. It has been remarked that Dante was only a few months old when Manfred died and so could scarcely be expected to recognize him, but Manfred cannot see Dante's face at this moment and so has no impression of his probable age.

106. *Io mi volsi*: Thus Dante does look back as requested, without halting. *guardail = lo guardai. fiso = fisamente*.

107. *biondo era e bello e di gentile aspetto*: See n. to vs. 112.

108. *ma l'un de' cigli un colpo avea diviso*: Nothing in the account given in *Purg*. XXV of the aerial body assumed by the soul in the afterlife will explain how it is that the diaphanous "body" of Manfred should bear wounds at all, his two "punte mortali," as they are called in vs. 119. But it may be noted that Augustine, for one, speaks of the desire that we the faithful have to see, in the heavenly kingdom, the marks of the wounds that the blessed martyrs received in the name of Christ, and he adds that possibly we shall see those wounds. See *De civ. Dei* XXII, xix, 3: "Non enim deformitas in eis, sed dignitas erit, et quaedam, quamvis in corpore, non corporis, sed virtutis pulchritudo fulgebit." ("For, in the martyrs, such wounds will not be a deformity; they will have a dignity and loveliness all their own; and, though this radiance will be spiritual and not physical, it will, in some way, beam from their bodies.") Thus the possibility of such wounds remaining in the "body" after death is somehow allowed. Manfred is no martyr—indeed, he died in contumacy of Holy Church. And yet, in spite of excommunication by the Church ("their malediction"), he is already a *spirito eletto*. But is there not something of the martyr about Manfred, with the curious twist to it that he has somehow been persecuted by "them," by the Church?

109. *disdetto*: "Denied." See Dante, *Conv*. IV, viii, 12.

111. *una piaga*: The other of the two mortal wounds referred to in vs. 119, which he points to, as if it might somehow serve to identify him.

112. *sorridendo*: Again (see *Purg*. II, 83), in greatest contrast with the attitude of souls in Hell, a soul smiles in this new realm; here it is to reassure Dante that the wound Manfred points to is no longer of any consequence, but merely bears witness to his violent death and "martyrdom" (see n. to vs. 108).

Manfredi: Manfred, natural son of the Emperor Frederick II by Bianca, daughter of Count Bonifazio Lancia, was born in Sicily *ca*. 1232. He was grandson of the Emperor Henry VI and of Constance of Sicily. At his father's death (1250) he was appointed regent of the so-called Regno (see n. to vs. 131) during the absence of his half-brother Conrad IV. On the death of Conrad in 1254, Conrad's son, Conradin, the rightful successor to the throne of Sicily, was only a young child; Manfred, at the invitation of the Sicilian barons, once more assumed the regency.

Having made himself nominal master of the kingdom on behalf of Conradin, on a rumor of the death of the latter in 1258 he was entreated to assume the crown, which he did at Palermo on August 10 in that year amid universal rejoicing. But the pope could not tolerate a Ghibelline and infidel on the throne; Manfred was excommunicated in 1258 by Alexander IV, and again by Urban IV, by whom the forfeited crown was offered to Louis IX of France and then, on his refusal, to his brother, Charles of Anjou. Urban's offer having been confirmed by his successor, Clement IV, Charles advanced into Italy with a large force in 1265 and entered Rome, where, after being elected senator in opposition to Manfred, he was crowned king on January 6, 1266, and immediately set out to take possession of his kingdom.

Urban IV having proclaimed a crusade against Manfred, Charles persuaded his followers that since they fought for the Catholic faith against an excommunicated heretic and a Saracen, they would receive the reward due to those engaged in a holy war. On February 26, 1266, the two armies met on the plain of Grandella near Benevento. Manfred's Germans and Saracens fought with desperate valor, but were outnumbered by the French. Manfred accordingly ordered the Apulian barons to charge, but they, through either treachery or cowardice, instead of obeying, turned and fled from the field. With a handful of troops who still remained faithful, Manfred resolved to die rather than seek safety in flight, and plunging into the thickest of the fight, he fell dead in the midst of the enemy. To the request of some of his followers that Manfred's body should receive honorable burial, Charles replied that he would willingly have granted it, had Manfred not been excommunicated (Villani, VII, 9). For this reason he would not have him laid in consecrated ground, but caused him to be buried at the foot of a bridge over the Calore, near Benevento. Upon his grave was made a great pile of stones, each one of the army throwing one upon it as he passed. Subsequently, it is said by command of Clement IV, the archbishop of Cosenza caused the body to be disinterred from its resting place in Church territory and had it cast unburied upon the banks of the river Verde, outside the limits of the kingdom (see n. to vs. 131).

Dante's description of Manfred's personal appearance is borne out by the old chroniclers. The following description of Manfred by Saba Malaspina is quoted in Gmelin: "Homo flavus, amoena facie, aspectu placibilis, in maxillis rubeus, per totum niveus, statura mediocris." ("He was blond, fair of face, placid of countenance with reddish cheeks, in general, fair and of medium height.")

Like his father, whom Dante places among the heretics in Hell (*Inf.* X, 119), Manfred was accused of being an Epicurean and unbeliever, doubtless on account of his dealings with the Saracens and his fondness for eastern ways. The account of him given by Villani (VI, 46) expresses the opinion of his character current in Dante's time:

> Il detto re Manfredi fu nato per madre d'una bella donna de' marchesi Lancia di Lombardia, con cui lo 'mperadore ebbe affare, e fu bello del corpo, e come il padre, e più, dissoluto in ogni lussuria: sonatore e cantatore era, volentieri si vedea intorno giocolari e uomini di corte, e belle concubine, e sempre vestìo di drappi verdi; molto fu largo e cortese e di buon aire, sicchè egli era molto amato e grazioso; ma tutta sua vita fu epicuria, non curando quasi Iddio nè santi, se non a diletto del corpo. Nimico fu di santa Chiesa, e de' cherici e de' religiosi, occupando le chiese come il suo padre, e più ricco signore fu, sì del tesoro che gli rimase dello 'mperadore e del re Currado suo fratello, e per lo suo regno ch'era largo e fruttuoso, e egli, mentre che vivette, con tutte le guerre ch'ebbe colla Chiesa, il tenne in buono stato, sicchè 'l montò molto di ricchezze e in podere per mare e per terra.

This King Manfred was the son of a beautiful lady, of

the [family of the] Marquises Lancia of Lombardy, with
whom the emperor had an affair. He was a handsome
man, but just as dissolute as his father, or even more.
He played music and sang, and liked to see jugglers,
courtiers, and beautiful concubines around him. Man-
fred always dressed in green. He was generous, courte-
ous, and debonair, so that he was much loved and en-
joyed great favor. But his whole life was Epicurean; he
cared neither for God nor for the saints, but only for the
delights of the flesh. He was an enemy of the Holy
Church, of priests, and of monks. Like his father, he oc-
cupied the churches; and he became even richer, for he
had inherited the treasure of the emperor and of his
brother, King Conrad. Moreover he had a large and
prosperous kingdom, which, despite the wars with the
Church, he kept in good state as long as he lived, in-
creasing its riches and power on land and on sea.

The confession Dante puts into Manfred's mouth (vs. 121)
is fully justified by the above account; but still graver charges
were brought against him: that he murdered his father, his
brother Conrad, and two of his nephews, and attempted to
murder his nephew Conradin. These crimes, which the hatred
of his enemies imputed to him, are gravely recorded by his
contemporary the Guelph Brunetto Latini (*Tresor* I, xcvii,
1-9).

113. *nepote di Costanza imperadrice*: See n. to vs. 112. On
the manner in which Manfred chooses to identify himself by
his paternal grandmother, Lana comments: "Perchè fu fi-
gliuolo naturale non volle tòrre il sopranome del padre, ma
fassi nipote di sua ava." ("Because he was a natural son, he
did not want to take his father's name. Instead, he identifies
himself by way of his grandmother.") Similarly, in the *Con-
vivio* (IV, xxv, 10) Dante writes of Polynices, son of
Oedipus:

Quando Polinice fu domandato da Adrasto rege del suo
essere, ch'elli dubitò prima di dicere, per vergogna del
fallo che contra lo padre fatto avea, e ancora per li falli
d'Edippo suo padre, chè paiono rimanere in vergogna

59

del figlio; e non nominò suo padre, ma li antichi suoi e la terra e la madre.

When Polynices was questioned by King Adrastus of his origin, he hesitated before speaking, for shame of the fault he had committed against his father, and further for the faults of Œdipus his father, which seemed to leave their trace in the shame of the son. And he did not mention his father, but his ancestors and his land and his mother.

Costanza: Constance (1154-98), daughter of Roger II, king of Naples and Sicily, and wife of Henry VI, by whom she became the mother of Frederick II. She is called "la gran Costanza" in *Par.* III, 118. Manfred named his daughter, whom he mentions in vss. 115 and 143, after her.

114. *quando tu riedi*: "When you return" to the world of the living.

115. *vadi = vada.   mia bella figlia*: Constance (see vs. 143), daughter of Manfred and Beatrice of Savoy. In 1262 she married Pedro III of Aragon, by whom she became the mother of Alfonso (king of Aragon, 1285-91), James (king of Sicily, 1285-95; king of Aragon, 1291-1327), and Frederick (king of Sicily, 1296-1337). It was through his marriage with Constance that Pedro III claimed the crown of Sicily, which he assumed in 1282 after the Sicilian Vespers. Constance died at Barcelona in 1302, having outlived both her husband and her eldest son.

115–16. *genitrice de l'onor di Cicilia e d'Aragona*: The "honor" of Sicily (for the form *Cicilia*, see *Inf.* XII, 108) is Frederick, the third son of Constance and Pedro (see n. to vs. 115). The "honor" of Aragon could be either Alfonso, their eldest son, or James, their second son, who, when Alfonso died in 1291, succeeded him in Aragon, leaving the government of Sicily in the hands of his younger brother, Frederick, who became king of Sicily in 1296. In *Purg.* VII, 119-20 Dante expresses a poor opinion of the worth of both Frederick and James, but (if we assume that James rather than Alfonso is here intended) it should be remembered that

it is their grandfather who speaks of them here as "honors."
For the view advanced by Tobler that "onor" may mean sim-
ply *signoria* or, in this case, "sovereigns," see E. G. Parodi
(1901), p. 52.

117. *dichi = dica.*   *'l vero*: That I was saved by repent-
ing in the last moment, and that I am in Purgatory.
   s'altro si dice: That I am among the damned for my
"horrible sins."

119–20. *mi rendei . . . perdona*: I turned to God (cf. *Inf.*
XXVII, 83, and vs. 123 of the present canto: "ciò che si
rivolge a lei"). See Thomas Aquinas, *Summa theol.* III,
q. 85, a. 3, resp.: "unde poenitens recurrit ad Deum"
("wherefore the penitent has recourse to God"). On Man-
fred's reported conversion before his death, see F. Novati
(1898), pp. 3-13.

120. *piangendo*: With true contrition of the heart (*contritio
cordis*) for his horrible sins. See *Purg.* XXX, 145.

121. *Orribil furon li peccati miei*: See n. to vs. 112.

122. *ma la bontà infinita ha sì gran braccia*: The metaphor
represents a variation of such expressions as "amplissimos
sinus caritatis." Citing a gloss by Augustine on Luc. 15:18,
Bonaventura in his *Sermones de tempore (Dominica vige-
sima post Pentecosten* I, 1) writes:

   Unde Augustinus super illud Lucae decimo quinto:
   *Surgam et ibo ad patrem meum et dicam ei: Pater, pec-
   cavi in caelum et coram te* etc.: "Quaecumque neces-
   sitas cogat peccatorem ad poenitentiam, non peccati
   quantitas nec vitae enormitas nec hominis extremitas
   excludit a venia, si perfecta fuerit immutatio voluntatis;
   sed in amplissimos sinus caritatis misericordia filios suos
   prodigos suscipit revertentes."

   Thus Augustine on Luke 15 ("I shall arise and go to my
   father and I shall say to him: Father, I have sinned
   against heaven and against thee"): "Whatever need
   drives a sinner to penitence, neither the number of his
   sins nor the scandal of his life nor the depth to which he

has fallen will exclude him from forgiveness if only there be a complete change of his will; but God receives into the ample bosom of His love His prodigal sons who turn back to Him."

124. *Cosenza*: Town in northern Calabria about twelve miles inland from the Tyrrhenian Sea. The bishop ("pastor") in question was probably not Bartolomeo Pignatelli, archbishop of Cosenza, as many commentators affirm, but Tommaso d'Agni, his successor.

126. *avesse in Dio ben letta questa faccia*: The literal meaning of the word *faccia* is "face," and this whole phrase lends itself to differing interpretations, of which the two most common are: (1) "Faccia" here means the face of a page in a book, and therefore the reference is to a page of God's book, the Holy Scriptures, or to all the many pages (taken figuratively as one page) of the Bible where God's mercy is named; (2) "Faccia" is God's "face" in the sense that God's two "faces" would be His justice and His mercy (see *Inf.* III, 50). But these are, of course, referred to on many pages of His book, and we know them through His book, the Bible. Hence the two meanings are in essence one, and the possibility of God's mercy in Manfred's case is what the pastor of Cosenza failed to consider.

127. *sarieno = sarebbero.*

128. *in co = in capo*. Cf. *Inf.* XX, 76; XXI, 64.   *del ponte*: The bridge over the river Calore, which flows by Benevento.

129. *sotto la guardia de la grave mora*: On the burial of Manfred, see n. to vs. 112 and F. Maggini (1927); and, on the term *mora*, see M. Barbi (1921a), where Barbi cites in a document of 1255 in Latin the phrase "una mora lapidum." Porena reminds us of the term *morena* (English "moraine"), the accumulation of rocky debris formed by a glacier.

130. *Or le bagna la pioggia e move il vento*: Here Dante clearly echoes the *Aeneid* (VI, 362), the verse in which Vir-

gil has Palinurus speak of his own unburied remains: "Nunc me fluctus habet versantque in litore venti." ("Now the wave holds me, and the winds toss me on the beach.")

131. *di fuor dal regno*: *Regno* was the name often used to indicate the kingdom of Naples (which included the whole of the southern extremity of Italy extending as far north as the Tronto on the Adriatic and, roughly, the Garigliano on the Mediterranean), as well as the island of Sicily. In 1282, the year of the Sicilian Vespers, the insurrection of the Sicilians against the house of Anjou, then in possession of the kingdom of Naples and Sicily, had led to the separation of the island of Sicily and the kingdom of Naples.

It was the custom to exhume the bodies of those who had been excommunicated and to cast them outside a city when it fell into the hands of papal forces. Torraca comments:

> Quando Forlì, nel 1283 . . . aprì le porte all'esercito pontificio, un cardinale mandato dal papa "fece cavare da' sepolcri ed estrarre i morti nella detta guerra, e le loro ossa portare fuori della città, alle fosse, perchè erano stati scomunicati e interdetti dal papa, a cagione della detta guerra e della loro disubbidienza." *Ann. maggiori di Parma.* Cfr. *Conti morali* IV: "La terra fue iscomunicata: onde . . . quando moriva alcuno, era portato fuore de la terra. . . . Quando la terra fue ricomunicata, tutti i parenti de' morti recarono i loro a le chiese."

> In 1283, when Forlì . . . opened its gates to the papal army [see *Inf.* XXVII, 43], a cardinal sent by the pope "had all those who had died in this war removed from their graves and had their bones taken to ditches outside the city; for they had been excommunicated and interdicted by the pope on account of that war and their disobedience." *Ann. maggiori di Parma.* Cf. *Conti morali* IV: "The city was excommunicated, and so . . . when someone died, he was taken outside the city. . . . When the excommunication was lifted from the city, all the dead people's relatives brought them back to the churches."

In the case of Manfred, in place of a city it is the whole realm from which his bones must be removed. *il Verde*: A name commonly applied to one of the principal rivers of southern Italy, known to the ancients as the Liris, now called the Liri from its source to its junction with the Rapido, and the Garigliano from there to its mouth.

132. *a lume spento*: It was the custom to bury the bodies of the excommunicated and of heretics with candles extinguished.

133-34. *Per lor maladizion . . . amore*: Excommunication is referred to as a *maledictio* by Bonaventura, *Comm. Sent. Petri Lombardi IV* XVIII, ii, a. 1, q. 2, contra 1: "Excommunicatio sive anathematizatio est maledictio" ("Excommunication or being anathematized is a curse") and by Thomas Aquinas, *Summa theol.* III, Suppl., q. 21, a. 2, obj. 1: "Excommunicatio maledictio quaedam est." ("Excommunication is a kind of curse.") See the following interesting passage in Bonaventura, *Comm. Sent. Petri Lombardi IV* XVIII, ii, a. 1, q. 1, ad 1, which applies to the doctrine in question:

> Dicendum, quod communio triplex est: quaedam *spiritualis omnino*, et haec est quantum ad dilectionem interiorem; quaedam *corporalis*, et haec est quantum ad exteriorem conversationem; quaedam *medio modo*, et haec est quantum ad Sacramentorum susceptionem, et praecipue quantum ad Sacramentum altaris. Dico ergo, quod a *prima* nullus potest nec debet excludi, quamdiu est viator, nec excommunicatio dicit privationem illius communionis.

> We must say that communion is threefold: one is entirely spiritual and this refers to interior love; another is corporeal, and this regards external converse; while still another is between these two, and this regards the reception of the sacraments, and especially the sacrament of the altar. I assert that no one ought or can be excluded from the first as long as he is in this life, nor does excommunication mean the privation of that communion.

Dante's shift to "lor" seems to carry a certain note of disdain, setting "ecclesiastics" off as a class.

134. *l'etterno amore*: Sanctifying grace and charity, without which no one is saved.

135. *mentre che la speranza ha fior del verde*: See n. to vss. 133-34 and Bonaventura's words "quamdiu est viator," i.e., as long as there is life and the possibility of repentance. Green is the color of hope, hence the phrase may in this way refer to hope itself, by its own color. Some would understand the expression to derive from the custom of dyeing the base of candles green, so that *il verde* is the part last to be burned, the last remnant. Compare the modern expression *essere al verde*, "to be broke."

136. *quale*: "Whosoever."   *in contumacia*: In willful disregard of ecclesiastical authority and censure, such as exclusion from communion.

137. *ancor ch'al fin si penta*: Even if the excommunication is unjust (which is not claimed in the case of Manfred), the excommunicated should obey; for, although the interdict will have no effect, still the sentence itself remains, and this obedience will redound to his merit. See Thomas Aquinas, *Summa theol.* III, Suppl., q. 21, a. 4, resp.:

> Excommunicatio potest dici iniusta dupliciter: uno modo ex parte excommunicantis; sicut cum ex odio, vel ex ira aliquis excommunicat et tunc excommunicatio nihilominus habet effectum suum, quamvis ille qui excommunicat peccet, quia iste iuste patitur, quamvis ille iniuste faciat. Alio modo ex parte ipsius excommunicationis, vel quia causa excommunicationis est indebita, vel quia fertur sententia, iuris ordine praetermisso: et tunc si sit talis error ex parte sententiae, qui sententiam nullam esse faciat, non habet effectum, quia non est excommunicatio; si autem talis error non annullet sententiam, habet effectum suum; et debet excommunicatus humiliter obedire (et erit ei ad meritum), et vel ad superiorem iudicem recurrere, vel petere ab excom-

municante absolutionem. Si autem contemneret, eo ipso mortaliter peccaret.

An excommunication may be unjust for two reasons. First, on the part of its author, as when anyone excommunicates through hatred or anger, and then, nevertheless, the excommunication takes effect, though its author sins, because the one who is excommunicated suffers justly, even if the author act wrongly in excommunicating him. Secondly, on the part of the excommunication, through there being no proper cause, or through the sentence being passed without the forms of law being observed. In this case, if the error, on the part of the sentence, be such as to render the sentence void, this has no effect, for there is no excommunication; but if the error does not annul the sentence, this takes effect, and the person excommunicated should humbly submit (which will be credited to him as a merit), and either seek absolution from the person who has excommunicated him, or appeal to a higher judge. If, however, he were to contemn the sentence, he would *ipso facto* sin mortally.

In the case of disobedience, then, there would be this penalty of exclusion—but the duration of such a penalty appears to be of Dante's own invention.

138–40. *star li convien . . . presunzion*: In conceiving this penalty for the contumacious, Dante seems to have been inspired by *Aen.* VI, 325-30, where Virgil tells of the unburied (Manfred is one such), who are rejected by Charon:

haec omnis, quam cernis, inops inhumataque turba est;
portitor ille Charon; hi, quos vehit unda, sepulti;
nec ripas datur horrendas et rauca fluenta
transportare prius quam sedibus ossa quierunt.
centum errant annos volitantque haec litora circum;
tum demum admissi stagna exoptata revisunt.

All this crowd thou seest is helpless and graveless; yonder warden is Charon; those whom the flood carries are the buried. Nor may he bear them o'er the dreadful

banks and hoarse-voiced waters ere their bones have
found a resting-place. A hundred years they roam and
flit about these shores; then only are they admitted and
revisit the longed-for pools.

138. *li = gli.   questa ripa*: The cliff, which has also
been called a "parete," or wall, in vs. 99.

139–40. *per ognun tempo . . . presunzion*: Why thirty-fold?
Dante does not appear to be following any established doc-
trine in conceiving such a period of time. In the case of Man-
fred, Torraca calculates that since he was excommunicated
in 1257 (according to Torraca's calculation) and died under
excommunication in 1266, he is, after the year 1300, doomed
to remain outside the wall 236 years more (unless, as he says,
he is helped by prayers).

140–41. *se tal decreto . . . diventa*: The good prayers must,
of course, be said by someone living in grace. Cf. *Purg.* IV,
133-34.

142. *oggimai = oramai*, "now," i.e., after what I have told
you.

143. *la mia buona Costanza*: The daughter, first spoken of
as "fair," is now "good," an expression of the father's confi-
dence that she will respond to his request and will pray for
him.

144. *come m'hai visto*: The good news that I am in Purga-
tory among the "spiriti eletti."   *e anco esto divieto*: The
prohibition that would keep him another 236 years here out-
side the wall.

145. *qui*: In Purgatory.   *per quei di là molto s'avanza*:
For the accepted doctrine respecting the efficacy of prayers
for souls in Purgatory, see Thomas Aquinas, *Summa theol.*
III, Suppl., q. 71, a. 2, resp.:

Charitas, quae est vinculum Ecclesiae membra uniens,
non solum ad vivos se extendit, sed etiam ad mortuos,
qui in charitate decedunt. Charitas enim, quae est vita

animae, sicut anima est vita corporis, non finitur, 1 Cor. 13, 8: *Charitas nunquam excidit.* . . . Et sic suffragia vivorum mortuis dupliciter prosunt, sicut et vivis, et propter charitatis unionem, et propter intentionem in eos directam. Non tamen sic eis valere credenda sunt vivorum suffragia, ut status eorum mutetur de miseria ad felicitatem, vel e converso; sed valent ad diminutionem poenae, vel aliquid huiusmodi, quod statum mortui non transmutat.

Charity, which is the bond uniting the members of the Church, extends not only to the living, but also to the dead who die in charity. For charity which is the life of the soul, even as the soul is the life of the body, has no end: *Charity never falleth away* (1 Cor. xiii. 8). . . . Hence the suffrages of the living profit the dead in two ways even as they profit the living, both on account of the bond of charity and on account of the intention being directed to them. Nevertheless, we must not believe that the suffrages of the living profit them so as to change their state from unhappiness to happiness or *vice versa*; but they avail for the diminution of punishment or something of the kind that involves no change in the state of the dead.

Also see *Summa theol.* III, Suppl., q. 71, a. 6, resp.: "Et ideo quia . . . opera unius possunt valere alteri ad satisfactionem, sive vivus, sive mortuus fuerit, non est dubium quin suffragia per vivos facta existentibus in purgatorio prosint." ("Consequently, since . . . the works of one person can avail for another's satisfaction, whether the latter be living or dead, the suffrages of the living, without any doubt, profit those who are in purgatory.") See II Mach. 12:46: "Sancta ergo et salubris est cogitatio pro defunctis exorare, ut a peccatis solvantur." ("It is therefore a holy and wholesome thought to pray for the dead, that they may be loosed from sins.")

CANTO IV

1–12. *Quando per dilettanze . . . sciolta*: The *potenze* ("potencies") of the soul, according to accepted technical terminology, are its "powers," which are variously classified, but in a major way always as three and as such are sometimes called "souls" (*animae*), namely, the vegetative, the sensitive, and the rational, or intellective. But the *potenze* are also the several functions or operations of these three "souls," being distinguished according to the several objects of these functions; thus, according to Thomas Aquinas (*Summa theol.* I, q. 77, a. 3, resp.), "alia potentia sensitiva est coloris, scilicet visus; et alia soni, scilicet auditus." ("There is one sensitive power with regard to color, namely, the sight, and another with regard to sound, namely, hearing.") An example of an intellective power is the free will ("liberum arbitrium," *Summa theol.* I, q. 83, a. 2, resp.). Such subordinate powers are also *virtutes* or *vires* (see quotation from the *Convivio* below).

The particular psychological phenomenon which Dante expounds in these verses is noted by Thomas Aquinas, among others. See Aquinas (*Summa theol.* I-II, q. 37, a. 1, resp.) on the effects of pain:

> Quia omnes potentiae animae in una essentia animae radicantur, necesse est quod quando intentio animae

vehementer trahitur ad operationem unius potentiae, retrahatur ab operatione alterius; unius enim animae non potest esse nisi una intentio: et propter hoc si aliquid ad se trahat totam intentionem animae, vel magnam partem ipsius, non compatitur secum aliquid aliud quod magnam attentionem requirat. Manifestum est autem quod dolor sensibilis maxime trahit ad se intentionem animae, quia naturaliter unumquodque tota intentione tendit ad repellendum contrarium, sicut etiam in rebus naturalibus apparet.

Since all the powers of the soul are rooted in the one essence of the soul, it must needs happen, when the intention of the soul is strongly drawn towards the action of one power, that it is withdrawn from the action of another power: because the soul, being one, can only have one intention. The result is that if one thing draws upon itself the entire intention of the soul, or a great portion thereof, anything else requiring considerable attention is incompatible therewith.

Now it is evident that sensible pain above all draws the soul's attention to itself; because it is natural for each thing to tend wholly to repel whatever is contrary to it, as may be observed even in natural things.

And, similarly, on pleasure Aquinas (*Summa theol.* I-II, q. 33, a. 3, resp.) says:

Sed delectationes corporales impediunt usum rationis triplici ratione: primo quidem ratione distractionis, quia . . . ad ea in quibus delectamur, multum attendimus. Cum autem intentio fortiter inhaeserit alicui rei, debilitatur circa alias res, vel totaliter ab eis revocatur.

On the other hand bodily pleasures hinder the use of reason in three ways. First, by distracting the reason. Because . . . we attend much to that which pleases us. Now when the attention is firmly fixed on one thing, it is either weakened in respect of other things, or it is entirely withdrawn from them.

The major division into three powers is based on the authority of Aristotle's *De anima* II. Thus, in *Conv.* III, ii, 11-16, Dante writes:

Dico adunque che lo Filosofo nel secondo de l'Anima, partendo le potenze di quella, dice che l'anima principalmente hae tre potenze, cioè vivere, sentire e ragionare: e dice anche muovere; ma questa si può col sentire fare una, però che ogni anima che sente, o con tutti i sensi o con alcuno solo, si muove; sì che muovere è una potenza congiunta col sentire. E secondo che esso dice, è manifestissimo che queste potenze sono intra sè per modo che l'una è fondamento de l'altra; e quella che è fondamento puote per sè essere partita, ma l'altra, che si fonda sopra essa, non può da quella essere partita. Onde la potenza vegetativa, per la quale si vive, è fondamento sopra 'l quale si sente, cioè vede, ode, gusta, odora e tocca; e questa vegetativa potenza per sè puote essere anima, sì come vedemo ne le piante tutte. La sensitiva sanza quella essere non puote, e non si truova in alcuna cosa che non viva; e questa sensitiva potenza è fondamento de la intellettiva, cioè de la ragione: e però ne le cose animate mortali la ragionativa potenza sanza la sensitiva non si truova, ma la sensitiva si truova sanza questa, sì come ne le bestie, ne li uccelli, ne' pesci e in ogni animale bruto vedemo. E quella anima che tutte queste potenze comprende, e perfettissima di tutte l'altre, è l'anima umana, la quale con la nobilitade de la potenza ultima, cioè ragione, participa de la divina natura a guisa di sempiterna intelligenzia; però che l'anima è tanto in quella sovrana potenza nobilitata e dinudata da materia, che la divina luce, come in angelo, raggia in quella: e però è l'uomo divino animale da li filosofi chiamato. In questa nobilissima parte de l'anima sono più vertudi, sì come dice lo Filosofo massimamente nel sesto de l'[Etica]; dove dice che in essa è una vertù che si chiama scientifica, e una che si chiama ragionativa, o vero consigliativa: e con quest[e] sono certe vertudi – sì come in quello medesimo luogo Aristotile dice – sì come la vertù inventiva e giudicativa. E tutte queste

nobilissime vertudi, e l'altre che sono in quella eccellen-
tissima potenza, sì chiama insieme con questo vocabulo,
del quale si volea sapere che fosse, cioè mente.

I say then that the Philosopher in the second *Of the
Soul,* when analysing its powers, says that the soul has
in the main three powers, to wit, life, sense and reason;
and he also mentions motion, but this may be united
with sense, for every soul that has sense (either with all
the senses or some one of them only), has motion also;
so that motion is a power inseparable from sense. And,
as he says, it is quite plain that these powers are so re-
lated to each other that one is the foundation of the
other. And that which is the foundation may exist by it-
self apart; but the other, which is founded upon it, may
not exist apart from it. Wherefore the vegetative power,
whereby things live, is the foundation upon which rests
the sensitive life, to wit, sight, hearing, taste, smell and
touch; and this vegetative power may constitute a soul
in itself, as we see in all the plants. The sensitive power
cannot exist without this; there is nothing that feels,
without being alive. And this sensitive power is the
foundation of the intellectual power, to wit the reason;
and therefore, amongst mortal things that have life, the
rational power without the sensitive is not to be found;
but the sensitive power is to be found without the other,
as we see in the beasts and in the birds and in the fishes
and in every brute animal. And that soul which em-
braces all these powers is the most perfect of all the
rest. And the human soul, which is associated with the
nobility of the highest power, to wit reason, participates
in the divine nature after the fashion of an eternal in-
telligence; because the soul is so ennobled, and stripped
of material, in this sovran power, that the divine light
shines in it as in an angel; and therefore man has been
called by the philosophers the divine animal. In this
most noble part of the soul exist many faculties, as says
the Philosopher, especially in the sixth of the *Ethics,*
where he says that there is a capacity in it which is called

the scientific, and another which is called the ratiocinative or counselling; and together with this are certain faculties, as Aristotle says in that same place, such as the inventive faculty and the judicial. And all these most noble faculties, and the rest that abide in this excellent power, are called collectively by this name, as to the meaning of which we were inquiring, to wit, mind.

1. *Quando per dilettanze o ver per doglie*: In the light of the foregoing general statement, it is clear that "dilettanze" or "doglie" relegates the particular phenomenon here observed to the *potenza sensitiva*, i.e., to one of the physical senses, called "virtù" in the following verse.

2. *che alcuna virtù nostra comprenda*: The sense, as a "virtù" or function of the *potenza sensitiva,* is viewed as being passive in its operation: it receives or takes in ("comprenda") the delight or pain.

3. *l'anima bene ad essa si raccoglie*: The soul attends wholly ("bene") to this one sensation.

4. *par ch'a nulla potenza più intenda*: The soul seems to pay no attention to any (other) power; i.e., being entirely absorbed in this one sensation of pleasure or pain, the soul suspends all other conscious operations. See n. to *Purg.* II, 108, and the quotation there from the *Convivio*; also see Thomas Aquinas, *Summa theol.* I-II, q. 37, a. 1, resp. (quoted in n. to vss. 1-12), and *Summa theol.* I-II, q. 4, a. 1, ad 3: "Et dum uni vehementer intendimus, necesse est quod ab alio intentio retrahatur." ("And when we are very attentive to one thing, we must needs be less attentive to another.")

5-6. *e questo è contra . . . s'accenda*: See Thomas Aquinas, *Summa contra Gentiles* II, 58, entitled "Quod nutritiva, sensitiva et intellectiva non sunt in homine tres animae" ("that in man there are not three souls, nutritive, sensitive, and intellective"), and among the arguments adduced:

Amplius, Diversae vires quae non radicantur in uno principio, non impediunt se invicem in agendo, nisi forte

earum actiones essent contrariae; quod in proposito non
contingit. Videmus autem quod diversae operationes
animae impediunt se: cum enim una est intensa, altera
remittitur. Oportet igitur quod istae actiones, et vires
quae sunt eorum proxima principia, reducantur in unum
principium. Hoc autem principium non potest esse
corpus; tum quia aliqua actio est in qua non communi-
cat corpus, scilicet intelligere; tum quia, si principium
harum virium et actionum esset corpus, in quantum
huiusmodi, invenirentur in omnibus corporibus, quod
patet esse falsum. Et sic relinquitur quod sit principium
earum forma aliqua una per quam hoc corpus est tale
corpus, quae est anima. Relinquitur igitur quod omnes
actiones animae quae sunt in nobis ab ipsa una pro-
cedunt; et sic non sunt in nobis plures animae.

Furthermore, diverse powers that are not rooted in one
principle do not hinder one another in acting, unless,
perhaps, their action be contrary; and this is not so in
the present case. Now, we observe that the diverse ac-
tions of the soul hinder one another, for when one is in-
tense another is remiss. Therefore, these actions and the
powers that are their proximate principles must be re-
ferred to one principle. But this principle cannot be the
body, both because there is an action in which the body
does not share, namely, understanding, and because, if
the body, as such, were the principle of these powers
and actions, they would be found in all bodies; which
is clearly false. It therefore remains that their principle
is some one form, by which *this* body is *such* a body.
And this principle is the soul. It follows, then, that all
the actions of the soul which are in us proceed from the
one soul. Thus, there are not several souls in us.

The whole matter of there being *one* soul in us, for Thomas
Aquinas and a certain school of scholastic thought, hinged
on the fact that the soul was the *form* of the body, and the is-
sue between Plato and Aristotle rested on this, as Aquinas
and others commonly state it. See *Summa theol.* I, q. 76, a.
4, resp.:

Si poneretur anima intellectiva non uniri corpori ut
forma, sed solum ut motor, ut Platonici posuerunt,
necesse esset dicere, quod in homine esset alia forma
substantialis, per quam corpus ab anima mobile in suo
esse constitueretur.

Sed si anima intellectiva unitur corpori ut forma sub-
stantialis . . . impossibile est quod aliqua alia forma sub-
stantialis praeter eam inveniatur in homine.

If we suppose that the intellectual soul is not united to
the body as its form, but only as its motor, as the
Platonists maintain, it would necessarily follow that in
man there is another substantial form, by which the
body is established in its being as movable by the soul.
If, however, the intellectual soul be united to the body
as its substantial form . . . it is impossible for another
substantial form besides the intellectual soul to be found
in man.

6. *sovr' altra*: According to the hierarchy of the powers. See
n. to vss. 1-12.   *s'accenda*: Cf. *Purg.* XVIII, 71: "ogne
amor che dentro a voi s'accende."

7. *però = perciò.   quando s'ode cosa o vede*: The argu-
ment narrows to the particular experience in question: Dante
has been listening to Manfred and gazing in wonder at him.

8. *che tegna*: The subjunctive continues the hypothetical
proposition.   *volta*: Cf. "si raccoglie" in the general
statement, vs. 3.

9. *vassene = se ne va.   l'uom*: Cf. the French *on.*

10. *ch'altra potenza = ché (perché) altra potenza.   altra
potenza è quella che l'ascolta*: Dante is using "potenza" here
in the more restricted meaning of a single sense or faculty
(namely, the hearing, "quella che l'ascolta") of one of the
major *potenze* of the soul. Thus: "It is one faculty which
heeds it," i.e., the passing of time. The use of "ascolta" in this
case has caused some perplexity among the commentators,
and E. G. Parodi (1957, pp. 368-69) has judged it a lax use,

in part dictated by the rhyme. We should remember, how-
ever, that in Dante's day time was commonly told by the ring-
ing of bells, which makes appropriate the verb *to hear*. It is
essential, in any case, to understand that "l'" (*lo*) here refers
to the passing of time ("vassene 'l tempo," vs. 9) and that
the faculty in question is that faculty which perceives the
passing of time, by observing the position of the sun, by
hearing bells, or howsoever.

10–11. *altra . . . altra*: Cf. the Latin *alter . . . alter*, "one
. . . another."

11. *e altra è quella c'ha l'anima intera*: "And another
[power] is that which holds the whole soul [concentrated on
it]," as in vss. 3-4. The reference, in this particular case, is
to Dante's complete absorption in Manfred.

12. *questa è quasi legata*: The power which holds the whole
soul is absorbed ("legata") in listening and looking (as is the
case here) and accordingly pays no attention to the power
that observes the passing of time, which would be the *esti-
mativa*, a function of the *intellectiva*.   *e quella è sciolta*:
And the faculty which notes the passing of time (the *estima-
tiva*) is inoperative, unengaged. See M. Barbi (1934b),
pp. 219-21, and Ristoro d'Arezzo, *Della comp.* II, 1:
"Stando uomo attento a udire non vede; e se l'uomo mira ben
fiso come 'l dipintore, suona la campana e non l'ode, e non
se ne addae." ("A man who is attentively listening does not
see; and if a man looks very fixedly at something, as does a
painter, a bell may ring and he will not hear it and will take
no notice of it.") See also *Purg.* II, 115-17.

14–16. *udendo quello spirto . . . accorto*: This particular
experience thus bears out the general psychological truth.
Dante has been so absorbed in listening to Manfred, marvel-
ing to see him there (see vss. 7-8), that he has not noticed
how high the sun has climbed.

15–16. *ché ben cinquanta gradi . . . lo sole*: In its twenty-
four-hour revolution the sun traverses fifteen degrees in one
hour, hence three hours and twenty minutes have passed

since sunrise, the encounter with Manfred taking only the last part of that time. It is now about 9:30 in the morning.

17–18. *venimmo ove quell' anime . . . a noi*: Meanwhile, the troop of souls, with Dante and Virgil ahead of them, have continued on their way.

17. *ad una*: *Voce* is understood ("ad una voce").

18. *gridaro = gridarono. vostro dimando*: "What you ask," i.e., where the mountain slopes in such a way as to provide a means of ascent (*Purg.* III, 76-77).

19. *aperta = apertura. impruna*: Verb based on *pruno,* "thornbush."

21. *l'uom de la villa*: "The man of the farm." *quando l'uva imbruna*: When the grape turns purple (ripens) and hence is more likely to be stolen, and the thorn hedges must be in good repair. Benvenuto refers to this homely simile as a *comparatio domestica*; it is typical of Dante's art (cf. *Inf.* XXIV, 1-15) and of the various ways he finds by which to keep his style a *sermo humilis et remissus* (see *Epist.* XIII, 31). Typical as well is the symbolic dimension of this simple rustic scene, namely, the allusion it bears to a familiar passage of the Scriptures, Matt. 7:13-14: "Intrate per angustam portam, quia lata porta et spatiosa via est quae ducit ad perditionem, et multi sunt qui intrant per eam. Quam angusta porta et arcta via est quae ducit ad vitam, et pauci sunt qui inveniunt eam!" ("Enter by the narrow gate. For wide is the gate and broad is the way that leads to destruction, and many there are who enter that way. How narrow the gate and close the way that leads to life! And few there are who find it.") This symbolism of the "arcta via" will be brought out more than once. See *Purg.* X, 16.

22. *la calla*: I.e., *apertura*. Cf. *Purg.* IX, 123, where the term is used of the entrance to Purgatory proper (which likewise connects with the *angusta porta* of the Scriptures). See "callaia," used later of a very narrow and difficult passageway (*Purg.* XXV, 7). *onde*: I.e., *per la quale. saline*:

Cf. "partìne" in rhyme (vs. 24). The ending *-ne* was often attached to verb forms ending in an accented vowel. Cf. "pòne" for *può* in *Inf.* XI, 31, and "féne" for *fé* (*fece*) in *Inf.* XVIII, 87. See E. G. Parodi (1957), pp. 243-44.

25-26. *Vassi . . . discendesi . . . montasi = si va . . . si discende . . . si monta.*

25. *Sanleo*: San Leo, chief town of the mountainous district of Montefeltro in the ancient duchy of Urbino, not far from San Marino, in the northern part of the modern region of the Marches. It is situated on an extremely steep and rugged hill and is difficult of access (see Plate 1, facing). According to Benvenuto, San Leo, which was a strong place, was almost deserted in his day:

> Sanctus Leo est civitas Romandiolae in Montefeltro, iam satis deserta tempore nostri poetae, et hodie plus; in altissimo monte sita, montibus altissimis aggregatis circumcincta, ita quod colligit intra fortilitium fructus et omnia necessaria ad victum et substentationem humanae vitae, sicut et Samarinum castrum naturali situ munitissimum et optimum distans a Sancto Leone per quatuor milliaria, et ab Arimino per decem, mirabile fortilitium.

> San Leo is a city of Romagna in Montefeltro, sparsely populated in the times of the poet, and now more so; it lies on top of a mountain, surrounded by a circle of high peaks, so that it contains crops and all the necessaries of life within the bounds of the fortress just as San Marino is a town wonderfully well protected by its location, about four miles from San Leo and ten from Rimini, a wonderful fortress.

Noli: Town in Liguria, on the Gulf of Genoa, about ten miles southwest of Savona on the Riviera di Ponente. The only approach to Noli by land, in Dante's time, was a precipitous descent from the mountains behind. Benvenuto says: "Noli est quaedam terra antiqua in riperia Ianuae supra mare, subiecta monti altissimo scabroso, ad quam est difficillimus descensus." ("Noli is an ancient place along the

1. San Leo

2. Pietra di Bismantova

Genoese coast, above the sea; it lies beneath a very high and rocky mountain, which it is very difficult to descend.")

26. *Bismantova*: Former hamlet in Emilia on a steep mountain of the same name about twenty miles south of Reggio and not far distant from Canossa. In the Middle Ages it was strongly fortified and was a place of some importance. Nothing now remains except the huge sheer semicircular rock itself, known as the Pietra di Bismantova. Benvenuto describes it as having a sort of plateau at the summit, which seems to have been cultivated at times. He says it could be approached only by a single tortuous pathway, which became very steep toward the top. To his fancy the mountain presented a striking resemblance in many particulars to the mountain of Purgatory. (See Plate 2, facing.)

Thus "montasi su Bismantova in cacume" would mean "one climbs above [the village of] Bismantova to the summit" of the so-called Pietra di Bismantova. This reading of the verse seems more acceptable than the variant "montasi su in Bismantova e 'n Cacume," which Petrocchi and other editors accept, in which case the reference would be to a mountain in the Lepini Mountains, not far from Frosinone. See Petrocchi's note on this, where he grants that the reading "in cacume" is also acceptable, according to the manuscript evidence.

27. *con esso i piè*: "With one's own feet." Cf. the Latin *ipsis pedibus*. Cf. *Purg.* XXIV, 98; for "esso" used with a preposition, see *Inf.* XXIII, 54 and *Purg.* II, 10.   *om*: Cf. the French *on*.

29–30. *di retro a quel condotto . . . lume*: "Condotto" may be construed either as a noun or as a past participle, but it seems best to understand it as the latter and to take "quel" as a demonstrative pronoun indicating Virgil. See E. G. Parodi (1957), pp. 369-70.

Whenever Virgil is designated as a "light," the poem provides a momentary glimpse of its main allegory, which is thus gradually disclosed. Here one may note, in fact, the easy shift from "om" (vs. 27) to the first person "mi" of vs. 30, from any man who might attempt such an ascent, to Dante, who is attempting it.

31. *'l sasso rotto*: "The cloven rock," i.e., the cleft in the rock.

32. *ne = ci.   lo stremo*: The sides of the cleft, literally, the surface of the sides. On the significance of the narrowness of the way, see n. to vs. 21.

33. *e piedi e man volea il suol di sotto*: "Suol" is the subject. *volea = voleva*.

34–35. *in su l'orlo suppremo de l'alta ripa*: The narrow passageway leads to the top of the cliff and the beginning there of the "scoperta piaggia" ("open hillside") which must now be climbed.

35. *piaggia*: "Slope." For "piaggia" in this meaning, see *Inf.* I, 29. This "piaggia" will also be termed a "costa," as in *Inf.* II, 40.

37. *Nessun tuo passo caggia*: Of course Virgil does not really think that Dante might turn back and descend the slope, but he enjoins him not to choose some way to the right or left that would be less steep than the more difficult direct way up the mountain. "Caggia" (*cada*) thus means "turn" or "fall" to one side or the other of the straight way up the slope.

38. *pur su al monte*: For "al monte" indicating ascent of the mountain, see n. to *Purg.* II, 60.

39. *n' = ne (ci).   alcuna scorta saggia*: Someone who is familiar with the way. See "saggi" in *Purg.* V, 30.

40. *vincea = vinceva*.

41. *la costa*: The "piaggia," as it has been called (vs. 35). *superba*: "Steep." Cf. *Inf.* XXI, 34.

42. *che da mezzo quadrante a centro lista*: A line ("lista") drawn from the center of a circle to the middle of one of its

quadrants would describe an angle of 45° at the center, since the angle of the quadrant itself at that point is 90°. Thus the "piaggia" here, rising at an even sharper inclination, is very steep indeed.

45. *se non restai = se non ristai*, "if you do not stay your steps."

46. *infin quivi*: The words imply a gesture.   *ti tira =* *tìrati* (imperative).

47. *balzo*: Circling ledge. Cf. *Inf.* XI, 115; XXIX, 95 (where it is used for the circles of Hell).   *sùe*: The addition of *-e* to words ending in an accented vowel and followed by a pause was common practice in early Italian, as it still is in Florentine speech. Cf. "fue" in vs. 51 and "giùe" in *Inf.* XXXII, 53.

48. *che da quel lato il poggio tutto gira*: "Tutto" here signifies as much of the ledge as Dante can see from the side on which he is climbing. The "balzo" may circle the whole mountain, but this he cannot see here, of course.

50. *carpando*: Crawling on hands and knees. Cf. "carpone," *Inf.* XXV, 141.

51. *'l cinghio*: The encircling ledge.   *fue = fu.* See "sùe" in vs. 47.

53-54. *vòlti a levante . . . altrui*: "Che" has as antecedent the notion contained in the phrase "ond' eravam saliti": it always cheers a man to look back over the (difficult) way he has climbed. Some commentators (see M. Barbi, 1934b, pp. 246-47) take "che" to refer to "vòlti a levante" and argue, with examples that are not hard to find, that east was the direction toward which one faced in prayer and toward which churches were "oriented." But, true though this certainly is, it is not a meaning that seems to fit here. Dante first looks all the way down to the "bassi liti," to the farthest point whence he and Virgil have come.

53. *ond'*: From which part.

57. *che da sinistra n'eravam feriti*: Dante now dramatizes his puzzlement and wonder over the fact that the sun at mid-morning is not in the southeast, where an observer in Europe would see it at this season, but in the northeast quarter of the sky. See Lucan, *Phars.* III, 247-48: "Ignotum vobis, Arabes, venistis in orbem / Umbras mirati nemorum non ire sinistras." ("The Arabs entered a world unknown to them, and marvelled that the shadows of the trees did not fall to the left.") See also *Phars.* IX, 538-39: "At tibi, quaecumque es Libyco gens igne dirempta, / In Noton umbra cadit, quae nobis exit in Arcton." ("But the shadow of people, if such there be, who are separated from us by the heats of Libya falls to the South, whereas ours falls northwards.")

59. *stupido = stupito.* *tutto*: "Utterly." *al carro de la luce*: The chariot of the Sun. See vs. 72.

60. *tra noi e Aquilone*: Between us and the north (Aquilo, the north wind, commonly serves to indicate the north). *intrava*: "Was passing."

61-66. *Se Castore e Poluce . . . vecchio*: Virgil's explanation is paraphrased by M. A. Orr (1956, p. 218) as follows:

"If Castor and Pollux (stars in Gemini) were in company with that Mirror (the sun) which carries his light up and down (*i.e.* goes north and south alternately), you would see the glowing zodiac (that part in which the sun is) revolving still closer to the Bears." Gemini is literally nearer to the constellations of the Bears than Aries, but this is not the sense of Virgil's statement: he means merely to indicate the north in general.

The reader is expected to remember that the sun is in Aries (from March 21 until April 20) when Dante makes his journey (see *Inf.* I, 38-40), and that it will be "in company with" Gemini from May 21 through June 21, the summer solstice, when the sun reaches its northernmost point. In Aries, or more exactly, about March 21, the sun rises and sets due east and west, i.e., is on the equator, making day and night equal all over the earth (M. A. Orr, 1956, pp. 23-24).

61. *Castore e Poluce*: Pronounced *Càstore* and *Polùce*. Castor and Pollux, the Dioscuri. According to one version of the myth, Leda, having been visited by Jupiter in the form of a swan, brought forth two eggs, from one of which issued Helen, and from the other Castor and Pollux. At their death Jupiter placed the twin brothers among the stars to form the constellation of Gemini.

62. *quello specchio*: The sun, mirror of light, luminous and shining as it is.

63. *che sù e giù del suo lume conduce*: Which leads its light during one half of the year on this side of the equator, to the north or above it, and during the other half leads it on that side, to the south or below it.

64. *il Zodiaco rubecchio*: The zodiac is a zone or belt of the heavens eighteen degrees in breadth, extending nine degrees on either side of the ecliptic (the great circle apparently described by the sun in the course of a year), within which, according to the Ptolemaic system, the moon, Mercury, Venus, the sun, Mars, Jupiter, and Saturn perform their annual revolutions. It is divided into twelve equal parts of thirty degrees each, called signs, which are named from the constellations lying within them. The "ruddy Zodiac" is that part where the sun is; hence it here denotes the sun itself. (See Fig. 1, p. 33.)

65. *ancora a l'Orse più stretto rotare*: Since "the Bears" serve merely to designate the north in general (see n. to vss. 61-66), Virgil means that Dante, in that case, would see the sun circling even farther north, if the time were nearer the summer season.

66. *se non uscisse fuor del cammin vecchio*: The old (i.e., wonted) path of the sun is the ecliptic, in which, on June 21, it reaches its northernmost point. The "if" clause seems to allow for something quite impossible; yet the myth of the misguiding of the Sun's chariot by Phaëthon (recalled by Virgil in vs. 72) easily prompts such a turn of phrase.

68. *dentro raccolto*: If you will collect your thoughts within.

Siòn: Mount Zion, name of one of the two hills upon which is situated the old city of Jerusalem, here serves to indicate the city itself, which it does most appropriately, since its position is being compared with that of another mountain, Mount Purgatory. "Siòn," "orizzòn" (vs. 70), and "Fetòn" (vs. 72) are *rime tronche*. Cf. *Inf*. IV, 56.

70-71. *sì, ch'amendue . . . emisperi*: Dante is asked to conceive the real geographical situation. Mount Zion (Jerusalem) being at the exact center of the northern hemisphere, and Mount Purgatory at the center of the southern hemisphere ("diversi emisperi"), the two mountains are on directly opposite sides of the earth and thus have a common horizon ("un solo orizzòn") midway between them, which passes through Ganges in the east and Gibraltar in the west. It is assumed that Dante character (and the reader) will have in mind the fact that Zion is north of the Tropic of Cancer and Mount Purgatory is south of the Tropic of Capricorn.

70. *orizzòn*: From the Latin nominative *horizon*.

71. *la strada*: The ecliptic ("cammin vecchio," vs. 66) of the sun.

72. *che mal non seppe carreggiar Fetòn*: The myth of Phaëthon is dealt with in the n. to *Inf*. XVII, 107. For the construction with "mal," see *Inf*. IX, 54: "mal non vengiammo in Teseo l'assalto"; for the accent on "Fetòn" (note another nominative form, "orizzòn," in vs. 70), see E. G. Parodi (1957), p. 370.

73-74. *vedrai come . . . fianco*: The ecliptic passes between Mount Purgatory and Mount Zion; and since the sun moves "up and down" (vs. 63), i.e., is half the year above the equator and half the year below, it follows that the more the sun is south of Jerusalem, the less it is north of Purgatory.

73. *costui*: This mountain.

74. *colui*: Mount Zion.

76. *unquanco*: Cf. *Inf.* XXXIII, 140: "unquanche."

78. *manco*: "Insufficient," "inadequate."

79. *'l mezzo cerchio del moto superno*: The middle circle of the celestial motion—the revolution of the spheres—is the celestial equator. See F. Angelitti (1911), p. 33:

> L'equatore celeste da Gherardo è chiamato *equator diei*; da Dante è denotato con varie locuzioni, come *il cerchio che s'intende nel mezzo dei primi poli* (*Conv.* III, 5), il *cerchio diritto* secondo la denominazione degli astronomi greci (*Par.* X, 19 e *Conv.* II, 3), *il mezzo cerchio del moto superno*, aggiungendo *che si chiama equatore in alcun'arte* (*Purg.* IV, 79-80). In quest'ultima locuzione *mezzo cerchio* è detto nel senso latino di *circulus medius motus superni*: in questo stesso senso Dante usa (*Conv.* III, 5) la frase *cerchio del mezzo*, e Gherardo dice *cingulus primi motus*. Dante, che aveva tradotta letteralmente la parola *aggregazione* poco chiara, avrebbe qui potuto opportunamente adottare le locuzioni *equatore del dì* e *cingolo*. E si noti che per Dante *equatore* è parola generica: ogni cielo ed ogni sfera che gira, ha due poli ed ha il proprio equatore, che è il cerchio egualmente in ogni sua parte distante dai poli (*Conv.* II, 4), ed anche quello che massimamente gira (*Conv.* III, 5).

The celestial equator is called by Gherardo the "equator diei"; Dante refers to it by various locutions, such as "il cerchio che s'intende nel mezzo dei primi poli" (*Conv.* III, 5 [*Conv.* III, v, 8]), the "cerchio diritto" according to the designation of the Greek astronomers (*Par.* X, 19 and *Conv.* II, 3 [*Conv.* II, iii, 5]), "il mezzo cerchio del moto superno," adding "che si chiama equatore in alcun'arte" (*Purg.* IV, 79-80). In this latter phrase "mezzo cerchio" is used in the sense of the Latin *circulus medius motus superni*; Dante uses the phrase "cerchio del mezzo" in this same sense, and Gherardo calls it "cingulus primi motus." Dante, who had translated literally the word *aggregazione*, which was not very clear, could have adopted here opportunely the phrases *equatore del dì* and *cingolo*. And it should be noted that for Dante *equatore* is a generic term: every heaven and every sphere that turns has two poles and has its own equator, which is the circle equidistant from the poles in its every part (*Conv.* II, 4 [*Conv.* II, iii, 13]) and is also that which turns the widest (*Conv.* III, 5 [*Conv.* III, v, 8]).

80. *in alcun' arte*: In a certain art, i.e., astronomy, one of the four "arts" of the quadrivium—arithmetic, music, geometry, and astronomy.

81. *e che sempre riman tra 'l sole e 'l verno*: Winter is always on the other side of the equator from the sun. The sun crosses the equator at the autumnal equinox.

82. *quinci*: From this mountain. *si parte*: "Is distant from."

83. *quanto*: Some editors prefer "quando," which seems to fit the context less well.

84. *vedevan*: The Hebrews living in Jerusalem used to see the sun so, before they were dispersed. *lui*: The sun. *verso la calda parte*: To the south.

86. *avemo = abbiamo*.

88–89. *Questa montagna . . . grave*: Clearly Virgil's statement has a spiritual meaning. As, on the successive terraces of Purgatory proper, the burden of the "scoglio" left by sin (*Purg.* II, 122-23) is gradually put off through purgation, the souls, and Dante wayfarer, find that the climbing is easier; but this is particularly true of the living man, and the point primarily concerns the allegory of the "cammin di nostra vita" (*Inf.* I, 1) as represented by Dante wayfarer. Cf. *Purg.* XII, 124-26. Later, when Dante ascends with Beatrice from the summit, and asks how this is possible, a similar "gravitational" figure explains the matter (*Par.* I, 136-38).

90. *e quant' om più va sù, e men fa male*: The second "e"

here is not the usual conjunction, but serves to stress the words which follow.

91. *Però = perciò.*

92. *fia = sarà.*

93. *a seconda giù*: Downstream, following (*secondando*) the current.

96. *Più non rispondo, e questo so per vero*: It is as if now Virgil were following the exhortation he addressed to mankind (*Purg.* III, 37): "State contenti, umana gente, al *quia.*"

97. *sua parola = le sue parole.*

98. *Forse*: There is a gentle thrust of irony in this "perhaps" (the more apparent for its being in the emphatic rhyme position), addressed to the panting Dante, who was so glad to sit down and rest from his first climb. For "forse" in a similar function, see *Inf.* X, 63.

99. *in pria = in prima*, i.e., before you arrive at the summit.
    distretta: "Necessity."

100. *Al suon di lei*: At the sound of the voice.

101. *a mancina = a sinistra.*

102. *del qual né io né ei prima s'accorse*: On reaching the ledge, Virgil and Dante immediately faced toward the east, and so until the voice causes them to turn toward it they have taken no notice of the boulder itself. "Prima" thus refers to the time that has passed since their arrival there or in their approach to the ledge, not to the sound of the voice itself.
    s'accorse = s'era accorto.

104. *si stavano a l'ombra*: The midmorning sun is already hot (though this is not said). The rock which casts the shade is to the left of Dante and Virgil as they face east, and hence it is to the north of them. Its shade would therefore be toward them. "Si" here is an example of the so-called pleonastic reflexive in its "distancing" function. Cf. *Inf.* VII, 94, 96.

105. *come l'uom per negghienza a star si pone*: Lounging about in lazy posture, such as the one described. "Negghienza," popular form of *negligenza,* proves to be the significant term (cf. "negligente," vs. 110) for these are indeed the "negligent." *negghienza = negligenza.*

106. *sembiava = sembrava.* *lasso*: The shade appears "weary" without having any special reason for being so.

109. *adocchia*: "Look closely at." Cf. *Inf.* XV, 22; XVIII, 123.

111. *serocchia*: From the Latin *sororcula,* "little sister." *Serocchia* is a more popular form than *sorella,* but with the same meaning, the original sense of the diminutive having been lost.

112. *si volse a noi*: The following verse tells how he turns, i.e., turning only his face without raising his head, which he continues to hold down between his knees. *puose mente*: I.e., to us.

113. *movendo 'l viso pur su per la coscia*: "Pur" modifies "viso"; the soul moves only its glance, being too lazy to raise its head.

114. *Or va tu sù, che se' valente*: The thrust of the words is evident, referring as they do to the fact that Dante has but now sat down to rest and is still somewhat out of breath (vss. 115-16). *valente: Bravo* in modern Italian.

115. *Conobbi allor chi era*: Dante recognizes the soul by the lazy and derisive words it utters. *angoscia*: "Exertion."

116. *avacciava*: Cf. "avaccio," *Inf.* X, 116. *la lena*: Cf. *Inf.* I, 22: "come quei che con lena affannata."

117-18. *e poscia . . . pena*: Not until Dante actually stands before him does the soul trouble to raise its head, and then only slightly.

119-20. *Hai ben veduto . . . mena?* This second thrust, also ironical and gently derisive, is conveyed in large part by the "ben." Porena comments:

Con la sua domanda questo spirito pigro mette un po'
in burla Dante che s'è tanto interessato di comprendere
come mai il Sole sia alla sua sinistra; e rivela con ciò una
negligenza non solo materiale ma anche spirituale: egli
non ha di tali pungenti curiosità! E non ha sentito
neanche quella di sapere come mai sia lì un vivo che
deve ascendere il monte.

With this question, the lazy spirit makes a little fun of
Dante, who is trying so hard to understand how the sun
can be on his left; and with that he reveals not only ma-
terial, but spiritual negligence as well: he has no curios-
ity of that sort! He has not even felt the curiosity to find
out why a living man should be there climbing the
mountain.

120. *da l'omero sinistro*: The words refer to Dante's posi-
tion as he sat with Virgil, facing east. Clearly the soul has
overheard Virgil's explanation of the phenomenon that
caused Dante to wonder, but all the while he has kept his
head down between his knees.

121. *Li atti suoi pigri e le corte parole*: Dante began by sin-
gling out this soul because of its lazy posture in the shade,
then recognized it by its lazy movements and "short words,"
as they are now called. One is tempted to translate "corte
parole" with "curt words," but this is not exact. Belacqua, in
his laziness, is as sparing of words as he is of any physical
exertion; his words are "short" in this sense, because of his
laziness, which prompts Dante's smile.

122. *mosser = mossero.   le labbra mie un poco a riso*:
Here we see Dante smile for the first time.

123. *Belacqua*: Little or nothing is known of this acquaint-
ance of Dante's. The early commentators say that he was a
maker of musical instruments, noted for his indolence. He
can perhaps be identified, as has been suggested (see S. De-
benedetti, 1906), with one Duccio di Bonavia, of Florence,
who was still living in 1299 but who was dead by March
1302, and so might have died before 1300.

123-24. *a me non dole di te omai*: Now that I see you here in Purgatory, and know that you are saved, I shall not sorrow for you as for one who might have died unrepentant and so be among the damned of Hell.

124. *assiso = seduto.*

125. *quiritto*: The adverb, which originally meant more emphatically "right here," probably has here no more force than a simple *qui*. Cf. *Purg.* XVII, 86.   *attendi tu iscorta*: This part of Dante's question seems to allow, charitably, for such a possibility, though it seems most unlikely that any guide would be awaited here.

126. *t'ha' ripriso = ti sei ripreso.* Although Petrocchi's text has "t'ha' ripriso," other editors have "t'ha ripriso," construing the "modo usato" as subject rather than object of the verb.

127. *O frate*: Torraca comments: "Come *amico, compare* e simili, nel linguaggio familiare, *fratello* ha talvolta l'uffizio di preparar l'uditore a udire cosa, che non lo può interamente soddisfare, un rimprovero, un'obbiezione, anche, come qui, una rettificazione." ("In familiar speech, the word *fratello* [*frate*, brother], just like *amico* [friend], *compare* [chum], and similar expressions, sometimes has the function of preparing the listener for something he may not quite expect to hear —a rebuke, an objection, or even, as is the case here, a correction.") Cf. *Purg.* XI, 82; XIII, 94; XVI, 65.   *che porta?* "What does it avail?"

128. *ire*: I.e., *andare.*   *a' martìri*: I.e., of Purgatory proper.

129. *l'angel di Dio che siede in su la porta*: An angel of God will indeed be seen seated at the gate of Purgatory when Dante reaches it.

130. *il ciel*: The heavenly spheres.   *m'aggiri = giri intorno a me.*

131. *di fuor da essa*: Of Purgatory proper.   *quanto fece*

in vita: For as long as the heavens revolved about me during my lifetime.

132. *al fine*: *In extremis.*   *sospiri*: Buti comments: "li pentimenti e rimordimenti de la penitenzia, che inducono sospiri" ("the regret and remorse of penitence, which bring forth sighs").

133–34. *se orazione . . . viva*: Unless prayer aid me first (before I serve so long a time), prayer arising from a heart living in grace. Cf. Manfred's "buon prieghi" (*Purg.* III, 141) and his last words, "ché qui per quei di là molto s'avanza" (*Purg.* III, 145). See Iac. 5:16: "Multum enim valet deprecatio iusti assidua." ("For the unceasing prayer of a just man is of great avail.")

135. *l'altra*: Prayer arising from a heart not in grace. *che 'n ciel non è udita*: See Ioan. 9:31: "Scimus autem quia peccatores Deus non audit; sed si quis Dei cultor est et voluntatem eius facit, hunc exaudit." ("Now we know that God does not hear sinners; but if anyone is a worshipper of God, and does his will, him he hears.")

137. *Vienne = vieni* (imperative) + *ne.*   *tocco = toccato.*

137–38. *vedi ch'è tocco meridian dal sole*: The sun is at the meridian; it is high noon. Two and a half hours have passed since Dante and Virgil departed from Manfred and the troop of souls.

138–39. *e a la riva . . . Morrocco*: It is nightfall in Morocco (here equivalent to Gibraltar), which is at the extreme western horizon of Jerusalem and 90° distant from both Mount Zion and Mount Purgatory, or midway between them. In this way the two hemispheres are again brought in (see vss. 70-71). Morocco is the most western of the Barbary states, occupying the northwest corner of Africa. See Ovid, *Metam.* II, 142-43: "Dum loquor, Hesperio positas in litore metas / umida nox tetigit; non est mora libera nobis!" ("While I am speaking dewy night has reached her goal on the far western shore. We may no longer delay.")

CANTO V

1. *quell' ombre*: Belacqua and the other negligent.

3. *di retro a me*: Where the souls sit in the shade of the boulder.   *drizzando 'l dito*: Since Dante does not turn to look until he hears the voice, presumably he then sees the soul still pointing its finger at him and so, in afterknowledge, reports what, strictly speaking, he could not have seen at the moment. For other examples of this, see *Purg.* II, 39-42, and especially *Purg.* XXI, 10-12.

4. *una gridò*: This negligent soul gives evidence of having somewhat more energy and curiosity, certainly, than Belacqua seemed to have.   *Ve' = vedi*. The soul speaks to one companion only, not to the group.

4-5. *non par che luca . . . sotto*: As Dante climbs on up the steep slope of the mountain, he is facing west—and here in this hemisphere the sun is to the north. Therefore his shadow falls to his left, as the souls now see. When he first approached them, having turned to the north (*Purg.* IV, 101: "a mancina") to proceed to where Belacqua sat, his shadow was falling more or less directly behind him and was therefore less noticeable.

6. *e come vivo par che si conduca*: The repetition of "par"

stresses the incredibility of what the spirit *seems* to see. One sign of the fact that Dante is alive would be his very noticeable effort in climbing.

8. *vidile = le vidi.*   *guardar per maraviglia*: But one can hardly imagine that lazy Belacqua is one of these, even now!

9. *pur me, pur me*: For the stress on persistence and intensity which "pur" makes here, the more so by repetition, see *Purg.* VIII, 48.   *rotto*: Cf. *Purg.* III, 17, 88.

12. *che ti fa ciò che quivi si pispiglia?* The souls are now talking among themselves about the discovery of Dante's shadow. "Pispiglia," however, is already leading to "lascia dir le genti," in vs. 13, a moral injunction that would apply to Dante in this life and as such may be compared with the moral injunctions in *Inf.* XXIV, 46-51, and XXX, 145-48.

14–15. *sta come torre . . . venti*: For the background of the metaphor, cf. Virgil, *Aen.* VII, 586, and X, 693-96—though there the figure is of a cliff rather than a tower.

17–18. *da sé dilunga il segno . . . insolla*: He puts the target (i.e., the attainment of the goal) ever farther from himself, because the new thought weakens the force (the resolution) of the first.

18. *insolla*: Cf. the adjective *sollo* in *Inf.* XVI, 28, and *Purg.* XXVII, 40.

20. *Dissilo = lo dissi.*

20–21. *del color . . . degno*: The blush of shame.

21. *talvolta*: Buti comments: "Et anco non sempre la vergogna fa l'omo degno di perdono, che sono certi peccati che richiedeno altro che vergogna." ("Moreover, shame does not always make a man worthy of forgiveness; for there are certain sins that require more than shame.")

22–23. *per la costa . . . poco*: These souls, somewhat higher up on the slope, are circling the mountain in what proves to be the "proper" direction in Purgatory, i.e., to the right, or counterclockwise, for anyone facing the mountainside. Their path is crosswise to Dante's, and they are on his left, or to the south of him, when they notice that he casts a shadow; for, as noted, Dante's shadow falls on his left side as he climbs, facing west, since the sun here is to the north.

24. *Miserere*: The fiftieth psalm, one of the seven penitential psalms, which prays for forgiveness of sin and for cleansing from sin. See Ps. 50:3-5[51:1-3]:

> Miserere mei, Deus, secundum magnam misericordiam tuam; et secundum multitudinem miserationum tuarum dele iniquitatem meam. Amplius lava me ab iniquitate mea, et a peccato meo munda me. Quoniam iniquitatem meam ego cognosco, et peccatum meum contra me est semper.

> Have mercy on me, O God, in your goodness; in the greatness of your compassion wipe out my offense. Thoroughly wash me from my guilt and of my sin cleanse me.

> For I acknowledge my offense, and my sin is before me always.

Thus, in the words of this psalm, the souls pray that they may be admitted to Purgatory (proper) above, where they are to cleanse themselves of their "gravi offese," as vs. 72 has it.

a verso a verso: This probably means that two groups sing the verses alternately. Buti comments: "come cantano li chierici in coro" ("just as priests sing in choir").

27. *mutar = mutarono.   in un "oh!" lungo e roco*: The *Anonimo fiorentino* comments: "una voce roca, ciò è fioca et spaventata" ("a hoarse voice, that is, a weak and frightened voice"). The exclamation thus registers something of the same wonder, touched with awe, that was evidenced by the pallor of the first group encountered (*Purg.* II, 69).

28. *messaggi = messaggeri*. Cf. *Purg.* XXII, 78. As is then indicated (vs. 32), the two are chosen by the group as messengers, hence "in forma di" ("delegated as").

29. *dimandarne = ci domandarono.*

30. *fatene = fateci.   saggi*: "Informed," "aware."

32. *mandaro = mandarono.*

34. *per veder = per aver veduto.   restaro = restarono.*

35. *assai*: Cf. the French *assez* and "assai" in *Inf.* XXXIV, 72.

36. *fàccianli onore = gli facciano onore*. Cf. *Inf.* IV, 93.
    ed esser può lor caro: "And it may profit them," since Dante, when he returns to the world of the living, can ask their dear ones to pray for their advancement here.

37–39. *Vapori accesi . . . agosto*: Grandgent explains that "*vapori accesi* comprise both meteors and lightning. Meteors, cleaving the clear sky in the early night, and lightning, cleaving the August clouds at sunset, move less swiftly than the messengers." "Vapori accesi" is understood as the subject of the verb "fender"; "sereno" and "nuvole" are the objects.

38. *di prima notte*: Early night is a time when we commonly gaze at the stars.   *fender sereno*: Cleave the heavens. *sereno*: Clear sky.

39. *sol calando*: "Sol calando" is modeled on an ablative absolute construction (Latin *occidente sole*).

40. *che color non tornasser suso in meno*: The comparison is in terms of the "sì tosto" of vs. 37. But, no matter how swiftly the two messengers may run back up the slope, and even though these are spirits, the hyperbole seems somewhat extreme, to say the least.

41. *dier = diedero.*

42. *come schiera che scorre sanza freno*: The comparison denotes a mounted troop that charges with loose rein.

43. *che preme a noi*: "That crowds towards us."

44. *vegnonti a pregar = vengono a pregarti.*

45. *però = perciò.   in andando*: Cf. the French *en allant.*

46. *che vai per esser lieta*: "Who go to be happy" in Heaven.

47. *con quelle membra con le quai nascesti*: This connects with "che vai," of the preceding verse, and does not depend on "esser lieta."

48. *venian = venivano*.

49. *unqua*: Cf. *Purg.* III, 105: "unque."

50. *di là*: In the world of the living (cf. "tra ' vivi," vs. 103).   *novella = notizia*.

51. *deh, perché vai? deh, perché non t'arresti?* Clearly Dante is following Virgil's bidding and continuing on up the slope, listening as he goes (vs. 45).

52. *Noi fummo tutti*: Group movement, so characteristic of Purgatory, is now matched by choral speech.   *già*: The adverb defies translation in this context. It serves to reinforce the absoluteness of the past tense of the verb "fummo," but also distributes the time referred to: "we were slain, each in his time." Without the "già" there might somehow be the suggestion that all were slain at one and the same time.   *per forza*: Cf. *Inf.* XI, 34.   *morti*: *Morire* as a transitive verb was common in early Italian. Cf. *Purg.* VII, 95.

53. *e peccatori infino a l'ultima ora*: Sinners to the very end, even as were those of the other two groups in this Antepurgatory; yet these, having been slain by violence, are distinct, as yet another and third group.

54. *quivi*: In the last hour.   *lume del ciel*: The light of grace from Heaven.   *ne = ci*.

55. *pentendo = pentendoci*. Cf. *Inf.* XXVII, 119.   *perdonando*: Cf. the Lord's Prayer (Matt. 6:12), "et dimitte nobis debita nostra, sicut et nos dimittimus debitoribus nostris" ("and forgive us our debts, as we also forgive our debtors"), which is then repeated by Jesus (Matt. 6:14-15): "Si enim dimiseritis hominibus peccata eorum, dimittet et vobis Pater vester caelestis delicta vestra; si autem non di-

miseritis hominibus, nec Pater vester dimittet vobis peccata vestra." ("For if you forgive men their offenses, your heavenly Father will also forgive you your offenses. But if you do not forgive men, neither will your Father forgive you your offenses.") Cf. also *Purg.* XV, 112-13.   *fora = fuori.*

56. *a Dio pacificati*: Reconciled with God. Cf. *Purg.* XIII, 124: "Pace volli con Dio in su lo stremo."

57. *che del disio di sé veder n'accora*: God gives to these souls a longing to see Him, which saddens them ("accora") because of the time they are obliged to wait in Purgatory, here and also higher up, before that desire may be fulfilled, in Heaven with Him. Thus their condition here reflects that of the Christian "pilgrim" who must live out his time on this earth, even though he longs to be with God. Cf. *Purg.* II, 12, "che va col cuore e col corpo dimora," and see n. to *Purg.* II, 11-12. For "accora," cf. *Inf.* XIII, 84; XV, 82.   *n' = ne (ci).*

58. *Perché . . . guati*: "Though I gaze."

60. *ben nati*: Born to good, since these souls will one day see God (cf. *Purg.* III, 73); even as, by contrast, souls in Hell were termed *mal nati* (see *Inf.* V, 7; XVIII, 76; XXX, 48).

61. *voi dite*: Imperative with emphatic subject pronoun.
    per quella pace: Dante swears by that which is most dear to him, even as this first spirit to speak knows (vs. 65). Dante too is seeking peace with God, through realm after realm of the afterlife, guided by Virgil first through Hell, now through Purgatory, at the summit of which he will attain to a first, if imperfect, peace (see *Purg.* XXVII, 115-17).

63. *cercar mi si face*: The peace, which is the goal, is said to inspire the pilgrim with desire for itself, even as God gives the souls a desire to see Him.   *face = fa.*

64. *E uno incominciò*: This soul who speaks "before the others" (vs. 67) is not named, but from the details of the story he tells of his own violent death he can readily be identified as Jacopo del Cassero, member of a noble family of

Fano, who was born *ca.* 1260. He incurred the enmity of
Azzo VIII d'Este by his opposition to the designs of the lat-
ter upon Bologna, of which city Jacopo was *podestà* in 1296.
In revenge Azzo had him assassinated at Oriago, between
Venice and Padua, while he was on his way (in 1298) to as-
sume the office of *podestà* at Milan at the invitation of Matteo
Visconti. He appears to have gone by sea from Fano to
Venice, and thence to have proceeded toward Milan by way
of Padua; but while he was still among the lagoons, he was
waylaid and stabbed.

66. *pur che 'l voler nonpossa non ricida*: "Provided lack of
power [inability on your part] does not thwart your [good]
will." "Nonpossa" ("possa" here is a noun) is on the model
of such words as *nonchalance* and the scholastic *non posse*;
cf. "nonpoder," *Purg.* VII, 57. Benvenuto translates: "dum-
modo impotentia non impediat voluntatem" ("so long as im-
potence does not inhibit the will"). Dante has just said (vs.
60): "cosa ch'io possa."   *ricida*: Infinitive *ricidere*, "to
cut off."

67. *Ond' io, che solo innanzi a li altri parlo*: This spirit
seems somewhat apologetic for venturing to speak thus alone
and for standing out in front of the rest of the group. The
touch serves to make the scene more concrete and vivid.

68–69. *quel paese . . . Carlo*: The March of Ancona (Marca
Anconitana), a former province of Italy situated between
Romagna and the kingdom of Naples. It corresponds roughly
to the *compartimento* now known as the Marches.

70–71. *di tuoi prieghi cortese in Fano*: Kind enough to ask
those who live in Fano and who love me to pray for me here.

71. *Fano*: Town of the March of Ancona, on the Adriatic
coast between Pesaro and Ancona, subject in Dante's time
to the Malatesta of Rimini.   *sì che ben per me s'adori*:
That good prayers may be said for me, i.e., by persons living
in grace. Cf. "buon prieghi," *Purg.* III, 141.

72. *pur ch'i' possa purgar le gravi offese*: The "grievous sins" will be purged higher up, in Purgatory proper, to which good prayers will hasten his admission.

73–75. *Quindi fu' io; ma . . . Antenori*: Freely (to account for "ma" here): I was born in Fano, *but* I did not die there; I met violent death in another place. Cf. vs. 134: "Siena mi fé, disfecemi Maremma."

74. *ond' uscì 'l sangue in sul quale io sedea*: Benvenuto comments: "Idest, vivebam, quia sanguis est sedes animae." ("That is to say, I lived; for the blood is the seat of the soul.") See Lev. 17:14: "anima enim omnis carnis in sanguine est" ("since the life of every living body is in its blood"). The spirit speaks here as the soul, which was "seated on its blood" when in the body. See M. Barbi (1934b), pp. 278-79, and E. G. Parodi (1917), p. 31, n. 2.

75. *fuoro = furono.   in grembo a li Antenori*: In the territory of the Paduans. The phrase suggests the great treachery on the part of the Paduans, called Antenori for being, according to the legend, the descendants of the Trojan Antenor, who was said to have founded Padua and who in the Middle Ages was believed to have betrayed Troy to the Greeks, whence a division of Cocytus is named after him (*Inf.* XXXII, 88). The name thus makes a pointed allusion to the treacherous complicity of the Paduans in the murder of Jacopo.

76. *là dov' io più sicuro esser credea*: Benvenuto comments: "quia inter Venetias et Paduam . . . ubi solet iter esse tutissimum" ("because the route between Venice and Padua . . . was normally quite safe"). Moreover, Jacopo had no reason to suspect that there would be any complicity on their part.

77. *quel da Esti*: Azzo VIII d'Este, who in 1293 succeeded his father, Obizzo II, as marquis of Este. See the probable reference to him in *Inf.* XII, 112, and XVIII, 56, where he is referred to as *il marchese.   fé = fece.*

78. *assai più là che dritto non volea*: Far beyond any right-ful claim, i.e., far exceeding any good reason he might have had for hating me. According to the early commentators, Jacopo had excited the animosity of Azzo not only by his political opposition (see n. to vs. 64) but also by his personal abuse of the marquis; thus Lana, commenting on vs. 70, says:

> Non li bastava costui fare de' fatti contra li amici del marchese, ma elli continuo usava villanìe volgari contra di lui: ch'elli giacque con sua matrigna, e ch'elli era disceso d'una lavandara di panni, e ch'elli era cattivo e codardo; e mai la sua lingua non saziavasi di villaneg-giare di lui. Per li quali fatti e detti l'odio crebbe sì al marchese, ch'elli li trattò la morte in questo modo.

> He was not satisfied with doing things to hurt the friends of the marquis, but he would continually indulge in vul-gar vilification of him, saying he had slept with his step-mother, that he was the son of a washerwoman, that he was evil and cowardly. His tongue never tired of abusing him. These words and deeds caused such great hatred in the marquis, that he had him killed in this way.

It should be recalled that Jacopo must have died *forgiving* the marquis and his henchmen. Thus here he speaks fairmindedly and objectively, granting that "he of Este" had cause to hate him, but not cause enough to justify his murdering him in this way.

79. *fosse = fossi.* *la Mira*: Small town between Padua and Venice on the banks of the Brenta canal.

80. *Oriaco*: Now Oriago, a village between Padua and Ven-ice, close to the lagoons. The main highway leading from Venice passed near Oriago and continued to La Mira. The marquis' henchmen did not "overtake" Jacopo at Oriago in the sense of capturing him there, but only of surprising him there and entering into pursuit of him as he then ran toward the swamp.

81. *ancor sarei di là dove si spira*: I.e., I should still be among the living—apparently implying that he would have

been helped by the townsfolk of La Mira, or would have found some refuge or defense there, or might have escaped from his assailants by continuing along the high road through La Mira.

82–84. *Corsi al palude . . . laco*: Jacopo may well mean that he was mounted and fleeing on horseback and that his horse became entangled in the reeds and mud, so that he fell and was overtaken and slain.

83. *impigliar = impigliarono*.

84. *laco = lago*.

85–86. *Deh, se quel disio . . . monte*: The familiar formula of adjuration, appealing to that which is most dear to the person spoken to (cf. *Inf.* X, 82; *Purg.* II, 16). Dante had sworn by his own desire for peace. See nn. to vss. 61 and 63.

86. *tragge = trae.*   *a l'alto monte*: Here again (cf. *Purg.* II, 60; IV, 38) this phrase means the ascent to the summit and to that goal to which Virgil leads, which is declared to be peace (see *Purg.* XXVII, 115-17).

87. *con buona pietate aiuta il mio*: "With gracious pity do you help my" desire for peace, i.e., by requesting the living to pray for me, that I may enjoy a speedier entrance into Purgatory proper.

88. *Io fui di Montefeltro, io son Bonconte*: "Montefeltro" is here meant as part of a famous family name, not as a statement of geographical origin. There is thus some pride of family in this first declaration, but it is relegated to the past, by the verb in the past absolute; and there is a becoming humility in the simple: "I *am* Bonconte." Buonconte da Montefeltro was the son of Guido da Montefeltro (*Inf.* XXVII, 19-132) and like his father a leader of the Ghibelline party. In June 1287 he helped the Ghibellines to expel the Guelphs from Arezzo, an event which was the beginning of the war between Florence and Arezzo (Villani, VII, 115); in 1288 he helped command the Aretines when they defeated the Sienese at Pieve del Toppo (VII, 120); and in 1289 he

was appointed captain of the Aretines and led them against the Guelphs of Florence, by whom they were totally defeated (June 11) at Campaldino, among the slain being Buonconte himself (VII, 131), whose body, however, was never discovered on the field of battle.

89. *Giovanna*: The widow of Buonconte.   *o altri*: Buonconte was also survived by a daughter and a brother.

90. *con bassa fronte*: The soul hangs its head in sadness, and perhaps in shame, at being quite forgotten among the living.

91. *Qual forza o qual ventura*: The two terms, by juxtaposition, suggest the meaning "what *deliberate* violence or what *blind* chance."

92. *Campaldino*: Small plain in the Casentino, between Poppi and Bibbiena, which was the scene of the battle, fought June 11, 1289, in which Buonconte was slain. See n. to vs. 88 and *Inf.* XXII, 4.

94. *Casentino*: District in Tuscany comprising the upper valley of the Arno and the slopes of the Tuscan Apennines. Cf. *Inf.* XXX, 65.

95. *Archiano*: Torrent which rises in the Apennines above Camaldoli and, traversing the Casentino valley at its "foot," falls into the Arno just above Bibbiena.

96. *l'Ermo = l'eremo*. "The Hermitage" is the monastery of Camaldoli, perched high in the mountains above the Casentino not far from the peak of Falterona, about thirty miles from Florence, founded in the early eleventh century by Romuald for his order of reformed Benedictines. One branch of the Archiano does in fact rise above the Hermitage, and Dante must have considered this to be its main source.

97. *Là 've 'l vocabol suo diventa vano*: When the Archiano flows into the Arno, some two and a half miles from Campaldino, its name "becomes useless" or "is lost."

99. *fuggendo a piede*: We must imagine him clad in armor and thus fleeing on foot with great difficulty.

100. *Quivi*: At the confluence of the Archiano and Arno.

103. *Io dirò vero*: For this sort of pointer to some remarkable or almost incredible thing which is about to be told, see *Inf.* XVI, 124-30; XXV, 46-48; XXVIII, 112-18.   *e tu 'l ridì = e tu ridìllo.* "Ridì" is an imperative.

104-5. *l'angel di Dio . . . gridava*: This is not the incredible part of the scene as recounted by Buonconte, for it was a common belief that angels and devils would come for the soul at death and would struggle for possession of it, or, in the case of a Franciscan, that St. Francis would come, instead of the angel, as for Buonconte's father, Guido (*Inf.* XXVII, 112-23). See Bonaventura, *Comm. Sent. Petri Lombardi IV* XX, i, a. 1, q. 5, resp.:

> Credendum est enim, quod in egressu animae a corpore assistunt et spiritus bonus et spiritus malus, unus vel plures, et tunc secundum veritatem ferri sententiam; et si bona est, per ministerium boni Angeli vel adduci in caelum, vel in purgatorium, quousque, postquam purgata fuerit, per eius ministerium educatur . . . ; si vero sit mala, per ministerium daemonum deduci ad infernum.

> For we must believe that when the soul leaves the body, the good and the evil spirits stand by, one or more, and then a true sentence is passed; if the soul is judged to be good, he is led away to Heaven in the company of a good angel, or else to Purgatory, from which, after he has been cleansed, he will be led out by the same escort . . . ; if, however, the soul is judged to be evil, he will be led by the devil into Hell.

This belief had scriptural support; in his *Sermones de Sanctis*, Bonaventura (*De Sanctis Angelis* V, *collatio*, p. 630) cites Apoc. 12:7: "factum est proelium magnum in caelo" ("there was a battle in heaven"), commenting: "[Hoc proelium] fit quotidie in morte cuiuslibet, quia nituntur daemones animas secum portare." ("This battle also takes place daily, whenever a man dies, because devils seek to carry off the souls.") Bonaventura also cites Luc. 16:22, explaining: "Daemones portaverunt divitem, Angeli mendicum." ("Devils carried away the rich man, while an angel bore off the soul of the beggar.")

106-7. *Tu te ne porti . . . lagrimetta*: The devil, by his vehement protest, dramatizes the situation, seizing as he does on the external and material "*little* tear." Tears would of course accompany sincere repentance, as Manfred indicated (*Purg.* III, 119-20). But true contrition for one's sins and the pardoning of those who offend us is an essential part of the final "conversion" by which the soul is reconciled with God —as perhaps the devil knows, but chooses not to acknowledge. Preachers, legends, and miracle plays might also dramatize the salvation of someone by "one little tear." See Fra Giordano da Rivalto, *Prediche inedite* IV: "E quì, cioè in questo mondo, solo una lagrima che vegna di buon cuore, di contrizione di suoi peccati, è di grande vertude; chè spegne e disfà il peccato, e quanti n'avessi, e scàmpati dalle pene del ninferno, e merita vita eterna." ("Here, that is, in this world, a single tear from a goodhearted person, contrite for his sins, is a thing of great virtue. It extinguishes and erases sins, be they ever so many, it saves you from the pains of Hell, and it merits eternal life.")

108. *l'altro*: The body.

109-10. *Ben sai come . . . riede*: Cf. Virgil, *Georg.* I, 322-24:

> saepe etiam immensum caelo venit agmen aquarum
> et foedam glomerant tempestatem imbribus atris
> collectae ex alto nubes . . .

Often, too, there appears in the sky a mighty column of waters, and clouds mustered from on high roll up a murky tempest of black showers.

111. *tosto che sale dove 'l freddo il coglie*: Cf. Dante, *Conv.* IV, xviii, 4: "Lo freddo è generativo de l'acqua." ("It is cold that begets water.")

112-13. *Giunse quel . . . 'ntelletto*: "Quel" (the devil), a demonstrative pronoun here, is the subject of "giunse," and "mal voler" is the object. Angels, whether good or bad, have the faculties of will and intellect. See Thomas Aquinas, *De malo* q. 16, a. 1, ad 14: "In Angelo aut daemone, si incorporei ponantur, non est alia potentia neque operatio, nisi intellectus et voluntas." ("In an angel or a devil, considered as being incorporeal, there is no power or operation if not the intellect and the will.") The devil makes use of both faculties, joining evil will, which seeks only evil, with intellect (intelligence), to call up the storm and "make other disposal" (vs. 108) of the body.

113. *il fummo*: The "umido vapor" while it is still mist and before it condenses to fall as rain.

114. *per la virtù che sua natura diede*: It was generally acknowledged that devils and angels had power over the elements. See Thomas Aquinas, *Summa theol.* I, q. 112, a. 2, resp.: "Sed et Angeli boni et mali possunt aliquid in istis corporibus operari praeter actionem caelestium corporum, condensando nubes in pluvias, et aliqua huiusmodi faciendo." ("Moreover both good and bad angels can work some effect in these bodies independently of the heavenly bodies, by the condensation of the clouds into rain, and by producing some such effects.") See also Eph. 2:2, where the devil is termed *princeps potestatis aeris* ("the prince of the power of the air").

115-23. *Indi la valle . . . ritenne*: For a description of storms, see Virgil, *Georg.* I, 324-27 (continuing the passage quoted in the n. to vss. 109-10):

> . . . ruit arduus aether,
> et pluvia ingenti sata laeta boumque labores
> diluit; implentur fossae et cava flumina crescunt
> cum sonitu fervetque fretis spirantibus aequor.

Down falls the lofty heaven, and with its deluge of rain washes away the gladsome crops and the labours of oxen. The dykes fill, the deep-channelled rivers swell and roar, and the sea steams in its heaving friths.

115. *la valle*: The Casentino.   *come 'l dì fu spento*: The devil waits for night to fall, as he has more power in the dark air.

116. *Pratomagno*: The mountain ridge which forms the southwestern barrier of the Casentino.   *al gran giogo*: The main ridge of the Apennines, forming the northeastern barrier of the valley.

117. *intento*: Ready to pour forth its vapors as rain. According to Dino Compagni's *Cronica* (I, 10), on the day of the battle of Campaldino "l'aria era coperta di nuvoli." ("The air was covered with clouds.")

118. *si converse = si convertì.*

119-20. *a' fossati venne . . . sofferse*: See Virgil's "implentur fossae" quoted in the n. to vss. 115-23.

120. *ciò che la terra non sofferse*: That part which the ground could not absorb.

122. *lo fiume real*: The Arno. Buti comments: "Chiamano li Poeti fiumi reali quelli che fanno capo in mare, come fa l'Arno; l'altri no." ("The poets call 'royal rivers' those that flow into the sea, like the Arno; not other rivers.") But this was an established term for rivers that flow into the sea and not merely one used by "poets." See M. Barbi (1934b), p. 247.

123. *si ruinò*: Cf. Virgil's "ruit" in the quotation in the n. to vss. 115-23 and *Inf.* I, 61, "rovinava," where many texts have "ruinava."

124-25. *Lo corpo mio gelato . . . sospinse*: "Corpo" is the object of "trovò," "l'Archian" the subject; the construction continues with "quel" as the object and "Archiano" the subject of "sospinse." For "rubesto" ("raging"), see *Inf.* XXXI, 106.

127. *ch'i' fe' = che io feci.*   *'l dolor*: Physical pain (which Buonconte knows will prove mortal) and also pain

of remorse, which brings him to fold his arms devoutly upon his breast in the sign of the cross.

128. *voltòmmi = mi voltò*. The subject is still the "Archiano," or the Arno, which it has now become.

129. *di sua preda*: The river's "spoil" is the debris it carries with it, particularly at flood stage.

131. *e riposato de la lunga via*: Only when Dante has rested from the long way will the third spirit have him take any thought of her; and he is not asked to turn to others to request that they pray for her, but only to "remember" her himself: tenderness, compassion, and a sense of sad loneliness impress these words of hers on every reader's mind and heart.

133. *ricorditi*: "Ricorditi" is here the impersonal verb, in the subjunctive, with the pronoun in the dative. Cf. *Inf.* XXVIII, 73: "rimembriti."   *la Pia*: The use of the article with a first name adds a touch of intimacy or familiarity, Pia repeating in this way the *la* which other people used in speaking *of* her, not *to* her. Pia was a lady of Siena who, according to some accounts, was the daughter of Buonincontro Guastelloni and wife, first of Baldo di Ildobrandino de' Tolomei (who died in 1290) and secondly of Nello or Paganello de' Pannocchieschi of Castello della Pietra in the Sienese Maremma. The *Anonimo fiorentino* and Benvenuto, on the other hand, state that she was herself a member of the Tolomei family and married Nello, by whom she was put to death (in 1295); the mode of her death is disputed, some saying that she was killed so secretly that no one knew how it was done, while Benvenuto and others relate that she was by Nello's orders thrown out of a window of his castle in the Maremma:

> Ista anima fuit quaedam nobilis domina senensis de stirpe Ptolomaeorum, quae fuit uxor cuiusdam nobilis militis, qui vocatus est dominus Nellus de Panochischis de Petra, qui erat potens in maritima Senarum. Accidit ergo, quod dum coenassent, et ista domina staret ad fenestram palatii in solatiis suis, quidam domicellus de mandato Nelli cepit istam dominam per pedes et prae-

cipitavit eam per fenestram, quae continuo mortua est.
. . . Ex cuius morte crudeli natum est magnum odium
inter dictum dominum Nellum, et Ptolomaeos consortes
ipsius dominae.

This soul was a certain noble lady of Siena of the family
of the Tolomei, and she was the wife of a distinguished
soldier, called Lord Nello de' Pannocchieschi della Pie-
tra, and he was powerful in the coastal area controlled
by Siena. One day, while they were dining and she stood
for a time at a window of the palace with her maid serv-
ants, a servant, at Nello's bidding, took her by the feet
and threw her out of the window, and she died on strik-
ing the ground. . . . Because of this her cruel death
there arose a great enmity between Nello and her fam-
ily, the Tolomei.

According to C. Loria (1872, p. 413) a tradition, said to be
still current in the neighborhood, identifies the scene of the
murder with a spot known as the Salto della Contessa. Nello's
motive for the crime is supposed to have been his desire to
marry the Countess Margherita degli Aldobrandeschi, widow
of Guy de Montfort. Nello, who was captain of the Tuscan
Guelphs in 1284, and *podestà* of Volterra (1277) and Lucca
(1313), was still living in 1322, in which year he made his
will. See B. Aquarone (1889), pp. 79-84.

The identification of La Pia with Pia the wife of Baldo de'
Tolomei has been disproved by L. Banchi, who shows from
documents discovered in the Sienese archives that the latter
was still alive, as the widow of Baldo, eighteen years after the
assumed date of Dante's journey through the afterlife. See
L. Banchi (1883), p. 523:

Questa Pia dei Comentatori era ancor viva nel 1318,
vale a dire solo tre anni avanti la morte di Dante . . . è
certo che nel 18 mantenevasi vedova di Baldo Tolomei.
Senza dubbio ell'era già molto innanzi con gli anni; e lo
stesso Nello della Pietra che ne fu sin qui creduto il
marito e il carnefice, nel 1318 toccava la settantina;
erano ambedue per conseguenza non più in età da
amori, da gelosie, da romanzi.

Questi ed altri argomenti proveranno che la vedova
di Baldo Tolomei non fu la Pia che Dante cantò.

See W. Mercer (1886) for the translation of Banchi's
statement:

> This Pia of the commentators was still alive in 1318—
> that is to say just three years before the death of Dante
> . . . it is certain that in 1318 she continued widow of
> Baldo Tolomei. Without doubt she was then well ad-
> vanced in years; and the veritable Nello della Pietra,
> who was believed till now to be her husband and mur-
> derer, was close upon seventy years old in the year
> 1318. They were both, therefore, past the age of love,
> jealousy, and romance. These and other facts will dem-
> onstrate that the widow of Baldo Tolomei was not the
> Pia whom Dante celebrated.

Also see M. Barbi (1894); F. Maggini (1910), pp. 124-26;
G. Ciacci (1935), pp. 303-34.

134. *Siena mi fé, disfecemi Maremma*: Cf. Virgil's epitaph
in the n. to *Purg.* III, 27: "Mantua me genuit, Calabri
rapuere." *fé = fece.   disfecemi = mi disfece.*

135. *salsi = se lo sa*, the so-called pleonastic reflexive being
(here, as usual) not pleonastic at all. It serves to reinforce
the subject, bringing the verbal statement back upon it, as
though to say "he knows it *well in his very own conscience.*"

135-36. *che 'nnanellata pria . . . gemma*: Who had ringed
me in wedlock with his gem. "Pria" defies translation. F. Ci-
polla (1894-95, p. 642) finds this to say about the elusive lit-
tle adverb in the present context: "Non indica un antecedente
a qualche cosa di determinato, che segua a quello: indica sol-
tanto l'inizio d'una serie, d'una condizione, che dopo dura."
("It does not indicate an antecedent of something determi-
nate that follows upon it; rather, it only indicates the begin-
ning of a series, of a condition that then perdures.") And he
also points to a kind of equivalent in the "primus" of the
opening verses of the *Aeneid*:

> Arma virumque cano, Troiae qui primus ab oris
> Italiam fato profugus Laviniaque venit
> litora . . .

which, to be sure, may be translated:

> Arms I sing and the man who first from the coasts of
> Troy, exiled by fate, came to Italy and Lavinian shores.

But "first," in such a context, gives quite the wrong meaning. Cipolla has also pointed to the fact that Annibal Caro, in his famous translation of Virgil's poem, rendered this "primus" precisely with a *pria*.

Thus, the "pria" spoken by Pia points to the first act of a whole sequence which led to her murder, but the term does not imply a *second* specific event, but precisely the whole sequence, which ended with her death.

In the words "che 'nnanellata . . . m'avea con la sua gemma" Pia refers to the common marriage custom of the day whereby, with or without witnesses, it was enough for the man to place a ring upon the woman's finger, and for the two to declare that they took one another for husband and wife. See M. Barbi (1934b), pp. 279-80. The so-called *nozze*, or public celebration of marriage, with a banquet and merry-making, then followed, after a varying period of time, and took place in the house of the new husband, whither the bride was led on this occasion, this ceremony being commonly referred to as *menare la donna*. For several excellent examples of the practice, see Boccaccio, *Decam.* II, 3, and V, 4 (vol. I, pp. 84-92, 367-72), and X, 8 (vol. II, pp. 275-91). For a defense of another reading of the verses, see G. Crocioni (1953).

CANTO VI

1. *si parte*: "Is over." *Partire* is used here in the sense of "end," "break up." Cf. Boccaccio, *Decam.* III, 1 (vol. I, p. 187, ll. 31-32): "Ma poi, partito il lor ragionamento, cominciò Masetto a pensare che via dovesse tenere." ("But then, when their conversation was ended, Masetto began to think how he should set about the matter.")   *il gioco de la zara*: L. Zdekauer (1886, pp. 24-25) has the following account of this game of dice:

> I due gruppi principali del giuoco di fortuna nel medio evo sono adunque il giuoco de' dadi, e quello delle tavole. Il tipo del primo è il giuoco a zara. Molto si è detto su questa parola, senza arrivare ad una conclusione soddisfacente. Dagli statuti pertanto risulta questo, ch'esso si giocava con 3 dadi, e generalmente senza tavoliero, sopra un banco od un piano qualunque, liscio, ("*discum pollitum*," Firenze, St. d. 1285; v. Docum IV. Padova l. c. 785, ed altrove); e che, durante il giuoco, secondo certe combinazioni, la parola "azar" veniva proferita dai giuocatori stessi. Quali fossero queste combinazioni, lo dice Iacopo della Lana, nel Commento di Dante, Purgat. VI, 1: cioè tre e quattro, i numeri più bassi, e 17 e 18, i più alti. Il particolare di questi tratti si è, che essi non valgono; essi non vengono contati

come numeri ("non sono computati"), ma soltanto come "zari" ("sono computati zari"). Di fronte a questi numeri peggiori stanno quelli, che hanno maggior probabilità, come i migliori. "Quello numero" dice l'Ottimo nel commento al passo sopracitato del Purg., "che in più modi può venire, è detta migliore volta di ragione." Risulta dunque, che qui non si tratta di vincere col numero più grande, essendo peggiori i numeri colla minima probabilità, anche se fossero alti ed invece migliori quelli, che possono venire in più modi.—Ma oltre di questo è certo, che non soltanto nel caso della "zara," ma ad ogni trar di dado proferivano un numero. "Se io non avessi chiamato XI," dice il perditore nel commento di Iacopo della Lana "non avrei perduto." E poi: "Io chiamavo cotal numero, che era ragionevole a dovere venir."— Ora il computo della probabilità ci dice, che i numeri colla massima probabilità fra le combinazioni di tre dadi, segnati ognuno dal N.º 1 fino al N.º 4 sono i numeri 10 e 11; 3 e 4, 17 e 18 invece sono le combinazioni, che hanno la minima probabilità, a venire. Atteso dunque, che il numero da farsi venne gridato prima di gettare i dadi, e che il miglior numero fosse quello che aveva la maggior probabilità a venire, concludiamo che la zara sia un giuoco di dadi, in cui vinceva colui, che facesse il numero già proclamato ad alta voce da lui stesso, prima di gettare i dadi. La particolarità sta in questo, che i numeri della minore probabilità sono chiamati e contati zeri. Così si spiega, come la parola "zara" potette acquistare il significato della combinazione sfavorevole, e del danno in generale.

The two main forms of gambling in the Middle Ages were the game of dice and the game of *tavole*. The first takes the form of the game *a zara*. Much has been said about this word, but no satisfactory conclusion has been reached. From the statutes, we learn that it was played with three dice, generally without a board, on a bench or on any smooth surface ("discum pollitum," Florence, St. d. 1285; cf. Docum. IV, Padua, l. c. 785, and elsewhere). In the course of the game the players would say

the word *azar* whenever certain combinations came out.
Jacopo della Lana, in his commentary on Dante (*Purg.
VI, 1*) tells us what these combinations were: three and
four, the lowest numbers, and seventeen and eighteen,
the highest. The important thing about these throws is
that they do not count. They are not counted as numbers
("not computed") but only as *zari* ("computed *zari*").
These are the worst numbers; then there are the best,
which are the numbers of highest probability. The *Ot-
timo*, in the commentary to the passage in *Purgatory*
cited earlier, says: "The number that can come in many
ways is said to be the best number." Clearly, then, the ob-
ject is not to win with the highest number, since the worst
are those with the minimum probability, even if they are
high. And the best are those that can come in several
ways. Furthermore, it is certain that they called a num-
ber at every throw of the dice, not only in the case of
zara. "If I had not called eleven," says the loser in the
commentary of Jacopo della Lana, "I should not have
lost." And later: "I called that number because it was
due to come up." Now, according to the laws of prob-
ability, the numbers that have the best chance of being
thrown by the three dice, each marked from one to four,
are ten and eleven; on the other hand, three and four,
and seventeen and eighteen have the minimum prob-
ability of turning up. Since the number the thrower
hoped would turn up was announced before throwing
the dice, and since the best number was the one that had
the highest probability of coming out, we conclude that
zara was a game of dice in which the winner was the one
who made the number which he had called aloud before
throwing the dice. There is this special feature: that the
numbers of least probability are called and counted
zero. That explains why the word *zara* could acquire the
meaning of an unfavorable combination, and of harm
in general.

N. Tamassia (1893, p. 456) calls attention to the following
passage in Odofredo, Bolognese doctor in jurisprudence, who
died in 1265: "Item sicut videmus in lusoribus ad taxillas vel

similem ludum, nam multi stare solent ad videndum ludum, et quando unus lusorum obtinet in ludo, illi instantes solent petere aliquid sibi dari de lucro illo in ludo habito, et illi lusores dare solent." ("Likewise we observe that, when people are playing games of chance such as with dice, there will be a group standing to watch the game, and when one of the players wins, they will ask for a share of his profits and the players will always give it to them.")

2. *colui che perde*: This figure of the loser, though serving to make the whole scene more graphic, finds no correspondence in the second term of the simile.   *si riman*: The so-called pleonastic reflexive once more, in its usual function of setting off the subject.

3. *repetendo le volte*: "Repeating the throws" to see how he might have come out if he had had another chance. Lana imagines the loser saying: "Se io non avessi chiamato XI, non avrei perduto." ("If I had not called eleven, I should not have lost.") See the quotation from L. Zdekauer in n. to vs. 1.   *e tristo impara*: But learns all too late.

4. *con l'altro*: With the winner.   *tutta la gente*: All the onlookers.

6. *li si reca a mente*: Calls himself to his attention. Cf. *Inf.* XI, 106.   *li = gli*.

7. *el*: The winner.   *intende*: "Gives heed to." Vs. 11, in the second term of the simile, makes this clear.

8. *a cui*: A relative pronoun—*colui* or *quello*—is understood: "quello a cui porge la man, più non fa pressa."

11. *volgendo a loro, e qua e là, la faccia*: Dante is obeying Virgil's previous order of *Purg.* V, 45: "però pur va, e in andando ascolta."

12. *promettendo*: I.e., that he will ask their loved ones among the living to pray for their speedier advance to Purgatory proper.

13-14. *l'Aretin . . . morte*: This is a reference to Benincasa da Laterina (Laterina is in the upper Val d'Arno), a judge who, according to the early commentators, while acting as assessor for the *podestà* of Siena, sentenced to death a brother (or uncle) of Ghino di Tacco. In revenge Ghino murdered him while he was sitting in the papal audit office at Rome. The murder probably took place around 1297.

14. *Ghin di Tacco*: Famous highwayman. Although the date of his death is uncertain, he is thought to have died *ca.* 1303. See P. Toynbee (1968), pp. 313-14. Boccaccio, who tells a story of him in the *Decameron* (X, 2), calls Ghino "per la sua fierezza e per le sue ruberie uomo assai famoso" ("a man very famous on account of his fierceness and his thefts") in *Decam.* X, 2 (vol. 2, p. 241, ll. 8-9).

15. *e l'altro ch'annegò correndo in caccia*: This soul is identified by the early commentators as Guccio de' Tarlati of the Tarlati of Pietramala in the territory of Arezzo, in which city they were the chiefs of the Ghibelline party. According to Benvenuto, he was the uncle of the celebrated Guido Tarlati, bishop of Arezzo, and was drowned in the Arno, his horse having run away with him, while he was in pursuit of some of the Bostoli, Guelph exiles from Arezzo. Other accounts, however, state that he was drowned while trying to escape from the Bostoli (after the battle of Campaldino, say some). The phrase "in caccia," in fact, lends itself to either interpretation, "in flight" or "in pursuit"; see M. Barbi (1934b), p. 222, and the phrase as used by Dino Compagni in his *Cronica* (I, 10): "[Gli Aretini] furono messi in caccia, uccidendoli." ("[The Aretines] were pursued and killed.")

17. *Federigo Novello*: One of the Conti Guidi, son of Guido Novello (hence he is Frederick junior of Guido junior). He is said to have been killed near Bibbiena in 1289 or 1291 by one of the Guelph Bostoli of Arezzo, while helping the Tarlati of Pietramala against the latter.   *quel da Pisa*: The son of Messer Marzucco (see n. to vs. 18).

18. *Marzucco*: This personage was of an ancient noble family originally from Scorno, and like his father, Scornigiano,

he held the title of judge and was charged with many delicate offices within and without the city of Pisa (for more details, see P. Toynbee, 1968, pp. 434-35). In 1258 he married (for the second time), and in April 1286 he declared himself a novice in the Franciscan convent of Pisa, from which he seems to have passed to the convent of Santa Croce in Florence. In Florence he served as a witness to documents dated October 10, 1291, August 17, 1293, September 1, 1295, and July 26, 1298, always with the name *Frater Marzuccus de Pisis* or *teste Fratre Marzucho pisano*. Marzucco thus appears to have lived his last years in Florence at a time when Dante could have known him. His wife also entered a religious order, as is witnessed by a document of October 28, 1301, in which she appears as "uxor olim domini fratris Marzucci Scornigiani," which clearly witnesses the fact that Marzucco was no longer living at that date.

The commentators differ as to the details of the circumstance alluded to by Dante; they are, however, for the most part agreed upon one point, viz. that Marzucco had a son who was murdered, and that he showed his fortitude in forgiving, instead of avenging, the murder.

The true facts of the incident referred to, in which "the good Marzucco showed himself strong," are not available. Strong evidence points to the murder, in 1287, of one Gano Scornigiani by Nino, known as "il Brigata" (see *Inf.* XXXIII, 89), grandson of Count Ugolino, and by certain others who joined in with Nino della Gherardesca. However, the documents do not mention any son of Marzucco by the name of Gano; they mention only a son named Gallo by his first wife. In any event, Gano was slain in 1287, and Marzucco was already a novice in the Franciscan order in 1286. Did Marzucco as a Friar Minor "show himself strong"? The extant documents give no answer.

19. *conte Orso*: Orso degli Alberti della Cerbaia, son of Count Napoleone degli Alberti. According to Benvenuto he was killed by his cousin Alberto, son of Count Alessandro degli Alberti: "Iste comes Ursus fuit filius comitis Neapoleonis de Acerbaia, qui acerbe fuit interfectus velut ursus

tractatu comitis Alberti de Mangona consobrini." ("This
Count Orso, the son of Count Napoleone of Cerbaia, was
viciously murdered by the 'bear mauling' of his cousin Al-
berto da Mangona.") Pietro di Dante gives a similar account,
but without specifying the name of the murderer: "Comes
Ursus occisus proditorie a suis consortibus et propinquis, fuit
de Comitibus Albertis." ("Count Orso, foully murdered by
his friends and relatives, was one of the Alberti.") The mur-
der of Count Orso by his cousin Alberto took place before
1286 and was doubtless, as Casini-Barbi suggests, a con-
tinuance of the blood-feud which had existed between the
fathers of the two cousins, Napoleone and Alessandro, who
killed each other. See *Inf.* XXXII, 55-58, and n. to
Inf. XXXII, 57.

20. *inveggia = invidia.* The form is probably a Proven-
çalism, from *enveia.* See E. G. Parodi (1957), p. 227.

21. *com' e' dicea*: A soul in Purgatory would tell the truth,
of course.   *commisa = commessa*: Cf. "miso" for *messo*
in *Inf.* XXVI, 54.

22. *Pier da la Broccia*: Although according to tradition
Pierre de la Brosse was a surgeon of low birth, he was ac-
tually a gentleman of Touraine of honorable extraction, who
was chamberlain and, for a time, favorite of Philip III of
France. He had already held the office of chamberlain
to Philip's father, Louis IX. On the sudden death in 1276 of
the heir to the throne (Louis, Philip's son by his first wife,
Isabella of Aragon), an accusation was brought against the
queen, Marie of Brabant, of having poisoned Louis in order
to secure the succession of her own son. Among her accusers
was Pierre de la Brosse.

In 1278 Pierre was suddenly arrested by order of the king,
and was hanged in that year. The suddenness and ignominy
of his execution appear to have caused great wonder and con-
sternation, especially as the charge on which he was
condemned was not made known. According to the popular
account he had been accused by the queen of an attempt
upon her chastity. The truth seems to be that he was hanged

on a charge of treasonable correspondence with Alfonso X, king of Castile, with whom Philip was at war, the intercepted letters on which the charge was based having, it is alleged, been forged at the instance of the queen. It is at any rate certain that Pierre was an object of envy and hatred to the great nobles of Philip's court, and it is likely enough that they made common cause with the queen in bringing about his fall.
qui: Here on earth, among the living.   *proveggia* = *proveda*.

23. *Brabante*: Brabant, ancient duchy of the Netherlands, covering the territory of what is now the southern Netherlands and central and northern Belgium; now the name of a province in central Belgium. Dante thus urges Marie (see n. to vs. 22) to repent of having caused Pierre's death while she yet has time (vss. 22-24). She died in 1321, in the same year as Dante, and thus could have read this warning.

24. *sì che però non sia di peggior greggia*: That she not find herself in a far worse flock (i.e., among the damned of Hell) than this in which Pierre is, in Purgatory. Clearly Marie, should she die unrepentant of this sin and accordingly be sentenced by Minos, might well find herself in company with Potiphar's wife, in the tenth ditch of Malebolge (*Inf.* XXX, 97).   *però* = *per ciò*.

26. *pregar* = *pregarono*.   *pur*: "Only," i.e., for nothing else. Cf. vs. 31.   *altri*: A singular pronoun that is, in the context, plural in meaning.   *prieghi*: Present subjunctive of *pregare*.

27. *sì che s'avacci lor divenir sante*: "Lor divenir sante" is the subject of the verb. They pray that their becoming blessed (in Paradise) may be hastened. For another example of *avacciare,* see *Purg.* IV, 116.

28. *El*: An impersonal subject pronoun, sometimes called pleonastic.

28-30. *El par che tu . . . pieghi*: The reference is to Virgil, *Aen.* VI, 337-83, where Aeneas encounters the shade of

Palinurus, who prays, as one whose body has not received
burial, to be taken across the Stygian waves that he may find
a quiet resting-place. The Sibyl (termed "vates" in vs. 372)
answers (*Aen.* VI, 373-76):

> . . . unde haec, o Palinure, tibi tam dira cupido?
> tu Stygias inhumatus aquas amnemque severum
> Eumenidum aspicies ripamve iniussus adibis?
> desine fata deum flecti sperare precando.

> Whence, O Palinurus, this wild longing of thine? Shalt
> thou, unburied, view the Stygian waters and the Furies'
> stern river, and unbidden draw near the bank? Cease to
> dream that heaven's decrees may be turned aside by
> prayer.

29. *o luce mia*: Later in this canto Beatrice is called a
"lume" (vs. 45).   *in alcun testo*: Cf. *Inf.* XX, 113: "in
alcun loco"; *Purg.* IV, 80: "in alcun' arte."

30. *che decreto del cielo orazion pieghi*: "Decreto del ciel"
is the object of the verb, "orazion" is the subject.

31. *pur*: Cf. vs. 26.

32. *sarebbe dunque loro speme vana*: The hope of these
souls is expressed in vss. 26-27.

34. *La mia scrittura è piana*: For *piano* in this sense, see
Purg. XVIII, 85.

35. *non falla*: "Is not fallacious."

37. *ché cima di giudicio non s'avvalla*: Grandgent trans-
lates this "the summit of justice (*apex iuris*) is not over-
turned" and recalls Shakespeare, *Measure for Measure,* Act
II, sc. ii, ll. 75-77:

> . . . How would you be
> If he which is the top of judgment should
> But judge you as you are? . . .

s'avvalla: Virgil's verb is "flecti" (see quotation in n. to vss.
28-30); Dante phrases it as "pieghi" (vs. 30).

38. *perché foco d'amor compia*: "Though fire of love ful-
fill." The debt owed the Deity is essentially a debt of love, as
this verse suggests. In praying for those in Purgatory, the liv-
ing can (provided they are *in grazia*) contribute "payments"
toward the satisfaction of this debt.   *in un punto*: "In a
moment" posits the extreme or limiting case, hence "perché"
("though"). If enough love were contributed toward the debt
by the living, it might in one moment, or instantly, absolve
it. It follows from this that it can also be satisfied gradually,
by installments.

39. *de' = deve.   s'astalla*: "Has his *stallo*" (cf. *Inf.*
XXXIII, 102), or place of sojourn, here.

40. *fermai*: Cf. *Purg.* XXI, 99.

41–42. *non s'ammendava . . . disgiunto*: Palinurus, to
whose prayers in *Aen.* VI, 363-71 Virgil here refers, was a
pagan, living in the period between the Fall and the Redemp-
tion, a time, that is, in which God's grace (with notable ex-
ceptions) was withdrawn from mankind. See *Par.* XXXII,
82, "ma poi che 'l tempo de la grazia venne," i.e., when grace
returned to man through Christ's sacrifice, which, by clear
implication, makes the time before Christ a time "without
grace." See also *Purg.* IV, 133-35.

43. *Veramente*: Nevertheless.   *alto sospetto*: Deep ques-
tion, i.e., one involving matters such as grace, which tran-
scend Virgil's understanding. Virgil will continue to refer to
Beatrice along the way of the purgatorial journey: see *Purg.*
XV, 76-78; XVIII, 46-48.

45. *che lume fia tra 'l vero e lo 'ntelletto*: When Beatrice
came to him in Limbo (*Inf.* II), Virgil recognized her as that
lady through whom mankind transcends all that lies beneath
the moon. Now she is said to be a light between the truth and
the intellect. Again and again she will be termed a light: all
of which serves to point to Beatrice's meaning in allegory.
Virgil also is frequently referred to as a light, as in vs. 29,
above.

47-48. *tu la vedrai . . . monte*: Through such verses as these, Beatrice is seen as the goal at the summit of the mountain, and the journey thither thus becomes a journey to Beatrice. See C. S. Singleton (1958).

48. *ridere e felice*: M. Barbi (1934a, pp. 39-41) offers a justification of this rather unusual construction in which an infinitive and an adjective can both depend on a verb, as on *vedere* here. See *Purg.* XII, 35.

51. *e vedi omai che 'l poggio l'ombra getta*: Virgil and Dante are climbing the mountain on its eastern slope and therefore in the early afternoon are on its shady side.

52. *con questo giorno innanzi*: For as long as day lasts.

54. *ma 'l fatto è d'altra forma che non stanzi*: In fact, if Virgil knows how long it will take him and his charge to climb this mountain, he would appear to be deliberately withholding this discouraging fact from Dante. And yet Virgil does not seem to know the entire "fact" himself, i.e., that there is actually no climbing the mountain at night. See *Purg.* VII, 49-51.   *stanzi*: "Think," "judge." Cf. *Inf.* XXV, 10, where the word bears the meaning "decree."

56. *colui che già si cuopre de la costa*: The sun.

57. *sì che ' suoi raggi tu romper non fai*: Dante, being now in the shadow of the mountain, no longer intercepts the rays of the sun.

59. *sola soletta*: The repetition of the adjective begins the stress on the apartness of this spirit, as does the fact that it is seated, for all the other souls seen in this area of Antepurgatory have been moving about in groups. Moreover, the suffix *–etta* adds a touch as of endearing sentiment.

60. *la via più tosta*: The quickest way, which suggests that it is still necessary for Virgil and Dante to make their way across rough terrain.

61. *o anima lombarda*: The exclamation is uttered by the poet as he sees again, in memory, this soul seated alone on

the slope. The apostrophe which then follows (vss. 76-151) is voiced out of this same focus on the figure.

62. *come ti stavi*: "Ti" here is an excellent example of the "distancing" reflexive. Cf. *Inf.* VII, 94; VIII, 48; and *passim*.
altera e disdegnosa: Landino comments:

> In nostra lingua diciamo altiero, e disdegnoso colui, che per eccellentia d'animo non risguarda, nè pon pensiero, a cose vili, nè quelle degna. Sì che dimostra una certa schifezza generosa, e senza vitio. Perciò che quando uno sprezza non per grandezza d'animo, ma per troppa alterigia, non altiero, ma superbo si chiamerà.

> In our language, we use the words *altiero* (lofty) and *disdegnoso* (disdainful) of the man whose excellence of spirit is such that he completely ignores vile things and will not stoop to them. Such a man shows fastidiousness that is generous and without taint. But if a man is scornful not out of magnanimity but out of arrogance we call him not *altiero*, but *superbo* (haughty).

63. *e nel mover de li occhi onesta e tarda*: Cf. *Inf.* IV, 112: "Genti v'eran con occhi tardi e gravi"; also see *Purg.* III, 10-11.

65. *lasciavane gir = ci lasciava andare*.   *sguardando*: The verb *sguardare* suggests gazing rather than direct, intent looking.

66. *a guisa di leon quando si posa*: The simile may have a literary source for Dante. Cf. Gen. 49:9: "Requiescens accubuisti ut leo." ("He crouches and couches as a lion.") But it could well come from the direct observation of a lion in a cage as it lies gazing distantly at or beyond the human creatures who stand looking at it. Lions were kept in several city zoos in Italy at the time and are known to have been kept in Florence in Dante's time and later.

67. *Pur*: May mean either "only" (i.e., Virgil advances, leaving Dante somewhat behind) or "nonetheless" (i.e., in spite of this soul's "distant" attitude), which seems more probable.

68. *ne = ci.*

70. *de la vita*: Of our former condition among the living. The soul has not perceived that Dante is here in the flesh, since now, in the shade of the mountain, no shadow is cast by his body.

71. *ci 'nchiese = ci inchiese (ci richiese).*   *e 'l dolce duca incominciava*: The charge of sentiment which soon will run so high, in the scene of the embrace, is already showing itself in the adjective "dolce" and in the fact that the scene itself is framed descriptively, by the verb in the imperfect, rather than in the narrative past absolute—and so on to the climax "abbracciava," vs. 75.

72. *Mantua . . .* : No doubt Virgil would have said "Mantua fu la mia patria," thus answering the first part of the question addressed to him. Benvenuto, in his Latin, can think that he would have said "Mantua me genuit," thus echoing the epitaph written for Virgil: see n. to *Purg.* III, 27.   *tutta in sé romita*: Cf. vss. 58-59; now, by this effective touch, the physical apartness is made a psychological apartness: the soul was "in sé romita" ("in himself recluse") and now rises out of such a condition *and* out of the *place* where it is (the physical place, vs. 73) to embrace Virgil.

74. *Sordello*: Sordello, one of the most distinguished among the Italian poets who elected to write in Provençal rather than in their mother-tongue, was born at Goito, some ten miles from Mantua, about the year 1200. He led a chequered and wandering life, the latter portion of which was devoted to the service of Charles of Anjou, by whom he was well rewarded. The latest record of him that has come down to us is dated 1269. To the Dante student one episode of Sordello's life and one of his poems are of special interest. Between the years 1227-29, while staying at Treviso with Ezzelino III da Romano, he had a liaison with the latter's sister Cunizza (see *Par.* IX, 25-36), who was the wife of Count Riccardo di San Bonifazio, but whom Sordello had abducted (for political reasons) at the request of her brother. When the latter dis-

covered the intrigue, Sordello was forced to flee to Provence. About the year 1240 he wrote a very fine *planch* (or song of lamentation) on the death of Blacatz, himself a poet and one of the barons of Count Raymond Berenger IV. In this poem the leading sovereigns and princes of Europe are exhorted to eat of the dead man's heart, so that their courage may increase, and they be fired on to noble deeds. These verses may have indirectly inspired the patriotic outburst for which the appearance of Sordello is made the pretext; and they certainly induced Dante to assign to Sordello the task of pointing out the princes in the following canto. There is a reference to Sordello in *De vulg. eloqu.* I, xv, 2.

This information is provided by the Temple Classics edition of the *Purgatorio*; see P. Toynbee (1968), pp. 585-88, for further details. Of the office assigned to Sordello, Benvenuto, commenting on *Purg.* VII, 69, says:

> Nota quod poeta pulcre fingit quod Sordellus duxerat istos poetas ad videndum istos viros illustres, quia fuit homo curialis et curiosus investigator et admirator omnium valentum sui temporis et omnium virtutes et mores sciebat et referebat.

We should notice how beautifully the poet portrays Sordello's bringing the poet to visit these illustrious men; he did so because he was a courtier and a diligent observer and admirer of the great men of his times, and he knew and related all about the virtues and conduct of his contemporaries.

75. *e l'un l'altro abbracciava*: Cf. n. to vs. 71; the following apostrophe thus arises out of this descriptive focus, out of this "picture" as relived in memory by the poet now.

76. *serva Italia*: Italy, formerly "mistress of provinces," would be free if she were ruled by an emperor, as God intended. In *De mon.* I, xii, 6-8, Dante writes:

> Hoc viso, iterum manifestum esse potest quod hec libertas sive principium hoc totius libertatis nostre, est maximum donum humane nature a Deo collatum: quia per ipsum hic felicitamur ut homines, per ipsum alibi

felicitamur ut dii. Quod si ita est, quis erit qui humanum genus optime se habere non dicat, cum potissime hoc principio possit uti? Sed existens sub Monarcha est potissime liberum.

When we see this we may further understand that this freedom (or this principle of all our freedom) is the greatest gift conferred by God on human nature; for through it we have our felicity here as men, through it we have our felicity elsewhere as deities. And if this be so, who would not agree that the human race is best disposed when it has fullest use of this principle? But it is under a monarch that it is most free.

See also Dante's letter addressed to the infamous Florentines who resist the Emperor Henry VII (*Epist.* VI, 5):

Vos autem divina iura et humana transgredientes, quos dira cupiditatis ingluvies paratos in omne nefas illexit, nonne terror secunde mortis exagitat, ex quo, primi et soli iugum libertatis horrentes, in romani Principis, mundi regis et Dei ministri, gloriam fremuistis, atque iure prescriptionis utentes, debite subiectionis officium denegando, in rebellionis vesaniam maluistis insurgere?

But you, who transgress divine and human law, whom a dire rapaciousness hath found ready to be drawn into every crime,—doth not the dread of the second death pursue you? For ye first and alone, shunning the yoke of liberty, have murmured against the glory of the Roman prince, the king of the world and the minister of God, and on the plea of prescriptive right have refused the duty of the submission which ye owed, and have rather risen up in the insanity of rebellion!

77. *nave sanza nocchiere*: The helmsman is the emperor. See *Conv.* IV, iv, 5-7, where Dante says:

Sì come vedemo in una nave, che diversi offici e diversi fini di quella a uno solo fine sono ordinati, cioè a prendere loro desiderato porto per salutevole via: dove, sì come ciascuno officiale ordina la propria operazione nel proprio fine, così è uno che tutti questi fini considera,

e ordina quelli ne l'ultimo di tutti; e questo è lo noc-
chiero, a la cui voce tutti obedire deono. Questo vedemo
ne le religioni, ne li esserciti, in tutte quelle cose che
sono, come detto è, a fine ordinate. Per che manifesta-
mente vedere si può che a perfezione de la universale
religione de la umana spezie conviene essere uno, quasi
nocchiero, che considerando le diverse condizioni del
mondo, ne li diversi e necessarii offici ordinare abbia del
tutto universale e inrepugnabile officio di comandare.
E questo officio per eccellenza Imperio è chiamato,
sanza nulla addizione, però che esso è di tutti li altri
comandamenti comandamento. E così chi a questo
officio è posto è chiamato Imperadore, però che di tutti
li comandamenti elli è comandatore, e quello che esso
dice a tutti è legge, e per tutti dee essere obedito e ogni
altro comandamento da quello di costui prendere vigore
e autoritade.

Even as we see in a ship that the divers offices and divers
ends of it are ordained to one single end, to wit the mak-
ing of the desired port by a prosperous voyage; wherein,
like as each officer regulates his proper function to its
proper end, there is one who considers all these ends
and regulates them with a view to the final end; and he
is the shipmaster, whose voice all are bound to obey.
And we see the same thing in religious orders, and in
armies, and in all things which are ordained, as afore-
said, to some end. Whereby it may be manifestly seen
that for the perfection of the universal religious order
of the human race it behoves that there should be one,
as shipmaster, who, considering the diverse conditions
of the world, and ordaining the diverse and necessary
offices, should have the universal and indisputable office
of commanding the whole. And this office is called by
pre-eminence empire, without any qualification, because
it is the command of all the other commands. And hence
he who is appointed to this office is called emperor be-
cause he is the commander who issues all the com-
mands. And what he says is law to all, and he ought to

be obeyed by all, and every other command draws its strength and authority from his.

78. *non donna di provincie*: See Lam. 1:1: "Quomodo sedet sola civitas plena populo! facta est quasi vidua domina gentium; princeps provinciarum facta est sub tributo." ("How doth the city sit solitary that was full of people! How is the mistress of the Gentiles become as a widow: the princes of provinces made tributary!") For the phrase as traditionally applied to Italy, derived from the *Corpus iuris civilis* of Justinian (see n. to vss. 88-89), see the quotation provided by F. Ercole (1913, p. 172, n. 2): "L'Italia non può essere tributaria di alcuno, perchè sta scritto nelle leggi: *non est provincia* etc." ("Italy cannot be the tributary of anyone, because it is written in the laws: it is not a province, etc.") Cf. Ristoro d'Arezzo, *Della comp.* VII, iv, 6 (p. 216): "La nobile provincia d'Italia: la quale è donna di tutte le provincie, che per la sua nobiltà ingeneraro la grande Roma, la quale signoreggiò e fu donna di tutte le città." ("The noble province of Italy is mistress of all the provinces, which through her nobility gave birth to the great city of Rome, which ruled and was mistress of all the cities.")

ma bordello: Literally, *bordello* is a house of prostitution, but in this context the term denotes, metaphorically, a prostitute. Cf. Isa. 1:21: "Quomodo facta est meretrix, civitas fidelis, plena iudicii?" ("How is the faithful city, that was full of judgment, become a harlot?") See *Conv.* I, ix, 5: "l'hanno fatta di donna meretrice" ("have made her a harlot instead of a lady").

81. *quivi*: In Purgatory, among the dead, as is made clear by the contrasting "in te" of the following verse.

83. *li vivi tuoi*: In contrast with the two Mantuan souls there, among the dead.

85-86. *intorno da le prode le tue marine*: The regions near your shores.

86. *e poi ti guarda in seno*: And then consider your regions within.

88–89. *Che val perché . . . Iustiniano*: Justinian, emperor of Constantinople from 527 to 565. He appointed a commission of jurists to draw up a complete body of law, which resulted in the compilation of two great works; one, called *Digesta* or *Pandectae* (533), in fifty books, contained all that was valuable in the works of preceding jurists; the other, called *Codex constitutionum*, consisted of a collection of the imperial constitutions. To these two works was subsequently added an elementary treatise in four books, under the title of *Institutiones* (533); and at a later period Justinian published various new constitutions, to which he gave the name of *Novellae constitutiones* (534-65). These four works, under the general name of *Corpus iuris civilis*, form the Roman law as received in Europe, and it is to this work that Dante here makes special allusion. Cf. *Par.* VI, 12.

89. *se la sella è vòta*: Cf. *Conv.* IV, ix, 10, where (after a direct reference to the *Digesta*—"Vecchio Digesto"—of Justinian) Dante continues:

> Sì che quasi dire si può de lo Imperadore, volendo lo suo officio figurare con una imagine, che elli sia lo cavalcatore de la umana volontade. Lo quale cavallo come vada sanza lo cavalcatore per lo campo assai è manifesto, e spezialmente ne la misera Italia, che sanza mezzo alcuno a la sua governazione è rimasa!

> Wherefore we may in some sort say of the emperor, if we wish to figure his office by an image, that he is the rider of the human will. And how that horse courses over the plain without the rider is manifest enough, and especially in the wretched Italy which, without any mediator at all, has been abandoned to her own direction.

90. *Sanz' esso*: Without the bridle, which Justinian had "refitted."

91–92. *Ahi gente . . . sella*: In denouncing the cause of Italy's woeful plight the poet turns first to the "people" of the Church, popes and ecclesiastics in power, who ought to be "devout," that is, heed the precepts of God (vs. 93); on this, see the whole thesis of the third book of the *De monarchia*.

93. *se bene intendi ciò che Dio ti nota*: Cf. Matt. 22:21: "Tunc ait illis: Reddite ergo quae sunt Caesaris Caesari, et quae sunt Dei Deo." ("Then he said to them, 'Render, therefore, to Caesar the things that are Caesar's, and to God the things that are God's.' ")

94. *fiera*: The metaphor of the horse continues.   *fella*: See vs. 98: "indomita e selvaggia."

97. *Alberto tedesco*: Albert I of Austria, son of Rudolf I of Habsburg, was emperor (but never crowned), 1298-1308. He was elected after he had defeated and, it was rumored, slain his predecessor, Adolf of Nassau, in a battle at Göllheim. Finally, in 1303, his election was recognized by Boniface VIII in consideration of the advantages of his alliance against the pope's mortal enemy, Philip the Fair of France. On May 1, 1308, he was assassinated by his nephew John.

100-102. *giusto giudicio da le stelle . . . n'aggia*: What this judgment might be is left obscure, nor is it possible to ascertain that the poet, writing after the assassination of Albert (1308) or the death of his eldest son the year before, would be alluding to those calamities. On Dante's chronological perspective, see E. G. Parodi (1920), pp. 453-54:

> Ricordiamoci che Dante, nemmeno nel canto sesto, nell'invettiva che fa in nome proprio, non si allontana dalla sua finzione cronologica del 1300, ossia, come mi sono già espresso "si colloca idealmente, anche qual narratore del proprio viaggio, in un punto di tempo che gli permette di considerare il presente o il non lontano passato come futuro, e allo scrittore non toglie del tutto i preziosi vantaggi di cui godeva il pellegrino dei regni oltremondani!"

Let us remember that Dante never departs from the chronological fiction of 1300—not even in the sixth canto, during that invective delivered in his own name. As I have said before, even as the narrator of his own voyage, he places himself ideally at a point in time that allows him to view the present or the not very distant past as future. He does not completely take away from the writer those precious advantages enjoyed by the pilgrim in the world beyond.

102. *tuo successor*: Albert's successor was Henry VII, emperor from 1308 to 1313, but if, as advocated by E. G. Parodi (see quotation in preceding note), we hold to the point of view adopted by the poet as he utters this invective, this fact is not yet known.   *aggia = abbia*.

103. *ch' = ché (perché)* or *che* without the accent in an attenuated "because," translatable by "for" in English.
'l tuo padre: Rudolf I, emperor from 1273 to 1291. For the reproach, as it applies to him, see *Purg.* VII, 94-96.

104. *per cupidigia = da cupidigia*.   *costà*: Up there, in Germany, where Albert is. See Villani, VII, 146: "Sempre intese a crescere suo stato e signoria in Alamagna, lasciando le 'mprese d'Italia per accrescere terra e podere a' figliuoli." ("Always intent upon augmenting his power and lordship in Germany, he undertook nothing in Italy, so that he might increase the lands and possessions of his sons.")

106. *Montecchi*: The Montecchi family gave its name to the imperial party, or faction of the Monticoli (Dante has Tuscanized the name), which was headed, from *ca.* 1235 to 1259, by Ezzelino III da Romano in his attempt to conquer Lombardy. Thus the Monticoli, as the name of a party, became synonymous with "friends of Ezzelino." The focal point of the struggle between the imperial and anti-imperial parties passed (*ca.* 1247) to Cremona, where the anti-imperial party had long borne the name of Cappelletti.
    The Monticoli, originally a merchant family, by the acquisition of vast estates became politically very powerful; by 1195, their name already designates a faction in the political life of Verona. And, as the faction of the Monticoli was absorbed into that of Ezzelino, it gradually extended the theater of its interests into all of Lombardy. By 1291, the Monticoli party was dead in Verona, the Della Scala family having gained control after the death of Ezzelino (1259).

In his invective against "servile Italy" Dante sarcastically invites the Emperor Albert to come and see the Montecchi and the Cappelletti, who are already "tristi" (vs. 108). The meaning of these verses was the subject of extensive debate until a thorough study of the question by F. Ghisalberti (1935) placed the entire matter in its proper historical focus. In his conclusion, Ghisalberti observes (p. 67):

> Infatti sulla fine del secolo XIII la lotta che aveva dilaniato l'alta Italia era venuta assumendo un altro aspetto. I partiti erano finiti come tali, e il loro programma si poteva considerare fallito. Monticoli e Cappelleti non erano ormai più che nomi di vinti. Ambedue avevano agitato nelle loro origini le aspirazioni del popolo e della borghesia mercantile, assertori entrambi della libertà e autonomia del Comune. Ma nel processo degli avvenimenti avevano finito per lasciarsi attirare nella sfera di interessi signorili, e troppo tardi s'erano accorti d'essersi dati dei padroni. . . .
>
> Così verso il 1300 Dante poteva benissimo considerare che i colori di quelle fazioni fossero affatto cancellati dalla carta politica di Lombardia, e dire quindi ad Alberto tedesco:
>
>> Vieni a veder Montecchi e Cappelletti,
>>   Monaldi e Filippeschi, uom sanza cura:
>>   color già tristi, e questi con sospetti!
>
> invitandolo così sarcasticamente a fare un viaggio per constatare gli effetti della sua colpevole assenza.

In fact, toward the end of the thirteenth century, the struggle that was tearing apart northern Italy had taken on a different aspect. The factions were finished as such, and their program could be considered a failure. Monticoli and Cappelletti were by now nothing more than the names of the vanquished. Both, when they started out, had excited the hopes of the people and of the merchant bourgeoisie, which in turn were the forces behind the liberty and autonomy of the commune. But in the course of events, they allowed themselves to be drawn into the

sphere of aristocratic interests; and when they realized
they had subjugated themselves, it was too late. . . .

And so, in about the year 1300, Dante could easily
consider the colors of those factions quite erased from
the political map of Lombardy. Thus he could say to
Alberto Tedesco: "Come, you that have no care, and
see Montecchi and Cappelletti, Monaldi and Filippeschi,
those already wretched and these in dread"—sarcas-
tically inviting him to take a trip, to view the effects of
his reprehensible absence.

Luigi da Porto's *Historia novellamente ritrovata di due nobili
amanti, con la lor pietosa morte* (published at Venice *ca.*
1530; adapted from a story by Masuccio Salernitano, *Novel-
lino* 33 published at Naples in 1476), with its setting in Ve-
rona and its young protagonists named Romeo and Giulietta,
of the feuding families of the Montecchi and Cappelletti (Da
Porto thus misconstruing the meaning of Dante's verses), be-
came, through Matteo Bandello's version (1554), Shake-
speare's source for *Romeo and Juliet.*

Cappelletti: A Guelph party of Cremona (not, as has
commonly been supposed, a Cremonese family). There is
frequent mention of this party in the chronicles, between
1249 and 1266, and of their struggles against the Monticoli
party for political supremacy in Lombardy.

The Cappelletti party was ultimately victorious over the
Emperor Henry VII. Although in control of Cremona from
1300 to 1321, it was, by 1290, greatly on the wane as the
anti-imperial party throughout Lombardy and accordingly,
together with the Monticoli, was designated as "tristi."

107. *Monaldi*: Guelph family of Orvieto, otherwise known
as Monaldeschi.   *Filippeschi*: Ghibelline family of Or-
vieto. These two families were the leaders, respectively, of the
Ghibellines and Guelphs in Orvieto, and were in consequence
continually at variance. In April 1312, the Filippeschi, em-
boldened by the approach of the Emperor Henry VII, at-
tacked the Monaldi, but were worsted and expelled from the
city with the rest of the Ghibellines. Subsequently, in 1337,
the tyranny of the Monaldi led to their own expulsion.

109. *la pressura*: Cf. Luc. 21:23: "Erit enim pressura magna super terram." ("For there will be great distress over the land.")

110. *d'i tuoi gentili*: Buti comments: "cioè de' conti, marchesi et altri gentili omini e signori d'Italia" ("that is, of counts, marquises, and other lords and gentlemen of Italy").

111. *Santafior*: Santafiora, county and town in Sienese territory, just under Monte Amiata, at the head of the river Fiora, which from the ninth century down to 1300 belonged to the powerful Ghibelline family of the Aldobrandeschi, who thence took their title of counts of Santafiora. It was formerly an imperial fief, but at the time Dante wrote it was in the hands of the Guelphs of Siena. See G. Ciacci (1935), pp. 335-59. Also see F. Ghisalberti (1935), pp. 68-69:

> Che se poi il sacro imperatore avesse voluto rendersi conto di quei nobili che da lui avevan ricevuto solenne investitura, ecco:
>
> > Vien, crudel vieni, e vedi la pressura
> > de' tuoi gentili, e cura lor magagne;
> > e vedrai Santafior com'è oscura.
>
> Anche qui un esempio solo che schiude un'altra vista disastrosa, e scopre un altro aspetto della multiforme anarchia: i diritti gentilizi calpestati, la nobiltà "battuta e punta" e magagnata. Là dove un giorno s'apriva ai sovrani lo splendido feudo del superbo e fiero Omberto Aldobrandeschi, avrebbe visto un'oscura terra, ridotta alle estreme difese dalla cupidigia dei potenti vicini (e la mano di Bonifazio anche qui non era stata inoperosa) e soprattutto dalla Signoria popolare di Siena.
>
> For if the holy emperor had wanted to find out what happened to those noblemen who received solemn investiture at his hands, behold: "Come, cruel one, come and see the distress of your nobles and cure their hurts; and you will see how forlorn Santafiora is!" Here, too, a single example unveils another disastrous vista, and uncovers another aspect of the multiform anarchy: noble privilege trampled upon, the nobility "vanquished and

wounded" and in decay. In the place of what was once the splendid fief of the proud and fierce Omberto Aldobrandeschi, he would now have seen a dark land, reduced to extremity by the greed of its powerful neighbors (nor had the hand of Boniface been idle there), above all by the middle-class *signoria* of Siena.

See G. Fatini (1922), pp. 42-46.

113. *vedova e sola*: See n. to vs. 78.   *chiama*: Cf. the Latin *clamat*.

114. *accompagne* = *accompagni*.

116. *nulla* = *nessuna*. "Nulla" modifies "pietà."

117. *a vergognar ti vien* = *vieni a vergognarti*.

118. *o sommo Giove*: Jove means Christ, as is made evident by the following verse.

120. *li giusti occhi tuoi*: If God's justice now prevailed, the emperor would rule and order would be restored. See *Purg.* XX, 94-96.

123. *l'accorger nostro scisso*: "Cut off," i.e., inaccessible to our understanding.

125. *tiranni*: See n. to *Inf.* XXVII, 38.   *Marcel*: Marcellus, Roman consul and determined opponent of Julius Caesar. There were three consuls named Marcellus who were opponents of Caesar, viz., Marcus Claudius Marcellus, consul 51 B.C., who was pardoned by Caesar (46 B.C.) on the intercession of the senate (the subject of Cicero's *Pro Marcello*), and was afterwards murdered by one of his own attendants in Greece; Gaius Claudius Marcellus, brother of Marcus, consul 49 B.C., when the civil war broke out; and Gaius Claudius Marcellus, first cousin of the preceding, consul 50 B.C. However, it is certainly to the first, Marcus Claudius Marcellus, that Dante refers. He is the "Marcellus loquax" of Lucan (*Phars.* I, 313), who mentions him, together with Cato and Pompey, as being among Caesar's bitterest enemies. Benvenuto says:

Loquitur . . . de Marcello illo consule qui fuit audacis-
simus Pompeianus infestus semper Caesari, qui iudicavit
ipsum hostem, ut patet apud Suetonium libro I; contra
quem dicit Caesar, ut Lucanus scribit: *Marcellusque
loquax et nomina vana Catonis.* Vult ergo poeta dicere
tacite, quod sicut olim Marcellus ex magna affectione
praesumpsit et insurrexit contra Caesarem primum im-
peratorem, ita hodie omnis castellanus et villanus prae-
sumit et insurgit contra imperatorem.

He means . . . Marcellus, the consul, who as a devoted
follower of Pompey was always opposed to Caesar, who
considered him his enemy, as is clear from Book I of
Suetonius. Against whom, as Lucan has it, Caesar said:
"talkative Marcellus and the empty titles of Cato." The
poet is here hinting that, just as Marcellus, out of his at-
tachment [to Pompey], deliberately rebelled against
Caesar, the first emperor, so today every owner of a cas-
tle and every villager would deliberately rebel against
an emperor.

126. *parteggiando*: Organizing a faction (*parte* in Italian)
or placing himself at the head of one.

127. *Fiorenza mia*: In *Conv.* IV, xxvii, 11 Dante exclaims:
"Oh misera, misera patria mia! quanta pietà mi stringe per
te, qual volta leggo, qual volta scrivo cosa che a reggimento
civile abbia rispetto!" ("Oh, my wretched, wretched country!
What pity for thee constrains me whensoever I read, when-
soever I write, of aught that hath respect to civil govern-
ment.") The whole "digression" here is bitterly ironical. See
Inf. XXVI, 1-12.

129. *si argomenta*: Cf. *Inf.* XXII, 21.

130. *Molti*: "Many," i.e., in other cities.   *e tardi scocca*:
It is let fly (as an arrow) slowly. "Arco" in the next verse
continues the metaphor.

133. *lo comune incarco*: Public office.

135. *sanza chiamare*: For the construction with the infinitive, see *Purg.* V, 65.

136. *ti fa = fatti*, an imperative.

137. *tu ricca, tu con pace e tu con senno*: Porena comments: "Il verso è ironico, ma di due generi d'ironia. *Tu con pace tu con senno* dicono il contrario di ciò che è, ed è ironia di concetto. Ma che Firenze fosse ricca, è vero; onde nel *tu ricca* l'ironia è invece di sentimento." ("The verse is ironic, but contains two different kinds of irony. 'You at peace, you wise' state the opposite of the truth and constitute irony of conception. But it was true that Florence was rich, so that 'you rich' is irony of sentiment.")

138. *S'io dico 'l ver, l'effetto nol nasconde*: Porena continues: "Si riferisce al *tu con senno*, chè quanto segue è appunto una dimostrazione del quanto poco assennati sieno i Fiorentini." ("It refers to 'you with sense,' for what follows is precisely a demonstration of how little sense the Florentines had.")

139. *Atene e Lacedemona*: See F. Torraca (1912, p. 184, n. 2), who quotes from the *Institutiones* of Justinian: "Origo eius [iuris civilis] ab institutis duarum civitatium, Athenarum scilicet et Lacaedemonis, fluxisse videtur." ("It would appear that the civil law takes its origin from the institutions of two cities, Athens, that is, and Sparta.") Lacedaemon, or Sparta, was the capital of ancient Laconia and chief city of the Peloponnesus. The allusion is to the legislation of Lycurgus there, and to that of Solon at Athens.   *fenno = fecero*.

141. *al viver bene*: The good, well-ordered life of the city-state.

142. *verso di te*: "Compared to you."   *sottili*: In a double sense of "clever" and "weak."

143–44. *ch'a mezzo novembre . . . fili*: The provision is such that the laws which Florence spins in October do not last till mid-November. The choice of these two months, as I. Del Lungo (1888, p. 159) suggests, may have been prompted by the fact that the political changes which took place in Florence from October to November of 1301 brought about the downfall of the Bianchi and Dante's exile.

145. *rimembre = rimembri.*

147. *e rinovate membre*: And renewed your citizens, i.e., by exiling them and then recalling them from exile. For *membre* used for *membri*, see E. G. Parodi (1957), p. 249.

149–51. *vedrai te somigliante . . . scherma*: Cf. Augustine, *Conf.* VI, 16: "Vae animae meae audaci, quae speravit, si a te recessisset, se aliquid melius habituram! versa et reversa in tergum et in latera et in ventrem, et dura sunt omnia, et tu solus requies." ("Woe unto that audacious soul of mine, which hoped that had she forsaken thee, she should have had some better thing! Turned she hath, and turned again, upon back, sides, and belly, yet found all places to be hard; and that thou art her rest only.")

CANTO VII

1. *oneste*: "Courteous." See *Conv.* II, x, 8, where Dante says: "Cortesia e onestade è tutt'uno." ("Courtesy and honour are all one.")

2. *furo = furono.*   *iterate = ripetute.* "Iterate" is from the Latin *iterare.*   *tre e quattro volte*: See Virgil, *Aen.* I, 93-96:

> ingemit et duplicis tendens ad sidera palmas
> talia voce refert: "O terque quaterque beati,
> quis ante ora patrum Troiae sub moenibus altis
> contigit oppetere! ..."

He groans and, stretching his two upturned hands to heaven, thus cries aloud: "O thrice and four times blest, whose lot it was to meet death before their fathers' eyes beneath the lofty walls of Troy!"

Also see *Aen.* IV, 589: "Terque quaterque manu pectus percussa decorum" ("thrice and four times she struck her comely breast with her hand") and *Georg.* I, 410-11: "Tum liquidas corvi presso ter gutture voces / aut quater ingeminant." ("Then the rooks, with narrowed throat, thrice or four times repeat their soft cries.") Clearly the expression is an established one, suggesting a small but indefinite number of times.

3. *si trasse*: "Stood back," i.e., from Virgil, whom he has just embraced. *Voi, chi siete?* Sordello asks the question in the plural; but he has only to hear that this is Virgil and he does not ask further about Dante. Later he will be much surprised to learn that Dante is a living man. Sordello, also addressing both Dante and Virgil, previously asked about the origin and condition of these two wayfarers (*Purg.* VI, 70-71).

4. *Anzi che = prima che.*

4–5. *fosser volte l'anime degne di salire a Dio*: See *Inf.* IV, 62-63: "dinanzi ad essi, / spiriti umani non eran salvati" ("essi" are the souls which Christ harrowed from Limbo). Thus Adam and the others there named as being taken from Limbo were directed ("volte") to Purgatory, which, from the time of Satan's fall, had stood as an empty mountain (see *Inf.* XXXIV, 124-26). These were made worthy of salvation by their faith in the Redeemer, and through the power of His Passion they were delivered (see Thomas Aquinas, *Summa theol.* III, q. 52, a. 5).

6. *fur = furono.* *per = da.* *Ottavian*: Octavian, i.e., Augustus, the first Roman Emperor, was born in 63 B.C. and died in A.D. 14. His original name was Gaius Octavius, which, after his adoption by his great-uncle Julius Caesar, was changed to Gaius Julius Caesar Octavianus. Augustus was a title of veneration conferred upon him by the Roman senate and people, 27 B.C., eight years before Virgil's death in 19 B.C.

7. *rio*: "Wickedness."

8. *per non aver fé*: I.e., for not having had implicit faith in the Redeemer. See *Inf.* IV, 37-42. This verse is a *verso tronco*, as are also vss. 10 and 12.

15. *abbracciòl = lo abbracciò.* *là 've 'l minor s'appiglia*: The exact nature of this second and more respectful embrace by Sordello is not clear. While some early commentators understand the embrace to be about the knees or feet, the

Anonimo fiorentino comments: "ciò è dal petto in giù, sotto le braccia di Virgilio, dov'è d'usanza ch'abbracci il minore in dignità o in tempo" ("that is, below the chest, under Virgil's arms, where one who is of lesser dignity or age is wont to embrace"). Cf. *Purg.* XXI, 130-31; *Inf.* XVI, 46-48.

16. *O gloria di Latin*: The glory of the ancient Romans, whose language was Latin, and of modern Italians and other Romance peoples, whose languages are the living survivors of Latin (Sordello wrote in Provençal). *per cui*: "Through whom," i.e., through whose achievement in poetic language.

17. *la lingua nostra*: "Lingua nostra," as here used by Sordello, embraces Latin and all its Romance derivatives and regards them as one language—to which a patriotic "nostra" attaches.

18. *del loco ond' io fui*: Mantua or its territory. Both poets were born near Mantua.

19. *qual merito o qual grazia*: Any merit would be Sordello's, the grace would be from God.

21. *chiostra*: Circle (cf. *Inf.* XXIX, 40).

23. *lui = a lui.   di qua = qua.*

24. *virtù del ciel mi mosse*: Cf. *Inf.* II, 52-54; *Purg.* I, 68-69.   *con lei*: With this heaven-sent power.

25. *Non per far*: Not through the commission of any actual sin.   *ma per non fare*: I.e., because he did not worship God worthily, as was said in *Inf.* IV, 37-41. For such a "defect" he is lost.

26. *a veder = di vedere.   l'alto Sol che tu disiri*: God, as seen by the blessed in that beatific vision which all souls desire, but which souls in Limbo desire in vain, without hope; this is their only torment (see *Inf.* IV, 40-42). Compare the sun as the symbol of God's light in *Inf.* I, 17-18 and *passim*, as well as an established symbol of Christ in medieval

thought. Virgil did not know Christ, since he died nineteen years before His Advent, and so he knew of the true God only after his death when Christ came to Limbo in the harrowing (*Inf.* IV, 52-63)—too late for Virgil's salvation.

28–30. *Luogo è là giù . . . sospiri*: Limbo. Cf. *Inf.* IV, 25-30.

28. *non tristo di martìri* = *non attristato da martiri*.

29. *ma di tenebre solo*: *Tristo* is understood ("ma tristo di tenebre soltanto").

30. *guai*: Outcries of pain. Cf. *Inf.* V, 48.   *ma son sospiri*: The souls, in vain longing, sigh for the beatific vision, which is forever denied them.

31. *Quivi sto io*: Virgil makes no mention of the special privilege that he and the other virtuous pagans enjoy, namely, the hemisphere of light and the noble castle which is their abode.   *coi pargoli innocenti*: Dante has made the *Limbus puerorum* (recognized in theology) and the *Limbus* of the virtuous pagans one and the same place. The "pargoli" are children innocent of any actual or personal sin (*Inf.* IV, 34: "ei non peccaro"). See *Inf.* IV, 34-36.

32. *dai denti morsi de la morte*: Cf. Osee 13:14: "De manu mortis liberabo eos, de morte redimam eos; ero mors tua, o mors, morsus tuus ero, inferne." ("I will deliver them out of the hand of death. I will redeem them from death. O death, I will be thy death; O hell, I will be thy bite.")

33. *da l'umana colpa essenti*: I.e., before they were exempted, through baptism, from the guilt of original sin. Cf. *Inf.* IV, 35-36.   *essenti = esenti*.

34–36. *con quei . . . quante*: These must be the souls of adults; in fact, Virgil means virtuous pagans of antiquity, his companions in Limbo.

34–35. *le tre sante virtù*: The three theological virtues—faith, hope, and charity—which are *infused* virtues given only with sanctifying grace. It did not generally lie within the power of pagans to "clothe" themselves in such grace and virtues, for such a possibility was established by Christ's coming and His death for mankind upon the Cross. This "defect" of virtue (referred to in *Inf.* IV, 40) informs the notion of "non fare" (vs. 25, above), for without the infused theological virtues and sanctifying grace, which unite men to God (as His sons), no man can do the good that is above human powers and merits salvation.

35. *vestiro = vestirono.*

35–36. *e sanza vizio conobber l'altre*: The "other" virtues are in general all the moral and intellectual virtues known to the pagans, but especially the four cardinal virtues—prudence, temperance, justice, and fortitude. Virgil draws no fine line here between these four as the *acquired* virtues, as distinguished from the four *infused* cardinal virtues. He and his pagan companions in Limbo were all denied the infused virtues and could attain and follow only the acquired.

36. *seguir = seguirono.*

37. *Ma se tu sai e puoi*: The coupling of these two verbs in such cases is common, and "puoi" need not be taken to mean that permission might be required (as some commentators understand it). Cf. *Par.* I, 6: "né sa né può chi di là sù discende."

38. *noi = a noi.*

39. *là dove purgatorio ha dritto inizio*: I.e., where Purgatory (as distinguished from Antepurgatory) has its true and proper beginning. See Belacqua's reference to this point in *Purg.* IV, 127-29.

40. *Loco certo non c'è posto*: Cf. Virgil, *Aen.* VI, 672-75:

> atque huic responsum paucis ita reddidit heros:
> "nulli certa domus; lucis habitamus opacis
> riparumque toros et prata recentia rivis
> incolimus. . . ."

And to her the hero thus made brief reply: "Fixed home hath none. We dwell in shady groves, and live on cushioned river-banks and in meadows fresh with streams."

And soon now Sordello is to lead Dante and Virgil to the meadows of the princes. Remembering this, we may suppose that the princes have wandered about on the slope during the day, but have now gathered in their little valley for the night, as is their wont. It is never made clear to which group Sordello belongs, if any. It is perhaps implied that, like the princes, he also was too much absorbed in worldly cares; but since he is not a prince, but a judge of princes, he is seen as dwelling apart and alone, "sola soletta" (*Purg.* VI, 59). *posto = imposto.*

41. *suso*: That is, as far up the slope as the entrance to Purgatory proper, but no farther.   *intorno*: Going round about the slope of Antepurgatory, as we have seen other souls doing, group after group.

42. *a guida = come guida.*

43. *dichina = declina.*

44. *puote = può.*

45. *però = per ciò.*

46. *a destra*: To proceed in this direction means to circle the mountain in the proper direction, i.e., counterclockwise.
    qua: The adverb implies a gesture: Sordello points.
remote: As a group.

47. *merrò = menerò.*

48. *fier = saranno.*

50. *fora = sarebbe.*

50–51. *impedito d'altrui*: I.e., prevented from climbing by someone else.

143

51. *sarria = salirebbe.* *ché non potesse*: "Because he had not the power [himself]." The question thus admits of two possibilities, of either external or internal hindrance.

52–54. *E 'l buon Sordello . . . partito*: Cf. Ioan. 8:6, 8: "Iesus autem inclinans se deorsum, digito scribebat in terra. . . . Et iterum se inclinans, scribebat in terra." ("But Jesus, stooping down, began to write with his finger on the ground. . . . And again stooping down, he began to write on the ground.") Sordello draws the line above them on the slope.

54. *partito = tramontato.*

55. *non però ch' = non perciò che.* *desse*: The imperfect subjunctive form of the verb is determined by the conditional "varcheresti" of the preceding verse. *briga*: "Hindrance," "opposition."

57. *nonpoder*: Cf. "nonpossa," *Purg.* V, 66. *intriga*: "Entangles," "impedes."

58. *poria = potrebbe.* *lei*: The "notturna tenebra" of vs. 56.

60. *mentre che = finchè.* *l'orizzonte il dì tien chiuso*: Cf. *Aen.* I, 374: "ante diem clauso componet Vesper Olympo" ("sooner would heaven close and evening lay the day to rest"). The horizon is said to lock out the sun for the night.

61. *quasi ammirando*: "As one who marvels." The fact continues to be stressed that Virgil is a complete stranger here in Purgatory. Cf. *Purg.* II, 61-63.

62. *Menane = menaci* (pronounced *mènaci*).

64. *allungati = allontanati.* Cf. *Purg.* XIII, 32. *di lici = di lì.* Cf. E. G. Parodi (1957), p. 261, who points to corresponding forms *laci* and *quaci* in early prose texts.

66. *vallon*: *Vallone* is used to denote the *bolge* of the eighth circle of Hell: see *Inf.* XIX, 133; XXIII, 135. *li*:

I monti.   *quici = qui*, in the northern hemisphere, the world of the living. For the form, see E. G. Parodi (1957), p. 261.

70. *Tra erto e piano era un sentiero schembo*: The path, neither steep nor level, leads obliquely across the slope.

71. *ne = ci.*   *lacca*: Cf. *Inf.* VII, 16; XII, 11.

72. *là dove più ch'a mezzo muore il lembo*: The banks of the valley merge finally with the slope, hence they are said to "die."

73–75. *Oro e argento . . . fiacca*: The colors here named must all be such as might be seen in some beautiful flowery meadow, but are also (at least in part) pigments used by artists—hence the appropriateness of "dipinto," vs. 79.

73. *fine*: Pure.   *cocco*: "Cochineal" (from the Latin *coccum*) or "chermes," from which a scarlet pigment was commonly made.   *biacca*: "White lead," used as a white pigment.

74. *indaco legno lucido e sereno*: As pointed out by M. P. Cook (1903, p. 356), several interpretations of this verse have been proposed: one is that "indaco" and "legno" are two different colors, and "indaco," taken by itself, means "indigo"; another is that the words "indaco legno" taken together mean "amber," the tree gum that sometimes comes from India. The most persuasive interpretation advanced so far is that "legno" means *lychnis* (or *lignis*), termed *lignus* in medieval Latin, mentioned as a bright purple gem by Pliny, Solinus, and Isidore of Seville (see H. D. Austin, 1922). "Indaco" in the present translation is construed as an adjective modifying "legno," and accordingly Petrocchi's punctuation, which places a comma after "indaco," has been removed. The passage in Pliny (*Nat. hist.* XXXVII, xxix, 103) is as follows:

> Ex eodem genere ardentium est lychnis appellata a lucernarum accensu, tum praecipuae gratiae. nascitur circa Orthosiam totaque Caria ac vicinis locis, sed pro-

batissima in Indis. quidam remissiorem carbunculum esse dixerunt, secundam bonitate quae similis esset Iovis appellatis floribus. et alias invenio differentias: unam quae purpura radiet, alteram quae cocco.

To the same class of fiery red stones belongs the "lychnis," so called from the kindling of lamps, because at that time it is exceptionally beautiful. It is found around Orthosia and throughout Caria and the neighbouring regions, but occurs at its finest in India. "Mild carbuncle" is the term sometimes applied to "lychnis" of the second grade resembling the so-called "Flower of Jove." I find that there are other varieties as well, one of which has a purple and the other a scarlet sheen.

76–78. *da l'erba . . . meno*: Each of the above-named colors, if placed within that valley, would be surpassed by the grass and the flowers there, as the less is surpassed by the greater. It seems better to construe "posti" as referring to the colors and not to the grass and flowers, particularly because of the verb ("saria") in the conditional tense.

78. *il meno*: "The lesser thing," i.e., the inferior.

79–81. *Non avea pur natura . . . indistinto*: The stress falls on "pur" and "dipinto" (on "dipinto" here, see n. to vss. 73-75); that is, nature has not only painted all these bright colors, but has also made of the many different scents of flowers a single blended and mysterious fragrance.

82. *Salve, Regina*: This well-known antiphon, which is a prayer to the Virgin Mary, our advocate in Heaven, is recited at dusk and is thus appropriately sung here, since now it is that time of evening in Purgatory. Moreover, as a prayer it is addressed to Mary by those who are exiles in this "vale of tears"—and indeed these souls in Purgatory have in fact gathered in a vale for the night. On the figure of the Exodus which thus emerges here, see C. S. Singleton (1965). The text of the hymn, with a translation, may be found in M. Britt (1955), p. 67:

Salve, Regina, mater misericordiæ;
Vita, dulcedo et spes nostra, salve.
Ad te clamamus exsules filii Hevæ.

Ad te suspiramus gementes et flentes in hac
    lacrimarum valle.
Eia ergo, advocata nostra,
Illos tuos misericordes oculos ad nos converte.

Et Iesum, benedictum fructum ventris tui,
Nobis post hoc exsilium ostende.
O clemens, o pia, o dulcis Virgo Maria.

Hail, Holy Queen, Mother of Mercy; our life, our sweet-
ness, and our hope. To thee we cry, poor banished chil-
dren of Eve. To thee we send up our sighs, mourning
and weeping in this valley of tears. Turn then, most
gracious Advocate, thine eyes of mercy upon us and
after this our exile show unto us the blessed fruit of thy
womb, Jesus. O clement, o loving, o sweet Virgin Mary.

Aeneas also saw shades chanting in chorus, but theirs was a
joyous song. See Virgil, *Aen.* VI, 656-58:

    conspicit ecce alios dextra laevaque per herbam
    vescentis laetumque choro paeana canentis
    inter odoratum lauri nemus . . .

Lo! others he sees, to right and left, feasting on the
sward, and chanting in chorus a joyous paean within a
fragrant laurel grove . . .

It may be noted that the words from the *Aeneid* quoted in
the n. to vs. 40 come soon after these verses.

83. *quindi*: Connects with "vidi" in the same verse, thus
referring to the place from which Dante observes the scene.

84. *di fuori = dal di fuori.* The little valley is deep enough
to hide the souls until Dante comes to the edge and can look
down into it.

85. *Prima che 'l poco sole omai s'annidi*: The sun is about
to set, hence is termed "poco"; and its setting is called a set-
tling into its nest.

86. *ci avea vòlti*: "Had turned us," "had directed us" thither, around the mountain slope.

89. *tutti quanti*: Each and every one.

90. *che ne la lama giù tra essi accolti*: Better than Dante might see them, were he down among them on the floor of the little dale. See "lama" in this sense in *Inf*. XX, 79; XXXII, 96.

92. *d'aver negletto ciò che far dovea*: These, like the other souls already encountered in Antepurgatory, are guilty of negligence; and this emperor particularly is guilty of having neglected to come into Italy and rule her, as was his duty.

94. *Rodolfo*: Rudolf I, emperor from 1273 to 1291. He was born in 1218 and was the son of Albert IV, count of Habsburg, and the founder of the imperial house of Austria. In 1273 he was elected emperor, in preference to Ottokar, king of Bohemia, and to Alfonso X of Castile. Ottokar refused to acknowledge him as emperor; but Rudolf, supported by powerful allies, made war upon him and compelled him to sue for peace, which was granted only upon condition that he should cede Austria, Styria, Carinthia, and Carniola. A few years later Ottokar again rebelled, and was finally defeated and slain near Vienna in August 1278. Villani (VII, 55) says of him: "Questo re Ridolfo fu di grande affare, e magnanimo, e pro' in arme, e bene avventuroso in battaglie, molto ridottato dagli Alamanni e dagl'Italiani; e se avesse voluto passare in Italia, sanza contasto n'era signore." ("This King Rudolf was a man of great deeds. He was magnanimous, skilled in arms, and very brave in battle, so that he was much feared by the Germans and by the Italians. If he had wanted to invade Italy, he could have become its lord without opposition.") Villani (VII, 146) continues:

> Sempre intese a crescere suo stato e signoria in Alamagna, lasciando le 'mprese d'Italia per accrescere terra e podere a' figliuoli, che per suo procaccio e valore di piccolo conte divenne imperadore, e acquistò in proprio il ducato d'Osterich, e gran parte di quello di Soavia.

Since he was always intent upon increasing his power
and lordship in Germany, he abstained from any Italian
enterprise, so that he might increase the lands and the
power of his sons. By his energy and valor he rose from
a petty count to become emperor. He acquired for him-
self the duchy of Austria and a large part of the duchy
of Swabia.

potea = avrebbe potuto.

95. *le piaghe c'hanno Italia morta*: The many divisions and
the internal strife (see *Purg.* VI, 106-26). *Morire* has the
transitive meaning here, "to slay."

96. *sì che tardi per altri si ricrea*: Present tense for the fu-
ture: "she will not soon be revived." For such a use of the
present, common in prophecies, see *Purg.* XIV, 66.
tardi: *Troppo* is understood ("troppo tardi").   *per al-
tri*: Some commentators see this as a reference to the Em-
peror Henry VII, who first crossed the Alps into Italy in
1310.

97. *L'altro*: Ottokar, named in vs. 100, who in life was
Rudolf's enemy, now appears to comfort him here. So it was
with former enemies in Virgil's Elysian fields (*Aen.* VI,
824-27):

> Quin Decios Drusosque procul saevumque securi
> aspice Torquatum et referentem signa Camillum.
> illae autem, paribus quas fulgere cernis in armis,
> concordes animae nunc . . .

Nay, see apart the Decii and Drusi, and Torquatus of
the cruel axe, and Camillus bringing home the stand-
ards. But they whom thou seest gleaming in equal arms,
souls harmonious now . . .

98–99. *la terra . . . porta*: Bohemia, in the southwest part
of which rises the "Molta," the river Moldau (Czech
Vltava), which, after flowing southeast for some distance,
turns north and, passing through Prague, enters the "Albia,"
the Elbe (Czech Labe), about twenty miles north of Prague.

The Elbe then flows west-northwest through Germany into the North Sea.

100. *Ottacchero*: Ottokar II was king of Bohemia from 1253 to 1278. He refused to recognize Rudolf I as emperor, and the latter in consequence made war on him and defeated him at Marchfeld near Vienna, Ottokar being slain in the battle, on August 26, 1278. He was succeeded by his son Wenceslaus II. Villani (VII, 55) gives the following account of his defeat by Rudolf and of the humiliation of his son:

> Negli anni di Cristo 1277, essendo grande guerra tra 'l re Ridolfo della Magna e lo re di Boemia per cagione che nol volea ubbidire nè fare omaggio, per la qual cosa il re Ridolfo eletto imperadore con grandissima oste andò sopra il detto re di Boemia, il quale gli si fece incontro con grandissima cavalleria, e dopo la dura e aspra battaglia che fu tra così aspre genti d'arme, come piacque a Dio il detto re di Boemia nella detta battaglia fu morto, e la sua gente sconfitta, nella quale innumerabile cavalleria furono morti e presi, e quasi tutto il reame di Boemia Ridolfo ebbe a sua signoria. E ciò fatto, col figliuolo del detto re di Boemia fece pace, faccendolsi prima venire a misericordia: e stando il re Ridolfo in sedia in uno grande fango, e quello di Boemia stava dinanzi a lui ginocchione innanzi a tutti i suoi baroni; ma poi riconciliato, il re Ridolfo gli diede la figliuola per moglie, e rendègli il reame.

> In the year of Christ 1277 there was a great war between King Rudolf of Germany and the king of Bohemia, who did not want to obey him or do him homage. For this reason, when King Rudolf was elected emperor, he went with a large army to attack the king of Bohemia, who came to meet him with a very large force of cavalry. After a hard and bitter battle between these two fierce armies, the king of Bohemia was slain in battle, as it pleased God, and his army was defeated. Innumerable knights were killed or captured, and Rudolf gained possession of nearly the entire kingdom of

Bohemia. When that was done, he made peace with the
son of the king of Bohemia; but first he made him come
to ask for mercy. King Rudolf was seated on a throne
in a quagmire, and the king of Bohemia kneeled there
before him and all his barons. But later, when they were
reconciled, King Rudolf gave him his daughter in mar-
riage and restored the kingdom to him.

100–102. *ne le fasce . . . pasce*: Ottokar, the father, is said
to have been better when he was a child in swaddling clothes
than is his son as a grown ("bearded") man.

101. *Vincislao*: Wenceslaus II, son and successor of Otto-
kar and son-in-law of the Emperor Rudolf, was king of Bo-
hemia from 1278 to 1305. In the heaven of Jupiter he is re-
ferred to as "quel di Boemme" (*Par.* XIX, 125) and as one
"who never knew valor nor wished it."

102. *cui lussuria e ozio pasce*: The verb in the singular
serves a dual subject: both lust and idleness nurture
Wenceslaus.

103. *quel nasetto*: This "small-nosed" one is Philip III,
the Bold, born in 1245 and king of France from 1270 until
his death in 1285. He was the son and successor of Louis IX
and nephew of Charles of Anjou. In 1262 Philip married
Isabella, daughter of James I of Aragon, by whom he had,
among other children, Philip, who succeeded him as Philip
IV, the Fair, termed "il mal di Francia" in vs. 109. After the
Sicilian Vespers in 1282 and the loss of Sicily by his uncle,
Charles of Anjou, Philip, with the assistance of James of
Majorca, made war upon Pedro III of Aragon, whose crown
had been offered him for his son by Pope Martin IV. After
a long siege he captured Gerona, but, his fleet having
been destroyed in the Gulf of Rosas by Ruggiero di Loria,
Pedro III's admiral, and his supplies being thus cut off, he
was forced to retreat. Sick with fever and vexation at this
reverse, he was carried as far as Perpignan, where he died
in October of 1285. A few days later Gerona was recaptured
by Pedro of Aragon, who himself died before the close of the
year.

104. *colui c'ha sì benigno aspetto*: Henry I, surnamed the Fat, king of Navarre from 1270 to 1274. He was the son of Thibaut I and brother of Thibaut II ("il buon re Tebaldo," *Inf.* XXII, 52), whom he succeeded. His daughter Jeanne married Philip the Fair; hence he is styled (vs. 109) "father-in-law of the plague of France," which causes his melancholy and his sighs here in Purgatory, as vss. 110-11 make clear.

105. *il giglio*: The royal emblem of France, three lilies or on a field azure.

107. *L'altro*: Henry of Navarre.

107-8. *ha fatto a la guancia . . . letto*: A standard posture expressing grief. Cf. G. L. Hamilton (1921).

109. *del mal di Francia*: Philip IV, the Fair, king of France from 1285 to 1314, was the son of Philip III, whom he succeeded, and brother of Charles of Valois. Philip is not mentioned by name in the *Divine Comedy*. He was referred to by Pope Nicholas III, in the third *bolgia* of the eighth circle of Hell, as "chi Francia regge" (*Inf.* XIX, 87), and he is bitterly denounced elsewhere in the poem for his relations with the papal see (imprisonment of Boniface VIII), his persecution of the Order of the Templars, his debasement of the French coinage, and many another misdeed.

112-14. *Quel che par sì membruto . . . corda*: Pedro III, king of Aragon from 1276 to 1285. He married (in 1262) Constance, daughter of King Manfred of Sicily, and thus had a claim on the crown of Sicily, which he assumed after the massacre of the Sicilian Vespers in 1282 and retained until his death in 1285, in spite of all the efforts of Charles of Anjou (including even a challenge of his rival to a duel), backed by Pope Martin IV (who excommunicated Pedro), to regain his lost kingdom. Dante's estimate of Pedro of Aragon is borne out by Villani (VII, 103): "Il sopraddetto Piero re d'Araona fu valente signore e pro' in arme, e bene avventuroso e savio, e ridottato da' cristiani e da' saracini altrettanto o più, come nullo re che regnasse al suo tempo." ("The above-mentioned Pedro of Aragon was a worthy lord, skilled in arms, very brave and wise. He was more feared by Christians than any king of that time, and as much or more by Saracens.")

113. *colui dal maschio naso*: Charles I, king of Naples and Sicily, count of Anjou and Provence, son of Louis VIII of France and Blanche of Castile, and brother of Louis IX (St. Louis), was born in 1226. In 1246 he married Beatrice, youngest daughter of Count Raymond Berenger IV of Provence, in whose right he became count of Provence; after the death of Beatrice in 1267, he married Margaret of Burgundy, daughter of Eudes, duke of Burgundy, in 1268. In 1266, after the defeat of Manfred at Benevento, he became king of Naples and Sicily; he died January 7, 1285. Charles and Pedro of Aragon were bitter foes in life, but now sing in harmony together in Purgatory.

Villani (VI, 89) speaks of him in the most glowing terms: "Il più sofficiente principe di prodezza d'arme e d'ogni virtù che fosse al suo tempo." ("In his time he was the prince who excelled in feats of arms and in every virtue as well.") Villani (VII, 95) continues: "Il più temuto e ridottato signore, e il più valente d'arme e con più alti intendimenti, che niuno re che fosse nella casa di Francia da Carlo Magno infino a lui, e quegli che più esaltò la Chiesa di Roma." ("He was the most feared and redoubtable lord, the most valiant in arms, and the most lofty in his aims of any king of the house of France, from Charlemagne down to him. And he was the one who most exalted the Church of Rome.") In describing his person, the chronicler (VII, 1) mentions his large nose: "Grande di persona e nerboruto, di colore ulivigno, e con grande naso, e parea bene maestà reale più ch'altro signore." ("He was large and strong limbed, of olive complexion, and with a large nose, and he was more regal in aspect than any other lord.") In vs. 124 Dante again refers to Charles by his nose, as "il nasuto."

114. *d'ogne valor portò cinta la corda*: Cf. *Inf.* XVI, 106. The metaphor is biblical in origin. See Isa. 11:5: "Et erit

iustitia cingulum lumborum eius, et fides cinctorium renum eius." ("And justice shall be the girdle of his loins: and faith the girdle of his reins.") Also see Prov. 31:17: "Accinxit fortitudine lumbos suos." ("She is girt about with strength.") Torraca comments: "L'imagine fa pensare alla cintura, che si cingeva al nuovo cavaliere, simboleggiante 'ogni nettezza e ogni cortesia, tutte virtù e tutte buone opere.'" ("The image makes one think of the belt that was put on a new knight, symbolizing 'every purity, every courtesy, all virtues, and all good deeds.'")

116. *lo giovanetto*: The reference is probably to Pedro, the last-born son of Pedro III of Aragon. See M. Amari (1886), p. 442. Some commentators have understood the reference to be to Alfonso III of Aragon, the eldest son of Pedro III. But Alfonso did actually become king after his father, reigning from 1285 to 1291.

117. *ben andava il valor di vaso in vaso*: Cf. Ier. 48:11: "nec transfusus est de vase in vas" ("and hath not been poured out from vessel to vessel"). Porena comments: "Quanto all'*andava di vaso in vaso* ecc. non può intendersi come un 'passava di padre in figlio,' perchè tale passaggio di virtù c'era realmente stato; sarà dunque da intendere 'passava di sovrano in sovrano.'" ("So far as the 'passing from one vessel to another' is concerned, it cannot be interpreted as 'passing from father to son,' because there really had been just such a transferral of virtue. It must be interpreted, then, as 'passing from one sovereign to another.'") Porena continues: "Invece questo passaggio non c'è stato con gli altri eredi: Jacopo d'Aragona e Federigo di Sicilia." ("That transferral did not take place with the other heirs: James of Aragon and Frederick of Sicily.")

118. *rede = eredi*.

119. *Iacomo*: James II, the Just, king of Sicily from 1285 to 1295 and king of Aragon from 1291 to 1327, was the second son of Pedro III of Aragon. On the death of Pedro III, king of Aragon and Sicily, in 1285, his eldest son, Alfonso

III, became king of Aragon, while James succeeded to the crown of Sicily. When Alfonso died in 1291, James succeeded him in Aragon, leaving the government of Sicily in the hands of his younger brother Frederick II. A few years later, however, James, ignoring the claims of Frederick, agreed to cede Sicily to the Angevin claimant, Charles II of Naples, whose daughter Blanche he married (1295). The Sicilians, on learning of this agreement, renounced their allegiance to James, and proclaimed his brother Frederick king in his stead (1296). Charles and James thereupon made war upon Frederick, but in 1299 James withdrew his troops, and in 1302 his brother was confirmed in possession of the kingdom of Sicily, under the title of king of Trinacria. James, who by his own subjects was surnamed the Just, died at Barcelona, November 2, 1327.

Federigo: Frederick II, king of Sicily from 1296 to 1337, was born in 1272, the third son of Pedro III of Aragon. For additional details, see the preceding section of this note. Frederick is alluded to by his grandfather Manfred in *Purg.* III, 116 as "l'onor di Cicilia" even as his brother James is styled "l'onor . . . d'Aragona." From this fond judgment Dante differs notably.

120. *del retaggio miglior nessun possiede*: Neither James nor Frederick possesses the better heritage, i.e., the goodness of their father, Pedro.

121-23. *Rade volte . . . chiami*: Cf. *Conv.* IV, xx, 5, where Dante writes: "Chè 'l divino seme non cade in ischiatta, cioè in istirpe, ma cade ne le singulari persone, e . . . la stirpe non fa le singulari persone nobili, ma le singulari persone fanno nobile la stirpe." ("For the divine seed [of nobility] falls not upon the race, that is the stock, but falls upon individuals and . . . the stock does not ennoble individuals, but individuals ennoble the stock.") Dante continues (*Conv.* IV, xx, 7): "Dio solo porge questa grazia a l'anima di quelli cui vede stare perfettamente ne la sua persona, acconcio e disposto a questo divino atto ricevere." ("God alone gives this grace to the soul of that man whom he sees perfectly balanced in his person and ready and disposed to receive this divine

act.") Thus worthiness is not transmitted by heredity, but is
God-given only, in order that it may be prayed for from Him.
Cf. Chaucer, *The Wife of Bath's Tale,* vs. 1117: "Crist wole
we clayme of hym oure gentillesse." See Iac. 1:17: "Omne
datum optimum et omne donum perfectum desursum est,
descendens a Patre luminum." ("Every good gift and every
perfect gift is from above, coming down from the Father of
Lights.")

121. *risurge*: A. D'Ancona (1901, p. 33) observes:
"[Dante] dice *risurge*, risale, dacchè negli alberi genealogici
si andò per lungo tempo di sotto in su, mentre ora nel fi-
gurarli si comincia dall'alto." ("[Dante] says *risurge* [rises],
'comes up again,' because it was long the custom to draw
genealogical trees as proceeding from the bottom to the top,
whereas nowadays they are drawn to be read from the top
down.")

124. *Anche al nasuto*: I.e., to Charles of Anjou, "colui dal
maschio naso," vs. 113. Torraca comments: "Ha del dis-
pregiativo; ed è degno di nota che Sordello, il quale visse nella
corte di Carlo d'Angiò . . . non lo indichi a nome, nè la prima
volta, nè ora, che nomina *Pier*, il nemico di lui." ("It con-
tains a derogatory note. It is noteworthy that Sordello, who
lived at the court of Charles of Anjou . . . does not mention
him by name, either the first time or now, when he names
his enemy Pedro.")   *vanno mie parole*: I.e., my words
are to be understood as referring to Charles of Anjou as well,
who did not transmit his worth to his successor, Charles II.

126. *Puglia e Proenza già si dole*: Again a plural subject
with the verb in the singular. Apulia and Provence are said
to lament having passed under the rule of Charles' son,
Charles II, who on his father's death (in 1285) became king
of Naples (Apulia) and count of Provence ("Proenza");
but being at the time a prisoner in Spain, where he was de-
tained until 1288, he was not crowned until May 29, 1289.
He died in May of 1309. He was mentioned in *Purg.* V, 69,
and will be referred to in *Par.* XIX, 127, as the "Ciotto di
Ierusalemme" (Cripple of Jerusalem)—he being lame, and

the title of Jerusalem being attached to the crown of Naples
—and as being very degenerate. He is also denounced in
Conv. IV, vi, 20; see *De vulg. eloqu.* I, xii, 5.

127–29. *Tant' è del seme . . . vanta*: Grandgent offers the
following explanation: "Charles II is as much inferior to
Charles I as Charles I is to Peter III. Beatrice of Provence
and Margaret of Burgundy were the successive wives of
Charles I, Constance (daughter of Manfred) was the wife of
Peter." Grandgent goes on to paraphrase these verses: "The
plant (the son) is inferior to the seed (the father) to the
same extent that Constance boasts of her husband (Peter)
more than Beatrice and Margaret boast of theirs (Charles)."

129. *ancor*: Constance and Margaret were both living in
1300, hence "ancor." Cf. *Purg.* III, 115.

131. *Arrigo d'Inghilterra*: Henry III, who was king of Eng-
land from 1216 to 1272, succeeded his father John and
reigned for fifty-six years. He married Eleanor, daughter of
Raymond Berenger IV, count of Provence. Eleanor's sister
Sancha married Henry's brother, Richard of Cornwall.
Villani, who makes Henry the son of Richard Coeur de Lion
(in which error he is followed by Benvenuto), describes
him (V, 4) as "semplice uomo e di buona fè e di poco
valore" ("a simple man of good faith, but of little worth")
and (VII, 39) "uomo di semplice vita, sicchè i baroni
l'aveano per niente" ("a man of simple life, so that the bar-
ons considered him nil"). Henry III is one of the princes
mentioned by Sordello in his celebrated lament for Blacatz,
in which he reproaches the sovereigns of Europe for their
degeneracy.

133–36. *Quel che più basso . . . Canavese*: Guglielmo VII
(or V), surnamed Spadalunga ("Longsword"), was marquis
of Montferrat from 1254 to 1292. Shortly after his accession
to power Guglielmo took advantage of internal dissensions
in several of the independent Lombard cities to reduce them
to subjection. In 1264 he made an alliance with Charles of
Anjou and aided him in his descent into Italy (Villani, VII,

4); but he vigorously opposed him later, when Charles, after the defeat of Manfred and the conquest of the kingdom of Naples, attempted the subjugation of Lombardy. In 1281 Guglielmo was at the head of a powerful Ghibelline league which included Milan, Vercelli, Novara, Tortona, Alessandria, Asti, Como, and Pavia; in consequence, however, of the expulsion of his vicar from Milan, in 1282, by Ottone Visconti, archbishop of Milan, several of these towns, Vercelli, Tortona, and Pavia, seceded from the league and joined the Guelphs. By the help of his son-in-law, the emperor of Constantinople, he reduced Tortona; and Vercelli and Pavia submitted to him soon after. In 1290 he marched against Alessandria to quell a rising which had been fostered by the people of Asti, but he was taken prisoner by the Alessandrians, and placed in an iron cage, in which he died in February of 1292, after having been exhibited like a wild beast for seventeen months. In order to avenge his death, his son and successor, Giovanni I, declared war against Alessandria, but the Alessandrians, with the help of Matteo Visconti, invaded the territory of Montferrat and took possession of Trino, Pontestura, Moncalvo, and several other places. It is to this war that Dante alludes here.

135–36. *Alessandria e la sua guerra . . . Canavese*: The phrase "Alessandria e la sua guerra" is the subject of "fa," and "Monferrato" and "Canavese" are objects of that verb.

136. *Monferrato e Canavese*: Montferrat, extending from the Ligurian Apennines to the river Po, and Canavese, stretching from the Pennine and Graian Alps to the Po, constituted the marquisate of Guglielmo VII.

CANTO VIII

1. *Era già l'ora*: The hour of dusk, of Compline, when the "Salve, Regina" (*Purg.* VII, 82) and the "Te lucis ante" (vs. 13, below) are sung.

1–2. *che volge il disio ai navicanti*: Turns homeward their desire, which during the day (this the first day of their voyage) was set on their destination.

2. *ai navicanti*: The preposition "a" expresses "of." *navicanti = naviganti*.

3. *lo dì*: The article here keeps the force of the Latin demonstrative from which it derives. It is *the* day on which they have said farewell to their sweet friends.

4. *lo novo peregrin*: *Peregrino* is one who travels by land. Following on the "navicanti" by sea, the poet brings in the land-traveler, and he thus presents both as being homesick as the first night falls on their outward journey.

4–5. *d'amore punge = punge d'amor*, "pricks with love" (matching the "melts their heart" of vs. 2).

5. *squilla*: The bell of Compline (Italian *compieta*, Latin *dies completa*). Cf. Dante's *canzone* "Così nel mio parlar,"

Rime CIII, 69: "Con esse passerei vespero e squille." ("I would pass with them Vesper and evening bells.")

6. *che paia il giorno pianger*: The subjunctive here is not that of hypothesis, but the subjunctive that projects the sentiment as subjective on the part of the "new pilgrim," in this moment of nostalgia.   *che si more*: The so-called pleonastic "si" here serves to reinforce the subjective focus of the sentiment; without it, the "che more" would simply present the fact objectively.

7–8. *quand' io incominciai . . . l'udire*: Dante no longer hears what Sordello is saying, nor does he hear any other sound, having suddenly become completely absorbed in the sight he now describes. This concentration of the whole attention through one faculty was set forth, as a psychological phenomenon, in *Purg.* IV, 1-12. Cf. also *Purg.* XV, 82-84; *Par.* III, 7-9.

9. *surta*: The souls in the valley are all seated (*Purg.* VII, 83).   *che l'ascoltar chiedea con mano*: With a gesture, the soul signals for attention. Cf. Actus 13:16: "surgens autem Paulus, et manu silentium indicens, ait . . ." ("then Paul arose, and motioning with his hand for silence, said . . .").

10. *giunse e levò ambo le palme*: The soul clasps and raises both its hands, in the familiar gesture of prayer; the prayer is the hymn which it then sings.

11. *ficcando li occhi verso l'oriente*: See Bonaventura, *Comm. Sapien.* XVI, 28: "versus orientem . . . quia . . . omne melius est Deo tribuendum; unde quia oriens est melior pars caeli, ideo ad orientem est adorandum" ("toward the east . . . because . . . what is best is to be referred to God; wherefore, since the east is the best part of the heaven, we should pray facing the east"). Also see *Il libro di Sidrach* CCCXLI (a passage to which M. Barbi, 1934b, p. 246, calls attention): "Altressì dei dire al mattino, quando ti levi; e lo volto dei tenere verso oriente, ch'è lo volto del mondo; e la **grazia** di Dio viene di là." ("Also you must say [this prayer]

in the morning when you get up, and you must keep your
face turned toward the east, which is the face of the world,
and the grace of God comes from there.") We have only to
think of the way in which churches were formerly oriented,
so that the faithful, when they prayed, would face east in fac-
ing the altar, and of medieval maps of the world, in which
east is "up," with Christ the *sol oriens* or *sol iustitiae* fre-
quently pictured over the world at the top. It should be noted
that the soul "officiating" here looks to the east as if speak-
ing to God, while the rest look *up*, as vs. 18 clearly implies.
Meanwhile, in the west the light is fading.

12. *calme = mi cale.*

13. *Te lucis ante*: The entire hymn, usually attributed to
Ambrose, is as follows (from M. Britt, 1955, p. 8):

> Te lucis ante terminum,
> Rerum Creator, poscimus,
> Ut pro tua clementia
> Sis præsul et custodia.
>
> Procul recedant somnia,
> Et noctium phantasmata;
> Hostemque nostrum comprime,
> Ne polluantur corpora.
>
> Præsta, Pater piissime,
> Patrique compar Unice,
> Cum Spiritu Paraclito
> Regnans per omne sæculum.
>
> Before the ending of the day,
> Creator of the world, we pray
> That, with Thy wonted favor, Thou
> Wouldst be our guard and keeper now.
>
> From all ill dreams defend our eyes,
> From nightly fears and fantasies;
> Tread under foot our ghostly foe,
> That no pollution we may know.
>
> O Father, that we ask be done,
> Through Jesus Christ, Thine only Son,

Who, with the Holy Ghost and Thee,
Doth live and reign eternally.

14. *uscìo = uscì.*

15. *che fece me a me uscir di mente*: I.e., rapt, as in ecstasy.

16. *dolcemente e devote*: This matches "devotamente" (vs. 13) and "con sì dolci note" (vs. 14), said of the song as sung by the one soul. Thus *concordia*, the keynote of Purgatory, is again observed here in choral singing.

17. *seguitar = seguitarono.* *per tutto l'inno intero*: The stress on "intero" obviously invites the reader to go over the entire hymn in his memory (see text in n. to vs. 13) and thus come to the all-important second stanza and the verse "hostemque nostrum comprime," which, as we are to see, signals what is to come.

18. *superne rote*: The revolving heavenly spheres. The angels who are to come are expected to come from there. See vs. 11, where the soul leading the hymn is seen to look toward the east. It is clearly implied, though not declared, that this whole episode is repeated every evening at dusk, as a kind of devotional service.

19-21. *Aguzza qui, lettor . . . leggero*: On the allegorical meaning signaled by this address to the reader, see C. S. Singleton (1965).

20. *ché 'l velo è ora ben tanto sottile*: It is the *event,* the literal happening here, that is to be viewed as disclosing now, in the mode of scriptural allegory, a "true" meaning. See *Inf.* IX, 61-63.

21. *certo che = che certamente.* *'l trapassar dentro*: "The passing within," i.e., to the true meaning (as if the literal event were a kind of cortex that contained the true or allegorical meaning).

22. *quello essercito gentile*: On the connotation of the term "army" as applied to these souls gathered here in this valley,

awaiting the coming of the two angels as sentinels, see
C. S. Singleton (1965), pp. 116-17.

23. *sùe* = *su*. Cf. "giùe" for *giù* in vs. 25.

24. *quasi aspettando*: As if waiting for something.
palido = *pallido*. They are "pallid" in fear of the "adversary"
who is to come (cf. *Inf.* IX, 1-3).   *umìle*: They are
"humble" as they wait upon the Lord. See C. S. Singleton
(1965), pp. 119-21.

26. *due angeli con due spade affocate*: The flaming sword
is reminiscent of that of the Cherubim set to guard Eden after
the Fall. See Gen. 3:24: "Eiecitque Adam et collocavit ante
paradisum voluptatis Cherubim et flammeum gladium atque
versatilem, ad custodiendam viam ligni vitae." ("He drove
out the man; and before the Paradise of Delight he placed
the Cherubim, and the flaming sword, which turned every
way, to guard the way to the tree of life.") Another remind-
er of Eden and the Fall will soon come, with the serpent,
vss. 94-99.

27. *tronche e private de le punte sue*: For the symbolism
of this detail, see C. S. Singleton (1965), p. 117.

28–30. *Verdi come fogliette . . . ventilate*: These are the
only *green* angels that appear anywhere in Dante's works.
Green is the color of hope (cf. *Purg.* XXIX, 124-25) and
connects with the humility of these souls, who wait upon
the Lord.

28. *pur mo nate*: "Just now born."

29. *veste*: Plural of *vesta*, an archaic form.

30. *percosse traean dietro e ventilate*: "Veste" is the object
of "percosse traean" and of "ventilate."

31. *poco sovra noi*: The angels take up their posts on the
edges (*sponde*) of the valley, a little higher up than the point
where Dante, Virgil, and Sordello stand.

33. *sì che la gente in mezzo si contenne*: Again the image of an army camped at night and guarded by sentinels is dominant.

34. *discernea = discernevo*.

35. *smarria = smarriva*.

36. *come virtù ch'a troppo si confonda*: The "virtù" in question is the power or faculty of sight (cf. "virtù" in this sense, *Purg.* IV, 2).   *troppo*: "Excess" of light. Dante was dazzled in this way before (*Purg.* II, 39-40) and will be again (*Purg.* XV, 22-30).

37. *grembo di Maria*: Clearly the angels of hope have been sent by the Virgin Mary, our advocate in Heaven, a touch that recalls the movement of mercy and grace that brought help to Dante on the dark slope where he struggled to cope with the beasts (*Inf.* II, 94-114). For the expression "grembo di Maria," cf. "sinum Abrahae" ("Abraham's bosom") in Luc. 16:22.

39. *per*: "On account of."   *lo serpente*: It should be recalled (see n. to vs. 13) that in the second stanza of the hymn "Te lucis ante" the prayer is that our adversary be driven back ("hostemque nostrum comprime"), and the serpent will now be called "our adversary," vs. 95.   *vie via = via via*. On the precise meaning of the adverb thus repeated (a common construction), see M. Barbi (1934b), p. 247: "*Via via* piuttosto che 'a momenti,' che accenna a indugio per quanto breve, vale 'tosto, incontanente.'" ("*Via via* [shortly] rather than *a momenti* [before long], which indicates a delay, brief though it be, has the force of *tosto* [at once] or *incontanente* [immediately].") In support of Barbi's view, see the examples cited by him.

40. *per qual calle*: "By which way" the serpent would come.

42. *tutto gelato*: Dante is chilled in fear. Cf. *Inf.* XXXIV, 22 (though on that scene there was actually a very cold wind blowing).   *a le fidate spalle*: Dante moves close up behind Virgil, for protection.

43. *anco = ancora.*

44. *grandi ombre*: The shades in the valley were great in life. This touch may remind the reader of the "great shades" of Limbo (*Inf.* IV, 83, 119). A certain correspondence between the two groups is surely intended by the poet.

45. *grazioso = gradito.   fia = sarà.   lor = a loro.*
   vedervi: The subject of the verb "fia."   *assai*: Modifies "grazioso."

46. *Solo tre passi credo ch'i' scendesse*: This detail should be connected with *Purg.* VII, 72. The side or bank of the hollow is to be conceived as being quite low at the point where Dante and the other two have been standing.   *scendesse = scendessi.*

47. *e fui di sotto*: The past absolute tense has its usual narrative force here: "And I reached the bottom."

48. *pur me*: Cf. *Purg.* V, 9: "pur me, pur me."

49–51. *Temp' era . . . serrava*: The darkening air has concealed until now the features of Dante and of the soul who gazes so fixedly at him. But they are now so close to each other that one can recognize the other, despite the growing darkness.

51. *pria = prima.*

52. *Ver' = verso.   Ver' me si fece: Farsi verso qualcuno* means "to approach someone."   *fei = feci.*

53. *giudice Nin gentil*: Nino (i.e., Ugolino) de' Visconti of Pisa, judge (*giudice*) of the district (*giudicato*) of Gallura in Sardinia, was the son of Giovanni Visconti. His mother was a daughter of Count Ugolino della Gherardesca. In 1285, Nino was called to share with the count, his grandfather, the office of *podestà* and *capitano del popolo* of Pisa in a government then dominantly Guelph. For the friction between Nino and his grandfather, see n. to *Inf.* XXXIII, 17-18. Following Ugolino's betrayal of him, Nino fled from

Pisa in July 1288 and joined the Guelph league in warring against Pisa (which had now returned to its traditional Ghibellinism). He became, in 1293, captain general of the league. He later went to Genoa, which did him the honor of making him a citizen, and from there he went to his lands in Sardinia. It was during this time, apparently, that he inflicted summary punishment on his deputy, Fra Gomita, for his misdeeds during Nino's absence (see n. to *Inf.* XXII, 81). He died in 1296. His heart, in accordance with his wishes, was removed to Lucca and entombed in the church of San Francesco.

It should be noted that, after Nino's escape to Florence in 1288 and during his sojourn in the city, there was ample occasion for Dante to have made the personal acquaintance with him that is witnessed here.

54. *quando ti vidi non esser tra ' rei*: Dante, the poet returned, recalls now how pleased he was to find Nino in Purgatory and thus to know that he is not among the damned ("rei") of Hell. But the exclamation on the part of the poet should not be taken to mean that Dante was surprised because he would have assumed that Nino would certainly be in Hell. The question of salvation, from the limited human point of view, is always open. Cf. *Inf.* VI, 79-84.

55. *Nullo bel salutar tra noi si tacque*: No fair greeting ("salutar," the infinitive used as a noun, is the object of "si tacque").

56-57. *Quant' è che tu venisti . . . acque?* Although Nino, after gazing intently at Dante, has been able to recognize him, the dark air prevents his seeing that Dante is here in the flesh, for his question clearly assumes that Dante would have come to Purgatory as a soul, in the angel's boat. Cf. *Purg.* II, 41-45.

57. *per le lontane acque*: Cf. "le larghe onde," vs. 70 below, and "tra liti sì lontani," *Purg.* II, 33.

58. *lui = a lui.*

60. *l'altra*: Eternal life in Heaven. Elsewhere in the *Purgatorio* the purpose of Dante's journey through the other-world is so indicated. See *Purg.* I, 61-66; V, 61-63.

62. *Sordello ed elli in dietro si raccolse*: Plural subject with verb in the singular.

63. *come gente di sùbito smarrita*: "Smarrita" suggests that these souls grow pale in their bewilderment. As seen before (*Purg.* II, 69), souls in Purgatory do this when they realize that they are in the presence of living flesh. Sordello has not known till now that Dante is a living man, because the sun was already so low in the west when Dante first approached him on the slope (and of course the air grew increasingly dark thereafter) that Dante's body did not cast the telltale shadow. To be sure, Sordello put his question, "chi siete?" (*Purg.* VII, 3), to the two wayfarers in the plural, but Virgil answered for himself and so amazed Sordello that he then inquired no further about Dante's identity.

64. *L'uno*: Sordello.   *l'altro*: Nino.

65. *Currado*: See n. to vs. 118.

66. *che = ciò che.*   *volse = volle.*

67. *grado*: "Gratitude."

68. *dei = devi.*   *colui*: God.

68-69. *sì nasconde . . . guado*: God's first purpose is so hidden in the abyss of His counsel that there is no fording to it, no crossing to it, that is, it is not given to human reason to know God's reasons. See *Purg.* III, 34-36, and note the verb "trascorrer" used in vs. 35 there.

69. *li = vi*, adverb, meaning "there." Cf. *Inf.* XXIII, 54; *Purg.* I, 62.

70. *di là da le larghe onde*: Yonder, in the world of the living.

71. *Giovanna*: Daughter (born *ca.* 1291) of Nino Visconti of Pisa and Beatrice d'Este. In 1296, while still an infant,

she was entrusted by Boniface VIII to the guardianship of the town of Volterra, as the daughter of a Guelph who had deserved well of the Church, but she was deprived of all her property by the Ghibellines, and, after living with her mother at Ferrara and Milan, was married to Rizzardo da Camino, lord of Treviso. After the death of her husband in 1312, she seems to have been reduced to poverty; in 1323, she was living in Florence, where a grant of money was made her in consideration of the services of her father. The date of her death is uncertain, but she was almost certainly dead in 1339. *chiami*: From the biblical Latin *clamare*. Cf. *Purg.* VII, 123.

72. *là dove a li 'nnocenti si risponde*: In Heaven where the prayers of those who are in grace (*Purg.* IV, 133-35) and the prayers of "the innocent," i.e., children, are heard. Giovanna was a mere child, about eight years old, in 1300.

73. *la sua madre*: Beatrice, daughter of Obizzo II d'Este and sister of Azzo VIII. She was married first to Nino Visconti of Pisa, by whom she had a daughter, Giovanna, and afterwards (at Modena in June 1300) to Galeazzo Visconti of Milan. It appears that before her marriage to the latter she had already been betrothed to a son of Alberto Scotto of Piacenza, but Matteo Visconti of Milan, being anxious for an alliance with the house of Este, managed to secure her as the wife of his son Galeazzo. Beatrice, after her marriage, came to reside in Milan, but within two years (in 1302) the Visconti were expelled thence by the Torriani (aided by Alberto Scotto, who thus avenged the slight passed upon him). Although Galeazzo died in 1328, Beatrice lived to return to Milan, her son Azzo having regained the lordship, and died there in 1334. Tommaseo comments: "Il chiamarla non *moglie mia* ma *sua madre* è rimprovero pieno di pietà." ("To call her not 'my wife' but 'her mother' is a reproof, full of pity.")

74. *poscia che trasmutò le bianche bende*: In Dante's day it was the custom for widows to dress in black, save for white bands worn over the head (see R. Davidsohn, 1929, pp. 651-

52). Nino refers, of course, to Beatrice's marriage to Galeazzo Visconti, which probably took place in June 1300 (as stated in the n. to vs. 73) and hence after the imagined date of Dante's journey through Purgatory, in the spring of 1300. But this does not necessarily mean that the poet was confused about or forgot the exact date of this second marriage (it is also possible that such was the case), since Beatrice may have doffed the white bands of widowhood some time before the wedding.

75. *le quai convien che, misera!, ancor brami*: Nino now passes to dire prophecy: Beatrice will have good cause to regret her marriage to Galeazzo. The Visconti, as indicated in the n. to vs. 73, were expelled from Milan in 1302, two years after this marriage, and Galeazzo died in poverty. Thus Beatrice will have reason to wish that she had never married a second time.

77. *quanto in femmina foco d'amor dura*: Cf. Virgil, *Aen.* IV, 569-70: "Varium et mutabile semper / femina." ("A fickle and changeful thing is woman ever.")

79-80. *Non le farà . . . la vipera*: The heraldic device of the Visconti of Milan was a blue viper swallowing a red Saracen, which, says Nino, will not be such a fine adornment on Beatrice's tomb as his own device, the cock, would have been.

80. *che Melanesi accampa*: Petrocchi argues persuasively for this reading rather than "che 'l Melanese accampa." (See his note for the relevant bibliography on this much-discussed phrase.) As he points out, the article is often omitted before "ethnic" names ("Melanesi" = *i Milanesi*). If the plural "Melanesi" is to stand, the verb in the singular must have "la vipera" as subject. In Dante's time the Milanese, when at war, never pitched their camp until they had hoisted the Visconti banner, the *vipera*; thus Lana comments: "Sì è giurisdizione di quella arma che sempre quando li milanesi vanno in oste, dove si pone quella insegna, si pone il campo." ("It is a prerogative of that device that, whenever the

Milanese take the field, the camp is set up wherever that emblem has been placed.") F. Novati (1899, pp. 153-60) argues, with good supporting evidence, for such an interpretation.

81. *avria = avrebbe.* *il gallo di Gallura*: The emblem of the Visconti of Pisa was a cock; Nino, as mentioned in the n. to vs. 53, was judge of Gallura, in Sardinia.

83. *zelo*: "Zelo" is used here in a sense frequent in the Vulgate Bible in the Latin *zelus*, "indignation"; "dritto zelo" is thus righteous indignation.

85. *Li occhi miei ghiotti*: Elsewhere Dante's eyes are said to be always eager to behold new things (*Purg.* III, 13; X, 103-5).

85-86. *pur . . . pur là*: Dante keeps looking heavenward, completely intent on this certain quarter.

86-87. *dove le stelle . . . stelo*: Toward the Antarctic pole, where, as with the parts of a wheel nearest the axle, the stars revolve the slowest.

88. *guarde = guardi.*

89. *quelle tre facelle*: See *Purg.* I, 25, where the four stars which these have replaced are called "fiammelle." On the symbolic meaning, see C. S. Singleton (1958), pp. 159-83.

90. *'l polo di qua*: The Antarctic pole.

91-92. *Le quattro chiare stelle . . . staman*: See *Purg.* I, 22-27.

92. *son di là basse*: The four stars are no doubt still above the horizon, but are invisible now because they are hidden by the mountain.

94. *Com' ei parlava = mentre egli parlava.* *e Sordello*: The "e" has more force than the simple conjunction; it amounts to an *ecco che*, as Porena observes. *a sé il trasse*: Sordello draws Virgil to himself, a gesture expressive of his apprehension on seeing the serpent.

95. *'l nostro avversaro*: Cf. I Pet. 5:8: "adversarius vester diabolus" ("your adversary the devil"). *avversaro = avversario*. See also *Purg.* XI, 20.

97–98. *Da quella parte . . . biscia*: The lower side of the hollow, where it merges with the slope and accordingly has no bank and so is said to present no hindrance to the serpent.

99. *forse qual diede ad Eva il cibo amaro*: "Forse" prompts the reader to consider that this serpent may be the same that tempted Eve in Eden, i.e., may be the devil in the form which he there assumed. On the "bitter food," see the lament over the four stars in *Purg.* I, 26-27. Death (of the body) was a consequence of original sin, death which is "so bitter" (*Inf.* I, 7).

100. *venìa = veniva. la mala striscia*: The verb *strisciare*, which might have been used to describe the crawling of the serpent, very effectively becomes a noun referring to the serpent himself.

101–2. *volgendo ad ora ad or . . . leccando*: Scartazzini-Vandelli comments: "Il leccarsi e lisciarsi della biscia figura l'astuzia del tentatore che s'avanza con atteggiamento di noncuranza per tutto ciò che ha d'intorno, senza neppur guardare chi già pensa di assalire, sicchè nulla trapeli delle sue male intenzioni." ("The viper licking and sleeking itself represents the wile of the tempter, who comes with an air of nonchalance toward everything about him. He does not even look at those he already contemplates attacking, so that his evil intention may not be revealed at all.")

103. *però = perciò. dicer = dire.*

104. *li astor celestiali*: The *astore*, or *nibbio*, is said to prey on snakes.

106. *a le verdi ali = da le verdi ali.*

107. *dier volta = diedero volta.* Cf. *Purg.* V, 41.

108. *suso a le poste rivolando iguali*: "Iguali" suggests that the angels are stationed as sentinels and guards directly op-

posite one another on the bank of the hollow. Thus, though the two banks are not high, "suso" indicates the posts of the angels on those banks. So Benvenuto comments: "idest, ad utramque spondam montis, ubi primo stabant ad custodiam" ("that is to say, to both ridges of the mountain where first they stood guard"). To understand "suso" as meaning *al cielo*, as some commentators do, seems wrong. Surely the angels must stand guard throughout the night, for then the serpent can always come.   *poste*: See "posta" in this sense in *Inf*. XIII, 113.

109. *L'ombra*: Corrado, the shade to whom Nino called (vs. 65).

111. *punto non fu da me guardare sciolta*: Although the serpent comes every night (or so it would seem) and is always driven back by the angels, the fact that this shade has not taken its eyes off Dante all the while witnesses its complete absorption and interest in him, as a living man who can bring news of the world.

112–14. *Se la lucerna . . . smalto*: Grandgent comments: "The meaning is: 'As thou hopest that illuminating grace (the lantern which leads thee up) may find in thy free will the responsive spirit (the wax, food for the flame) that is needed to take thee to the Earthly Paradise.'"

115. *ella*: "It," the soul (feminine).   *novella =notizia*.

116. *Val di Magra*: The valley of the river Magra, which flows through Lunigiana, the territory of the Malaspina family (see the reference to Moroello Malaspina in *Inf*. XXIV, 145). Here was the castle of Villafranca, the home of Corrado's father, Federigo I, marquis of Villafranca.

118. *Currado Malaspina*: Corrado II, called "il Giovane," son of Federigo I, marquis of Villafranca, and grandson of Corrado I, "l'antico" of vs. 119. He died *ca*. 1294. According to Boccaccio, who introduces Corrado and his daughter Spina in the *Decameron* (II, 6), he was a Ghibelline.

119. *l'antico*: Corrado I, called "l'antico," member of the Spino Secco branch of the Malaspina family. He was the son of Obizzone and the grandfather of Franceschino, who was Dante's host in Lunigiana in 1306, as well as of Corrado II. Corrado, who was a warm supporter of his father-in-law, the Emperor Frederick II, died about the year 1255.

120. *qui*: In Purgatory. Pride of family, in fact, will be seen later as one of the forms of pride which are purged in Purgatory (*Purg.* XI, 58-72).   *raffina = si raffina*, "is purified."

121. *lui = a lui.   li vostri paesi*: The lands of the Malaspina family. Cf. "la vostra casa," vs. 124.

122. *già mai non fui*: Dante went to Lunigiana in 1306 (see n. to vs. 119), probably for the first time.

123. *ei*: Those places, Val di Magra and the territory of the Malaspina.   *palesi*: Well known.

125. *grida i segnori e grida la contrada*: Celebrates the lords and their domains.

127. *s'io di sopra vada*: The *si* clause of asseveration: "As I hope to go above."

128. *vostra gente*: Cf. "la vostra casa," vs. 124.   *non si sfregia*: "Does not divest itself" (as of an ornament, *fregio*) of worthy liberality ("pregio de la borsa") or of prowess of arms ("pregio . . . de la spada"). For *cortesia e valor* used as corresponding terms, see *Inf.* XVI, 67; *Purg.* XVI, 116.

130. *Uso e natura*: Habitual virtue and natural inclination. The first is acquired, the second is given by nature. See *Conv.* I, xi, 7: "L'abito di vertude, sì morale come intellettuale, subitamente avere non si può, ma conviene che per usanza s'acquisti." ("The habit of a virtue, whether moral or intellectual, may not be had of a sudden, but must needs be acquired by practice.")

131. *il capo reo*: Rome, the seat of a corrupt papacy (Boniface VIII) is probably meant. *il mondo torca*: Rome "twists" it, that is, from the *dritta via*. See *Purg.* XVI, 106-14; *Par.* XVIII, 126.

133. *Or va*: The expression is hard to translate. "Va" is not to be taken literally, as the imperative of *andare*. The phrase probably means "now, let me say this to you," "now, rest assured that," "now, be sure that." *si ricorca*: The verb *ricorcarsi* means literally "to bed itself down again." Though used here in the present tense, it clearly implies a future, this being a prophecy.

133–39. *'l sol non si ricorca . . . s'arresta*: This soul, like others, can see into the future. It is to be noted that Corrado gives no sign that he knows who Dante is; yet, in making such a prophecy, it is clear that he does know.

133–35. *'l sol non si ricorca . . . inforca*: The sun will not return seven times to the sign of Aries, the Ram, where it is at this time (see *Inf.* I, 38-40); that is, seven years will not pass. As observed in nn. to vss. 119 and 122, Dante was in Lunigiana in 1306 and there served as *procuratore* of the Malaspina.

136. *oppinione = opinione*.

137. *fia = sarà*.   *chiavata = inchiodata*.

138. *chiovi = chiodi*.   *d'altrui sermone*: Others' report. Dante will know directly by experience what he now knows only by report.

139. *corso di giudicio*: The course of events—in this case, future events—as ordained by God. Obviously, a course ordained by Him will not be arrested. Cf. "cima di giudicio," *Purg.* VI, 37.

CANTO IX

1–9. *La concubina di Titone . . . l'ale*: Tithonus, son of Laomedon, was loved by Aurora and by her intercession was made immortal. Since she neglected to ask for him eternal youth, he shriveled up in his old age, until at last Aurora changed him into a grasshopper. Aurora, as the goddess of dawn, is represented in mythology as rising at the close of each night from the couch of her spouse, Tithonus, and ascending to Heaven from the ocean to herald the approach of day. See Virgil, *Aen.* IV, 584-85 (repeated in *Aen.* IX, 459-60): "Et iam prima novo spargebat lumine terras / Tithoni croceum linquens Aurora cubile." ("And now early Dawn, leaving the saffron bed of Tithonus, was sprinkling her fresh rays upon the earth.") See also *Georg.* I, 446-47: "aut ubi pallida surget / Tithoni croceum linquens Aurora cubile" ("or when Aurora rises pale, as she leaves Tithonus' saffron couch").

Dante appears to be alone in calling Aurora the "concubine" of Tithonus. His use of this term may be taken to mean that he is referring not to the Aurora of the sun (i.e., the wife of Tithonus), but to the Aurora of the moon. Tithonus, moreover, is qualified by Dante not as Aurora's spouse, but as her lover ("amico," vs. 3). That Dante is here speaking of the lunar Aurora as it comes on in Purgatory, where Dante is, is an interpretation that is cogently defended by E. Moore (1887), pp. 77-98, and (1903), pp. 75-84. Moore refers (1903, p. 75) to the opening verses of this canto as a "veritable *crux interpretum*" and summarizes his understanding of these lines (p. 81): "The Aurora before moonrise was lighting up the eastern sky (ll. 1-3); the brilliant stars of the constellation Scorpio were on the horizon (ll. 4-6); and, finally, it was shortly after 8.30 p.m. (ll. 7-9)." Moore (1903, pp. 81-82) argues as follows for the interpretation of Dante's reference as being to the lunar rather than to the solar Aurora:

> But the question is to be mainly settled on the ground of the better suitability of one or the other of these interpretations to the passage, when viewed in connexion with other related passages giving data of time. From this point of view I assert most unhesitatingly that this is the case with the lunar Aurora. In the first place, following the usual popular computation, and assuming that we are right in determining this to be the evening of Easter Sunday, April 10, the third night after the full moon, then moonrise would occur about nine p.m. or soon after, and the phenomenon of the lunar Aurora about half an hour before. Further, allowing the same daily retrogradation for the moon of about 13° of space, which is equivalent to about fifty minutes of time, she would have fallen back either from the first point of Libra, or from whatever point in that sign we might rather take as the *terminus a quo* of the full Moon, say, about 40°. That would obviously bring her into Scorpio, and probably somewhere about the middle of that constellation. It will be also remembered that the bright band of stars, with Antares among them, are those that rise first. . . .
>
> Let us next point out how entirely this harmonizes with the other data of time in this part of the poem. In viii. 1 it was just the hour of sunset. In viii. 49 the air was growing dark, say from seven to 7.30. Then occurs the incident of the serpent driven away by the angel

guards (ll. 95 *seqq.*), and the conversation with Conrad Malaspina, &c. The present passage then follows, indicating an hour or more later, when Dante, weary with "the burden of the flesh" (l. 10), lies down to sleep. It will be found that the position of the moon on the following night, which is given in another passage of some obscurity in xviii. 79 . . . is consistent with that here described.

More recent interpretations of vss. 1-6 (by Porena, Sapegno, and others) understand them to refer not to the lunar Aurora as it takes place in Purgatory at the hour stated by Moore above, but to the solar Aurora as it would be seen in Italy, in contrast with the nocturnal phenomenon of vss. 7-9 which occurs in Purgatory, "nel loco ov' eravamo." Such a view was known to Moore, who argues persuasively against it as follows (1903, p. 83):

> It is argued with misplaced ingenuity that, if it were 2½ hours after nightfall in Purgatory, it would be 2½ hours after sunrise in Jerusalem, and consequently in Italy, 45° of longitude west of Jerusalem (according to Dante's system of geography), there would be three hours' difference of time, so that it would be half an hour before sunrise. But . . . it would surely be preposterous to suppose that all this brilliant description refers to an absent and invisible phenomenon.

For a further defense of this whole view of the meaning of vss. 1-9, see M. A. Orr (1956), pp. 252-54.

2. *s'imbiancava*: "Was whitening." Cf. Virgil's "pallida surget" in *Georg.* I, 446. Some commentators (Torraca, Sapegno, and others) have taken the view that "s'imbiancava" here means that Aurora, personified as a woman, is imagined as "whitening" her face with make-up, but this would seem to materialize the image too much.   *balco = balcone.*

balco d'oriente: Benvenuto comments: "a fenestra orientis, sicut mulier pulcra alba surgens de lecto facit se ad fenestram" ("from the window facing east; just as a beautiful woman arising, pale from her bed, comes to the window").

4-6. di gemme . . . gente: E. Moore (1903, pp. 78-79) comments:

> Granting, as seems most natural, that some sign of the zodiac is referred to, one may again ask, apart from any reference to the interpretation of the passage, to which of these signs does such a description seem most appropriate? Would not any one at once say, the Scorpion? It is the only one whose tail is conspicuously an object of terror; and besides, there are two passages in Ovid which may have suggested this description of the Scorpion to Dante.

Moore then quotes *Metam.* XV, 371, "scorpius exibit caudaque minabitur unca" ("a scorpion will come forth threatening with his hooked tail"), and *Fasti* IV, 163-64, "elatae metuendus acumine caudae / Scorpios" ("the Scorpion, the tip of whose winged tail strikes fear"), and continues:

> Indeed, as far as I know, no one has even thought of suggesting any other of the signs of the zodiac except Pisces, which, though it would correspond with the solar Aurora, and though it would suit the epithet *freddo*, is at once excluded by three considerations: (α) the singular, "freddo animale," would be rather out of place: (β) there are no conspicuous stars in that sign, so that the beautiful description in l. 4,
>
> > "Di gemme la sua fronte era lucente,"
>
> becomes unmeaning: (γ) the reference to the formidable tail in l. 6 would be simply ridiculous. . . .
>
> But if, as is more probable, he is referring to the scorpion itself, the epithet *freddo* can be justified by several lines of association between it and coldness. First, it is an invertebrate and cold-blooded animal; next, its *habitat* is in cold and shady places; and further, its venom produces cold. As Brunetto Latini says when speaking of poisonous serpents: "Tutti i veneni sono freddi." ["All poisons are cold."]

See Apoc. 9:5: "Et cruciatus eorum ut cruciatus scorpii cum percutit hominem." ("And their torment was as the torment of a scorpion when it strikes a man.") Also see *Inf.* XVII, 26-27.

7-9. *e la notte . . . l'ale*: E. Moore (1903, p. 76) comments:

> I think, then, that we can scarcely have any doubt that the "passi con che la notte sale" are the hours from six p.m. to midnight, and consequently that the precise time indicated by the words which follow, viz. that two of these steps were already made, and the third was now beginning to droop its wings (the metaphors, it must be admitted, are a little mixed), would be shortly after 8.30 p.m. or between 8.30 and nine.

See also his review here (pp. 77-78) of other interpretations that have been given of the verse.

10-11. *quand' io . . . inchinai*: Cf. *Purg.* XI, 43-45. The climb has been wearisome for Dante, who is here in the flesh.

10. *quel d'Adamo*: The body.

11. *inchinai = m'inchinai.* Dante, who was seated on the grass and flowers (as indicated in vs. 12), reclines to sleep.

12. *tutti e cinque*: Dante, Virgil, Sordello, Nino, and Corrado.

13-14. *Ne l'ora . . . rondinella*: Cf. Albertus Magnus, *De animalibus* XXIII, xxiv, 56: "Garrula est et diem praenuntiando praecinit." ("The chattering swallow salutes the coming of the day in song.")

13-18. *Ne l'ora . . . divina*: It was generally believed that dreams which come in the early morning hours at or just before dawn are likely to be prophetic, for the reasons stated in vss. 16-17 (see n. to *Inf.* XXVI, 7). In *Conv.* II, viii, 13 Dante notes: "Ancora, vedemo continua esperienza de la nostra immortalitade ne le divinazioni de' nostri sogni, le quali essere non potrebbono se in noi alcuna parte immortale non fosse." ("Further we witness constant experience of our immortality in the divinations of our dreams, which might not be if there were not some immortal part in us.") On the whole notion, see Thomas Aquinas, *De veritate* q. 8, a. 12, ad 3:

> Sicut Augustinus narrat . . . quidam posuerunt quod anima in se ipsa quamdam divinationis vim habet. Sed hoc Augustinus ibidem reprobat; quia si per se ipsam posset futura praedicere, esset praescia futurorum; nunc autem videmus, quod non sit in potestate sua cognitio futurorum quandocumque voluerit, quamvis aliquando praesciat; unde oportet quod hoc adiutorio alicuius eveniat quod futura cognoscat. Adiuvatur autem aliquo superiori spiritu, creato vel increato, bono vel malo. Et quia mole corporis aggravatur, et dum sensibilibus intendit, minus est intelligibilium capax; ideo quando a sensibus abstrahitur vel per somnium vel per aegritudinem, vel quocumque alio modo, fit ex hoc magis idonea ad impressionem superioris spiritus recipiendam. Et ideo dum praedicto modo a nexibus corporis absolvitur, futura praenoscit, aliquo spiritu revelante, qui ea futura revelare potest quae ipse praescit vel naturali cognitione, vel in Verbo, ut dictum est, in corp. art.

As Augustine tells us, some asserted that "the soul has powers of divination in itself." He refuted this opinion on the grounds that, if the soul could foretell the future by its own means, it would always know future events; but we know that, even if the soul does have foreknowledge at some times, it is unable to know the future whenever it wishes. Consequently, it must need some help in order to know the future. It can be helped by a higher spirit, created or uncreated, good or evil. Moreover, while it is burdened with the weight of a body and fixes its attention on sense-objects, it is less capable of receiving such thoughts. Hence, when it withdraws from the senses, either in sleep or in sickness or by any other way, it thereby becomes more susceptible to the influence of the higher spirit. So, being severed in this manner from its physical connections, the soul foreknows the future with the help of a revelation by a higher spirit, who can reveal these future things, because, as has been said [see *De veritate* q. 8, a. 12, *resp.*], he knows them either by his natural knowledge or in the Word.

For the quotation from Augustine, see his *De Genesi ad litteram* XII, xii, 27. See also Cicero, *De senectute* XXII, 81: "Atqui dormientium animi maxime declarant divinitatem suam; multa enim, cum remissi et liberi sunt, futura prospiciunt." ("And yet it is when the body sleeps that the soul most clearly manifests its divine nature; for when it is unfettered and free it sees many things that are to come.") The prophetic dreams of the *Vita nuova* are termed *visioni* (see C. S. Singleton, 1949, pp. 14-15 and *passim*). It was a popular idea that false dreams came before, and true dreams after, midnight. On the prophetic morning dream, see C. Speroni (1948) and N. Busetto (1905), both of whom cite, among others, Albertus Magnus, *De apprehen.* III, 9:

Illae quidem imaginationes . . . ad organum sensus communis deferuntur: et per easdem imaginationes futuros effectus ad quos disponunt coelestes motus, advertere possunt, praecipue si ab occupationibus quieti fuerint, et carnis deliciis quae ad exteriora evocant, ne coelestes impressiones perpendant. Et ideo huiusmodi praecipue sentiuntur in dormiendo, et maxime in nocte et circa horam digestionis completae.

Such acts of the imagination . . . are carried to the organ of central perception and through them future effects, toward which heavenly movements impel, can be recognized, especially if the persons are resting from activities and are free from carnal delights, which turn us toward external things unless heavenly impressions prevail. And so, such experiences of the imagination are generally had in sleep, and especially at night about the time when digestion is completed.

See also F. D'Ovidio (1906), pp. 526-28.

15. *forse a memoria de' suo' primi guai*: Dante alludes here to the legend of Philomela and Procne. Procne, having been

married to Tereus, to whom she bore a son, was desirous of seeing her sister Philomela, from whom she was parted. At her request, therefore, Tereus set out for Athens to fetch Philomela. On the way back to Thrace he ravished her and, to prevent her revealing what had happened, cut out her tongue and abandoned her, informing Procne on his return that her sister was dead. Philomela, however, contrived to weave her story into a piece of cloth and thus conveyed the truth to Procne. The latter in fury killed her son and served up his flesh to his father Tereus, who partook of it, unconscious that he was feeding on his own child. Learning from Procne what she had done, Tereus pursued her and Philomela with an axe and was about to slay them, when in answer to the prayers of the two sisters all three of them were metamorphosed into birds, Procne becoming a nightingale, Philomela a swallow, and Tereus a hoopoe. According to some versions, Procne became a swallow, Philomela a nightingale, and Tereus a hawk. See *Metam.* VI, 412-674, where Ovid tells the story.

16. *e che = e in cui.*

19. *in sogno mi parea*: Typically, the verb *parere* is repeated in later verses (vss. 28, 31) continuing to stress the fact that this is indeed a dream.

20. *aguglia = aquila.*   *con penne d'oro*: See "fulvis . . . alis" in the passage quoted from Statius in the n. to vss. 22-24, and also see *Aen.* XII, 247-48: "Namque volans rubra fulvus Iovis ales in aethra / litoreas agitabat avis." ("For, flying through the ruddy sky, Jove's golden bird was chasing the fowls of the shore.")

21. *intesa = intenta.*

22-24. *ed esser mi parea . . . consistoro*: Ganymede was the son of Tros and Callirrhoe and brother of Assaracus, who was one of the forefathers of Aeneas. He was the most beautiful of mortals and, according to one version of the story, was carried off by an eagle while hunting with his companions on Mount Ida in Mysia, so that he might take

his place among the immortals as the cup-bearer of Jupiter.
See Virgil, *Aen.* V, 252-57:

> intextusque puer frondosa regius Ida
> velocis iaculo cervos cursuque fatigat,
> acer, anhelanti similis; quem praepes ab Ida
> sublimem pedibus rapuit Iovis armiger uncis;
> longaevi palmas nequiquam ad sidera tendunt
> custodes, saevitque canum latratus in auras.

Inwoven thereon the royal boy, with javelin and speedy
foot, on leafy Ida tires fleet stags, eager, and like to one
who pants; him Jove's swift armour-bearer has caught
up aloft from Ida in his talons; his aged guardians in
vain stretch their hands to the stars, and the savage
barking of dogs rises skyward.

See also Statius, *Theb.* I, 548-51:

> hinc Phrygius fulvis venator tollitur alis,
> Gargara desidunt surgenti et Troia recedit,
> stant maesti comites, frustraque sonantia lassant
> ora canes umbramque petunt et nubila latrant.

Here the Phrygian hunter is borne aloft on tawny wings,
Gargara's range sinks downwards as he rises and Troy
grows dim beneath him; sadly stand his comrades, in
vain the hounds weary their throats with barking and
pursue his shadow or bay at the clouds.

24. *al sommo consistoro*: Cf. *Georg.* I, 24-25: "deorum /
concilia" ("company of the gods").

30. *suso infino al foco*: Upward all the way to the sphere
of fire which was thought to exist above the sphere of air and
just below the sphere of the moon.

31. *ardesse*: Singular verb with plural subject.

32. *lo 'ncendio imaginato*: "The dreamed-of fire." The
phrase already takes a position outside the dream, as some-
thing remembered.

33. *che 'l sonno si rompesse*: Cf. *Inf.* IV, 1.

34–38. *Non altrimenti Achille . . . braccia*: In his youth Achilles was instructed by Chiron the centaur, from whose charge he was withdrawn by his mother, who conveyed her son in his sleep to the island of Skyros to prevent his going to the Trojan War. See Statius, *Achilleid* I, 104-241. For Achilles' awakening, see *Achilleid* I, 247-50:

> cum pueri tremefacta quies oculique patentes
> infusum sensere diem. Stupet aere primo,
> quae loca, qui fluctus, ubi Pelion? Omnia versa
> atque ignota videt dubitatque agnoscere matrem.

> . . . when the boy's sleep was stirred, and his opening eyes grew conscious of the inpouring day. In amaze at the light that greets him he asks, where is he, what are these waves, where is Pelion? All he beholds is different and unknown, and he hesitates to recognize his mother.

36. *dove si fosse*: The so-called pleonastic reflexive is frequently used after *non sapere*.

39. *là onde poi li Greci il dipartiro*: After Achilles' mother had taken her son to the island of Skyros, he remained there in hiding, dressed like a woman, among the daughters of Lycomedes, until Ulysses visited the island, disguised as a merchant, and offered women's dresses for sale, among which he had concealed some arms. The arms were eagerly seized by Achilles, who, having thus disclosed his sex, was persuaded by Ulysses to accompany him to the Greek army, which was on its way to Troy. Diomedes also took part in the crafty deed. See *Inf.* XXVI, 55-57, and n. to *Inf.* XXVI, 62. *il dipartiro = lo dipartirono.*

41–42. *e diventa' ismorto . . . agghiaccia*: See *Aen.* III, 259-60: "At sociis subita gelidus formidine sanguis / deriguit." ("But my comrades' blood chilled and froze with sudden fear.") See also Matt. 28:4: "Prae timore autem eius exterriti sunt custodes, et facti sunt velut mortui." ("And for fear of him the guards were terrified, and became like dead men.") Note, too, Statius, *Theb.* X, 621-22: "Stupet anxius alto / corda metu glaciante pater." ("He is benumbed by anguish, and an icy dread assails the father's heart.") Cf. *Purg.* VIII, 42; *Inf.* XXXIV, 22.

44. *'l sole er' alto già più che due ore*: It is past 8:00 A.M. on the morning of Easter Monday. Dante and Virgil are still on the eastern side of the mountain.

47. *fatti*: The imperative *fa* with the usual doubling of the initial consonant of the word attached to a monosyllabic imperative.   *sicur = sicuro.   semo = siamo.*

48. *non stringer, ma rallarga*: "Do not bridle, but give reins to." The two verbs are commonly used in this sense.

50. *il balzo che 'l chiude dintorno*: See *Purg.* IV, 47-48. A low cliff or steep face of rock girds the mountain, marking the boundary of Purgatory proper. It is high enough to oblige any who would ascend farther to enter through the gate, which is no doubt the only break in this wall.

52. *procede al giorno = precede il giorno.*

53. *quando l'anima tua dentro dormia*: "Dentro" stresses the withdrawal of the mind in sleep from all outward experience of the senses, and such a passing touch again points to the fact that Dante is here in the flesh ("quel d'Adamo," vs. 10), so that both body and soul are the subject of the verb and can be said to be asleep.

53-55. *quando l'anima tua . . . donna*: Petrocchi's text has a comma after "dormia," instead of after "addorno," which would make Lucy's coming, rather than the sleeping Dante, be upon the flowers. This is possible, but the other meaning seems preferable.

54. *ond' è là giù addorno*: "The place," i.e., the hollow, is understood as subject.

56. *lasciatemi pigliar costui che dorme*: Lucy addresses the four who are with Dante (Sordello and the others), not Virgil alone, and "costui" points to the sleeping Dante as being near them in the group.

58. *forme*: Souls. Cf. *Inf*. XXVII, 73.

59. *e come 'l dì fu chiaro*: Apparently even Lucy must respect the rule that there can be no climbing the mountain by night (*Purg*. VII, 52-57).

60. *sen = se ne.*

61. *dimostraro = dimostrarono.*

62. *li occhi suoi belli*: The touch is especially appropriate, this being St. Lucy, who, according to the well-known legend, plucked out her eyes when they were admired by a noble suitor. They were then restored to her more beautiful than before, and she became thereby the special patroness of those who suffer from ailments of the eyes.   *quella intrata aperta*: The opening in the *balzo* mentioned in vs. 51. The fact that it is closed by a portal is not yet apparent.

63. *poi ella e 'l sonno ad una se n'andaro*: Lucy vanishes as suddenly and mysteriously as she appeared. It must have taken her more than two hours to climb from the valley of the princes to the gate of Purgatory bearing the sleeping Dante, which stresses the great distance of that stretch of the journey. We realize the distance when we learn later (*Purg*. XXI, 40-54) that the boundary of Purgatory proper is indeed so high that above it there is no atmospheric change.   *andaro = andarono.*

66. *li = gli.*

68. *su per lo balzo*: Up *toward* the cliff (vs. 50), not up *over* it, of course.

74–76. *là dove pareami . . . porta*: The portal is recessed in the rock and was not visible before (see vs. 62).

76–78. *una porta . . . motto*: The door is closed and guarded, and the entrance is not wide, all in striking contrast with the entrance to Hell, which is always wide open and is not guarded (*Inf*. VIII, 125-26).

80. *vidil = lo vidi.   grado sovrano*: This uppermost "grado" is also the threshold itself (vss. 104-5).   *sovrano = supremo*.

81. *tal*: I.e., so resplendent. See *Purg*. II, 38-39; VIII, 35-36; and Matt. 28:3: "Erat autem aspectus eius sicut fulgur." ("His countenance was like lightning.")

82. *e una spada nuda avea in mano*: The sword, as the early commentators observe, is the sign of one who has authority to pronounce sentence. See, for example, Benvenuto: "sicut sedet iudex in alto tribunali ad examinandam causam et ferendam sententiam iuste; ideo dat sibi ensem in manu" ("just as a judge, when he sits on the bench to examine a case and to pass a just judgment, takes a sword in his hand"). But it is also reminiscent of the Cherubim with the flaming sword that were placed to guard Eden after Adam and Eve were driven forth, as becomes clear especially when we learn that Eden is indeed situated inside this gate, Eden being at the summit of the mountain, and this being the way thereto. See n. to *Purg*. VIII, 26.

85. *Dite costinci*: "Say from where you are." Cf. *Inf*. XII, 63.

86. *ov' è la scorta?* The angel's challenge recalls Cato's question in *Purg*. I, 43: "Chi v'ha guidati?" It should not be taken to mean, of course, that the souls, when they come up to enter through the gate, are escorted to it. Indeed, the angel can see that Dante and Virgil are not souls who come in the usual way.

87. *Guardate che 'l venir sù non vi nòi*: An admonition which can, in its very different way, remind us of Minos' "non t'inganni l'ampiezza de l'intrare" (*Inf*. V, 20). For *noiare* in this sense, cf. *Inf*. XXIII, 15.

90. *ne = ci*.

91. *avanzi*: Cf. *Inf*. IV, 78; XIX, 71.

97. *tinto più che perso*: Darker than perse, hence very dark (cf. *Inf.* V, 89; *Conv.* IV, xx, 2).

98. *petrina*: Torraca comments: "Il diminuitivo allude alla qualità della pietra, che *ruvida* e tutta *crepata,* pareva piuttosto una conglomerazione di pietruzze." ("The diminutive alludes to the quality of the stone. Being rough and all cracked, it seemed more like a conglomeration of small stones.") Thus, this step is not only cracked, but is of a weak and crumbling stone, features which clearly have symbolic meaning.

100. *s'ammassiccia*: Torraca continues: "A differenza del secondo, scabro e frastagliato, il terzo 'scaglione' è tutto una massa compatta e soda." ("In contradistinction to the second, rough and irregular, the third 'step' is one compact and hard mass.")

102. *come sangue che fuor di vena spiccia*: A comparison that not only further defines the color of the third step but suggests its symbolic value, as having to do with our redemption by Christ's blood. For *spicciare* in this sense, cf. *Inf.* XIV, 76-78.

105. *sembiava = sembrava.* *pietra di diamante*: Since this is the "grado sovrano," or threshold, of the entrance to Purgatory, upon which the vicar of Peter sits as the symbol of ecclesiastical authority, "pietra" here brings to mind Christ's words to Peter (Matt. 16:18): "Tu es Petrus, et super hanc petram aedificabo Ecclesiam meam." ("Thou art Peter, and upon this rock I will build my Church.")

106. *di buona voglia*: This refers to Dante's eagerness to enter the gate.

107-8. *Chiedi umilemente . . . scioglia*: See *Inf.* VIII, 126, where the portal of Hell is said to be "sanza serrame."

108. *umilemente*: We recall that Dante, before he began his ascent of the mountain, was girt with the rush of humility. See *Purg.* I, 133-36.

110. *misericordia chiesi e ch'el m'aprisse = chiesi la misericordia di aprirmi. La porta* is understood as the object of "aprisse."

111. *ma tre volte nel petto pria mi diedi: Darsi nel petto* means "to smite one's breast." Thrice implies that Dante says, as he does this: "Mea culpa, mea culpa, mea maxima culpa," expressing remorse for his sins of thought, word, and deed.

112–14. *Sette P . . . disse:* The seven P's (from the Latin *peccatum,* "sin") stand for the sins that are somehow to be purged on the seven terraces of Purgatory. Here Dante is in the figure of Everyman, of course. See L. Cicchitto (1935), p. 114:

> Essi pertanto, pur non rappresentando propriamente i peccati, che come tali sono già stati rimessi dalla potestà delle chiavi, si riferiscono però certamente alle colpe e significano quelle *sequelae* che, anche dopo rimesso e cancellato, il peccato lascia nell'anima, e cioè la *pronitas ad malum* e la *difficultas ad bonum.*

> In any case, these [P's] do not properly represent the sins, for as such they have been absolved by the power of the keys. But they quite certainly refer to faults, and they signify those consequences which are left in the soul even after the sin has been forgiven and erased. It is a "tendency toward evil" and a "resistance toward good."

On this point Cicchitto cites Bonaventura, who states in his *Sermones de Sanctis (De Sanctis Apostolis Petro et Paulo* I, 1): "Difficultas ad bonum et pronitas ad malum . . . sunt in sequela peccati." ("Resistance toward the good and tendency toward evil . . . are among the consequences of sin.") It seems important to conceive of the P's in this way, since, as we are to see, they are nowhere said to be inscribed upon the forehead of the *souls* of Purgatory who enter through the gate, but only on the forehead of the living man, Dante, and hence must find their meaning in terms of the general allegory of the poem, of man in this life, *in via.* They correspond, moreover, to those sinful inclinations (*vulnera*) which were represented in the prologue scene of the poem by the three beasts that prevented Dante's ascent of the mountain, and thus they are part of the correspondence between that first failure to climb and this present successful ascent.

The P's should also be conceived as representing the penance that is imposed upon the sinner after absolution and their removal as the *satisfactio operis*, "satisfaction by works," which is the third essential part of the sacrament, following *contritio cordis*, "contrition of the heart," and *confessio oris*, "confession by the lips." See Thomas Aquinas, *Summa theol.* III, Suppl., q. 18, a. 3, ad 1: "Illud residuum poenae ad quod obligat, est medicina purgans peccati impuritatem." ("The remainder of the punishment to which the priest binds the penitent is the medicine which cleanses the latter from the blemish of sin.") In this sense the P's as wounds ("piaghe") correspond to the stains which the souls themselves bear into Purgatory and of which they must cleanse themselves. For other references and a general discussion of the P's, see G. R. Sarolli (1957).

114. *piaghe*: The term echoes the biblical *vulnera*, or *plagae*. See Ps. 38:11[39:10]: "Amove a me plagas tuas." ("Take away your scourge from me.") Also see Lev. 26:24-25: "Ego quoque contra vos adversus incedam, et percutiam vos septies propter peccata vestra, inducamque super vos gladium ultorem foederis mei." ("I, too, will defy you and will smite you for your sins seven times harder than before. I will make the sword, the avenger of my covenant, sweep over you.")

115. *Cenere, o terra*: Ashes and earth are both symbols of humility. *che secca si cavi*: The verb *cavare* is in the hypothetical subjunctive.

116. *fora = sarebbe*.

117. *due chiavi*: Christ said to Peter (Matt. 16:18-19):

Et ego dico tibi, quia tu es Petrus, et super hanc

petram aedificabo Ecclesiam meam, et portae inferi
non praevalebunt adversus eam. Et tibi dabo claves
regni caelorum; et quodcumque ligaveris super terram,
erit ligatum et in caelis; et quodcumque solveris super
terram, erit solutum et in caelis.

And I say to thee, thou art Peter, and upon this rock
I will build my Church, and the gates of hell shall not
prevail against it. And I will give thee the keys of the
kingdom of heaven; and whatever thou shalt bind on
earth shall be bound in heaven, and whatever thou
shalt loose on earth shall be loosed in heaven.

Peter will be seen in Paradise, at what is, symbolically, a
kind of entrance thereto (*Par.* XXIV). In *Par.* XXIII, 139,
he is referred to as "colui che tien le chiavi di tal gloria," but
he is never shown actually holding the keys.

On the power of the keys, see Thomas Aquinas, *Summa
theol.* III, Suppl., q. 17, treated under the sacrament
of penance; note, especially, a. 3, resp.:

Et secundum hoc distinguuntur duae claves, quarum
una pertinet ad iudicium de idoneitate eius qui absol-
vendus est; et alia ad ipsam absolutionem. Et hae duae
claves non distinguuntur in essentia auctoritatis, quia
utrumque ex officio eis competit; sed ex comparatione
ad actus quorum unus alium praesupponit.

Accordingly we may distinguish two keys, the first of
which regards the judgment about the worthiness of
the person to be absolved, while the other regards the
absolution.

These two keys are distinct, not in the essence of au-
thority, since both belong to the minister by virtue of
his office, but in comparison with their respective acts,
one of which presupposes the other.

121–23. *Quandunque l'una . . . calla*: See Thomas Aquinas,
Summa theol. III, Suppl., q. 17, a. 2, ad 4: "ita sacerdos
dicitur excludere, non quod impedimentum ad intrandum
ponat, sed quia impedimentum positum non amovet; quia
ipse amovere non potest, nisi prius Deus amoverit" ("so a

priest is said to exclude, not as though he placed an obstacle to entrance, but because he does not remove an obstacle which is there, since he cannot remove it unless God has already removed it"). It is God, therefore, who opens the gate, and if on the part of the priest there is a failure of true discernment or authority, the gate is not opened, i.e., the absolution he gives is not valid.

123. *calla*: A passageway (cf. *Purg.* IV, 22).

124–26. *Più cara è l'una . . . digroppa*: "L'una" is the golden key and "l'altra" the silver key. Porena comments:

> Qui si torna ad accennare alla funzione del confessore. La chiave d'oro simboleggia l'autorità di assolvere, che proviene da Dio, e quindi è cosa di natura superiore ma inerente, diciam così, alla qualità sacerdotale in astratto. La chiave d'argento simboleggia l'atto concreto dell'assoluzione (*disgroppa*, cioè scioglie, il nodo del peccato) e richiede grande capacità psicologica del sacerdote nel comprendere se il peccatore sia veramente pentito e se meriti l'assoluzione.

> Here he indicates the function of the confessor. The golden key symbolizes the authority to absolve, which comes from God, and is therefore by nature superior but inherent, so to speak, in the sacerdotal quality in the abstract. The silver key symbolizes the concrete act of absolution (it disentangles, that is, unties, the knot of sin); and it requires great psychological capacity on the part of the priest, in understanding whether the sinner has really repented and merits absolution.

127. *Da Pier le tegno*: "Tegno" expresses the idea of receiving in custody, by virtue of which the angel is Peter's vicar.   *dissemi = mi disse.*

129. *pur che la gente a' piedi mi s'atterri*: Again the stress is on the necessity of humility.

130. *l'uscio*: The door proper.   *porta*: The doorway.   *sacrata = sacra* (see vs. 134).

131. *facciovi* = *vi faccio*. The angel continues to address the two wayfarers without distinguishing Dante the living man from Virgil, a soul.

132. *di fuor torna chi 'n dietro si guata*: See Gen. 19:17, the order given to Lot. On this also see Augustine, *De civ. Dei* XVI, 30:

> Post hanc promissionem liberato de Sodomis Lot, et veniente igneo imbre de coelo, tota illa regio impiae civitatis in cinerem versa est, ubi stupra in masculos in tantam consuetudinem convaluerant, quantam leges solent aliorum factorum praebere licentiam. Verum et hoc eorum supplicium specimen futuri iudicii divini fuit. Nam quo pertinet quod prohibiti sunt qui liberabantur ab Angelis retro respicere, nisi quia non est animo redeundum ad veterem vitam, qua per gratiam regeneratus exuitur, si ultimum evadere iudicium cogitamus?

> This promise was followed by the rescue of Lot from the Sodomites and the rain of fire from heaven which reduced the whole territory of that wicked city to ashes. It was a place where the practice of unnatural lust had become as much sanctioned by custom as other forms of wickedness are elsewhere permitted by law. The point of their particular kind of punishment was that it provided a foretaste of the divine judgment to come, just as the command of the angels bidding those who were rescued not to look back was a reminder to us all, who hope to escape that ultimate doom, not to allow our wills to look back to the old life we put off when we put on the new life of grace.

Also see Luc. 9:62: "Nemo mittens manum suam ad aratrum et respiciens retro, aptus est regno Dei." ("No one, having put his hand to the plow and looking back, is fit for the kingdom of God.")

136–38. *non rugghiò . . . macra*: Tarpeia, the Tarpeian Rock (Tarpeius mons) at Rome on which, in the temple of Saturn, was placed the Roman treasury. The reference is to the violation of the treasury by Julius Caesar in 49 B.C. after the vain attempt of the tribune Metellus, an adherent of Pompey, to defend it. See Lucan, *Phars.* III, 153-57, 167-68:

> Protinus abducto patuerunt templa Metello.
> Tunc rupes Tarpeia sonat magnoque reclusas
> Testatur stridore fores; tum conditus imo
> Eruitur templo multis non tactus ab annis
> Romani census populi . . .
> . . . tristi spoliantur templa rapina,
> Pauperiorque fuit tunc primum Caesare Roma.

Metellus was drawn aside and the temple at once thrown open. Then the Tarpeian rock re-echoed, and loud grating bore witness to the opening of the doors; then was brought forth the wealth of the Roman people, stored in the temple vaults and untouched for many a year. . . . Dismal was the deed of plunder that robbed the temple; and then for the first time Rome was poorer than a Caesar.

138. *macra*: Despoiled of the treasure (see "pauperior" in *Phars.* III, 168, quoted in preceding note).

139. *Io mi rivolsi attento al primo tuono*: Dante faced toward the angel while he spoke. Now, at the first sound made by the door as it opens, he turns his whole attention forward to that note. For the "tuono" made by the door, see Lucan's "magno . . . stridore" in *Phars.* III, 154-55, quoted in n. to vss. 136-38.

140. *Te Deum laudamus*: A hymn which has been called by J. Julian (1892, p. 1119) "the most famous non-biblical hymn of the Western Church." It has been traditionally ascribed to Ambrose and Augustine, who were said to have uttered it extemporaneously on the occasion of the latter's baptism, but it is now thought to have been composed in the early fifth century by Nicetas. It is written in the kind of accented prose known as the *cursus leoninus*, which began to

come into use in the fourth century and lasted until the time of Dante. Buti comments that the hymn "si suole cantare da' cherici quando uno omo esce del mondo, e va a la religione" ("is generally sung by priests when a man departs from this world and enters a religious order"). The following text and translation of the hymn may be found in M. Britt (1955), pp. 14-16:

Te Deum laudamus: te Dominum confitemur.
Te æternum Patrem omnis terra veneratur.
Tibi omnes Angeli, tibi Cæli, et universæ Potestates:
Tibi Cherubim et Seraphim incessabili voce
    proclamant:
Sanctus,
Sanctus,
Sanctus Dominus Deus Sabaoth.
Pleni sunt cæli et terra maiestatis gloriæ tuæ.
Te gloriosus Apostolorum chorus,
Te prophetarum laudabilis numerus,
Te Martyrum candidatus laudat exercitus.
Te per orbem terrarum sancta confitetur Ecclesia,
Patrem immensæ maiestatis;
Venerandum tuum verum et unicum Filium;
Sanctum quoque Paraclitum Spiritum.
Tu Rex gloriæ, Christe.
Tu Patris sempiternus es Filius.
Tu, ad liberandum suscepturus hominem, non
    horruisti Virginis uterum.
Tu, devicto mortis aculeo, aperuisti credentibus
    regna cælorum.
Tu ad dexteram Dei sedes, in gloria Patris.
Iudex crederis esse venturus.
Te ergo quæsumus, tuis famulis subveni, quos
    pretioso sanguine redemisti.
Æterna fac cum Sanctis tuis in gloria numerari.
Salvum fac populum tuum, Domine, et benedic
    hereditati tuæ.
Et rege eos, et extolle illos usque in æternum.
Per singulos dies benedicimus te;

Et laudamus nomen tuum in sæculum, et in
    sæculum sæculi.
Dignare, Domine, die isto sine peccato nos
    custodire.
Miserere nostri, Domine, miserere nostri.
Fiat misericordia tua, Domine, super nos,
    quemadmodum speravimus in te.
In te, Domine, speravi: non confundar in æternum.

We praise Thee, O God: we acknowledge Thee to
    be the Lord.
All the earth doth worship Thee, the Father
    everlasting.
To Thee all the Angels cry aloud, the Heavens and
    all the Powers therein:
To Thee the Cherubim and Seraphim continually
    do cry:
Holy,
Holy,
Holy Lord God of Hosts.
Heaven and earth are full of the majesty of
    Thy glory.
The glorious choir of the Apostles praise Thee.
The admirable company of the Prophets
    praise Thee.
The white-robed army of Martyrs praise Thee.
The holy Church throughout the world doth
    acknowledge Thee,
The Father of infinite majesty,
Thy adorable, true, and only Son,
And the Holy Spirit the Comforter.
Thou art the King of glory, O Christ.
Thou art the everlasting Son of the Father.
Thou, when Thou wouldst take human nature to
    deliver man, didst not disdain the
    Virgin's womb.
When Thou hadst overcome the sting of death,
    Thou didst open to believers the kingdom of
    heaven.

Thou sittest at the right hand of God, in the glory
   of the Father.
We believe that Thou shalt come to be our Judge.
We beseech Thee, therefore, help Thy servants,
   whom Thou hast redeemed with Thy precious
   Blood.
Make them to be numbered with Thy Saints in
   glory everlasting.
O Lord, save Thy people, and bless
   Thine inheritance.
Govern them, and lift them up forever.
Day by day we bless Thee;
And we praise Thy name forever, yea, forever
   and forever.
Vouchsafe, O Lord, this day to keep us without sin.
Have mercy upon us, O Lord, have mercy upon us.
Let Thy mercy be upon us, O Lord, as we have
   hoped in Thee.
O Lord, in Thee have I hoped, let me not be
   confounded forever.

141. *al dolce suono*: The "tuono" made by the hinges is
mysteriously "dolce," like organ music, as the following
simile suggests.

142–45. *Tale imagine . . . parole*: Dante hears the "Te
Deum laudamus" sung as by voices within, mingled with the
sweet music that is made by the opening of the door, just as
voices are heard singing to organ music.

CANTO X

1. *Poi = poi che.   soglio*: Cf. *Inf*. XVIII, 14. *Soglio* is a synonym of *soglia* and *sogliare*; see *Inf*. XIV, 87, where "sogliare" is used of the portal to Hell.

2. *'l mal amor de l'anime*: The whole phrase is the subject of the verb "disusa," which is transitive here and has for its object the relative "che" (i.e., "porta").

3. *perché fa parer dritta la via torta*: Such a deception, caused by evil love, will be enacted later in a significant dream (*Purg*. XIX, 1-24).

4. *sonando la senti' esser richiusa*: Dante knows by the sound alone that the door is closed behind him; but, obeying the angel, he does not look back. Again the hinges resound, as they did when the door was opened (*Purg*. IX, 133-38), but they do so this time with the clear suggestion that they have somehow grown rusty from "disuse," the consequence of evil love, which brings but few souls to enter here. Love, good and bad, is the keystone to the whole purgatorial system, as will be explained in *Purg*. XVII-XVIII (see *Purg*. XVII, 91 - XVIII, 75), at the center of the poem.

5-6. *e s'io avesse . . . scusa?* Dante's thought ("if I had turned back my eyes") underscores, from a position now within the portal of Purgatory proper, the rule that there may be no more backward glances, once this threshold is crossed (see *Purg.* IX, 131-32).

5. *avesse = avessi.*

6. *fora = sarebbe.*

7-16. *Noi salavam . . . cruna*: The account of this climb through the very narrow passageway (ending so significantly in the rhyme word "cruna") stresses the fact that beyond the portal itself this narrow way marks a kind of entrance to Purgatory proper and, unlike the gate of Hell, which is very wide (see *Inf.* V, 20) and is "denied to none" (*Inf.* XIV, 87), the gate here is narrow. The whole passage, indeed, would call to mind precisely the "angusta porta et arcta via," and the few who enter, of the Gospel. See Matt. 7:13-14: "Intrate per angustam portam, quia lata porta et spatiosa via est quae ducit ad perditionem, et multi sunt qui intrant per eam. Quam angusta porta et arcta via est quae ducit ad vitam, et pauci sunt qui inveniunt eam!" ("Enter by the narrow gate. For wide is the gate and broad is the way that leads to destruction, and many there are who enter that way. How narrow the gate and close the way that leads to life! And few there are who find it.") For "cruna," see the "foramen acus" in Christ's words to the disciples (Matt. 19:24): "Et iterum dico vobis, facilius est camelum per foramen acus transire, quam divitem intrare in regnum caelorum." ("And further I say to you, it is easier for a camel to pass through the eye of a needle, than for a rich man to enter the kingdom of heaven.")

8-9. *che si moveva . . . s'appressa*: The cleft is zigzag, projecting here and receding there, and so narrow that the climbers must cling now to the one side and now to the other. On the whole passage, cf. *Purg.* IV, 31-33.

13. *fece i nostri passi scarsi*: Cf. *Inf.* VIII, 117, and vs. 100 of the present canto: "i passi radi."

14-15. *lo scemo de la luna . . . ricorcarsi*: "Lo scemo de la luna" is the waning moon. See *Inf.* XX, 127, where it is said that the moon was full over the dark wood on the preceding Thursday night. It is now three and a half days later, which would give a retardation of about three hours, and the moon would be passing toward its last quarter. It should be noted that the moon is said to be at the point of setting when Dante and Virgil come forth from the cleft—and it is, therefore, not possible to determine the time exactly. But since the waning moon sets later than the full moon, and when Dante awoke outside the gate, the sun was "more than two hours high" (*Purg.* IX, 44), it must now be several hours after sunrise. For the figure of speech involving *letto* and *ricorcarsi*, see *Purg.* VIII, 133-34.

16. *cruna*: See n. to vss. 7-16.

17. *liberi e aperti*: Liberated from the narrow passage and in the open now.

18. *sù dove il monte in dietro si rauna*: Dante and Virgil have come to the first terrace of Purgatory, which is said to be formed by the mountain's "gathering itself back."

19. *io stancato*: The diaeresis is most effective, by its peculiar stress distinguishing Dante, who must climb with the "weight of Adam" (*Purg.* IX, 10), from Virgil, who as a spirit does not labor under any such burden. *amendue incerti*: The two wayfarers still must seek their way, as they have done from the beginning of Purgatory, for Virgil has never been in this place before and is a pilgrim here. See *Purg.* II, 61-63; III, 52-57.

20. *restammo = ristemmo.*

20–21. *un piano solingo . . . diserti*: The circling terrace is strangely deserted, which must arouse a certain suspense in the reader: must not such a way (*strada*) round the mountain serve some purpose here in Purgatory proper? So it was (yet how different!) when the wayfarers arrived over a certain ditch of Malebolge (*Inf.* XXI, 19-21). It will be noted that, in the next canto, a verse in the paraphrase of the Lord's Prayer (*Purg.* XI, 14) echoes the notion of desert here expressed.

22. *ove confina il vano*: *Piano* is understood as the subject. For *vano* in this sense, see *Inf*. XVII, 25.

23. *al piè de l'alta ripa che pur sale*: As indicated in vs. 30, the bank rises very abruptly; at a certain height, of course, it continues (as "pur" suggests) to form the rising slope of the mountain.

24. *misurrebbe = misurerebbe.   in tre volte un corpo umano*: The width of the terrace, from its outer edge to the base of the inner wall of rock, is three times the length of a human body, about sixteen to eighteen feet. Presumably the other terraces of Purgatory have more or less this same width. Other such precise measurements are given in *Inferno*, of a giant's body (*Inf*. XXXI, 61-66) and of a ditch in Malebolge (*Inf*. XXX, 86-87).

25–27. *e quanto l'occhio . . . cotale*: The terrace is of an equal width all the way round.

25. *quanto l'occhio mio potea trar d'ale*: "As far as my eye could reach" (literally, "as far as my eye could fly with its wings").

27. *cotale*: Of such width.

28–29. *Là sù non eran mossi . . . conobbi*: Virgil and Dante have arrived on the terrace but have not yet taken a step in either direction.

28. *anco = ancora*.

29. *quella ripa intorno*: The bank to the right.

30. *che, dritta, di salita aveva manco*: The meaning of this verse has been much discussed, and its reading questioned by many commentators: Should it read "dritto" or "dritta"? If "dritta," modifying "ripa," one might punctuate it "che, dritta, di salita aveva manco," meaning "which, being perpendicular, lacked means of ascent." Or, if "dritto" is the correct reading, then that adjective may be taken to modify "manco" (and to be the more emphatic in being so separated from its noun), and the meaning would be: "which provided

no means of ascent whatsoever."As long as we have no auto-
graph manuscript of the poem, such problems cannot be
settled.

32. *Policleto*: Polycletus was a celebrated Greek sculptor
(*ca.* 452-412 B.C.), a contemporary of Phidias, but some-
what younger. He was supposed to be unsurpassed in carv-
ing images of men, as Phidias was in making those of gods,
and is so acclaimed by Cicero, Pliny, Quintilian, and others.
He is mentioned as follows by Aristotle in his *Nicomachean
Ethics* (see *Eth. Nicom.* VI, 7, 1141^a in Aquinas, *Opera
omnia*, Vol. XXI, p. 204, or R. M. Spiazzi, 1964, p. 321):
"Sapientiam autem in artibus certissimis assignamus, puta
Phydiam latomium sapientem, Polycletum statuificum. Hic
quidem igitur nihil aliud significantes sapientiam, quam
quoniam virtus artis est." ("We attribute 'wisdom' to the
most certain arts; accordingly we call Phidias a wise sculptor,
and Polycletus a wise statuary. Here then by wisdom we
mean nothing more than the excellence of the art.") Thomas
Aquinas (*Exp. Eth. Nicom.* VI, lect. 5, n. 1180) comments
on this as follows:

> Et secundum hunc modum dicimus Phydiam fuisse
> sapientem laterum et lapidum incisorem, et Polycletum
> sapientem statuificum, idest factorem statuarum: ubi
> nihil aliud dicimus sapientiam, quam virtutem artis,
> idest ultimum et perfectissimum in arte, qua scilicet
> aliquis attingit ad id quod est ultimum et perfectissi-
> mum in arte.

> In this way we say Phidias was a wise sculptor and
> Polycletus a wise statuary, i.e., a carver of statues. Here
> we call wisdom nothing other than the excellence of the
> art (i.e., its ultimate perfection) by which a man at-
> tains what is ultimate and most perfect in the art.

33. *ma la natura lì avrebbe scorno*: Nature looks up to the
eternal ideas of God in practicing her art, and the human
artist looks to Nature in practicing his (thus human art is
as grandchild to God, as stated in *Inf.* XI, 105). Now these
carvings are God's art, fashioned directly by Him. It follows,

therefore, that both of His imitators (Nature directly and a human artist indirectly) would be quite put to scorn here, since they would be greatly surpassed by such a Master.

34–45. *L'angel che venne . . . pace*: The first *intaglio* represents the familiar scene of the angel Gabriel's announcement of the Incarnation to the Virgin Mary. In presenting Mary as the first of these "images of humilities so great," as they are called in vs. 98, this *intaglio* initiates what will prove to be a constant pattern in Purgatory, i.e., Mary always comes first in the series of virtues and in this way is proclaimed to be the keystone of them all. For the Annunciation, see Luc. 1:26-38. Mary's great humility was expressed in her reply to Gabriel (Luc. 1:38): "Ecce ancilla Domini; fiat mihi secundum verbum tuum." ("Behold the handmaid of the Lord; be it done to me according to thy word.") Mankind had wept and longed for peace with God ever since that peace had been lost by Adam's sin. Gabriel thus brings to earth the glad tidings that peace with Him is now restored.

36. *ch'aperse il ciel del suo lungo divieto*: With Adam's sin, the door to Heaven was closed to mankind. Those who were one day to enter Heaven went to Limbo, there to await the Redeemer (see *Inf.* IV, 52-63). This was the long "ban." See Thomas Aquinas, *Summa theol.* III, q. 49, a. 5, resp.:

> Clausio ianuae est obstaculum quoddam prohibens homines ab ingressu. Prohibebantur autem homines ab ingressu regni caelestis propter peccatum, quia, sicut dicitur Isa. 35, 8, *Via illa santa vocabitur, et non transibit per eam pollutus*. Est autem duplex peccatum impediens ab ingressu regni caelestis. Unum quidem commune totius humanae naturae, quod est peccatum primi parentis; et per hoc peccatum praecludebatur homini aditus regni caelestis.

> The shutting of the gate is the obstacle which hinders men from entering in. But it is on account of sin that men were prevented from entering into the heavenly kingdom, since, according to Isa. XXXV.8: *It shall be called the holy way, and the unclean shall not pass over*

it. Now there is a twofold sin which prevents men from entering into the kingdom of heaven. The first is common to the whole race, for it is our first parents' sin, and by that sin heaven's entrance is closed to man.

37. *pareva* = *appariva*.

39. *sembiava* = *sembrava*.

40. *saria* = *sarebbe*.

42. *ch'ad aprir l'alto amor volse la chiave*: Heaven was "opened" at the Annunciation; hence Mary can be said to have turned the key that opened God's love, which then descended to mankind.

43-45. *e avea in atto . . . suggella*: Mary can be "seen" to reply to Gabriel, as distinctly as an image is impressed in wax by a seal.

43. *esta* = *questa*.

46. *Non tener pur ad un loco la mente*: Virgil will not allow Dante to linger too long, even though here he is gazing upon God's art.

47-48. *che m'avea . . . gente*: Dante is now standing on Virgil's left.

49-52. *e vedea . . . storia*: Mary is to the far right as Dante faces the bank, and he now looks farther to the right, beyond Virgil ("colui che mi movea"), to see the next *intaglio*. "Storia" here is used in the sense suggested later by "storiata" (vs. 73), i.e., a depiction in art, even as stained-glass windows or initial letters in manuscripts or frescoed walls were said to be "historiated."

53. *varcai Virgilio*: Dante crosses past Virgil, going toward the right. The "stories" are thus leading him in the proper direction for movement in Purgatory, as we know.   *fe'mi* = *mi feci*.

54. *a li occhi miei disposta*: I.e., spread before his eyes. See Fra Giordano, *Prediche inedite* VII: "Questo iscrive santo

Gregorio, quando dispone il Giobbo." ("That is what St. Gregory writes when he expounds Job.")   *disposta = esposta.*

55–69. *Era intagliato lì . . . trista*: The second of the "images of humilities so great" shows King David, "the humble Psalmist," dancing before the ark of the covenant. See II Reg. 6:2-17, especially vss. 12, 14, 16:

> Erant cum David septem chori et victima vituli. . . . Et David saltabat totis viribus ante Dominum. Porro David erat accinctus ephod lineo. . . . Cumque intrasset arca Domini in civitatem David, Michol filia Saul prospiciens per fenestram vidit regem David subsilientem atque saltantem coram Domino, et despexit eum in corde suo.
>
> And there were with David seven choirs and calves for victims. . . . And David danced with all his might before the Lord. And David was girded with a linen ephod. . . . And when the ark of the Lord was come into the city of David, Michol the daughter of Saul, looking out through a window, saw king David leaping and dancing before the Lord: and she despised him in her heart.

55. *nel marmo stesso*: In that same white marble, which continuing round the bank is the material in which these carvings are made.

57. *per che si teme officio non commesso*: The reference is to Uzzah (Oza), one of the sons of Abinadab, in whose house the ark had rested for twenty years. Uzzah and his brother Ahio accompanied the ark when David undertook its removal to Jerusalem. On the way, the oxen of the cart in which it was being borne stumbled, and Uzzah, who was walking by the side, put out his hand and steadied the ark to prevent its falling, whereupon for his presumption and profanation he was struck dead (II Reg. 6:3-7; I Par. 13:6-10).

In his letter to the Italian cardinals, Dante deprecates the comparison of himself with Uzzah, for his interference in the affairs of the Church, on the ground that Uzzah laid his hand on the ark itself, while he desires only to admonish the oxen who are straying from the right path (*Epist.* XI, 9, 12).

58. *Dinanzi parea gente*: "Dinanzi" seems to suggest that Dante is taking in the whole scene and sees the people there on his far right heading the procession. Even the figures in a carving, those who walk before the ark, are thus seen to move in the proper direction for Purgatory.   *parea = appariva.*

58–60. *e tutta quanta . . . canta*: The two senses are Dante's sight and his hearing. The ear says "no," of course, and the eye says "yes."

59. *in sette cori*: As in the Vulgate Bible, quoted in n. to vss. 55-69 (these do not appear, however, in the King James Bible).

61. *Similemente*: As with the two senses of sight and hearing, so now with sight and smell.   *fummo = fumo.*

63. *al sì e al no*: For similar expressions, see *Inf.* VIII, 111; *Purg.* IX, 145.   *fensi = si fecero.*

64. *al benedetto vaso*: The ark of the covenant.

65. *trescando*: The *trescone* is a lively, jumping sort of dance (see *Inf.* XIV, 40), and the corresponding verb would imply as much of David's dance, thus marking the similarity to the biblical text (II Reg. 6:14): "Et David saltabat totis viribus ante Dominum." ("And David danced [jumped] with all his might before the Lord.") See n. to vss. 55-69.
alzato: A touch which seems to have been suggested by Michal's scornful words (II Reg. 6:20): "Quam gloriosus fuit hodie rex Israel, discooperiens se ante ancillas servorum suorum; et nudatus est quasi si nudetur unus de scurris." ("How glorious was the king of Israel today, uncovering himself before the handmaids of his servants, and was naked, as if one of the buffoons should be naked.") David was

dressed in a linen ephod, which he had girt up, in order to dance better.   *l'umile salmista*: David's great humility, evidenced by his dance, was finally expressed by him in his reply (II Reg. 6:21-22) to Michal's sarcastic and scornful words: "Dixitque David ad Michol: Ante Dominum, qui elegit me potius quam patrem tuum et quam omnem domum eius . . . et ludam et vilior fiam plus quam factus sum; et ero humilis in oculis meis, et cum ancillis de quibus locuta es gloriosior apparebo." ("And David said to Michol: Before the Lord, who chose me rather than thy father, and than all his house . . . I will both play and make myself meaner than I have done. And I will be little in my own eyes: and with the handmaids of whom thou speakest, I shall appear more glorious.") See Gregory, *Moral.*, pars quinta XXVII, xlvi, 77:

Et tamen cum arcam Dei in Ierusalem revocat ([II Reg.] vi, 14), quasi oblitus praelatum se omnibus, admistus, populis ante arcam saltat. Et quia coram arca saltare, ut creditur, vulgi mos fuerat, rex se in divino obsequio per saltum rotat. Ecce quem Dominus cunctis singulariter praetulit, sese sub Domino et exaequando minimis, et abiecta exhibendo contemnit. Non potestas regni ad memoriam reducitur, non subiectorum oculis saltando vilescere metuit, non se honore praelatum caeteris ante eius arcam qui honorem dederat recognoscit. Coram Deo egit vilia vel extrema, ut illa ex humilitate solidaret quae coram hominibus gesserat fortia. Quid de eius factis ab aliis sentiatur ignoro; ergo David plus saltantem stupeo quam pugnantem. Pugnando quippe hostes subdidit, saltando autem coram Domino semetipsum vicit. Quem Michol filia Saul adhuc ex tumore regii generis insana, cum humiliatum despiceret, dicens: *Quam gloriosus fuit hodie rex Israel discooperiens se ante ancillas servorum suorum, et nudatus est, quasi si nudetur unus de scurris* (*Ibid.*, 20), protinus audivit: *Vivit Dominus, quia ludam ante Dominum, qui elegit me potius quam patrem tuum.* Ac paulo post ait: *Et ludam, et vilior fiam plus quam*

factus sum, eroque humilis in oculis meis (Ibid., 22).
Ac si aperte dicat: Vilescere coram hominibus appeto,
quia servare me coram Domino ingenuum per humilita-
tem quaero.

And yet, when he brings back the Ark of God to Jeru-
salem, he dances before the Ark [II Reg. 6:14], min-
gled with the people, as though forgetful that he had
been preferred to them all. And because, as is believed,
it had been the custom of the common people to dance
before the Ark, the king wheels round in the dance, in
service to God. Behold how he whom the Lord pre-
ferred specially above all, contemns himself beneath the
Lord, both by equalling himself with the least, and by
displaying abject behaviour. The power of his kingdom
is not recalled to his memory; he fears not to be vile
in the eyes of his people, by dancing; he remembers
not, before the Ark of Him Who had given him honour,
that he had been preferred in honour above the rest.
Before God he performed even the extremest vilenesses,
in order to strengthen, by his humility, the bold deeds
he had performed in the sight of men. What is thought
by others of his doings, I know not; I am more sur-
prised at David dancing, than fighting. For by fighting
he subdued his enemies; but by dancing before the Lord
he overcame himself. And when Michal, the daughter
of Saul, still mad with pride at her royal descent, de-
spised him when humbled, saying, *How glorious was the
king of Israel to-day, uncovering himself before the
handmaids of his servants, and made himself naked, as
though one of the buffoons were naked* [II Reg. 6:20]:
she immediately heard, *As the Lord liveth, I will play
before the Lord, Who hath chosen me rather than thy
father* [II Reg. 6:21]. And a little after he says, *And I
will play, and I will become more vile than I have been,
and I will be humble in mine own eyes* [II Reg. 6:22].
As if he plainly said, I seek to become vile before men,
because I seek to keep myself noble before the Lord,
through my humility.

208

66. *e più e men che re era in quel caso*: Before God David
was more than king in being so humble as to dance before
the ark; but in the eyes of men, he was, in so doing, less than
king. For the implied antithesis here, see in the prayer to the
Virgin in *Par.* XXXIII, 2, the verse which speaks of her as
being "umile e alta più che creatura." We recall that in the
Bible her humble words to Gabriel are followed, some time
later, by the Magnificat (Luc. 1:46-55):

> Magnificat anima mea Dominum, et exultavit spiritus
> meus in Deo salutari meo; quia respexit humilitatem
> ancillae suae; ecce enim ex hoc beatam me dicent omnes
> generationes, quia fecit mihi magna qui potens est, et
> sanctum nomen eius; et misericordia eius a progenie in
> progenies timentibus eum. Fecit potentiam in brachio
> suo: dispersit superbos mente cordis sui, deposuit
> potentes de sede, et exaltavit humiles, esurientes im-
> plevit bonis, et divites dimisit inanes. Suscepit Israel
> puerum suum, recordatus misericordiae suae, sicut
> locutus est ad patres nostros, Abraham et semini eius
> in saecula.

> My soul magnifies the Lord, and my spirit rejoices in
> God my Savior; Because he has regarded the lowliness
> of his handmaid; for, behold, henceforth all generations
> shall call me blessed; Because he who is mighty has
> done great things for me, and holy is his name; And his
> mercy is from generation to generation on those who
> fear him. He has shown might with his arm, he has scat-
> tered the proud in the conceit of their heart. He has
> put down the mighty from their thrones, and has exalted
> the lowly. He has filled the hungry with good things,
> and the rich he has sent away empty. He has given help
> to Israel, his servant, mindful of his mercy—Even as
> he spoke to our fathers—to Abraham and to his
> posterity forever.

67. *Di contra*: The palace from which Michal is looking on
is across the street, as it were, from the place where Dante
stands as spectator.

67–68. *vista d'un gran palazzo*: See "vista," meaning "opening," in *Inf.* X, 52. Dante has added the touch "d'un gran palazzo" and thus made this a town scene. Michal would surely be at the window of a royal palace, since she was the daughter of Saul and the first wife of David. She was punished with sterility for her haughtiness on this occasion (II Reg. 6:23).

68. *Micòl ammirava*: Michal looks on in amazement at what she considers such ignominious conduct on the part of a king.

69. *dispettosa*: "Contemptuous." The adjective may have been suggested by the verb "despexit" of the biblical text (II Reg. 6:16): "Et despexit eum in corde suo." ("And she despised him in her heart.")

72. *di dietro a Micòl*: Michal, as noted, appears to the far right of Dante, as did Mary in the preceding scene ("di retro da Maria," vs. 50). *mi biancheggiava*: "Was gleaming white to me," that is, the third scene is carved in that same marble (vs. 55).

73–96. *Quiv' era storiata . . . si trova*: The third and "longest" of the scenes depicts a great act of humility on the part of Trajan (Marcus Ulpius Traianus), Roman Emperor from A.D. 98 to 117. Legend has it that the emperor was setting out for the wars when a poor widow stopped him and demanded redress for the death of her son and that when he tried to put her off, she constrained him to accede to her demand. The legend appears in the life of Gregory in the ninth century by John the Deacon (*Sancti Gregorii Magni vita* II, 44) and is thereafter found in many compilations of *exempla*.

Dante was probably indebted for his version of the story of Trajan and the widow to the account given in the *Fiore di filosofi* (a compilation wrongly attributed to Brunetto Latini), which in its turn was based upon that given by Vincent of Beauvais in the *Speculum historiale* (see A. Graf, 1923, pp. 374-406). In the *Fiore* (pp. 58-60) the story, which corresponds in several striking details with Dante's version, runs as follows:

Trajano fue imperatore molto giusto. Essendo un dì
salito a cavallo per andare alla battaglia con la sua
cavalleria, una femina vedova se gli fece dinanzi e pre-
segli il piede piangendo molto teneramente, e diman-
dogli che li facesse ragione di coloro che gli aveano
morto un suo figliuolo ch'era giustissimo e sanza colpa.
Lo imperatore le parlò, e disse: "Io ti satisfarò alla mia
tornata." E quella disse: "E se tu non torni?" Ed egli
rispuose: "Lo successore mio ti sodisfarae." E quella
disse: "Io come lo soe? e pognamo ch'elli lo faccia,
a te che farà se quegli farà bene? Tue mi se' debitore,
e secondo l'opere tue serai meritato: frode è non volere
rendere quello che l'uomo dee. Lo successore tuo a
quelli che hanno ricevuto e riceveranno ingiuria, sarà
tenuto per sè. L'altrui giustizia non libera te; e bene
starà lo successore tuo, se elli libera sè medesimo." Per
queste parole l'imperatore discese da cavallo ed esaminò
immantenente la vicenda di questa femina, e fece gius-
tiziare costoro ch'aveano morto il figliuolo di questa
femina, e poscia rimontò e andoe alla battaglia, e
sconfisse gli suoi nimici.

Trajan was a very just emperor. One day, when he had
mounted to go off to war with his cavalry, a woman, a
widow, weeping piteously, came to him and taking hold
of his foot, asked him to bring to justice the men who
had murdered her innocent son, who was a very just
man. The emperor spoke to her and said, "I will satisfy
you when I return." And she said, "But suppose you do
not return?" Whereupon he answered, "My successor
will satisfy you." And she said, " How do I know that?
But even if he does, what does it avail you if he does
the right thing? You are in my debt, and you will be
judged by your deeds. It is fraudulent not to give what
you ought to give. Your successor will be responsible
on his own account for those who have been wronged
or who will be wronged. The justice done by another
does not exonerate you; your successor will do well if
he saves himself." Moved by these words, the emperor
got off his horse and forthwith looked into the case of

this woman and had justice done to those who had killed her son, and then he remounted and went off to the battle and defeated his enemies.

See G. Paris (1878); R. Davidsohn (1929), p. 479; C. Cipolla di Vallecorsa (1906).

73. *storiata*: See n. to vss. 49-52.   *l'alta gloria*: Since this was an act of humility, we feel here the same antithesis of *alto* and *umile* as above (see n. to vs. 66).

74. *principato* = *principe*.

74-75. *il cui valore . . . vittoria*: A victory over death and damnation in Hell.

75. *Gregorio*: Gregory I, the saint, called Gregory the Great, was born at Rome, of a noble family, *ca.* 540 and was pope from 590 to 604. The legend, alluded to by Dante (here and in *Par.* XX, 106-17), that the Emperor Trajan was recalled to life from Hell, through the intercession of Gregory the Great, in order that he might have room for repentance, was widely believed in the Middle Ages and is repeatedly recounted by medieval writers.

Thomas Aquinas, who cites this case of Gregory's intercession for Trajan, attempts to reconcile it with the orthodox doctrine that prayer is of no avail for those in Hell. In *Summa theol.* III, Suppl., q. 71, a. 5, obj. 5 he says: "Damascenus . . . narrat quod Gregorius pro Traiano orationem fundens, audivit vocem sibi divinitus dicentem: *Vocem tuam audivi et veniam Traiano do*; cuius rei, ut Damascenus dicit in dicto sermone, *testis est Oriens omnis et Occidens*. Sed constat, Traianum in inferno fuisse." ("The Damascene . . . relates that Gregory, while praying for Trajan, heard a voice from heaven saying to him: *I have heard thy voice, and I pardon Trajan*: and of this fact the Damascene adds in the same sermon, *the whole East and West are witnesses*. Yet it is clear that Trajan was in hell.") Aquinas continues (*Summa theol.* III, Suppl., q. 71, a. 5, ad 5):

De facto Traiani hoc modo potest probabiliter aestimari, quod precibus B. Gregorii ad vitam fuerit revocatus, et ita gratiam consecutus sit, per quam remissionem peccatorum habuit, et per consequens immunitatem a poena: sicut etiam apparet in omnibus illis qui fuerunt miraculose a mortuis suscitati, quorum plures constat idololatras et damnatos fuisse. De omnibus talibus enim similiter dici oportet quod non erant in inferno finaliter deputati, sed secundum praesentem propriorum meritorum iustitiam: secundum autem superiores causas, quibus praevidebantur ad vitam revocandi, erat aliter de eis disponendum.

Vel dicendum, secundum quosdam, quod anima Traiani non fuit simpliciter a reatu poenae aeternae absoluta; sed eius poena fuit suspensa ad tempus, scilicet usque ad diem iudicii.

Concerning the incident of Trajan it may be supposed with probability that he was recalled to life at the prayers of blessed Gregory, and thus obtained the grace whereby he received the pardon of his sins and in consequence was freed from punishment. The same applies to all those who were miraculously raised from the dead, many of whom were evidently idolaters and damned. For we must needs say likewise of all such persons that they were consigned to hell, not finally, but as was actually due to their own merits according to justice: and that according to higher causes, in view of which it was foreseen that they would be recalled to life, they were to be disposed of otherwise.

Or we may say with some that Trajan's soul was not simply freed from the debt of eternal punishment, but that his punishment was suspended for a time, that is, until the judgment day.

77. *li* = *gli* (dative of possession).

79. *Intorno a lui*: The area around him. The phrase is the subject of "parea" (*appariva*).

80. *l'aguglie ne l'oro*: Scartazzini-Vandelli notes that this refers to "le aquile romane effigiate nere in campo d'oro nelle bandiere" ("the Roman eagles, portrayed in black on

a field or on the flags"), going on to comment: "D. si figura le insegne dell'esercito di Traiano come quelle del tempo suo; mentre le insegne militari degli antichi romani erano d'oro e d'altre materie, e fissate in capo a un'asta." ("Dante imagines the insignia of Trajan's army to be like those of his time. But the military insignia of the ancient Romans were made of gold and other materials, and affixed to the end of a pole.") Clearly these must indeed be banners, to move so in the wind; accordingly, the reading "ne l'oro" seems preferable to "de l'oro," as some editors would have it.

81. *sovr' essi*: I.e., over Trajan and his whole retinue. *movieno = movevano.*

82. *La miserella*: Here, as in "vedovella" in vs. 77, the suffix *–ella* expresses compassion and sympathy.   *intra tutti costoro*: By virtue of this touch the poor woman seems even more lowly and alone.

83. *vendetta*: The widow demands justice, of course, but for her this justice will be a revenge.

84. *mio figliuol ch'è morto*: In early Italian the verb *morire* can be used in a transitive sense. Cf. *Par.* XVI, 137: "per lo giusto disdegno che v'ha morti."   *m'accoro*: Cf. *Purg.* V, 57.

85. *ed elli a lei rispondere*: The infinitive depends on "pareva," vs. 83.

86. *Segnor mio*: "Mio" now adds something to the poor woman's plea, showing that her grief is indeed urgent (as the next verse affirms: "come persona in cui dolor s'affretta").

88. *fia = sarà.   dov'io*: In my place.

89. *la ti farà = te la farà.   L'altrui bene*: "Altrui" is the possessive here.

90. *a te che fia*: How will it be to your credit? How will it be counted among your good works?   *fia = sarà.*
'l tuo: Your own welldoing.

91. *ti conforta = confòrtati* (imperative).   *ei convene*:
Impersonal, "it behooves that." The "alta gloria" (vs. 73)
of Trajan consists in this yielding to a poor woman's prayer
and is a great act of humility on the part of an emperor.

92. *anzi ch'i' mova*: The verb *muovere* is often used in-
transitively. Cf. *Inf.* II, 67.

93. *giustizia vuole*: Here Trajan speaks as the emperor who
recognizes his duty.   *e pietà mi ritene*: And here he
speaks as a man and with that humility which Gregory
deemed a *valore*. Note that these words come emphatically
at the end of the *storia*.

94. *Colui che mai non vide cosa nova*: God, to whom noth-
ing can be new, since He sees all things in His eternal light.

95. *esto = questo.   visibile parlare*: Thus the conceit
of this miraculous art continues: Dante while gazing at the
reliefs has mysteriously heard all the words spoken in the
scenes.

96. *qui*: Among the living.

98. *l'imagini di tante umilitadi*: The phrase prompts the
reader to look back upon all three stories, beginning with
the Annunciation, as examples of great humility and to do
this just before he is to learn that pride is indeed the vice
punished on this first terrace, for from these scenes we now
turn to see the proud as they come round the bend.
tante: "Tante" here is the equivalent of the Latin *tantae*.

99. *lo fabbro loro*: God.

100–101. *Ecco di qua . . . genti*: The words "ecco di qua"
imply a gesture by Virgil, who has looked back (as one who
is not intent upon the carvings, but who is ever anxious con-
cerning the way, and who seeks guidance) to see these souls
come into view from his side (he is now on Dante's left, vs.
53), moving to the right or counterclockwise.

102. *ne 'nvieranno = ci invieranno.*

106-8. *Non vo' però . . . paghi*: The poet would not have the reader be turned from his good resolve ("buon proponimento") to make amends because of any despair over the harsh punishments of Purgatory, of which this is our first glimpse. It is particularly significant that Dante makes this point here because everyone, every sinner, will have a debt to pay for pride. For *smagare* in this sense (vs. 106), cf. *Purg.* XXVII, 104.

107. *per udire*: "For hearing" (as we are now to do).

108. *'l debito*: As will be made clear later, this debt to God can always be stated in terms of a debt of love to Him. Here, specifically, it is the purgatorial punishment ("martìre," vs. 109) to which the proud are subjected that straightens the will bent by the sin of pride.

109. *martìre* = *martirio*.

110. *la succession*: That which shall follow upon the punishment, i.e., eternal beatitude in Paradise.

110-11. *pensa ch'al peggio . . . ire*: In any case the punishment will cease at the Judgment Day, for then the purgations of Purgatory will stop, and all souls there, even as souls in Hell, will return for their bodies and hear the judgment, "that which resounds to all eternity" (*Inf.* VI, 97-99); but souls who happen to be in Purgatory at the time will proceed to their reward in Heaven, of course, and those of Hell will return to their eternal punishment there.

112. *veggio* = *vedo*.

113. *muovere* = *muoversi*. *sembian* = *sembrano*. *persone*: Human figures. In pointing out these figures to Dante, Virgil referred to them as "genti" (vs. 101), and Dante is trying to see them as people.

114. *nel veder vaneggio*: I look in vain, confusedly, with such uncertain vision.

117. *pria = prima.   n'ebber tencione*: Cf. "tenciona,"
Inf. VIII, III. Virgil's eyes at first had a "struggle" or "con-
troversy" in discerning what is coming.

118. *fiso = fisamente, fissamente.   disviticchia*: "Disvitic-
chia" (from the Latin *vitis,* "vine") here suggests "un-
winding," as the tendrils and canes of a vine from its sup-
port, hence "separating one thing from another," as stone
from person here. Cf. the antonym *avviticchiare,* used in
Inf. XXV, 60.

120. *come ciascun si picchia*: Virgil points to that which
most distinguishes them as persons, i.e., their act of penance,
of obedience and humility (cf. *Purg.* IX, III). Some com-
mentators, taking the image of vss. 130-32 too strictly, have
argued that these souls would not be able to beat their
breasts, obliged as they are to hold up their stones with both
hands, and have advanced some very curious alternative
meanings. See E. G. Parodi (1957), p. 372.

121. *O superbi cristian*: The address is to us, the living, sin-
ful mankind in general.   *miseri lassi*: Cf. *Inf.* XXXII, 21.

122. *de la vista de la mente infermi*: Blinded in the mind's
vision by actual sins, all of which arise from pride, which is
the beginning of all sins. See *Par.* VII, 25-33, where it is ex-
plained that as a result of Adam's sin (a sin of pride) man-
kind "lay sick below in great error [blindness] for many ages,
till it pleased the word of God to descend [in humility]" and
become flesh.

123. *fidanza avete ne' retrosi passi*: The proud are said to
place their trust in backward steps, that is, in those affections
which cause them to fall back. See *Purg.* XI, 13-15, in the
paraphrase of the Lord's Prayer:

> Dà oggi a noi la cotidiana manna,
> sanza la qual per questo aspro diserto
> a retro va chi più di gir s'affanna.

124. *vermi*: The term *vermo* echoes scriptural usage, as in
Iob 25:6: "et filius hominis vermis" ("the son of man, who

is only a worm") and Ps. 21:7[22:6]: "ego autem sum vermis et non homo." ("But I am a worm, not a man.") See also Augustine, *In Ioan.* I, 13: "Omnes homines de carne nascentes, quid sunt nisi vermes? et de vermibus Angelos facit." ("All men who are born of the flesh, what are they if not worms? And from worms [God] makes angels.")

125–26. *l'angelica farfalla . . . schermi*: On this image, see *Purg.* XII, 95-96.

126. *che vola a la giustizia sanza schermi*: Finally the soul, if it does not go downward to Hell, will rise upward to God the Judge and will stand before the light of His truth without any shield or defense such as it might have attempted to hold up against that light when it was putting its trust in its own strength, in pride. Thus Augustine (*Sermones ad populum* CCCLXV, 5) comments: "Qualem noctem? Conscientiae tuae caliginosae, cuius tenebris involutus velles, si posses, his quasi clypeum adversus lumen veritatis obtendere, et de fortitudine tua bene sperare." ("What night? The night of the mists of your conscience, being enveloped in whose shadows you desire, if you can, to hold these [shadows] as a shield against the light of truth and to put your trust in your own strength.")

127. *in alto galla*: "Mounts aloft." Cf. *Purg.* XII, 70-72. Note "galli" as it is used in *Inf.* XXI, 57.

128. *poi = poi che.   quasi*: "Like."   *antomata*: Petrocchi prefers this form; other editors have "entomata." Grandgent observes: "The Greek word is ἔντομον, pl. ἔντομα. Dante probably found *entoma* in his Latin version of Aristotle, and, taking it for a singular, formed a plural on the model of *poema poemata*, and other words."

129. *falla*: Grandgent comments: "*Falla*, 'is lacking.' Albertus Magnus speaks of the incompleteness of caterpillars and such creatures: *De Animalibus*, XVII, Tract. ii, Cap. I."

130–32. *Come per sostentar . . . petto*: For this very com-

3. Detail of the episcopal chair in the basilica of San Nicola of Bari

mon figure in medieval art, which the poem would thus call
to the reader's mind, see Plate 3.

130. *solaio*: "Loft."

134. *così fatti*: Thus bent over.

136–37. *Vero è che . . . dosso*: The phrase concedes that
not all the souls are equally doubled over, as the comparison
with the single figure might suggest, but they are more or
less crushed down ("contratti") by their weights. So was
the punishment graduated at certain places in Hell (cf. *Inf.*
XII, 103-32).

138. *pazienza*: It seems best to understand "pazienza" here
as *patimento*, "suffering."

CANTO XI

1–21. *O Padre nostro . . . sprona*: This expanded para-phrase of the Lord's Prayer (Matt. 6:9-13), a verse or clause of which is rendered by each tercet, occupies seven tercets, which correspond in number to the seven terraces of Purga-tory, to the seven sins that are purged thereon, and to the seven virtues that oppose those sins. This is the only prayer in the poem which is recited in its entirety.

1–3. *O Padre nostro . . . hai*: God has His abode in Heaven not because He is circumscribed by the space of the material universe, as the human creature is on earth, even though His city and His high throne are there (*Inf.* I, 128), but because of His love for His "first works," the angels and the heavens.

2. *non circunscritto*: On circumscription by space, cf. *Purg.* XXV, 88, and see Thomas Aquinas, *Summa theol.* I-II, q. 102, a. 4, ad 1: "Ipse igitur Deus qui colitur nullo cor-porali loco clauditur; unde propter ipsum non oportuit spe-ciale tabernaculum fieri aut templum. Sed homines ipsum colentes corporales sunt." ("Accordingly God, who is wor-shipped, is confined to no bodily place: wherefore there was no need, on His part, for a tabernacle or temple to be set up. But men, who worship Him, are corporeal beings.") In *Par.* XXII, 67, the Empyrean heaven, God's abode, is said not

to be "in loco," and in *Par.* XIV, 30, it is said that the Trinity is "non circunscritto, e tutto circunscrive." See Dante's statement in *Conv.* IV, ix, 3: "Dunque la giurisdizione de la natura universale è a certo termine finita—e per consequente la parziale—; e anche di costei è limitatore colui che da nulla è limitato, cioè la prima bontade, che è Dio, che solo con la infinita capacitade infinito comprende." ("Therefore the jurisdiction of universal nature is bounded by certain limits, and by consequence so is the particular. Moreover, he doth bound her who is bounded by nought, to wit the prime excellence, which is God, who alone with infinite capaciousness comprehends infinitude.")

2–3. *ma per più amore . . . hai*: The "primi effetti," or "first works" of God, are the angels and the heavens, the former called "prime creature" in *Inf.* VII, 95, and their turning of the heavenly spheres spoken of in *Inf.* VII, 96. See *Par.* XXIX, 28-32. On God's greater love for the angels, see Thomas Aquinas, *Summa theol.* I, q. 20, a. 3, resp.:

> Respondeo dicendum quod cum amare sit velle bonum alicui, duplici ratione potest aliquid magis vel minus amari. Uno modo ex parte ipsius actus voluntatis, qui est magis vel minus intensus; et sic Deus non magis quaedam aliis amat, quia omnia amat uno et simplici actu voluntatis, et semper eodem modo se habente. Alio modo ex parte ipsius boni, quod aliquis vult amato; et sic dicimur aliquem magis alio amare, cui volumus maius bonum, quamvis non magis intensa voluntate; et hoc modo necesse est dicere quod Deus quaedam aliis magis amat. Cum enim amor Dei sit causa bonitatis rerum, ut dictum est art. praec., non esset aliquid alio melius, si Deus non vellet uni maius bonum quam alteri.

> *I answer that,* Since to love a thing is to will it good, in a twofold way anything may be loved more, or less. In one way on the part of the act of the will itself, which is more or less intense. In this way God does not love some things more than others, because He loves all things by an act of the will that is one, simple, and always the same. In another way on the part of the good

itself that a person wills for the beloved. In this way we are said to love that one more than another, for whom we will a greater good, though our will is not more intense. In this way we must needs say that God loves some things more than others. For since God's love is the cause of goodness in things, as has been said ([*Summa theol.* I, q. 20] a. 2), no one thing would be better than another, if God did not will greater good for one than for another.

Also see *Summa theol.* I, q. 20, a. 4. As Porena observes: "C'è in questo esordio un umile riconoscimento che Deo ama l'uomo meno degli angeli." ("There is, in this exordium, the humble recognition that God loves man less than the angels.")

4. *laudato sia 'l tuo nome*: This corresponds to the "sanctificetur nomen tuum" ("hallowed be thy name") of the Lord's Prayer (Matt. 6:9). *'l tuo valore*: "Thy power" (omnipotence); the prayer is addressed to God the Father. Cf. *Inf.* III, 5.

5-6. *com' è degno . . . vapore*: See II Thess. 1:3: "Gratia agere debemus semper Deo pro vobis, fratres, ita ut dignum est." ("We are bound to give thanks to God always for you, brethren. It is fitting that we should.") See also the Preface to the Canon of the Mass: "Vere dignum et iustum est, aequum et salutare, nos tibi semper et ubique gratias agere: Domine sancte, Pater omnipotens, aeterne Deus." ("It is truly meet and just, right and profitable, for us, at all times, and in all places, to give thanks to Thee, O Lord, the holy One, the Father almighty, the everlasting God.")

6. *al tuo dolce vapore*: "To Thy sweet emanation." See Sapien. 7:25: "Vapor est enim virtutis Dei, et emanatio quaedam est claritatis omnipotentis Dei sincera; et ideo nihil inquinatum in eam incurrit." ("For she [Wisdom] is an aura of the might of God and a pure effusion of the glory of the Almighty; therefore nought that is sullied enters into her.") The opening verses of the *Paradiso* present the emanation in terms of glory (*Par.* I, 1-3).

7. *Vegna ver' noi la pace del tuo regno*: See the comparable phrase in the Lord's Prayer (Matt. 6:10): "Adveniat regnum tuum." ("Thy kingdom come.") But it is particularly peace which these souls pray for, the peace of God, which is His sanctifying grace.

8–9. *ché noi ad essa . . . ingegno*: The amplification touches on the insufficiency of human powers and so expresses humility and our need to wait upon the Lord. In *Summa theol.* II-II, q. 83, a. 15, resp. Thomas Aquinas notes: "Humilitas autem est necessaria ex parte ipsius petentis, qui suam indigentiam recognoscit." ("Humility is necessary on the part of the person praying, who recognizes his neediness.") See *De mon.* III, xvi, 7, where Dante speaks of "beatitudinem vite eterne, que consistit in fruitione divini aspectus ad quam propria virtus ascendere non potest, nisi lumine divino adiuta" ("the blessedness of eternal life, which consists in the fruition of the divine aspect, to which [man's] power may not ascend unless assisted by the divine light").

8. *potem* = *possiamo*.

10–12. *Come del suo voler . . . suoi*: See Matt. 6:10: "Fiat voluntas tua sicut in caelo et in terra." ("Thy will be done on earth, as it is in heaven.") With "angeli" the poet has rendered the "in caelo" of the Lord's Prayer, and with "uomini," the "in terra."

10. *suo* = *loro*.

11. *cantando osanna*: For the angels' hosanna to the Lord, cf. *Par.* XXVIII, 118.

12. *suoi* = *loro*.

13. *Dà oggi . . . manna*: See Luc. 11:3: "Panem nostrum quotidianum da nobis hodie." ("Give us this day our daily bread.") Appropriately the poet has converted "panem" to "manna," which signifies grace, or spiritual food, since bread, in any literal sense, is obviously no longer needed by these souls; God's grace, however, is needed by them as by the living.

14. *questo aspro diserto*: "Desert" following "manna" clearly evokes the figure of the Exodus, which applies not only to Christians in their life on earth and to the souls of Antepurgatory, but to the souls here who move round and round their terrace, which was first seen as being "solingo più che strade per diserti" (*Purg.* X, 21). The figure applies both to Antepurgatory and to Purgatory proper, in respect to the time which souls have to spend here in waiting and in purgation, even as the Israelites had to wander for forty years in the desert. See C. S. Singleton (1965).

15. *a retro va chi più di gir s'affanna*: See the n. to *Purg.* X, 123, on "retrosi passi." See also Bernard's prompting of Dante to his final prayer in *Par.* XXXII, 145-47.

16–17. *E come noi . . . ciascuno*: In Matt. 6:12, this verse of the Lord's Prayer reads: "Et dimitte nobis debita nostra, sicut et nos dimittimus debitoribus nostris." ("And forgive us our debts, as we also forgive our debtors.")

17. *e tu perdona*: Hortatory, the "e" having the force of the *sicut et* in the Latin.

18. *benigno, e non guardar lo nostro merto*: Again the extension of the Lord's Prayer expresses humility and lack of merit on our part, so that, if God pardons us, it will be of His loving-kindness alone.

19–21. *Nostra virtù . . . la sprona*: See Matt. 6:13: "Et ne nos inducas in tentationem, sed libera nos a malo." ("And lead us not into temptation, but deliver us from evil.") The verses with which Dante renders this verse of the prayer begin with the recognition of our weakness: "our strength, which is easily overcome."

19. *s'adona*: "Is subdued." Cf. *Inf.* VI, 34.

20. *con l'antico avversaro*: The reader will recall that the serpent, which came at night to the valley of the princes (*Purg.* VIII, 94-99), figuring as the last of the "temptations" of Antepurgatory, is called "nostro avversaro" in *Purg.* VIII, 95, and in the hymn sung by the souls in the valley he is

called *hostis noster* (see n. to *Purg.* VIII, 13). Cf. *Purg.*
XIV, 146. This touch replaces the "a malo" of the scriptural
text.

21. *ma libera da lui*: I.e., free our strength ("virtù") from
him, the devil.   *che sì la sprona*: "Who so spurs it" to
evil.

22-24. *Quest' ultima preghiera . . . restaro*: Commentators
disagree as to whether the reference is limited to what is ex-
pressed in the preceding tercet (vss. 19-21), which pertains
both to the living and to the souls in Antepurgatory, or in-
cludes the prayer from the words "cotidiana manna" (vs. 13)
on, this being the part that pertains mainly to our life on
earth and to our needs there. Any interpretation will depend
on what is understood by "color che dietro a noi restaro,"
but since the "Our Father," in its extensions and amplifica-
tions here (e.g., Exodus, manna), has already been phrased
in terms that apply not only to the souls who recite it on the
diserta strada (*Purg.* X, 21) of this first circle, but also to
the living and to the souls of Antepurgatory, it seems best to
understand "color che dietro a noi restaro" to mean both
the living and the souls of Antepurgatory, who must still hope
for protection from "our adversary" (*Purg.* VIII, 95), and
to understand "quest' ultima preghiera" as referring to what
has just been expressed in vss. 19-21. To be sure, as is im-
mediately evident from the "noi" of vs. 25 and of vs. 31, the
prayer is first of all for us the living, but since the souls of
Antepurgatory continue to be subject to temptation also in
a certain sense, and their condition is an image of our life,
which is an exodus, the prayer is also for them.

23. *già non*: The Latin *iam non*. Cf. *Purg.* XII, 46.

25. *ramogna*: This is a very puzzling word, since only two
other instances of its use are known, and the contexts in
which these occur do not make the meaning wholly clear (see
E. G. Parodi, 1957, p. 283; M. Porena, 1946-47). Uncer-
tain though the meaning is, it would seem to amount to some-
thing like "good speed" (in the context even "Godspeed"),

i.e., "good progress" in the "cammin di nostra vita" and the desert that we must cross in this life. Grandgent comments: "*Ramogna*, according to several of the early commentators, signifies 'journey'; the meaning of the word is not otherwise known." Grandgent notes that the meaning may be "fortune" and calls attention to E.G.P. (1899).

26. *'l pondo*: From the Latin *pondus*, literally, "weight."

27. *quel che talvolta si sogna*: The incubus. See Virgil, *Aen*. XII, 908-12:

> ac velut in somnis, oculos ubi languida pressit
> nocte quies, nequiquam avidos extendere cursus
> velle videmur et in mediis conatibus aegri
> succidimus; non lingua valet, non corpore notae
> sufficiunt vires, nec vox aut verba sequuntur . . .

And as in dreams of night, when languorous sleep has weighed down our eyes, we seem to strive vainly to press on our eager course, and in mid effort sink helpless: our tongue lacks power, our wonted strength fails our limbs, nor voice nor words ensue.

Also see Macrobius, *Comm. in somn. Scip*. I, iii, 7.

28. *disparmente angosciate*: The souls are tormented, some more, some less, by their burden, some having heavier weights than others. Cf. *Purg*. X, 136-37.　　*a tondo*: Cf. *Inf*. VI, 112.

29. *e lasse*: Cf. *Purg*. X, 121.

30. *purgando la caligine del mondo*: "Caligine" implies a thick mist, i.e., the mist of sin (compare the "dark wood," or darkness of sin, of *Inf*. I, 2). Souls bring this "sully" to Purgatory, to be purged away, even as the "note" of vs. 34. Cf. "nebbia," *Purg*. XXX, 3, which is said to hide the seven-fold Spirit of the Lord from us. Thus both "caligine" and "nebbia," as obstructions to be removed, may be compared with the "scoglio" or "skin" which must be shed in this second realm (*Purg*. II, 122).

31–32. *si dice . . . dire*: Prayer is implied in both cases, as welldoing and works of piety (attending Mass, giving of alms) are by the "far" of vs. 32. See Thomas Aquinas, *Summa theol.* III, Suppl., q. 71.

32. *di qua*: Among the living.

33. *quei c'hanno al voler buona radice*: Those whose wills are "rooted" in charity and who are in grace (*Purg.* IV, 133-35). See Thomas Aquinas, *Summa theol.* II-II, q. 83, a. 15, resp.: "Oratio autem, sicut et quilibet alius actus virtutis, habet efficaciam merendi, in quantum procedit ex radice charitatis." ("Now prayer, like any other virtuous act, is efficacious in meriting, insofar as it proceeds from charity as its root.")

34. *atar = aiutare.   le note*: Cf. the Latin *nota* meaning "spot," "mark," also "brand," as on the body of a bad slave. These are the marks left by sin (borne from the world) which must be purged away. The seven P's that Dante wears inscribed on his forehead (*Purg.* IX, 112-14) are a token of the "note" he brings here and correspond to those marks which the souls must wash away.

35. *portar = portarono.   quinci*: From this world of the living.   *mondi*: "Cleansed."   *lievi*: "Light," when cleansed of the "marks."

36. *uscire a le stellate ruote*: They may issue forth from Purgatory, as from their "desert," to the promised land or Empyrean heaven, passing through the heavens, i.e., the "starry wheels" or spheres of the planets and fixed stars, as they ascend to eternal beatitude with God. Cf. *Purg.* VIII, 18: "le superne rote."

37. *se giustizia e pietà vi disgrievi*: A dual subject with a singular verb. This is the familiar formula of adjuration with the verb in the subjunctive. This "liberation" (as in vss. 35-36) will come through God's justice and mercy. See Thomas Aquinas, *Summa theol.* I, q. 21, a. 4, resp.: "Opus autem divinae iustitiae semper praesupponit opus miseri-

cordiae, et in eo fundatur." ("Now the work of divine justice always presupposes the work of mercy, and is founded thereupon.") Cf. *Inf.* III, 50.   *disgrievi = disgravi (alleggerisca)*.

38–39. *sì che possiate . . . lievi*: This extends the image of the upward flight (vss. 35-36). Cf. *Purg.* X, 125-26; IV, 28-29: "l'ale snelle . . . / del gran disio."

39. *vi lievi = vi sollevi, vi innalzi*.

40. *da qual mano*: On which side, whether to the right or to the left.

41. *varco*: A "crossing," i.e., from one terrace to the next, a passageway, a stairway.

42. *ne = ci.   'nsegnate = insegnate.   che men erto cala*: The path that descends least steeply.

43–44. *per lo 'ncarco . . . veste*: Cf. *Purg.* IX, 10.

44. *onde si veste*: "In which he is clad."

45. *contra sua voglia*: See *Purg.* VI, 49, where Dante expresses his eagerness to make haste.   *parco = limitato*, "limited," hence "slow."

46. *Le lor parole*: The words in vss. 49-51 are apparently uttered by the entire group, whereas in the continuation of the reply to Dante one person only (Omberto Aldobrandeschi) speaks now in vss. 52-72.   *rendero = renderono*, i.e., "answered."

47. *colui cu' io seguiva*: Virgil.

48. *fur = furono.   da cui = da chi.   venisser manifeste*: Porena comments: "La costruzione regolare sarebbe stata 'non fu manifesto'; ma per la rima il verbo è accordato con *parole*." ("The normal construction would have been: 'non fu manifesto.' But for the sake of the rhyme, the verb is made to agree with 'parole.' ")

49-50. *A man destra . . . venite*: This is in reply to Virgil's question (vs. 40) "on which hand," the "con noi" of vs. 50 making quite clear the intended direction, which is, of course, the proper direction in Purgatory.

49. *per la riva*: Along the *piano*, which may be called a "bank" in the sense that it "borders the void" (*Purg.* X, 19-22).

50. *il passo*: The "varco" that Virgil speaks of in vs. 41.

51. *possibile a salir persona viva = per cui persona viva possa salire*. Cf. *Purg.* III, 76-77.

53. *la cervice mia*: The expression is common in biblical contexts, in reference to pride. See, for example, Exod. 32:9: "Cerno quod populus iste durae cervicis sit." ("I see how stiff-necked this people is.") Also see Exod. 34:9; Deut. 9:6, 13; Actus 7:51.

54. *convienmi = mi conviene*.

55. *cotesti = costui.   e non si noma*: The meaning may be either "is not named" or "does not name himself." Sapegno comments that this is not a reproach, but "un invito a parlare e a manifestarsi" ("an invitation to speak and show himself").

57. *e per farlo pietoso a questa soma*: Porena remarks: "Fine tocco psicologico: lo sguardo doloroso di chi soffre rivolto verso di noi, accresce la nostra pietà." ("A fine psychological touch: the doleful look of a suffering person, turned towards us, increases our pity.") Unlike the next soul, then, this one never looks at Dante, being prevented by the huge stone which he carries from turning his head even so much. Dante himself, moreover, is not yet so bowed over as in a moment he will be with Oderisi.

58. *Io fui latino e nato d'un gran Tosco*: The speaker, who will identify himself in vs. 67, is Omberto Aldobrandeschi, the second son of Guglielmo and lord of the stronghold of

Campagnatico, one of the many fortified castles of the Aldo-
brandeschi. The Sienese, with whom the Aldobrandeschi
were constantly at war, sent an expedition against Omberto
in 1259, and Omberto was slain. Benvenuto tells of Omber-
to's death as follows: "Fuit iste Humbertus, qui hic loquitur,
iuvenis quidem strenuus et animosus valde: qui cum exivis-
set probiter contra inimicos . . . interfectus fuit in campo
apud unum suum castellum, quod dicitur Campagnaticum."
("Omberto, who is here speaking, was a lusty and vigorous
young man. Laudably, he went off on an expedition against
his enemies . . . and he was killed in the field near one of his
fortified castles, called Campagnatico.") On Omberto's
death, see F. Maggini (1910), pp. 127-28. For further par-
ticulars, see P. Toynbee (1968), p. 475.   *latino = italia-
no*. See *Inf.* XXII, 65, and *passim*.   *e nato d'un gran
Tosco*: Torraca comments: "Come suona *gran*! Che vampo
in tutta la frase! Certo, le 'note,' che questo peccatore ha
portate dal mondo, tarderanno a 'lavarsi.' " ("How that *gran*
resounds! The whole sentence is ablaze! Certainly, the
'marks' this sinner brought from the world require some time
to be washed away.") And, on the name of the father in the
following verse, he adds: "E il nome veramente 'sonante e
forte,' del padre, con che tono esce dalle sue labbra!" ("With
what tones does that truly 'resounding and strong' name of
his father come forth from his lips!")   *Tosco*: Cf. *Inf.*
X, 22.

59. *Guiglielmo Aldobrandesco*: Count of Santafiora in the
Sienese Maremma. Owing to his animosity against the
Sienese, Guglielmo apparently abandoned the Ghibelline
principles of his house and allied himself with the Florentines
and Tuscan Guelphs. He was included in the peace that was
arranged between Florence and Siena in 1254 and died
shortly after. See G. Ciacci (1935), pp. 65-119.

60. *non so se 'l nome suo già mai fu vosco*: I.e., "I do not
know if you ever heard his name." The soul addresses both
Virgil and Dante. The modest tone is in striking contrast with
the tone of the two preceding verses.   *vosco = con voi*.

61. *L'antico sangue*: The Aldobrandeschi were an ancient and powerful Ghibelline family, counts of Santafiora in the Sienese Maremma, where they had been settled since the ninth century. Dante mentions Santafiora, whence the counts took their title, in *Purg.* VI, 111. Benvenuto says they were so powerful in Tuscany at one time that they used to boast that they had as many strongholds as there are days in the year. He adds that they were nearly extinct in his day. According to Casini-Barbi (see the gloss on vs. 58), they reached the height of their power with Count Ildebrando, who died in 1208. See G. Ciacci (1935), pp. 25-63.

62. *miei maggior*: Cf. *Inf.* X, 42.   *fer* = *fecero.*

63. *la comune madre*: Mother earth, to which we all return at death. See Ecclus. 40:1: "Occupatio magna creata est omnibus hominibus, et iugum grave super filios Adam, a die exitus de ventre matris eorum, usque in diem sepulturae in matrem omnium." ("A great anxiety has God allotted, and a heavy yoke, to the sons of men; from the day one leaves his mother's womb to the day he returns to the mother of all the living.")

64. *ogn' uomo* = *ognuno.*   *ebbi in despetto*: Cf. *Inf.* X, 36.

64-66. *ogn' uomo . . . fante*: Omberto may mean that his scorn provoked the Sienese to attack him or that he fought with such reckless scorn that it resulted in his death.

66. *sallo* = *lo sa.*   *fante*: Cf. *Purg.* XXV, 61; *Par.* XXXIII, 107.

68. *superbia*: "Superbia" is the subject of "fa."   *consorti*: Relatives. Cf. *Inf.* XXIX, 33; *Par.* XVI, 139.

68-69. *tutti miei consorti . . . malanno*: Buti elaborates on this as follows: "e sì in questa vita che li à fatti periculare e morire innanti ora, e sì nell'altra che li à posti in pena" ("both in this life, because it exposed them to danger and made them die before their time, and in the other life, because it subjected them to punishment").

71. *per lei*: "Because of it [pride]." *tanto che a Dio si sodisfaccia*: I.e., until the debt to God (*Purg.* X, 108) is paid.

72. *poi ch'io nol fe' tra ' vivi, qui tra ' morti*: See Thomas Aquinas, *Summa theol.* III, Suppl., q. 71, a. 6, resp.: "Poena purgatorii est in supplementum satisfactionis quae non fuerat plene in corpore consummata." ("The punishment of purgatory is intended to supplement the satisfaction which was not fully completed in the body [in life, while living].") *fe' = feci.*

75. *il peso che li 'mpaccia*: "Li" ("them") is the direct object plural and is not a form of *gli*, the indirect object.

76. *e videmi e conobbemi e chiamava*: Porena considers this a "verso affannoso con tutti quegli *e*" ("a panting verse, with all those *ands*"). *videmi = mi vide. conobbemi = mi conobbe. chiamava*: "Called out" to me.

77. *tenendo li occhi con fatica fisi*: Torraca comments: "Altra pennellata da maestro: impacciato dal peso, non potendo alzare il capo, lo spirito costringeva gli occhi a guardare di sotto in su, e, nonostante la *fatica*, *li teneva fisi*, fissi per lo stupore, fissi per la commozione." ("Another master stroke: burdened by the weight, unable to raise his head, the spirit forced his eyes to look upward from below; and despite the difficulty, he kept them fixed, out of amazement, out of emotion.") Thus this soul, recognizing Dante here, is "exclaiming" with his eyes, as Dante in his turn will do in words.

78. *chin = chino*. "This stooping," comments Norton, "as if burdened like the sinners, is the symbol of Dante's consciousness of pride as his own besetting sin; see Canto xiii. 136-138."

79. *Oderisi*: Oderigi or Oderisi da Gubbio, miniature-painter and illuminator of whom little is known. Vasari, who quotes vss. 79-84, says in his *Life* of Giotto (pp. 384-85)

that Oderisi was a friend of Giotto and that Oderisi and
Franco of Bologna, whom Oderisi is to mention in vs. 83,
were both employed by Boniface VIII to illuminate manu-
scripts in the papal library at Rome. Vasari adds that he had
in his possession specimens of the work of both of them, and
that Franco was decidedly the better artist of the two.

The early commentators have little to say of Oderisi be-
yond what may be gathered from Dante's own words. Ben-
venuto remarks: "Iste Odorisius fuit magnus miniator in
civitate Bononiae tempore autoris, qui erat valde vanus iacta-
tor de arte sua non credens habere parem; ideo Dantes, qui
optime noverat animum eius avidum laudis et gloriae, de
industria commendat eum super omnes, ut experiatur si de-
posuit ventum, quo solebat esse inflatus." ("This Oderisi
was a great miniature-painter in Bologna at the time of our
author, and he was very vain and boastful about his artistic
talents, quite sure that he had no peer. Dante, who was well
aware of his hunger for praise and glory, deliberately praised
him as being without equal, to see if he had lost the wind that
formerly inflated him.")

According to later researches, Oderisi was born *ca.* 1240,
the son of Guido da Gubbio, and was in residence in Bologna
in 1268, 1269, and again in 1271, in which year he received
a commission from a member of the Lambertazzi family to
illuminate some eighty pages of an antiphonary. He is said
to have gone to Rome in 1295 and to have died there in
1299; at any rate, he must have been dead in 1300, the as-
sumed date of the journey. It appears from the text (vss. 76-
80) that he and Dante were acquainted or at least knew each
other by sight. See P. D'Ancona (1925), pp. 15-19;
P. Toesca (1927), pp. 1066 and 1134, n. 14.

80. *l'onor d'Agobbio e l'onor di quell' arte*: "Onor" is strik-
ingly repeated in a context of pride-humility and serves as
a test to the soul thus addressed. Will the soul feel pride at
these words?   *Agobbio*: Gubbio, town of central Italy
on the slopes of the Apennines in northern Umbria, about
twenty miles northeast of Perugia.   *l'onor di quell' arte*:
Cf. *Inf.* I, 87: "lo bello stilo che m'ha fatto onore."

81. *alluminar*: The Italian verb that is normally used for the art of decorating manuscripts is *miniare* (whence *miniatura*), from the Latin *minium*, a red lead used as pigment, but, as P. Toynbee (1902, pp. 266-67) points out, "alluminar" is used here to represent the French *enluminer*, the *al-* reflecting a typical mispronunciation of the nasal sound. Cf. the English *limn*. *Parisi = Parigi* (Latin *Parisii*). *Parisi* is found in early Italian.

82. *Frate*: The tone is familiar and intimate. Cf. *Purg.* IV, 127; Beatrice will so address Dante in *Purg.* XXXIII, 23. *Frate* is often used in the poem to begin a moral discourse of one sort or another (cf. *Purg.* XVI, 65 and *passim*).
più ridon le carte: The vivid colors used in the art of miniature are appropriately said to "smile" in their radiance. Cf. *Purg.* I, 20.

82-84. *più ridon le carte . . . parte*: Thus Oderisi does not respond with a "Yes, I am indeed the glory of Gubbio," but turns all the honor (or *almost* all!) to his rival in the art, Franco: greater humility can no artist show!

83. *Franco Bolognese*: Very little is known of this Franco of Bologna. It would appear from this reference to him that he was still living in 1300.

84. *l'onore è tutto or suo, e mio in parte*: Torraca comments: "*È tutto, or, suo*: detto con forza. Segue molto più lento e a stento, quasi concessione, che faccia dopo avervi riflettuto: *e, mio, in parte*." (" 'It is now all his': that is said with force. Then follows, a little slower and more laboriously, as though it were a concession made after some reflection: 'and mine in part.' ") But the point is that Oderisi does reserve some part of the honor for himself. As Butler observes: "It is hard not to suppose that the *e mio in parte* is a little natural touch; the old instinct of pride has not yet quite yielded to the purificatory discipline." It would indeed appear that Oderisi still has some time to serve here!

86-87. *per lo gran disio de l'eccellenza*: The phrase reflects a standard definition of pride. See the definition of Thomas

Aquinas in *Summa theol.* II-II, q. 162, a. 3, ad. 4: "Superbia dicitur esse *amor propriae excellentiae,* inquantum ex amore causatur inordinata praesumptio alios superandi, quod proprie pertinet ad superbiam." ("Pride is said to be *love of one's own excellence,* inasmuch as [this] love makes a man presume inordinately on his superiority over others, and this belongs properly to pride.") See *Purg.* XVII, 115-17.

87. *ove = alla quale.*

88. *il fio:* The "debito" (*Purg.* X, 108), the penalty; cf. *Inf.* XXVII, 135.

89–90. *e ancor non sarei qui . . . Dio:* He would still be in Antepurgatory, among the negligent, if he had put off the good sighs until the last, as Belacqua and the others had done (*Purg.* IV, 132).

90. *possendo = potendo.   possendo peccar:* While still alive, when I could still have sinned.   *mi volsi a Dio:* I was "converted," as even a pope will say of himself later (*Purg.* XIX, 106).

91. *Oh vana gloria:* The poet thus brings into this canto a term which was commonly used of the first or gravest of the mortal sins: vainglory.   *umane posse:* Cf. *Inf.* XXXI, 56.

92–93. *com' poco verde . . . grosse:* Fame lasts but a short while if it is not followed by ignorant times in which excellence remains unsurpassed, that is, green or living.

92. *com' = come.* Cf. *Inf.* XXVI, 12. This apocopated form was also used in prose.   *poco verde in su la cima dura:* Porena comments: " 'Quanto poco dura verde sul ramo': vi è implicita la similitudine fra la gloria e una foglia verde che tosto dissecca. Si guardi dunque di non intendere *cima* nel senso di altezza, sommità, ecc." (" 'How little the green lasts on the branch.' Implicit is the similarity between glory and a green leaf that soon shrivels. We must be careful not to interpret *cima* in the sense of 'height,' 'summit,' etc.") But grass, or any green plant, is probably underlying the image by way of familiar verses of the Scriptures, which fit this

whole context very well. See, for example, Isa. 40:6: "Omnis caro foenum, et omnis gloria eius quasi flos agri" ("All flesh is grass, and all the glory thereof as the flower of the field") and Ps. 89:6[90:5-6]: "Mane sicut herba transeat, mane floreat et transeat; vespere decidat, induret et arescat." ("The next morning they are like the changing grass, which at dawn springs up anew, but by evening wilts and fades.") See also Ecclus. 14:18: "Omnis caro sicut foenum veterascet." ("All flesh withers like grass.") *cima*: See *Inf.* XIII, 44, where "cima" means the tip of a branch.

93. *guinta*: I.e., *sopraggiunta*, "overtaken." Cf. *Inf.* VIII, 18; XXII, 126. *da l'etati grosse*: By rude and barbarous times.

94. *Cimabue*: Cenni di Pepo, known as Giovanni Cimabue, the great Florentine painter and mosaicist and master of Giotto, commonly regarded because of his departure from the Byzantine tradition as the regenerator of painting in Italy. He was born *ca.* 1240 and died, not in 1300, as Vasari states in his *Life* of Cimabue (p. 256), but probably *ca.* 1302. He is proved by documentary evidence to have been painting in Pisa in 1302.

95. *tener lo campo*: "To hold [i.e., keep] the field," a military metaphor. *e ora ha Giotto il grido*: *Avere il grido* means to have the general acclaim for mastery and surpassing excellence. *Giotto*: Giotto di Bondone, the great Florentine artist, was born probably in 1266 or 1267 (one or two years after the birth of Dante, whose intimate friend he is said to have been), either in Colle, near Vespignano, north of Florence, or in Florence. He died in Florence on January 8, 1337.

97–98. *Così ha tolto . . . lingua*: Guido Cavalcanti has taken the glory of eloquence in the vulgar tongue (i.e., poetry) from Guido Guinizzelli, whom Dante will call his father and the father of "li altri miei miglior che mai / rime d'amor usar dolci e leggiadre" in *Purg.* XXVI, 97-99. See *Inf.* X, 60, where it is indicated that Guido Cavalcanti was

still living at the time of this journey. It seems highly unlike-
ly that the first Guido (chronologically) would be Guittone
d'Arezzo, as some commentators would understand it.

98–99. *forse è nato . . . nido*: We must not forget that it
is Oderisi who says this, and that excellence in both painting
(Giotto) and poetry (Guido Cavalcanti) is spoken of. The
"chi" here would seem to imply, therefore, two persons, the
artist (who is perhaps born) who will win the field from
Giotto and the poet who will win it from Guido. We have
no inkling as to who the former might be, and the indefinite
"chi" and the "forse" suggest that Oderisi has no particular
candidate in mind for poetry, but it is hard not to think that
he intends Dante himself as the poet. In this way Oderisi
would, so to speak, be returning the compliment to his friend,
who had termed him the "honor" of his own art (vs. 80).

99. *nido*: Torraca feels that *"nido* risveglia l'idea di dimora
propria, tranquilla, cara, alla quale non si rinunzia senza
dolore." *("Nido* [nest] suggests the idea of one's own home,
a peaceful, beloved place that one cannot renounce without
pain.")

100. *romore*: See Boethius, *Consol. philos.* II, vii, ll. 62-
65: "Vos autem nisi ad populares auras inanesque rumores
recte facere nescitis et relicta conscientiae virtutisque
praestantia de alienis praemia sermunculis postulatis." ("But
without popular blasts and vain rumours you know not how
to do well, and, rejecting the excellency of a good conscience
and of virtue, you choose to be rewarded with others'
tattling.")

100–101. *un fiato di vento*: Cf. *Aen.* VII, 646: "Ad nos vix
tenuis famae perlabitur aura." ("To us scarcely is wafted
some scant breath of fame.")

102. *e muta nome perché muta lato*: Porena comments: "Il
vento si chiama scirocco se soffia da un lato, libeccio se da
un altro, e così via: la stessa mutevolezza hanno i nomi dif-
fusi dalla fama." ("The wind is called *scirocco* [sirocco] if
it blows from one side, *libeccio* if it comes from the other,

and so on. The names borne by fame are subject to the same changes.") "Lato" is the quarter from which the wind blows.

103. *voce*: Renown.

103-4. *se vecchia scindi da te la carne*: I.e., if you die old.

104-5. *che se fossi morto . . . "dindi"*: I.e., than if you had died young, before you left off childish prattle. "Pappo" for *pane* and "dindi" for *danari* is baby talk.

106. *pria che passin mill' anni*: "Before a thousand years shall pass."

106-8. *ch'è più corto spazio . . . torto*: Which (i.e., a thousand years) is a shorter time compared with eternity than is the twinkle of an eye compared with the time required for the heaven of the fixed stars (the eighth heaven) to make one revolution from west to east (precession of the equinoxes), which in the astronomy of Dante's day was calculated to take 36,000 years. See *Conv.* II, xiv, 10, where Dante, referring to the heaven of the fixed stars, mentions "lo movimento ne lo quale ogni die si rivolve, e fa nova circulazione di punto a punto" ("the movement wherewith it revolveth day by day, and maketh a fresh return from point to point") and "lo movimento quasi insensibile, che fa da occidente in oriente per uno grado in cento anni" ("the almost insensible movement which it makes from west to east, at the rate of a degree in a hundred years"). It is the movement of the eighth heaven that is meant in vs. 108, that heaven being the outermost of the "stellate ruote" (vs. 36). In the other, or diurnal, movement, from east to west (the motion of the planets more commonly referred to), the speed of the revolution is greater in proportion to the distance from the center. For the moral reflection, see Boethius, *Consol. philos.* II, vii, ll. 45-62.

109. *Colui*: This shade is Provenzan (pronounced Provenzàn) Salvani, a prominent Ghibelline of Siena who was born *ca.* 1220. His family, the Salvani, were descendants of the Cacciaconti, feudal lords of Scialenga. Provenzan's father, Ildebrando, and his paternal grandfather, Salvano (who gave

his name to his descendants), were both prominent Ghibel-
lines. Provenzan himself begins to appear in the records in
1247, when he was named "Provveditore alla Biccherna,"
and from 1249 his political activities can be followed fairly
well. After the battle of Montaperti (September 4, 1260)
he was virtual dictator of Siena, and it was he who at the
council of Empoli after the battle advocated the destruction
of Florence, which was averted by the firmness and patriot-
ism of Farinata (*Inf.* X, 91-93). He was *podestà* of Monte-
pulciano in 1261 and was elected *podestà* of Arezzo in 1262-
63, but did not serve; but after the battle of Benevento (Feb-
ruary 1266) his power, along with that of the Ghibellines
generally, was on the wane. He met his death in an engage-
ment with the Florentines at Colle in the Val d'Elsa, in June
of 1269, when he was taken prisoner and beheaded by one
Cavolino de' Tolomei. See F. Tempesti (1936).   *che del
cammin sì poco piglia*: I.e., goes so slowly, because he car-
ries a heavier weight than most (see "disparmente angoscia-
te," vs. 28).

109–10. *Colui che del cammin . . . sonò*: "Colui" is the
object of "sonò," and "Toscana" is the subject.

110. *Toscana sonò tutta*: How immense little Tuscany
sounds in this verse!

111. *ora*: I.e., only thirty-one years after his death.   *sen
= se ne.*   *pispiglia*: In contrast with "sonò," vs. 110.

112. *ond' era sire*: Siena was a republic, and Provenzan
was a private citizen, but he had become chief in authority,
or, as Villani (VI, 78) says: "Era il maggiore del popolo di
Siena." ("He was the first among the citizens of Siena.")
In his presumption he sought to "get all Siena into his hands"
(vs. 123), private citizen though he was, and for this he pays
the fee here. According to Villani (VII, 31) "fu grande
uomo in Siena al suo tempo dopo la vittoria ch'ebbe a Mon-
taperti, e guidava tutta la città, e tutta parte ghibellina di
Toscana facea capo di lui, e era molto presuntuoso di sua
volontà." ("He was an important man in Siena in his time,

after the victory of Montaperti. He controlled the whole city, and the entire Ghibelline faction of Tuscany looked to him as its leader. He was very imperious in manner.")

112–13. *quando fu distrutta la rabbia fiorentina*: The reference is to the battle of Montaperti, disastrous defeat for the Florentines (see *Inf*. X, 85-86). Villani may be echoing Dante's verse when he writes of the battle (VI, 79): "Così s'adonò la rabbia dell'ingrato e superbo popolo di Firenze." ("And thus was the arrogance of the ungrateful and haughty Florentine people abashed.")

114. *com' ora è putta*: See "putti" in this sense in *Inf*. XIII, 65.

115. *La vostra nominanza*: The plural refers this judgment to all the living. *è color d'erba*: Oderisi thus returns to the theme of vss. 91-92, for which see the biblical references given in the n. to vs. 92.

116. *quei*: The sun. Even as the color of grass is determined by the sun and the seasons, so is our earthly fame subject to the passage of time.

117. *acerba*: Immature, unripe. "Acerba" modifies "ella," i.e., "erba." See n. to *Inf*. XXV, 15.

118–19. *Tuo vero dir m'incora bona umiltà*: "Your true words inspire my heart with good humility."

119. *e gran tumor m'appiani*: The swelling of pride was commonly referred to as a *tumor*. See Augustine's use of the word in *Conf*. VII, 7: "Et haec de vulnere meo creverant, quia humiliasti tamquam vulneratum superbum, et tumore meo separabar abs te, et nimis inflata facies claudebat oculos meos." ("And all these had grown out of my wound; for thou hast humbled the proud like as him that is wounded, and through my own swelling was I set further off from thee; yea, my cheeks, too big swollen, even blinded up mine eyes.") See also *Conf*. VII, 8: "Et residebat tumor meus ex occulta manu medicinae tuae." ("Thus, by the secret hand of thy medicining was my swelling abated.")

125. *poi che morì = da quando morì.*

125–26. *cotal moneta rende a sodisfar*: Again the metaphor of the debt and the fee that must be paid.

126. *oso*: "Bold," "overweening" (note "presuntuoso," vs. 122). Cf. the Latin *ausus*.

127–28. *Se quello spirito . . . la vita*: Such was Belacqua, *Purg.* IV, 132.

129. *qua giù*: In Antepurgatory, where Belacqua and those who were negligent must serve time equal to their lifetime. The expression implies a gesture on Dante's part.   *qua sù*: In Purgatory proper, where Dante now is.

130. *se buona orazion lui non aita*: Dante seems to assume, by his question, that Provenzan has not been helped out of Antepurgatory by "good prayers."

132. *la venuta*: His coming here into Purgatory proper.
   lui largita: "Mercifully granted him." Thirty-one years have passed since Provenzan died, and he was about forty-nine years of age at his death.

133. *Quando vivea più glorïoso*: Torraca comments that "la dieresi dà maggiore spicco alla parola e al concetto." ("The diaeresis makes the word and the concept stand out even more.")

133–38. *Quando vivea . . . vena*: The incident here alluded to is related by the *Ottimo Commento*, in the gloss on vs. 142, as follows:

> Avendo il re Carlo in prigione uno suo amico caro, puosegli di taglia fiorini dieci mila d'oro (chè era stato contra lui con Curradino nella sconfitta a Tagliacozzo), ed assegnogli brieve termine a pagare, o a morire. Quelli ne scrisse a messer Provenzano. Dicesi, che messer Provenzano fece porre uno desco, susovi uno tappeto, nel campo di Siena, e puosevisi suso a sedere in quello abito, che richiedea la bisogna; domandava alli Sanesi vergognosamente, che lo dovessono aiutare a quella

sua bisogna di moneta, non sforzando alcuno, ma umilmente domandando aiuto; d'onde li Sanesi vedendo costui, che solea essere loro signore e tanto superbo, domandare così pietosamente, furono commossi a pietade, e ciascuno, secondo sua facultade, diede aiuto; sicchè, anzi che 'l termine spirasse, fu ricomperato l'amico.

King Charles had a friend of his [Provenzan's] in prison, on whom he put a ransom of 10,000 gold florins. (He had fought with Conradin against Charles in the defeat at Tagliacozzo.) When the king gave him only a short time to pay or die, he appealed to Messer Provenzan. It is said that Messer Provenzan had a bench with a carpet over it put up in the square of Siena, and then sat on it in clothes that the occasion required. Bashfully, he asked the Sienese to help him in his need of money, forcing no one, just humbly asking for help. When the Sienese saw this man, whom they thought of as their lord, usually so proud, begging so pitifully, they were moved to pity. Everyone helped, according to his means. So that, before the time had expired, he was able to buy his friend's release.

Torraca points out that begging for money to pay fines, though prohibited by law, was common in the Middle Ages.

134. *liberamente*: "Freely," which renders it a meritorious act. *nel Campo di Siena*: The famous oval piazza before the Palazzo Pubblico in Siena.

135. *ogne vergogna diposta*: This construction is modeled on an ablative absolute. *s'affisse*: Took his stand.

138. *si condusse a tremar per ogne vena*: For *condursi a* in this sense, see Torraca, who provides the following quotation from a work attributed to Brunetto Latini: "E tennero el castello . . . conducendosi a mangiare i topi e rodere i cuoi di tavolacci." ("And they held the castle . . . reduced to eating mice and chewing the leather on the shields.") Cf. *Inf.* I, 90.

139. *e scuro so che parlo*: "Tremar per ogne vena" are the obscure words, since the reason for trembling so is not stated, but is only implied.

140–41. *ma poco tempo andrà . . . chiosarlo*: No great while shall pass till your fellow-citizens will act in such a way (by exiling you) as to enable you to interpret those dark words. For similar prophecies, see *Inf.* XV, 89; *Par.* XVII, 94. That is, in the humiliation of exile, begging his bread, Dante will learn what it means to "tremble in every vein." In *Conv.* I, iii, 3 Dante laments: "Nè io sofferto avria pena ingiustamente, pena, dico, d'essilio e di povertate." ("Nor should I have unjustly suffered penalty, the penalty I mean of exile and of poverty.") He continues (*Conv.* I, iii, 4): "Poi che fu piacere de li cittadini de la bellissima e famosissima figlia di Roma, Fiorenza, di gittarmi fuori del suo dolce seno . . . per le parti quasi tutte a le quali questa lingua si stende, peregrino, quasi mendicando, sono andato, mostrando contra mia voglia la piaga de la fortuna." ("Since it was the pleasure of the citizens of the most beauteous and the most famous daughter of Rome, Florence, to cast me forth from her most sweet bosom . . . through well-nigh all the regions whereto this tongue extends, a wanderer, almost a beggar, have I paced, revealing, against my will, the wound of fortune.")

140. *vicini*: For *vicino* in this sense, cf. *Inf.* XVII, 68; *Par.* XVII, 97.

142. *li = gli.   tolse quei confini*: Buti explains: "cioè lo stare . . . fuor del purgatorio a purgare la negligenzia" ("that is, staying . . . outside of Purgatory and purging negligence").

CANTO XII

1. *Di pari*: Modifies "m'andava," indicating that Dante is keeping even pace with Oderisi and goes along bent over with him.   *come buoi che vanno a giogo*: The comparison with oxen suggests the most patient submission to the yoke, i.e., humility. Thus Dante shares in the painful purgation on this terrace (see vs. 9).

2. *carca = carica*.

4. *varca*: Cf. *Purg.* X, 53.

5. *con l'ali e coi remi*: Cf. the Latin *velis remisque contendere*.

7. *dritto*: "Upright."   *come andar vuolsi = come si vuole andare*, "as a man should walk."

8. *avvegna che*: "Albeit."

8–9. *avvegna che i pensieri . . . scemi*: As if Dante's thoughts remain bent over in humility, as his person has been, and emptied, deflated, of pride. The metaphor of the *tumore* is latent here (cf. "gran tumor m'appiani" in *Purg.* XI, 119). Dante thus has undergone a kind of purgation and deserves to have a P removed from his forehead, the P of pride, this first and most besetting sin of all.

4. Pavement
tomb of the old
church of
Santa Reparata
in Florence

11–12. *e amendue . . . leggeri*: Virgil, being a spirit, is always "light," of course; and now that Dante has purged himself of the heavy burden of pride, he has become light, too. "Amendue," in the emphatic rhyme position, serves to set off Virgil and Dante from the laden souls, as the two wayfarers now pass on ahead of them.

13. *Volgi li occhi in giùe*: A standing injunction, a corrective for pride, is "look down" (see vs. 71), though there is here a special reason for doing so.

14. *per tranquillar la via*: "To ease your way." See Dante, *Rime* LX, 1-6.

15. *lo letto de le piante tue*: "Letto" continues the figure suggested by "tranquillar."

16. *di lor*: Of the buried dead, vs. 17.

17. *le tombe terragne*: Tombs set in the floor (*terra*), of churches or cloisters. (See Plate 4, facing.)

18. *segnato quel ch'elli eran pria*: Buti elaborates on this as follows: "Cioè lo sepolto co la soprascrizione co l'arme, co la figura corporale a mo' di iudici o di medico o di cavallieri, secondo ch'è stato ne la vita." ("That is, the buried person, with the inscription, with the arms, with the image, as a judge, doctor, or knight, depending upon what he was in life.") Often the sculptured image will show family arms or professional dress. *quel ch'*: "That which." *elli*: The dead.

19. *lì*: Over the sculptured image. *si ripiagne*: There is weeping again and again.

20. *per la puntura*: Because of the prick. "Puntura" introduces the metaphor of the spur, which continues in the following verse in the phrase *dar de le calcagna*, "to give of the heels (*calcagna*)," i.e., "to dig in with the spurs, worn at the heel."

21. *solo a' pii*: Only the faithful (those faithful to a memory) are spurred by such a reminder.

24. *quanto per via di fuor del monte avanza*: The whole floor of the terrace, i.e., all that juts out from the mountain to form a roadway.

25–63. *Vedea . . . mostrava*: On the anaphora that begins with vs. 25 and ends with the tercet of vss. 61-63, see n. to vss. 61-63.

25–27. *colui che fu . . . lato*: Lucifer, "la creatura ch'ebbe il bel sembiante" of *Inf.* XXXIV, 18. See *Par.* XIX, 46-47. He was the highest of the Seraphim (the highest of the angelic orders), hence his six wings, mentioned in *Inf.* XXXIV, 46-47.

27. *folgoreggiando scender*: See Luc. 10:17-18: "Reversi sunt autem septuaginta duo cum gaudio, dicentes: Domine, etiam daemonia subiiciuntur nobis in nomine tuo. Et ait illis: Videbam Satanam sicut fulgur de caelo cadentem." ("Now the seventy-two returned with joy, saying, 'Lord, even the devils are subjects to us in thy name.' But he said to them, 'I was watching Satan fall as lightning from heaven.'") See *Inf.* XXXIV, 121-26; Isa. 14:12.

28–30. *Vedea Briareo . . . gelo*: Cf. *Inf.* XXXI, 98: "lo smisurato Briareo." Briareus, or Aegaeon, son of Heaven (Uranus) and Earth (Gaea), was one of the giants who warred against Olympus. According to some accounts, he was slain by Jupiter with a thunderbolt and buried under Mount Etna. Virgil (*Aen.* X, 565-68) represents him with a hundred arms and fifty heads:

> Aegaeon qualis, centum cui bracchia dicunt
> centenasque manus, quinquaginta oribus ignem
> pectoribusque arsisse, Iovis cum fulmina contra
> tot paribus streperet clipeis, tot stringeret ensis . . .

Even as Aegaeon, who, men say, had a hundred arms and a hundred hands, and flashed fire from fifty mouths and breasts, what time against Jove's thunders he clanged with as many like shields, and bared as many swords.

See Statius, *Theb.* II, 595-601:

non aliter—Geticae si fas est credere Phlegrae—
armatum immensus Briareus stetit aethera contra,
hinc Phoebi pharetras, hinc torvae Pallados anguis,
inde Pelethroniam praefixa cuspide pinum
Martis, at hinc lasso mutata Pyracmone temnens
fulmina, cum toto nequiquam obsessus Olympo
tot queritur cessare manus . . .

Not otherwise—if Getic Phlegra be worthy credence—
stood Briareus vast in bulk against embattled heaven,
contemning on this hand Phoebus' quiver, on that the
serpents of stern Pallas, here Mars' Pelethronian pine-
wood shaft, with point of iron, and yonder the thunder-
bolts oft changed for new by weary Pyracmon, and yet
complaining, though combated in vain by all Olympus,
that so many hands were idle.

In this passage from Statius, it will be noted, Apollo, Pallas,
and Mars are mentioned, as in vs. 31 below.

Briareus, on the principle of concordance between the
biblical and non-biblical examples of the sin being purged
on each terrace, corresponds, in the extra-biblical line, to
Satan cast forth from Heaven. He is depicted "da l'altra
parte," i.e., alongside Satan, in the first of the series of six
pairs of reliefs set in the floor.

28-29. *fitto dal telo celestial*: Jupiter's weapon was the *ful-
men*, a thunderbolt, but "telo" here may denote an arrow, as
the visual symbol of his lightning. Cf. *Inf.* XXXI, 44-45: "li
orribili giganti, cui minaccia / Giove del cielo ancora quando
tuona."

31. *Timbreo*: Thymbraeus, epithet of Apollo, derived from
Thymbra in the Troad, where there was a celebrated temple
dedicated to him. Dante would be familiar with the term from
its frequent use by Statius in the *Thebaid* (I, 643, 699; III,
513, 638; IV, 515) and from Virgil (*Georg.* IV, 323; *Aen.*
III, 85).   *Pallade*: Pallas, surname of the Greek goddess
Athena, whom the Romans identified with Minerva.

32. *al padre loro*: Jupiter.

33. *mirar le membra d'i Giganti sparte*: With the use of "grave" in vs. 30 and "sparte" in this verse, it is as if Dante were deliberately echoing Ovid, *Metam.* X, 150-51: "Cecini plectro graviore Gigantas / sparsaque Phlegraeis victricia fulmina campis." ("I have sung the giants in a heavier strain, and the victorious bolts hurled on the Phlegraean plains.") See *Inf.* XXXI, 44-45.   *Giganti*: The giants of mythology, who, according to Hesiod (*Theogony*, vs. 185), were said to have sprung from the blood that fell from Heaven (Uranus) upon the earth, whence Earth (Gaea) was regarded as their mother. They made an attack upon Olympus, the abode of the gods, armed with huge rocks and trunks of trees, but the gods with the aid of Hercules destroyed them all and buried them under Etna and other volcanoes.

34-36. *Vedea Nembròt . . . fuoro*: See *Inf.* XXXI, 77-78, and *Par.* XXVI, 126. Nimrod, who according to Gen. 10:8-9 was the son of Cush and "robustus venator coram Domino" ("a mighty hunter before the Lord"), was commonly supposed to have been the builder of the Tower of Babel, on the plain of Shinar. The origin of the tradition was probably Gen. 10:10: "Fuit autem principium regni eius Babylon et Arach et Achad et Chalanne in terra Sennaar." ("The beginning of his kingdom was Babylon, Arach and Acchad and Chalanne, all of them in the land of Sennaar.") For the building of the tower, see Gen. 11:1-9:

> Erat autem terra labii unius et sermonum eorundem. Cumque proficiscerentur de oriente, invenerunt campum in terra Sennaar, et habitaverunt in eo. Dixitque alter ad proximum suum: Venite, faciamus lateres et coquamus eos igni. Habueruntque lateres pro saxis, et bitumen pro caemento. Et dixerunt: Venite, faciamus nobis civitatem, et turrim cuius culmen pertingat ad caelum, et celebremus nomen nostrum antequam dividamur in universas terras.
>
> Descendit autem Dominus ut videret civitatem et turrim quam aedificabant filii Adam, et dixit: Ecce unus est populus et unum labium omnibus; coeperuntque hoc facere, nec desistent a cogitationibus suis, donec eas

248

opere compleant. Venite igitur, descendamus et confundamus ibi linguam eorum, ut non audiat unusquisque vocem proximi sui. Atque ita divisit eos Dominus ex illo loco in universas terras, et cessaverunt aedificare civitatem. Et idcirco vocatum est nomen eius Babel, quia ibi confusum est labium universae terrae, et inde dispersit eos Dominus super faciem cunctarum regionum.

The whole earth used the same language and the same speech. While men were migrating eastward, they discovered a valley in the land of Sennaar and settled there. They said to one another, "Come, let us make bricks and bake them." They used bricks for stone and bitumen for mortar. Then they said, "Let us build ourselves a city and a tower with its top in the heavens; let us make a name for ourselves lest we be scattered all over the earth." The Lord came down to see the city and the tower which men had built. And the Lord said, "Truly, they are one people and they all have the same language. This is the beginning of what they will do. Hereafter they will not be restrained from anything which they determine to do. Let us go down, and there confuse their language so that they will not understand one another's speech." So the Lord scattered them from that place all over the earth; and they stopped building the city. For this reason it was called Babel, because there the Lord confused the speech of all the earth. From there the Lord scattered them all over the earth.

35. *quasi smarrito*: Cf. *Inf.* XXXI, 74: "o anima confusa."
   e riguardar le genti: Some editors have simply "riguardar," in place of "e riguardar," taking "Nembròt" to be the subject. The scene matches that of vss. 31-33 more closely, however, if we understand "le genti" to be the subject of "riguardar." That is, Nimrod and all those who joined him in the proud enterprise now gaze upon the ruin of their work. Sapegno comments:

In questa prima serie, i bassorilievi sono concepiti secondo uno schema antitetico: al movimento rapido della

caduta di Lucifero si contrappone la pesante immo-
bilità del cadavere di Briareo; al gruppo degli dei, che
contemplano dall'alto i terribili effetti della loro cruenta
vittoria, l'altro gruppo di Nembròt e dei suoi compagni,
che contemplano smarriti i risultati del loro proposito
superbo vinto e confuso.

In this first series, the bas reliefs are conceived accord-
ing to an antithetic scheme: the rapid movement of
Lucifer's fall is counterbalanced by the heavy immobil-
ity of Briareus' cadaver; the group of the gods, con-
templating from on high the terrible effects of their
bloody victory, is counterbalanced by the other group
of Nimrod and his friends, who gaze bewildered at the
results of their proud intention, now beaten and
confused.

36. *superbi*: See Dante, *De vulg. eloqu.* I, vii, 4-5:

Presumpsit ergo in corde suo incurabilis homo, sub per-
suasione gigantis, arte sua, non solum superare naturam,
sed etiam ipsum naturantem, qui Deus est, et cepit
hedificare turrim in Sennear, que postea dicta est Babel,
hoc est confusio, per quam celum sperabat adscendere:
intendens, inscius, non equare, sed suum superare Fac-
torem. O sine mensura clementia celestis imperii! Quis
patrum tot sustineret insultus a filio? Sed exsurgens, non
hostili scutica, sed paterna, et alias verberibus assueta,
rebellantem filium pia correctione, nec non memorabili,
castigavit.

For incorrigible man, persuaded by the giant, presumed
in his heart to surpass by his own skill not only nature,
but even the very power that works in nature, who is
God; and he began to build a tower in Sennear, which
was afterwards called Babel, that is, confusion, by which
he hoped to ascend to heaven; purposing in his ignor-
ance, not to equal, but to surpass his Maker. O bound-
less clemency of the heavenly power! Who among
fathers would bear so many insults from a son? But
he arose, and, with a scourge which was not hostile
but paternal and had been wont at other times to smite,

he chastised his rebellious son with correction at once merciful and memorable.

fuoro = furono.

37–39. *O Niobè . . . spenti*: Niobe was the daughter of Tantalus and Dione and the wife of Amphion, king of Thebes. Being proud of the number of her children, she boasted herself superior to Latona, who had only two, Apollo and Diana, whereupon Latona persuaded Apollo and Diana to slay with their arrows Niobe's seven sons and seven daughters. Although Niobe was transformed into stone and carried away to her native Mount Sipylus in Lydia, tears continued forever to trickle down her marble cheeks. This story is told by Ovid (*Metam.* VI, 182-312), whom Dante has followed in putting the number of her children at seven sons and seven daughters. For Niobe's sin, clearly one of pride, see *Metam.* VI, 182-84, the words spoken by Niobe herself:

> . . . huc natas adice septem
> et totidem iuvenes et mox generosque nurusque!
> quaerite nunc, habeat quam nostra superbia causam . . .

> Add to all this that I have seven daughters and as many sons, and soon shall have sons- and daughters-in-law. Ask now what cause I have for pride.

37. *con che occhi dolenti*: The phrase focuses on the miraculous feature of the transformation, the fact that the marble sheds tears. See Ovid, *Metam.* VI, 310-12:

> flet tamen et validi circumdata turbine venti
> in patriam rapta est: ibi fixa cacumine montis
> liquitur, et lacrimas etiam nunc marmora manant.

> But still she weeps; and, caught up in a strong, whirling wind, she is rapt away to her own native land. There, set on a mountain's peak, she weeps; and even to this day tears trickle from the marble.

40–42. *O Saùl . . . rugiada*: Saul, the son of Kish of the tribe of Benjamin, was the first king of Israel. He was anointed by Samuel and was deposed by him in obedience to the command of God, for Saul had been proud in disobeying the Lord's command in sparing a life and allowing booty to be taken, wherefore God abandoned him (I Reg. 15:10-11). See E. Auerbach (1949), who points out that Saul's offense to God was commonly viewed as one of pride, Samuel's words to him being cited (I Reg. 15:17): "Nonne, cum parvulus esses in oculis tuis, caput in tribubus Israel factus es?" ("When thou wast a little one in thy own eyes, wast thou not made the head of the tribes of Israel?") Gregory (*In librum primum Regum* VI, ii, 2) comments: "Aperte ergo transgressor per inobedientiam exstitit, quia implere praeceptum Domini per superbiam recusavit." ("[Saul] stands clearly as the transgressor, because he refused through pride to fulfill the word of the Lord.")

40–41. *come in su la propria spada . . . Gelboè*: See I Reg. 31:3-4:

Totumque pondus proelii versum est in Saul, et consecuti sunt eum viri sagittarii et vulneratus est vehementer a sagittariis. Dixitque Saul ad armigerum suum: Evagina gladium tuum et percute me, ne forte veniant incircumcisi isti et interficiant me illudentes mihi. Et noluit armiger eius; fuerat enim nimio terrore perterritus. Arripuit itaque Saul gladium et irruit super eum.

And the whole weight of the battle was turned upon Saul: and the archers overtook him. And he was grievously wounded by the archers.

Then Saul said to his armourbearer: Draw thy sword, and kill me: lest these uncircumcised come, and slay me, and mock at me. And his armourbearer would not: for he was struck with exceeding great fear. Then Saul took his sword, and fell upon it.

41. *Gelboè*: Gilboa, mountain in Samaria.

42. *che poi non sentì pioggia né rugiada*: Such was David's lament and imprecation, on learning of King Saul's death. See II Reg. 1:17-21, especially vs. 21: "Montes Gelboe, nec ros nec pluvia veniant super vos." ("Ye mountains of Gelboe, let neither dew, nor rain come upon you.")

43-45. *O folle Aragne . . . fé*: Arachne (i.e., "spider") was the daughter of Idmon of Colophon, a dyer in purple. She excelled in the art of weaving and, proud of her skill, ventured to challenge Minerva to compete with her. Arachne produced a piece of cloth in which the amours of the gods were woven; and Minerva, unable to find fault with it, tore it in pieces. In despair Arachne hanged herself, but the goddess loosened the rope and saved her life, the rope being changed into a cobweb, and Arachne herself into a spider. See Ovid, *Metam.* VI, 5-145. In the *Metamorphoses* the story of Niobe follows directly upon that of Arachne.

44. *già mezza ragna*: Like Ovid, Dante loves to catch a metamorphosis at some intermediary point, *in fieri*.

45. *fé = fece*. This verse, like those in rhyme with it, are *versi tronchi*. Cf. *Inf.* IV, 56 and *passim*.

46-48. *O Roboàm . . . cacci*: Rehoboam was the son of Solomon by the Ammonite princess Naamah (III Reg. 14:21, 31). He succeeded his father as king of Israel, but, owing to his haughty refusal of the demand of the people for a remission of the heavy burdens imposed by Solomon, ten of the tribes revolted from him and acknowledged Jeroboam as their king, Judah and Benjamin alone remaining faithful to Rehoboam, who fled to Jerusalem. The incident referred to is related in III Reg. 12:18: "Misit ergo rex Roboam Aduram, qui erat super tributa; et lapidavit eum omnis Israel, et mortuus est. Porro rex Roboam festinus ascendit currum, et fugit in Ierusalem." ("Then king Roboam sent Aduram, who was over the tribute: and all Israel stoned him: and he died. Wherefore king Roboam made haste to get him up into his chariot, and he fled to Jerusalem.")

46. *già non*: "Già" reinforces the negative; cf. the Latin *iam non*. See *Purg.* XI, 23.

47. *segno*: Cf. the Latin *signum*, "image," "statue."

48. *nel porta = ne lo porta*, i.e., bears off the image. *il = lo*.

49. *Mostrava ancor lo duro pavimento*: "Pavimento" is the subject of "mostrava" not only in this verse, but also in vss. 52, 55, and 58. The floor is hard because it is of stone, of course; but it is also hard in that it shows such "hard" examples of the consequences of pride.

50-51. *Almeon a sua madre . . . addornamento*: Alcmaeon was the son of Amphiaraus the seer and Eriphyle. Amphiaraus, foreseeing that the expedition against Thebes would prove fatal to him, concealed himself in order to avoid joining it; but his wife Eriphyle, bribed by Polynices with the necklace of Harmonia, revealed his hiding-place, so that he went and met his death. Before he left Argos, however, he had enjoined Alcmaeon to slay Eriphyle in punishment for her betrayal of him; accordingly, Alcmaeon put his mother to death. See Statius, *Theb.* IV, 187-213; Virgil, *Aen.* VI, 445-46. Alcmaeon is mentioned again in the same connection in *Par.* IV, 103-5.

51. *lo sventurato addornamento*: Eriphyle's vanity in *desiring* to possess the necklace of Harmonia is, of course, the main point in this scene of punished pride, and her death at the hands of her son makes the "luckless ornament" seem to cost too much. The story of the "sventurato addornamento" is told by Statius, *Theb.* II, 265-305. One notes in *Theb.* II, 303, the judgment on Eriphyle's desire to have the necklace: "Quantas cupit impia clades!" ("To what ruin tend her impious wishes!") This is her "pride."

52-54. *Mostrava come . . . lasciaro*: Sennacherib, king of Assyria from 705 to 681 B.C., was the son of Sargon, whom he succeeded. He was himself succeeded by his own son, Esarhaddon. In the year 701 he sent an expedition against Hezekiah, king of Judah (IV Reg. 18:13-16); some time later he sent a second expedition against Hezekiah, and it was on this occasion that, according to IV Reg. 19:35, the Assyrian host, to the number of 185,000 men, was annihilated in a single night by an angel of the Lord. Sennacherib himself escaped and reached his capital in safety, where he was eventually assassinated by two of his sons.

See IV Reg. 19:36-37 (also related in Isa. 37:37-38): "Et reversus est Sennacherib rex Assyriorum, et mansit in Ninive. Cumque adoraret in templo Nesroch deum suum, Adramelech et Sarasar filii eius percusserunt eum gladio, fugeruntque in terrram Armeniorum." ("And Sennacherib king of the Assyrians departing went away: And he returned and abode in Ninive. And as he was worshipping in the temple of Nesroch his god, Adramelech and Sarasar his sons slew him with the sword. And they fled into the land of the Armenians.")

Sennacherib is punished for the arrogance of his demands upon Hezekiah and the Israelites, as declared by his envoys, in the face of which blasphemous threats Hezekiah prayed to the Lord for deliverance and through Isaiah was given assurance thereof, the Lord judging Sennacherib in these words in IV Reg. 19:22 (also to be found in Isa. 37:23): "Cui exprobrasti et quem blasphemasti? contra quem exaltasti vocem tuam et elevasti in excelsum oculus tuos? Contra sanctum Israel." ("Whom hast thou reproached, and whom hast thou blasphemed? Against whom hast thou exalted thy voice, and lifted up thy eyes on high? Against the holy one of Israel.")

55-57. *Mostrava la ruina . . . t'empio*: Tomyris (or Thamyris) was queen of the Massagetae, a Scythian people, by whom Cyrus was defeated and slain in 529 B.C. Tomyris had Cyrus' head cut off and thrown into a skin of human blood, and she mocked it, because he had treacherously slain her son. Dante's authority in this case was Orosius, who, after describing how Cyrus was slain in ambush by the queen, says (*Hist.* II, vii, 6): "Regina caput Cyri amputari atque in utrem humano sanguine oppletum coici iubet non muliebriter increpitans: Satio te, inquit, sanguine quem sitisti, cuius per annos triginta insatiabilis perseverasti." ("The Queen had the head of Cyrus cut off and thrown into a leather bottle full of human blood, mocking him in unwomanly fashion: 'I satisfy you,' she said, 'with the blood for which you thirsted, and of which for thirty years you have never had your fill.' ")

58-60. *Mostrava come . . . martiro*: Holofernes was the

general of the armies of Nebuchadnezzar, king of the Assyrians, and was slain by Judith. His pride resembles that of Sennacherib in that he attacked a city of the Israelites and hence offended their God, declaring that there was no god except Nebuchadnezzar (Iudith 6:2), while the besieged Israelites prayed in prostration before the Lord, as exhorted thereto by Judith, who pointed to the "superbia" of their enemies, the Assyrians. See Iudith 8:16-17:

> Et ideo humiliemus illi animas nostras, et in spiritu constituti humiliato, servientes illi, dicamus flentes Domino, ut secundum voluntatem suam sic faciat nobiscum misericordiam suam, ut sicut conturbatum est cor nostrum in superbia eorum, ita etiam de nostra humilitate gloriemur.

> And therefore let us humble our souls before him. And continuing in an humble spirit in his service.

> Let us ask the Lord with tears, that according to his will so he would shew his mercy to us: that as our heart is troubled by their pride, so also we may glorify in our humility.

See also Judith's prayer (Iudith 9:12): "Fac, Domine, ut gladio proprio eius superbia amputetur." ("Bring to pass, O Lord, that his pride may be cut off with his own sword.")

60. *le reliquie del martiro*: "Remnants of the slaying" would seem to refer to the body of Holofernes, whose head Judith had cut off, though "reliquie" may also include the booty left by the Assyrians and indeed the many Assyrians dead on the field. See Iudith 15:7: "Reliqui autem qui erant in Bethulia ingressi sunt castra Assyriorum; et praedam quam fugientes Assyrii reliquerant abstulerunt." ("And the rest that were in Bethulia went into the camp of the Assyrians, and took away the spoils, which the Assyrians in their flight had left behind them.") However, since this is an example of pride punished and the pride is Holofernes', his headless body would fittingly be part of the scene, his head having been carried back to Bethulia and placed on the walls of the city.

61–63. *Vedeva Troia . . . discerne*: Cf. *Inf.* I, 75: "poi che 'l superbo Ilión fu combusto"; also see *Inf.* XXX, 13-14: "E quando la fortuna volse in basso / l'altezza de' Troian che tutto ardiva." For the pride of Troy and the Trojans, see Virgil, *Aen.* III, 2-3: "Ceciditque superbum / Ilium et omnis humo fumat Neptunia Troia." ("Proud Ilium fell, and all Neptune's Troy smokes from the ground.")

This tercet closes the anaphora which began in vs. 25. The words "vedea," "o," and "mostrava," which each begin four consecutive tercets, also constitute the initial words of vss. 61, 62, and 63; allowing the *v* of "vedea" to be read as *u,* the initial letters of these three words form the acrostic VOM (UOM), "man." This is no doubt deliberate in the poet's design here, pointing emphatically to man in his lamentable pride, so strikingly exemplified in the carvings. The numerical pattern in this design is intended to be meaningful, for the numbers four, three, and twelve (plus one) are always meaningful in Dante's numerology. Four is the number of earth, of matter, of the heavy elemental world, of our flesh and our mortality. Three is the number of spirit.

61. *caverne*: The ruined houses and buildings, which without roofs appear as caverns.

63. *segno*: See preceding note.

64. *stile*: A style, either the sharp-pointed tool used in engraving or a kind of drawing pencil; or, simply a pencil or pen. Cf. *Par.* XXIV, 61.

65. *l'ombre*: "The masses."   *tratti*: "Lines."

66. *farieno = farebbero.*

68–69. *il vero, quant' io calcai*: I.e., the reality of all that which I trod upon (there in the carvings).

69. *givi*: Past absolute of *gire*. Cf. "audivi" in *Inf.* XXVI, 78. See E. G. Parodi (1957), p. 259.

70–72. *Or superbite . . . sentero*: This apostrophe to all proud Christians connects with *Purg.* X, 121-29. The tone is strongly sarcastic, with verbs in the imperative, "superbite" and the elliptical "via," i.e., "continue to go." For such a tone, see Virgil's words to Dante in *Inf.* XXX, 131: "Or pur mira."

70. *col viso altero*: Cf. the injunction to "turn down your eyes," in vs. 13.

71. *figliuoli d'Eva*: Eve was the first to sin in pride (Gen. 3:5-6). She was often opposed to Mary, in her humility, and the *Ave* spoken by Gabriel was read in reverse as *Eva*. Dante presents Mary as the first example of humility, in *Purg.* X, 34-45. The *Ottimo Commento* remarks: "E bene dice più proprio d'Eva, che d'Adamo, ch'ella disubbidì, come è scritto nel Genesi, terzo capitolo; ella fu prima travalicante il comandamento d'Iddio, volente essere simile a Dio." ("And he does well to say of Eve rather than of Adam, for she disobeyed, as it is written in the third chapter of Genesis. She was the first to trespass against God's commandment, wanting to be like God.")

72. *sentero = sentiero*.

73. *per noi = da noi*.

75. *l'animo non sciolto*: See *Purg.* IV, 1-16. Dante's mind was so absorbed in the floor-carvings that he was not "free" to pay attention to the passing of time.

76-77. *quando colui . . . andava*: Again we note that Virgil does not contemplate the works of art on this terrace, but continues to look ahead and be concerned about the way.

76. *innanzi*: I.e., "innanzi a noi."   *atteso*: See "attesi" in this sense in *Inf.* XIII, 109.

77. *Drizza la testa*: Cf. *Inf.* XX, 31.

78. *sospeso*: Absorbed in viewing the carvings.

80. *per venir verso noi*: This is the only guardian angel of Purgatory who comes to meet the wayfarers, and this, in view of the context, may be intended as a special gesture of humility.

80-81. *vedi che torna . . . sesta*: Dante would see this by looking at the sun. The hours were traditionally represented as goddesses in attendance upon the sun. See Ovid, *Metam.* II, 116-19:

> Quem petere ut terras mundumque rubescere vidit
> cornuaque extremae velut evanescere lunae,
> iungere equos Titan velocibus imperat Horis.
> iussa deae celeres peragunt . . .

> When Titan saw him setting and the world grow red, and the slender horns of the waning moon fading from sight, he bade the swift Hours to yoke his steeds. The goddesses quickly did his bidding . . .

Thus six hours of this second day on the mountain of Purgatory have passed: it is past noon. Dante and Virgil have spent about an hour in this circle (cf. *Purg.* X, 14-15), and, as Butler observes, "it will be found that of no other circle, except the 7th, does the passage occupy so short a time."

82. *addorna*: Imperative.

83. *i = gli*, i.e., the angel. "Lo 'nviarci in suso" is the subject of "diletti," subjunctive of *dilettare*.

86. *pur*: I.e., his *repeated* admonitions, as in *Inf.* XXIV, 52-57. Cf. *Purg.* III, 78.

87. *chiuso*: "Obscurely." Cf. *Par.* XI, 73, and compare the "obscure" poetry in Old Provençal written in the intentionally difficult style known as *trobar clus*.

88. *venìa = veniva*. See n. to vs. 80.

89. *biancovestito*: For angels robed in white, see *Purg.* II, 23; Matt. 28:3.

89-90. *e ne la faccia . . . stella*: Dante is able to gaze upon the face of this angel, as he was not able to do on that of another, *Purg.* II, 38-40.

91. *Le braccia aperse*: The angel had come forward to Dante, and now it welcomes him with open arms.

92. *qui son presso i gradi* = *qui presso sono i gradi.*

93. *agevolemente omai si sale*: I.e., now that you are purged of pride, the ascent will be easy.

94–96. *A questo invito . . . cadi?* Editors have been uncertain whether this tercet should be included in quotation marks. Does the angel speak these words, or does the poet? It seems best to understand, with Petrocchi, that they are spoken by the angel, since there is a special point in having it (winged creature that it is) speak of the human race as created to "fly upward" (a notion clearly reminiscent of the "angelic butterfly" image of *Purg.* X, 125-26).

94. *molto radi*: See Matt. 7:14: "Quam angusta porta et arcta via est quae ducit ad vitam, et pauci sunt qui inveniunt eam!" ("How narrow the gate and close the way that leads to life! And few there are who find it.") Also see Matt. 22:14: "Multi enim sunt vocati, pauci vero electi." ("For many are called, but few are chosen.")

96. *a poco vento*: At the slightest adversity.

97. *Menocci* = *ci menò.*

100–104. *Come a man destra . . . scalee*: The reference here is to the church of San Miniato al Monte, which dates mainly from the eleventh century and is situated on a hill, the Monte alle Croci, to the east of Florence beyond the Arno just above the bridge formerly known as the Rubaconte. The *Anonimo fiorentino* elaborates on "come a man destra": "Ciò è andando alla chiesa di santo Miniato a Monte, ch'è sopra il ponte Rubaconte, da Firenze dalla mano destra all'andare in su alla Chiesa, perchè la via è molto erta, si fece scaglioni di pietra per rompere la superba salita del monte." ("That is to say, going toward the church of San Miniato al Monte, which is above the Rubaconte bridge. On the right-hand side going from Florence to the church, steps of stone were built to break the hard ascent of the mountain, for the path up is very steep.") Villani (I, 57) comments: "Ma poi per lo comune di Firenze si compiè la detta chiesa, e si feciono le scalee de' macigni giù per la costa, e ordinaro sopra la detta opera di Santo Miniato i consoli dell'arte di Calimala, e che l'avessono in guardia." ("But then the commune of Florence had the church finished, and stone steps were built leading down the hill. The consuls of the Calimala guild were put in charge of the church of San Miniato, and they were to take care of it.")

100. *per salire al monte*: Cf. "gire al monte" in *Purg.* II, 60, and see the note to that verse.

102. *la ben guidata*: That is, "città," Florence. This is said in bitter irony.   *sopra Rubaconte*: Across and above the bridge known at one time as the Rubaconte. The Rubaconte was the old name for the bridge at Florence now known as the Ponte alle Grazie. Villani (VI, 26) records that it was built in 1237 and was named after the then *podestà*, during whose term of office also the streets of Florence were paved:

> Negli anni di Cristo 1237, essendo podestà di Firenze messer Rubaconte da Mandello da Milano, si fece in Firenze il ponte nuovo, e egli fondò con sua mano la prima pietra, e gittò la prima cesta di calcina; e per lo nome della detta podestà fu nomato il ponte *Rubaconte*. E alla sua signorìa si lastricarono tutte le vie di Firenze, che prima ce n'avea poche lastricate; se non in certi singulari luoghi, e mastre strade lastricate di mattoni; per lo quale acconcio e lavorio la cittade di Firenze divenne più netta, e più bella, e più sana.

> In the year of Christ 1237, while Messer Rubaconte da Mandello of Milan was *podestà* of Florence, the new bridge was built in Florence. He laid the first stone with his own hand and threw in the first hod of mortar. And the bridge was named Rubaconte after him. During his tenure all the streets in Florence were paved. Before that time, only a few of the streets were paved, except in certain particular neighborhoods and except for the main roads, which were paved with bricks. These repairs and this work made the city of Florence cleaner, more beautiful, and more healthy.

103. *si rompe*: Is made easier to climb.

104. *fero = fecero*.

104-5. *ad etade ch'era sicuro il quaderno*: This is an allusion to an incident involving one Niccola Acciaiuoli, a Florentine Guelph who, in 1299, together with Baldo d'Aguglione (*Par.* XVI, 56), in order to destroy the evidence of a fraudulent transaction in which, with the connivance of the *podestà*, he had been engaged, defaced a sheet of the public records of Florence. This scandal took place during the period of corruption and maladministration which followed the expulsion of Giano della Bella from Florence.

The following account of the incident, which appears to have been unknown to Benvenuto, is given by the *Anonimo fiorentino*:

Nel M.CC.LXXXXV., doppo la cacciata di Gian da la Bella, essendo Firenze in male stato, fu chiamato rettore di Firenze, a petizione di quelli che reggevono, uno povero gentile uomo chiamato messer Monfiorito della Marca Trivigiana, il quale prese la forma della terra, et assolvea et condennava sanza ragione, et palesemente per lui et sua famiglia si vendea la giustizia. Nol sostennono i cittadini, et compiuto l'ufficio, presono lui et due suoi famigli, et lui missono alla colla, et per sua confessione si seppono cose che a molti cittadini ne seguì grande infamia; et faccendolo collare due cittadini chiamati sopra a ciò, l'uno dicea *basta*, l'altro dicea *no*. Piero Manzuoli cambiatore, chiamato sopra ciò, disse: *Dàgli ancora uno crollo*; e 'l cavalieri ch'era in sulla colla disse: *Io rende' uno testimonio falso a messer Niccola Acciajoli, il quale non condannai*; non volea il Manzuolo che quella confessione fosse scritta, però che messer Niccola era suo genero; l'altro pure volle, et scrissesi; et saputo messer Niccola questo fatto, ebbe sì gran paura che il fatto non si palesasse, ch'egli se ne consigliò con messer Baldo Agulione, pessimo giudice ghibellino antico. Chiesono il quaderno degli atti al notajo, et ebborlo; et il foglio dov'era il fatto di messer

Niccola trassono del quaderno: et palesandosi per lo
notajo del foglio ch'era tratto, fu consigliato che si cer-
casse di chi l'avea fatto; onde il Podestà, non palesando
niente, prese messer Niccola, et messer Baldo fuggì.
Fu condennato messer Niccola in libre iij.ᵐ, et messer
Baldo in .ij.ᵐ et a' confini fuori della città, et del con-
tado per uno anno.

In the year 1295, after the expulsion of Giano della
Bella, Florence was in a bad state. By order of those
who governed, a poor gentleman named Messer Mon-
fiorito della Marca Trivigiana was called in as rector of
Florence. He took over the legal control of the city and
absolved and condemned people without reason; jus-
tice was openly sold by him and his staff. The citizens
did not tolerate this: when his term was over, he and
two of his staff were taken and put to the rope [i.e., tied
up and flogged with a rope's end]. His confession re-
vealed things that brought great shame to many citizens.
Of two citizens summoned, who were being tortured
in the interrogation, one kept saying "enough," and the
other kept saying "no." Piero Manzuoli, a money chang-
er, who was one of those in charge, said: "Give him
another taste of it." And the knight being tortured said:
"I rendered a false judgment when I did not condemn
Messer Niccola Acciaiuoli." Manzuoli did not want this
confession written down, because Messer Niccola was
his son-in-law. But the other man did, and so it was
written down. When Messer Niccola heard about it, he
was so terribly afraid the story would spread that he
went to get the advice of Baldo d'Aguglione, an elderly
and very bad Ghibelline judge.

They asked the notary for the notebook, and got it.
Then they tore out the page that contained the matter
concerning Messer Niccola. When the notary noticed
that the page was missing, it was advised that those re-
sponsible should be sought. Whereupon the *podestà,*
without saying anything, went and arrested Messer Nic-
cola, but Messer Baldo escaped. Messer Niccola was

condemned to pay a fine of three hundred lire; and
Messer Baldo condemned to pay two hundred lire, and
to a year's confinement outside the borders of the city
and its countryside.

Villani makes no mention of this incident, possibly because
the Acciaiuoli were Guelphs like himself. It is, however, re-
corded at length in the *Cronica* of Dino Compagni (I, 19),
whose account is substantially the same as that given above;
he adds that the corrupt *podestà,* whom he calls "messer
Monfiorito da Padova," was not only flogged but imprisoned
by the Florentines, who refused to release him in spite of
repeated applications from the Paduans. He finally effected
his escape by the help of the wife of one of the Arrigucci.
See A. Vital (1918).

105. *la doga*: A reference to a fraud perpetrated by a mem-
ber of the Chiaramontesi family, a certain Durante (or Do-
nato) de' Chiaramontesi who, when overseer of the salt
customs in Florence, used to receive the salt in a measure
of the legal capacity, but distributed it in a measure of small-
er capacity from which a stave had been withdrawn, and thus
made a large profit on the difference. The *Ottimo Commento*
says: "Essendo un ser Durante de' Chermontesi Doganieri
e Camarlingo della Camera del sale del Comune di Firenze,
trasse il detto ser Durante una doga dello staio, applicando
a sè tutto il sale, ovvero pecunia che di detto avanzamento
perveniva." ("Ser Durante de' Chiaramontesi was the cus-
toms agent and chamberlain of the salt chamber of the com-
mune of Florence. He took a stave off the bushel and then
would keep the salt or the money that he would have left
over.") The *Anonimo fiorentino* provides the following
account:

> Era usanza di mensurare il sale et altre cose con stara
> fatte a doghe di legname, come bigonciuoli; un cittadino
> della famiglia de' Chiaramontesi fu camerlingo a dare
> il sale; appresso questi, quando il ricevea dal comune,
> il riceveva collo stajo diritto; quando il dava al popolo
> ne trasse una doga picciola dello stajo, onde grossa-
> mente ne venia a guadagnare. Scopersesi il fatto; et

saputa la verità, questo cittadino fu condennato et
gravemente et vituperevolmente, onde poi i discendenti
suoi, che sono antichi uomini, essendo loro ricordato
arrossono et vergognonsi; et fessi di ciò in lor vergogna
una canzoncella che dicea: *Egli è tratta una doga del
sale, Et gli uffici son tutti salviati* ec.

It was customary to measure salt and other things in
bushels made of wooden staves, like buckets. A citizen
of the Chiaramontesi family was overseer of the salt.
When he received it from the commune, he would use
the right bushel, but when he passed it on to the peo-
ple, he removed a small stave from the bushel, so that
he made a great profit. This was discovered; and when
the truth was known, this citizen was punished severely,
to his disgrace. His descendants, who are an ancient
family, blush and are ashamed when they are reminded
of this. A ditty was composed, to their shame, and it
goes: "A stave has been taken off the salt, and the
offices are all saved" etc.

Benvenuto in his gloss on *Par.* XVI, 105 states that the cul-
prit was beheaded, and that to prevent similar frauds it was
ordained that for the future the measure should be of iron.
  Neither Villani nor Dino Compagni makes mention of
this particular fraud, which by Lana (see his n. on *Par.* XVI,
105), and one or two of the other early commentators, is
laid at the door, not of the Chiaramontesi, but of the
Tosinghi, who are said to have cheated in the distribution
not of salt, but of grain. The family is again referred to in
Par. XVI, 105, as "quei ch'arrossan per lo staio."

106. *così*: I.e., with such steps.   *la ripa che cade*: See
Purg. X, 23.

107. *ratta = rapida*, "steep."

108. *ma*: Although the steps make the bank easier to
ascend, the passage is narrow, like the one before (*Purg.* X,
7-9), so that the rock "presses close" on either side anyone
who climbs through it. See n. to vs. 94.

109. *Noi volgendo ivi le nostre persone*: This construction amounts to a kind of ablative absolute. Dante and Virgil have been moving counterclockwise, or to the right, around the terrace, and now turn to their left into the passageway.

110. *Beati pauperes spiritu*: This is the first of the beatitudes of the Sermon on the Mount (Matt. 5:3) and the antithesis of pride, which is the first of all sins, referred to as the "initium omnis peccati" in Ecclus. 10:15. See Augustine, *De sermone Domini in monte* I, i, 3:

> Quapropter recto hic intelliguntur *pauperes spiritu,* humiles et timentes Deum, id est, non habentes inflantem spiritum. Nec aliunde omnino incipere oportuit beatitudinem; siquidem perventura est ad summam sapientiam: *Initium autem sapientiae timor Domini (Eccli.* I, 16); quoniam et e contrario, *Initium omnis peccati superbia inscribitur* (Id. X, 15). Superbi ergo appetant et diligant regna terrarum: *Beati* autem *pauperes spiritu, quoniam ipsorum est regnum coelorum.*

> Here, therefore, the poor in spirit are rightly understood as the humble and the God-fearing—that is to say, those who do not have an inflated spirit. And it would be entirely unfitting for blessedness to take its beginning from any other source, since it is to reach the summit of wisdom, for "the beginning of wisdom is the fear of the Lord" [Ecclus. 1:16; Ps. 110(111):10], and on the other hand, pride is described as "the beginning of all sin" [Ecclus. 10:15]. Let the proud, therefore, strive after the kingdoms of the earth, and love them. But, *"Blessed are the poor in spirit, for theirs is the kingdom of heaven."*

This beatitude is thus most appropriate as the first of what will prove to be a series of seven, each of which is pronounced by an angel as the wayfarers leave a given circle. On the significance of the beatitudes as expressions of the virtues, see Thomas Aquinas, *Summa theol.* I-II, q. 69, a. 3, resp.

110-11. *voci cantaron*: Since in every other instance it is one angel only who pronounces the beatitude appropriate to the exit from a given circle, it is thought by most commentators that the angel here must sing "Beati pauperes spiritu," in which case the plural "voci" would be, as F. D'Ovidio (1906, p. 276) observes, "un plurale meramente stilistico" ("a merely stylistic plural") or, as Torraca comments, "il plurale pare che alluda a canto variamente modulato." ("The plural seems to allude to a song with various modulations.")

111. *diria = direbbe.*

112. *foci*: "Entrances," "passageways." Cf. *Inf.* XXIII, 129.

114. *per lamenti feroci*: See similar expressions in *Inf.* III, 22; IV, 26; and elsewhere throughout the *Inferno*.

115. *li scaglion*: The steps of the passageway.   *santi*: "Holy," since they lead upward to righteousness.

116. *troppo = molto.*

117. *lo pian*: The *piano* (*Purg.* X, 20) of the first terrace, which Dante has just left.   *davanti = dianzi.*

120. *per me = da me.*

121–26. *Quando i P . . . pinti*: We now understand from Virgil's explanation how the P's which were inscribed on Dante's forehead (*Purg.* IX, 112-14) will be removed (note vss. 134-35 below). In a token sort of way, Dante has now purged himself of pride, and the removal of the P registers that fact. Moreover, with the phrase "presso che stinti," said of the remaining P's, it is clearly suggested that the purging of pride, which is the beginning of all sin (see Ecclus. 10:15) and the deepest wound, has made the other wounds less burdensome, fainter. See Thomas Aquinas, *Summa theol.* II-II, q. 162, a. 7, resp.: "Et inde est quod superbia habet rationem primi peccati, et est etiam principium omnium peccatorum." ("Hence it is that pride fulfils the conditions of the first sin, and is *the beginning of all sins.*") Also see *Summa theol.* II-II, q. 162, a. 7, ad 4:

Et ideo superbia causat gravitatem aliorum peccatorum. Contingit ergo ante superbiam esse aliqua peccata leviora, quae etiam ex ignorantia vel infirmitate committuntur. Sed inter graviora peccata primum est superbia, sicut causa, per quam alia peccata aggravantur.

Hence pride is the cause of gravity in other sins. Accordingly previous to pride there may be certain less grievous sins that are committed through ignorance or weakness. But among the grievous sins the first is pride, as the cause whereby other sins are rendered more grievous.

124. *fier* = *saranno*.

126. *ma fia diletto loro esser sù pinti*: For this feature, see the explanation in *Purg.* IV, 88-96.   *fia* = *sarà*.

129. *cenni*: Such as gestures, smiles.   *altrui*: The possessive.   *sospecciar* = *sospettare*. Cf. *Inf.* X, 57.

133. *e con le dita de la destra scempie*: "Scempie" may mean "outspread," although this is not certain. Sapegno approves of Buti's comment, which is: "co le dita de la mano ritta, semplice sensa altro aiuto" ("with the fingers of his right hand, simply, without any other help").

134. *pur*: "Only."

135. *quel da le chiavi*: The angel at the gate of Purgatory, *Purg.* IX, 78.

CANTO XIII

1. *al sommo de la scala*: Dante and Virgil have come to the topmost step of the stairway and stand facing the wall of the bank of the second terrace.

2. *si risega*: "Is cut back" or "is sliced" to form another terrace.

3. *salendo altrui dismala*: "Salendo" is to be understood as a participle with the indefinite pronoun "altrui" as its implied subject; "altrui" in turn becomes the object of "dismala." The meaning is that the ascent of the mountain purifies, cleanses of evil, whosoever ascends it. *Dismalare* seems to be a verb coined by Dante (see E. G. Parodi, 1957, pp. 215, 266).

4. *lega*: The terrace "binds," as if it were a belt around the mountain.

5. *primaia*: An archaic form of *prima*. Cf. *Inf.* V, 1 and *passim*.

6. *l'arco suo più tosto piega*: Since the mountain is cone-shaped, each successive terrace in the ascent is smaller in circumference than the preceding, and so it is said that "its curve bends more sharply."

7-9. *Ombra non . . . petraia*: These verses focus upon the absence of what Dante at once came upon when he entered upon the first terrace: though seemingly deserted, that terrace showed first a bank of white marble with the carvings we know and then later the "tomb" carvings in its floor, in connection with which the terms *ombra* (*Purg.* XII, 65) and *segno* (*Purg.* XII, 47) were used. Accordingly "ombra" here does not seem to mean "shade" (i.e., soul), but "figure," even as "segno" means "image." Thus the verses focus on the "ripa" and the "via schietta" as not containing what the *ripa* and the *via* of the first terrace contained. Here only the livid color of the stone is seen, and in such a focus "livido" stands out the more by way of the absence of all else and anticipates (since it is envy's color) what is to be found on this second cornice.

7. *li = vi*. Petrocchi interprets this "li" as a "lì," but the emphatic adverb seems out of place in this position and in the rhythm of the verse. The choice is entirely an editor's in this case.   *si paia*: "Si" here is the familiar pleonastic reflexive, which is twice repeated in the next verse, in its common function of distancing, distinguishing, or setting off the subject. See n. to *Inf.* VII, 94.

8. *parsi = si pare.   schietta*: "Smooth." Neither the bank nor the roadbed contains carvings on its surface, as on the first terrace. Cf. *Inf.* XIII, 4-6; see "schietto" in *Purg.* I, 95.

9. *col livido color de la petraia*: Torraca comments: "La prima cornice (*Purg.* X, 31) era 'di marmo candido'! La voce dà rilievo a *livido*, s'indugia e fa uno sforzo a *petraia* —propriamente massa di pietre—che qui pare un dispregiativo." ("The first cornice [*Purg.* X, 31] was 'of white marble.' The voice sets off 'livido,' to emphasize, then makes an effort with 'petraia'—properly speaking, a mass of stones, which here sounds pejorative.") For "livid" as envy's color, see *Purg.* XIV, 84.

10-12. *Se qui per dimandar . . . eletta*: Virgil concludes

that no souls move about on this terrace, a fact which is soon to be confirmed.

12. *eletta*: The "choice" between proceeding to the right or to the left in order to reach the next stairway. As he says this, Virgil is still facing the bank at the top of the stairs.

13. *li occhi porse*: Cf. *Inf.* XVII, 52.

14-15. *fece del destro lato . . . torse*: Virgil, as he stands at the head of the stairs and faces the bank of the terrace, is facing west or southwest. It is now a little after noon, and the sun, which is in the north, is to Virgil's right. Then Virgil and Dante proceed in what is the proper direction in Purgatory, around to the right or counterclockwise, which, in this segment of the circling way at least, means that they go toward the sun. Its rays are therefore guides to them, as Virgil prays they may be.

16. *a cui fidanza = fidandomi del quale.*

17. *ne conduci = ci conduci* (imperative).

18. *si vuol*: "As is needful."   *quinc' entro*: On this terrace.

19. *Tu . . . tu*: The repetition sustains the tone of praise.

20. *ponta*: "Press." Petrocchi grants that "pronta" ("prompt") here, as allowed by other editors, is possible.

21. *dien* (pronounced *dièn*) = *devono.*

22. *di qua*: In the world of the living.   *migliaio = miglio.* In Latin *miliarium* denotes a milestone, i.e., a stone that marks the distance of a thousand paces; it was also used for the number one thousand. "Migliaio" counts as two syllables in this verse. Cf. "primaio" in *Purg.* XIV, 66.

26. *spiriti*: These spirits are not further explained, and since they are invisible to the shades, as we come to understand, even if they are visible to the visitors, they remain simply voices. As will become clear, the voices declare the examples of charity, the virtue which opposes the vice of envy.

26–27. *parlando a la mensa . . . inviti*: The normal word order would be "parlando cortesi inviti a la mensa d'amore." The metaphor anticipates the "vinum non habent" ("They have no wine," Ioan. 2:3) of Mary's words at the table, as it were, of the wedding feast of Cana, the first example of charity.

29. *Vinum non habent*: The first example of charity is represented by the words of loving solicitude which Mary addressed to Jesus at the feast of Cana. See Ioan. 2:1-7:

Et die tertia nuptiae factae sunt in Cana Galilaeae, et erat mater Iesu ibi. Vocatus est autem et Iesus et discipuli eius ad nuptias. Et deficiente vino, dicit mater Iesu ad eum: Vinum non habent. Et dicit ei Iesus: Quid mihi et tibi est, mulier? Nondum venit hora mea. Dicit mater eius ministris: Quodcumque dixerit vobis, facite.

Erant autem ibi lapideae hydriae sex positae secundum purificationem Iudaeorum, capientes singulae metretas binas vel ternas. Dicit eis Iesus: Implete hydrias aqua. Et impleverunt eas usque ad summum.

And on the third day a marriage took place at Cana of Galilee, and the mother of Jesus was there. Now Jesus too was invited to the marriage, and also his disciples. And the wine having run short, the mother of Jesus said to him, "They have no wine." And Jesus said to her, "What wouldst thou have me do, woman? My hour has not yet come." His mother said to the attendants, "Do whatever he tells you."

Now six stone water-jars were placed there, after the Jewish manner of purification, each holding two or three measures. Jesus said to them, "Fill the jars with water." And they filled them to the brim.

Whereupon Jesus turned the water to wine.

30. *e dietro a noi l'andò reiterando*: Apparently the "spiriti" fly round the circle in a clockwise direction, since they come toward the wayfarers here; the reiteration of the utterance behind them suggests that the voice continues to utter the words all the way round the terrace, as do the other voices.

It is not clear that any symbolic meaning is intended in this reversal of the correct direction for movement in Purgatory; the voices that declare the examples of envy will also move in this same "reversed" direction (see *Purg.* XIV, 132).

32. *Oreste*: When Orestes, the son of Agamemnon and Clytemnestra, was in danger of being slain for having avenged the murder of his father, his friend Pylades pretended that he was Orestes in order to save his life. Orestes, however, would not allow Pylades to risk his life for him and persisted in declaring who he was. Dante perhaps derived his knowledge of the incident, which he uses as the second example of charity, from the allusion of Cicero in the *De amicitia* (VII, 24) to a scene from the play of Pacuvius on the subject. See also Cicero, *De fin.* I, xx, 65; V, xxii, 63; Ovid, *Ex Ponto* III, ii, 69-96.

33. *anco non = neanche.   anco non s'affisse*: Neither did this voice stop.

36. *Amate da cui male aveste*: The word *coloro* is understood as the object of the verb "amate": "amate coloro da cui male aveste." By summarizing the familiar text in these few words, this voice would remind the envious of Christ's words enjoining charity. See Matt. 5:43-48:

> Audistis quia dictum est: Diliges proximum tuum, et odio habebis inimicum tuum. Ego autem dico vobis: Diligite inimicos vestros, benefacite his qui oderunt vos, et orate pro persequentibus et calumniantibus vos; ut sitis filii Patris vestri qui in caelis est, qui solem suum oriri facit super bonos et malos, et pluit super iustos et iniustos. Si enim diligitis eos qui vos diligunt, quam mercedem habebitis? nonne et publicani hoc faciunt? Et si salutaveritis fratres vestros tantum, quid amplius facitis? nonne et ethnici hoc faciunt? Estote ergo vos perfecti, sicut et Pater vester caelestis perfectus est.

> You have heard that it was said, "Thou shalt love thy neighbor, and shalt hate thy enemy." But I say to you, love your enemies, do good to those who hate you, and pray for those who persecute and calumniate you, so

that you may be children of your Father in heaven, who makes his sun to rise on the good and the evil, and sends rain on the just and the unjust. For if you love those that love you, what reward shall you have? Do not even the publicans do that? And if you salute your brethren only, what are you doing more than others? Do not even the Gentiles do that?

You therefore are to be perfect, even as your heavenly Father is perfect.

37. *Questo cinghio*: This second terrace. Cf. "cinghio" used in *Purg.* IV, 51. *sferza*: "Punishes," literally "lashes."

38. *però = perciò.*

38–40. *però sono tratte . . . sono*: The scourge, which goads the sinners toward the virtue that opposes envy, is made up of three thongs, three examples of love, of charity. The curb, which deters the sinners from envy and is opposed in its function to the scourge, is comprised of examples of envy and must be of a "contrary sound." Following the pattern established on the first terrace, these examples will be heard later, as Virgil surmises.

39. *ferza = sferza.*

40. *Lo fren = il freno.* *vuol esser*: "Needs must be."

42. *giunghi = giunga.* *al passo del perdono*: At the entrance to the way up to the next circle, where the angel will erase another P.

45. *la grotta*: The bank of the terrace. Cf. *Purg.* I, 48.

46. *li occhi apersi*: Cf. *Purg.* IX, 79.

47–48. *con manti . . . non diversi*: The envious wear cloaks that are of the color of envy, even as is the stone on and against which they sit. For this reason it is more difficult to make them out, hence Virgil's urging Dante to "direct your sight steadily."

50. *udia = udiva (udivo).*

50–51. *udia gridar . . . "Tutti santi"*: These souls seem to be reciting the Litany of the Saints, which begins with "Kyrie eleison," passes to "Sancta Maria, ora pro nobis" (Mary is invoked thrice), then to "Sancte Michael," on to "Sancte Petre" among other angels and saints, and eventually to "Omnes Sancti."

52. *per terra*: Among the living.   *ancoi*: From the Latin *hanc hodie*, "this very day." See E. G. Parodi (1957), pp. 261, 289. Dante uses "ancoi" only twice elsewhere (*Purg.* XX, 70; XXXIII, 96) and always in rhyme.

56. *li atti loro*: Their demeanor and condition.   *certi*: "Clear." Cf. *Inf.* VIII, 71.

57. *per li occhi fui di grave dolor munto*: Dante weeps for compassion, but this may also be seen as his token participation in the purgatorial punishment of this terrace.   *munto*: Past participle of *mungere*, "to milk." For this verb and the notion of milking tears as a punishment, see *Inf.* XII, 135-36.

58. *ciliccio*: Haircloth, made of horsehair, as Buti explains: "Si fa di setole di cavallo annodate; li quali nodi pungeno continuamente la carne, ed è freddissimo a tenere in dosso: imperò che è fatto a mallie come la rete." ("It is made of knotted horsehair, and the knots prick the skin continuously. It is a very cold thing to wear, because it is knit like a net.")

59. *sofferia = sofferiva*, "was holding up."

60. *sofferti*: The souls lean back against the bank, along the base of which they sit (vs. 45) in single file.

61. *a cui la roba falla*: "To whom sustenance is lacking." Cf. *Inf.* XXIV, 7.   *falla*: Cf. *Purg.* X, 129.

62. *stanno a' perdoni a chieder lor bisogna*: In Dante's time it was a familiar sight to see the blind begging at churches and shrines on the days when crowds gathered for special indulgences (pardons) granted to the faithful. Fairs, also

attracting many people, were held in these places on those occasions. *perdoni*: Cf. the French *pardon*.

63. *avvalla*: Cf. *Purg.* VI, 37.

64. *altrui*: Possessive. *si pogna = si ponga*.

66. *la vista*: "The sight," but especially the expression on the face, with the sightless eyes. *agogna*: Cf. *Inf.* VI, 28.

67. *li orbi*: *Orbo* is a synonym of *cieco*, "blind." Cf. the Latin *orbus*, "deprived." *non approda*: Literally, "does not arrive." "Approda" is from *approdare* ("to arrive at the shore"), based on *proda*, "shore." Thus even as the sun is "denied" to the blind among the living, so is the light of Heaven denied to these blinded souls in Purgatory. It is possible to understand "approda" as a form of *approdare* (from *prode*, deriving from the Latin *prodesse*), meaning *giovare*, "to help," "to please," but such a meaning does not fit the simile so well. The early commentators are divided in the matter, some holding for one meaning and some for the other.

69. *luce del ciel*: This is ambiguous, "ciel" having both a physical sense (the heavens) and a spiritual sense (Heaven), but the spiritual meaning of the phrase (God's light shed from Heaven) is the dominant one. *di sé largir*: "To give generously of itself."

70–72. *un fil di ferro . . . dimora*: The reference is to falcons that were taken in the woods when already grown and were therefore harder to domesticate. Their eyelids were stitched shut (were *cigliati*, as the sewing shut was termed) to force them to be quiet in the presence of their trainers. A wire, of course, would be more painful than a thread. The falcon's eyes were sewn with thread, not with wire.

71. *come a sparvier selvaggio*: Cf. "sparvier grifagno" in *Inf.* XXII, 139.

73–74. *A me pareva . . . veduto*: Dante's compassion and solicitude at this point, his empathy, is notable as a feeling that is the opposite of envy.

75. *per ch'io mi volsi al mio consiglio saggio*: Dante turns to Virgil to ask his permission to speak with the souls. *consiglio = consigliere*.

76. *lo muto*: Dante, who does not speak.

77. *però = per ciò*.

78. *sie = sia.   arguto*: "Clear," "precise." It is particularly important that Dante speak clearly since these souls are blind and must depend entirely on the spoken word for communication.

79. *venìa = veniva*. The verb suggests that Dante is now a little ahead of Virgil.

79-80. *da quella banda . . . si puote*: On Dante's right or toward the outside rim of the terrace, over which one could fall. Thus Virgil has taken a position that would protect his living charge, even as he did in Inferno, when he placed himself between Dante and Geryon's dangerous tail (*Inf*. XVII, 83-84).

81. *da nulla sponda s'inghirlanda*: The terrace is not "crowned," i.e., girded, by any parapet along its outer edge.

82. *da l'altra parte*: Along the bank, on Dante's left.

82-83. *le divote ombre*: The shades show their devoutness by reciting the Litany of the Saints and by submitting so patiently to the purgation of their stain of envy.

83-84. *per l'orribile costura premevan sì*: *Le lagrime* is understood as the object of "premevan." They are said to squeeze out their tears between their sewn eyelids.

83. *costura*: I.e., *cucitura*.

85. *Volsimi = mi volsi*.

85-87. *O gente sicura . . . cura*: A clear instance of *captatio benevolentiae* (see n. to *Inf*. II, 58-60), affirming that these souls, to whom now "the light of Heaven wills to deny its bounty" (vs. 69), shall one day see the high sun of the Empyrean and the light of glory which streams forth from God and makes it possible for the creature to see Him "face to face." This only do these souls now desire, the light of that sun; and in penance now they willingly endure privation of the light of the sun in the physical sense.

88-90. *se tosto grazia . . . il fiume*: The familiar hortatory formula, adjuring by that which is most dear or most desired (cf. *Inf.* X, 82 and *passim*), which is here stated as the completion of purgation for these souls. Envy has left a scum on their minds, over their mental vision, a residue resulting from sin, which is elsewhere referred to as "note" (*Purg.* XI, 34) or as a "scoglio" to be put off (*Purg.* II, 122). Envy is a spiritual blindness. This metaphor suggests purification, clarification of vision, by grace; even so, it is a rather curious figure.

91. *fia = sarà.*   *grazioso = gradito.*

92. *latina = italiana.* Cf. *Inf.* XXII, 65 and *passim.*

93. *lei = a lei* (i.e., to the "anima," feminine).   *lei sarà buon s'i' l'apparo*: Cf. *Purg.* XII, 5. It will be well for such a soul, since Dante, on returning to Italy, can ask the living there to pray for this soul in Purgatory and thus hasten its purgation.   *l'apparo = l'apprendo.* See *Rime* L, 25.

94-96. *O frate mio . . . peregrina*: One notes a striking change of outlook on the part of souls, as registered by this reaction to Dante's question. These souls, being already elect and inside the gate of Purgatory proper now, have their conversation in Heaven and no longer indulge in those lingering attachments to the world of the living that were characteristic of souls in Antepurgatory, outside the gate, who were as pilgrims. See C. S. Singleton (1965).

95. *una vera città*: The City of God. Cf. *Inf.* I, 126. See Eph. 2:17-22:

> Et veniens evangelizavit pacem vobis qui longe fuistis, et pacem iis qui prope; quoniam per ipsum habemus accessum ambo in uno Spiritu ad Patrem.

Ergo iam non estis hospites et advenae, sed estis
cives sanctorum et domestici Dei, superaedificati super
fundamentum apostolorum et prophetarum, ipso sum-
mo angulari lapide Christo Iesu; in quo omnis aedifi-
catio constructa crescit in templum sanctum in Domino,
in quo et vos coaedificamini in habitaculum Dei in
Spiritu.

And coming, he announced the good tidings of peace
to you who were afar off, and of peace to those who
were near, because through him we both have access in
one Spirit to the Father. Therefore, you are now no
longer strangers and foreigners, but you are citizens
with the saints and members of God's household: you
are built upon the foundation of the apostles and
prophets with Christ Jesus himself as the chief corner
stone. In him the whole structure is closely fitted to-
gether and grows into a temple holy in the Lord, in him
you too are being built together into a dwelling place for
God in the Spirit.

96. *peregrina*: See n. to *Purg.* II, 63 and Heb. 11:13-16.

99. *ond' io mi feci ancor più là sentire*: Dante now moves
on toward the soul that has spoken and thus makes himself
heard, i.e., makes his steps heard on the stone floor of the
terrace. The particular turn of phrase keeps the blindness of
the souls in mind, "feels" with them, since only by hearing
Dante come forward can they know of his approach.

100–101. *aspettava in vista*: "Was expectant in its look,"
an image that is rendered especially graphic by the following
verse, "lo mento a guisa d'orbo in sù levava." As Buti notes,
"cotale atto fanno li cechi, quando aspettano." ("That is
what blind men do when they are waiting for something.")

101. *se volesse alcun dir "Come?"* On this phrase and simi-
lar postulations of a question from some imagined interlocu-
tor, see M. Barbi (1934b), pp. 248-49.

103. *ti dome = ti domi*. The verb connects with the image
of the falcon, which is *domato* ("domesticated") by the cruel

means referred to in vss. 70-72. See "doma" in *Purg.* XI, 53.

105. *conto = cognito.* *o per luogo*: I.e., by your place of origin. The soul accordingly begins: "Io fui sanese."

107. *rimendo*: Petrocchi has "rimendo" ("I mend"); other editors have "rimondo" ("I purge," "I cleanse").

108. *lagrimando a colui che sé ne presti*: Supplicating God with tears of contrition that He manifest (show, give) Himself to us. Porena notes that "sé ne presti" is the Latin *praestet se nobis.* Cf. "di sé largir," vs. 69, and the "Light above" which is all that these souls desire to see (vss. 86-87). *ne = ci.*

109. *Savia . . . Sapìa*: The soul who speaks is indulging in a customary play on the etymology (apparent etymology at least) of names that is expressed in the dictum "nomina sunt consequentia rerum" ("names are the consequences of things") mentioned by Dante in *Vita nuova* XIII, 4. On the medieval predilection for such conceits, see E. G. Parodi (1957), pp. 388-90. See also *Vita nuova* XXIV, 4, where "Primavera" is construed as "prima verrà," thus showing the same indifference to accent as in "savia" and "Sapìa."
Sapìa: Sienese lady of the Salvani family, aunt of Provenzan Salvani, and wife of Ghinibaldo Saracini. Born *ca.* 1210, she was married *ca.* 1230 and became the mother of five children. At the time of the battle of Colle (June 17, 1269), to which she refers in vss. 115-19, she was a widow (her husband having died in 1268), living possibly at the family castle of Castiglioncello, close to the plain on which the battle of Colle was fought. Sapia was still living in 1274, as witnessed by a document of that year in which she made a donation to a hospital founded by her and her husband in 1265. Her death must have preceded that of Pier Pettinaio, whom she mentions in vss. 127-29 as having prayed for her and who died in 1289. See A. Lisini (1920); I. Sanesi (1923).

110-11. *de li altrui . . . mia*: In *Purg.* XVII, 118-20, envy is defined as chagrin at the good fortune of others. Here

Dante apparently turns the matter around, in having Sapia say that she rejoiced more at the misfortunes of others than at her own good fortune.

112. *E perché tu non creda ch'io t'inganni*: This amounts to saying "and to prove it to you."

113. *folle*: Here, as elsewhere in the poem, the term implies hubris. Cf. Ulysses' "folle volo" (*Inf.* XXVI, 125).

114. *già discendendo l'arco d'i miei anni*: Sapia means by this that she was well past the "mezzo del cammin di nostra vita," i.e., the age of thirty-five. She was, in fact, about sixty (see n. to vs. 109) and thus had reached a time when one should turn one's thoughts to God. See *Inf.* XXVII, 79-81. Ulysses and his companions were also old when they dared to sail into the unknown (*Inf.* XXVI, 106-7). On the "arco de la vita," see *Conv.* IV, xxiii, 6-11.

115. *Colle*: Town (modern Colle di Val d'Elsa) in Tuscany, in the Val d'Elsa, situated on a hill near San Gimignano, on the left bank of the Elsa, about fourteen miles northwest of Siena. It was the scene of a battle (June 17, 1269) in which the Sienese Ghibellines, with a mixed force of Germans and Spaniards, under Provenzan Salvani and Count Guido Novello, were defeated by the Florentine Guelphs with the help of some of the French troops of Charles of Anjou.

117. *e io pregava Iddio di quel ch'e' volle*: The Sienese suffered defeat in this battle because it was God's will, not because God granted Sapia's "envious" prayer that this should happen.

118. *fuor = furono*.

119. *veggendo la caccia*: Since Sapia's husband was lord of Castiglioncello, near Montereggioni (see n. to vs. 109), Sapia may have been at this castle when the rout took place and could actually have witnessed some part of it.

120. *letizia presi a tutte altre dispari*: Sapia's joy shows clearly how "folle" she was, rejoicing at the disastrous defeat

of her fellow-citizens in this battle, in which her own nephew, Provenzan Salvani, was slain.

122. *Omai più non ti temo*: Porena paraphrases this as follows: "Ho avuto tale gioia, che non m'importerà nulla di qualunque male tu possa mandarmi." ("I have known such joy that I don't care what you do to me.")

123. *come fé 'l merlo*: Buti comments:

Questo è uno uccello che teme molto lo freddo, e mal tempo, e quando è mal tempo sta appiattato; e come ritorna lo bono tempo, esce fuora e par che faccia beffe di tutti li altri, come si finge che dicesse ne la faula di lui composta; cioè: "Non ti temo, Domine, che uscito son del verno."

This bird is very afraid of the cold and of bad weather. When the weather is bad, it goes into hiding; then, when fair weather returns, it comes forth and seems to make fun of every other bird. As in the fable about this bird, it is made to say: "I do not fear you, Lord, for winter's over!"

See Sacchetti, *novella* CXLIX.   *per poca bonaccia*: At the slightest sign of good weather. See G. Agnelli (1895).

124–29. *Pace volli . . . increbbe*: Sapia repented only at the end of her life; and, for having waited so long, she would have been confined in Antepurgatory and would still be there with Belacqua and the others who similarly put off repentance to the end had Pier Pettinaio not prayed so effectively for her.

125–26. *e ancor non sarebbe . . . scemo*: I.e., even by serving out the time equal to her life, as the other negligent in this respect (see *Purg.* IV, 130-32).

126. *scemo*: "Emptied," "annulled."

128. *Pier Pettinaio*: Peter the comb-maker (or comb-seller) was a native of Campi in the Chianti district northeast of Siena. According to the commentators he was a hermit of the Franciscan order and dwelt in Siena, where he was renowned

for his piety and miracles. In his calling as comb-seller he was characterized by unusual honesty, refusing to sell any comb which had the smallest defect in it. He died in December of 1289 (documents suggest that he was 109 years old) and was buried at Siena in a handsome tomb erected at public expense. In 1328 the senate of Siena passed a resolution (the record of which is still extant) for the official commemoration of his annual festival. See A. Lisini (1920), pp. 80-81; E. G. Gardner (1913), pp. 214-15. See F. Ageno (1957), pp. 212-15, who gives a bibliography of studies on Pier Pettinaio and calls attention to a Sienese document of 1246 (in the *Libri della Biccherna*) which mentions a certain "Ventura Pieri pectinarius," who perhaps may be identified with Sapia's holy man.

129. *increbbe*: Past absolute of *increscere*, modern *rincrescere*.

131. *sciolti*: Not sewn shut.

132. *spirando*: Sapia, with the sharp hearing of the blind, has heard that Dante breathes as he speaks.

133. *fieno = saranno*.

136. *Troppa . . . più*: I.e., *molto più.*   *sospesa*: "Apprehensive," "fearful."

136–38. *Troppa è più . . . mi pesa*: Villani (IX, 136) comments on Dante's pride: "Questo Dante per lo suo savere fu alquanto presuntuoso e schifo e isdegnoso, e quasi a guisa di filosofo mal grazioso non bene sapea conversare co' laici." ("This Dante, because of his learning, was somewhat presumptuous, haughty, and disdainful, and being rude, as philosophers are, knew not how to speak with the unlearned.") Dante was aware, at least, that such was his most besetting sin.

138. *lo 'ncarco di là giù*: The heavy weight of stone.

139–40. *Chi t'ha dunque condotto . . . credi?* Sapia is puzzled, since she has not yet understood that a living man is speaking to her, although she has sensed that he breathes as he speaks (thus Dante must declare to her, "E vivo sono," vs. 142). Accordingly, she cannot understand how the man who speaks to her has come here, if he has yet to return below, to the first terrace. Clearly she has no inkling of the presence of Virgil, who does not breathe and did not make himself heard by his steps as he came forward with Dante, since he is a spirit. Dante, of course, speaks here of the purgation of pride which he will have to undergo when he passes this way again after death.

142. *però = perciò.*   *mi richiedi:* Imperative, "request of me."

143. *spirito eletto:* Cf. *Purg.* III, 73.

143-44. *se tu vuo' . . . piedi:* Dante is offering to seek out those close to Sapia and urge them to pray for her, in order to speed her on her way through Purgatory.

144. *mortai = mortali.*

145-47. *Oh, questa è a udir . . . giova:* Sapia, seeing that God loves Dante so much, now urges him to pray for her.

148. *cheggioti = ti chiedo.*   *per quel che tu più brami:* This something is left indefinite. It is simply that which Dante most desires, the usual basis for such adjuration.

149. *se mai calchi la terra di Toscana:* Curiously enough, Sapia seems not to have noticed from Dante's speech that he is Tuscan, or she would surely assume that he would return to that region.

150. *propinqui:* Kinsfolk, perhaps especially the Salvani, her own immediate family.   *mi rinfami:* Sapia asks Dante to restore her fame by telling her kinsfolk that she is among the *spiriti eletti* of Purgatory, despite her envious life and her tardy repentance.

151. *quella gente vana:* The Sienese. See *Inf.* XXIX, 121-32.

152. *Talamone:* Small seaport on the Tyrrhenian Sea, situated on a promontory in the southwestern extremity of the

Sienese Maremma, in Tuscany, about ten miles southeast of
the mouth of the Ombrone. It possesses a convenient anchor-
age, sheltered from the southwest gales by the island of
Giglio and by Monte Argentario, but the creek is liable to
become silted up. In 1303 the harbor of Talamone was pur-
chased by the Sienese from the abbot of San Salvatore for
8,000 gold florins. The deed of purchase, dated September 10
in that year, is still preserved at Siena. The Sienese were
eager for an outlet to the sea, but the enterprise was a failure
on account of the expense entailed by the constant dredging
operations to keep the entrance clear, and also because of the
unhealthiness of the situation, the place being infected with
malaria from the Maremma.   *a perderagli = vi perderà.*
Cf. "li" (or *gli*) used for *vi* in *Purg.* VIII, 69; XIII, 7; and
passim. The "gli" here corresponds to the "vi" of vs. 154.

153. *la Diana*: The name of a river which the Sienese be-
lieved to exist beneath their city and in the search for which
they spent large sums of money. At the time Dante wrote,
their search had been unsuccessful. The name of Diana was
given to the supposed subterranean river because of a tradi-
tion that a statue of that goddess had once stood in the mar-
ket place of Siena, just as that of Mars had stood on the
Ponte Vecchio in Florence.

154. *ma più vi perderanno li ammiragli*: Thus, by this jibe
at her fellow-townsmen, it is clear that Sapia can still be
malicious and still has time to serve on this terrace, purging
away such feelings. Though some early commentators under-
stand "ammiragli" to mean "contractors," i.e., in the build-
ing of the port, it seems likely that Sapia intends the term in
its proper sense of "admirals," as if the Sienese had, or hoped
to have, a vast fleet of ships, a navy, and these who aspire to
be its "admirals" will lose more hope than those who place
their hope in Talamone as an eventual port, since to be "ad-
miral" is a special and personal ambition. Thus "più" of vs.
154, modifying an understood *speranza*, connects with
"spera" of vs. 152, but has "speranza" of vs. 153 to refer to
as a noun and the basis of comparison.

CANTO XIV

1. *costui*: The demonstrative pronoun, normally used to point to a position near the person spoken to, expresses the "distance" of blindness itself, since Dante would seem to be standing right beside the two souls who speak here, and they know it (see vs. 5). *'l nostro monte*: The possessive serves to remove and distance even more the two souls, in their blindness.

2. *prima che morte li abbia dato il volo*: Cf. *Purg.* X, 125-26. *li = gli*.

3. *e apre li occhi a sua voglia e coverchia*: The soul remarks what is most to be wondered at, the power of sight, which he is deprived of.

4. *e' = ei (egli)*.

5. *domandal = domandalo* (pronounced *domàndalo*). The accusative for the person interrogated is commonly used with the verb *domandare* in early Italian. *che più li t'avvicini = che più gli sei vicino*.

6. *e dolcemente, sì che parli, acco'lo*: The *Ottimo Commento* paraphrases this as follows: "Fagli sì dolce accoglienza, ch'egli ti risponda." ("Receive him so kindly that he will respond.") *acco'lo = accòglilo* (imperative).

7. *l'uno a l'altro chini*: The posture of the two blind souls, leaning one to the other in intimate conversation, as if Dante were farther away from them than he is, continues to bring out the psychological distance and isolation of blindness which was expressed by the opening "costui." See n. to vs. 1.

8. *a man dritta*: Dante was facing Sapia as he spoke with her and so was facing the bank of the terrace. The souls are seated in single file along the base of the bank, and the two souls who speak now are therefore to the right of anyone facing the bank. Dante continues to move in the proper direction for Purgatory.

9. *fer = fecero.   supini*: The souls are seated, and Dante is standing, hence it would be natural for them to turn their faces "supine" to him; but the gesture is characteristic of the blind, and for any reader who has observed this it serves to evoke the image of the two figures most vividly, putting the focus of the poem on the sightless eyes in the upturned faces.

10. *O anima*: The souls address Dante as a "soul," even though they know that he is here in his body (as is immediately recognized in the words which follow).   *fitta*: Past participle of *figgere*, "to plant." Cf. *Inf.* XIX, 50.

11. *ten = te ne.*

12. *per carità*: The souls appeal to the virtue opposing envy.   *ne = ci.   ne ditta = ne di' (dicci)*. It is not uncommon for *dittare* to be used for *dire* in early Italian.

13. *onde vieni e chi se'*: Again, as with Sapia, the first question concerns one's place of origin, the second, one's name. Compare Dante's words to Sapia in *Purg.* XIII, 105: "o per luogo o per nome." Dante will answer both questions in the two tercets that follow.   *ne = ci.*

14. *tanto maravigliar de la tua grazia*: See vss. 79-80 and *Purg.* XIII, 145-46.   *la tua grazia*: The God-given grace that makes possible this extraordinary journey, which has caused great marvel before (*Purg.* VIII, 65-66).

16–19. *Per mezza Toscana . . . persona*: In reply to the question "onde vieni?" Dante brings in the course of the river Arno, from the river's source to the city of Florence, which "sits" on its banks. Compare Francesca's identification of herself in a similar way in *Inf.* V, 97-98, Virgil's discourse on the origin of Mantua in *Inf.* XX, 61-81, and Dante's identification of himself in *Inf.* XXIII, 94-95. Guido del Duca, who will be named in vs. 81, then traces the whole course of the river.

17. *un fiumicel*: The Arno is a great river, for Dante and all Tuscans, since it is the principal river of Tuscany, which, rising among the spurs of Monte Falterona in the Apennines, flows southeast through the Casentino, past Poppi, Bibbiena, Rassina, and Subbiano, to within four or five miles of Arezzo, where it makes a sudden sweep away to the northwest. Then with a more rapid descent it flows past Laterina, Montevarchi, Figline, and Pontassieve, receiving on its way the waters from Pratomagno on the right and from the Chianti hills on the left. Here it is joined by the Sieve and turning west flows through Florence; then, descending more gently, it winds between Montelupo and Capraia, and passing through the deep gorge of Pietra Golfolina enters the plain of Empoli, whence it flows through Pisa into the Mediterranean, after a course of approximately 150 miles, its mouth being about five miles below the city of Pisa. Villani (I, 43) traces the course of the Arno in his account of Tuscany:

> Questa provincia di Toscana ha più fiumi: intra gli altri reale e maggiore si è il nostro fiume d'Arno il quale nasce di quella medesima montagna di Falterona che nasce il fiume del Tevere che va a Roma; e questo fiume d'Arno corre quasi per lo mezzo di Toscana, scendendo per le montagne della Vernia, ove il beato santo Francesco fece sua penitenzia e romitaggio, e poi passa per la contrada di Casentino presso a Bibbiena e a piè di Poppi, e poi si rivolge verso levante vegnendo presso alla città d'Arezzo a tre miglia, e poi corre per lo nostro Valdarno di sopra, scendendo per lo nostro piano, e quasi passa per lo mezzo della nostra città di Firenze.

E poi uscito per corso del nostro piano, passa tra Montelupo e Capraia presso a Empoli per la contrada di Greti e di Valdarno di sotto a piè di Fucecchio, e poi per lo contado di Lucca e di Pisa, raccogliendo in se molti fiumi, passando poi quasi per mezzo la città di Pisa ove assai è grosso, sicchè porta galee e grossi legni; e presso di Pisa a cinque miglia mette in mare, e 'l suo corso è di spazio di miglia cento venti.

This province of Tuscany contains several rivers. The major one among them, our majestic river Arno, rises in the mountain of Falterona, which is also the source of the river Tiber that leads to Rome. The Arno runs almost through the middle of Tuscany, coming down the mountains of the Verna, where St. Francis lived as a hermit and did penance; then it passes through the countryside of the Casentino, near Bibbiena, and at the foot of Poppi. The river then turns eastward, flowing three miles from the city of Arezzo; then it runs along our upper Val d'Arno, descends to our plain, and passes almost through the center of our city of Florence. When it has flowed past our plain, it passes between Montelupo and Capraia near Empoli, through the countryside of Greti and the lower Val d'Arno, by the foot of Fucecchio. Then it goes through the countryside of Lucca and Pisa, receiving the waters of many rivers as it flows, and passes almost through the center of Pisa, where it becomes so large that it can take galleys and large ships. Five miles from Pisa, it flows into the sea. The river is 120 miles long.

(See C. S. Singleton, *Inferno Commentary,* Map 4, following p. 683.) Near its source on Monte Falterona the river is merely a small stream, which is why Dante uses the diminutive *fiumicello* here.

18. *e cento miglia di corso nol sazia*: The verb "sazia," in the singular, has "corso" as the subject. Villani, in the passage quoted in the preceding note, speaks of the river's length as being 120 miles, though it is actually closer to 150. There

is already a slight touch of personification in "sazia," as if the river desired an even longer course.

19. *Di sovr' esso*: See *Inf.* XXIII, 95 for this use of *sovra*. *rech' io questa persona*: I.e., there was I born.

20. *dirvi*: Dante speaks, in the plural, to both souls. *saria = sarebbe*.

20–21. *dirvi ch'i' sia . . . suona*: Dante's modesty regarding his own name is notable and suggests that the purging of his pride on the first terrace has been effective (compare Omberto Aldobrandeschi's modesty in the same way, *Purg.* XI, 60); yet clearly there remains a touch of pride, on the part of the poet, in the "ancor" here. The fact that Dante avoids naming himself should prompt the reader to reflect that in fact he has not been named as yet in the poem, although he has been recognized by many souls as Dante Alighieri.

22. *accarno*: Literally, "pierces the flesh of." Cf. the French *acharner*.

24. *quei = quegli* (singular).   *pria = prima*.

26. *questi*: Dante.   *il vocabol*: Il nome. Cf. *Purg.* V, 97.   *riviera*: Cf. *Inf.* III, 78.

27. *pur = proprio*.   *om*: Cf. the French *on*.

29. *si sdebitò così*: Literally, "paid his due thus."

29–30. *degno ben è*: It is only right.

30. *che 'l nome di tal valle pèra*: See Iob 18:17: "Memoria illius pereat de terra." ("His memory perishes from the land.") The "valle" is, of course, the Val d'Arno, which together with the river itself becomes the subject of the long discourse which follows.   *pèra = perisca*.

31. *dal principio suo*: From its source on Monte Falterona. *pregno*: Commentators, beginning with the earliest, are not agreed on the meaning of this adjective, some understanding it to mean "pregnant" in the sense of "abounding in water," others "pregnant" in the sense of "swollen" in

height and in its mass, like a mountain peak. Benvenuto com-
ments: "tumorosus vel altus" ("swollen or high"). See "in-
tumuit," in Benvenuto's sense of "tumorosus," in the follow-
ing verses from Lucan, *Phars.* II, 396-98, verses that are re-
called by Dante in *De vulg. eloqu.* I, x, 6:

> Umbrosis mediam qua collibus Appenninus
> Erigit Italiam, nulloque a vertice tellus
> Altius intumuit propiusque accessit Olympo.

. . . where Apennine raises up the centre of Italy
in wooded hills; nor is there any peak at which earth
rises [swells] higher and approaches closer to the sky.

32. *l'alpestro monte*: The entire range of the Apennines
viewed   as   one   chain.   *tronco = troncato.*   *Peloro*:
Pelorus (modern Punta del Faro or Cape Faro) is the pro-
montory at the northeastern extremity of Sicily. Benvenuto
repeats the tradition about the derivation of the classical
name from Pelorus, the pilot of Hannibal's ship, but as a
matter of fact the name is older than Hannibal's time and is
mentioned by Thucydides (IV, xxv, 3). The commentators
refer to Virgil (*Aen.* III, 410-19):

> ast ubi digressum Siculae te admoverit orae
> ventus et angusti rarescent claustra Pelori,
> laeva tibi tellus et longo laeva petantur
> aequora circuitu; dextrum fuge litus et undas.
> haec loca vi quondam et vasta convolsa ruina
> (tantum aevi longinqua valet mutare vetustas)
> dissiluisse ferunt, cum protinus utraque tellus
> una foret; venit medio vi pontus et undis
> Hesperium Siculo latus abscidit, arvaque et urbes
> litore diductas angusto interluit aestu.

But when, on parting thence, the wind has borne thee
to the Sicilian coast, and the barriers of narrow Pelorus
open out, make thou for the land on the left and the
seas on the left, long though the circuit be; shun the
shore and waters on the right. These lands, they say, of
old broke asunder, torn by force of mighty upheaval
—such vast change can length of time effect—when the

two countries were one unbroken whole. The sea came in might between, cut off with its waters the Hesperian from the Sicilian coast, and with narrow tideway laves fields and cities on severed shores.

Reference is also made by the commentators to Lucan (*Phars.* II, 437-38): "At postquam gemino tellus elisa profundo est, / Extremi colles Siculo cessere Peloro." ("But when the earth was crushed out by the two seas, that end of the Apennines was surrendered to Pelorus in Sicily.")

33. *che 'n pochi luoghi passa oltra quel segno*: Although this is not, strictly speaking, quite accurate, taking "pregno" in either of the above-mentioned senses (see n. to vs. 31), Dante may well have thought it to be the fact.

34-36. *per ristoro . . . loro*: The heavens (*il ciel*), by the heat of the sun, cause the water of the sea to evaporate and rise; this then falls as rain to replenish the rivers with water ("ciò che va con loro"), and the rivers in turn, with the water they bring to the sea, replace that which was lost through evaporation.

37. *vertù così per nimica si fuga*: Virtue, worth, worthiness, is shunned. On *fugare* (*fugarsi*) in this sense, see E. G. Parodi (1957), pp. 280, 374; M. Barbi (1934b), p. 281. For a similar conception, cf. *Purg.* XVI, 118-20.

38-39. *per sventura del luogo*: As if there were some curse on the place.

39. *per mal uso*: Because of vicious habit.   *che li fruga*: Which goads, drives, the inhabitants. Cf. "fruga" in *Purg.* III, 3, and *spronare* as another expression of the same notion in *Purg.* XI, 21.

40. *ond' hanno sì mutata lor natura*: They are so changed in nature. "Mutata" has the force of an adjective here, i.e., "hanno lor natura sì mutata." The construction is thus open to the suggestion that some Circe may have transformed them thus.

42. *Circe*: The enchantress Circe, daughter of Helios, god of the Sun, and Perse. She dwelt in the island of Aeaea (in Virgil's time, Circaeum Promontorium; modern Mount Circeo), on the north side of the Gulf of Gaeta, upon which Ulysses was cast (see Homer, *Odyssey* X, 133-50), and she had the power of transforming men into beasts.

43. *Tra brutti porci*: The river passes through the Casentino valley (see *Inf.* XXX, 65; *Purg.* V, 94), and by "porci" all its inhabitants may be intended, but the term may contain a special reference to the Conti Guidi particularly (note Dante's mention of members of this family in *Inf.* XVI, 38, and *Inf.* XXX, 77), with a play on the name of the Porciano branch of the family, who were lords of Porciano, a stronghold at the foot of Monte Falterona.   *galle*: "Acorns," on which swine were commonly fed in such wooded regions.

45. *dirizza prima il suo povero calle*: The river sets out, as it were, on its way, which is termed "poor" for the same reason that the river itself was called a "stream" at the beginning (see n. to vs. 17). The personification of the river, clearly suggested before, is now explicit and will remain so.

46. *Botoli*: The inhabitants of Arezzo. When the Arno leaves the Casentino it enters into the territory of Arezzo, but within four or five miles of that city it suddenly turns to the northwest toward Florence. On the term *botolo* Buti comments: "Botoli sono cani picculi da abbaiare più che da altro." ("*Botoli* are small dogs that do more barking than anything else.") The term was probably commonly applied to the Aretines in Dante's time, perhaps because they had adopted as an official motto the words which the *Anonimo fiorentino* recalls: "Et ancora perchè è scolpito nel segno loro: *A cane non magno saepe tenetur Aper.*" ("And furthermore because it says on their standard: oftentimes a small dog can hold down a boar.") This motto clearly boasts of their power ("possa," vs. 47) despite the fact that their city is quite small.

47. *chiede = richiede.*

48. *e da lor disdegnosa torce il muso*: From the Aretines the stream "twists its muzzle." The river (or rather the "valle," which "disdegnosa" modifies) with this turn of phrase enters into the animalesque personifications. As stated in the n. to vs. 17, when the Arno comes to within a few miles of Arezzo, it suddenly turns away to the northwest.

49. *Vassi = si va*. The so-called pleonastic reflexive supports the personification of the river and valley at this point ("fossa," of vs. 51, is the subject), making it, as it were, a conscious wayfarer.   *caggendo = cadendo*.

50. *di can farsi lupi*: As the river swells, the little dogs, the Aretines, become wolves, i.e., the Florentines.

51. *fossa*: "Fossa" is a touch pejorative here.

52. *per più pelaghi cupi*: There are deep hollows or pools where the river passes through the gorge known as the Pietra Golfolina, the *golfo*, i.e., "deep pool," of the name itself no doubt suggesting *pelago*, "deep."

53. *trova*: The verb is here used for the third time.   *le volpi*: As Buti comments, this refers to the inhabitants of Pisa, "li quali assimillia a le volpi per la malizia: imperò che li Pisani sono astuti, e co l'astuzia più che co la forsa si rimediano dai loro vicini" ("who resemble foxes, because they are sly; the Pisans are crafty, and their main defense against their neighbors is craft rather than force"). For the fox as a symbol of fraud, see *Inf.* XXVII, 75.

54. *ingegno*: Trap, snare, i.e., the astute and fraudulent designs of other rival cities.   *occùpi*: The normal stress is *òccupi*. The subjunctive form is the hypothetical, i.e., that any trap whatsoever will catch them.

55. *perch' altri m'oda*: The indefinite pronoun here refers to a definite person, i.e., to the other soul, Rinieri da Calboli (to be named in vss. 88-89), to whom Guido del Duca is speaking and who will be greatly grieved to hear the prophecy. For "altri" used in this way, see *Inf.* XXII, 63; XXVII, 56. On this usage, see M. Barbi (1920a).

56. *costui*: Dante (see n. to vs. 1). "Costui" is the dative here.

56–57. *buon sarà . . . disnoda*: It will be good for this Tuscan (the speaker does not know who Dante is) to bear in mind (*ammentarsi*) when he returns to the world of the living (*ancor*) what I am about to say prophetically, since this concerns grievous things for the city of Florence.

57. *vero   spirto*: See Ioan. 16:13: "Spiritus veritatis" ("Spirit of truth").   *mi disnoda*: "Unknots," "unties," i.e., from the dark future.

58. *veggio = vedo.*   *tuo nepote*: From vs. 88 we learn that the soul being addressed, to whom the following prophecy will cause grief, is Rinieri da Calboli. Rinieri's grandson, here referred to, is the degenerate and corrupt Fulcieri da Calboli, who was *podestà* of Florence in 1303, after the return of the Neri through the influence of Charles of Valois, and he proved himself a bitter foe of the Bianchi. Villani (VIII, 59) gives the following account of his proceedings:

> Nel detto anno 1302, essendo fatto podestà di Firenze Folcieri da Calvoli di Romagna, uomo feroce e crudele, a posta de' caporali di parte nera, i quali viveano in grande gelosia, perchè sentivano molto possente in Firenze la parte bianca e ghibellina, e gli usciti scriveano tutto dì, e trattavano con quegli ch'erano loro amici rimasi in Firenze, il detto Folcieri fece subitamente pigliare certi cittadini di parte bianca e ghibellini; ciò furono, messer Betto Gherardini, e Masino de' Cavalcanti, e Donato e Tegghia suo fratello de' Finiguerra da Sammartino, e Nuccio Coderini de' Galigai, il quale era quasi uno mentecatto, e Tignoso de' Macci, e a petizione di messer Musciatto Franzesi, ch'era de' signori della terra, vollero essere presi certi caporali di casa gli Abati suoi nimici, i quali sentendo ciò, si fuggiro e partiro di Firenze, e mai poi non ne furono cittadini: e uno massaio delle Calze fu de' presi, opponendo loro che trattavano tradimento nella città co' bianchi usciti,

o colpa o non colpa, per martorio gli fece confessare che doveano tradire la terra, e dare certe porte a' bianchi e ghibellini: ma il detto Tignoso de' Macci per gravezza di carni morì in su la colla. Tutti gli altri sopraddetti presi gli giudicò, e fece loro tagliare le teste, e tutti quegli di casa gli Abati condannare per ribelli, e disfare i loro beni, onde grande turbazione n'ebbe la città, e poi ne seguì molti mali e scandali.

In that year, 1302, Fulcieri da Calboli of Romagna, a fierce and cruel man, was made *podestà* of Florence, through the influence of the leaders of the Neri. They were very jealous of the power enjoyed by the Bianchi and the Ghibellines in Florence; moreover, they saw that the exiles were writing to their friends in Florence every day, and were plotting with them. Now Fulcieri quickly had certain of the Bianchi and Ghibellines arrested. They were Messer Betto Gherardini, Masino de' Cavalcanti, Donato and his brother Tegghia de' Finiguerra da Sammartino, Nuccio Coderini de' Galigai, who was almost an idiot, and Tignoso de' Macci. At the insistence of Messer Musciatto Franzesi, who was one of the priors, certain leaders of the Abati family, his enemies, were to be arrested. When they heard about it, they fled from Florence, never again to be counted among its citizens. A steward of the Calzi family was among those arrested, who were accused of plotting with the White exiles to betray the city. Whether he was really guilty or not, he was made to confess through torture that they were going to betray the city, and surrender certain gates to the Bianchi and the Ghibellines. Tignoso de' Macci, who was very much overweight, died under the rope torture. All those others who had been arrested were condemned by him [the *podestà*], and he had their heads cut off. He had all the members of the Abati family condemned as rebels and their possessions destroyed. All this caused great turmoil in the city, with evil and scandalous consequences.

The prophecy, styling Fulcieri as *cacciatore* (vs. 59), recalls Ugolino's prophetic dream in *Inf.* XXXIII, 28-36.

59–60. *in su la riva del fiero fiume*: At Florence.

60. *fiero fiume*: Even as the river takes on the nature of an animal as it passes among animals (vs. 48), it now, with "fiero," seems to partake of Fulcieri's savage ways.

61. *Vende la carne loro essendo viva*: Fulcieri sells his victims to their enemies, "on the hoof," as it were (the metaphor of beasts sold for slaughter is already evident). As Del Lungo observes, "mercanteggia della loro morte col Comune Nero; il quale, invece che solamente per il consueto patteggiato semestre, lo tenne suo Potestà per ambedue i semestri del 1303." ("He bargains over their lives with the Neri, who in turn kept him on as *podestà* for both semesters of 1303, instead of the usual one.")

62. *poscia li ancide come antica belva*: Then, after selling them alive, Fulcieri slaughters them like old cattle, i.e., like an ox too old to work, which is sold to the butcher. Del Lungo comments: " 'Belva' è qui, poeticamente, nel significato generico che ha, di 'animale grosso' (distintamente da quello di 'bestia feroce')." ("Here 'beast' is used poetically in its general significance of large animal, rather than ferocious animal.")

64. *Sanguinoso*: Covered with blood. The adjective returns to the metaphor of the *cacciatore* (vs. 59) as this "hunter" comes forth from the sorry forest which is so full of wolves, i.e., Florence.

65. *lasciala = la lascia*.

65–66. *tal, che di qui . . . rinselva*: As if the hunt so tears and breaks the trees and branches (cf. *Inf.* XIII, 112-17) that the forest will not recover from this, even in a thousand years. On the meaning here out of metaphor, see Villani as quoted in the n. to vs. 58.

66. *primaio*: The word counts as only two syllables here.

69. *l'assanni*: "May bite him," "may sink its fangs in him." Cf. "l'assannò" in *Inf.* XXX, 29 and "sanne" in *Inf.* VI, 23.

70. *l'altr' anima*: Rinieri (named in vs. 88), grandfather of Fulcieri.

72. *poi ch'ebbe la parola a sé raccolta*: When he had taken in the meaning of the other's words.

73. *la vista*: The face of Rinieri, disturbed and saddened.

74. *fer = fecero*.

75. *fei = feci*.

76. *parlòmi = parlommi (mi parlò)*.

77. *Tu vuo' ch'io mi deduca*: "You wish me to bring myself." The *de-* of "deduca" perhaps suggests a lowering, a condescending.

78. *non vuo'mi = non mi vuoi*.

79. *traluca*: "Shine forth" from within.

81. *Guido del Duca*: Gentleman of Bertinoro (see Guido's lament on Bertinoro in vss. 112-14). Our information concerning Guido del Duca is uncertain. He may have been the son of Giovanni del Duca of the Onesti family of Ravenna, who had settled in Bertinoro. The earliest mention of this Guido occurs in a document dated May 4, 1199, in which he is described as holding the office of judge to the *podestà* of Rimini. In 1218, Pier Traversaro (see n. to vs. 98) with the help of his Ghibelline friends, and especially of the Mainardi of Bertinoro, made himself master of Ravenna and expelled the Guelphs from the city. The latter, in revenge, seized Bertinoro, destroyed the houses belonging to the Mainardi, and drove out all Piero's adherents, among whom was Guido del Duca, who at this time apparently, together with his family, went to Ravenna, his father's native place, and resided there under the protection of Pier Traversaro. Some ten years later, in 1229, Guido's name appears as witness to a deed at Ravenna, and since this is the last mention of him that can be found, it is therefore supposed that he died after that date.

Benvenuto, in his discussion of the opening of this canto, describes Guido as "quidam nobilis vir et prudens romandiolus de Bretenorio" ("a noble and prudent Romagnole gentleman of Bertinoro") and relates, in his gloss on Arrigo Mainardi (vs. 97), that when Guido died, his friend Arrigo Mainardi of Bertinoro caused the bench on which they used to sit together to be sawn in two, since there was no one worthy to take his place: "Eo mortuo, fecit secari lignum per medium, in quo soliti erant ambo sedere, asserens quod non remanserat alius similis in liberalitate et honorificentia." ("When he died, his friend caused the bench on which they had been wont to sit together to be sawn in two, saying that his equal in nobility and honor no longer existed.") We know nothing of Guido's envy, which he is purging here.

82. *riarso*: Literally, "burned," i.e., consumed. The prefix *ri-* intensifies the verb (*ardere*, past participle *arso*).

83–84. *che se veduto . . . sparso*: The very definition of envy as *tristitia de alienis bonis* (see n. to *Purg.* XVII, 118-20) is reflected here. See Horace, *Epistles* I, ii, 57: "Invidus alterius macrescit rebus opimis." ("The envious man grows lean when his neighbour waxes fat.")

83. *avesse* = *avessi,* second person past subjunctive.

84. *di livore sparso*: On *livore* as the color of envy, see *Purg.* XIII, 9, and the note to that verse.

85. *Di mia semente cotal paglia mieto*: See Gal. 6:8-10 [7-10]:

Quae enim seminaverit homo, haec et metet. Quoniam qui seminat in carne sua, de carne et metet corruptionem; qui autem seminat in spiritu, de spiritu metet vitam aeternam.

Bonum autem facientes non deficiamus; tempore enim suo metemus, non deficientes. Ergo, dum tempus habemus, operemur bonum ad omnes. . . .

For what a man sows, that he will also reap. For he who sows in the flesh, from the flesh also will reap corruption. But he who sows in the spirit, from the spirit will reap life everlasting. And in doing good let us not grow tired; for in due time we shall reap if we do not relax. Therefore, while we have time, let us do good to all men. . . .

His sowing is his envious actions, the straw (and not grain) which he reaps is his punishment in Purgatory.

88. *Rinier*: Rinieri de' Paolucci da Calboli (pronounced Càlboli), member of an illustrious Guelph family of Forlì, was born probably at the beginning of the thirteenth century and was *podestà* of Faenza in 1247, of Parma in 1252, and of Ravenna in 1265 (the year of Dante's birth). For a full account of his very active political life and his many exploits, see P. Toynbee (1968), pp. 543-44.

89. *ove*: In which family (the Calboli).

90. *reda = erede* (cf. *Inf.* XXXI, 116).

91. *lo suo sangue*: His blood (i.e., his family).   *brullo*: "Bare," "destitute." The construction continues with "del ben," in vs. 93.

92. *tra 'l Po e 'l monte e la marina e 'l Reno*: This is a reference to Romagna, a former province of northern Italy, corresponding roughly to the eastern portion of the modern Emilia. Cf. *Inf.* XXVII, 29-30. According to Dante's definition, Romagna as a region extended from Bologna to Rimini and from the hills of Montefeltro to the plain of Ravenna. Tolosano, a chronicler of Faenza (who died in 1226), in a passage quoted by T. Casini (1894), p. 21, defines it as stretching from the Reno to the Foglia, which falls into the sea just above Pesaro, and from the Adriatic to the Alps. The Reno passes about two miles to the west of Bologna so that according to these limits Bologna was within the confines of Romagna, which is somewhat unusual by way of classification, though Bologna dominated Romagnole politics in part in Dante's day. Note that "Po," in this verse, means the Po di Primaro. (See Map 1, facing.)

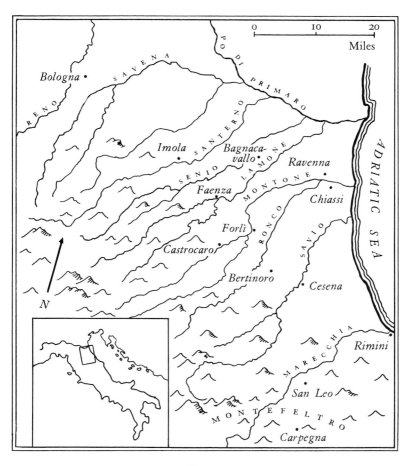

1. Romagna

93. *del ben richesto al vero e al trastullo*: Connects with "brullo" in vs. 91. This "good" is virtue in general or those virtues required in the serious business of life and in courtly pastimes. Cf. the French *agréments*. *Cortesia* in a broad sense means good manners and a gay life.

94. *dentro a questi termini*: The whole phrase may be taken as the subject of "è ripieno." See *Purg*. X, 79, where a prepositional phrase is also the subject of the verb.

95. *venenosi sterpi*: Cf. "sterpi" in *Inf*. XIII, 7. The whole figure expresses the idea of neglected fields that have been allowed to grow up in brush and become wild again. Thus, as indicated in vss. 95-96, it would now be too late to reclaim them, so far advanced is the growth.

97. *Ov' è*: There is a clear echo of the *ubi sunt* theme here, in this context.   *Lizio*: Lizio da Valbona, nobleman of Romagna, was born in the first half of the thirteenth century and was a contemporary of Rinieri. The date of his death is unknown. For his active political life, see P. Toynbee (1968), pp. 394-95. He figures in a charming story by Boccaccio, *Decam*. V, 4 (vol. I, pp. 367-72). The castle of Valbona, the headquarters of the family, was situated in the valley of the Bidente in the upper valley of the Savio, near Bagno di Romagna.

Arrigo Mainardi: Arrigo Mainardi, or Manardi, was a gentleman of Bertinoro. Little is known of him beyond the fact that he was a contemporary of Guido del Duca and Pier Traversaro and that he was taken prisoner with the latter by the Faentines in 1170. He is known to have been still alive in 1228, in which year he was present in Ravenna at the nomination of Paolo Traversaro to the procuratorship of the city. The *Ottimo Commento* says of him: "Fu da Brettinoro, cavaliere pieno di cortesia e d'onore volentieri mise tavola, donò robe e cavalli, pregiò li valentuomini, e sua vita tutta fu data a larghezza ed a bello vivere." ("He was from Bertinoro, a knight full of courtesy and honor. He set an abundant table, gave away clothes and horses, and knew how to value good men. His life was given to generosity and good living.")

98. *Pier Traversaro*: Member of the powerful Traversari family of Ravenna, Piero was born *ca.* 1145 and died, at the age of 80, in 1225. He was of great influence and authority in Ravenna, with the history of which he was closely identified for nearly fifty years. He was several times *podestà* of the city, an office which was filled by members of his house at least ten times in the forty years between 1180 and 1220. Piero, whose family were by tradition adherents of the Empire, was a staunch Ghibelline and enjoyed the confidence of the Emperor Frederick II. For further particulars concerning Piero and the Traversari, see P. Toynbee (1968), p. 619.

Guido di Carpigna: The Carpigna family, who boasted descent from one of the comrades of Odoacer (the Herulian king who extinguished the Roman Empire in the West, A.D. 476, and called himself king of Italy), appear to have been established in Romagna in the neighborhood of Montefeltro as early as the tenth century. Two members of the family bore the name of Guido, of whom the elder was already dead in 1221, while the younger, who was grandson of the other, died toward the end of the thirteenth century. Guido di Carpigna the elder had three sons, Rinieri (mentioned as late as 1249), Ugo (*podestà* of Rimini in 1249, alive in 1256), and Guiduccio; Rinieri, the eldest of the three, had two sons, Guido and Ugo, of whom the former, Guido di Carpigna the younger, is probably the person alluded to by Dante. This Guido was *podestà* of Ravenna in 1251; he is mentioned as late as 1270, but was dead before 1283, having left three sons, Guido, Rinieri, and Contuccio.   *Carpigna*: Now Carpegna, town in Romagna (in the present province of the Marches) in the district of Montefeltro, about fifteen miles northwest of Urbino, between the sources of the Marecchia and the Foglia.

99. *tornati in bastardi*: For *tornare* in the sense of "change into," see *Inf.* XIII, 69.

100. *un Fabbro*: The reference is to Fabbro de' Lambertazzi, Ghibelline of Bologna. Benvenuto, who was well

acquainted with Bologna, and who takes this opportunity of singing its praises as "nidus philosophorum et mater legum, omniumque bonorum fertilis, humanitatis piissima nutrix" ("the nest of philosophers and the mother of laws, replete with every good, most pious nurse of humanity"), says of Fabbro: "Iste fuit nobilis miles de Lambertacciis de Bononia, vir sapiens et magni consilii." ("He was a noble soldier of the Lambertazzi of Bologna, a man of prudence and wisdom.") The Lambertazzi were a noble family of Bologna, dating from the twelfth century, who boasted descent from the dukes of Ravenna. The head of the family at the beginning of the thirteenth century was Bonifazio di Guido di Guizzardo, who with Baruffaldino de' Geremei led the Bolognese crusaders in 1217 at Damietta and who, on his return home a few years later, was recognized as the head of the Ghibelline party in Bologna, a circumstance which led to the adoption by the Bolognese Ghibellines of the name of his family as their party designation, while the Guelphs, at whose head was the other crusading captain, Baruffaldino, assumed that of the Geremei. Bonifazio was succeeded in the leadership of the party by his son Fabbro, to whom Dante refers. The first mention of Fabbro in contemporary documents occurs in 1228, when he was in charge of the *carroccio* in the war between Bologna and Modena. Two years later (1230) he was *podestà* in Faenza, an office which he held in several cities of northern Italy. (For details concerning his public life, see P. Toynbee, 1968, p. 258.) Fabbro died in 1259, leaving several sons who shortly after his death were involved in a deadly conflict with the Geremei, which led to the ruin of the Lambertazzi and to the downfall of the Ghibelline party in Bologna.   *si ralligna*: To take root again and grow. The verb, normally used of plants in this sense, continues the latent metaphor of growth and good cultivation.

101. *un Bernardin di Fosco*: This Bernardo, son of Fosco, of Faenza, is said by the early commentators to have been of humble origin, but to have so distinguished himself as to be received on terms of equality by the nobles of his native city.

Beyond the indications afforded by Dante himself and the early commentators nothing is known of Bernardo di Fosco, except that he was *podestà* of Siena in 1249 (and probably of Pisa in 1248); and that he played a prominent part in the defense of Faenza against the Emperor Frederick II in 1240, during the *podestàship* of Michele Morosini of Venice, a defense which lasted nearly a year and was famous enough to be commemorated in a *sirventes* by Ugo di Sain Circ, who makes special mention of Bernardo (for a quotation from this *sirventes*, see T. Casini, 1897, p. 57).

102. *di picciola gramigna*: The reference is to his lowly origin (see preceding note). *gramigna*: "Grass," "weed."

104. *Guido da Prata*: Lana and several other early commentators state that Guido was a native of Forlì, while the *Ottimo Commento* and others make him a native of Prata, a village near Faenza. As a matter of fact, he appears to have belonged to Ravenna, where members of his family were domiciled in the middle of the twelfth century. Benvenuto, bearing in mind that Ugolino d'Azzo, with whom Guido is coupled, belonged to the Tuscan family of the Ubaldini, thinks Guido came from the Prata in Tuscany, which is about twenty-five miles southwest of Siena and about fifty miles from Florence. There is little doubt, however, that the Prata in question is the village (now called Prada) in Romagna, between Forlì, Faenza, and Ravenna, south of Russi. Guido da Prata, who is mentioned in documents in the years 1222, 1225, and 1228 (in the last year he was present with Arrigo Mainardi at a council in Ravenna), appears to have been a person of some importance in Ravenna and to have been possessed of considerable landed property in the neighborhood of that city; he died probably between 1235 and 1245, in which year he is mentioned as being no longer alive.

105. *Ugolin d'Azzo*: Probably Ugolino degli Ubaldini, son of Azzo degli Ubaldini da Senno, a member of the powerful Tuscan family of that name, to which Ubaldino dalla Pila (*Purg*. XXIV, 29), the famous Cardinal Ottaviano degli Ubaldini (*Inf*. X, 120), and the Archbishop Ruggieri degli

Ubaldini (*Inf.* XXXIII, 14) also belonged. This Ugolino, whose mother's name was Aldruda, is repeatedly mentioned in contemporary records, viz. in 1218, 1220, 1228, 1231, 1244, 1249, 1252 (in which year he was in Florence), 1257, 1274, and in 1280 (under which year his name appears among those who bound themselves to abide by the terms of peace proposed by the pacificator, Cardinal Latino). He married Beatrice Lancia, daughter of Provenzan Salvani of Siena, by whom he had three sons, Giovanni, Francesco, and Ottaviano. He made his will in 1285 and died at an advanced age in January 1293. He appears to have been a man of great wealth and landed property. His death is recorded, together with that of Guido Riccio da Polenta, in the contemporary chronicle of Pietro Cantinelli, a proof, as Casini (1897, p. 52) points out, that Ugolino d'Azzo degli Ubaldini was at that time well known in Romagna, so that Dante could, not long after, appropriately make Guido del Duca say of him "vivette nosco."

106. *Federigo Tignoso*: A noble of Rimini. Little is known of Federigo beyond the scanty notices given by the early commentators, who state that he was a native of Rimini and was noted for his wealth and hospitality. Benvenuto, for example, says: "Iste fuit vir nobilis et dives de Arimino, cuius domus erat domicilium liberalitatis, nulli honesto clausa; conversabatur laete cum omnibus bonis; ideo Dantes describit ipsum a societate sua, quae erat tota laudabilis." ("He was a rich nobleman of Rimini whose house was a fountain-head of liberality, its door closed to no honest man. He enjoyed conversation with all worthy men and so Dante characterizes him from the company he kept, an altogether admirable group.") The family of the Tignosi is mentioned in old records as having been of some importance in Rimini and the neighborhood from the eleventh century to the middle of the fourteenth century. The Federigo referred to by Dante probably lived in the first half of the thirteenth century; no mention of him occurs in documents, but it has been conjectured on plausible grounds that he belonged to or was connected with Longiano in the Riminese territory.   *e sua*

brigata: His company, in the sense of the many people he constantly entertained.

107. *la casa Traversara*: The Traversari family (usually mentioned in contemporary documents as *domus Traversariorum*), powerful Ghibelline house of Ravenna, where they first came into prominence about the middle of the tenth century. The most distinguished member of the family appears to have been Pier Traversaro, whom Guido has already mentioned (see n. to vs. 98). *Anastagi*: Noble Ghibelline family of Ravenna, next in importance to the Polentani and Traversari, with the latter of whom, as well as with the counts of Bagnacavallo, they were in close alliance. The Anastagi for a time played an important part in the politics of Romagna. In 1249, while Alberto de' Caccianemici of Bologna was *podestà* of Ravenna, the Anastagi and their friends rose upon the Polentani and their Guelph adherents and expelled them from the city, after deposing the *podestà*, who was the nominee of the Church. Soon after, however, the exiled Guelphs returned to Ravenna, replaced the *podestà* in his office, and in their turn expelled the Ghibellines, who were, moreover, threatened with excommunication by the famous Cardinal Ottaviano degli Ubaldini unless within a given time they submitted themselves to the Church. Eight or nine years later, the Anastagi made peace with their adversaries and were allowed to return to Ravenna, probably through the mediation of their allies, the counts of Bagnacavallo, one of whom was at this time (1258) *podestà* of Ravenna. From about this period the family of the Anastagi appears to have fallen rapidly into decay, and by the year 1300, the date of the journey, hardly a trace of them remained in Ravenna.

108. *diretata*: From the low Latin *deherito*.

109–10. *le donne e' cavalier . . . cortesia*: "Le donne e' cavalier" and "li affanni e li agi" constitute the object of the verb, the dual subject of which is "amore e cortesia."

109. *li affanni e li agi*: The labors (military exploits) and

the pastimes. The pair of terms corresponds to the "vero" and "trastullo" of vs. 93.

110. *ne 'nvogliava = ci invogliava.*

111. *là*: In Romagna.

112. *Bretinoro*: Now Bertinoro, small town in Romagna, between Forlì and Cesena. After being for a time under the lordship of the Malatesta of Rimini, the town passed toward the end of the thirteenth century into the hands of the Ordelaffi of Forlì, in whose possession it was at the date of the journey. According to the *Ottimo Commento*, whose account is repeated by Benvenuto, it was in its best days renowned for the hospitality of its nobles.

113. *poi che gita se n'è = poi che se n'è andata.   la tua famiglia*: The reference is perhaps to the Mainardi. The *Anonimo fiorentino* comments: "I Mainardi, che furono costì signori, et quella famiglia de' Manardi che tennono Bertinoro è spenta et venuta meno." ("The Mainardi, who were lords there, and that family of the Mainardi that held Bertinoro have disappeared and become extinct.")

114. *e molta gente per non esser ria?* And many other noble families (have departed) in order not to degenerate.

115. *Bagnacaval*: Bagnacavallo, town in Romagna, province of Ravenna, between the rivers Senio and Lamone, midway between Imola and Ravenna. In Dante's time it was a stronghold belonging to the Malvicini, who thence took their title of counts of Bagnacavallo. They were Ghibellines and in 1249 expelled Guido da Polenta and the Guelphs from Ravenna. Later they were in ill repute for often changing sides. Guido del Duca here implies that its counts were becoming extinct; they were in fact extinct by 1305 in the principal male line. This is the sense of "non rifiglia" of this verse.

116. *Castrocaro*: Formerly a strong castle, now a village, in Romagna, in the valley of the Montone, a few miles from Forlì. In the thirteenth century it belonged to the counts of

Castrocaro, who were Ghibellines but submitted in 1282 to the Church. Benvenuto speaks of them as being extinct in his day: "*Castrocaro*, nobile castrum, et vere carum, supra Forlivium in Valle Montorii, cuius comites hodie defecerunt. Sed tunc adhuc vigebant, sed degenerabant a nobilitate vicinorum." ("Castrocaro was a splendid castle, favored in name and fact, above Forlì in the valley of the Montone, but the family have by now become extinct. But, at that time, they were still alive, though fallen from their former state.") About the year 1300 the castle passed into the hands of the Ordelaffi of Forlì; subsequently it appears to have been purchased by the Florentines. It was for some years one of the principal Guelph strongholds in Romagna. *Conio*: Cunio, castle in Romagna, near Imola, now totally destroyed. Its counts appear to have been for the most part Guelphs. According to the *Anonimo fiorentino*, the counts of Conio styled themselves Conti da Barbiano. Though their castle was destroyed soon after 1295, Benvenuto records that a family bearing the title of counts of Conio was still in existence in his day.

117. *figliar*: Torraca comments: "detto di essi come di bestie" ("said of them as of animals").

118. *i Pagan*: The Pagani, noble Ghibelline family of Faenza (or, according to some, of Imola), who at the end of the thirteenth century were lords of Faenza, Forlì, and Imola. Benvenuto describes the Pagani as "nobilem . . . stirpem de Romandiola . . . qui habuerunt dominium in montibus supra Imolam et Faventiam, quorum territorium vocabatur *Podere Paganorum*" ("a noble . . . family of Romagna . . . who had their domain in the mountains above Imola and Faenza, which territory was called the Estate of the Pagani"). *da che*: From the moment when.

118–19. *'l demonio lor*: Maghinardo (or Mainardo) Pagano da Susinana, head of the Pagani family in Dante's time, was lord of Faenza in 1290, of Forlì in 1291, and of Imola in 1296. He is mentioned by Guido da Montefeltro in *Inf.* XXVII, 50, as "il lioncel dal nido bianco," a reference to his arms (see n. to *Inf.* XXVII, 50), and was commonly called "the Demon." He died in Imola in 1302. For further particulars, see P. Toynbee (1968), pp. 409-10.

119-20. *ma non però . . . testimonio*: But the death of Maghinardo will come too late to leave them an undefiled reputation. They should have become extinct before he came into existence.

121. *Ugolin de' Fantolin*: Ugolino de' Fantolini, gentleman of Faenza, whom Lana describes as "valorosa, virtudiosa e nobile persona" ("a valorous, virtuous, and noble person") and Benvenuto as "vir singularis bonitatis et prudentiae" ("a man of singular goodness and wisdom"), was born at the beginning of the thirteenth century. He was lord of several castles in the valley of the Lamone and belonged to the Guelph party. He was *podestà* of Faenza in 1253, but lived for the most part in retirement at Cerfugnano, without taking any active part in politics. He died in 1278, leaving two sons, Ottaviano, who was killed at Forlì in 1282, on the occasion of the repulse of the Guelphs and the French troops of Martin IV by Guido da Montefeltro (*Inf.* XXVII, 43-44), and Fantolino, who died before 1291. Because of his admirable reputation he is fortunate that he has no descendants left alive to sully his name.

123. *tralignando*: The term continues the metaphor of plant stock that degenerates. See Butler, who provides the following quotation from the Italian version of Crescentius, where the term is used of the apple: "Invecchia tosto, e nella sua vecchiezza traligna." ("It gets old fast and in old age degenerates.")

124. *Ma va via, Tosco*: To put it this way is to underscore the fact that the soul who speaks was a Romagnole, who has condemned his own in speaking to a Tuscan.   *omai* = *ormai*. I.e., I have said enough now.

124-25. *ch'or mi diletta . . . parlare*: "For now weeping pleases me far more ('troppo') than speaking."

126. *nostra ragion*: Our discourse. Guido is speaking, primarily, to Rinieri.   *la mente stretta*: See Virgil, *Aen.* IX, 294: "Atque animum patriae strinxit pietatis imago." ("And the picture of filial love touched his soul.")

127-29. *Noi sapavam che . . . confidare*: I.e., we knew that, since they could hear in which direction we were going, they would have told us if we were not going the most direct way to the stairway leading up to the next circle.

127. *sapavam = sapevamo.*

130. *Poi fummo . . . procedendo*: I.e., when we had proceeded on our way and were alone, having left the souls behind.

131-32. *folgore parve . . . contra*: "Voce che giunse di contra" is the subject of "parve." As at the beginning of the circle, with the examples of charity, these voices appear to circle the terrace clockwise.

133. *Anciderammi = mi ucciderà.   Anciderammi qualunque m'apprende*: These are the words of Cain, speaking to the Lord after he had slain his brother Abel. See Gen. 4:13-14: "Dixitque Cain ad Dominum: Maior est iniquitas mea, quam ut veniam merear. Ecce eiicis me hodie a facie terrae, et a facie tua. Abscondar et ero vagus et profugus in terra; omnis igitur qui invenerit me occidet me." ("Cain said to the Lord, 'My punishment is too great to bear. You are driving me today from the soil; and from your face I shall be hidden. And I shall be a fugitive and a wanderer on the earth, and whoever finds me will kill me.' ")

134-35. *e fuggì come tuon . . . scoscende*: The voice dies out, like a thunderclap after it has split the cloud. For the phenomenon here, see n. to *Inf.* XXIV, 145-50.

136. *Come da lei l'udir nostro ebbe triegua*: "Our hearing" may be said to "have truce" from the voice (i.e., "lei") of vs. 132, which was so loud that it hurt the ears.

137. *ed ecco l'altra*: The turn of phrase with the definite article suggests that this second voice was expected, doubtless because there were two examples of charity at the beginning, to be matched in opposition now by these.

138. *che somigliò tonar che tosto segua*: The second voice follows quickly on the first, as a second thunderclap may follow another.

139. *Aglauro*: Aglauros was the daughter of Cecrops, king of Athens. According to one legend, she was changed into a stone by Mercury, because she through envy tried to prevent him from visiting her sister Herse, whom he loved. This story is told by Ovid in *Metam*. II, 737-832. Since Aglauros is an example of envy, it is significant that in Ovid's account Minerva in fact repairs to the cave of Envy and has Envy infect Aglauros with her venom; see *Metam*. II, 797-813:

> sed postquam thalamos intravit Cecrope natae,
> iussa facit pectusque manu ferrugine tincta
> tangit et hamatis praecordia sentibus inplet
> inspiratque nocens virus piceumque per ossa
> dissipat et medio spargit pulmone venenum,
> neve mali causae spatium per latius errent,
> germanam ante oculos fortunatumque sororis
> coniugium pulchraque deum sub imagine ponit
> cunctaque magna facit; quibus inritata dolore
> Cecropis occulto mordetur et anxia nocte
> anxia luce gemit lentaque miserrima tabe
> liquitur, ut glacies incerto saucia sole,
> felicisque bonis non lenius uritur Herses,
> quam cum spinosis ignis supponitur herbis,
> quae neque dant flammas lenique tepore cremantur.
> saepe mori voluit, ne quicquam tale videret,
> saepe velut crimen rigido narrare parenti.

But, having entered the chamber of Cecrops' daughter, she [Envy] performed the goddess' bidding, touched the girl's breast with her festering hand and filled her heart with pricking thorns. Then she breathed pestilential, poisonous breath into her nostrils and spread black venom through her very heart and bones. And, to fix a cause for her grief, Envy pictured to her imagination her sister, her sister's blest marriage and the god in all his beauty, magnifying the excellence of everything. Maddened by this, Aglauros eats her heart out in secret misery; careworn by day, careworn by night, she groans and wastes away most wretchedly with slow decay, like ice touched by the fitful sunshine. She is consumed by envy of Herse's happiness; just as when a fire is set under a pile of weeds, which give out no flames and waste away with slow consumption. She often longed to die that she might not behold such happiness; often to tell it, as 'twere a crime, to her stern father.

The succession of examples from the Bible and those from pagan mythology continues to be observed.

140-41. *per ristrignermi . . . passo*: The voices are loud enough to frighten Dante, causing him to draw close to Virgil, who is on his right. Some texts read "indietro" instead of "in destro." Cf. M. Barbi (1934b), p. 249.

142. *aura = aria.*

143. *camo*: Cf. *freno* in *Purg.* XIII, 40. See Ps. 31[32]:9: "In camo et freno maxillas eorum constringe, qui non approximant ad te." ("With bit and bridle their temper must be curbed, else they will not come near you.") Also see Dante, *De mon.* III, xvi, 9.

144. *dovria = dovrebbe.*   *meta*: The bounds assigned to man by God.

145-46. *Ma voi prendete l'esca . . . tira*: See Eccles. 9:12: "Nescit homo finem suum, sed sicut pisces capiuntur hamo." ("Man no more knows his own time than fish taken in the fatal net.")

145. *voi*: You the living, mankind in general, beset by envy. See *Inf.* I, 111.

146. *l'antico avversaro*: The devil. Cf. *Purg.* VIII, 95; XI, 20.

147. *però = perciò.   freno o richiamo*: Dual subject of "val." The curb would be the examples of envy punished by God's justice; the lure, the examples of charity that have been rewarded by His justice. For "richiamo" as "lure," see *Inf.* III, 117.

148. *Chiamavi = vi chiama.*

151. *chi tutto discerne*: God.

1-2. *tra l'ultimar de l'ora terza . . . dì*: The "end of the third hour" is midmorning, or 9:00 A.M., and the span measured here is the first three hours of the day. It is precisely the end of this span that marks the significant point, for it is then that the office is said. See *Conv.* IV, xxiii, 15-16, where Dante explains why he measures the canonical divisions of the day backward from midday for the morning hours and forward from midday for the afternoon hours:

> Però che la sesta ora, cioè lo mezzo die, è la più nobile di tutto lo die e la più virtuosa, li suoi offici appressa quivi da ogni parte, cioè da prima e di poi, quanto puote. E però l'officio de la prima parte del die, cioè la terza, si dice in fine di quella; e quello de la terza parte e de la quarta si dice ne li principii.

> Because the sixth hour, which is midday, is the most noble of the whole day, and the most virtuous, she [the Church] approximates her offices thereto from each direction, that is to say before and after, as much as she may. And therefore the office of the first part of the day, that is Tierce, is said at the end of that, and that of the third part and of the fourth is said at the beginning.

2-3. *la spera . . . scherza*: One of the clearest explications of this much debated passage is the following by B. Nardi (1953, pp. 7-8):

Ma la spera del sole si muove di moto retrogrado intorno ad un asse inclinato sull'asse del mondo, con un periodo annuo che si compone col movimento diurno. Per questo la lucerna del mondo surge ogni giorno ai mortali da una foce sempre diversa; sì che nel suo annuo periodo la spera solare descrive quella spirale ascendente e discendente, chiusa fra i due tropici, e detta dai matematici "spirale di Eudosso" e dagli arabi "laulab," parola che i latini del medio evo tradussero coll'espressione di "giratio laulabina." Movendosi su questa spirale ascendente e discendente, il sole ora nasce sotto un segno zodiacale ora sotto un altro e si avvicina ora più al Tropico del Cancro ora più a quello del Capricorno. Per questo ritmico e continuo innalzarsi ed abbassarsi, ora sopra ora sotto l'equatore, il sole e la spera di cui è parte suscitano nell'immaginazione del Poeta l'idea di un fanciullo che giuochi, correndo di qua, correndo di là, senza mai stancarsi.

Now the sphere of the sun moves around its axis, which is inclined on the axis of the world, in a backward movement, the period of which is a year; and this [backward] movement is taking place together with the [sun's] diurnal movement. That is why mortals always see the lamp of the world rising at a different source. In its annual period, the solar sphere describes that ascending and descending spiral contained between the two tropics, called the "spiral of Eudoxus" by mathematicians and called "laulab" by the Arabs—a word which in medieval Latin was translated as *giratio laulabina*. Moving in this ascending and descending spiral, the sun rises now under one zodiacal sign, now under another; at one time it approaches the Tropic of Cancer, at another, the Tropic of Capricorn. Because of this rhythmic and continuous rise and fall, now above and now below the equator, the sun and the sphere of which it is a part give rise, in the poet's imagination, to the idea of a boy playing, running here and there, without ever getting tired.

4–6. *tanto pareva . . . era*: Porena quite rightly insists that "la spera" described in vss. 2-3 and the "sol" of vs. 5 are essentially identical (see *Purg*. XVII, 5-6: "la spera / del sol") and that those commentators who fail to recognize this find themselves in difficulties. However, it should be said that "la spera" in its spiral between the tropics is a fused notion, focusing on the sun as moving in the course of its entire annual revolution, whereas the sun with three hours' time remaining for its course on this particular day in Purgatory clearly presents a much narrower view of that disk. In the latter view it cannot be seen as a child at play at all, of course, but simply as the sun with $45°$ yet to descend to its setting.

Thus the reader is told that it is mid-afternoon now in Purgatory ("là"), the beginning of the fourth division of the day, Vespers, which extends from 3:00 to 6:00 P.M., and it is midnight in Italy ("qui"), where the poet presumably is as he writes his poem. It is therefore 3:00 A.M. in Jerusalem. (See C. S. Singleton, *Inferno Commentary*, Fig. 7, p. 640.)

7–9. *i raggi ne ferien . . . occaso*: It should be recalled that in this season, as seen from the mountain of Purgatory, the sun would set in the northwest (see *Purg*. III, 16-18, on the rising sun). "Occaso" should be understood not as the west, but as the place where the sun is to set, in the northwest in this instance. The wayfarers faced west when they began their climb up the mountain. But by going a certain distance to the right in Antepurgatory and on each of two terraces, they are now facing directly northwest as they walk on around the terrace, and accordingly the sun's rays strike them directly "on the nose."

7. *ne = ci.   ferien = ferivano.*

8. *per noi = da noi.* For this construction, see *Inf.* I, 126.

10–11. *quand' io senti' . . . prima*: Dante is suddenly obliged to lower his eyes, which are dazzled by an increase of light ("splendore" suggesting already more than a "natural" cause here), which for the moment remains mysterious since the sun would hardly have become suddenly so much brighter.

11. *a lo splendore = da lo splendore*. Sapegno comments: "È complemento d'agente, retto dalla preposizione *a*, in dipendenza di un verbo *sentiendi*." ("It is a complement of agent, ruled by the preposition *a* and depending on a verb of perception.")   *di prima = prima*.

12. *non conte*: I.e., not understood. Cf. "conto" in *Purg.* XIII, 105.

14. *fecimi = mi feci.   fecimi 'l solecchio*: *Farsi il solecchio* means to shade the eyes with the hand, as indicated.

15. *che del soverchio visibile lima*: "Visibile" is used here in the sense of "that which is seen." In *Conv.* III, ix, 10, Dante writes: "Veramente Plato e altri filosofi dissero che 'l nostro vedere non era perchè lo visibile venisse a l'occhio, ma perchè la virtù visiva andava fuori al visibile: e questa oppinione è riprovata per falsa dal Filosofo, in quello del Senso e Sensato." ("It is true that Plato and other philosophers declared that our seeing was not due to the visible coming into our eye, but to the visual power going out to the visible. And this opinion is refuted as false by the Philosopher in that *Of Sense and its Object*.") The shading of the eyes is thus said to remove (literally, "file down") the "excess" of that which is seen, here the excess of visible light.

16–21. *Come quando . . . arte*: The ray of light is conceived as falling on a horizontal surface, on water or on a mirror horizontally placed. Dante is of course unable to see that such is not the case here before him, as will soon be evident. (See Fig. 2, p. 318.)

18–19. *salendo su per lo modo . . . scende*: Rising back up at the same angle it descended. Norton observes: "The angle of reflection of a ray being equal to that of the angle of incidence, the distance of the direct or the reflected ray

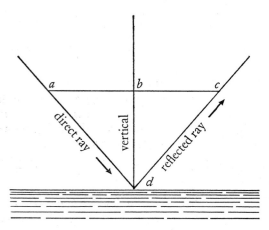

Figure 2. Direct and reflected rays of light

from the perpendicular—the fall of a plummet—at a given point is the same."

18. *parecchio = pari*. Cf. "pareglio" in *Par.* XXVI, 107 and 108, and the French *pareil*.

19. *e tanto si diparte*: That is, departs as much as the descending ray departs.

20. *dal cader de la pietra*: From the perpendicular or plumb line.   *in igual tratta*: At an equal space or distance. See Fig. 2 (above): points *a* and *c*, wherever taken, will always be equally distant from the perpendicular (*b*). B. Nardi (1953, p. 9) observes:

> Il fenomeno è ben noto a Dante, non tanto per l'esperienza comune che tutti n'abbiamo fatto, quanto perchè egli ha studiato il fenomeno della riflessione della luce sulla scorta di quella "arte che si chiama perspectiva" (*Conviv.*, II, III, 6) e che è "ancella della geometria" (ib. II, XIII, 26), della quale arte erano maestri ai contemporanei di Dante e l'arabo Alhazen ed Witelo ed altri, nei cui trattati si trova appunto dimostrata coll'espe-

rienza e col ragionamento la legge elementare del-
l'Ottica, che cioè l'angolo d'incidenza è uguale all'angolo
di riflessione, calcolati qui l'uno e l'altro in rapporto alla
verticale del piano sul quale il poeta cammina. . . .
(Witelo, *Perspec.* V, 10; cfr. Alhazen, *Optica* IV, cap.
3, n. 10; Eucl. *Catoptr.* th. 1; Tolomeo, *Catoptr.* I, th.
4).

Erudizione ingombrante? No; ma bisogno di preci-
sione da parte d'un uomo che ha contratto l'abito della
"subtilitas," ossia dell'acume e dell'esattezza nelle sue
osservazioni.

The phenomenon is well known to Dante, not just be-
cause it is an experience common to us all, but rather
because he had studied the phenomenon of reflection
of light in connection with that "art called perspective"
(*Conv.* II, iii, 6) which is "the handmaiden of geome-
try" (*Conv.* II, xiii, 26[27]). The masters of that art
in Dante's time were the Arab Alhazen, Witelo, and
others, in whose treatises we find demonstrated, through
experience and reason, the elementary law of the
Optics, i.e., that the angle of incidence is equal to the
angle of reflection. Here they are both calculated in re-
lation to a vertical line drawn to the plain on which the
poet is walking. . . . (Witelo, *Perspec.* V, 10; cf.
Alhazen, *Optica* IV, cap. 3, n. 10; Eucl. *Catoptr.* th. 1;
Tolomeo, *Catoptr.* I, th. 4).

Useless erudition? No. Rather, it is a necessity for
precision on the part of someone who has formed the
habit of *subtilitas,* that is to say, of discernment and
exactitude in his observations.

tratta: Archaic for *tratto,* the noun.

21. *sì come mostra esperienza e arte*: The singular verb
has a dual subject.   *esperienza*: I.e., a devised experience.

arte: Theoretical science (see the quotation from B. Nardi
in the preceding note and cf. *Par.* II, 95-96).

22. *da luce rifratta*: By reflected light. Since the increase
of light which dazzled Dante would not come suddenly from

the sun, he imagines that it must come from reflection, but how this can be is hidden from him. This is not meant to indicate that Dante conceives the light to be reflected back from the stone floor of the terrace or from any specific object, horizontal or otherwise, but is intended to introduce by simile the notion of reflected light, descending from above; when the light proves to be the radiance of an angel, that notion carries over to connote a refulgence that is both spiritual and physical, a "light of Heaven" (cf. *Purg.* XIII, 69).

24. *per che a fuggir la mia vista fu ratta*: The extreme brightness forces Dante to turn his eyes away from it (literally, forces his eyes to flee from it); presumably he turns toward Virgil.   *ratta = rapida.*

25. *a che = da cui.*

26. *schermar = schermire.   tanto che mi vaglia*: "So that it may avail me," i.e., that I may discern what it is.

27. *e pare inver' noi esser mosso*: Dante cannot see this, hence it "seems." But if he has any such impression, it must be that the dazzling light seems to become more intense and hence may in fact be drawing nearer.   *inver' = verso.*

28. *s'ancor t'abbaglia*: Dante has been dazzled by the radiance of angels before: *Purg.* II, 38-40.

29. *la famiglia del cielo*: Angels. Porena observes that *famiglia* implies here a notion not of consanguinity, but of dependence. Cf. *famiglia del podestà*, i.e., the police force of a medieval Italian city, commanded by the *podestà*.

30. *messo*: For the term as applied to angels, see *Inf.* IX, 85, and "messaggier" in *Purg.* XXX, 18.   *che viene ad invitar*: The angel of humility at the exit of the first circle came forward to meet the wayfarers in a similar manner. This second messenger shows its charity by so doing.   *ch'om saglia = che si salga.* Cf. the French *on.*

31-33. *Tosto sarà . . . dispuose*: This progress, promised to Dante in terms of an ability to endure such radiance, may

be compared to that which was vouchsafed him in the mat-
ter of his climbing's becoming progressively easier (see *Purg.*
IV, 88-94); and Virgil here, as there, means that this will
prove to be so by the time Dante reaches the summit. In fact
he is then able to look upon such heavenly messengers with-
out being dazzled (*Purg.* XXX, 16-21).

32. *fia = sarà.   fieti = ti sarà.*

33. *quanto natura a sentir ti dispuose*: Virgil speaks of a
natural disposition, though the effulgence of angels has, of
course, a supernatural source, as suggested in the verses
above which concern reflected light.

34. *Poi = poi che.*

35. *quinci = per qui*, words which could well be accom-
panied by a gesture.

36. *scaleo*: A flight of stairs.   *vie = via* (the adverb),
"far."

37. *linci*: "Thence," i.e., from the entrance to the stairway.
From the Latin *illinc*. See E. G. Parodi (1957), p. 261.

38. *Beati misericordes*: The fifth beatitude of the Sermon
on the Mount. See Matt. 5:7: "Beati misericordes, quoniam
ipsi misericordiam consequentur." ("Blessed are the merci-
ful, for they shall obtain mercy.") As usual, the first words
of the beatitude are meant to suggest the rest. None of the
beatitudes refers explicitly to charity (the virtue that opposes
envy), which a beatitude at the exit of this particular circle
would be expected to express. The poet has chosen the beati-
tude that speaks of mercy, meaning here a concern and com-
passion for others, which is indeed the opposite of envy, since
it signifies sadness for the evil suffered by others, as against
sadness for the good received by others, the standard defini-
tion of envy. See Thomas Aquinas, *Summa theol.* II-II, q. 36,
a. 3, resp.:

> Invidia autem secundum rationem sui obiecti contra-
> riatur charitati, per quam est vita animae spiritualis,

secundum illud 1 Ioan. 14: *Nos scimus quoniam trans-
lati sumus de morte ad vitam, quoniam diligimus fratres.*
Utriusque autem obiectum, et charitatis, et invidiae,
est bonum proximi; sed secundum contrarium motum;
nam charitas gaudet de bono proximi; invidia autem
de eodem tristatur.

And envy according to the aspect of its object is con-
trary to charity, whence the soul derives its spiritual
life, according to 1 Io. iii. 14, *We know that we have
passed from death to life, because we love the brethren.*
Now the object both of charity and of envy is our neigh-
bor's good, but by contrary movements, since charity
rejoices in our neighbor's good, while envy grieves over
it, as stated above.

Aquinas continues (ad 3):

Nam misericordiae opponitur directe, secundum con-
trarietatem principalis obiecti; invidus enim tristatur
de bono proximi; misericors autem tristatur de malo
proximi; unde invidi non sunt misericordes . . . nec e
converso. . . . Unde patet quod prima contrarietas est
magis directa quam secunda. Misericordia autem
quaedam virtus est, et charitatis proprius effectus. Unde
invidia misericordiae opponitur et charitati.

For it [envy] is directly contrary to pity, their princi-
pal objects being contrary to one another, since the
envious man grieves over his neighbor's good, whereas
the pitiful man grieves over his neighbor's evil, so that
the envious have no pity . . . nor is the pitiful man en-
vious. . . . Hence it is clear that the former contrariety
is more direct than the latter. Now pity is a virtue, and
an effect proper to charity: so that envy is contrary to
pity and charity.

39. *cantato retro*: The beatitude is chanted by the angel
standing at the foot of the stairway.   *Godi tu che vinci*:
This is not a paraphrase of the rest of the fifth beatitude, but
words of encouragement and comfort to the wayfarer who
now climbs the stair victoriously, having progressed to the

point of having another letter P removed from his forehead, though he and the reader learn only later (vs. 80) that this has happened. Cf. the conclusion to all the beatitudes, Matt. 5:12: "Gaudete et exultate, quoniam merces vestra copiosa est in caelis." ("Rejoice and exult, because your reward is great in heaven.") Thereby the angel further shows its charity, rejoicing in the good attained by Dante.

40–41. *soli amendue suso andavamo*: Dante and Virgil have left the angel behind and without other company are proceeding up the stairway.

41–42. *pensai, andando, prode acquistar*: Typically, Dante will take advantage of a moment when there are no other distractions and he can gain profit ("prode") from Virgil's words.

43. *dirizza'mi = mi dirizzai.*

44–45. *Che volse dir . . . menzionando?* This "planting" of a question by way of some turn of phrase uttered by a soul or by Virgil (or later, by Beatrice) will become more frequent in the poem, serving to make the wayfarer's journey a journey of the mind which passes certain major intellectual mileposts, the big questions.

44. *volse = volle.   lo spirto di Romagna*: Guido del Duca. Dante queries Virgil here on the question posed by Guido in *Purg.* XIV, 86-87.

46–47. *Di sua maggior magagna . . . danno*: Guido's greatest fault was envy (see *Purg.* XIV, 82-84), for which he has his eyes sewed shut in Purgatory. The "danno" referred to, however, is not the purgatorial punishment on the terrace of the envious, but the evil effects of envy for mankind, the living. Guido's words were, in fact, addressed to "gente umana."

46. *magagna*: "Fault," "vice." Cf. *Inf.* XXXIII, 152.

47. *però = perciò.   non s'ammiri*: "Let it not be wondered at."

48. *se ne riprende*: Guido's words were an admonition to us, the living, that we may correct our envious ways and so have less to weep for, both in life and here in Purgatory. "Riprende" therefore has human kind, the living, as its object, understood but not expressed; "ne" here is not *ci*, but has its more common sense, "for it."   *piagna = pianga*.

49. *Perché s'appuntano i vostri disiri*: With the plural "vostri" Virgil addresses us, the living, even as Guido did, since he now explains what Guido meant by stating the matter as he did.

50. *dove per compagnia parte si scema*: Where the share is made less through partnership.

51. *invidia move il mantaco a' sospiri*: Envy causes men to move their chests to sigh over the fact that there has to be any sharing of earthly goods. The chest and lungs constitute the metaphorical bellows.   *mantaco = mantice*.

52. *l'amor de la spera supprema*: The "highest sphere" is the Empyrean heaven, the abode of the elect, toward which, as toward our proper goal, our desires should be directed.

53. *torcesse*: "Torcesse" is in the contrary-to-fact subjunctive and suggests a certain violence: "twisted," "wrested."

54. *quella tema*: The fear of having to lose through sharing.

55–57. *ché, per quanti si dice . . . chiostro*: See Scartazzini-Vandelli for the following passage from Fra Giordano:

> Mistieri è che se io voglio arricchire, che molti ne 'mpoveriscano, imperò che le cose del mondo non si possono avere per tutti: pochi sono quelli che l'hanno, e ogni uomo le vuole. . . . Ma i beni di Paradiso i quali non *iscemano* perchè l'altro ne sia ricco—però che bastano e soperchiano etternalmente e infinitamente—e' non si possono occupare nè diminuire *per quantunque* siano quelli che ne diventano ricchi. E come vedi per esempio del sole, che allumina tutti e non manca il lume a nullo per la veduta dell'altro.

If I want to get rich, it is necessary that many others become poor, for not everyone can have the goods of this world. Those who have them are few; but everyone wants them. . . . But the goods of Paradise, which do not *diminish* because someone has lots of them—for they are infinitely and eternally sufficient and super-abundant—cannot be taken up or diminished *no matter how many* men are rich in those goods. They are like the sun, which illuminates things for everyone, and does not fail to shed its light on someone just because someone else is using that light.

In *Prediche inedite* LVIII, Fra Giordano says: "Per questa ragione vorrei che ogni uomo avesse quelli diletti; chè quanti più fossero quelli che n'avessero, più diletto avrei, cioè che avrei diletto di tutto il diletto degli altri." ("For this reason, I would like to see every man enjoy these [spiritual] pleasures; and the more men enjoyed them, the more pleased I would be, for I would derive pleasure from their pleasure.") He continues in the same sermon:

Tra santi di paradiso non può esser discordia o tencione nulla; perocchè 'l bene loro è sì comune, che abbiendolo io non lo scemo agli altri, nè gli altri a me, anzi ne cresce quello di catuno per lo bene c'hanno tutti; e però genera pace e dà amore di carità al prossimo.

There can be no discord or dispute among the saints in Paradise, for the nature of the good they enjoy in common is such that, if I have it, I do not decrease someone else's good, nor does someone else's possession of it decrease mine. In fact, each one's portion grows as everyone shares in it. And thus it generates peace and gives love of charity toward one's fellow man.

With Augustine it is *invidia* that divides the earthly and the heavenly cities from the beginning. See *De civ. Dei* XV, 5:

Sic enim condita est Roma, quando occisum Remum a fratre Romulo Romana testatur historia: nisi quod isti terrenae civitatis ambo cives erant. Ambo gloriam de Romanae reipublicae institutione quaerebant: sed ambo eam tantam, quantam, si unus esset, habere non poterant. Qui enim volebat dominando gloriari, minus utique dominaretur, si eius potestas vivo consorte minueretur. Ut ergo totam dominationem haberet unus, ablatus est socius: et scelere crevit in peius, quod innocentia minus esset et melius. Hi autem fratres Cain et Abel non habebant ambo inter se similem rerum terrenarum cupiditatem; nec in hoc alter alteri invidit, quod eius dominatus fieret angustior, qui alterum occidit, si ambo dominarentur (Abel quippe non quaerebat dominationem in ea civitate, quae condebatur a fratre): sed invidentia illa diabolica, qua invident bonis mali, nulla alia causa, nisi quia illi boni sunt, illi mali. Nullo enim modo fit minor accedente seu permanente consorte possessio bonitatis; immo possessio bonitas, quam tanto latius, quanto concordius individua sociorum possidet charitas. Non habebit denique istam possessionem, qui eam noluerit habere communem; et tanto eam reperiet ampliorem, quanto amplius ibi potuerit amare consortem.

For Rome began, as Roman history records, when Remus was killed by Romulus, his brother. However, in this case, both men were citizens of the earthly city. It was the ambition of both of them to have the honor of founding the Roman republic, but that was an honor that could not be shared; it had to belong to one or the other. For, no one who had a passion to glory in domination could be fully the master if his power were diminished by a living co-regent. One of the two wanted to have the whole of the sovereignty; therefore, his associate was removed. Without the crime, his position would have had less power, but more prestige. However, the crime made everything worse than before.

In the case of the brothers Cain and Abel, there was no rivalry in any cupidity for the things of earth, nor was there any envy or temptation to murder arising from a fear of losing the sovereignty if both were ruling together. In this case, Abel had no ambition for domination in the city that his brother was building. The root of the trouble was that diabolical envy which moves evil men to hate those who are good for no other reason than that they are good. Unlike material possessions, goodness is not diminished when it is shared, either momentarily or permanently, with others, but expands, and, in fact, the more heartily each of the lovers of goodness enjoys the possession the more does goodness grow. What is more, goodness is not merely a possession that no one can maintain who is unwilling to share it, but it is one that increases the more its possessor loves to share it.

57. *e più di caritate arde*: The Empyrean is a heaven of fire, the fire being love. *chiostro*: Porena remarks that the Empyrean is called a cloister perhaps because perfect charity is the model of what a cloister ought to be. Cf. *Purg.* XXVI, 128-29; *Par.* XXV, 127.

58. *digiuno*: Cf. *Inf.* XVIII, 42; XXVIII, 87.

59. *fosse* = *fossi*.

61. *puote* = *può*. *distributo* = *distribuito*.

62. *in più posseditor*: In many (not more) possessors—in contrast to "pochi" of vs. 63.

64. *Però* = *per ciò*. *rificchi*: The prefix *ri-* expresses persistence.

65. *pur*: Exclusively.

66. *di vera luce* = *da luce di verità*. *dispicchi*: Literally, "you pluck."

67. *Quello infinito e ineffabil bene*: God's goodness ("valore," vs. 72); now, metaphorically, His light.

69. *com' a lucido corpo raggio vene*: See Thomas Aquinas, *Summa theol.* I-II, q. 85, a. 2, resp.: "Sicut patet de diaphano corpore, quod quidem habet inclinationem ad susceptionem lucis ex hoc ipso quod est diaphanum." ("An example of this may be seen in a transparent body, which has an inclination to receive light, from the very fact that it is

transparent.") Also see Dante, *Conv.* III, xiv, 3: "Onde ve-
demo lo sole che, discendendo lo raggio suo qua giù, reduce
le cose a sua similitudine di lume, quanto esse per loro dis-
posizione possono da la [sua] virtude lume ricevere."
("Whence we see that the sun, when his ray descends down
here, reduces things to the similitude of light in so far as by
their dispositions they have the capacity for receiving light
from his power.") Thus, a luminous body was thought to
have an inclination, or disposition, to receive light, and there-
fore light came to it as to that which was disposed to receive
it.

70. *Tanto si dà quanto trova d'ardore*: To the extent that
it finds there the fire of charity in the elect, it gives itself.

72. *cresce sovr' essa l'etterno valore*: Grandgent comments:
"In other words, God's blessing corresponds to the measure
of affection of the loving soul, and is really added to it."

73-74. *E quanta gente . . . s'ama*: As many commentators
point out, *intendersi*, in old Provençal (*s'entender en*) and
early Italian, means "to love." Thus, the more souls there
are up there in the Empyrean who love God, the more right-
eous love ("bene amare") there is there, and the more lov-
ing (i.e., on the part of all) there is there ("vi s'ama").

75. *e come specchio l'uno a l'altro rende*: There is increase
of loving, as there would be increase of light (the glowing
of love) if as many mirrors as there are souls of the blessed
should give back the light that flows to them (vs. 69) as to
luminous bodies disposed to receive it. This amounts to a
veritable "chain reaction" of love.

76. *ragion* = *ragionamento*. *disfama*: "Satisfies your
hunger." This completes the metaphor of *essere digiuno* (vs.
58) and anticipates "brama" (vs. 78).

77-78. *vedrai Beatrice . . . brama*: Virgil seems to recog-
nize that his discourse has exceeded the range of his natural
understanding and were best left to Beatrice and the super-
natural enlightenment she stands for. Cf. *Purg.* VI, 43-45;
XVIII, 46-48.

79. *spente* = *spinte*, i.e., *sdipinte*. Torraca points out that *spente* is the contrary of *pente* (i.e., *pinte*, from *pingere*, *dipingere*) and that, in fact, *spegnere* was used to mean "to erase," "to remove," paintings or inscriptions on walls.

80. *come son già le due*: By this we learn that the angel of charity removed the second P from Dante's forehead when it came to meet him at the foot of the stairs.

81. *che si richiudon per esser dolente*: "Which are healed through being painful," i.e., through painful expiation here in Purgatory. Dante's token participation in the purgatorial punishment of each terrace is thus pointed to again. Cf. *Purg.* XII, 1-3, 8-9.

82. *m'appaghe'* = *m'appaghi*.

83. *vidimi giunto* = *mi vidi giunto*.   *in su l'altro girone*: Dante steps on to the third terrace.

84. *fer* = *fecero*.   *le luci vaghe*: Cf. *Purg.* X, 103-4. But his "eager eyes" see nothing, for at once he is caught up in an ecstatic vision.

86. *tratto*: "Drawn into."

87-92. *vedere in un tempio . . . cercavamo*: Here on the third terrace of Purgatory, as before, the first example of the virtue that opposes the vice being purged is taken from the life of Mary, an example now of gentleness, or *mansuetudo*: it is the scene in the temple when Mary and Joseph returned to Jerusalem in search of the child Jesus and found Him in the temple, sitting in the midst of the teachers (the "più persone"). See Luc. 2:40-48:

> Puer autem crescebat et confortabatur, plenus sapientia, et gratia Dei erat in illo. Et ibant parentes eius per omnes annos in Ierusalem in die solemni Paschae. Et cum factus esset annorum duodecim, ascendentibus illis Ierosolymam secundum consuetudinem diei festi, consummatisque diebus, cum redirent, remansit puer Iesus in Ierusalem, et non cognoverunt parentes eius.

Existimantes autem illum esse in comitatu venerunt iter diei; et requirebant eum inter cognatos et notos. Et non invenientes, regressi sunt in Ierusalem requirentes eum.

Et factum est, post triduum invenerunt illum in templo sedentem in medio doctorum, audientem illos et interrogantem eos. Stupebant autem omnes qui eum audiebant super prudentia et responsis eius. Et videntes admirati sunt. Et dixit mater eius ad illum: Fili, quid fecisti nobis sic? Ecce pater tuus et ego dolentes quaerebamus te.

And the child grew and became strong. He was full of wisdom and the grace of God was upon him.

And his parents were wont to go every year to Jerusalem at the Feast of the Passover. And when he was twelve years old, they went up to Jerusalem according to the custom of the feast. And after they had fulfilled the days, when they were returning, the boy Jesus remained in Jerusalem, and his parents did not know it. But thinking that he was in the caravan, they had come a day's journey before it occurred to them to look for him among their relatives and acquaintances. And not finding him, they returned to Jerusalem in search of him.

And it came to pass after three days, that they found him in the temple, sitting in the midst of the teachers, listening to them and asking them questions. And all who were listening to him were amazed at his understanding and his answers. And when they saw him, they were astonished. And his mother said to him, "Son, why hast thou done so to us? Behold, in sorrow thy father and I have been seeking thee."

88–89. *con atto dolce di madre*: Mary's attitude points up the gentleness of which this episode is the example.

93. *ciò che pareva prima = ciò che appariva prima*, i.e., the vision itself.   *dispario = disparì*.

94–105. *Indi m'apparve . . . condannato*: Dante's second

ecstatic vision, the second example of gentleness, is that of
Pisistratus, tyrant of Athens, whose story is related by Va-
lerius Maximus (doubtless deriving, directly or indirectly,
from him). See *Fact. dict. memor.* V, i, ext. 2:

> [Pisistratus Atheniensis tyrannus] cum adulescens
> quidam amore filiae eius virginis accensus in publico
> obviam sibi factam osculatus esset, hortante uxore ut
> ab eo capitale supplicium sumeret, respondit: "si eos,
> qui nos amant interficiemus, quid eis faciemus, quibus
> odio sumus?"

> [Pisistratus, tyrant of Athens,] when a youth in love
> with a daughter of his came up to her in the street and
> kissed her, and his wife urged that he be put to death
> for this, replied: "If we slay those who love us, what
> shall we do to those who hate us?"

Thus the device of alternating examples between biblical and
non-biblical (and, in the biblical, between Old Testament
and New Testament), as on the first and second terraces, is
continued, as is then evident from the third example, that of
St. Stephen.

94. *un'altra = un'altra donna.* This is the wife of Pisis-
tratus.   *acque*: Tears.

95. *che 'l dolor distilla*: Cf. *Inf.* XXIII, 97-98.

96. *quando di gran dispetto in altrui nacque*: Porena com-
ments: "Come si fa a distinguere nelle lagrime quale sia la
loro causa speciale? Evidentemente qui Dante, se pure lette-
ralmente le sue parole si riferiscano alle lagrime soltanto,
vuole accennare all'espressione che si dipinge su tutto il volto
della moglie di Pisistrato." ("How can anyone distinguish the
particular cause of those tears? Evidently, Dante here wants
to indicate all the expression depicted on the face of Pisis-
tratus' wife, even though literally his words refer only to the
tears.") In fact, the qualification amounts to a kind of
pseudo-simile. Cf. "dirò come colui che piange a dice" in
Inf. V, 126.

97. *e dir*: The wife speaks.   *sire de la villa*: Lord of the city of Athens. For "villa" meaning city, cf. *Inf.* XXIII, 95, where it refers to Florence.

98. *del cui nome ne' dèi fu tanta lite*: The reference is to the contest between the Greek goddess Athena and Poseidon as to who should give a name to the capital of Cecropia, the original name of Athens. According to the tradition, this contest took place in the reign of Cecrops, the first king. The decision rested with the other gods, who declared that their award would be given in favor of whichever of the two should confer the most useful gift upon mankind. Poseidon thereupon struck the ground with his trident, and straightway water or, according to another story, a horse appeared, while Athena planted an olive tree. The gods decided that the olive was the more useful to man and awarded the victory to Athena, whose name the city thenceforth bore. The contest is mentioned by Ovid (*Metam.* VI, 70-82) and described (after the account given by Varro) by Augustine (*De civ. Dei* XVIII, 9), from whom Dante may have got the story.

99. *e onde ogne scïenza disfavilla*: See Cicero, *De oratore* I, iv, 13:

> Atque ut omittam Graeciam, quae semper eloquentiae princeps esse voluit, atque illas omnium doctrinarum inventrices Athenas, in quibus summa dicendi vis et inventa est et perfecta: in hac ipsa civitate profecto nulla unquam vehementius, quam eloquentiae studia viguerunt.

> In fact, to say nothing of Greece, which has ever claimed the leading part in eloquence, and of Athens, that discoverer of all learning, where the supreme power of oratory was both invented and perfected, in this city of our own assuredly no studies have ever had a more vigorous life than those having to do with the art of speaking.

See also Augustine's reference in *De civ. Dei* XVIII, 9 to Athens as "mater ac nutrix liberalium doctrinarum, et tot tantorumque philosophorum" ("the mother and nurse of liberal studies and of so many great philosophers"). *dis-favilla*: "Sparkles forth," suggesting the shedding of light abroad.

100. *vendica te*: Porena comments: "Si noti come la donna vuol parere obiettiva, stimolando Pisistrato a vendicare *sè*, non anche lei!" ("Note how the woman wants to seem objective, urging Pisistratus to avenge himself, not herself as well!")

101. *abbracciar = abbracciarono*.

102. *E 'l segnor*: Pisistratus, the "sire" of vs. 97.

102–3. *benigno e mite . . . temperato*: As in the case of Mary in the preceding vision, there is stress on the quality of gentleness, the virtue here exemplified.

103. *lei = a lei*.

104–5. *Che farem noi . . . condannato?* Pisistratus speaks in the "plural of majesty."

104. *ne = ci*.

105. *quei = quegli* (singular).   *per noi = da noi*.

106–14. *Poi vidi genti . . . diserra*: The third ecstatic vision is of the stoning of St. Stephen, protomartyr, who was slain outside the gates of Jerusalem by the Jews on a charge of blasphemy. See Actus 7:54-59[54-60]:

> Audientes autem haec, dissecabantur cordibus suis, et stridebant dentibus in eum. Cum autem esset plenus Spiritu Sancto, intendens in caelum vidit gloriam Dei, et Iesum stantem a dextris Dei; et ait: Ecce video caelos apertos, et Filium hominis stantem a dextris Dei. Exclamantes autem voce magna, continuerunt aures suas, et impetum fecerunt unanimiter in eum. Et eiicientes eum extra civitatem lapidabant; et testes deposuerunt vestimenta sua secus pedes adolescentis, qui vocabatur Saulus. Et lapidabant Stephanum invocantem et dicentem: Domine Iesu, suscipe spiritum meum. Positis

autem genibus, clamavit voce magna dicens: Domine,
ne statuas illis hoc peccatum. Et cum hoc dixisset, ob-
dormivit in Domino. Saulus autem erat consentiens neci
eius.

Now as they heard these things, they were cut to the
heart and gnashed their teeth at him. But he, being full
of the Holy Spirit, looked up to heaven and saw the
glory of God, and Jesus standing at the right hand of
God; and he said, "Behold, I see the heavens opened,
and the Son of Man standing at the right hand of God."
But they cried out with a loud voice and stopped their
ears and rushed upon him all together. And they cast
him out of the city and stoned him. And the witnesses
laid down their garments at the feet of a young man
named Saul. And while they were stoning Stephen he
prayed and said, "Lord Jesus, receive my spirit." And
falling on his knees, he cried out with a loud voice, say-
ing, "Lord, do not lay this sin against them." And with
these words he fell asleep. And Saul approved of his
death.

107. *un giovinetto*: On the youthfulness of Stephen,
B. Nardi (1953, pp. 21-22) comments:

Questo appellativo di "giovinetto" fece un tempo arric-
ciare il naso allo Scartazzini. Il quale pretendeva, senz'
alcuna ragione, che quando Stefano fu lapidato, fosse
già "uomo maturo," magari con tanto di barba, e non
badò che proprio negli *Atti* (VI, 15), quei che sedevano
nel concilio, guardandolo, "viderunt faciem eius tan-
quam faciem angeli." Ora gli angeli, dalle figurazioni
evangeliche fino alla "Révolte des Anges" di Anatole
France, son sempre stati rappresentati come giovani im-
berbi. E giovane imberbe appare S. Stefano nella icono-
grafia ecclesiastica predantesca, come si vede nel bas-
sorilievo del timpano della porta laterale sud di Notre
Dame, del tempo di S. Luigi, nel codice vaticano della
Topografia Cristiana di Cosma del sec. XI, come ha
fatto rilevare Fedele Romani, e in un dipinto di scuola
giottesca della cattedrale di Prato. Orazio Bacci a

queste osservazioni aggiunge la testimonianza di un sermone attribuito a S. Agostino, ove si legge che il protomartire Stefano "in ipso flore juventutis decorem suae aetatis sanguine purpuravit"—nel fiore della gioventù rese purpurea di sangue la bellezza della sua età. Il sermone ricordato dal Bacci non pare di Agostino, ma esso è ugualmente assai antico e, quel che più conta, entrò nel Breviario Romano e servì a fissare l'iconografia del martirio di Stefano, della quale Dante ha accolto gli elementi più significativi e più patetici: la folla accesa in fuoco d'ira, cui fa contrasto la mansuetudine del giovinetto, chinato per la morte che lo aggrava, ma con lo sguardo rivolto al cielo in atto di pregare Dio perchè voglia perdonare ai suoi persecutori.

Del resto, è stato opportunamente notato che la parola "giovinetto" significa più spesso, in Dante, il finire dell' "adolescenza," a 25 anni, e l'inizio della "gioventù" che dai 25 anni si protrae fino ai 45. Così "giovinetti triunfaro Scipione e Pompeo," e "giovinetto in guerra del padre corse" San Francesco per amore di madonna Povertà.

The appellation "youthful" caused Scartazzini, at one time, to smirk somewhat contemptuously. Without any good reason, he claimed that Stephen was already a "mature man" with something of a beard when he was stoned. He seemed not to have noticed that precisely in Actus (6:15) those who sat in the council looking at him "saw his face as though it were the face of an angel." Now angels, from the evangelical depictions up to the *Revolt of the Angels* by Anatole France, have always been represented as beardless youths. In the pre-Dantesque ecclesiastical iconography, St. Stephen always appears as a beardless youth. Look at the bas-relief in the tympanum of the south side door of Notre Dame, done in the time of St. Louis; at the Vatican codex of the *Topographia Christiana* by Cosmas, of the eleventh century, as was observed by Fedele Romani; at a painting of the school of Giotto in the cathedral of Prato. To these observations, Orazio Bacci adds the testimony of a sermon attributed to St. Augustine, in which we read of the protomartyr Stephen who, "in the flower of youth, purpled with blood the beauty of his age." The sermon mentioned by Bacci does not seem to be by Augustine. Nevertheless it is very ancient, and, what is more, it entered the *Breviarium Romanum* and served to establish the iconography for the martyrdom of Stephen. Dante has chosen the most significant and the most pathetic elements of that martyrdom: the fiery anger of the mob, to which is contrasted the gentleness of the youth, bowed by the weight of death upon him, but with his gaze fixed toward heaven, in the act of begging God to forgive his persecutors.

Moreover, it has rightly been observed that Dante's use of the word *giovinetto* (young man) signifies, more often than not, the end of "adolescence," at twenty-five years, and the beginning of "youth," which extends from the age of twenty-five to forty-five. Thus "the young men Scipio and Pompey triumphed," and St. Francis, for love of our lady Poverty, "as a young man rushed into war with his father."

108. *a sé*: "To one another."   *pur*: "Repeatedly."

109. *vedea* = *vedevo*.

109-10. *per la morte . . . già*: See Ovid, *Metam.* IV, 145-46: "Ad nomen Thisbes oculos a morte gravatos / Pyramus erexit visaque recondidit illa." ("At the name of Thisbe, Pyramus lifted his eyes, now heavy with death, and having looked upon her face, closed them again.")

111. *ma de li occhi facea sempre al ciel porte*: See Actus 7:55: "intendens in caelum" ("looked up to heaven").

112-13. *orando a l'alto Sire . . . persecutori*: See Actus 7:59[60]. Also see *Purg.* V, 55-56. For "alto Sire," cf. *Inf.* XXIX, 56.

112. *in tanta guerra*: So fiercely assailed.

114. *con quello aspetto che pietà diserra*: Some commentators take this to mean that the countenance "unlocks compassion" in the agent himself, i.e., expresses pity. More probably the meaning is that the expression on his face "unlocks compassion" in the beholder, i.e., moves him to compassion. See M. Barbi (1934b), p. 249, who apparently wishes to have it both ways: "*Disserra* non può significare se non 'apre, sprigiona la Pietà,' sì che possa uscire a commuovere i cuori, sia pur chiusa in qualche angolo di essi." ("*Disserra* cannot mean anything but 'opens, releases pity,' so that it may come forth to move hearts, even though it is locked up in some corner of those hearts.")

115–17. *Quando l'anima mia . . . errori*: This tercet continues the conceit in which the examples of the first terrace were presented, where it was said that "he who saw the reality saw not better than I" in seeing these (*Purg.* XII, 68), and this is so because God made them. These three ecstatic visions are also God-given, and the same might be said of them, hence they can be termed "non falsi" and the poet can play on "errori" in the sense of "wanderings" of the mind from "the things that are real outside of it," i.e., external reality, to which Dante's mind returns when he comes out of his ecstasies. For the divine origin of these visions, see vs. 132 and *Purg.* XVII, 17-18; on the perception of external reality by the mind, see *Purg.* XVIII, 22-23. The visions are thus a subjective inner reality, but quite as real as are real things outside the mind.

119. *si slega*: "Unbinds himself."

120. *che non ti puoi tenere*: *Tenersi* means "to hold oneself" properly, to walk in a proper manner.

121. *più che mezza lega*: According to Jacopo della Lana, "lega" means a mile; but since the measure of a "league" varied so much from region to region, no exact meaning can be determined for the term as used by Virgil here.

123. *cui = colui cui*, or modern *chi*.

124. *ascolte* = *ascolti*.

127-29. *Se tu avessi . . . parve*: For Virgil's remark, cf. *Inf.* XVI, 118-26; XXIII, 25-27.

128. *sarian* = *sarebbero*.

129. *parve*: "Slight." From the Latin *parvae*.

130. *Ciò che vedesti*: I.e., in the three ecstatic visions.

130-31. *Ciò che vedesti . . . pace*: These things were given you to see so that henceforth you may not refuse to open your heart to the waters of peace.

131. *aprir lo core a l'acque*: The heart in question is of one who burns (or might burn) with wrath, which heats the blood about the heart. See Thomas Aquinas, *Summa theol.* I-II, q. 48, a. 2, resp.:

> Et quia motus irae non est per modum retractionis, cui proportionatur frigus, sed magis per modum insecutionis, cui proportionatur calor; consequenter fit motus irae causativus cuiusdam fervoris sanguinis et spirituum circa cor, quod est instrumentum passionum animae.

> And because the movement of anger is not one of recoil, which corresponds to the action of cold, but one of prosecution, which corresponds to the action of heat, the result is that the movement of anger produces fervor of the blood and vital spirits around the heart, which is the instrument of the soul's passions.

Aquinas continues (ad 1): "Fervor autem irae est cum amaritudine ad consumendum, quia tendit ad punitionem contrarii; unde assimilatur calori ignis et cholerae." ("On the other hand, the fervor of anger has a certain bitterness with a tendency to destroy, for it seeks to be avenged on the contrary evil: whence it is likened to the heat of fire and of the bile.") Dante's heart does not feel wrath in this moment; the examples of the opposing virtue, meekness or gentleness, are given to him, as to the souls of the wrathful of this terrace, that they may open his heart to that extinguishing virtue.

132. *da l'etterno fonte*: Cf. Ioan. 4:14: "fons aquae salien-
tis in vitam aeternam" ("a fountain of water, springing up
unto life everlasting"). The "eternal fountain" is God. Thus
it is clear that the visions are God-sent, even as the reliefs of
the first terrace were God-fashioned.

133–38. *Non dimandai . . . riede*: Commentators disagree
on the meaning of vss. 134-35. Some take the qualifying
phrase "che non vede . . . giace" to refer to Virgil and to
mean a mortal eye that can no longer see after the person in
question lies dead. But this seems far too banal a meaning.
The interpretation of Torraca, who understands the "corpo"
to be that of Dante in his ecstatic visions, seems preferable:

> Tenuto conto del valore di *per quel che face*, e conside-
> rando che Virgilio pone, di contro a *corpo, che giace
> disanimato*, i *pigri, lenti* a rimettersi al lavoro poi che
> si sono destati; mi pare che, per *corpo che giace disani-
> mato*, si debba intendere quello dell'uomo svenuto.

> Keeping in mind the import of "per quel che face," and
> considering that Virgil contrasts the body that lies in-
> sensible with those lazy ones who are slow to get to
> work after they have been roused, I think that the body
> that lies insensible must be understood to mean the
> body of a man who has fainted.

Torraca cites two good examples of such a use of *disanimato*
and continues:

> Ciò posto, altro è domandare: *Che hai?* a chi ha perduto
> i sensi, altro a chi è sveglio, ma s'indugia: nel primo
> caso, la domanda è oziosa, o sciocca addirittura, e suol
> farla chi guarda in modo da non vedere, da non
> accorgersi di parlare senz'essere udito; nel secondo caso,
> serve di sprone.

> It is, then, one thing to ask "che hai" of someone who
> lies senseless, and another thing to ask it of someone
> who is awake, but is slow in moving. In the first case
> the question is idle, or completely silly, and would be
> asked by someone who looks without seeing, without

noticing that he is speaking without being heard. In the
second case, it serves as a spur.

133. *face* = *fa*. In this construction "face" stands for the
main verb, *dimandare*.

137. *frugar*: "To prod." Cf. *Purg.* III, 3; XIV, 39.   *con-
viensi* = *si conviene*.

138. *vigilia* = *veglia*. Cf. *Inf.* XXVI, 114.

139. *lo vespero*: Cf. vs. 6.

142–43. *farsi verso di noi* = *venire incontro a noi*.

144. *né da quello era loco da cansarsi*: The smoke covers
the entire breadth of the terrace as it comes on, and there is
no escaping from it.

145. *ne* = *ci*.

CANTO XVI

1–2. *e di notte privata . . . cielo*: A dark night with no moon or other planet shining in the sky and with few if any stars. "Cielo," in this context, points specifically to the heaven of the fixed stars, which is the eighth heaven and is above the planetary spheres (see C. S. Singleton, *Inferno Commentary*, Fig. 1, p. 34). Benvenuto comments: "*Privata, quantum ad aspectum nostrum, d'ogni pianeta* . . . ideo bene dicit: *sotto povero cielo*, quantum in apparentia, quia coelum, quod est ditissimum tot gemmis lucentibus, tunc videtur pauperatum quando apparet privatum pretiosissimis ornamentis suis." ("Deprived, that is, insofar as we can see, of any planet . . . hence he is right in saying *sotto povero cielo,* as far as appearances go, because the heavens, so rich in so many gleaming gems, seem indeed barren, when deprived of their most precious ornaments.")

2. *pianeto = pianeta*. Cf. *Purg.* I, 19.

3. *quant' esser può di nuvol tenebrata*: Clearly there is intention of hyperbole here, with this privation of light added to the other.

4. *non fece*: The adverb *mai* is understood here: "non fece mai."   *grosso velo*: Cf. *Inf.* XXXII, 25.

5. *fummo* = *fumo*. *coperse*: "Covered," in the sense of enveloped.

6. *aspro*: The smoke stings the eyes. See the corresponding "fummo" of the irascible in Styx, there termed "acerbo" (*Inf.* IX, 75). *pelo*: The term continues the metaphor of "velo," denoting pile, as of a woven fabric.

7. *che*: "In such a way that."

8. *la scorta mia*: Virgil. Cf. *Purg.* IV, 39. *fida*: "Trustworthy."

8–9. *la scorta mia . . . m'offerse*: Virgil draws near to Dante and offers him his shoulder, that he may rest his hand on it and be guided, like a blind man. This does not mean that Virgil himself can see in the smoke. In fact, the closing verse of the preceding canto has it that the smoke "took from us our sight." Moreover, the spirits that are here being purged of wrath are surely blinded by the smoke. But Virgil as a wise guide has a way of "seeing" that is not purely physical and accordingly can lead Dante on around the terrace.

11. *dar di cozzo*: Literally, "to butt," i.e., to knock one's head against.

12. *cosa che 'l molesti, o forse ancida*: "Molesti" and "ancida" are hypothetical subjunctives. *ancida* = *uccida*. Cf. *Purg.* XIV, 133.

13. *m'andava io*: The so-called pleonastic reflexive, together with the subject pronoun in this case, serves to set off the subject Dante in his blind advance through smoke which is so painful to the eyes and so filthy that he cannot open them to see. *amaro*: See Virgil, *Aen.* XII, 588: "fumoque implevit amaro" ("and filled it with stinging smoke").

14–15. *diceva pur*: "Kept repeating."

15. *mozzo*: "Separated." Cf. *Inf.* IX, 95; XXVIII, 19.

16. *sentia* = *sentiva*.

17–19. *pregar per pace . . . essordia*: The voices are recit-
ing, perhaps chanting, the "Agnus Dei," a prayer in the sac-
rifice of the Mass. Addressed to the "Agnus Dei" ("Lamb
of God"), it implores the mercy and peace of God.
N. Gihr (1949, pp. 748-49) gives the following background:

> Pope Sergius I (687-701) is said to have been the first
> to order the singing of the Agnus Dei by the clergy and
> the people at the breaking of the host. The original rite
> differs in some respects from the present one, which
> was developed from the eleventh to the thirteenth cen-
> tury. At this time we meet everywhere the threefold
> repetition of the Agnus Dei, and instead of concluding,
> as previously, each with the same petition, *miserere
> nobis* ("have mercy on us"), the third petition,
> *dona nobis pacem* ("grant us peace"), began to be
> substituted.

Gihr adds (p. 749, n. 3): "The most ancient Roman
Ordines and the earliest liturgical writers say nothing with
regard to the repetition of the Agnus Dei. Gradually the rite
became fixed and general of singing, or reciting, it three
times."

Except for the change from "miserere nobis" to "dona
nobis pacem," the words of the prayer are unchanging
through the centuries, and Dante's verses clearly indicate
that the souls of the wrathful pray for peace, i.e., utter "dona
nobis pacem" in the third verse. Buti, in fact, comments:
"Li due primi dimandano misericordia, e lo terzo pace."
("The first two ask for mercy and the third for peace.") The
text intended, therefore, must be:

> Agnus Dei, qui tollis peccata mundi, miserere nobis.
> Agnus Dei, qui tollis peccata mundi, miserere nobis.
> Agnus Dei, qui tollis peccata mundi, dona nobis pacem.
>
> Lamb of God, who takest away the sins of the world,
> have mercy on us. Lamb of God, who takest away the
> sins of the world, have mercy on us. Lamb of God, who
> takest away the sins of the world, grant us peace.

Clearly the prayer for peace is most appropriately uttered
by those who in this life bore about within themselves the

fumes of wrath, which in Purgatory now envelop and blind them. Cf. "acque de la pace" in *Purg.* XV, 131.

18. *Agnel di Dio*: Christ as Lamb suggests innocence and gentleness, the opposite of wrath.   *le peccata*: Cf. *Inf.* V, 9.

19. *Pur*: "Repeatedly." Each of the verses of the prayer begins with the words "Agnus Dei."   *essordia*: From the Latin plural *exordia*. See E. G. Parodi (1957), p. 247.

20. *una parola in tutte era e un modo*: The souls recite the "Agnus Dei" in unison ("una parola") and with the same intonation, or perhaps the same chant.

21. *parea = appariva*.   *ogne concordia*: Such concord among the souls, the more notable in Purgatory by being so strikingly in contrast with the souls in Hell, is most significant here as manifested among the wrathful.

24. *iracundia*: A standard theological term in Latin for the sin of wrath, more or less interchangeable with *ira*. See n. to *Inf.* VII, 109-16.   *solvendo il nodo*: See Thomas Aquinas, *Summa theol.* III, q. 84, a. 3, resp.: "Nam peccata sunt quaedam vincula, secundum illud Proverb. 5, 22: *Iniquitates suae capiunt impium, et funibus peccatorum suorum quisque constringitur.*" ("Because sins are fetters, according to Prov. v. 22. *His own iniquities catch the wicked, and he is fast bound with the ropes of his own sins.*") In this sense, these souls are seeking liberty here (i.e., liberation from the bonds of sin), even as was said of Dante (*Purg.* I, 71). "Nodo" may also be conceived as something that shuts out, excludes, the "waters of peace" (*Purg.* XV, 131).

25. *'l nostro fummo*: The possessive here recalls that uttered by a soul on the preceding terrace (*Purg.* XIV, 1): "Chi è costui che 'l nostro monte cerchia?"   *'l nostro fummo fendi*: The soul notes that Dante's body cleaves the smoky air, which suggests not only that the smoke is very thick, but that the soul somehow perceives that a living body does this, as the airy shapes of souls do not.

26–27. *e di noi parli . . . calendi*: Dante's question to Virgil (vs. 22) has suggested that he himself is not a spirit.

26. *tue = tu.*

27. *calendi*: From the Latin *calendae*. See E. G. Parodi (1957), p. 248. In Dante's time the term was still used of the first day of the month. Cf. *Calendimaggio*, "May Day." Thus Dante is said to speak as the living do, dividing time into months. Benvenuto remarks that "mortui non dividunt tempus, quia tempus non currit eis." ("The dead know no division of time, since time does not pass for them.")

28. *per = da.   una voce*: The voice of Marco Lombardo, as the spirit itself soon declares.

30. *quinci*: "In this direction." Virgil is asking, as he has done before, which way is the shortest around the terrace for reaching the stairway that leads to the next circle. As usual, Virgil and Dante are proceeding to the right, or in a counterclockwise direction. The souls appear to move in the opposite direction, or clockwise about the circle, and are not permitted to leave the cloud of smoke, but must endure "blindness" as long as they are enveloped in it. Yet Marco can turn back and follow along with Dante and Virgil in the other direction, even as Brunetto Latini had been able to do (see n. to vs. 145). Can this mean that the souls "loosen the knot of anger," as it were (vs. 24), by reversing the usual, the proper direction for circling the mountain?   *sùe = su.* Cf. *Purg.* IV, 47.

31. *ti mondi*: Cf. "rimendo" in *Purg.* XIII, 107.

32. *per tornar bella a colui che ti fece*: To God, who breathes the soul into the body when it is formed (*Purg.* XXV, 70-75). See vss. 85-90. The soul is created directly by God and is His creature. "Ti mondi" and "tornar bello" recall *Purg.* II, 75 and 122-23, the image of the snake shedding its old skin.

33. *se mi secondi*: I.e., if you follow the sound of my voice and of my steps.

34. *quanto mi lece*: As we learn later (vss. 141-44), the spirits must remain inside the cloud of smoke.

36. *giunti = congiunti.*   *in quella vece*: Cf. *Inf.* XXI, 10.

37. *fascia*: Literally, "swathing band," i.e., the mortal body, as is made clear by the following verse.

38. *men vo = me ne vado.*

40–42. *E se Dio . . . uso*: Dante adjures the spirit by that "marvel" which he had promised it would hear if it followed him (vs. 33). Cf. *Purg.* VIII, 67-72.

40. *se Dio*: I.e., "se è vero che Dio."

41. *veggia = veda.*   *la sua corte*: Cf. *Inf.* II, 125, and, in that same canto, the courtly scene in Heaven as described by Beatrice, vss. 94-108.

42. *fuor del moderno uso*: Paul was caught up to Heaven and saw God's "court," and other contemplatives also had that experience in some measure, as the reader will learn in *Paradiso*. But the reader will also learn there that the upward way, the ladder, of contemplation which reaches to Heaven has been abandoned in modern times (*Par.* XXII, 64-75). "Fuor del moderno uso" points to this fact.

44. *dilmi = dimmelo.*   *al varco*: To the passage or stairway leading up to the next terrace. The passage here is metaphorically termed a "ford." Cf. *Inf.* XII, 26.

45. *fier = saranno.*   *scorte*: Cf. "scorta" in vs. 8.

46. *Lombardo fui, e fu' chiamato Marco*: Typically one's place of origin is declared before one's name. Cf. *Purg.* XIII, 106 and *passim*, and note the question as stated in *Purg.* XIV, 13: "onde vieni e chi se'." Marco was a Lombard (or Venetian) gentleman. The commentators differ as to the meaning of "Lombardo" as applied to Marco. The most natural inference is that he was so called because he was a native of Lombardy or of Lombard extraction; thus Benvenuto says:

Nota, quod iste denominat se a gente, quia fuit de Lombardia inferiori, quae dicitur Marchia Tarvisana; vel dic et melius, quod denominatus est Lombardus, quia familiariter conversabatur cum dominis Lombardiae tempore suo, inter quos tractabat saepe concordias, paces, affinitates, et confoederationes.

Notice that he identifies himself by his family since he was from lower Lombardy, which is called the March of Treviso; or, to put it more accurately, he is called a Lombard because he was on friendly terms with the lords of Lombardy in his times, and he often arranged agreements, pacts, treaties, and covenants between them.

It seems to be agreed that he was at any rate domiciled at Venice. "Fuit quidam miles curialis de nobili civitate Venetiarum" ("He was a certain noble knight of the illustrious city of the Venetians"), says Benvenuto. And some commentators assert that he belonged to the Lombardi of Venice and that "Lombardo" consequently was his family name. In the *Novelle antiche* (see LXXII) he is, on the other hand, described as "Marcho lonbardo," i.e., Marco of Lombardy. In the *Ottimo Commento* it is stated that he frequented Paris and that he was called Lombardo "alla guisa francesca parlando" ("after the French manner of speaking"), in which case the name would simply mean "Marco the Italian." Several stories are told of Marco. Benvenuto relates, as an indication of his temperament, how, when he had been taken prisoner and a ransom was demanded, he applied to Rizzardo da Camino for the required sum, and how, on learning that Rizzardo was raising contributions from the Lombard nobles, he declared he would sooner die in prison than be under such obligations, whereupon Rizzardo, abashed, paid the whole sum himself. Buti makes special mention of his liberality, and Villani (VII, 121) tells a story of how Marco foretold his misfortunes to Count Ugolino, who was then at the height of his power and prosperity.

For a discussion of the identity of this Marco, see F. Maggini (1925); see also G. Zaccagnini (1923), pp. 8-11. Zaccagnini cites a document, dated January 5, 1267, of the Archivio di Stato of Bologna in which a "dominus Marchus lombardus" is mentioned; he holds that Marco was born in the March of Treviso, which was at the time considered a part of "lower Lombardy," and that the designation *lombardo* was thus derived.

47. *del mondo seppi*: "I knew [the ways] of the world." The reader will remember Ulysses, who sought to become "del mondo esperto / e de li vizi umani e del valore" (*Inf.* XXVI, 98-99). *valore*: Virtue in general, as in Ulysses' words and also in Guido del Duca's in *Purg.* XIV, 37.

48. *disteso l'arco*: As frequently in the poem, the figure of the bow here expresses intention, purpose, aim. All have ceased to aim the bow at the virtues Marco had sought to cultivate.

49. *Per montar sù dirittamente vai*: I.e., yes, you are going in the right direction to come to the stair ("varco") by which you can mount to the next terrace. Marco is replying to Dante's question in vs. 44.

51. *quando sù sarai*: I.e., when you are in the court of Heaven.

52-53. *Per fede . . . chiedi*: This amounts to Dante's taking, as it were, a solemn oath to do what is promised, i.e., to say a prayer for Marco on high. Cf. the Latin *obligare,* meaning both "to bind" and "to oblige."

54. *s'io non me ne spiego*: "If I do not extricate myself from it."

55. *Prima era scempio*: Dante's doubt was "single" when it was first prompted by the words of Guido del Duca (*Purg.* XIV, 37-42) about how virtue had fled from the Val d'Arno and how its inhabitants had changed their nature to that of animals.

56. *ne la sentenza tua*: By what you say, by your pronouncement concerning the abandonment of virtue generally (vss. 47-48).

56–57. *che mi fa certo . . . l'accoppio*: Which assure me of that with which I couple it, i.e., of my persuasion (as stated in vss. 58-59) that virtue has departed from the world.

57. *qui*: In what you tell me.   *e altrove*: And by way of what another told me (i.e., Guido del Duca in *Purg.* XIV, 37-66).

58. *Lo mondo è ben così tutto diserto*: The "ben" is both emphatic and concessive.

59. *come tu mi sone*: "As you say to me."   *sone* = *suoni*, literally, "sound out."

60. *malizia*: "Evil," "depravity," the opposite of *virtù* in this context.   *gravido e coverto*: Pregnant within and covered without.

61. *addite* = *additi*.

62. *veggia* = *veda*.   *altrui*: To the living.

63. *nel cielo*: "Cielo" in this context means the heavens, i.e., the stars and planets in their respective spheres, which shed their influence on mortal creatures.   *nel cielo uno, e un qua giù la pone*: Some assign the cause to the heavens, others to men.   *qua giù*: In the living, in men.

64. *duolo*: Marco is grieved that mortals can be so blind as not to see the truth which he will now set forth.
   strinse: The sigh is "squeezed out" into an expression of sorrow and commiseration.   *uhi*: Some editors have preferred the form "hui." The *h* is silent in either case. Cf. the Latin *heu*.

65. *Frate*: See n. to *Purg.* IV, 127, and *Purg.* XIII, 94.

66. *lo mondo è cieco*: This judgment pronounced on mankind in general is reminiscent of Virgil's judgment in *Inf.* VII, 70-71: "Oh creature sciocche, / quanta ignoranza è quella che v'offende."   *e tu vien ben da lui*: And you certainly are from and of the world, to hold any such doubt.

67. *Voi che vivete*: You, all the living.

67–68. *ogne cagion recate pur suso al cielo*: Persist in assigning every cause to the heavens.

68. *pur come se*: "Just as if."

68–69. *pur come se . . . necessitate*: "As if they (the heavens) moved everything with them by necessity" (i.e., with an absolute determinism). See Dante's *Epist.* XI, 4: "Et, quod horribilius est, quod astronomi quidam et crude prophetantes necessarium asserunt quod, male usi libertate arbitrii, eligere maluistis." ("And, what is more horrible, certain astronomers, crudely prophesying, declare that to be of necessity which in truth ye, making ill use of the liberty of the will, have rather chosen.")

70. *fora = sarebbe*.

70–71. *fora distrutto libero arbitrio*: Free will would be done away with. The *locus classicus* of this question, one which Dante doubtless had in mind, is Boethius, *Consol. philos.* V, 2, ll. 1-27.

71–72. *non fora giustizia . . . lutto*: It would not be just that there should be any reward of happiness for welldoing, or of punishment for evil-doing. See Bonaventura, *Collationes de septem donis Spiritus Sancti* VIII, 18:

> Secundus error est de necessitate fatali, sicut de constellationibus: si homo sit natus in tali constellatione, de necessitate erit latro, vel malus, vel bonus. Istud evacuat liberum arbitrium et meritum et praemium: quia, si homo facit ex necessitate quod facit, quid valet libertas arbitrii? Quid merebitur?

> The second error is that of necessity determined by fate, as influenced by the stars; thus, if a man was born under a certain star, he will inevitably be a thief, whether he be good or bad. This view destroys free will as well as merit and reward, for, if a man does what he does under compulsion, what good is freedom of choice? What merit can he gain?

73. *Lo cielo i vostri movimenti inizia*: On this point, Thomas Aquinas (*Summa theol.* I-II, q. 9, a. 5, resp.) writes: "Appetitus intellectivus quodammodo movetur ab appetitu sensitivo, indirecte redundat motus caelestium corporum in voluntatem, inquantum scilicet per passiones appetitus sensitivi voluntatem moveri contingit" ("the intellectual appetite is moved, in a fashion, by the sensitive appetite, the movements of the heavenly bodies have an indirect bearing on the will; in so far as the will happens to be moved by the passions of the sensitive appetite"). Aquinas, referring to Aristotle's *De anima* and *Nichomachean Ethics*, elaborates as follows (*Summa theol.* II-II, q. 95, a. 5, resp.):

Secundo autem subtrahuntur causalitati caelestium corporum actus liberi arbitrii, quod est facultas voluntatis et rationis. Intellectus enim sive ratio, non est corpus, nec actus organi corporei, et per consequens nec voluntas, quae est in ratione, ut patet per Philosophum in 3 de Anima (text. 42). Nullum autem corpus potest imprimere in rem incorpoream. Unde impossibile est quod corpora caelestia directe imprimant in intellectum et voluntatem: hoc enim esset ponere intellectum non differre a sensu: quod Aristoteles in lib. 2 de Anima, (text. 150 et 151), imponit his qui dicebant quod *talis voluntas est in hominibus, qualem in diem inducit pater virorum deorumque*, scilicet sol vel caelum. Unde corpora caelestia non possunt esse per se causa operationum liberi arbitrii; possunt tamen ad hoc dispositive inclinare, inquantum imprimunt in corpus humanum, et per consequens in vires sensitivas, quae sunt actus corporalium organorum, quae inclinant ad humanos actus. Quia tamen vires sensitivae obediunt rationi, ut patet per Philosophum in 3 de Anima (text. 42 et 47), et 1 Ethic. (cap. ult., a med.), nulla necessitas ex hoc libero arbitrio imponitur; sed contra inclinationem caelestium corporum homo potest per rationem operari.

In the second place, acts of the free will, which is the faculty of will and reason, escape the causality of heavenly bodies. For the intellect or reason is not a body, nor the act of a bodily organ, and consequently neither is the will, since it is in the reason, as the Philosopher shows (*De Anima* iii. 4[429^a], 9[432^b]). Now no body can make an impression on an incorporeal body. Wherefore it is impossible for heavenly bodies to make a direct impression on the intellect and will: for this would be to deny the difference between intellect and sense, with which position Aristotle reproaches (*De Anima* iii. 3[427^a]) those who held that *such is the will of man, as is the day which the father of men and of gods,* i.e. the sun or the heavens, *brings on.* [Homer, *Odyssey* XVIII, 135-37.]

Hence the heavenly bodies cannot be the direct cause of the free will's operations. Nevertheless they can be a dispositive cause of an inclination to those operations, in so far as they make an impression on the human body, and consequently on the sensitive powers which are acts of bodily organs having an inclination for human acts. Since, however, the sensitive powers obey reason, as the Philosopher shows (*De Anima* iii. 11 [434^a]: *Ethic.* i. 13 [1102^b]), this does not impose any necessity on the free will, and man is able, by his reason, to act counter to the inclination of the heavenly bodies.

In *De veritate* q. 24, a. 1, ad 19 Aquinas explains:

Homines ex nativitate non consequuntur aliquam dispositionem immediate in anima intellectiva, per quam de necessitate inclinentur ad aliquem finem eligendum, nec a corpore caelesti, nec ab aliquo alio; nisi quod ex ipsa sui natura inest eis necessarius appetitus ultimi finis, scilicet beatitudinis, quod non impedit arbitrii libertatem, cum diversae viae remaneant eligibiles ad consecutionem illius finis; et hoc ideo quia corpora caelestia non habent immediatam impressionem in animam rationalem. Ex nativitate autem consequitur in corpore nati aliqua dispositio tum ex virtute corporum caelestium, tum ex causis inferioribus, quae sunt semen et materia concepta, per quam anima quodammodo ad aliquid eligendum prona efficitur, secundum quod electio animae rationalis inclinatur ex passionibus, quae sunt in appetitu sensitivo, qui est potentia corporalis consequens corporis dispositiones. Sed ex hoc nulla necessitas inducitur eis ad eligendum; cum in potestate animae rationalis sit accipere, vel etiam refutare passiones subortas.

Neither from the heavenly bodies nor from anything else do men acquire from birth immediately in the intellective soul any disposition by which they are inclined with necessity to choose any particular end; except that there is in them from their very nature a necessary appetite for their last end, happiness. But this does not prevent the freedom of choice, since different ways to attain that end remain open to choice. The reason for this is that the heavenly bodies do not have any immediate influence upon the rational soul.

There is acquired from birth, however, in the body of the child a certain disposition both from the power of the heavenly bodies and from inferior causes, which are the semen and the matter of the one conceived; and by it the soul is in some sense made prone to choose something inasmuch as the choice of the rational soul is inclined by the passions, which are in the sense appetite, a bodily power dependent upon the dispositions of the body. But no necessity in choosing is thereby introduced into it, since it is within the power of the rational soul to admit or to repress the passions which arise.

See also Thomas Aquinas, *Summa contra Gentiles* III, 85.

75. *lume v'è dato*: The light of rational discernment. See Thomas Aquinas, *Summa theol.* I-II, q. 19, a. 4, resp.:

In omnibus causis ordinatis effectus plus dependet a causa prima quam a causa secunda, quia causa secunda non agit nisi in virtute primae causae. Quod autem ratio humana sit regula voluntatis humanae, ex qua eius bonitas mensuretur, habet ex lege aeterna, quae est ratio divina; unde in Psal. 4, 6, dicitur: *Multi dicunt: Quis ostendit nobis bona? Signatum est super nos lumen vultus tui, Domine*; quasi diceret: Lumen rationis, quod in nobis est, intantum potest nobis ostendere bona, et nostram voluntatem regulare, inquantum est lumen vultus tui, idest, a vultu tuo derivatum. Unde manifestum est, quod multo magis dependet bonitas voluntatis humanae a lege aeterna quam a ratione humana; et ubi deficit humana ratio, oportet ad rationem aeternam recurrere.

Wherever a number of causes are subordinate to one another, the effect depends more on the first than on the second cause: since the second cause acts only in virtue of the first. Now it is from the eternal law, which is the Divine Reason, that human reason is the rule of the human will, from which the human will derives its goodness. Hence it is written (Ps. iv. 6, 7): *Many say: Who showeth us good things? The light of Thy countenance, O Lord, is signed upon us*: as though to say: "The light of our reason is able to show us good things, and guide our will, in so far as it is the light of (*i.e.*, derived from) Thy countenance." It is therefore evident that the goodness of the human will depends on the eternal law much more than on human reason: and when human reason fails we must have recourse to the Eternal Reason.

76. *e libero voler*: See Thomas Aquinas, *Summa theol.* I-II, q. 17, a. 1, ad 2:

Radix libertatis est voluntas sicut subiectum; sed sicut causa, est ratio; ex hoc enim voluntas libere potest ad diversa ferri, quia ratio potest habere diversas conceptiones boni. Et ideo philosophi definiunt liberum arbitrium, quod est *liberum de ratione iudicium*, quasi ratio sit causa libertatis.

The root of liberty is the will as the subject thereof; but it is the reason as its cause. For the will can tend freely towards various objects, precisely because the reason can have various perceptions of good. Hence philos-

ophers define the free will as being *a free judgment aris-
ing from reason*, implying that reason is the root of
liberty.

In *De mon.* I, xii, 2-4 Dante writes:

Propter quod sciendum quod primum principium nostre
libertatis est libertas arbitrii, quam multi habent in ore,
in intellectu vero pauci. Veniunt namque usque ad hoc,
ut dicant liberum arbitrium esse liberum de voluntate
iudicium; et verum dicunt: sed importatum per verba
longe est ab eis, quemadmodum tota die logici nostri
faciunt de quibusdam propositionibus, que ad exem-
plum logicalibus interseruntur; puta de hac: triangulus
habet tres duobus rectis equales. Et ideo dico quod
iudicium medium est apprehensionis et appetitus: nam
primo res apprehenditur, deinde apprehensa bona vel
mala iudicatur; et ultimo iudicans prosequitur sive fugit.
Si ergo iudicium moveat omnino appetitum et nullo
modo preveniatur ab eo, liberum est; si vero ab appetitu
quocunque modo preveniente iudicium moveatur, libe-
rum esse non potest, quia non a se, sed ab alio captivum
trahitur.

Wherefore be it known that the first principle of our
freedom is freedom of choice, which many have on their
lips but few in their understanding. For they get as far
as saying that free choice is free judgment in matters of
will; and herein they say the truth; but the import of the
words is far from them, just as is the case with
our teachers of logic in their constant use of certain
propositions, given by way of example in Logic; for in-
stance, "A triangle has three angles equal to two right
angles."
    Therefore I say that judgment is the link between
apprehension and appetite. For first a thing is appre-
hended, then when apprehended it is judged to be good
or bad, and finally he who has so judged it pursues or
shuns it. If, then, the judgment altogether sets the appe-
tite in motion, and is in no measure anticipated by it, it
is free. But if the judgment is moved by the appetite,

which to some extent anticipates it, it cannot be free, for it does not move of itself, but is drawn captive by another.

See also *Purg.* XVIII, 61-75; *Par.* V, 19-24.

76–77. che, se fatica . . . dura: On these struggles Thomas Aquinas (*Summa theol.* I, q. 115, a. 4, ad 3) comments:

> Plures hominum sequuntur passiones, quae sunt motus sensitivi appetitus, ad quas cooperari possunt corpora caelestia; pauci autem sunt sapientes, qui huiusmodi passionibus resistant. Et ideo astrologi ut in pluribus vera possunt praedicere, et maxime in communi, non autem in speciali, quia nihil prohibet aliquem hominem per liberum arbitrium passionibus resistere.

> The majority of men follow their passions, which are movements of the sensitive appetite, in which movements heavenly bodies can cooperate: but few are wise enough to resist these passions. Consequently astrologers are able to foretell the truth in the majority of cases, especially in a general way. But not in particular cases; for nothing prevents man's resisting his passions by his free will.

78. se ben si notrica: This means, Buti explains, "se l'omo s'alleva addottrinato et adusato a le virtù e buoni costumi" ("if man is well brought up and educated to virtue and good habits").   *notrica = nutrica.*

79. maggior forza . . . miglior natura: God.

80. liberi soggiacete: The apparent paradox of a *free* will subjected to a higher authority is a cardinal tenet of Christian doctrine. See Bonaventura, in *Comm. Sent. Petri Lombardi II* XXV, ii, a. 1, q. 4, resp.: "Hanc enim dignitatem habet liberum arbitrium, ut, in quantum liberum, soli Deo sit subiectum; et quia, in quantum liberum, nulli agenti creato subest, cum coactio sit a superiori, nullum agens creatum potest ipsum *cogere*." ("For this is the peculiar dignity of free will, that, precisely as being free, it is subject to God alone; because, insofar as it is free, the will is not under any created agent, and since compulsion must come from some higher source, no created agent can force the will.") Thomas Aquinas (*Summa contra Gentiles* III, 149) explains: "Attribuitur enim victoria duci, quae labore militum perpetratur; non ergo per huiusmodi verba excluditur liberum voluntatis arbitrium, sicut quidam male intellexerunt, quasi homo non sit dominus suorum actuum interiorum et exteriorum, sed ostenditur Deo esse subiectum." ("Thus, the victory is ascribed to the general even though it is accomplished by the work of the soldiers. Not that free choice of the will is excluded by these words, as some have wrongly understood them, as if man were not the master of his own internal and external acts; the text shows that man is subject to God.")

Basic to the whole notion is the concept of "yoke." See Matt. 11:29, where Jesus says: "Tollite iugum meum super vos, et discite a me, quia mitis sum et humilis corde; et invenietis requiem animabus vestris." ("Take my yoke upon you, and learn from me, for I am meek and humble of heart; and you will find rest for your souls.") In another context Dante refers to the "yoke of liberty," in his letter (*Epist.* VI, 5) to the Florentines who refused to submit to the emperor: "Vos autem divina iura et humana transgredientes . . . primi et soli iugum libertatis horrentes" ("but you, who transgress divine and human law . . . ye first and alone, shunning the yoke of liberty"). See *Epist.* VI, 23, where Dante states that "solis existentibus liberis qui voluntarie legi obediunt." ("They alone are free who of their own will obey the law.") Augustine, in the thirtieth chapter of the *Enchiridion*, speaks of the "slave of justice": "Unde ad iuste faciendum liber non erit, nisi a peccato liberatus esse iustitiae coeperit servus. Ipsa est vera libertas propter recti facti laetitiam, simul et pia servitus propter praecepti obedientiam." ("Wherefore, no one is free to do right who has not been freed from sin and begins to be the servant of justice. And such is true liberty because he has the joy of right-doing, and at the same time dutiful servitude because he obeys the precept.)
cria = crea.

81. *la mente*: The intellective soul.   *che 'l ciel non ha in sua cura*: Here, as throughout, "ciel" means the heavens and their movements. See n. to vs. 63. For *avere in cura*, cf. *Purg.* XIII, 87.

82. *Però = per ciò*.   *'l mondo presente*: Buti comments: "cioè li omini, che sono al presente nel mondo" ("that is, the men who are now in this world").   *disvia*: "Cioè esceno fuor de la via et abbandonano le virtù" ("that is, leave the path and abandon virtue"), explains Buti.

83. *in voi*: I.e., *qua giù* (see vs. 63), in the will of men. *cheggia = chieda*.

84. *vera spia*: A true investigator and informant.

85. *Esce di mano a lui*: "L'anima semplicetta" (vs. 88) is the subject of "esce." "Hand" suggests God's fashioning the soul, as it were, in creating it.

85–86. *la vagheggia prima che sia*: God is said to contemplate the existence of the soul fondly before He actually creates it.

86–87. *a guisa di fanciulla . . . pargoleggia*: The soul is innocent and pure.

88. *che sa nulla*: I.e., the mind is *tabula rasa*. See Thomas Aquinas (*Summa theol.* I, q. 79, a. 2, resp.), who, quoting Aristotle's *De anima*, says:

> Intellectus autem humanus, qui est infimus in ordine intellectuum, et maxime remotus a perfectione divini intellectus, est in potentia respectu intelligibilium; et in principio est *sicut tabula rasa, in qua nihil est scriptum,* ut Philosophus dicit, in 3 de Anima (text. 14). Quod manifeste apparet ex hoc quod in principio sumus intelligentes solum in potentia, postmodum autem efficimur intelligentes in actu. Sic igitur patet quod intelligere nostrum est quoddam pati, secundum tertium modum passionis; et per consequens intellectus est potentia passiva.

But the human intellect, which is the lowest in the order
of intelligence and most remote from the perfection of the
Divine intellect, is in potentiality with regard to things
intelligible, and is at first *like a clean tablet on which
nothing is written*, as the Philosopher says (*De Anima*
iii. 4[429^b–430^a]). This is made clear from the fact
that at first we are only in potentiality to understand,
and afterwards we are made to understand actually.
And so it is evident that with us to understand is *in a
way to be passive*; taking passion in the third sense. And
consequently the intellect is a passive power.

89. *salvo che*: This suggests that the soul's turning in this
sense is after all a kind of knowledge: it "knows" this much
at least.   *mossa*: "Mossa" suggests a "launching" of the
soul into existence.

89–90. *mossa da lieto fattore . . . trastulla*: The joy of the
Creator, in creating the soul He so fondly contemplates first
in idea, is communicated to it as a natural inclination, so that
it always seeks (turns to) that which can give it joy. See
Purg. XVIII, 55-60, and in general the argument of *Purg.*
XVII and XVIII.

91. *Di picciol bene in pria sente sapore*: At first the soul
enjoys the taste of some material good, which is "trifling"
compared with spiritual good.   *in pria = dapprima.*

92. *quivi*: "Therein."

92–93. *s'inganna, e dietro . . . amore*: The soul, in follow-
ing its natural inclination to seek joy, is really seeking to re-
turn to its Maker, the supreme Joy, though it does not know
this. The whole passage here is closely parallel to *Conv.* IV,
xii, 14-18, where Dante explains:

Lo sommo desiderio di ciascuna cosa, e prima da la
natura dato, è lo ritornare a lo suo principio. E però che
Dio è principio de le nostre anime e fattore di quelle
simili a sè (sì come è scritto: "Facciamo l'uomo ad
imagine e similitudine nostra"), essa anima massima-
mente desidera di tornare a quello. E sì come peregrino

ia per la quale mai non fue, che ogni
.gi vede crede che sia l'albergo, e non
.ssere, dirizza la credenza a l'altra, e così
sa, tanto che a l'albergo viene; così l'anima
ntanente che nel nuovo e mai non fatto cam-
uesta vita entra, dirizza li occhi al termine del
mo bene, e però, qualunque cosa vede che paia
vere alcuno bene, crede che sia esso. E perchè
i conoscenza prima è imperfetta, per non essere
rta nè dottrinata, piccioli beni le paiono grandi, e
.ò da quelli comincia prima a desiderare. Onde ve-
emo li parvuli desiderare massimamente un pomo; e
poi, più procedendo, desiderare uno augellino; e poi,
più oltre, desiderare bel vestimento; e poi lo cavallo,
e poi una donna; e poi ricchezza non grande, e poi
grande, e poi più. E questo incontra perchè in nulla
di queste cose truova quella che va cercando, e credela
trovare più oltre. Per che vedere si può che l'uno de-
siderabile sta dinanzi a l'altro a li occhi de la nostra
anima per modo quasi piramidale, che 'l minimo li
cuopre prima tutti, ed è quasi punta de l'ultimo deside-
rabile, che è Dio, quasi base di tutti. Sì che, quanto da
la punta ver la base più si procede, maggiori appari-
scono li desiderabili; e questa è la ragione per che, ac-
quistando, li desiderii umani si fanno più ampii, l'uno
appresso de l'altro. Veramente così questo cammino si
perde per errore come le strade de la terra.

The supreme longing of everything, and that first given
to it by nature, is to return to its first principle. And
inasmuch as God is the first principle of our souls, and
hath made them like to himself, even as it is written,
"Let us make man in our image and after our likeness,"
the soul itself most chiefly longs to return to him. And
like a pilgrim who is travelling on a road where he hath
never been before, who believes that every house which
he sees from afar is the hostel, and finding that it is not
directs his belief to another, and so from house to house
until he comes to the hostel; even so our soul, so soon

as it enters upon the new and never-yet-made journey
of life, directs its eyes to the goal of its supreme good,
and therefore whatever it sees that appears to have some
good in it, it thinks to be it. And because its knowledge
is at first imperfect, through having no experience or
instruction, little goods appear great to it; and therefore
it begins first from them in its longing. And so we see
little children intensely longing for an apple, and then
going on further, longing for a little bird, and then fur-
ther on longing for fine clothes, and then a horse, and
then a mistress, and then wealth, but not much, then
much and then enormous. And this comes to pass be-
cause in none of these things does he find that for which
he is ever searching, but believes he will find it further
on. Wherefore we may perceive that one desirable thing
stands in front of the other before the eyes of our soul,
something after the fashion of a pyramid, wherein the
smallest part first covers all the rest, and is as it were the
apex of the supreme object of longing, which is God, as
it were the base of all the rest. Wherefore, the further
we proceed from the apex towards the base, the greater
do objects of our longing appear; and this is why in the
process of acquisition the longings of men become more
capacious one after the other.

But in truth we may lose this way in error, just as we
may lose the paths of earth.

93. *se guida o fren non torce suo amore*: See Augustine,
De civ. Dei XXII, xxii, 1-2:

Verum haec hominum sunt malorum, ab illa tamen
erroris et perversi amoris radice venientia, cum qua
omnis filius Adam nascitur. Nam quis ignorat cum
quanta ignorantia veritatis, quae iam in infantibus mani-
festa est; et cum quanta abundantia vanae cupiditatis,
quae in pueris incipit apparere, homo veniat in hanc
vitam, ita ut si dimittatur vivere ut velit, et facere quid-
quid velit, in haec facinora et flagitia quae commemo-
ravi, et quae commemorare non potui, vel cuncta vel
multa perveniat?

Sed divina gubernatione non omni modo deserente damnatos, et Deo non continente in ira sua miserationes suas (*Psal.* LXXVI, 10), in ipsis sensibus generis humani prohibitio et eruditio contra istas, cum quibus nascimur, . . . plenae tamen etiam ipsae laborum et dolorum.

It is true that it is wicked men who do such things, but the source of all such sins is that radical canker in the mind and will that is innate in every son of Adam. For, our infancy proves with what ignorance of the truth man enters upon life, and adolescence makes clear to all the world how full we are of folly and concupiscence. In fact, if anyone were left to live as he pleased and to do what he desired, he would go through practically the whole gamut of lawlessnesses and lust—those which I have just listed and, perhaps, others that I refrained from mentioning.

Yet, for all this blight of ignorance and folly, fallen man has not been left without some ministries of Providence, nor has God, in His anger, shut up His mercies [see Ps. 76:10(77:9)]. There are still within the reach of man himself, if only he will pay the price of toil and trouble, the twin resources of law and education, with which we are born.

Thus, in Augustine's view, fallen man in a state of nature (without grace) is corrupt and requires such institutions as the Church and the state, which would not have been necessary had there been no original sin. Dante, however, does not bring the matter of original sin and the Fall into the argument here, but passes directly into the collective focus, the social order instead of the individual soul, hence the need of law and a temporal ruler.

94. *Onde*: "Wherefore." *convenne legge per fren porre*: The laws, that is, as codified by Justinian (see *Purg.* VI, 88-89; *Par.* VI, 10-12).

95. *convenne rege aver*: The king (in Dante's view the universal monarch) is needed as a guide, the laws enforced by him serving as the *freno*, or "curb."

95-96. *che discernesse . . . la torre*: The image transposes the notion of the soul guided by reason in its "pilgrimage" in this life (see the quotation from the *Convivio* in n. to vss. 92-93) to that of mankind collectively engaged in a pilgrimage. The goal, or "city," for mankind collectively (and following Dante's ideas as set forth in *De monarchia*, particularly in *De mon.* III, xvi, 7-11) is universal justice, which under the perfect rule of the monarch should prevail, and is synonymous with temporal felicity, the goal to which the emperor is ordained to lead. For this view of human society as being engaged in a pilgrimage toward a goal, see Dante's *Epist.* XI, 26: "pro tota civitate peregrinante in terris" ("for the whole estate of those on pilgrimage on earth") and *passim* in *De monarchia*.

This "true city" should not be understood as the eternal happiness in Heaven mentioned in *De mon.* III, xvi, 7, since it is the Church that leads to the heavenly goal. Here it is strictly a question of guidance by the emperor, who leads to a temporal goal. The image of the tower, indeed, is calculated to suggest a goal on this earth, since a band of travelers approaching a real city in the Middle Ages would see first a tower on the horizon, and the leader would bear on that. The tower in this case might well be that of some *palazzo di giustizia* or *palagio de la ragione*.

97. *le leggi son*: The laws exist, codified by Justinian. See n. to vs. 93. *ma chi pon mano ad esse*: The laws are the check or bridle, as for a horse, but there is no one now to take the bridle in hand. Cf. *Purg.* VI, 88-89.

98. *Nullo = nessuno*. In Dante's view Italy had had no imperial guidance since the death of the Emperor Frederick II in 1250. See *Conv.* IV, iii, 6: "Federigo di Soave, ultimo imperadore de li Romani—ultimo dico per rispetto al tempo presente." ("Frederick of Swabia, the last emperor of the Romans—I say the last up to the present time.")

98-99. *però che 'l pastor . . . fesse*: Spiritual rule is symbolized by "chewing the cud," which had come to signify meditation, and temporal rule by "having cloven hoofs," signifying the making of distinctions, in an established allegorical interpretation of Lev. 11:3: "Omne quod habet divisam ungulam et ruminat in pecoribus comedetis." ("Any animal that has hoofs you may eat, provided it is cloven-footed and chews the cud.") See also Deut. 14:6. The pope confounds the two rules or divinely ordained governances by usurping the office of temporal guide without being a competent horseman who holds the reins in his hand, i.e., who enforces the law (for that is not his proper office as decreed by God). Pietro di Dante comments:

> Dicta duo requiruntur in praelatis, et etiam in omnibus aliis regentibus, scilicet ruminare, hoc est sapere et habere discretionem, quod figuratur in ungulis fissis. Et sic praesentes pastores, licet sint sapientes, et sic ruminant, tamen non habent ungulas fissas in discernendo et dividendo temporalia a spiritualibus, et sic temporalem iurisdictionem occupando, quae penitus debet esse divisa.

> These two things are required in prelates and also in all others who rule, that is, *ruminare*, which is to know, and *habere discretionem*, which is figured in cloven hoofs. And thus modern-day pastors, though they be *sapientes* and thus ruminate, yet they do not have cloven hoofs in discerning and separating temporal things from spiritual things, and thus they assume temporal jurisdiction which should be wholly separate.

99. *rugumar = ruminar*.

100–102. *per che la gente . . . chiede*: The image is of the pastor, as guide, who is out in front of his flock as it moves on its earthly pilgrimage and who snatches at material goods along the way, goods for which the flock itself is greedy, since like the individual soul, which needs guidance, the flock runs after trivial material goods by natural inclination (vss. 91-92); and with no check or guide to correct or lead it aright, the flock feeds only on such goods and forgets spiritual goods.

103. *la mala condotta*: "Bad guidance." The emperor, not the pope, should be guiding the *civitas peregrinans*, in respect to temporal goods.

104. *'l mondo ha fatto reo*: For the world as made evil in consequence of the pope's ill guidance, see *Purg.* VIII, 131.

105. *e non natura che 'n voi sia corrotta*: The argument lays the entire blame on "ill guidance" and does not view the flock as being responsible for its straying; for, like the simple little soul that turns to whatever pleases it, the people quite naturally run after material goods and simply must be curbed and guided. Meanwhile the corruption of human nature resulting from original sin (which in Augustine's view was what necessitated the coercive institutions of Church and empire in the first place) is nowhere brought into the argument—a remarkable omission indeed!

106. *Roma, che 'l buon mondo feo*: Rome "made the good world" by bringing it to universal peace and justice under Augustus. That ideal condition was the good disposition to which Christ came, as to a place prepared to receive Him. See *De mon.* I, xvi, 1-2, where Dante says:

> Rationibus omnibus supra positis experientia memorabilis attestatur, status videlicet illius mortalium quem Dei Filius, in salutem hominis hominem assumpturus, vel expectavit vel cum voluit ipse disposuit. Nam si a lapsu primorum parentum, qui diverticulum fuit totius nostre deviationis, dispositiones hominum et tempora recolamus, non inveniemus nisi sub divo Augusto monarcha, existente Monarchia perfecta, mundum undique fuisse quietum. Et quod tunc humanum genus fuerit felix in pacis universalis tranquillitate, hoc ystoriographi omnes, hoc poete illustres, hoc etiam scriba mansuetudinis Christi testari dignatus est; et denique Paulus "plenitudinem temporis" statum illum felicissimum appellavit. Vere tempus et temporalia queque plena fuerunt, quia nullum nostre felicitatis ministerium ministro vacavit.

All the reasons set forth above are confirmed by a memorable experience; namely, of that state of mortal things which the Son of God, when about to become man for man's salvation, either awaited, or, when he would, produced. For if we go through all the states and periods of man, even from the fall of our first parents, which was the point at which we turned aside on our wanderings, we shall find that the world was never quiet on every side except under divus Augustus, the monarch, when there was a perfect monarchy. And that in truth the human race was then blessed in the tranquillity of universal peace is witnessed by all the historians, witnessed by illustrious poets. To this the scribe of the gentleness of Christ has likewise deigned to bear witness; and finally Paul has called that most happy state the "fulness of time." Verily the time and all temporal things were full, for no ministry to our felicity was then vacant of its minister.

In *Conv.* IV, v, 3-8 Dante writes:

Volendo la 'nmensurabile bontà divina l'umana creatura a sè riconformare, che per lo peccato de la prevaricazione del primo uomo da Dio era partita e disformata, eletto fu in quello altissimo e congiuntissimo consistorio de la Trinitade, che 'l Figliuolo di Dio in terra discendesse a fare questa concordia. E però che ne la sua venuta nel mondo, non solamente lo cielo, ma la terra convenia essere in ottima disposizione; e la ottima disposizione de la terra sia quando ella è monarchia, cioè tutta ad uno principe, come detto è di sopra; ordinato fu per lo divino provedimento quello popolo e quella cittade che ciò dovea compiere, cioè la gloriosa Roma. E però [che] anche l'albergo, dove il celestiale rege intrare dovea, convenia essere mondissimo e purissimo, ordinata fu una progenie santissima, de la quale dopo molti meriti nascesse una femmina ottima di tutte l'altre, la quale fosse camera del Figliuolo di Dio: e questa progenie fu quella di David, del qual [di]scese la baldezza e l'onore de l'umana generazione, cioè Maria. E però è scritto in Isaia: "Nascerà virga de la

radice di Iesse, e fiore de la sua radice salirà"; e Iesse
fu padre del sopra detto David. E tutto questo fu in uno
temporale, che David nacque e nacque Roma, cioè che
Enea venne di Troia in Italia, che fu origine de la cittade
romana, sì come testimoniano le scritture. Per che assai
è manifesto la divina elezione del romano imperio, per
lo nascimento de la santa cittade che fu contemporaneo
a la radice de la progenie di Maria. E incidentemente
è da toccare che, poi che esso cielo cominciò a girare,
in migliore disposizione non fu che allora quando di là
su discese Colui che l'ha fatto e che 'l governa; sì come
ancora per virtù di loro arti li matematici possono ritro-
vare. Nè 'l mondo mai non fu nè sarà sì perfettamente
disposto come allora che a la voce d'un solo, principe
del roman popolo e comandatore, [si descrisse], sì come
testimonia Luca evangelista. E però [che] pace univer-
sale era per tutto, che mai, più, non fu nè fia, la nave
de l'umana compagnia dirittamente per dolce cammino
a debito porto correa.

When the immeasurable divine goodness willed to re-
conform to itself the human creature (which was parted
from God by the sin of the disobedience of the first man,
and thereby deformed), it was appointed in the most
lofty and united divine consistory of the Trinity that the
Son of God should descend to earth to effect this har-
mony. And inasmuch as at his coming into the world it
was meet that not only heaven but earth should be in
its best disposition,—and the best disposition of earth
is when it is a monarchy, that is to say, when it is all
subject to one prince, as aforesaid,—therefore that peo-
ple and that city who were destined to bring this about,
(to wit the glorious Rome), were ordained by the divine
providence. And because the abode wherein the celestial
king must enter ought to be most clean and pure there
was likewise ordained a most holy family from the
which after many merits should be born a woman su-
premely good amongst all the rest, who should be the
treasure house of the Son of God. And this family is that
of David. And the triumph and honour of the human

race, Mary to wit, was born from it. Wherefore it is written in Isaiah [11:1] "a rod shall spring out of the root of Jesse and a flower shall spring up from his root." And Jesse was the father of the above-said David. And it was all at the same point of time wherein David was born and Rome was born, that is to say Æneas came into Italy from Troy, which was the origin of the most noble city of Rome, as testify the scriptures. Whereby the divine election of the Roman empire is manifest enough; to wit by the birth of the holy city being at the same time as the root of the family of Mary. And incidentally we may note that since the heaven itself began to roll it ne'er was in better disposition than at the time when he who made it and who rules it came down below; as even now by virtue of their arts the mathematicians may retrace. Nor was the world ever so perfectly disposed, nor shall be again, as then when it was guided by the voice of one sole prince and commander of the Roman people, as Luke the evangelist beareth witness. And therefore there was universal peace which never was before nor shall be, and the ship of the human fellowship was speeding straight to the due port in tranquil voyage.

See C. S. Singleton (1958), pp. 86-100.   *feo = fece.*

107. *due soli aver*: In the fourth chapter of *De mon.* III Dante argues against those who interpreted the sun and the moon made by God to mean, allegorically, the two regimens, the spiritual and the temporal, the Church and the empire, for he would not have the moon stand for the empire and therefore have no light except that from the sun, i.e., the Church. This was a standard allegory widely accepted and debated. The poet's image of "two Suns" is highly significant against such a background, for he has thereby affirmed the independence and autonomy of empire and Church. In *Epist.* XI, 21, Dante refers to "Romam urbem, nunc utroque lumine destitutam" ("the city of Rome, now destitute of either light"). See E. H. Kantorowicz (1951), especially p. 219:

For centuries, ever since the age of Gregory VII, a dangerous image had gained influence on the political theory of the papacy: Sun and Moon as symbols of Church and Empire. Although the sheer coexistence of two celestial luminaries of unequal size proved, all by itself, less than nothing in view of the relations of *regnum* and *sacerdotium*, the metaphor had yet been taken as evidence for the inferiority of the Moon-Empire to which only some reflected light was granted from the Sun-Papacy. Dante, in the *Monarchia* [see III, iv, 12-22], had denied and ridiculed the validity of the Sun-Moon symbol as an evidence in political matters. Now, in the *Comedy*, he abolishes it, and no more than two words are needed to do away with that specter: *due soli*. Pope and Emperor, to Dante two coördinate and equal powers with different tasks, no longer reflect a major and a minor light: they are "Two Suns" which jointly illuminate the world to lead the human race to the two goals which "Providence, that ineffable, has set before man": the terrestrial paradise and the celestial.

Kantorowicz concludes (p. 231):

He actually reinstates the emperor in his proper place as the *Sol mundi,* in full agreement with the trends of thought of his time, and he does so without denying to the papal *Vicarius Christi* the representation of the Sun of the World.

In short, the lines of the Lombard Marco are not simply a whim, or a flash of poetic inventiveness (though they are that as well); they are an act of reinstatement of the emperor in his old rights. It is the language of his own time, it is the then customary solar apostrophes of the imperial power, which have led Dante to his duplication of the Sun and to his seemingly strange and irrational metaphor of Rome's *due soli.*

109–10. *L'un l'altro ha spento . . . pasturale*: The pope as one "Sun" has "quenched" the other by assuming the powers over temporal affairs that rightly belong to the emperor, thus uniting the emperor's "sword" to the ecclesiastical "crook." See n. to vs. 98.

109. *giunta = congiunta*.

111. *per viva forza*: "Viva" reinforces the standing phrase "per forza." *mal convien che vada*: The normal word order would be "convien che vada male," a singular subject (it, the guidance) being understood. *Convenire*, as it often does, states necessity here.

112. *però che = perciò che*. *giunti = congiunti*, "united," in the one office of the papacy. *l'un l'altro non teme*: The sword does not fear the crook and vice versa; there is no balance of powers.

113. *pon = poni* (imperative). *la spiga*: "The ear of grain," i.e., the fruit, or result. Cf. Luc. 6:43-44: "Non est enim arbor bona quae facit fructus malos, neque arbor mala faciens fructum bonum. Unaquaeque enim arbor de fructu suo cognoscitur." ("For there is no good tree that bears bad fruit, nor is there a bad tree that bears good fruit. For every tree is known by its fruit.")

114. *ogn' erba*: With "spiga" the image is of some grain, such as wheat, which can be called a kind of "erba" or grass.

115. *In sul paese ch'Adice e Po riga*: This, in a general way, designates Lombardy, which, in the old sense, meant most of northern Italy, that part specifically referred to as watered by the Adige being the March of Treviso (Marca Trevigiana or Marca Trivigiana). Marco Lombardo therefore is standing in judgment now on his own land. In fact the three persons he will single out as samples of the virtue of former times are respectively from Brescia, Treviso, and Reggio nell'Emilia. *riga = irriga*.

116. *solea = soleva*. The verb has the dual subject "valore e cortesia," the principal virtues of knights, of courtiers, and of political life in the city-state. Cf. *Inf.* XVI, 67; *Purg.* VIII, 127-29; XIV, 90.

117. *prima che Federigo avesse briga*: The expression *aver briga* views the matter from the standpoint of the emperor. In the struggle of the papacy against Frederick II, last of the emperors according to Dante (see n. to vs. 98), the papacy took up the sword, which it should not have done.

118-20. *or può sicuramente . . . d'appressarsi*: Anyone who, because he is evil and degenerate, would seek to avoid the company of good men may now pass through Lombardy without risk of encountering any good men. For the construction *per* with agent, see *Inf.* I, 126. *Lasciare* in this use, meaning "to avoid" or "to eschew," is commonly found in early Italian. Compare the judgment on this region with that on Romagna in *Purg.* XIV, 91-96.

121. *èn = enno (sono)*. The plural is formed on the singular *è*, by analogy with such verbs as *sta, stanno.*   *tre vecchi ancora*: These men serve, in their rare virtue, as a living reproach to the modern generation. "Three elders" singled out thus remind one of the "giusti son due" of *Inf.* VI, 73.

122. *par lor tardo*: The three long to depart this life and pass to their reward in Heaven.

123. *ripogna = riponga*, the *ri-* expressing a return, of the soul to God.

124. *Currado da Palazzo*: Corrado, a member of an old family of Brescia, was a Guelph and acted as vicar for Charles of Anjou in Florence in 1276 (see M. Barbi, 1920b, p. 137). He was *podestà* of Piacenza in 1288. The *Ottimo Commento* says of him: "Messer Currado portò in sua vita molto onore, dilettossi in bella famiglia, ed in vita polita, in governamenti di cittadi, dove acquistò molto pregio e fama." ("Messer Corrado was much honored during his life. He took pleasure in having a fine household and engaging in political activity, in the governing of cities, in which he acquired great esteem and fame.") Benvenuto tells a story of how Corrado, while bearing the standard in battle, had both his hands cut off, but clasped the staff with the stumps of his arms rather than abandon it.   *e 'l buon Gherardo*: The

371

son of Biaquino da Camino and India da Camposampiero, Gherardo was born *ca.* 1240. He was a citizen of Padua and held vast estates around Belluno and Cadore, was captain of Belluno and Feltre, and in 1283 became captain-general of Treviso, an office he held until his death in March 1306, when he was succeeded by his son Rizzardo (*Par.* IX, 50-51). In his discussion of the nature of nobility in the *Convivio* (IV, xiv, 12) Dante singles out Gherardo as an illustrious instance of true nobility:

> Pognamo che Gherardo da Cammino fosse stato nepote del più vile villano che mai bevesse del Sile o del Cagnano, e la oblivione ancora non fosse del suo avolo venuta: chi sarà oso di dire che Gherardo da Cammino fosse vile uomo? e chi non parlerà meco dicendo quello essere stato nobile? Certo nullo, quanto vuole sia presuntuoso, però che egli fu, e fia sempre la sua memoria.

> Let us suppose that Gherardo da Cammino had been the grandson of the basest churl that ever drank of the Sile or the Cagnano, and that oblivion of his grandfather had not yet come about; who should dare to say that Gherardo da Cammino would have been a base man? And who would not agree with me and say that he was noble? Of a surety no one, howsoever presumptuous he might be; for noble he was, and so will his memory be for ever.

That Gherardo's name was familiar in Tuscany is evident from the fact, pointed out by I. Del Lungo (1880, pp. 596-97 and n. 6), that he is mentioned in one of the *Cento novelle antiche* (see *Il Novellino* LXXXIV) as having shortly before his death lent to Corso Donati, who was later on (in 1308) *podestà* of Treviso, a sum of "quattromila libbre per aiuto alla sua guerra" ("4,000 pounds in support of his war"). The *Ottimo Commento* remarks that Gherardo "si dilettò non in una, ma in tutte cose di valore" ("delighted not in one sort but in all sorts of valor"), and Benvenuto says of him: "Iste fuit nobilis miles de Tarvisio, de nobilissima domo illorum de Camino, qui saepe habuerunt principatum illius civitatis. Hic fuit vir totus benignus, humanus, curialis, liberalis, et amicus bonorum: ideo antonomastice dictus est bonus." ("He was a noble military man of Treviso of the very noble house of Camino, which often held the rule of that city. He was a man most benign, humane, courtly, and liberal and a friend of good men: wherefore antonomastically he is termed good.") On the Camino family, and on Gherardo in particular, see G. Biscaro (1928).

125. *Guido da Castel*: A gentleman of Reggio nell'Emilia, Guido was born in 1235 and was still living in 1315. Dante mentions Guido in the *Convivio* (IV, xvi, 6) in his discussion of the nature of nobility, where he says that if mere notoriety constituted a claim to nobility, "Asdente, lo calzolaio da Parma, sarebbe più nobile che alcuno suo cittadino; e Albuino de la Scala sarebbe più nobile che Guido da Castello di Reggio: che ciascuna di queste cose è falsissima" ("Asdente the cobbler of Parma would be nobler than any of his fellow-citizens; and Alboino della Scala would be more noble than Guido da Castello of Reggio; whereas every one of these things is most false"). Benvenuto says Guido belonged to the Castello branch of the Roberti family and adds that he was an accomplished poet in the vulgar tongue. *mei = meglio*.

126. *francescamente*: In the manner of the French, referring to the qualification "semplice" (from the French *simple*), which at the time was commonly used as a term of approbation, meaning honest, upright, trusty. Cf. *Purg.* VII, 130. Perhaps Marco, in coupling "semplice" with "Lombardo," intends a witticism, since in French the word *lombart* was often used in a deprecatory sense, to refer to Italians (of whatever region of Italy) who came so frequently into France to practice usury. Boccaccio, in *Decam.* I, 1, refers to "questi lombardi cani" ("these Lombard dogs"), which two Florentine usurers expect to be called by the Burgundians among whom they practice their profession.

127. *Dì oggimai*: The tone is familiar, and the meaning is, freely, "henceforth you can speak out and declare to the world the truth, what the true consequence of all this is."

128-29. *per confondere in sé . . . soma*: See vss. 109-11. The Church has confounded (that is, confused in the sense of fused) two rules by usurping that of the emperor, and this is too great a burden for her, so that she falls in the mire and sullies not only herself (i.e., in her own proper function) but also the burden of temporal guidance which she has taken on.

130. *O Marco mio*: Del Lungo notes that this is an affectionate vocative indicating personal relationship, but that here it only denotes cordial agreement.

131-32. *e or discerno . . . essenti*: The Levites, members of the tribe of Levi, served as subordinate ministers of the temple and are often spoken of as priests, although, strictly speaking, they were distinct from the "sons of Aaron," who were priests. Here the exclusion of the Levites from the inheritance of Israel is referred to. Cf. Num. 18:20-24.

132. *essenti = esenti*.

133-34. *per saggio . . . rimaso*: "Has remained as an example," a sample.

135. *in rimprovèro*: Cf. vss. 121-22. Some editors have "rimprovèrio," but "rimprovèro" is possible. Cf. *vitupèrio* and *vitupèro.*   *secol selvaggio*: The adjective seems to echo the image Guido del Duca used in speaking of degenerate Romagna as "ripieno / di venenosi sterpi" in *Purg.* XIV, 94-95. Cf. *Inf.* I, 5: "selva selvaggia."

136. *O tuo parlar m'inganna*: No intent to deceive on Dante's part is implied, of course; the meaning is simply "either I am misled by what you say."   *el*: I.e., your speech.   *mi tenta*: "Would test me," or perhaps "would draw me out," "would lead me on."

137. *tosco = toscano*, as often in the poem. That is, to judge from his speech Dante is clearly a Tuscan, and yet . . .

138. *par che del buon Gherardo nulla senta*: "It seems that you have never heard of the good Gherardo." *Sentire* is used here in the sense of "to know of."

139–40. *Per altro sopranome . . . Gaia*: "Sopranome" is used here in both the senses it can have in Italian, as its equivalent can in English: an epithet added to a person's name, especially one deriving from his birthplace (such as Marco Lombardo) or indicating some quality (such as "il buon Gherardo"); the name a person bears in common with the other members of his family, as distinct from his Christian name. In this latter sense Marco turns to Gherardo's family, but, instead of a family name, chooses that of his daughter Gaia, with a jibe at her fall from virtue, a further sad example of the general thesis concerning degeneration.

140. *Gaia*: Gaia was the daughter of Gherardo da Camino by his second wife, Chiara della Torre of Milan, and sister of Rizzardo (*Par.* IX, 50). She married a relative, Tolberto da Camino, and died in August of 1311. She was buried at Treviso, where, according to N. Barozzi (1865, p. 804), the remains of her tomb outside the church of San Niccolò were still to be seen in the eighteenth century. The commentators differ as to what is meant by the reference to the daughter. Some, such as the *Anonimo fiorentino* (followed by Buti, Landino, and others), state that she was famed for her beauty and virtue: "Gaja fu una bella giovane et constumata, simigliante al padre quasi in ogni cosa, et di lei et de' costumi suoi si ragionava non solamente in Trevigj, ma per tutta la marca Trevigiana." ("Gaia was a beautiful and well-mannered girl resembling her father in almost everything, and people talked about her and her ways not only in Treviso but throughout the whole March of Treviso.") On the other hand, the *Ottimo Commento*, Benvenuto, and others state that she was notorious on account of her loose conduct. Benvenuto, who writes as if he were well acquainted with her history, says:

> Ista enim erat famosissima in tota Lombardia, ita quod ubique dicebatur de ea: Mulier quidem vere gaia et vana; et ut breviter dicam, Tarvisina tota amorosa; quae dicebat domino Rizardo fratri suo: Procura tantum mihi iuvenes procos amorosos, et ego procurabo tibi puellas formosas.

For she was famous in all Lombardy and everywhere.
It was said of her: a truly gay and frivolous woman; in
short, a woman of Treviso all given to love who said to
Rizzardo, her brother: "Procure amorous young suitors
for me, and I will procure beautiful girls for you."

Lana's comment may be interpreted either way: "Fu donna
di tale reggimento circa le delettazioni amorose, ch'era
notorio il suo nome per tutta Italia." ("She was a lady who
so indulged in amorous pleasures that her name was notori-
ous throughout Italy.") It seems probable that Dante meant
to imply that Gaia's reputation was a bad one, and that he
mentions her by way of contrast to her father, in ironical al-
lusion, as elsewhere used by Dante (cf. *Inf.* XXI, 41; XXIX,
125-32).   *nol = non lo.*

141. *Dio sia con voi, ché più non vegno vosco*: Marco now
returns to the terse manner of speech he gave evidence of
when he first spoke (see vss. 46-49).   *vosco = con voi.*

142-43. *Vedi l'albor . . . biancheggiare*: The light of the
setting sun shines through the smoke enough to "whiten" it.

143. *già biancheggiare*: They now approach the edge of the
cloud of smoke which had overtaken them, and the light of
the sun increases in "whiteness." (This is not the radiance
of the angel, as some commentators choose to understand it.)
Marco must remain within the smoke and so must now turn
back. The angel is stationed on ahead and would see Marco
if he emerged from the smoke.   *me = a me.*

144. *prima ch'io li paia*: "Before I become visible to him."
li = gli.

145. *Così tornò, e più non volle udirmi*: One is somehow
reminded of Brunetto Latini at this point, for he too first
turned back with Dante, reversing the normal direction of his
circling about the plain, as Marco has done here around this
terrace, and was then obliged to quit Dante's company
abruptly, for a different, but analogous, reason. See *Inf.* XV,
31-33; 115-20.

CANTO XVII

1. *Ricorditi* = *ti ricordi*. The verb is impersonal, in the third person; *ti* is dative. Cf. "rimembriti" in *Inf.* XXVIII, 73, and "ricorditi" in *Purg.* V, 133.   *alpe*: Compare the use of this word in *Inf.* XIV, 30.

2. *ti colse*: "Overtook you," "surprised you."

3. *non altrimenti che per pelle talpe*: See Virgil, *Georg.* I, 183. It was commonly believed in Dante's time that the mole is blind, but this is actually not true. See Brunetto Latini, *Tresor* I, 197: "Et bien sachez que taupe ne voit goute, car nature ne volt pas ouvrir la pel qui est sur les yauz, et einsi ne *valent* ele neent, porce que il ne sont descouverz." ("And you know well that the mole cannot see at all, for nature will not open the membrane that is over its eyes, so that these are worthless, because they are covered.")

5. *cominciansi* = *si cominciano*.

5–6. *la spera del sol*: Cf. *Purg.* XV, 2.

7. *fia* = *sarà*.   *imagine* = *imaginativa*, the image-forming (and image-receiving) faculty. Cf. vss. 13, 21, and "l'imaginar mio" in vs. 43.

377

7–8. *leggera in giugnere a veder*: "Quick in coming to see."

9. *in pria = in prima.*   *corcar = coricare.*

10–11. *Sì, pareggiando i miei . . . maestro*: Dante has been walking like a blind man, with his hand on the trusty shoulders of Virgil. He walks beside him again now and keeps pace with him.

12. *ne' bassi lidi*: The shores of the island of Purgatory, which, apparently, are still visible from this height. The rays of the setting sun no longer strike the lower slopes of the mountain.

13. *O imaginativa*: The poet now addresses his own image-receiving faculty, called "fantasia" in vs. 25. Cf. *Par.* XXXIII, 142.   *ne rube = ci rubi.*

13–15. *O imaginativa . . . tube*: Compare the case in reverse described in *Purg.* IV, 1-12.

13–18. *O imaginativa . . . scorge*: In scholastic psychology, deriving from Aristotle's *De anima*, the *imaginativa* or *phantasia* is conceived as one of the interior senses, the specific function of which is to store or retain in the mind the forms or images that are received through the exterior senses. See Thomas Aquinas, *Summa theol.* I, q. 78, a. 4, resp.: "Ad harum autem formarum retentionem aut conservationem ordinatur *phantasia*, sive *imaginatio,* quae idem sunt; est enim phantasia sive imaginatio quasi thesaurus quidam formarum per sensum acceptarum." ("But for the retention and preservation of these forms, the *phantasy* or *imagination* is appointed; which are the same, for phantasy or imagination is as it were a storehouse of forms received through the senses.")

The question of vs. 16, "chi move te, se 'l senso non ti porge," envisages the uncommon experience of receiving into the *imaginativa* images that are not received from any exterior sense (the "senso," in this context). And the answer which follows recognizes that this by-passing of the exterior senses is possible if a light from above "rains down" (vs. 25) directly into the phantasy, bringing such images as Dante now sees in the three scenes described in the following verses.

These images, like the bas-reliefs of the first cornice, have God as their maker and are of the nature of those ecstatic visions of gentleness which Dante experienced when he entered upon this third terrace and which were termed "non falsi errori" in *Purg.* XV, 117. (See n. to *Purg.* XV, 115-17.) Thus, of the two possibilities granted by the answer in vss. 17-18, it is the second that applies here: the images descend into the mind directly from God, whose will directs them downward. The other possibility, that of a light formed in the physical heavens and descending directly into the mind, is excluded, though this is acknowledged as the other way by which such suprasensory experiences may be had. On this, see B. Nardi (1949), p. 174:

L'azione della luce dei corpi celesti o quella delle intelligenze motrici che nei corpi celesti suggellano l'immagine della mente profonda, suscitano talvolta nella fantasia quelle misteriose intuizioni, onde

... la mente nostra, peregrina
più da la carne e men da' pensier presa,
a le sue vision quasi è divina.

La qual dottrina non è precisamente aristotelica, ma ha piuttosto un'origine platonica; sviluppata poi dai neo-platonici, fu tramandata agli scolastici da Avicenna, da Apuleio e dai libri ermetici.

The action of the light of the heavenly bodies, or that of the motor intelligences, which imprint the image of the profound mind on the heavenly bodies, sometimes arouses those mysterious intuitions in the imagination, wherefore "our mind more a wanderer from the flesh and less prisoned by thoughts, in its visions is almost divine" [*Purg.* IX, 16-18].

This doctrine is not exactly Aristotelian, but rather Platonic in origin. It was then developed by the Neoplatonists and passed on to the Scholastics by Avicenna, Apuleius, and the Hermetic books.

See *Conv.* II, viii, 13.

14. *di fuor = dal di fuori.*   *om*: Cf. the French *on.*

15. *perché*: "Even though."   *suonin = suonino* (hypothetical subjunctive).   *tube*: From the Latin *tubae.*

16. *chi move te*: The *imaginativa* receives and forms images and in this sense is said to be moved.   *se 'l senso non ti porge*: The image in this case is not "offered" to the *imaginativa* by the exterior sense of sight.

17. *Moveti = ti move.*

18. *per sé*: This connects with the verb "move," to say how, i.e., by which agency, the light descends to move the phantasy—here, by astral influence. As an answer to the question "chi" (a personal pronoun), the presence of the Intelligences that move the spheres is understood; but as an operation of the heavens, this influence may be viewed as natural, hence "per sé" ("of itself"), without God's direct intervention.
o per voler che giù lo scorge: See n. to vss. 13-18. In this context "cielo" now must include the Empyrean heaven, where God is, since in this case it is His will that directs, "guides" such images downward.   *scorge*: Cf. the noun *scorta.*

19-20. *De l'empiezza . . . diletta*: The first of three examples of wrath and its punishment, which correspond to the examples of pride and envy of the two preceding terraces, is that of Procne, daughter of King Pandion of Athens, wife of Tereus, and sister of Philomela. For the story of Procne's slaying of her son, in connection with which Dante introduces her here, see n. to *Purg.* IX, 15.

21. *l'imagine*: As in vs. 7, "l'imagine" here is the *imaginativa*. It is termed "fantasia" in vs. 25.

22. *e qui fu la mia mente sì ristretta*: See vss. 13-15.

23. *venìa = veniva.*

24. *ricetta*: From the Latin *recepta*. See "porge" ("offer") in vs. 16: the sense offers, the phantasy receives.

25. *piovve*: The verb denotes the downward guidance (vs. 18) of these images by God's will. Cf. *Par*. III, 90, and *passim* in that *cantica*.   *l'alta fantasia*: The phantasy, or *imaginativa*, is "lofty" because of the experience of a vision coming from such a source. For this adjectival usage, cf. "la morta poesì," *Purg*. I, 7; "la scritta morta," *Inf*. VIII, 127; "alto ingegno," *Inf*. II, 7; and again "alta fantasia" in *Par*. XXXIII, 142.

26–30. *un crucifisso . . . intero*: The second example of wrath and its punishment is that of Haman (Aman), chief minister of Ahasuerus, who was enraged that the Jew Mordecai did not bow down to him (Esther 3:5) and obtained from Ahasuerus a decree that all the Jews in the Persian Empire should be put to death (Esther 3:8-15). After the failure of this attempt to compass the destruction of the Jews, Haman, through the intervention of Esther and Mordecai, was hanged on the gibbet he had prepared for Mordecai (Esther 7:7-10). Dante's use of the term "crucifisso," as applied to Haman, is explained by the Vulgate (Esther 5:14), where the word translated "gibbet" is represented by the Latin *crux*: "Iussit excelsam parari crucem." ("He commanded a high gibbet to be prepared.") The same term is employed by Brunetto Latini in *Tresor* I, 58: "[Hester] crucifia Amam ki voloit destruire le peuple Israel." ("Hester crucified Haman, who was seeking to destroy the Israelites.") The scene of this crucifixion with Haman on the cross "dispettoso e fero," and the others standing about, is Dante's own conception and is not from the Bible.

26. *dispettoso*: See Esther 5:9-10, where it is said of Haman that "indignatus est valde" ("he was exceedingly angry") but "dissimulata ira" ("dissembling his anger").

27. *e cotal si moria*: Haman is unchanged in his torment and even on the cross is fierce and wrathful. Cf. Capaneus,

Inf. XIV, 47. The "si" is the so-called pleonastic reflexive, which serves both to distance and to put the matter "subjectively." *moria = moriva*.

28. *il grande Assuero*: Ahasuerus, "qui regnavit ab India usque Aethiopiam super centum viginti septem provincias" ("who reigned from India to Ethiopia, over a hundred and twenty-seven provinces"), according to Esther 1:1. The book of Esther begins with mention of the great feast he held that, as stated in Esther 1:4, "ostenderet divitias gloriae regni sui, ac magnitudinem atque iactantiam potentiae suae" ("he might shew the riches of the glory of his kingdom, and the greatness, and boasting of his power").

29. *Estèr*: Esther was the cousin or niece of Mordecai, by whom she was adopted when her parents died. She pleased Ahasuerus when, among many other maidens, she was brought before him. According to Esther 2:17 "adamavit eam rex plus quam omnes mulieres; habuitque gratiam et misericordiam coram eo super omnes mulieres, et posuit diadema regni in capite eius, fecitque eam regnare." ("The king loved her more than all the women: and she had favour and kindness before him above all the women. And he set the royal crown on her head, and made her queen.") *'l giusto Mardoceo*: Mordecai the Jew, who saved the Jews from the destruction planned by Haman. Dante here describes Mordecai as "the just," an appellation by which he is continually designated in the Targum on the book of Esther, although the expression is not used of him in the biblical text. The same epithet is applied to him in the prologue to the Wycliffe versions of Esther. See T. Silverstein (1938).

31. *imagine*: Here not the *imaginativa*, but in the more usual meaning of "image." *rompeo = ruppe*.

32. *bulla = bolla*.

33. *cui manca l'acqua*: "Cui" is dative here, absorbing the *a* of *mancare a*. The water is said to fail the bubble when it bursts. *sotto qual si feo*: The bubble is formed as air enclosed in a spherical film of water. *feo = fece*.

34. *surse*: Referring to "surse" and other verbs used by Dante in this passage—"apparve," "piovve," "rompeo"— Momigliano observes the power with which Dante renders the sudden appearance and vanishing of the visions and their airy texture. One might note the further stress on this in "di butto," vs. 40, applied to the breaking of sleep.   *in mia visione*: "In my seeing." Cf. *Par.* XXXIII, 61-62: "quasi tutta cessa / mia visione." Of course the seeing in this instance is a *visione estatica* in itself. Cf. *Purg.* XV, 85-86.

34-39. *surse in mia visione . . . ruina*: For the third example of wrath and its ill consequences, Dante returns to a non-biblical case, in the usual alternation. Amata, wife of Latinus and mother of Lavinia, believing mistakenly that Turnus, to whom Lavinia had been betrothed, had been killed in battle, hanged herself in fury and despair, fearing that Lavinia would then marry Aeneas, a match to which Amata was opposed. Dante has clearly added to the scene in this case, as in that of Haman above; the episode is narrated by Virgil, but Dante supplies the words to which Virgil only alludes in *Aen.* XII, 593-607:

> Accidit haec fessis etiam fortuna Latinis,
> quae totam luctu concussit funditus urbem.
> regina ut tectis venientem prospicit hostem,
> incessi muros, ignis ad tecta volare,
> nusquam acies contra Rutulas, nulla agmina Turni,
> infelix pugnae iuvenem in certamine credit
> exstinctum et, subito mentem turbata dolore,
> se causam clamat crimenque caputque malorum,
> multaque per maestum demens effata furorem,
> purpureos moritura manu discindit amictus
> et nodum informis leti trabe nectit ab alta.
> quam cladem miserae postquam accepere Latinae,
> filia prima manu floros Lavinia crinis
> et roseas laniata genas, tum cetera circum
> turba furit; resonant latae plangoribus aedes.

This further fate befell the labouring Latins, and shook the whole city to her base with grief. When from her palace the queen sees the foe approach, the walls as-

sailed, flames mounting to the roofs, yet nowhere
Rutulian ranks, no troops of Turnus to meet them, alas!
she thinks her warrior slain in combat, and, her mind
distraught by sudden anguish, cries out that she is the
guilty source and spring of sorrows, and uttering many
a wild word in the frenzy of grief, resolved to die, rends
her purple robes, and from a lofty beam fastens the
noose of a hideous death. Soon as the unhappy Latin
women learned this disaster, first her daughter Lavinia,
her hand tearing her flowery tresses and roseate cheeks,
then all the throng around her, madly rave; the wide
halls ring with lamentations.

In his *Letter to the Emperor Henry VII* (*Epist.* VII, 24),
Dante compares the city of Florence to Amata: "Hec Amata
illa impatiens, que, repulso fatali connubio, quem fata
negabant generum sibi adscire non timuit, sed in bella furia-
liter provocavit, et demum, male ausa luendo, laqueo se
suspendit." ("She is that passionate Amata who rejected the
wedlock decreed by fate, and feared not to summon to her-
self the son-in-law that fate denied her; who called him forth
to war, in her madness, and at last, expiating her evil deeds,
hanged herself in the noose.")

36. *per ira*: A special pointer to the example of the vice
which this exemplifies.   *nulla*: Feminine of the adjective
nullus. Cf. the Latin *nullus sum*, meaning "I am dying," "I
exist no more."

37. *Ancisa t'hai = ti sei uccisa.*   *per non perder Lavina*:
Had Turnus been dead, as Amata believed, then Lavinia
would have been wed to Aeneas and in that sense Amata
would have "lost" her. *Lavina* for Lavinia was common in
early Italian.

38. *or m'hai perduta*: "Now," by taking your own life, "you
have lost me."   *essa*: Cf. the Latin *ipsa*.   *lutto*: "I
weep," "I lament." From the archaic *luttare*. See the exam-
ples of this word afforded by M. Barbi (1934b), p. 281.

39. *l'altrui ruina*: "Another's ruin," i.e., the death of
Turnus, believed by Amata to be a fact.

40. *ove*: *Quando*.   *di butto = di botto*. Cf. *Inf.* XXII, 130; XXIV, 105.

41. *il viso chiuso*: Literally, "the closed sight."

42. *che fratto*: Referring to "il sonno" of vs. 40.   *fratto*: Past participle of *frangere*.   *guizza pria che muoia tutto*: "Quivers" or "twitches" with the last movements of life, "before it dies completely" ("tutto"). The background image is probably that of a fish or other animal in the last throes of death.

43. *l'imaginar mio*: The act of receiving these images in my *imaginativa*.   *cadde giuso*: "Fell away."

45. *maggior assai che quel ch'è in nostro uso*: I.e., much greater than the light of the sun.

46. *per veder ov' io fosse*: This refers to Dante's coming out of his trance, not to his being dazzled by the bright light. *fosse = fossi*.

47. *una voce*: That of the angel, as the reader gathers from this repeated experience of the dazzling light.

48. *che da ogne altro intento mi rimosse*: Again the phenomenon of complete attention to one thing, to the exclusion of all others. Cf. vss. 23-24. The voice claims all his attention.

49-51. *e fece la mia voglia . . . raffronta*: Cf. *Purg.* XVIII, 31-33. The expression is elliptical: desire is rendered so intense that it must attain its object (the sight of the cause, in this case) else it will never rest. To be sure, Dante never actually sees the angel, and his desire in this case is not satisfied.

52. *Ma come al sol che nostra vista grava*: Cf. *Purg.* XV, 10.

53. *e per soverchio*: Cf. *Purg.* XV, 15, and vs. 57, below.

54. *virtù*: The power of sight.

55. *ne la*: One of the rare "weak" rhymes in the poem. Cf. *Par.* XI, 13: "ne lo."

56. *ne = ci.*   *sanza prego*: Without any request from us.

57. *e col suo lume sé medesmo cela*: This corresponds to vs. 53. Cf. Ps. 103[104]:2: "amictus lumine sicut vestimento" ("robed in light as with a cloak").

58. *come l'uom si fa sego*: Most commentators, including some of the earliest, understand this in a simple reflexive meaning: "as a man does with himself," i.e., loving himself, without need of asking himself. But such a meaning seems both banal and inapplicable to the present case. More probably the meaning is reciprocal, as Landino takes it to be, "cioè, l'un huomo con l'altro" ("as one man to another"), where "man" is in contradistinction to "angel." That is, the angel, this "divine spirit," anticipates the desire of the wayfarers, even as men in their charity do with one another (see vss. 59-60). The "si" is thus the pleonastic reflexive setting off the subject man, in this case, from angel.   *sego = seco (con sè)*.

59-60. *ché quale aspetta prego . . . nego*: See *Conv.* I, viii, 16, where Dante explains:

> La terza cosa, ne la quale si può notare la pronta liberalitade, si è dare non domandato: acciò che 'l domandato è da una parte non vertù ma mercatantia, però che lo ricevitore compera, tutto che 'l datore non venda. Per che dice Seneca che "nulla cosa più cara si compera che quella dove i prieghi si spendono."

> The third thing wherein zealous liberality may be noted is giving without being asked; because when a thing is asked for, then the transaction is, on one side, not a matter of virtue but of commerce, inasmuch as he who receives buys, though he who gives sells not; wherefore Seneca saith "that nothing is bought more dear than that on which prayers are spent."

In *De beneficiis* II, i, 3-4, Seneca writes: "Optimum est antecedere desiderium cuiusque, proximum sequi. Illud melius,

occupare ante quam rogemur." ("The best course is to antici-
pate each one's desire; the next best, to indulge it. The first
is the better—to forestall the request before it is put.")
Seneca continues, in a passage frequently cited by others:
"Non tulit gratis, qui, cum rogasset, accepit, quoniam
quidem, ut maioribus nostris gravissimis viris visum est, nulla
res carius constat, quam quae precibus empta est." ("The
man who receives a benefit because he asked for it, does not
get it for nothing, since in truth, as our forefathers, those
most venerable men, discerned, no other thing costs so dear
as the one that entreaty buys.") See Thomas Aquinas,
Summa theol. II-II, q. 83, a. 2, obj. 3: "Liberalius est dare
aliquid non petenti, quam dare petenti: quia, sicut Seneca
dicit . . . *nulla res,* etc." ("It is more liberal to give to one
that asks not, than to one who asks, because, according to
Seneca . . . *no other thing,* etc.")

61. *a tanto invito*: To an invitation from a being of a high-
er order than man. With this turn of phrase, the distinction
between angels and men continues.

63. *ché poi non si poria, se 'l dì non riede*: This fact was
first made plain by Sordello. See *Purg.* VII, 44-60.   *poi*:
After dark.   *poria = potrebbe.*

66. *al primo grado*: Dante stands at the first step, at the foot
of the stair.

67. *senti'mi presso = vicino a me sentii.*

68. *e ventarmi nel viso*: The angel erases another P from
Dante's forehead, brushing it away with a stroke of its wing.

68–69. *Beati pacifici*: See Matt. 5:9: "Beati pacifici, quoniam
filii Dei vocabuntur." ("Blessed are the peacemakers, for
they shall be called children of God.")

69. *ira mala*: See Thomas Aquinas, *Summa theol.* II-II, q.
158, a. 2, resp., on the distinction between *bona ira* and *mala
ira*:

> Ira . . . proprie nominat quamdam passionem. Passio
> autem appetitus sensitivi intantum est bona, inquantum

ratione regulatur; si autem ordinem rationis excludat, est mala. Ordo autem rationis in ira potest attendi quantum ad duo: primo quidem quantum ad appetibile in quod tendit, quod est vindicta. Unde si aliquis appetat quod secundum ordinem rationis fiat vindicta, est laudabilis irae appetitus: et vocatur ira per zelum. Si autem aliquis appetat quod fiat vindicta qualitercumque contra ordinem rationis, puta si appetat puniri eum qui non meruit, vel ultra quam meruit, vel etiam non secundum legitimum ordinem, vel non propter debitum finem, qui est conservatio iustitiae et correctio culpae, erit appetitus irae vitiosus; et nominatur ira per vitium.

Anger . . . is properly the name of a passion. A passion of the sensitive appetite is good in so far as it is regulated by reason, whereas it is evil if it set the order of reason aside. Now the order of reason, in regard to anger, may be considered in relation to two things. First, in relation to the appetible object to which anger tends, and that is revenge. Wherefore if one desire revenge to be taken in accordance with the order of reason, the desire of anger is praiseworthy, and is called *zealous anger*. On the other hand, if one desire the taking of vengeance in any way whatever contrary to the order of reason, for instance if he desire the punishment of one who has not deserved it, or beyond his deserts, or again contrary to the order prescribed by law, or not for the due end, namely the maintaining of justice and the correction of defaults, then the desire of anger will be sinful, and this is called *sinful anger*.

70–72. *Già eran sovra noi . . . lati*: The rays of the setting sun now strike only upon the higher reaches of the mountain, the sun itself being already below the horizon, so that here and there stars are becoming visible in the sky.

72. *da più lati*: Literally, "on several sides."

73. *O virtù mia*: Dante addresses his own strength, which in this instance Buti terms his "potenzia . . . andativa," his power to climb. Cf. vs. 75, "la possa de le gambe."

dilegue = dilegui. There is no climbing the mountain at night, as Sordello explained before (*Purg.* VII, 43-57), since the darkness of night "hampers the will with lack of power" (*Purg.* VII, 57).

75. *la possa*: Cf. *Inf.* XXXI, 56 and *Purg.* XXVII, 75. *posta in triegue*: Literally, "put in truce."

76–78. *Noi eravam dove . . . arriva*: Virgil and Dante reach the last step of the stairway and stand facing toward the next terrace, the fourth, just like a ship that touches shore (i.e., reaches a goal). That is, they reach the *edge* of this central terrace, so that, as they look ahead, facing toward the fourth terrace, they have that terrace and three beyond it ahead of them. This is very carefully planned by the poet, for it serves, by exact position, to group the sin purged on this fourth terrace, sloth, with the sins purged in upper Purgatory, even as vs. 96 will do in the general statement of the matter.

78. *pur*: "Pur" reinforces the comparison.

79–80. *E io attesi . . . girone*: Already it is too dark for Dante to see anything on the terrace before them, hence he listens.

82. *offensione*: Sin. Cf. *Inf.* XI, 83-84, "e come incontenenza / men Dio offende," and *Inf.* XI, 25-26, "frode . . . / più spiace a Dio."

83. *nel giro dove semo*: Dante and Virgil stand on the very edge of the terrace, facing in toward it; hence Dante now speaks as if they were in or on this central *girone*.   *semo = siamo*.

84. *stea = stia*.

85–86. *L'amor del bene, scemo del suo dover*: The sin ("offense") of sloth, *accidia*. Any reader mindful of the traditional list of the seven capital vices in their established order from pride "upwards" would be expecting the sin purged on the fourth terrace to be precisely sloth. Thomas Aquinas (*Summa theol.* I, q. 63, a. 2, ad 2) defines this sin in the following way: "Acedia vero est quaedam tristitia qua homo redditur tardus ad spirituales actus propter corporalem laborem." ("Sloth is a kind of sadness, whereby a man becomes sluggish in spiritual exercises because they weary the body.") See vs. 96, "per poco di vigore," and vs. 101, "o con men [cura] che non dee corre nel bene."

86. *quiritta:* "Right here." Cf. *Purg.* IV, 125. *si ristora:* The verb suggests a debt of love which is paid here, i.e., a deficiency which is compensated for in a special mode of purgation not yet disclosed.

87. *qui si ribatte il mal tardato remo:* The metaphor applies, of course, to the voyage of this life in which we seek to reach a good port. In *Conv.* IV, xxviii, 2, Dante writes: "Ella ritorna a Dio, sì come a quello porto onde ella si partio quando venne ad intrare nel mare di questa vita." ("She [the soul] returns to God, as to that port whence she departed when she came to enter upon the sea of this life.") Cf. *Purg.* XII, 5-6. The slothful have "rested on their oars," to their spiritual detriment, and now must ply them anew to make up for their indolence. *il mal tardato remo:* Cf. *Inf.* XV, 114: "li mal protesi nervi."

88. *aperto = apertamente,* "openly," "plainly." *intendi = intenda.*

90. *alcun buon frutto di nostra dimora:* The general exposition of the purgatorial system is thus made at a point in the journey when the wayfarers are obliged to pause, even as was the case (*Inf.* XI, 10-15) when the punitive system of Hell was expounded.

91-92. *Né creator né creatura . . . amore:* Virgil begins with the all-inclusive general statement that love is always found not only in the Creator but in all His creatures, which include plants and animals, as well as stones and flames (see *Par.* I, 109-17). In *Summa theol.* I, q. 20, a. 1 and a. 2, Thomas Aquinas states that God is love and loves all things. In *Summa theol.* I-II, q. 28, a. 6, resp., Aquinas notes that "omne agens agit propter finem aliquem" ("every agent acts for an end") and continues: "Finis autem est bonum desideratum et amatum unicuique. Unde manifestum est quod omne agens, quodcumque sit, agit quamcumque actionem ex aliquo amore." ("Now the end is the good desired and loved by each one. Wherefore it is evident that every agent, whatever it be, does every action from love of some kind.") In *Conv.* III, iii, 2-5 Dante elaborates as follows:

Onde è da sapere che ciascuna cosa, come detto è di sopra, per la ragione di sopra mostrata ha 'l suo speziale amore. Come le corpora simplici hanno amore naturato in sè a lo luogo proprio, e però la terra sempre discende al centro; lo fuoco ha [amore a] la circunferenza di sopra, lungo lo cielo de la luna, e però sempre sale a quello. Le corpora composte prima, sì come sono le minere, hanno amore a lo luogo dove la loro generazione è ordinata, e in quello crescono e acquistano vigore e potenza; onde vedemo la calamita sempre da la parte de la sua generazione ricevere vertù. Le piante, che sono prima animate, hanno amore a certo luogo più manifestamente, secondo che la complessione richiede; e però vedemo certe piante lungo l'acque quasi c[ontent]arsi, e certe sopra li gioghi de le montagne, e certe ne le piagge e dappiè monti: le quali se si transmutano, o muoiono del tutto o vivono quasi triste, sì come cose disgiunte dal loro amico. Li animali bruti hanno più manifesto amore non solamente a li luoghi, ma l'uno l'altro vedemo amare. Li uomini hanno loro proprio amore a le perfette e oneste cose. E però che l'uomo, avvegna che una sola sustanza sia, tuttavia [la] forma, per la sua nobilitade, ha in sè e la natura [d'ognuna di] queste cose, tutti questi amori puote avere e tutti li ha.

Wherefore be it known that everything, as said above, and for the reason above set forth, hath its specific love, as, for example, the simple bodies have a love which has an innate affinity to their proper place; and that is why earth ever drops to the centre; but the love of fire is for the upper circumference, under the heaven of the moon, and therefore it ever riseth thereto.

Primary compound bodies, like the minerals, have a love for the place where their generation is ordained; and therein they grow, and thence draw vigour and power. Whence we see the magnet ever receive power from the direction of its generation.

Plants, which are the primary living things, have a more manifest love for certain places, according as their composition requires; and therefore we see certain plants almost always gather along watercourses, and certain on the ridges of mountains, and certain on slopes and at the foot of hills, the which, if we transplant them, either die altogether or live as if in gloom, like things parted from the place dear to them.

As for the brute animals, not only have they a more manifest love for their place, but we see that they love one another.

Men have their proper love for perfect and comely things. And because man (though his whole form be one sole substance) has in himself, by his nobility, something of the nature of each of these things, he may have all these loves, and has them all indeed.

93. *o naturale o d'animo*: There are two kinds of love, however, natural and elective. See nn. to vss. 94 and 95.

94. *Lo naturale è sempre sanza errore*: Natural love is of the end, for all things, all creatures, are inclined by their nature toward their proper place, their *finis* or goal. Natural love is the desire each creature has for its own perfection; in angels and men, it is love for the supreme good, which is God. In *Summa theol.* I, q. 60, a. 5, ad 4, Thomas Aquinas says: "Deus, secundum quod est universale bonum, a quo dependet omne bonum naturale, diligitur naturali dilectione ab unoquoque." ("God, in so far as He is the universal good, from Whom every natural good depends, is loved by everything with natural love.") Angels and men, as well as creatures of a lower order, have natural love, and, in the case of angels and men, this is the principle of their elective love. See *Summa theol.* I, q. 60, a. 1, resp.:

Necesse est in Angelis ponere dilectionem naturalem.

Ad cuius evidentiam considerandum est quod semper
prius salvatur in posteriori. Natura autem prior est
quam intellectus; quia natura cuiuscumque rei est es-
sentia eius. Unde id quod est naturae, oportet salvari
etiam in habentibus intellectum. Est autem hoc com-
mune omni naturae, ut habeat aliquam inclinationem,
quae est appetitus naturalis, vel amor; quae tamen
inclinatio diversimode invenitur in diversis naturis, in
unaquaque secundum modum eius. Unde in natura
intellectuali invenitur inclinatio naturalis secundum vo-
luntatem; in natura autem sensitiva, secundum appeti-
tum sensitivum; in natura vero carente cognitione, se-
cundum solum ordinem naturae in aliquid. Unde cum
Angelus sit natura intellectualis, oportet quod in vo-
luntate eius sit naturalis dilectio.

We must necessarily place natural love in the angels. In
evidence of this we must bear in mind that what comes
first is always sustained in what comes after it. Now na-
ture comes before intellect, because the nature of every
subject is its essence. Consequently whatever belongs
to nature must be preserved likewise in such subjects
as have intellect. But it is common to every nature to
have some inclination; and this is its natural appetite or
love. This inclination is found to exist differently in dif-
ferent natures; but in each according to its mode. Conse-
quently, in the intellectual nature there is to be found
a natural inclination coming from the will; in the sensi-
tive nature, according to the sensitive appetite; but in
a nature devoid of knowledge, only according to the
tendency of the nature to something. Therefore, since
an angel is an intellectual nature, there must be a nat-
ural love in his will.

This inclination or instinct in all creatures is planted in them
by God, it is a part of the nature of each, and, God-given as
it is, it cannot err. On natural love as being "without error,"
see *Summa theol.* I, q. 60, a. 1, ad 3:

Sicut cognitio naturalis semper est vera, ita dilectio
naturalis semper est recta; cum amor naturalis nihil

aliud sit quam inclinatio naturae indita ab auctore naturae. Dicere ergo quod inclinatio naturae non sit recta, est derogare auctori naturae.

⌐As natural knowledge is always true, so is natural love well regulated; because natural love is nothing else than the inclination implanted in nature by its Author. To say that a natural inclination is not well regulated, is to derogate from the Author of nature.⌐

See also *Purg.* XVIII, 57-60; *Par.* I, 109-20.

95. *ma l'altro puote error*: Elective love can err, since it involves choice, as natural love does not. Only those creatures that have free will can have elective love, hence this love is given only to angels and men. But angels are confirmed forever in their choice, i.e., the vision of God, even as are the elect who see Him face to face. Therefore, as the argument passes here to elective love, it narrows to a focus on man in this life.

Natural love is of the end, but elective love is of the means to the end, as Thomas Aquinas points out. See *Summa theol.* I, q. 82, a. 1, ad 3, where Aquinas, quoting Aristotle (see *Eth. Nicom.* III, 2, 1111^b), notes that "sumus domini nostrorum actuum, secundum quod possumus hoc vel illud eligere. Electio autem non est de fine, sed de his quae sunt ad finem." ("We are masters of our own actions by reason of our being able to choose this or that. But choice regards not the end, but *the means to the end*.") Aquinas concludes: "Unde appetitus ultimi finis non est de his quorum domini sumus." ("Wherefore the desire of the ultimate end does not regard those actions of which we are masters.")

Natural love or natural appetite "tends to good existing in a thing," whereas elective love "tends to a good which is apprehended." In *Summa theol.* I-II, q. 8, a. 1, resp., Aquinas, citing Aristotle (*Physica* II, 3, 195^a), says on this:

Sed considerandum est, quod cum omnis inclinatio consequatur aliquam formam, appetitus naturalis consequitur formam in natura existentem; appetitus autem sensitivus, vel etiam intellectivus, seu rationalis, qui dicitur *voluntas,* sequitur formam apprehensam. Sicut igitur id in quod tendit appetitus naturalis, est bonum existens in re, ita id in quod tendit appetitus animalis, vel voluntarius, est bonum apprehensum. Ad hoc igitur quod voluntas in aliquid tendat, non requiritur quod sit bonum in rei veritate, sed quod apprehendatur in ratione boni; et propter hoc Philosophus dicit in 2 Physic. (text. 31), quod *finis est bonum, vel apparens bonum.*

But it must be noted that, since every inclination results from a form, the natural appetite results from a form existing in the nature of things: while the sensitive appetite, as also the intellective or rational appetite, which we call the will, follows from an apprehended form. Therefore, just as the natural appetite tends to good existing in a thing; so the animal or voluntary appetite tends to a good which is apprehended. Consequently, in order that the will tend to anything, it is requisite, not that this be good in very truth, but that it be apprehended as good. Wherefore the Philosopher says (*Phys.* ii. 3) that *the end is a good, or an apparent good.*

And in the apprehension of the good lies precisely the possibility of choice, as the argument proceeds to point out (here and in the following canto), on the principle that "malum nunquam amatur nisi sub ratione boni" ("evil is never loved except under the aspect of good"), as stated by Aquinas in *Summa theol.* I-II, q. 27, a. 1, ad 1.

95–96. *per malo obietto . . . vigore:* The three forms of erring elective love are purged on the seven terraces of Purgatory, as will be explained: love of an evil object (apprehended as good) on the first three, lower, terraces; a love of the good which is not vigorous enough (sloth), on this central terrace; and excessive love of a secondary good on the three upper terraces. The purgatorial system is thus tripartite, even as the punitive system of Hell is. See *Inf.* XI, 16-84. But we may note that, according to the object of love, whether good or bad, Purgatory proper may be viewed as divided into two parts rather than three, as Hell is. It has been observed in the n. to vss. 76-78 that such a division into two parts places the central or fourth terrace in upper Purgatory, even though in another sense it is itself the dividing line between lower and upper Purgatory.

97. *Mentre ch'elli è nel primo ben diretto*: So long, that is, as elective love is in accord with natural love, which is always directed on the Primal Good, God. See *Purg.* XVIII, 55-60.

98. *e ne' secondi sé stesso misura*: And so long as elective love observes due measure in seeking secondary goods, such as money, food, pleasure.

99. *esser non può cagion di mal diletto*: It cannot occasion sinful delight.

100. *ma quando al mal si torce*: "Torce" implies a kind of violence. When elective love turns to an evil object, it operates unnaturally, in that it is not in accord with natural love, which is always of the good and cannot err.

100–101. *o con più cura . . . bene*: This means excessive or deficient love of the good, and the verb "corre" (replacing "si torce") suggests a more natural operation than inclining toward evil. When we see that the slothful must ply "the too slack oar" by running constantly, we see the principle of *contrapasso* as it applies to them.

101. *dee = deve.*

102. *contra 'l fattore adovra sua fattura*: Every creature is the *fattura* or *effetto* of the Creator, since it is made by Him. He gives it a natural inclination to seek its proper end (see n. to vs. 94). But, as noted in n. to vs. 95, the argument here concerns man in this life, who has elective love, whereby he can choose a bad object or indulge in inordinate love, in doing which he works against his Creator and His providential order. Thus he sins and offends God.

It is, of course, not possible to love the First Good, God, too much. See Mar. 12:30: "Et diliges Dominum Deum tuum ex toto corde tuo, et ex tota anima tua, et ex tota mente

tua, et ex tota virtute tua: hoc est primum mandatum."
("'And thou shalt love the Lord thy God with thy whole
heart, and with thy whole soul, and with thy whole mind, and
with thy whole strength.' This is the first commandment.")
Excessive love is possible only with secondary goods, where-
as slack love is of the Creator, the First Good. Thomas
Aquinas (*Summa theol.* I-II, q. 64, a. 4, resp.) states: "Unde
nunquam potest homo tantum diligere Deum, quantum diligi
debet, nec tantum credere aut sperare in ipsum, quantum
debet. Unde multo minus potest ibi esse excessus." ("So that
never can we love God as much as He ought to be loved, nor
believe and hope in Him as much as we should. Much less
therefore can there be excess in such things.")

103–5. *esser convene amor . . . pene*: Thomas Aquinas
(*Summa theol.* I-II, q. 27, a. 4, resp.) explains:

> Nulla alia passio est quae non praesupponat aliquem
> amorem. Cuius ratio est, quia omnis alia passio animae
> importat motum ad aliquid vel quietem in aliquo. Omnis
> autem motus ad aliquid vel quies in aliquo ex aliqua
> connaturalitate vel coaptatione procedit, quae pertinet
> ad rationem amoris. Unde impossibile est quod aliqua
> alia passio animae sit causa universaliter omnis amoris.

> There is no other passion of the soul that does not pre-
> suppose love of some kind. The reason is that every
> other passion of the soul implies either movement to-
> ward something, or rest in something. Now every move-
> ment toward something, or rest in something, arises
> from some kinship or aptness of that thing; and in this
> does love consist. Therefore it is not possible for any
> other passion of the soul to be universally the cause of
> every love.

See the quotation from Aquinas in n. to vss. 91-93. Also see
Summa theol. I-II, q. 41, a. 2, ad 1, "omnes passiones ani-
mae derivantur ex uno principio, scilicet ex amore, in quo
habent ad invicem connexionem" ("all the passions of the
soul arise from one source, viz., love, wherein they are con-
nected with one another"), and *Summa theol.* I-II, q. 46,

a. 1, resp.: "Sed per hunc modum potest dici generalis passio amor, ut patet per Aug. in 14 de Civ. Dei, cap. 7 et 9. Amor enim est prima radix omnium passionum." ("But in this way love may be called a general passion, as Augustine declares [*De Civ. Dei* xiv. 7, 9], because love is the primary root of all the other passions.") Love is thus the cause of every good act ("ogne virtute") and of every bad act ("ogne operazion che merta pena").

105. *merta* = *merita*.

106–8. *Or, perché mai non può . . . tute*: Augustine (*De doct. Chris*. I, xxiv, 24) says: "Nemo ergo se odit. Et hinc quidem nulla cum aliqua secta quaestio fuit." ("Consequently, no one hates himself; there has never been any dispute on this point with any sect.") In *Summa theol*. I-II, q. 29, a. 4, resp., Thomas Aquinas explains:

> Impossibile est quod aliquis, per se loquendo, odiat seipsum. Naturaliter enim unumquodque appetit bonum, nec potest aliquid sibi appetere nisi sub ratione boni; nam malum est praeter voluntatem, ut Dionysius dicit, 4 cap. de divin. Nom., lect. 22. Amare autem aliquem est velle ei bonum, ut supra dictum est (quaest. 26, art. 4). Unde necesse est quod aliquis amet seipsum; et impossibile est quod aliquis odiat seipsum, per se loquendo.

> Properly speaking, it is impossible for a man to hate himself. For everything naturally desires good, nor can anyone desire anything for himself, save under the aspect of good: for *evil is outside the scope of the will*, as Dionysius says (*Div. Nom*. iv). Now to love a man is to will good to him, as stated above (q. 26, a. 4). Consequently, a man must, of necessity, love himself; and it is impossible for a man to hate himself, properly speaking.

In this same article (ad 2) Aquinas goes on to consider the case of the suicide:

> Nullus sibi vult et facit malum, nisi inquantum apprehendit illud sub ratione boni. Nam et illi qui interimunt

seipsos, hoc ipsum quod est mori, apprehendunt sub ratione boni, inquantum est terminativum alicuius miseriae vel doloris.

No man wills and works evil to himself, except he apprehend it under the aspect of good. For even they who kill themselves apprehend death itself as a good, considered as putting an end to some unhappiness or pain.

See *Inf.* XIII, 71. Also see Eph. 5:29: "Nemo enim umquam carnem suam odio habuit." ("For no one ever hated his own flesh.")

107. *subietto*: *Subiectum* in scholastic usage means the substance in which accidents inhere (as we say, "the thinking subject"). Love is an accident, and the "subietto" of love, in this sense, is the loving subject, i.e., the person who loves. It is axiomatic, therefore, that no one can turn away from loving—i.e., desiring—his own welfare ("salute").

108. *le cose*: Specifically, men, in this case.   *tute*: "Immune." This is a Latinism, from *tutus,* past participle of *tueor.*

109–11. *e perché intender . . . deciso*: In *Conv.* III, ii, 7-8, Dante writes:

E però che naturalissimo è in Dio volere essere—però che, sì come ne lo allegato libro si legge, "prima cosa è l'essere, e anzi a quello nulla è"—, l'anima umana essere vuole naturalmente con tutto desiderio; e però che 'l suo essere dipende da Dio e per quello si conserva, naturalmente disia e vuole essere a Dio unita per lo suo essere fortificare. E però che ne le bontadi de la natura e de la ragione si mostra la divina, viene che naturalmente l'anima umana con quelle per via spirituale si unisce, tanto più tosto e più forte quanto quelle più appaiono perfette: lo quale apparimento è fatto secondo che la conoscenza de l'anima è chiara o impedita.

And since it is most germane to the nature of God to will to be (because, as we read in the aforesaid book, "being comes first of all, and before that there is nought"), the human soul naturally desires, with the whole force of its longing, to be. And because its being depends on God, and by him is preserved, it naturally desires and wills to be united to God, in order to fortify its own being. And because it is in the excellences of nature [and of reason] that the divine principle reveals itself, it comes to pass that the human soul naturally unites herself with them in spiritual fashion, the more swiftly and the more mightily in proportion as they appear more perfect. And they so appear in proportion as the soul's power of recognition is clear or obstructed.

See Thomas Aquinas, *Summa theol.* II-II, q. 34, a. 1, resp.:

Odium est quidam motus appetitivae potentiae, quae non movetur nisi ab aliquo apprehenso. Deus autem dupliciter ab homine apprehendi potest; uno modo secundum seipsum, puta cum per essentiam videtur; alio modo per effectus suos, cum scilicet *invisibilia Dei per ea quae facta sunt intellecta conspiciuntur.* Deus autem per essentiam suam est ipsa bonitas, quam nullus habere odio potest, quia de ratione boni est ut ametur; et ideo impossibile est quod aliquis videns Deum per essentiam, eum odio habeat.

Sed effectus eius aliqui sunt qui nullo modo possunt esse contrarii voluntati humanae; quia *esse, vivere et intelligere* est et appetibile et amabile omnibus; quae sunt quidam effectus Dei. Unde etiam secundum quod Deus apprehenditur ut auctor horum effectuum, non potest odio haberi. Sunt autem quidam effectus Dei qui repugnant inordinatae voluntati, sicut inflictio poenae, et etiam cohibitio peccatorum per legem divinam; quae repugnant voluntati depravatae per peccatum; et quantum ad considerationem talium effectuum, ab aliquibus Deus odio haberi potest, inquantum scilicet apprehenditur peccatorum prohibitor, et poenarum inflictor.

Hatred is a movement of the appetitive power, which power is not set in motion save by something apprehended. Now God can be apprehended by man in two ways; first, in Himself, as when He is seen in His Essence; secondly, in His effects, when, to wit, *the invisible things* of God . . . *are clearly seen, being understood by the things that are made* (Rom. i. 20). Now God in His Essence is goodness itself, which no man can hate —for it is natural to good to be loved. Hence it is impossible for one who sees God in His Essence to hate Him.

Moreover some of His effects are such that they can nowise be contrary to the human will, since *to be, to live, to understand,* which are effects of God, are desirable and lovable to all. Wherefore again God cannot be an object of hatred if we consider Him as the Author of such like effects. Some of God's effects, however, are contrary to an inordinate will, such as the infliction of punishment, and the prohibition of sin by the Divine Law. Such like effects are repugnant to a will debased by sin, and as regards the consideration of them, God may be an object of hatred to some, in so far as they look upon Him as forbidding sin, and inflicting punishment.

Thus, the damned, who suffer torment in Hell, can hate God and do hate Him: recall Capaneus in *Inf.* XIV and Vanni Fucci in *Inf.* XXV. But the argument has it that creatures *in this life* do not hate Him.

110. *dal primo*: I.e., "dal primo essere," God. *Essere* is a noun here.

111. *ogne effetto*: Cf. *Purg.* XI, 3.   *è deciso*: "Is cut off."

112. *Resta*: Cf. the Latin *restat* and *relinquitur*, standard terms in scholastic argument.   *se dividendo bene stimo*: "If I proceed correctly in my distinctions."

113–14. *'l mal che s'ama . . . limo*: This love of evil for one's neighbor, which is purged in the three circles of lower Purgatory, is said to be "triforme" (vs. 124).

113. *del prossimo*: "Of one's neighbor."

114. *in vostro limo*: See Gen. 2:7: "Formavit igitur Dominus Deus hominem de limo terrae." ("Then the Lord God formed man out of the dust of the ground.") "Idest," explains Benvenuto, "in vobis hominibus, quia primus homo factus est de limo terrae." ("That is, in [all] men, because the first man was made from the slime of the earth.")

115–17. *È chi . . . messo*: The three modes of the love of evil manifest themselves in the sins of pride, envy, and anger, and each has an evil object, which is harm to one's neighbor. He who suffers from pride, *amor propriae excellentiae* (see n. to *Purg.* XI, 86-87)—the sin described in this tercet—hopes to excel "through abasement of his neighbor." Thomas Aquinas (*Summa theol.* II-II, q. 162, a. 4, resp.) states: "Superbia importat immoderatam excellentiae appetitum, qui scilicet non est secundum rationem rectam." ("Pride denotes immoderate desire of one's own excellence, a desire, to wit, that is not in accord with right reason.")

117. *el*: His neighbor.

118–20. *è chi . . . ama*: The sin of envy, which is *tristitia de alienis bonis*. See n. to *Purg.* XIII, 110-11. Thomas Aquinas (*Summa theol.* I, q. 63, a. 2, resp.) observes: "Invidus autem ex hoc de bono alterius dolet, inquantum bonum alterius aestimat sui boni impedimentum." ("Now the envious man repines over the good possessed by another, inasmuch as he deems his neighbor's good to be a hindrance to his own.") Also see *Summa theol.* II-II, q. 36, a. 1, resp., where Aquinas, referring to Aristotle's *Rhetoric,* defines envy as a kind of *tristitia*:

> Secundum hoc de bono alieno potest esse tristitia. Sed hoc contingit dupliciter: uno modo quando quis tristatur de bono alicuius, inquantum imminet sibi ex hoc periculum alicuius nocumenti, sicut cum homo tristatur de exaltatione inimici sui, timens ne eum laedat; et talis tristitia non est invidia, sed magis timoris effectus, ut Philosophus dicit in 2 Rhetor. (cap. 9, paulo a princ.).
>
> Alio modo bonum alterius aestimatur ut malum proprium, inquantum est diminutivum propriae gloriae

vel excellentiae; et hoc modo de bono alterius tristatur invidia; et ideo praecipue de illis bonis homines invident in quibus est gloria, et in quibus homines amant honorari et in opinione esse, ut Philosophus dicit in 2 Rhetor. (cap. 10, parum a princ.).

In this way sorrow can be about another's good. But this happens in two ways: first, when a man is sorry about another's good, in so far as it threatens to be an occasion of harm to himself, as when a man grieves for his enemy's prosperity, for fear lest he may do him some harm: such like sorrow is not envy, but rather an effect of fear, as the Philosopher states (*Rhet.* ii. 9 [1386^{b}]).

Secondly, another's good may be reckoned as being one's own evil, in so far as it conduces to the lessening of one's own good name or excellence. It is in this way that envy grieves for another's good: and consequently men are envious of those goods in which a good name consists, and about which men like to be honored and esteemed, as the Philosopher remarks (*Rhet.* ii. 10 [1387^{b}-1388^{a}]).

120. *onde s'attrista sì che 'l contrario ama*: In *Summa theol.* II-II, q. 36, a. 2, resp., Thomas Aquinas states: "Quarto modo aliquis tristatur de bonis alicuius, inquantum alter excedit ipsum in bonis: et hoc proprie est invidia; et istud semper est pravum . . . quia dolet de eo de quo est gaudendum, scilicet de bono proximi." ("Fourthly, we grieve over a man's good, in so far as his good surpasses ours; this is envy properly speaking, and is always sinful . . . because to do so is to grieve over what should make us rejoice, viz. over our neighbor's good.")

121-23. *ed è chi . . . impronti*: Each form of this "triforme amor" (as it is referred to in the next verse), which has harm of one's neighbor as its object, is closely related to the other. Thus Thomas Aquinas, in discussing the sin of anger, which is defined in this tercet, brings in envy, to distinguish one from the other. See *Summa theol.* II-II, q. 158, a. 1, resp.:

Est autem hoc considerandum circa passiones animae,

quod dupliciter potest in eis malum inveniri: uno modo
ex ipsa specie passionis, quae quidem consideratur
secundum obiectum passionis; sicut invidia secundum
suam speciem importat quoddam malum; est enim tris-
titia de bono aliorum, quod secundum se rationi re-
pugnat; et ideo invidia mox nominata sonat aliquid mali,
ut Philosophus dicit in 2 Ethic. (cap. 6, a med.) Hoc
autem non competit irae, quae est appetitus vindictae:
potest enim vindicta et bene et male appeti.

Now with regard to the passions of the soul, it is to be
observed that evil may be found in them in two ways.
First by reason of the passion's very species, which is
derived from the passion's object. Thus envy, in respect
of its species, denotes an evil, since it is displeasure at
another's good, and such displeasure is in itself con-
trary to reason: wherefore, as the Philosopher remarks
(*Ethic.* ii. 6 [1107ᵃ]), *the very mention of envy denotes
something evil.* Now this does not apply to anger, which
is the desire for revenge, since revenge may be desired
both well and ill.

Thus anger can be termed *tristitia,* as envy commonly is. The
wrathful man (says Aquinas in *Summa theol.* II-II, q. 158,
a. 2, ad 3) "tristatur de iniuria, quam aestimat sibi illatam;
et ex hac tristitia movetur ad appetendum vindictam" ("is
displeased . . . with the injury which he deems done to him-
self: and through this displeasure he is moved to seek ven-
geance"). See also *Summa theol.* II-II, q. 158, a. 4, resp.,
where Aquinas continues to dwell on the distinction between
envy and wrath:

Appetit enim ira malum poenae alicuius sub ratione
boni, quod est vindicta: et ideo ex parte mali quod ap-
petit convenit peccatum irae cum illis peccatis quae
appetunt malum proximi, puta cum invidia et odio; sed
odium appetit absolute malum alterius, inquantum
huiusmodi; invidus autem appetit malum alterius prop-
ter appetitum propriae gloriae; sed iratus appetit malum
alterius sub ratione iustae vindictae. Ex quo patet quod
odium est gravius quam invidia, et invidia quam ira:

quia peius est appetere malum sub ratione mali, quam
sub ratione boni; et peius est appetere malum sub ra-
tione boni exterioris, quod est honor, vel gloria, quam
sub ratione rectitudinis iustitiae.

For anger desires the evil of punishment for some per-
son, under the aspect of a good that is vengeance. Hence
on the part of the evil which it desires the sin of anger
agrees with those sins which desire the evil of our neigh-
bor, such as envy and hatred; but while hatred desires
absolutely another's evil as such, and the envious man
desires another's evil through desire of his own glory,
the angry man desires another's evil under the aspect
of just revenge. Wherefore it is evident that hatred is
more grievous than envy, and envy than anger: since
it is worse to desire evil as an evil, than as a good; and
to desire evil as an external good such as honor or glory,
than under the aspect of the rectitude of justice.

Aquinas (*Summa theol.* I-II, q. 46, a. 1, resp.) states:

Non enim insurgit motus irae, nisi propter aliquam tris-
titiam illatam, et nisi adsit desiderium et spes ulciscendi;
quia ut Philosophus dicit in 2 Rhet. (cap. 2 circa
princ.), *iratus habet spem puniendi*; appetit enim vin-
dictam ut sibi possibilem.

Because the movement of anger does not arise save on
account of some pain inflicted, and unless there be de-
sire and hope of revenge: for, as the Philosopher says
(*Rhet.* ii. 2 [1378^{a-b}]), *the angry man hopes to punish;
since he craves for revenge as being possible.*

Aquinas concludes: "Unde, si fuerit multum excellens per-
sona quae nocumentum intulit, non sequitur ira, sed solum
tristitia." ("Consequently if the person, who inflicted the in-
jury, excel very much, anger does not ensue, but only sor-
row.") In *Summa theol.* I-II, q. 46, a. 2, resp. he says:

Ira respicit unum obiectum secundum rationem boni,
scilicet vindictam quam appetit, et aliud secundum
rationem mali, scilicet hominem nocivum, de quo vult
vindicari; et ideo est passio quodammodo composita
ex contrariis passionibus.

Anger regards one object under the aspect of good, viz., vengeance, which it desires to have; and the other object under the aspect of evil, viz., the noxious person, on whom it seeks to be avenged. Consequently it is a passion somewhat made up of contrary passions.

In *Summa theol.* I-II, q. 46, a. 3, ad 3, Aquinas says that "ira dicitur componi ex tristitia et desiderio." ("Anger is said to be composed of sorrow and desire.") We may note how Dante has caught these two aspects in this tercet, the *tristitia* in "aonti" and the *desiderium* in "si fa de la vendetta ghiotto."

121. *aonti = adonti.* Cf. *Inf.* VI, 72.

123. *e tal convien che 'l male altrui impronti*: The construction may be easier to understand if taken in normal prose order: "e convien che tale [i.e., the person who is made greedy for vengeance] impronti [prepare, make ready] il male altrui," where "altrui" is the possessive.

124. *Questo triforme amor*: See vss. 113-14. *qua giù di sotto*: On the three lower terraces already left behind.

125-26. *or vo' che tu . . . corrotto*: The argument now passes to love of good that errs in being either excessive or deficient, "o per troppo o per poco di vigore" (vs. 96), now restated as being a love "che corre al ben con ordine corrotto."

125. *intende = intenda.*

127-29. *Ciascun confusamente . . . contende*: Three stages in love, as will be explained in the next canto, are represented in this tercet: perception, desire of the object, and attainment of the object. See *Purg.* XVIII, 22-33.

127. *Ciascun confusamente un bene apprende*: This first principle concerning love of the good rests on the assumption that "there is a common and confused knowledge of God which is found in practically all men" (see the quotation from the *Summa contra Gentiles* below), and since the good is conceived as apprehended, the love in question is elective

love. But as such it corresponds in its object to natural love, for in men natural love has as its object the contemplation of God. See n. to vs. 94; *Purg.* XVIII, 55-60. Thomas Aquinas (*Summa contra Gentiles* III, 38) writes:

> Est enim quaedam communis et confusa Dei cognitio, quae quasi omnibus hominibus adest; sive hoc sit per hoc quod Deum esse sit per se notum, sicut alia demonstrationis principia, sicut quibusdam videtur . . . sive (quod magis verum videtur) quia naturali ratione statim homo in aliqualem Dei cognitionem pervenire potest.

> For there is a common and confused knowledge of God which is found in practically all men; this is due either to the fact that it is self-evident that God exists, just as other principles of demonstration are—a view held by some people . . . or, what seems indeed to be true, that man can immediately reach some sort of knowledge of God by natural reason.

And in *Summa theol.* I, q. 2, a. 1, ad 1, Aquinas says:

> Cognoscere Deum esse in aliquo communi sub quadam confusione, est nobis naturaliter insertum, in quantum scilicet Deus est hominis beatitudo; homo enim naturaliter desiderat beatitudinem; et quod naturaliter desideratur ab homine, naturaliter cognoscitur ab eodem. Sed hoc non est simpliciter cognoscere Deum esse, sicut cognoscere venientem non est cognoscere Petrum, quamvis sit Petrus veniens; multi enim perfectum hominis bonum, quod est beatitudo, existimant divitias; quidam vero voluptates, quidam autem aliquid aliud.

> To know that God exists in a general and confused way is implanted in us by nature, inasmuch as God is man's beatitude. For man naturally desires happiness, and what is naturally desired by man must be naturally known to him. This, however, is not to know absolutely that God exists; just as to know that someone is approaching is not the same as to know that Peter is approaching, even though it is Peter who is approaching; for many there are who imagine that man's perfect

good, which is happiness, consists in riches, and others
in pleasures, and others in something else.

128. *nel qual si queti l'animo*: Every man apprehends in a
vague way the fact that there must be some good in which the
soul (specifically, the will) might come to rest, i.e., find com-
plete satisfaction. This would be perfect happiness—viewed
subjectively, the object of desire, or viewed objectively, the
vision of God, the beatitude of eternal life. This is natural
love in man (the natural desire for God), which is an *in-
clinatio* implanted in all things causing them to seek their
own perfection (see n. to vs. 94).   *si queti*: The verb in
the subjunctive represents the questing for some such good,
the possible existence of which is dimly apprehended.

129. *per che di giugner lui*: "Wherefore to attain it." "Lui"
is not primarily a personal pronoun here, but since it is un-
derstood that such a good, for man, is God, it can reflect the
personal, which becomes more evident in the next verse.
contende: From the Latin *contendit*, "strives," "struggles."

130. *lento amore*: Slothful love. See vss. 85-87.   *a lui
veder*: "Lui" is still the impersonal pronoun, the antecedent
of which is "un bene," vs. 127. But now, coupled with
"veder" here and "acquistar" in the next verse, it more plain-
ly connotes the personal, i.e., God, since only in the vision
of Him, face to face, is man's desire quieted, and since ulti-
mate beatitude consists not only in seeing Him (an operation
of the intellect) but in attaining Him (an operation of the
will). As Thomas Aquinas (*Summa theol.* I-II, q. 3, a. 4,
resp.) says: "Essentia beatitudinis in actu intellectus con-
sistit. Sed ad voluntatem pertinet delectatio beatitudinem
consequens." ("The essence of happiness consists in an act
of the intellect: but the delight that results from happiness
pertains to the will.") See *Purg.* XVIII, 31-33.

132. *dopo giusto penter*: "After duly repenting." All souls
who reach Purgatory must have repented before death or at
the moment of death, else they would be in Hell. Compare,
in *Inf.* XXVII, the case of Guido da Montefeltro, who did

not repent before dying, and, in *Purg.* V, that of his son Buonconte, who repented at the last moment.   *penter* = *pentire*. Pronounced *pentèr*.

133. *Altro ben*: Any one of the *secondi beni* mentioned in vs. 98.   *che non fa l'uom felice*: Secondary goods are incapable of satisfying man's natural appetite for the good. Man must not desire such goods as ends and must have a "measured" love of them (vs. 98). Cf. the "picciol bene" of *Purg.* XVI, 91.

134–35. *non è felicità . . . radice*: No secondary good can give man perfect happiness; for it is not the essence and true source of happiness, which is God alone.

135. *d'ogne ben frutto e radice*: Cf. *Inf.* I, 78: "principio e cagion di tutta gioia." The terms are reversed here, "frutto" being the beatific vision of God, the cause of man's perfect happiness, and "radice" the principle of such Good, i.e., its source.

136. *L'amor ch'ad esso troppo s'abbandona*: Cf. vss. 96 and 100-101.

137. *si piange*: Is expiated. Cf. vs. 125.

138. *tripartito*: This excessive love of secondary goods is one love, which manifests itself in three modes, according to three kinds of objects—even as the other love, love of an evil object, is "triforme" (vs. 124).

139. *tacciolo* = *lo taccio.*   *acciò che tu per te ne cerchi*: "Ne" here (instead of *lo*) reflects the *di* which would follow "cerchi" if another verb, such as *capire* ("to understand"), depended on "cerchi": *cercare di capire.*

2. *l'alto dottore*: The adjective bears the suggestion of both "lofty" and "deep," i.e., qualities of the discourse that Virgil has just concluded.

3. *ne la mia vista*: Literally, "in my eyes."

4. *cui*: Direct object.   *frugava*: Cf. *Inf.* XXX, 70; *Purg.* III, 3; XV, 137.

5. *tacea = tacevo*.   *dicea = dicevo*.

6. *li = gli*.   *grava*: "Annoys." Cf. *Inf.* III, 80: "temendo no 'l mio dir li fosse grave."

8. *del timido voler che non s'apriva*: Cf. *Inf.* II, 81.

11. *sì nel tuo lume*: Further on in this canto Virgil will distinguish between his own "light," in this sense, and the light of understanding that will be shed by Beatrice. See vss. 46-48.

12. *la tua ragion*: See vs. 1: "al suo ragionamento."
parta o descriva: Both forms are in the subjunctive, as required by "quanto," meaning "all."   *parta*: "May formulate."   *descriva*: "May distinguish."

13. *Però = per ciò*.

14. *che mi dimostri amore*: Dante desires to understand the psychology of love, how love operates in each individual.

14–15. *a cui reduci . . . contraro*: To which you refer every moral act, good or bad, as to its foundation and first principle. See *Purg.* XVII, 103-5. Thomas Aquinas (*Summa theol.* I, q. 3, a. 5, resp.) writes:

> Aliquid est in genere dupliciter; uno modo simpliciter, et proprie, sicut species, quae sub genere continetur; alio modo per reductionem, sicut principia, et privationes; sicut punctus et unitas reducuntur ad genus quantitatis sicut principia; caecitas autem et omnis privatio reducuntur ad genus sui habitus.

> A thing can be in a genus in two ways; either absolutely and properly, as a species contained under a genus; or as being reducible to it, as principles and privations. For example, a point and unity are reduced to the genus of quantity, as its principles; while blindness and all other privations are reduced to the genus of habit.

16. *ver'* = *verso.*   *agute* = *acute.*

17. *fieti* = *ti sarà.*

18. *l'error de' ciechi*: This error is explicitly stated in vss. 34-39.   *che si fanno duci*: See Matt. 15:14: "Caeci sunt et duces caecorum: caecus autem, si caeco ducatum praestet, ambo in foveam cadunt." ("They are blind guides of blind men. But if a blind man guide a blind man, both fall into a pit.") Dante elaborates on this in *Conv.* I, xi, 4-6.

19–21. *L'animo, ch'è creato . . . desto*: These three verses state succinctly the entire operation of love as this is then presented in four tercets, vss. 22-33.

19–20. *L'animo, ch'è creato . . . piace*: "L'animo," the intellective soul, created by a happy and loving Creator and breathed into the fully formed foetus, is ready and disposed to love whatever offers it pleasure. See *Purg.* XVI, 85-90, and compare vss. 89-90 of that canto, "mossa da lieto fattore, / volentier torna a ciò che la trastulla," with the words "ad ogne cosa è mobile che piace" here. The mind or soul naturally desires happiness and everything that seems to promise it. This will be referred to as the "inclination to the primary objects of appetite" in vs. 57. It is essentially natural love, in the sense that was intended in the preceding canto, vs. 94.

21. *tosto che dal piacere in atto è desto*: The complacency of the mind in the thing that seems to offer it pleasure awakens love, as is stated more fully in vss. 31-32.

22. *Vostra*: Virgil generalizes, in the plural, about us, the living. *apprensiva*: The faculty of perception. The term is standard in the psychology deriving from Aristotle, as are a number of other terms in this general exposition of love.

da esser verace: From something that has real objective existence outside the mind. See *Purg.* XV, 116, "le cose che son fuor di lei vere," and *Rime* CXVI, 35, "colà dov'ella è vera" ("where, in verity, is she herself").

23. *tragge intenzione*: The faculty of perception takes from the object an image or conception, known in scholastic terminology as *intentio*. The psychology is basically Aristotelian; see, in Aquinas, *Opera omnia*, vol. XX, p. 130, or in A. M. Pirotta (1936), p. 256, the following from Aristotle, *De anima* III, 8, 431[b]: "Non enim lapis in anima est, sed species." ("No stone is in the soul, but only its form.") For the meaning of *intentio*, see *Conv.* III, ix, 7: "Queste cose visibili, sì le proprie come le comuni in quanto sono visibili, vengono dentro a l'occhio—non dico le cose, ma le forme loro—per lo mezzo diafano, non realmente ma intenzionalmente, sì quasi come in vetro transparente." ("These visible things, both proper and common, in so far as they are visible, pass into the eye,—I do not mean the things themselves, but their forms—through the diaphanous medium—not in reality but in intention—much as in transparent glass.") And see, among the many passages that might be chosen from the works of Thomas Aquinas in this regard, *Summa contra Gentiles* I, 53:

Intellectus per speciem rei formatus intelligendo format

in seipso quamdam intentionem rei intellectae, quae est ratio ipsius, quam significat definitio. Et hoc quidem necessarium est, eo quod intellectus intelligit indifferenter rem absentem et praesentem; in quo cum intellectu imaginatio convenit. Sed intellectus hoc amplius habet, quod etiam intelligit rem ut separatam a conditionibus materialibus, sine quibus in rerum natura non existit; et hoc non posset esse, nisi intellectus intentionem sibi praedictam formaret.

The intellect, having been informed by the species of the thing, by an act of understanding forms within itself a certain intention of the thing understood, that is to say, its notion, which the definition signifies. This is a necessary point, because the intellect understands a present and an absent thing indifferently. In this the imagination agrees with the intellect. But the intellect has this characteristic in addition, namely, that it understands a thing as separated from material conditions, without which a thing does not exist in reality. But this could not take place unless the intellect formed the abovementioned intention for itself.

T. Gilby (1949, pp. 50-51) explains:

Conceptions involve a double existence, *duplex esse.* First, there is cheese really and physically existing, cheese in its natural being, in *esse naturali,* and secondly, there is cheese perceptually and mentally repeated in my consciousness, cheese in its significant being, in *esse intentionali.* The word comes from *intendere,* to stretch out, to direct towards, which indicates that the mental form or concept of cheese must be treated not as a thing and a final term of direct knowledge, but as an open relation and a medium. Through its passion or affection the mind conceives a similitude or likeness. The form is not opaque, but transparent; the mind does not stay there, but looks through it to the thing that is signified.

23–26. *e dentro a voi la spiega . . . amor*: The apprehending faculty brings the image of the thing inside the mind and

there "unfurls" it, causing the mind to turn its full attention
to it, and to form a judgment of it; and since we are here con-
cerned with moral action, the judgment will, in this instance,
be in terms of good or bad. Does it offer happiness and pleas-
ure, or not? If it does, the mind will incline toward it, and
such an inclination is *amor*, the first stage in the operation of
love, which in the accepted view is followed by two other
stages. Thomas Aquinas, citing Aristotle (see *De anima* III,
10, 433[b]), explains this in *Summa theol.* I-II, q. 26, a. 2,
resp.:

> Sic etiam ipsum appetibile dat appetitui primo quidem
> quamdam coaptationem ad ipsum, quae est quaedam
> complacentia appetibilis, ex qua sequitur motus ad ap-
> petibile. Nam *appetitivus motus circulo agitur*, ut dicitur
> in 3 de Anima (text. 55). Appetibile enim movet ap-
> petitum, faciens quodammodo in eo eius intentionem,
> et appetitus tendit in appetibile realiter consequendum,
> ut sit ibi finis motus ubi fuit principium.
>
> Prima ergo immutatio appetitus ab appetibili vocatur
> *amor*, qui nihil est aliud quam complacentia appetibilis;
> et ex hac complacentia sequitur motus in appetibile, qui
> est desiderium; et ultimo quies, quae est gaudium.

In the same way the appetible object gives the appetite
first a certain adaptation to itself, which consists in
complacency in that object; and from this follows move-
ment towards the appetible object. For *the appetitive
movement is circular,* as stated in *De Anima* iii. 10;
because the appetible object moves the appetite, intro-
ducing itself, as it were, into its intention; while the ap-
petite moves towards the realization of the appetible
object, so that the movement ends where it began. Ac-
cordingly, the first change wrought in the appetite by
the appetible object is called *love*, and is nothing else
than complacency in that object; and from this com-
placency results a movement towards that same object,
and this movement is *desire*; and lastly, there is rest
which is *joy*.

24. *face* = *fa*.

25. *inver' di = verso di.*

26. *quel piegare è amor*: In *Summa theol.* I-II, q. 26, a. 2, ad 3, Aquinas adds: "Amor, etsi non nominet motum appetitus tendentem in appetibile, nominat tamen motum appetitus, quo immutatur ab appetibili, ut ei appetibile complaceat." ("Although love does not denote the movement of the appetite in tending towards the appetible object, yet it denotes that movement whereby the appetite is changed by the appetible object, so as to have complacency therein.") Love as the first stage is not yet movement, but is complacency in the appetible object, and "piegare" here means to convey this.

26–27. *quell' è natura . . . si lega*: A most illuminating discussion of the conception of natural love is found in *Par.* I, 109-20, where we are told that all things have an inclination toward their source, an innate instinct that bears fire upward toward its source, for instance, as we are to be told in a simile now in vss. 28-30. Fire thus has this natural inclination, but it cannot be said to know that it has it, since it does not have cognition. In the case of human creatures, however, there is perception or awareness, as we have seen when the faculty of perception takes the image of some particular object into the mind and presents it there, and the mind bends toward it in complacency. Thomas Aquinas affords a fuller statement in these terms (*Summa theol.* I, q. 80, a. 1, resp.):

> Necesse est ponere quamdam potentiam animae appetitivam.
>
> Ad cuius evidentiam considerandum est quod quamlibet formam sequitur aliqua inclinatio; sicut ignis ex sua forma inclinatur ad superiorem locum, et ad hoc quod generet sibi simile. Forma autem in his quae cognitionem participant, altiori modo invenitur quam in his quae cognitione carent. In his enim quae cognitione carent, invenitur tantummodo forma ad unum esse proprium determinans unumquodque, quod etiam naturale uniuscuiusque est. Hanc igitur formam naturalem se-

quitur naturalis inclinatio, quae appetitus naturalis vocatur. In habentibus autem cognitionem sic determinatur unumquodque ad proprium esse naturale per formam naturalem, quod tamen est receptivum specierum aliarum rerum: sicut sensus recipit species omnium sensibilium, et intellectus omnium intelligibilium. Et sic anima hominis fit omnia quodammodo secundum sensum et intellectum, in quo cognitionem habentia ad Dei similitudinem quodammodo appropinquant, in quo omnia praeexistunt, sicut Dionysius dicit (cap. 5 de div. Nom., lect. 1). Sicut igitur formae altiori modo existunt in habentibus cognitionem supra modum formarum naturalium, ita oportet quod in eis sit inclinatio supra modum inclinationis naturalis, quae dicitur appetitus naturalis. Et haec superior inclinatio pertinet ad vim animae appetitivam, per quam animal appetere potest ea quae apprehendit, non solum ea ad quae inclinatur ex forma naturali.

It is necessary to assign an appetitive power to the soul. To make this evident, we must observe that some inclination follows every form: for example, fire, by its form, is inclined to rise, and to generate its like. Now, the form is found to have a more perfect existence in those things which participate knowledge than in those which lack knowledge. For in those which lack knowledge, the form is found to determine each thing only to its own being—that is, to its nature. Therefore this natural form is followed by a natural inclination, which is called the natural appetite. But in those things which have knowledge, each one is determined to its own natural being by its natural form, in such a manner that it is nevertheless receptive of the species of other things: for example, sense receives the species of all things sensible, and the intellect of all things intelligible, so that the soul of man is, in a way, all things by sense and intellect: and thereby, those things that have knowledge, in a way, approach to a likeness to God, *in Whom all things pre-exist*, as Dionysius says (*Div. Nom.* v).

Therefore, as forms exist in those things that have knowledge in a higher manner and above the manner of natural forms, so must there be in them an inclination surpassing the natural inclination, which is called the natural appetite. And this superior inclination belongs to the appetitive power of the soul, through which the animal is able to desire what it apprehends, and not only that to which it is inclined by its natural form.

This can help bring into proper focus Virgil's exposition at this particular point. It should be recalled that in *Purg.* XVII, 127-28, it is said that "every one confusedly apprehends a good in which the mind may be at rest." This is the natural inclination or love in man at the first level of consciousness, a natural love by which man is "bound."

Now Virgil is explaining how man perceives a particular object and bends toward the image of it when brought into the mind, and this is said to be nature which is bound in him anew through pleasure. "Di novo" here can mean "for the first time" and is so interpreted by several modern commentators. But it seems well to allow it to have a meaning that will do justice to the above considerations and therefore to see that "di novo" here would have another meaning. The natural appetite was said to perceive dimly that there must be some object in which it would find rest and to be inclined or bent toward that object in a general way (this being natural love, which will be called a "primal will" in vs. 59). Now, as the mind bends toward some particular object, or toward and through its image in the mind, it may be said to become bound *again*. The key phrase in this regard, in the passage here repeated from the preceding quotation from Aquinas, is at the end: "Et haec superior inclinatio pertinet ad vim animae appetitivam, per quam animal appetere potest ea quae apprehendit, non solum ea ad quae inclinatur ex forma naturali." ("And this superior inclination belongs to the appetitive power of the soul, through which the animal is able to desire what it apprehends, and not only that to which it is inclined by its natural form.") The form, the desire, the love of all creatures and things, including stones and flames, which inclines them to their proper ends is fundamental in their natures. But there is the category of higher creatures who *perceive* their ends and the objects of their desire, and the human creature may be said to do this in two ways. First, dimly or vaguely, and this is the natural appetite in operation at a first general stage; and second, in a specific and concrete way, when a particular object is desired, as Virgil is now explaining. Since these are two moments or levels of awareness and of love, the phrase "di novo" comes in to register the moment of the second "binding." See Thomas Aquinas, *De veritate* q. 24, a. 15, resp.: "et sic, cum homo se ad gratiam incipit praeparare, de novo voluntatem suam convertendo ad Deum" ("thus, when a man begins to prepare himself for grace by turning his will again to God").

28–30. *Poi, come 'l foco . . . dura*: See the following in the passage from Thomas Aquinas quoted in the preceding note: "sicut ignis ex sua forma inclinatur ad superiorem locum." The place to which fire rises is the elemental circle of fire which was thought to lie inside and nearest to the sphere of the moon. A flame seeks to rise to that, as to its proper place. Cf. *Par.* I, 115. "Nata" here clearly implies natural love.

28. *movesi* = *si move*.

30. *là dove più in sua matera dura*: B. Nardi (1925, p. 94) observes that "il concetto, a cui Dante fa chiara allusione, ebbe tra i filosofi medievali validi sostenitori. Si tratta della *virtus conservandi locata*, che alcuni di essi attribuiscono al *locus naturalis* dei quattro elementi." ("The concept to which Dante clearly alludes had some able spokesmen for it among the medieval philosophers. It is the *virtus conservandi locata* [virtue of conserving that which is located in place] which some of them attributed to the *locus naturalis* [natural place] of the four elements.") See a significant passage from Albertus Magnus cited by Nardi (1925, pp. 94-95), who also cites Thomas Aquinas, *Exp. Phys.* IV, lect. 1, n. 412: "Locus habet quamdam virtutem conservandi locata; et propter hoc locatum tendit in suum locum desiderio suae conservationis." ("Place has a certain power of conserving that which is lo-

cated in place. And because of this, that which is located in place tends toward its own place by a desire for its own conservation.") Nardi mentions Albertus Magnus' statement in *De coelo et mundo* IV, ii, 1 (text. et com. 21) that "loca illa ad quae moventur corpora simplicia, sunt perfectiones ipsorum." ("Those places toward which simple bodies are moved are really their true perfections.") Nardi concludes:

> *In altura*, cioè nel suo *luogo naturale*, in *concavo lunae*, il fuoco ha la sua *virtus formativa* et *perfectiva* nel raggior delle stelle, che in quella parte del mondo, e non in altra, hanno impressa la forma del fuoco nella materia. Il luogo naturale, mercè la virtù celeste che in esso opera costantemente, ha la proprietà di conservare più a lungo le cose da esso contenute. E per ciò dicono comunemente i filosofi medievali, che ogni corpo tende verso il suo luogo naturale come verso la propria perfezione.

> Upward, that is to say, in its natural place *in concavo lunae* (within the moon), the fire has its *virtus formativa et perfectiva* (formative and perfecting virtue), through the light of the stars, which impressed the form of fire into matter in that part of the world, and in no other. Because of the celestial virtue constantly operative in it, natural place has the property of preserving the things it contains for a longer time. That is why medieval philosophers commonly say that every body tends toward its natural place as toward its own perfection.

31. *così l'animo preso entra in disire*: This is the second stage in love, which Thomas Aquinas terms *desiderium* (see the quotation from Aquinas in n. to vss. 23-26). Although it is a movement of the mind, we must not think that the movement is toward the image or *intentio* of the object. The movement of desire is toward "every thing that pleases" (see vs. 20), the real thing, not the image of it, even as Aquinas explains in *Summa theol.* I-II, q. 26, a. 2, resp.: "Appetitus tendit in appetibile realiter consequendum, ut sit ibi finis motus ubi fuit principium." ("The appetite moves toward

the realization of the appetible object, so that the movement ends where it began.") See the quotation from T. Gilby (1949) in n. to vs. 23. *Preso* ("enamored") belongs to the vocabulary of the love lyric and appears in the first verse of the first poem of the *Vita nuova*, "a ciascun'alma presa e gentil core" ("to every captive soul and gentle heart"). But it is implied in the notion of *legato*, as the mind is said to be at the first stage.] ⟶opposite of courtly love

32–33. *e mai non posa . . . gioire*: Aquinas' statement of the third and last stage of love is: "Et ultimo quies, quae est gaudium" (see quotation from the *Summa theologica* in n. to vs. 23). "Posa" here corresponds to the "quies" of Aquinas, and "gioire" to "gaudium," by which we see that the poet has followed exactly the accepted presentation of the operation of love. At the third stage the circle of love is complete, as Aquinas, following closely his Aristotle, observes (see the quotation in the preceding note). The end of the movement is possession and fruition of the object.

33. *il = lo.*

34. *puote = può.   apparer = apparire.*

35–36. *la gente ch'avvera . . . cosa*: Those who maintain this are the Epicureans, termed "ciechi" in vs. 18. Their erroneous doctrine, their "blindness," is now declared.

37–38. *però che forse . . . buona*: The "matera" of love, that is, the innate potentiality, the disposition to love, is good, because it is implanted in him by God. The "forse" is not intended to suggest that there might be an exception to this, but only invites us to consider that such is the case. Vs. 39 restates or grants this fact.

38–39. *ma non ciascun segno è buono*: That is, not every object of love is good. The metaphor is of a stamp or seal that may be applied to wax and make its imprint on it. Through the metaphor we see love as something that is "offered to us from without," as vs. 43 states it. Just so Thomas Aquinas (see the quotation from *Summa theol.*

I-II, q. 26, a. 2, resp., in the n. to vs. 23) has the circle of
love beginning outside, with the real object. The image of the
thing, the *intentio*, is in fact, from this point of view, often
termed an *impressio* in the mind.

40. *'l mio seguace ingegno*: My mind, which has followed
your discourse attentively.

41. *lui = a lui.*

42. *ma ciò m'ha fatto di dubbiar più pregno*: "Dubbiar"
is to be construed as an infinitive here used as a substantive.
Cf. *Purg.* XV, 60.

43. *ché, s'amore è di fuori a noi offerto*: Love is a passion,
and the lover is one who undergoes an effect originating with
some "esser verace," an object which stamps his mind, as the
image of the seal and wax has suggested. This is true of both
natural and elective love: the circle of love begins outside
the mind, with the object. Thomas Aquinas, referring to
Aristotle's *Eudemian Ethics* (see VIII, 2, 1248[a]), writes
(*Summa theol.* I-II, q. 9, a. 4, resp.):

> Respondeo dicendum, quod secundum quod voluntas
> movetur ab obiecto, manifestum est quod moveri potest
> ab aliquo exteriori.
>
> Sed eo modo quo movetur quantum ad exercitium
> actus, adhuc necesse est ponere voluntatem ab aliquo
> principio exteriori moveri. Omne enim quod quandoque
> est agens in actu, et quandoque in potentia, indiget
> moveri ab aliquo movente. Manifestum est autem, quod
> voluntas incipit velle aliquid, cum hoc prius non vellet.
> Necesse est ergo quod ab aliquo moveatur ad volendum.
> Et quidem, sicut dictum est, art. praeced., ipsa movet
> seipsam inquantum per hoc quod vult finem, reducit
> seipsam ad volendum ea quae sunt ad finem. Hoc autem
> non potest facere nisi consilio mediante. Cum enim
> aliquis vult sanari, incipit cogitare quomodo hoc con-
> sequi possit; et per talem cogitationem pervenit ad hoc
> quod potest sanari per medicum, et hoc vult. Sed quia
> non semper sanitatem actu voluit, necesse est quod in-

ceperit velle sanari ab aliquo movente. Et si quidem ipsa moveret seipsam ad volendum, oportuisset quod mediante consilio hoc ageret ex aliqua voluntate praesupposita. Non autem est procedere in infinitum. Unde necesse est ponere quod in primum motum voluntatis voluntas prodeat ex instinctu alicuius exterioris moventis, ut Aristoteles concludit in quodam cap. Eth. Eudemicae.

I answer that, As far as the will is moved by the object, it is evident that it can be moved by something exterior. But in so far as it is moved in the exercise of its act, we must again hold it to be moved by some exterior principle.

For everything that is at one time an agent actually, and at another time an agent in potentiality, needs to be moved by a mover. Now it is evident that the will begins to will something, whereas previously it did not will it. Therefore it must, of necessity, be moved by something to will it. And, indeed, it moves itself, as stated above (a. 3), in so far as through willing the end it reduces itself to the act of willing the means. Now it cannot do this without the aid of counsel: for when a man wills to be healed, he begins to reflect how this can be attained, and through this reflection he comes to the conclusion that he can be healed by a physician: and this he wills. But since he did not always actually will to have health, he must, of necessity, have begun, through something moving him, to will to be healed. And if the will moved itself to will this, it must, of necessity, have done this with the aid of counsel following some previous volition. But this process could not go on to infinity. Wherefore we must, of necessity, suppose that the will advanced to its first movement in virtue of the instigation of some exterior mover, as Aristotle concludes in a chapter of the *Eudemian Ethics.*

44. *e l'anima non va con altro piede*: This is the lesson of the preceding canto and the central lesson of the whole poem: all movements of the soul are to be seen as movements

of love, and "neither Creator nor any creature . . . was ever without love" as *Purg.* XVII, 91-92, states it. For the metaphor of the foot, or feet, of the soul, see n. to *Inf.* I, 30.

45. *se dritta o torta va*: Cf. *Inf.* I, 3; *Par.* XXVI, 62.
non è suo merto: "Merto" (*merito*) is "desert" of punishment or of reward; cf. vs. 60, "merto di lode o di biasmo," and "meritare" as used in vs. 65. See Dante's *Letter to Can Grande* (*Epist.* XIII, 25), where this principle of reward and punishment is referred to as the allegorical subject of the poem: "Subiectum est homo prout merendo et demerendo per arbitrii libertatem iustitie premiandi et puniendi obnoxius est." ("The subject is 'man, as by good or ill deserts, in the exercise of the freedom of his choice, he becomes liable to rewarding or punishing justice.'")

46. *Quanto ragion qui vede, dir ti poss' io*: Virgil here declares that he speaks within the limits of reason or philosophy (see reference to the philosophers in vs. 67), as distinct from theology or Christian revelation. Thus he carries his argument as far as he can within the declared range of natural reason, then refers it on to Beatrice.

47. *da indi in là*: Beyond the scope of natural reason.
t'aspetta: "Look to," rely only ("pur") on.

48. *ch'* = *ché* (*perché*); the antecedent is "da indi in là" taken as meaning "that which lies beyond," i.e., beyond the confines of natural reason. The meaning of Virgil and Beatrice in the allegory is rather clearly disclosed through these verses.   *opra* = *opera*.

49. *Ogne forma sustanzial*: "Substantial form," in scholastic terms, is that which gives to something its separate existence, and this, in man, is the intellective soul. Thomas Aquinas (*Summa theol.* I, q. 76, a. 4, resp.) explains:

> Unde dicendum est, quod nulla alia forma substantialis est in homine nisi sola anima intellectiva, et quod ipsa sicut virtute continet animam sensitivam et nutritivam,

ita virtute continet omnes inferiores formas, et facit ipsa
sola quidquid imperfectiores formae in aliis faciunt.

Whence we must conclude, that there is no other sub-
stantial form in man besides the intellectual soul; and
that the soul, as it virtually contains the sensitive and
nutritive souls, so does it virtually contain all inferior
forms, and itself alone does whatever the imperfect
forms do in other things.

49-50. *che setta è da matera . . . unita*: This qualification
specifies the substantial form as being that of the human soul,
the intellective soul, distinguishing it from angels, which are
separate substances not joined to any matter, being
incorporeal.

49. *setta*: Literally, "cut off" (Latin *secta*).

51-54. *specifica vertute . . . vita*: This substantial form—
that is, the intellective soul—contains a *virtù* which is com-
posed of two faculties, intellect and will (note "the cognition
of primary ideas" and "the inclination to the primary objects
of appetite" in vss. 55-57). The argument here takes these
together as one *virtù* or power and as such regards them as
being specific to the intellective soul. But the argument will
not lose sight of the fact that this one *virtù* is actually two, in-
tellect and will: hence cognition and inclination. (Cf. *Purg.*
XXI, 105, where the will is referred to as "la virtù
che vuole.")

This doctrine connects closely with that of *Purg.* XVII,
which also had its central focus on the operation of the intel-
lect—"ciascun confusamente un bene apprende"—and that
of the will—"per che di giugner lui ciascun contende" (see
Purg. XVII, 127-29). Yet here, as there, the operation of the
will is the major concern, since moral action is reduced to
that, and love, an operation of the will, is the principle of all
moral acts "sementa in voi d'ogne virtute / e d'ogne opera-
zion che merta pene" (*Purg.* XVII, 104-5). The intellect,
however, must present the object to the will, when it is a
question of natural appetite in the rational soul. Moreover,
the argument will bring the whole matter around to focus on

free will as the principle by which merit is determined in human actions; and free will, as will be noted, involves also the intellect. The end or final principle of the intellect is within the mind or soul, the end of the will is outside the mind, being the object. It will be noted that this fact is kept before us in these verses. The *virtù* is said to be unperceived by the mind except in operation, and perception pertains to intellect; and it is said to manifest itself only in its effect, which pertains to the will and outward action or manifestation, as "life in a plant by green leaves." The operation of these two faculties is the life of the intellective soul. It will be noted that the comparison with the manifestation of life in a plant, as with the natural tendency of fire to rise, continues to point to a natural phenomenon, i.e., what is in us by nature.

53. *mai che = se non che* (Latin *magis quam*). Cf. *Inf.* IV, 26 and *passim*.

55–56. *Però, là onde vegna . . . sape:* Virgil, as is indicated in vss. 46-48, confines his argument to that which is understandable through reason, as distinct from revelation, and natural reason cannot know of itself the source of innate knowledge and primal desires. We know naturally only through effect (cf. "*quia,*" *Purg.* III, 37), or we know within ourselves only "confusedly" in these matters. See Thomas Aquinas (*De veritate* q. 18, a. 4, resp.) on the twofold knowledge which Adam had and the limits of his natural knowledge (in the perfect state of innocence, before the Fall):

In Adam duplex fuit cognitio; scilicet naturalis, et gratiae. Cognitio autem naturalis humana ad illa potest se extendere quaecumque ductu naturalis rationis cognoscere possumus. Cuius quidem naturalis cognitionis est accipere principium et terminum. Principium autem eius est in quadam confusa cognitione omnium; prout scilicet homini naturaliter inest cognitio universalium principiorum, in quibus, sicut in quibusdam seminibus, virtute praeexistunt omnia scibilia quae ratione naturali cognosci possunt. Sed huius cognitionis terminus est quando ea quae virtute in ipsis principiis sunt, explicantur in actum; sicut cum ex semine animalis, in quo virtute praeexistunt omnia membra animalis, producitur animal habens distincta et perfecta omnia membra, dicitur esse terminus generationis animalis.

Adam had a twofold knowledge: one natural and one due to grace. Natural human knowledge can extend to those things which we can know under the guidance of natural reason. And there is a beginning and a term of this natural knowledge. It has its beginning in a kind of confused knowledge of all things, in so far as man naturally has within him a knowledge of the general principles in which, as in seeds, there virtually pre-exist all the objects of knowledge which can be known by natural reason. This knowledge reaches its term when the things which are virtually in the principles are expressed in act, as animal generation is said to reach its term when the animal, with all its members perfect and distinct, is developed from the seed of the animal in which all its members pre-existed virtually.

See the "vertute" of vs. 51 and the "operar" and "effetto" of vss. 52 and 53.

56. *le prime notizie*: Thomas Aquinas speaks of "primary ideas" in *Summa theol.* I, q. 2, a. 1, resp., "sicut patet in primis demonstrationum principiis, quorum termini sunt quaedam communia, quae nullus ignorat, ut ens, et non ens, totum, et pars, et similia" ("as is clear with regard to the first principles of demonstration, the terms of which are common things that no one is ignorant of, such as being and non-being, whole and part, and such like"), and *Summa theol.* I, q. 63, a. 8, ad 1, "ut patet maxime in primis conceptionibus, quas quisque probat auditas" ("as is especially evident with regard to primary concepts, *which everyone accepts directly they are heard*"), quoting here from Boethius (see his *Quomodo substantiae*, p. 40). B. Nardi (1949, p. 193, n. 66) affords several quotations containing definitions of this.   *sape = sa.*

57. *de' primi appetibili*: See Aquinas, *Summa theol.* I-II, q. 10, a. 1, resp.:

> Alio modo dicitur natura quaelibet substantia, vel quodlibet ens; et secundum hoc illud dicitur esse naturale rei quod convenit ei secundum suam substantiam, et hoc est quod per se inest rei.
>
> In omnibus autem ea quae non per se insunt, reducuntur in aliquid quod per se inest sicut in primum. Et ideo necesse est quod hoc modo accipiendo naturam, semper principium in his quae conveniunt rei, sit naturale. Et hoc manifeste apparet in intellectu; nam principia intellectualis cognitionis sunt naturaliter nota. Similiter etiam principium motuum voluntariorum oportet esse aliquid naturaliter volitum.
>
> Hoc autem est bonum in communi, in quod voluntas naturaliter tendit, sicut etiam quaelibet potentia in suum obiectum, et etiam ipse finis ultimus, qui hoc modo se habet in appetibilibus, sicut prima principia demonstrationum in intelligibilibus; et universaliter omnia illa quae conveniunt volenti secundum suam naturam. Non enim per voluntatem appetimus solum ea quae pertinent ad potentiam voluntatis, sed etiam ea quae pertinent ad singulas potentias et ad totum hominem. Unde naturaliter homo vult non solum obiectum voluntatis, sed etiam alia quae conveniunt aliis potentiis; ut cognitionem veri, quae convenit intellectui; et esse et vivere, et huiusmodi alia, quae respiciunt consistentiam naturalem; quae omnia comprehenduntur sub obiecto voluntatis, sicut quaedam particularia bona.

In another sense nature stands for any substance, or even for any being. And in this sense, that is said to be natural to a thing which befits it in respect of its substance. And this is that which of itself is in a thing. Now all things that do not of themselves belong to the thing in which they are, are reduced to something which belongs of itself to that thing, as to their principle. Wherefore, taking nature in this sense, it is necessary that the principle of whatever belongs to a thing, be a natural principle. This is evident in regard to the intellect: for the principles of intellectual knowledge are naturally known. In like manner the principle of voluntary movements must be something naturally willed.

Now this is good in general, to which the will tends naturally, as does each power to its object; and again it is the last end, which stands in the same relation to things appetible, as the first principles of demonstrations to things intelligible: and, speaking generally, it is all those things which belong to the willer according to his nature. For it is not only things pertaining to the will that the will desires, but also that which pertains to each power, and to the entire man. Wherefore man wills naturally not only the object of the will, but also other things that are appropriate to the other powers; such as the knowledge of truth, which befits the intellect; and to be and to live and other like things which regard the natural well-being; all of which are included in the object of the will, as so many particular goods.

58–59. *che sono in voi . . . mele*: B. Nardi (1949, p. 194, n. 69) argues for the reading "che sono in voi," as Petrocchi has it, rather than "ch'è solo in voi," the reading followed by Vandelli and others. In the case of "che sono," clearly the antecedent subjects would be "lo 'ntelletto de le prime notizie" and "l'affetto de' primi appetibili," which would seem to fit the developing argument better than "ch'è," in which case the antecedent subject would be "l'affetto de' primi appetibili." Of course, as noted, the two faculties are being considered together as one specific *virtù*, which could well suggest a singular verb with a dual subject; moreover, the two faculties are called a "prima voglia" in vs. 59, which would seem to support a verb in the singular, also with a dual subject.

Either interpretation of the intended subject must be justified in terms of the simile of the bees' zeal to make honey: is their zeal to do this a matter of volition only, or does it involve a certain cognition? See *Par*. XVIII, 109-11. The zeal of bees to make honey is an operation of this same nat-

ural *virtù*, which is implanted by God in the creature, and
that operation, even in bees, involves cognition and desire.
"Studio" suggests both calculation and endeavor. The corre-
sponding primal will of the human creature (or of his intel-
lective soul) involves both *intelletto* and *affetto*, as we have
already been told (see n. to vss. 51-54).

It should be noted that Dante, in three similes, has drawn
on fire (inanimate nature) in vss. 28-30, plants (animate
nature) in vs. 54, and now bees (sentient nature) following
a progression from lower to higher orders.

59-60. *e questa prima . . . cape*: See *Purg.* XVII, 94: "the
natural [love] is always without error." Through similes
drawn on nature, the argument has now come to the identi-
fication of natural love or natural appetite in man with the
primal will, but this primal will includes intellect, cognition
of the end, though the accent is on the will or appetite, as
"voglia" indicates. We have a dim awareness of a good that
would quiet our desire (see n. to *Purg.* XVII, 127), and we
strive to attain to this good (*Purg.* XVII, 129). It may be
helpful to consider a statement by Aquinas on the matter of
the end or good that man naturally desires (*Summa theol.*
I, q. 60, a. 2, resp.):

> Et hoc apparet in homine quantum ad intellectum, et
> quantum ad voluntatem. Intellectus enim cognoscit
> principia naturaliter: et ex hac cognitione causatur in
> homine scientia conclusionum, quae non cognoscuntur
> naturaliter ab homine, sed per inventionem, vel doctri-
> nam. Similiter autem in voluntate, finis hoc modo se
> habet sicut principium in intellectu, ut dicitur in 2
> Physic. (text. 89). . . . Unde voluntas naturaliter tendit
> in suum finem ultimum; omnis enim homo naturaliter
> vult beatitudinem. Et ex hac naturali voluntate causan-
> tur omnes aliae voluntates, cum quidquid homo vult
> velit propter finem. Dilectio igitur boni quod homo
> naturaliter vult sicut finem, est dilectio naturalis; dilectio
> autem ab hac derivata, quae est boni quod diligitur
> propter finem, est dilectio electiva.

⌐This is clearly evident in man, with respect to both his
intellect and his will. For the intellect knows principles
naturally; and from such knowledge in man comes the
knowledge of conclusions, which are known by him not
naturally, but by discovery, or by teaching. In like man-
ner, the end acts in the will in the same way as the prin-
ciple does in the intellect, as is laid down in *Phys.* ii,
text. 89. Consequently the will tends naturally to its
last end; for every man naturally wills happiness: and
all other desires are caused by this natural desire; since
whatever a man wills he wills on account of the end.
Therefore the love of that good, which a man naturally
wills as an end, is his natural love; but the love which
comes of this, which is of something loved for the end's
sake, is the love of choice.⌐

See Aristotle, *Physica* II, 9, 200ᵃ.

60. *merto = merito.*   *biasmo = biasimo.*   *cape*: Pres-
ent indicative of *capere*, "to contain," "to admit of." From
the Latin *capit*.

61–63. *Or perché a questa . . . soglia*: The "questa" here
is the "voglia," the natural appetite or the will, which is di-
rected to the ultimate end and concerning which man has no
choice, for choice is of the means and not of the end. Thomas
Aquinas (*Summa theol.* I, q. 83, a. 1, ad 5) says: "Qualitas
hominis est duplex, una naturalis, et alia superveniens. Na-
turalis autem qualitas accipi potest vel circa partem intellec-
tivam, vel circa corpus et virtutes corpori annexas. Ex eo
igitur quod homo est aliqualis qualitate naturali, quae at-
tenditur secundum intellectivam partem, naturaliter homo
appetit ultimum finem, scilicet beatitudinem. Qui quidem ap-
petitus naturalis est, et non subiacet libero arbitrio." ("Qual-
ity in man is of two kinds: natural and adventitious. Now
the natural quality may be in the intellectual part, or in the
body and its powers. From the very fact, therefore, that man
is such by virtue of a natural quality which is in the intellec-
tual part, he naturally desires his last end, which is happiness.
Which desire, indeed, is a natural desire, and is not subject

to free will.") All other desires ("ogn' altra"), therefore, concern the means to the end—or away from it, if in error— and these are subject to choice. Free will, now termed an innate virtue, is the power of choice as to means and involves both the apprehensive power and the will. Thus here we have a correspondence and proportion between the perception of the first principles and discursive reason, on the one hand, and the will of the end (natural appetite) and the elective power known as free will, on the other. Thus Thomas Aquinas (*Summa theol.* I, q. 83, a. 4, resp.) states:

Potentias appetitivas oportet esse proportionatas potentiis apprehensivis, ut supra dictum est, quaest. 64, art. 2, et qu. 80, art. 2. Sicut autem ex parte apprehensionis intellectivae se habent intellectus et ratio; ita ex parte appetitus intellectivi se habent voluntas et liberum arbitrium, quod nihil aliud est quam vis electiva. Et hoc patet ex habitudine et obiectorum et actuum. Nam intelligere importat simplicem acceptionem alicuius rei; unde intelligi dicuntur proprie principia quae sine collatione per seipsa cognoscuntur. Ratiocinari autem proprie est devenire ex uno in cognitionem alterius. Unde proprie de conclusionibus ratiocinamur, quae ex principiis innotescunt. Similiter ex parte appetitus velle importat simplicem appetitum alicuius rei; unde voluntas dicitur esse de fine, qui propter se appetitur. Eligere autem est appetere aliquid propter alterum consequendum; unde proprie est eorum quae sunt ad finem. Sicut autem se habet in cognitivis principium ad conclusionem, cui propter principia assentimur; ita in appetitivis se habet finis ad ea quae sunt ad finem, quae propter finem appetuntur. Unde manifestum est quod sicut se habet intellectus ad rationem, ita se habet voluntas ad vim electivam, id est ad liberum arbitrium. Ostensum est autem supra, qu. 79, art. 8, quod eiusdem potentiae est intelligere et ratiocinari, sicut eiusdem virtutis est quiescere et moveri: unde etiam eiusdem potentiae est velle et eligere. Et propter hoc voluntas et liberum arbitrium non sunt duae potentiae, sed una.

The appetitive powers must be proportionate to the apprehensive powers, as we have said above (q. 64, a. 2). Now, as on the part of the intellectual apprehension we have intellect and reason, so on the part of the intellectual appetite we have will, and free will which is nothing else but the power of choice. And this is clear from their relations to their respective objects and acts. For the act of *understanding* implies the simple acceptation of something; whence we say that we understand first principles, which are known of themselves without any comparison. But to *reason*, properly speaking, is to come from one thing to the knowledge of another: wherefore, properly speaking, we reason about conclusions, which are known from the principles. In like manner on the part of the appetite to *will* implies the simple appetite for something: wherefore the will is said to regard the end, which is desired for itself. But to *choose* is to desire something for the sake of obtaining something else: wherefore, properly speaking, it regards the means to the end. Now, in matters of knowledge, the principles are related to the conclusion to which we assent on account of the principles: just as, in appetitive matters, the end is related to the means, which is desired on account of the end. Wherefore it is evident that as the intellect is to reason, so is the will to the power of choice, which is free will. But it has been shown above (q. 79, a. 8) that it belongs to the same power both to understand and to reason, even as it belongs to the same power to be at rest and to be in movement. Wherefore it belongs also to the same power to will and to choose; and on this account the will and the free will are not two powers, but one.

62–63. *la virtù che consiglia . . . soglia*: "Consiglia" and "assenso" reflect operation on the part of the reason and of the will respectively, of judgment and election; on human freedom, i.e., freedom of choice or free will, see *De mon.* I, xii, 2-4, 6, where Dante states: "Propter quod sciendum quod primum principium nostre libertatis est libertas arbi-

trii." ("Wherefore be it known that the first principle of our
freedom is freedom of choice.") He continues: "Et ideo dico
quod iudicium medium est apprehensionis et appetitus: nam
primo res apprehenditur, deinde apprehensa bona vel mala
iudicatur; et ultimo iudicans prosequitur sive fugit. Si ergo
iudicium moveat omnino appetitum et nullo modo prevenia-
tur ab eo, liberum est." ("Therefore I say that judgment is
the link between apprehension and appetite. For first a thing
is apprehended, then when apprehended it is judged to be
good or bad, and finally he who has so judged it pursues or
shuns it. If, then, the judgment altogether sets the appetite
in motion, and is in no measure anticipated by it, it is free.")
Dante draws the conclusion that "hoc viso, iterum manifes-
tum esse potest quod hec libertas sive principium hoc totius
libertatis nostre, est maximum donum humane nature a Deo
collatum." ("When we see this we may further understand
that this freedom, or this principle of all our freedom, is the
greatest gift conferred by God on human nature.") On this
same matter Aquinas (*Summa contra Gentiles* III, 10) says:

> In actionibus autem moralibus inveniuntur per ordinem
> quatuor activa principia: Quorum unum est virtus exe-
> cutiva, scilicet vis motiva, qua moventur membra ad
> exequendum imperium voluntatis; unde haec vis a
> voluntate movetur, quae est aliud principium, voluntas
> vero movetur a iudicio virtutis apprehensivae, quae
> iudicat hoc esse bonum vel malum, quae sunt volunta-
> tis obiecta, unum ad prosequendum, aliud ad fugiendum;
> ipsa autem vis apprehensiva movetur a re apprehensa.
> Primum igitur activum principium in actionibus morali-
> bus est res apprehensa: secundum, vis apprehensiva;
> tertium, voluntas; quartum, vis motiva quae exequitur
> imperium rationis.

> Now, in moral actions we find four principles arranged
> in a definite order. One of these is the *executive power*,
> the moving force, whereby the parts of the body are
> moved to carry out the command of the will. Then this
> power is moved by the *will*, which is a second princi-
> ple. Next, the will is moved by the *judgment* of the ap-

prehensive power which judges that this object is good
or bad, for the objects of the will are such that one
moves toward attainment, another moves toward avoid-
ance. This apprehensive power is moved, in turn, by the
thing apprehended. So, the first active principle in moral
actions is the thing that is cognitively apprehended, the
second is the apprehensive power, the third is the will,
and the fourth is the motive power which carries out the
command of reason.

63. *de' = deve.   tener la soglia*: The metaphor is plain-
ly one of guarding a door or entranceway, so as to prevent
bad loves on the part of the object from entering or bad loves
on the part of the subject from going forth. "To hold the
threshold of assent" may be understood in either way or in
both. The metaphor is an established one, as the following
two passages from Gregory's *Moralia* suggest; one of them
is all the more striking because it contains the notion of win-
nowing, which will turn up immediately in vs. 66. See, first,
Moral., pars prima, IV, xxvi, 47: "Cubicula quippe ingredi-
mur, cum secreta nostrae mentis intramus. Ostia autem clau-
dimus, cum desideria illicita coercemus. Haec itaque con-
cupiscentiae carnalis ostia, dum consensus noster aperuit,
ad innumera nos mala corruptionis pertraxit." ("For we
'enter our chambers,' when we go into the recesses of our
own hearts. And we 'shut the doors,' when we restrain for-
bidden lusts; and so whereas our consent set open these
doors of carnal concupiscence, it forced us to the countless
evils of our corrupt state.") Also see *Moral.*, pars prima, I,
xxxv, 49 (which contains a quotation from II Reg. 4:5-6):

Sed haec agere nesciunt, nisi hi qui priusquam cogita-
tiones ad opus prodeant, internos suos motus sollicite
circumspicientes frenant; haec agere nesciunt, nisi qui
virili custodia munire mentem noverunt. Unde recte
inopinata morte exstinctus Isboseth dicitur, quem et
Scriptura sacra non in domo ostiarium, sed ostiariam
habuisse testatur, dicens: *Venientes filii Remmon
Berothitae, Rechab et Banaa, ingressi sunt fervente die*

domum Isboseth, qui dormiebat super stratum suum
meridie. Ingressi sunt autem domum; et ostiaria domus
purgans triticum obdormivit. Assumentes spicas tritici,
latenter ingressi sunt, et percusserunt eum in inguine.
(II Reg. IV, 5.) Ostiaria triticum purgat, cum mentis
custodia discernendo virtutes a vitiis separat. Quae si
obdormierit, in mortem proprii Domini insidiatores ad-
mittit; quia cum discretionis sollicitudo cessaverit, ad
interficiendum animum malignis spiritibus iter pandit.
Qui ingressi spicas tollunt, quia mox bonarum cogita-
tionum germina auferunt. Atque in inguine feriunt, quia
virtutem cordis delectatione carnis occidunt. In inguine
quippe ferire, est vitam mentis delectatione carnis per-
forare. Nequaquam vero Isboseth iste hac morte suc-
cumberet, si non ad ingressum domus mulierem, id est,
ad mentis aditum mollem custodiam deputasset. Fortis
namque virilisque sensus praeponi cordis foribus debet,
quem nec negligentiae somnus opprimat, nec ig-
norantiae error fallat. Unde bene et Isboseth appellatus
est, qui custode femina hostilibus gladiis nudatur.
Isboseth quippe vir confusionis dicitur. Vir autem con-
fusionis est, qui forti mentis custodia munitus non est;
quia dum virtutes se agere aestimat, subintrantia vitia
nescientem necant. Tota itaque virtute muniendus est
aditus mentis, ne quando eam insidiantes hostes pene-
trent foramine neglectae cogitationis.

But none know how to do this saving those, who, be-
fore their thoughts proceed to deeds, restrain with anx-
ious circumspection the inward motions of their hearts.
None know how to do this saving they who have learnt
to fortify their soul with a manly guard. Hence Ish-
bosheth is rightly said to have perished by a sudden
death, whom holy Scripture at the same time testifies
to have had not a man for his doorkeeper but a woman,
in these words; *And the sons of Rimmon the Beerothite,*
Rechab and Baanah, went and came about the heat of
the day to the house of Ishbosheth, who lay on a bed
at noon; and they came thither into the midst of the

435

house, and the portress of the house was fallen asleep,
winnowing wheat. And they came privily into the house
fetching ears of wheat, and they smote him in the groin.
The portress winnows the wheat, when the wardkeep-
ing of the mind distinguishes and separates the virtues
from the vices; but if she falls asleep, she lets in con-
spirators to her master's destruction, in that when the
cautiousness of discernment is at an end, a way is set
open for evil spirits to slay the soul. They enter in and
carry off the ears, in that they at once bear off the germs
of good thoughts; and they smite in the groin, in that
they cut off the virtue of the soul by the delights of the
flesh. For to smite in the groin is to pierce the life of
the mind with the delights of the flesh. But this Ish-
bosheth would never have perished by such a death, if
he had not set a woman at the entrance to his house,
i.e. set an easy guard at the way of access to the mind.
For a strong and manly activity should be set over the
doors of the heart, such as is never surprised by sleep
of neglect, and never deceived by the errors of
ignorance; and hence he is rightly named Ishbosheth,
who is exposed by a female guard to the swords of his
enemies, for *Ishbosheth* is rendered "a man of confu-
sion." And he is "a man of confusion," who is not pro-
vided with a strong guard over his mind, in that while
he reckons himself to be practising virtues, vices steal-
ing in kill him unawares. The entrance to the mind then
must be fortified with the whole sum of virtue, lest at
any time enemies with insidious intent penetrate into it
by the opening of heedless thought.

64–65. *Quest' è 'l principio . . . voi*: Thus Virgil comes to
the conclusion which is the answer to Dante's main point,
expressed in vs. 45. See *Conv.* IV, ix, 7, where Dante writes:

Sono anche operazioni che la nostra [ragione] considera
ne l'atto de la volontade, sì come offendere e giovare,
sì come star fermo e fuggire a la battaglia, sì come stare
casto e lussuriare, e queste del tutto soggiacciono a la
nostra volontade; e però semo detti da loro buoni e rei,

perch'elle sono proprie nostre del tutto, perchè, quanto la nostra volontade ottenere puote, tanto le nostre operazioni si stendono.

There are also operations which our reason considers as they exist in the act of will, such as attacking and succouring, standing ground or fleeing in battle, abiding chaste or wantoning; and these are entirely subject to our will, and therefore we are considered good or bad on their account, because they are properly ours in their entirety; for, so far as our will can have its way, so far do operations that are really ours extend.

66. *accoglie e viglia*: See n. to vs. 63 and the second passage from Gregory quoted there, with its notion of winnowing. Each of the two verbs would seem to look in a different direction from the "threshold of assent," with "accoglie" denoting a receiving from without and "viglia" a winnowing of impulses within as they move outward toward the object of desire. Cf. "ritener" in vs. 72.   *viglia = vaglia.*

67–69. *Color che ragionando . . . mondo*: Ancient philosophers, such as Plato and Aristotle, who "went to the root" of the matter and left us the science of morality, or ethics.

70–71. *poniam che . . . s'accende*: "Poniam che" means "let us grant that," i.e., let it be granted for purposes of the argument that . . . (cf. Marco Lombardo's similar concession in *Purg.* XVI, 74). What Virgil says must be granted, of course, since the soul "ad ogne cosa è mobile che piace" (vs. 20).

72. *di ritenerlo è in voi la podestate*: Each and every love may be awakened in us of necessity, but it lies within our power to check it, at the first stage of love, and before the inclination and complacency in the object which is properly so termed becomes a desire and moves toward possession of the object, thus crossing the "threshold of assent."

73. *La nobile virtù*: Free will may be properly termed so, for it is God's most precious gift to man. See the quotation from *De monarchia* in the n. to vss. 62-63.

73–74. *Beatrice intende per lo libero arbitrio*: Here, in referring the matter on to Beatrice, Virgil means that beyond this point ("da indi in là," vs. 47) the matter involves elements that exceed the scope of natural reason ("quanto ragion qui vede," vs. 46). It is not exactly clear why this should be if not that, in its effective operation, free will involves, in the apprehensive part, a light of discernment which is given us from above, i.e., a light of grace, such as is meant by Marco Lombardo (who is not confining himself to any such limits as Virgil is here) when he says in *Purg.* XVI, 75: "lume v'è dato a bene e a malizia."

75. *s'a parlar ten prende*: Beatrice does in fact go beyond all that reason sees when she discourses on the subject in *Par.* V, 19-24, speaking there of free will as God's greatest gift to man.

76–78. *La luna, quasi a mezza notte tarda . . . arda*: The meaning of these verses is much debated. E. Moore, who fits their meaning into his whole view of the time system of the poem, grants that the references may be to the moon's rising (1887, p. 101):

> The majority of Commentators have assumed (as it appears to me quite needlessly), that this must refer to the actual hour of Moon-*rise*, which would certainly be, according to the principle we have been advocating, about 10 p.m. or perhaps 10.30, since the Moon is already well up, and producing a sensible effect in quenching the lesser stars.

But he proposed another interpretation, as follows (pp. 102-3):

> The effect here indicated of the quenching of the lesser stars by the light of the gibbous or pitcher-shaped moon (as it is graphically described in l. 78) would be much more striking if it were some little time above the horizon than if it were just rising. I think it probable that the whole passage is only a poetical and slightly elaborate way of saying that the *hour* was approaching midnight, described, as usual, by some striking visible

aspect of the fact. . . . It is surely quite a natural (poetical) description of such an hour (it being allowed that the Moon was up as a fact), to say, "And now the Moon, as it were towards midnight late, shaped like a pitcher all afire, was making the stars appear to us more rare."

Moore goes on to find other objections to the understanding that moonrise is indicated. I have therefore adopted his understanding of the puzzling verses and have translated accordingly. The important indication is that it is almost midnight, and therefore may be exactly midnight when the slothful come running around the terrace.

78. *com' un secchion che tuttor arda*: A *secchione* is a pot-shaped bucket, usually of copper, which when polished could be said to glow ruddy. M. Barbi (1921b) has pointed out that the verb *ardere* commonly had the meaning "to shine new" when applied to such things. But it must be granted that *ardere* can have here its more common meaning "to burn," which in this case would mean that a shining new copper bucket could appear to glow, as if from heat.   *tuttor*: Petrocchi has "tuttor," thus departing from Vandelli and Casella, who have "tutto." "Tuttor" makes for a smoother verse, as Petrocchi claims, and the meaning can be "which goes on glowing."

79-81. *e correa contra 'l ciel . . . cade*: E. Moore (1887, pp. 104-5) observes:

The words which follow in l. 79 describe evidently the backing of the moon through the signs from west to east, which causes the daily retardation to which we have so often referred: and more particularly he says that she was in that path of the Zodiac which is illuminated by the Sun, when the people of Rome see him setting between Sardinia and Corsica. This is stated by Mr. Butler, no doubt correctly, to be towards the end of November, when the Sun sets west by south. If so the Sun would be then in Sagittarius, and that is precisely where the Moon's Right Ascension would bring her on this night, as is pointed out by Della Valle.

See also Moore (1903), pp. 71-73, where he restates this conclusion at greater length and cites the description in Orosius of the position of Corsica and Sardinia (neither of which can actually be seen from Rome, of course). Regarding Sardinia Orosius (*Hist.* I, ii, 102) says: "Habet ab oriente et borea Tyrrhenicum mare quod spectat ad portum urbis Romae." ("To the east and northeast of the island is the Tyrrhenian Sea, which faces toward the harbor of the city of Rome.") Moore notes that "this would imply a line about south-west, or west-south-west, from Rome," and he concludes: "Dante's statement comes in effect to something like this: 'the moon on that night was about where the sun is in November.' "

80. *quel da Roma*: An inhabitant of Rome.

83. *Pietola*: Pronounced *Piètola*. This village, now known as Pietole, is about three miles south of Mantua and is commonly identified with the ancient Andes, the birthplace of Virgil.   *più che villa mantoana*: The words lend themselves to two possible interpretations: more famous than any other Mantuan town; or more famous than Mantua itself. The first seems preferable.

84. *del mio carcar diposta avea la soma*: Virgil had put off the burden of discourse, which Dante was bearing before and had laid on him by his questions.   *carcar = caricare,* infinitive used as a noun.

85. *la ragione aperta e piana*: Virgil's "ragione," or "ragionamento," as it was called in vs. 1, which has answered all of Dante's questions, his "dubbiar" (vs. 42).

86. *ricolta*: "Gathered in," "brought to bear."

87. *vana*: As used here, "vana" means "wanders in thought." Cf. *vaneggiare*, the frequentative of *vanare* that became the more common form. See E. G. Parodi (1957), p. 268.

89–90. *dopo le nostre spalle*: Dante and Virgil had arrived at the topmost step of the stairway leading up to this fourth terrace and had stopped there "like a ship that arrives at the shore" (*Purg.* XVII, 78). But they have surely not been standing all this time, since they know that they cannot proceed on their way until day returns (*Purg.* VII, 62-63). We may well imagine that they have been seated on the edge of the terrace, facing away from the wall, to look out over the slope of the mountain and the sea or up at the stars. Thus the souls who come running are said to come "dopo le nostre spalle" in the sense that Dante and Virgil have their backs turned to the terrace on which those spirits run.

90. *era già volta*: Had already rounded the curve of the terrace.

91–93. *E quale Ismeno . . . uopo*: "Quale" modifies "furia e calca" ("such a rush and crowd as"). The reference is to the famous Bacchic orgies, invoking the god. Ismenus and Asopus are small rivers of Boeotia; the first flows through Thebes, the second near the city. According to tradition Thebes was the birthplace of Bacchus, whose mother, Semele, was a Theban.

93. *pur che*: Literally, "if only."

94. *cotal*: I.e., *cotal furia e calca*.   *suo passo falca*: Literally, "sickles its way."

95. *per quel ch'io vidi*: Judging from what I saw, i.e., by the light of the moon.   *venendo = che venivano*.

95–96. *color . . . cui*: A compound relative, direct object of "vidi."

96. *buon volere e giusto amor cavalca*: "Volere" and "amor" are the subjects of "cavalca" (literally, "rides"). Cf. *Conv.* IV, xxvi, 6: "Veramente questo appetito conviene essere cavalcato da la ragione." ("But this appetite must needs be ridden by reason.")

97. *Tosto fur sovr' a noi*: The throng comes on so fast that it is quickly "upon" Dante and Virgil.   *fur = furono*.

100. *Maria corse con fretta a la montagna*: As usual, the examples of the virtue opposing the vice in question begin with Mary and follow an alternation between biblical and non-biblical. Cf. Luc. 1:39-40: "Exurgens autem Maria in diebus illis abiit in montana cum festinatione, in civitatem Iuda. Et intravit in domum Zachariae, et salutavit Elisabeth." ("Now in those days Mary arose and went with haste into the hill country, to a town of Juda. And she entered the house of Zachary and saluted Elizabeth.") Gmelin notes that in the *Speculum Beatae Mariae Virginis*, which he attributes to Bonaventura, Mary's hastening to Elisabeth is seen as an example of *sedulitas*.

101-2. *E Cesare . . . Ispagna*: On his way to Lérida (ancient Ilerda) in Catalonia in Spain, Caesar besieged Marseilles and then left part of his army there under Brutus to complete the task and hurried on. Lucan, who likens Caesar to a thunderbolt (*Phars*. I, 151-54), mentions this in *Phars*. III, 453-55, as does Orosius in *Hist*. VI, xv, 6.

103. *Ratto, ratto*: "Quickly, quickly."

104. *per poco amor*: See *Purg*. XVII, 130.

105. *che = così che*. "Che" depends on "ratto, ratto." *rinverda*: Subjunctive of *rinverdire*. *Rinverdire grazia* means "to make grace green again," that is, to have it renewed again and so to advance toward the completion of purgation when, with grace fully restored, the soul may proceed on its way to God.

106-8. *O gente in cui . . . messo*: Virgil states the exact nature of the sin of sloth which these souls are purging here, and the "forse" simply bears a touch of courtesy, to make his diagnosis less blunt.

107. *ricompie*: "Compensates for."

442

109. *non vi bugio = non vi dico bugia.* See E. G. Parodi (1957), pp. 264, 374. Virgil's declaration here to these souls that Dante is alive becomes all the more emphatic for this touch, but these souls, driven by just love and good will, have no time to marvel over the fact that Dante is alive, as do souls in other circles.

110. *ne = ci.*

111. *però = per ciò.   ne dite = diteci,* imperative.   *il pertugio:* The opening or passageway to the next circle.

113. *Vieni:* Virgil, in his haste, had spoken in the plural and had said that his companion was a living man. This spirit disregards this amazing fact and quickly answers Virgil in the singular.

114. *di retro a noi:* The throng dashes round the circle counterclockwise; hence when Dante and Virgil proceed as here directed, they will be going in the proper direction for Purgatory.

116. *potem = possiamo.   però = perciò.*

117. *giustizia:* Their purgatorial punishment, which is to run so fast without ever pausing.

118. *Io fui abate in San Zeno a Verona:* Nothing is actually known of this abbot, though he has been identified with a certain Gherardo II, who was abbot of the church of San Zeno in Verona in the time of the Emperor Frederick I and who died in 1187. The famous church and cloister of San Zeno (Zeno was bishop of Verona in the fourth century), which are very old, are but a short distance outside the old city.

119. *del buon Barbarossa:* Cf. the similar reference to Augustus in *Inf.* I, 71. The term means merely "worthy." Thus Benvenuto says: "Vocat Fridericum bonum, quia fuit vir virtuosus, strenuus, largus triumphator et corpore pulcer." ("He calls Frederick good, because he was a man of virtue, strong, a great conqueror, and very handsome of body.")

120. *di cui dolente ancor Milan ragiona*: Milan was de-stroyed by the Emperor Frederick Barbarossa in 1162; the walls were razed to the ground and the site plowed and sown with salt, according to Villani (V, 1). Dante in *Epist.* VI, 20 cites the destruction of Milan as a warning to the Florentines.

121. *E tale*: "And a certain one."

121–26. *E tale . . . vero*: How much time this sprinting abbot has for such observations and dire prophecies! The veiled reference is to Alberto della Scala, who was an old man in 1300, the fictional date of this encounter, and died on September 10, 1301. Besides Giuseppe, the illegitimate son now referred to, whose tenure of the abbacy of San Zeno (1292-1313) coincided in part with Dante's sojourn at Verona, he had three legitimate sons who succeeded him one after the other in the lordship of Verona, among whom was Can Grande, Dante's host at Verona.

122–26. *che tosto piangerà . . . pastor vero*: Momigliano comments:

> Il fatto è ricordato da Gherardo con un tono acerbissimo, come se egli risentisse in se stesso l'offesa fatta al suo monastero: i sei versi (121-6) tempestano implacabil-mente contro Alberto e suo figlio. I primi tre manifes-tano replicatamente una rude impazienza di vedere quella prepotenza punita; i due seguenti fanno del figlio di Alberto uno spietato, irruente ritratto, e riversano sul figlio una parte dello sdegno dovuto al padre.

> Gherardo tells the story in a very bitter tone, as though he felt within himself the injury done to his monastery. The six lines (121-26) rage implacably against Alberto and his son: the first three repeatedly manifest an im-patience to see that insolence punished; the next two give a pitiless, vehement portrait of Alberto's son, heap-ing upon him some of the scorn that was due the father.

123. *fia = sarà.* *possa*: Power over the church of San Zeno and the monastery.

124. *suo figlio*: Giuseppe was born in 1263 and died in 1313.
mal del corpo intero: He was lame. See Lev. 21:17-21.

125. *de la mente peggio*: Benvenuto comments: "Erat pra-
vus animo . . . lupus raptor; fuit enim homo violentus, de
nocte discurrens per suburbia cum armatis, rapiens multa, et
replens meretricibus locum illum." ("He was a mean man
. . . a rapacious wolf, a violent man, roaming the outskirts
of the city by night with armed companions, destroying
much and filling the place with harlots.")   *che mal
nacque*: He was born out of wedlock.

126. *in loco di suo pastor vero*: Who this legitimate pastor
might have been we are not told.

131. *Volgiti qua*: "Turn round this way," i.e., toward me.
If Virgil and Dante are seated on the last step, or on the
floor of the terrace, and remain so all the while, they must
turn round to watch the souls run by and to listen to the ab-
bot. Apparently Virgil is seated on Dante's right (as they
face away from the mountain and toward the sea), for the
two souls bringing up the rear, whom he would now have
Dante see, come from the side on which Virgil sits, since all
run counterclockwise around the terrace. Dante was looking
at the abbot as he ran on, to Dante's left, and so would have
to turn, as Virgil bids, to see the two who bring up the rear.

132. *dando a l'accidia di morso*: Biting (*mordendo*), i.e.,
denouncing, sloth with their examples. See "morso" in *Purg.*
III, 9.

134. *la gente a cui il mar s'aperse*: The Israelites, who were
sluggish and recalcitrant in crossing the desert after the Lord
had caused the waters of the Red Sea to divide so that they
marched across it as on dry land, while the Egyptians per-
ished in it.

135. *che vedesse Iordan le rede sue*: See Num. 14:1-39,
especially vs. 23: "Non videbunt terram pro qua iuravi pa-
tribus eorum; nec quisquam ex illis qui detraxit mihi in-
tuebitur eam." ("Not one shall see the land which I prom-

ised on oath to their fathers. None of these who have spurned me shall see it.") Joshua and Caleb were the two exceptions; aside from them, only those Israelites who had been born in the desert reached the Promised Land.

136–38. *E quella che . . . offerse*: The examples as usual follow the alternation of biblical and extra-biblical. The examples in both cases have to do with providential history, the line of the Hebrews and that of the Romans and their Trojan ancestors. The reference in this second instance is to those of Aeneas' band who chose to remain in Sicily with Acestes and so avoid the hardship of the journey. See *Aen.* V, 604-40, especially vs. 617: "Taedet pelagi perferre laborem." ("Weary are they of bearing the ocean-toil.") For "sé stessa a vita sanza gloria offerse," see *Aen.* V, 751: "animos nil magnae laudis egentes" ("souls with no craving for high renown"). They were *accidiosi* in shunning such hardship and (though they were doubtless quite unaware of it) were refusing to take part in a great and glorious pattern of providential history. For those who did take part, see *Inf.* I, 106-8; IV, 121-28.

139. *fuor = furono.*

140. *potiersi = si poterono.* Cf. "sediero," *Purg.* II, 45.

143. *vaneggiai*: Cf. "vana," vs. 87.

144. *vaghezza*: "Wool-gathering" is the translation suggested by Grandgent.

CANTO XIX

1–6. *Ne l'ora . . . bruna*: The dream that Dante is about to relate is his second and, like the first, comes just before dawn (see *Purg.* IX, 13-18), which suggests that it will prove to be prophetic, as did the other. See *Inf.* XXVI, 7, where Dante refers to early-morning dreams as being true. At that hour the heat of the day avails least against the cold that was believed to be shed by the moon. Buti comments: "La Luna non è fredda in sè; ma è effettiva di freddo coi raggi del Sole che percuoteno in essa, et ella li reflette giuso; e la reflessione che viene di su giù cagiona freddo, come quella che è di giù su cagiona caldo, e però la Luna la notte raffredda l'aire e la terra." ("The moon is not cold in itself, but produces cold with the rays of the sun which beat upon it and which it reflects downward. Reflection that moves downward causes cold, just as that which moves upward causes warmth. And therefore the moon at night cools the air and the earth.")

1. *che = in cui.*

3. *vinto da terra, e talor da Saturno*: The reference is to the natural cold of the earth and the cold that was believed to be shed by the planet Saturn (whenever it is above the horizon at night, hence "at times"). For other references to the cold of Saturn, see Dante's *Rime* C, 7, "e quel pianeta

447

che conforta il gelo" ("and that planet that strengthens the cold"), and *Conv.* II, xiii, 25, "la freddura di Saturno" ("the cold of Saturn"), as well as Virgil's *Georg.* I, 336, "frigida Saturni sese quo stella receptet" ("whither Saturn's cold star withdraws itself").

4–6. *quando i geomanti . . . bruna*: Geomancy is the art of divination by means of figures constructed on points set down at random, which can then be seen to correspond to the configuration of certain stars (see L. Thorndike, 1923, pp. 837-38). One of these figures, called *fortuna maior* ("greater fortune"), is based on the last stars of Aquarius and the first of Pisces, constellations that would be seen in the east, in the northern hemisphere as well as the southern, just before sunrise at the time of Dante's journey, since they immediately precede Aries, in which the sun appears at this time of the year (see *Inf.* I, 38-40). See *Inf.* XI, 113 for another reference to Pisces.

6. *per via che poco le sta bruna*: The "path" by which *fortuna maior* rises "does not long remain dark for it" because, as Grandgent points out, "the sun, following close after, makes the stars fade."   *le*: "To it," i.e., to the figure of *fortuna maior*.

7–9. *mi venne in sogno una femmina . . . scialba*: This woman, symbolizing the sins of the flesh, the *malo amor* that is purged in the three upper circles of Purgatory, could not be more ugly or deformed than this tercet suggests, defective as she is in speech and vision, lame, her hands maimed, her complexion sickly pale.

7. *balba* = *balbuziente*.

10–15. *Io la mirava . . . colorava*: The dreamer's gaze now transforms the figure (which was first seen objectively in all her ugliness) into an apparent good and a seductive one.

10–11. *e come 'l sol . . . aggrava*: Cf. *Inf.* II, 127-29. Clearly the cold of night suggested by the opening verses carries over into this simile.

12–15. *così lo sguardo mio . . . colorava*: The dream continues to be presented in a double focus, objective and subjective. The transformation now recorded matches exactly the order in which the deformed features were presented (vss. 7-9).

15. *com' amor vuol*: The color that "love desires" is no doubt a blend of rose and white. Compare the words of Guido Guinizzelli (vs. 5 of his sonnet beginning "Vedut' ho la lucente stella diana" in G. Contini, 1960, vol. II, p. 469): "viso de neve colorato in grana" ("a snow-white face tinged with red"). For the psychology of the transformation, see Andreas Capellanus, *De amore* I, 6 (p. 75): "Amor enim personam saepe degenerem et deformem tanquam nobilem et formosam repraesentat amanti et facit, eam plus quam omnes alias nobilem atque pulcherrimam deputari." ("For love often makes a man think that a base and ugly woman is noble and beautiful and makes him class her above all other women in nobility and beauty.") Also see Giacomo da Lentini (in G. Contini, 1960, vol. I, p. 90):

> Amor è un[o] desio che ven da core
> per abondanza di gran piacimento;
> e li occhi in prima genera[n] l'amore
> e lo core li dà nutricamento.

Love is a desire which comes from the heart through a great abundance of pleasure; and the eyes first generate love, then the heart gives it nourishment.

16. *disciolto*: The verb suggests that the woman, as first seen, was tongue-tied.

18. *intento*: "Attention." But the term seems to reflect something of the technical use of the word *intenzione* in the psychology of love (see *Purg.* XVIII, 23).

19–24. *Io son . . . l'appago*: Momigliano comments:

> *Io son . . . io son*: musicalmente rilevata da *cantava* che la intramezza; le molli allitterazioni del v. 20 e la vaga eco fra *marinari* e *mar*; e l'ombra di mollezza che ancora avvicina, nell'ultimo verso, *piacere* e *piena*. Evi-

dentemente Dante ha intonato questi versi come un canto, quasi ne sentisse dentro di sè le note.

I am . . . I am: musically pointed up by "cantava" [she sang], which comes between them. The soft alliterations of vs. 20, and the gentle echo between "marinari" [sailors] and "mar" [sea]; the shadow of softness that also draws together "piacere" [pleasure] and "piena" [full] in the last line. Evidently Dante composed these lines as a song, almost as though he felt the notes within himself.

19. *serena* = *sirena*.

20. *che ' marinari* = *che i marinari.*   *in mezzo mar* = *in mezzo al mare.* Cf. *Inf.* XIV, 94, and the Latin *medio in mare.*   *dismago*: Cf. *Inf.* XXV, 146; *Purg.* III, 11.

21. *a sentir* = *ad esser sentita.*

22. *Io volsi Ulisse*: See *Inf.* XXVI, where Dante tells of Ulysses' voyage. Dante did not know the *Odyssey* directly and so may not have known that the hero, in Homer's account, resisted the Sirens by having himself tied to the mast (*Odyssey* XII, 153-200). E. Moore (1896, p. 264) comments:

It is commonly objected that, according to the Homeric legend, [Ulysses] resisted the Sirens, though he yielded to Circe (see Inf. xxvi. 91, 2). Hence commentators have charged Dante either with confusing the two narratives, or of supposing Circe to be a Siren. I think it is probable that Dante may have derived his ideas, not from Homer (whom in any case he did not know directly), but from Cicero, de Fin. V. xviii. § 49, a work familiar to him, as the Index shows. Cicero thus translates a passage in Homer:

O decus Argolicum, quin puppim flectis, Ulixes,
Auribus ut nostros possis agnoscere cantus!
Nam nemo haec umquam est transvectus caerula cursu,
Quin prius astiterit vocum dulcedine captus,

Post, variis avido satiatus pectore Musis,
Doctior ad patrias lapsus pervenerit oras.

For a translation of the passage from Cicero quoted by
Moore, see the following afforded by the Loeb Classical Li-
brary edition of *De finibus*:

Ulysses, pride of Argos, turn thy bark
And listen to our music. Never yet
Did voyager sail these waters blue, but stayed
His course, enchanted by our voices sweet,
And having filled his soul with harmony,
Went on his homeward way a wiser man.

See E. G. Parodi (1957), p. 375, for his interpretation of
this verse, and for a discussion of the question see E. S. Hat-
zantonis (1959-60). Clearly, in this dream the Siren (later
termed an old witch) can represent any aspect of the seduc-
tive *malo amor* that is purged in upper Purgatory. Cf. *Purg.*
XXXI, 45.   *vago*: "Vago" is variously understood by the
commentators. Some (see M. Barbi, 1934b, p. 228) take it
to refer to Ulysses himself and so to mean "eager" to con-
tinue on his way; others (Del Lungo, Momigliano) under-
stand it to modify "cammin" and so to mean "wandering,"
"errant."

23. *s'ausa = si adusa.* Cf. *Inf.* XI, 11.

24. *rado = raramente.   sen = se   ne.   tutto l'appago*:
The Siren promises complete satisfaction or joy, i.e., the final
stage in the operation of love as set forth in *Purg.* XVIII,
31-33 (see n. to *Purg.* XVIII, 32-33). But she never fulfills
her promise, of course, since no secondary good can wholly
satisfy our natural desire. See *Purg.* XVII, 133-35.

26. *una donna*: This now is a "lady," not a *femmina*, a
"woman." For the meaning of this little allegorical drama,
the reader will do well to recall the lesson in love and in the
operation of love which he has just had set forth to him at
the center of the poem (*Purg.* XVI, XVII, XVIII). This
lesson began with Marco Lombardo's discourse on the light
that is given to enable us to distinguish between good and

bad, and free will (*Purg.* XVI, 75-76). The holy lady who now comes is the personification of that light of discernment, and Virgil, in this dream, assumes the role of the will which acts upon that discernment, i.e., the awareness that the love of this Siren is a *bad* love. We should also recall the lesson on the operation of love as set forth in *Purg.* XVIII, 22-66, which comes finally to speak of a "virtue that counsels and that ought to hold the threshold of assent" (*Purg.* XVIII, 62-63) and of the winnowing of good and bad loves. The holy lady and Virgil act out the guarding of this threshold and the winnowing. The lady comes from above, surely, since she is "holy." She is the *lume dato* (*Purg.* XVI, 75), and Virgil performs the winnowing that can take place when this light shines in us, as it should. See, then, Virgil's declaration of the meaning of this dream, vss. 58-60.

27. *lunghesso me*: Cf. *Vita nuova* XXXIV, 1: "Vidi lungo me uomini." ("I beheld alongside me men.") *Esso* (Latin *ipsum*) adds emphasis: "right there beside me," "close beside me." Cf. *Inf.* XXIII, 54; *Purg.* IV, 27.

28. *O Virgilio, Virgilio, chi è questa?* The question is clearly rhetorical and is simply aimed at calling upon Virgil to do what he then does, for the *donna santa* knows full well who this Siren is.

29. *venìa*: The descriptive "venìa" (*veniva*) focuses upon the scene as a continuing action in a way that a narrative tense (*venne*) would not. Note that the descriptive tense continues in the verbs which have Virgil as the subject, but shifts back abruptly to the narrative with "svegliò," vs. 33.

30. *pur*: "Only." Virgil does not take his eyes off the *donna santa* and acts according to her "light."

31. *apria = apriva.*

32. *mostravami = mi mostrava.*

33. *n'uscia = ne usciva.*

34. *Io mossi li occhi*: The expression seems at first a little surprising, since we might expect "io apersi li occhi," but it serves precisely to suggest the moment of awakening, when Dante, without yet moving his head (he is still recumbent, of course), opens his eyes and turns them this way and that to try to see where he is. See the comparable moment in *Purg.* IX, 34-36.   *Almen tre*: Cf. *Inf.* VII, 28 for a similarly weak rhyme.

35. *messe*: Literally, "sent," i.e., in Dante's direction.

36. *aperta = apertura.   entre = entri* (subjunctive).

39. *col sol novo a le reni*: Dante and Virgil are on the north side of the mountain and are walking toward the west, hence the new sun (the sun of this new day) is behind them.

41. *carca = carica.*

42. *che fa di sé un mezzo arco di ponte*: Scartazzini-Vandelli comments: "L'immagine apparirà tanto più conveniente, se si ricordi che gli archi de' ponti erano di solito nel medioevo a sesto acuto." ("If we remember that the arches of bridges in the Middle Ages were generally ogives, the image will appear to be even more appropriate.")

43. *qui si varca*: Cf. "varco," *Purg.* XVI, 44.

45. *marca*: "Region." Cf. *Purg.* XXVI, 73. The term implies a border region, however, and may even bear such a suggestion here, thus distancing the world of the living from this world of the dead. See *Purg.* XIII, 94-96, where something of the same effect is achieved in another way.

46. *parean = parevano.*

47. *volseci = ci volse.   parlonne = ci parlò.*

48. *tra due pareti del duro macigno*: Other editors have "tra i due pareti," construing *parete* as masculine in this case, as *paries, parietis* in Latin. This is possible, but somewhat

unusual since *parete* is feminine elsewhere in the poem (cf. *Purg.* III, 99). I have followed Petrocchi, in agreement with Sapegno (see his commentary), in not having the article here, which leaves *parete* feminine and in turn calls for an explanation of the article in "del duro macigno." However, as Sapegno points out, this use of the article is frequent enough in early Italian and has in fact occurred already in *Purg.* X, 80, where "l'aguglie ne l'oro" = *le aguglie di oro.* Thus here "del duro macigno" = *di duro macigno.* Sapegno terms this a "complemento di materia."

49. *ventilonne* = *ci ventilò.* One more P is thus erased from Dante's brow.

50. *Qui lugent:* "They that mourn." Cf. Matt. 5:5[4]: "Beati qui lugent, quoniam ipsi consolabuntur." ("Blessed are they who mourn, for they shall be comforted.") The beatitude here applies to those who have purged themselves of the sin of sloth. See Thomas Aquinas, *Summa theol.* I-II, q. 69, a. 3, resp.: "A sequela vero passionum concupiscibilis retrahit virtus, moderate huiusmodi passionibus utendo; donum vero eas, si necesse fuerit, totaliter abiiciendo; quinimmo, si necessarium fuerit, voluntarium luctum assumendo. Unde tertia beatitudo ponitur: *Beati qui lugent.*" ("From following the concupiscible passions, man is withdrawn—by a virtue, so that man uses these passions in moderation, and by a gift, so that, if necessary, he casts them aside altogether; nay more, so that, if need be, he makes a deliberate choice of sorrow; hence the third beatitude is: *Blessed are they that mourn.*") Thus this beatitude praises those who, unlike the slothful, have the fortitude to endure pain.

51. *ch'avran di consolar l'anime donne:* Literally, "who shall have their souls mistresses of consolation," i.e., when they have their heavenly reward. "Consolar" is the infinitive used as a noun.

52. *Che hai che pur inver' la terra guati?* Virgil knows the answer to this question, of course. Cf. *Purg.* XV, 120. *inver'* = *verso.*

54. *poco amendue . . . sormontati*: A kind of ablative construction, in which "sormontati" is intransitive (cf. *Purg.* XVII, 119).   *da l'angel*: I.e., "da dove stava l'angelo."

55. *sospeccion*: "Perplexity" and apprehension in this case. What bodes this dream? Dante does not yet know.   *fa irmi = mi fa ire.*

56. *novella vision*: The dream just had. The words serve to remind the reader that this is another or second prophetic vision experienced during the ascent of the mountain. Cf. "vision" in *Purg.* IX, 18, where it implies that the first prophetic dream is properly understood as a vision.   *a sé mi piega*: Dante is "bent" inwardly, as well as outwardly.

58. *quell'antica strega*: The term suggests the bewitching seductiveness of *malo amor* which the figure symbolizes, a love as old as the human race and Adam's sin.

59. *che sola sovr' a noi omai si piagne*: The witch symbolizes the triform love that is purged (is wept for) on the three terraces of upper Purgatory.

60. *vedesti come l'uom da lei si slega*: The meaning of the dream is now declared. It was "prophetic" in the sense that it revealed to the wayfarer sins to be purged on the three circles yet to be traversed. And it is didactic in that it has shown him how a man frees himself from the enchantment of the old witch.   *si slega*: Cf. "si lega," said of the operation of love, *Purg.* XVIII, 27.

61. *Bastiti = ti basti.* I.e., let the vision, and the lesson that it holds, suffice you now, and come along.   *e batti a terra le calcagne*: Cf. *Purg.* XV, 136.

62–63. *li occhi rivolgi . . . rote magne*: God whirls the great wheels of the heavens to call us up there, even as the falconer whirls a lure ("logoro") to call the falcon down. Not the least impressive part of the figure is this reversal of direction which it expresses. God "lures" us upwards (cf. *Purg.* XIV, 148-50). So does Dante's poem at many a point in its argument and imagery; we should consider that each of its canticles—*Inferno, Purgatorio, Paradiso*—ends with the word "stelle," which bears in itself the injunction "look up." For *logoro*, see n. to *Inf.* XVII, 128 and Fig. 5 of the *Inferno Commentary*, p. 309.

64–66. *Quale 'l falcon . . . tira*: This second simile drawn on falconry has puzzled many commentators because they have failed, first of all, to note the impressive reversal presented by the first simile (vss. 62-63) and accordingly do not come into proper focus through that. The first simile has plainly implied that the proper direction for us to look is up, even as it is the right direction for the upward flight of our love (this being the central injunction of the whole poem). Now Dante, urged by Virgil, quickens the pace of his upward climb, drawn on by his desire to be up there, and in this can be compared to the falcon when it soars up, at the cry of the falconer, to take the quarry aloft.

64. *che prima a' piè si mira*: A passing touch of realism, no doubt, for anyone who has seen a falcon in the moment when it is expecting to be released from the wrist of the falconer, to which it is bound by the jesses. This corresponds in the terms of the first simile to the figure of Dante bent over like a half-arch of a bridge.

65. *indi si volge al grido*: The shout, or cry, is that of the falconer urging the falcon on to the quarry.   *e si protende*: The falcon is now seen to look up and spread its wings just before it is released from the wrist of the falconer for its flight to the prey aloft; only so can there be a true correspondence with the feature in the second term of the first simile, i.e., with Dante in the moment he feels the desire to move on upward, hence "tal mi fec' io" (vs. 67). The falcon is released and soars toward its prey, and correspondingly Dante moves eagerly upward through the passage in the rock.

66. *per lo disio del pasto che là il tira*: Part of the bird taken by the falcon was given to it to eat. This was called the "falcon's share." The falcon is said to be drawn up there ("là") by the desire it has for its share of the prey. For the notion

of desire "drawing," cf. *Inf.* V, 82: "colombe dal disio chiamate."

69. *n'andai infin dove 'l cerchiar si prende*: Dante thus continues to climb up the stairway through the rock, looking upward, i.e., toward the lure of the heavens, until he reaches the fifth terrace, "where the circling begins," i.e., is resumed.
    si prende = si riprende.

70. *dischiuso*: After being closed in by the rock walls of the narrow passageway.

71. *per esso*: Along the floor of the terrace.

73. *Adhaesit pavimento anima mea*: This is from Ps. 118[119]:25, translated "I lie prostrate in the dust," but the Latin with "anima mea" as uttered by prostrate souls is even more appropriate here.

74. *sentia = io sentivo.*   *alti sospiri*: "Deep sighs."

76. *O eletti di Dio*: Cf. *Purg.* III, 73.   *soffriri*: The infinitive used as a plural noun. Cf. "saliri," vs. 78.

76–77. *li cui soffriri . . . duri*: The sufferings are made less painful by the knowledge that they are justly imposed and by the certain expectation that they will not endure forever.

77. *giustizia e speranza*: Plural subject of the singular verb "fa."

78. *li alti saliri*: Some editors have preferred to read "li altri saliri." I have followed Petrocchi with "alti," having found his justification persuasive. As he points out, this repeats a use of the word *alti* already encountered in *Purg.* X, 102, "li alti gradi," and here ("saliri" being the infinitive used as a noun in the plural) would mean "the steps for climbing higher."

79. *Se voi venite dal giacer sicuri*: The soul who speaks assumes that the "souls" who have asked the way to the exit are newly arrived on this terrace (otherwise they would know where the stairway is) and that they do not have to remain

there, but may proceed at once on their upward way. This is the first glimpse we have of the fact that this can happen in Purgatory. Later Statius will join the company of Dante and Virgil and move through the last two terraces with them, exempt from the punishments there. However, such exemption is perhaps rare enough to make the soul wonder who these souls can be. The one who speaks now does not yet know that Dante is alive. He will learn this later (vs. 96).

81. *le vostre destre sien sempre di fori*: Dante and Virgil are thus told to proceed in the usual counterclockwise direction.   *fori = fuori*. See E. G. Parodi (1957), p. 225.

83. *ne = ci*.

83-84. *per ch'io . . . l'altro nascosto*: The speaker's face, turned to the ground, cannot be seen, but Dante is able to make out which soul it is who speaks, as if he had recognized the hidden face.

87. *la vista del disio*: My look of desire, i.e., which expressed my desire.

89. *trassimi = mi trassi.   sovra*: Dante approaches and stands over the soul who lies face down.

90. *le cui parole pria notar mi fenno*: "Notar" has no expressed object here, but a *cui* is understood as the direct object, as implied by the possessive "cui" of "le cui parole."   *pria = prima.   fenno = fecero*.

92. *quel sanza 'l quale a Dio tornar non pòssi*: Purification.   *a Dio tornar*: The soul is created by God (*Purg.* XVI, 85) and will return to Him after it is made pure by purgation here.   *pòssi = si può*.

93. *tua maggior cura*: Your great concern to do penance for your sin and, in this way, to "ripen" (vs. 91) the purgation.

95. *e se vuo'*: "Mi dì" is understood as repeated here.

458

95–96. *se vuo' ch'io t'impetri cosa di là*: To obtain prayers from those who live in grace to lessen the time spent in Purgatory.

96. *ond' io vivendo mossi*: Dante thus makes known to the spirit that he is a living man and will return to the world of the living.

97–99. *Perché i nostri diretri . . . Petri*: The spirit answers Dante's requests in the order in which he made them and so first tells who he is.

99. *scias quod ego fui successor Petri*: "Know that I was a successor of Peter." This soul, who was a pope, appropriately declares that fact in the language of the Church.

99–114. *ego fui successor Petri . . . punita*: This is Adrian V (Ottobuono de' Fieschi of Genoa), who was elected pope, in succession to Innocent V, on July 11, 1276, and died at Viterbo thirty-eight days later on August 18 before he had been crowned. He was a nephew of Innocent IV and had been sent by Clement IV to England as legate in 1265-68, in which capacity he helped to bring about the restoration of peace after the Barons' War and preached the Crusade of 1270, which was joined by Prince Edward.

No historical evidence has been found to bear out either Pope Adrian's avarice or his conversion in so brief a time in office. Dante appears to have attributed to Adrian V words which John of Salisbury had put in the mouth of Pope Adrian IV (1154-59). In *Policraticus* VIII, 23, 814[b-c], John of Salisbury writes: "Spinosam dicit cathedram Romani pontificis, mantum acutissimis usquequaque consertum aculeis tantaeque molis ut robustissimos premat terat et comminuat humeros." ("He said that the chair of Peter was very uncomfortable; the cope is completely studded with spikes, and it is of such a weight that it presses upon, wears away, and breaks down even the strongest shoulders.") He continues: "Cum de gradu in gradum a claustrali clerico per omnia officia in pontificem summum ascenderit, nichil umquam felicitatis aut tranquillae quietis vitae priori adiectum est ab ascensu." ("[He often told me that] as he rose, step by step, from cloistered monk through various positions until he finally became pope, his rise never added one whit to the happiness or peace of his former life.") The passage in the *Policraticus* was known to Dante by an indirect tradition, even as it was to Petrarch, who at first made the same confusion of the two popes, but later corrected it. See U. Bosco (1942), pp. 136-43.

100. *Intra Siestri e Chiaveri*: Sestri Levante (so called to distinguish it from Sestri Ponente, a few miles west of Genoa) and Chiavari (formerly also Chiaveri), pronounced Chiàvari, are towns in Liguria on the Riviera di Levante east-southeast of Genoa.   *s'adima*: *Adimarsi* is apparently a verb coined by Dante, formed on *imo*, "deep." Cf. *Par.* I, 138.

100-101. *s'adima una fiumana bella*: The beautiful river (actually a *torrente* which is dry part of the year) is the Lavagna, which falls into the Gulf of Genoa between the two towns named. The Fieschi family took from it their title of counts of Lavagna.

102. *lo titol del mio sangue fa sua cima*: My family's title adorns or "crests" itself with the name of that river. Del Lungo paraphrases this as follows: "Il cognome della mia famiglia . . . ha Lavagna per suo predicato comitale; si fregia, si nobilita ('fa sua cima'), del titolo di Conti di Lavagna." ("The surname of my family . . . has Lavagna as its predicate of nobility; it adorns itself, it ennobles itself, 'it crests itself' with the title counts of Lavagna.")

104. *il gran manto*: Cf. *Inf.* XIX, 69.   *a chi dal fango il guarda*: Cf. *Purg.* XVI, 129.

106. *La mia conversione*: When a *pope* can speak of his *late* conversion, we realize what the term can mean for Dante and what it can mean in the theology of his time, i.e., any turning to God. See C. S. Singleton (1958), pp. 39-41. Adrian's conversion was indeed late, and yet he has not had to spend much time in Antepurgatory, due no doubt to the

intense love for heavenly things that had been kindled in him
(vs. 111).

108. *scopersi la vita bugiarda*: The "lying life" (i.e., deceit-
ful, false life) was well symbolized by the *serena* or *strega* of
the dream, who never fulfills her promises (see vss. 23-24),
and the dream itself showed how her falsity is uncovered.

109. *lì*: In the papal chair, the supreme office. The promise
of the Siren is false, for she does not quiet the heart as she
claims to do. Cf. *Conv.* IV, xii, 3-5:

> E per questo modo le ricchezze pericolosamente nel
> loro accrescimento sono imperfette, che, sommettendo
> ciò che promettono, apportano lo contrario. Promet-
> tono le false traditrici sempre, in certo numero adunate,
> rendere lo raunatore pieno d'ogni appagamento; e con
> questa promissione conducono l'umana volontade in
> vizio d'avarizia. E per questo le chiama Boezio, in quel-
> lo De Consolatione, pericolose, dicendo: "Ohmè! chi
> fu quel primo che li pesi de l'oro coperto, e le pietre
> che si voleano ascondere, preziosi pericoli, cavoe?"
> Promettono le false traditrici, se bene si guarda, di torre
> ogni sete e ogni mancanza, e apportare ogni saziamento
> e bastanza; e questo fanno nel principio a ciascuno
> uomo, questa promissione in certa quantità di loro ac-
> crescimento affermando: e poi che quivi sono adunate,
> in loco di saziamento e di refrigerio danno e recano sete
> di casso febricante intollerabile; e in loco di bastanza
> recano nuovo termine, cioè maggiore quantitade a de-
> siderio e, con questa, paura grande e sollicitudine sopra
> l'acquisto. Sì che veramente non quietano, ma più dan-
> no cura, la qual prima sanza loro non si avea.

> And it is in this fashion that riches are dangerously im-
> perfect in their growth; for, submitting certain things
> to us which they promise, they actually bring the con-
> trary. The false traitoresses ever promise to make him
> who gathers them full of satisfaction when they have
> been amassed up to a certain sum; and with this prom-
> ise they lead the human will to the vice of avarice. And

this is why Boethius in that of *Consolation* calls them perilous, saying: "Ah me, who was he who first dug out the weights of hidden gold, and the stones that sought to hide themselves, those precious perils?" The false traitresses promise (if it be well considered) to remove every thirst and every want and to bring satiety and sufficiency; for this is what they do at first to every man, confidently fixing this promise at a certain measure of their growth; and then, when they are amassed to that point, in place of satiety and of refreshment, they give and produce the thirst of a feverish bosom and not to be endured; and in the place of sufficiency they offer a new limit, that is to say, a greater quantity to long for; and together with it fear and great concern for what has already been acquired so that verily they "give no quiet," but "multiply care," which, without them, was not there before.

On the reference to Boethius in the above quotation, see *Consol. philos.* II, v, vss. 27-30. Cf. *Purg.* XVII, 133-35.

110. *potiesi* (pronounced *potìesi*) = *si poteva*.

111. *questa*: Of the eternal life, to which a soul in Purgatory has been admitted. Cf. *Purg.* XIII, 94-95.

112-13. *partita da Dio*: "Separated from God," i.e., turned away from Him.

115. *Quel ch'avarizia fa*: What the effects of avarice on the soul are in life. Now the soul replies to Dante's second request (vss. 94-95) and indicates that avarice is the sin being punished here. Clearly, by the principle of *contrapasso* (cf. *Inf.* XXVIII, 142), the form of punishment sustained by these souls on the fifth terrace is most fitting for the avaricious, but not particularly for the prodigal, who, as in *Inferno*, are punished together with the avaricious.

116. *in purgazion de l'anime converse*: There is irony in the *contrapasso*. Adrian was "converted" late, i.e., it was late when he turned *to* God. He now must lie turned away ("con-

verted") *from* God, as must the other souls who lie face down.

118–26. *Sì come l'occhio nostro . . . distesi*: The principle of *contrapasso* in the purgatorial punishment which these souls must endure is clearly affirmed in these three tercets with an obvious parallelism between the first and second, in the repetition of "così giustizia."

118. *s'aderse*: Past absolute of *adergersi,* "to raise oneself."

120. *il merse = lo merse. Merse* is the past absolute of *mergere* (= *sommergere*). Cf. *sommerso* in *Inf.* VI, 15, and XX, 3. Peter Chrysologus (*sermo* XXIX) writes of gold: "Aurum natura grave, gravius fit avaritia nimis. Hinc est quod plus habentem deprimit quam ferentem, et vehementius aggravat corda quam corpora." ("Though gold is naturally heavy, avarice makes it heavier still; consequently it weighs more heavily on the one who owns it than on one who merely carries it, and it is a greater burden to the heart than to the body.") He notes that "alta mentium semper in terrena demergit." ("It always submerges the highest aspirations of the mind in worldly things.")

121–22. *avarizia spense a ciascun bene . . . perdési*: The doctrine of love's operation that was expounded in the preceding canto may serve as a gloss here. In the operations of the soul love is the sole motive force (*Purg.* XVIII, 44), and the soul that has entered into desire for the object (in this case, earthly possessions and riches) is *preso* ("bound"), even as it is here in the punishment, on the principle of *contrapasso* (see vs. 123, "stretti," and vs. 124, "legati e presi"). That is, in life the avaricious man is so intent upon attaining his object that he can attend to nothing else and never rests until the desired thing is possessed (*Purg.* XVIII, 32-33). "Ciascun bene," in this context, must therefore mean every other good or kind of good, and "operar" every other operation or movement in the soul. The avaricious soul knows only one object and engages in but one operation with respect to that object.

122. *perdési = si perdé.*

123. *ne = ci.*

125. *fia = sarà.   del giusto Sire:* Cf. *Inf.* XXIX, 56; *Purg.* XV, 112; *Par.* XIII, 54.

129. *solo ascoltando:* The soul, hearing Dante's voice come closer now, surmises that he has kneeled.   *mio reverire:* My act of reverence, in kneeling.

131. *Per vostra dignitate:* This shift from the second person singular (*tu*) to the second person plural (*voi*) is another form of reverence and stands in striking contrast to Dante's manner as he addressed the simoniac pope in Inferno, where he did *not* kneel (*Inf.* XIX, 49-120).

132. *dritto:* This is variously interpreted by the commentators. Del Lungo explains it as follows: "La coscienza del mio dovere verso il pontefice mi si fece senz'altro ('dritto,' avverbiale per 'dirittamente, per via diritta') sentire, 'mi rimorse,' s'io non mi fossi, come feci, inchinato." ("The consciousness of my duty toward the pontiff made itself felt in me straightway—*dritto*, direct, in the adverbial sense of *dirittamente*, directly, or *per via diritta*, by a direct path; it stung me, had I not kneeled, as I did.") Some of the early commentators, including Benvenuto, read it as "dritta," modifying "coscienza," meaning "good conscience." Some (Scartazzini-Vandelli, Grandgent, and others) understand it to mean "my conscience stung me *for standing*." Given the context, this seems the most probable meaning.

133. *frate:* Cf. *Purg.* XI, 82, and XIII, 94-96, where Sapia says something not unlike this, using such a "leveling" term of address to introduce it.

134-35. *conservo sono teco . . . podestate:* You and I are servants of one Power, as are these others. Cf. Apoc. 19:9-10:

Et dixit mihi: Scribe: beati qui ad cenam nuptiarum Agni vocati sunt. Et dixit mihi: Haec verba Dei vera sunt. Et cecidi ante pedes eius ut adorarem eum, et dicit

mihi: Vide ne feceris; conservus tuus sum, et fratrum
tuorum habentium testimonium Iesu: Deum adora; tes-
timonium enim Iesu est spiritus prophetiae.

And he said to me, "Write: Blessed are they who are
called to the marriage supper of the Lamb." And he
said to me, "These are true words of God." And I fell
down before his feet to worship him. And he said to
me, "Thou must not do that. I am a fellow-servant of
thine and of thy brethren who give the testimony of
Jesus. Worship God! for the testimony of Jesus is the
spirit of prophecy."

The *cena nuptiarum Agni* may be seen to connect with the
"nubent" of vs. 137. See also Actus 10:25-26: "Et factum
est cum introisset Petrus, obvius venit ei Cornelius; et pro-
cidens ad pedes eius, adoravit. Petrus vero elevavit eum, di-
cens: Surge; et ego ipse homo sum." ("And as Peter entered,
Cornelius met him and, falling at his feet, made obeisance to
him. But Peter raised him up, saying, 'Get up, I myself also
am a man.'")

136–37. *Se mai quel santo evangelico suono . . . intendesti*:
See Matt. 22:23-30:

In illo die accesserunt ad eum sadducaei, qui dicunt
non esse resurrectionem; et interrogaverunt eum, di-
centes: Magister, Moyses dixit: Si quis mortuus fuerit
non habens filium, ut ducat frater eius uxorem illius, et
suscitet semen fratri suo. Erant autem apud nos septem
fratres; et primus, uxore ducta, defunctus est, et non
habens semen reliquit uxorem suam fratri suo. Simi-
liter secundus et tertius, usque ad septimum. Novissime
autem omnium et mulier defuncta est. In resurrectione
ergo, cuius erit de septem uxor? Omnes enim habuerunt
eam. Respondens autem Iesus ait illis: Erratis, nes-
cientes scripturas neque virtutem Dei. In resurrectione
enim neque nubent, neque nubentur; sed erunt sicut
angeli Dei in caelo.

On that same day some of the Sadducees, who say there
is no resurrection, came to him, and questioned him,

saying, "Master, Moses said, 'If a man die without hav-
ing a son, his brother shall marry the widow and raise
up issue to his brother.' Now there were among us seven
brothers. And the first, after having married a wife,
died, and having no issue, left his wife to his brother.
In like manner the second, and the third down to the
seventh. And last of all the woman also died. At the
resurrection, therefore, of which of the seven will she
be the wife? For they all had her."

But Jesus answered and said to them, "You err be-
cause you know neither the Scriptures nor the power of
God. For at the resurrection they will neither marry
nor be given in marriage, but will be as angels of God
in heaven."

Thus, as Sapia said (*Purg.* XIII, 94-96), souls in Purgatory
(proper) are already citizens of a true city, and what Jesus
said of the elect in Heaven already applies to them.

137. *intendesti*: "Have understood," that is, as Grandgent
explains, "in the broader sense, as meaning that earthly rela-
tions are not preserved in the spiritual world."

139. *vo' = voglio.*

141. *col qual maturo ciò che tu dicesti*: Cf. vss. 91-92.

142. *Nepote ho io di là*: Adrian now responds to Dante's
"e se vuo' ch'io t'impetri / cosa di là" (vss. 95-96), to de-
clare that there is indeed someone in the world of the living
who can pray for him. See *Purg.* IV, 133-35.   *c'ha nome
Alagia*: Alagia de' Fieschi was the daughter of Niccolò de'
Fieschi, imperial vicar in Italy, the niece of Pope Adrian V,
and the wife of Dante's friend Moroello Malaspina, by whom
she had three sons. She had two sisters, one of whom, Fiesca,
married Alberto Malaspina, while the other, Giacomina,
married Obizzo II d'Este. Benvenuto says that Dante means
to imply that "mulieres illorum de Flisco fuerunt nobiles
meretrices." ("The women of the house of Fiesco were noble
prostitutes.") Some of the early commentators think that

Alagia is the "femmina" of *Purg.* XXIV, 43. Of Alagia the *Anonimo fiorentino* says:

> Ebbe nome . . . di gran valore et di gran bontà; et l'Auttore che stette più tempo in Lunigiana con questo Morello de' Malespini, conobbe questa donna, et vidde che continuamente faceva gran limosine, et facea dire messe et orazioni divotamente per questo suo zio; et però l'Auttore, come uomo che l'udì, et vedea, et sapea la fama buona ch'ella avea, gli rendè questa testimonianza.

> She had the reputation . . . of being a person of great merit and goodness. The author, who spent quite some time in Lunigiana with this Moroello Malaspina, became acquainted with her. He saw that she continually and generously gave alms, and devotedly had masses and orations said for her uncle. That is why the author, who heard, saw, and knew her good reputation, rendered her this testimonial.

143–44. *pur che la nostra casa . . . malvagia*: Apparently the Fieschi were not distinguished for their virtue. In the next circle (*Purg.* XXIV, 29-30) we are to meet one of the family who was a great glutton. On the women of the house, Benvenuto comments: "Et vide, quod iste sacerdos loquitur honeste et caute: dicit enim quod neptis est bona, nisi imitetur exemplum aliarum de domo sua. Per hoc enim dat intelligi caute, quod mulieres illorum de Flisco fuerunt nobiles meretrices." ("We should notice that that priest is speaking with care and honesty: he says that his niece is good, provided she does not follow the example of other women of her house. He is here speaking with great care, since the women of the house of Fiesco were noble prostitutes.")

144. *essempro = esempio.*

145. *e questa sola di là m'è rimasa*: I.e., his niece is the only one whose prayers would avail him, as one who "lives in grace." Cf. *Purg.* IV, 134.   *rimasa = rimasta.*

CANTO XX

1. *Contra miglior voler voler mal pugna*: The "better will" is that of Adrian's to continue his penance (*Purg*. XIX, 139-41). Dante's desire, of course, is to hear more from him.

2. *piacerli = piacergli.*

3. *trassi de l'acqua non sazia la spugna*: Buti comments: "Fa qui similitudine, cioè che la volontà sua era come una spugna, e che li desidèri, ch'elli avea di sapere altre cose da quello spirito, rimaseno non sazi, come rimane la spugna quando si cava dell'acqua, inanti che sia tutta piena." ("This is a simile. His will is like a sponge, and his desire to know other things from that spirit remained unsatiated, just as the sponge is when it is taken out of the water before it is full.")

4. *Mossimi = mi mossi.*   *per li*: For this type of weak rhyme, cf. *Inf*. VII, 28; *Purg*. XVII, 55.

5. *luoghi spediti*: The spaces where no soul is lying. *spediti*: "Unoccupied."   *pur lungo = sempre lungo.* *la roccia*: The wall of the terrace.

6. *come si va per muro stretto a' merli*: Grandgent explains: "The poets step carefully along on the inner side of the cornice, close to the upright cliff, just as soldiers march on

the top of a narrow rampart, close to the battlements. Such battlemented walls still surround Carcassonne and Aigues-Mortes, and may be seen also at Avignon and Florence."
stretto: Adverb.

7. *fonde a goccia a goccia*: *Fondere* suggests a melting, as of ice. See *Purg.* XXX, 85-90.

8. *il mal che tutto 'l mondo occupa*: Avarice (and not prodigality). Just as avarice possesses the whole world, these souls "occupy" the whole terrace, as the following verse indicates. It will be remembered that there was also stress on the great numbers of the avaricious in their respective circle of Hell (see *Inf.* VII, 25). Torraca notes the possible connection between the last words in the following passage from Prudentius (*Psychomachia*, vss. 480-82, 493-94) and "tutto 'l mondo occupa":

> talia per populos edebat funera victrix
> orbis Avaritia, sternens centena virorum
> millia vulneribus variis . . .
> omne hominum rapit illa genus, mortalia cuncta
> occupat interitu . . .

Such the slaughter that Greed, the conqueress of the world, was dealing among the nations, laying low myriads of men with diverse wounds. . . . The whole race of men she seizes upon, all mortality she destroys before it can help itself.

occupa: Grandgent comments: "For the accentuation, cf. *occùpi, collòca, perpètra*. Petrarch has *implìca*; Lorenzo de' Medici, *riplìca* and *s'esplìca*; Ariosto, *esplìco*; Cavalcanti, *s'umilìa*."

9. *s'approccia = s'avvicina*. The souls lie too close to the outer edge of the terrace to leave a passageway there.

10. *Maladetta sie tu, antica lupa*: This clearly recalls the prologue scene and the she-wolf of covetousness which this wolf represents there, the most troublesome of the three beasts; it also brings to mind Plutus' being called "maladetto

lupo" in *Inf.* VII, 8. It should be noted that "antica lupa"
echoes significantly the "antica strega" of *Purg.* XIX, 58. The
she-wolf is indeed old, since she represents one of the vices
(concupiscence) which are a consequence of the fall of our
first parents.

11. *che più che tutte l'altre bestie hai preda*: The "other
beasts" are other sins and vices. One recalls the *lonza* and the
lion at the beginning of the poem and the verse in the
prophecy of the "veltro" where it is said that the she-wolf
mates with many other beasts (*Inf.* I, 100-102), a matter
now echoed in these verses. Note the repetition of the rhyme
-eda in vss. 11, 13, and 15, which connects with another such
prophecy and rhyme scheme in *Purg.* XXXIII, 35, 37, and
39. The she-wolf takes more souls than any other beast,
hence the great numbers of the avaricious both here and in
Hell.

12. *per la tua fame sanza fine cupa*: Cf. *Inf.* I, 98-99.
cupa: "Hollow," "deep." Cf. *Purg.* XIV, 52, and note the
rhyme scheme in *Inf.* VII, 8, 10, 12.

13–15. *O ciel . . . disceda?* The heavens are addressed as
the determining influence and mediate cause, but beyond
them is God's providence working through them. The
prophetic question looks to the advent of that temporal mon-
arch about whom Dante composed his treatise *De monarchia*,
the same that was called the "veltro" in the first canto of the
Inferno and whose birth (i.e., advent) was to be "between
felt and felt" (see n. to *Inf.* I, 105), that is, under the sign of
Gemini.

13. *par che si creda*: "Par" (*pare*) here is not intended to
reflect any doubt on the poet's part. Dante believed that con-
ditions on earth were determined by the heavens, of course,
as did most men of his time, but the turn of phrase recognizes
the mystery of this fact. For the phrase, cf. *Inf.* XII, 42.

14. *le condizion di qua giù*: The apostrophe is uttered by
the poet and concerns the condition of the living.

15. *quando verrà per cui questa disceda*: For the meaning, see *Inf.* I, 109-11.   *per cui = colui per cui,* "he through whom."   *disceda*: From the Latin *discedat,* "shall depart."

16. *lenti e scarsi*: "Slow and short" because Dante and Virgil must step carefully so as not to tread on the prostrate souls; for this reason Dante is especially "attentive" to the shades, as will be indicated in the following verse.

19. *Dolce Maria*: As usual, Mary serves as the first example of the virtue that opposes the vice in question, in this case exemplifying the largess that opposes avarice. Compare *Speculum beatae Mariae Virginis* IV (p. 45), formerly attributed to Bonaventura, but now to Conrad of Saxony: "Maria contra avaritiam *tenuissima* per paupertatem." ("Mary against avarice is very lowly through poverty.")

20-21. *chiamar così nel pianto . . . sia*: See Isa. 26:17: "Sicut quae concipit, cum appropinquaverit ad partum dolens clamat in doloribus suis." ("As a woman with child, when she draweth near the time of her delivery, is in pain and crieth out in her pangs.") Cf. *Par.* XV, 133.

22. *seguitar*: Infinitive depending on "udi'," vs. 19.
Povera: The key term, poverty, focusing on the virtue which opposes avarice, is thus given the initial position in what is then said.

23. *quello ospizio*: The humble stable of Bethlehem.

24. *sponesti = deponesti* (cf. "spuose," *Inf.* XIX, 130).
portato: See Luc. 2:7: "Et peperit filium suum primogenitum; et pannis eum involvit, et reclinavit eum in praesepio, quia non erat eis locus in diversorio." ("And she brought forth her firstborn son, and wrapped him in swaddling clothes, and laid him in a manger, because there was no room for them in the inn.") *Portato* was commonly used in this sense. See, for example, Torraca, who provides the following quotation from *Laude cortonesi* XLIV: "Elisabet . . . sei mesi fe' 'l portato." ("Elizabeth . . . bore her burden for six months.")

25–27. *Seguentemente intesi*: *"O buon Fabrizio . . . vizio"*:
The usual alternation between a biblical and a non-biblical
example is now observed, the second example of largess be-
ing Gaius Fabricius Luscinus, famous Roman hero, consul
in 282 and 278 B.C., and censor in 275. During the invasion
of Italy by Pyrrhus, king of Epirus, he was sent to the latter
to negotiate an exchange of prisoners. Pyrrhus used every
effort, including rare gifts, to gain him over, but Fabricius
refused all his offers. On a later occasion he sent back
to Pyrrhus the traitor who had offered to poison him, after
which he succeeded in arranging terms for the evacuation of
Italy by the former. During his censorship he severely re-
pressed the growing luxury of the Romans, and he died in
such poverty that the state had to pay for his funeral. Roman
writers take pride in recording how Fabricius lived on his
farm and refused the rich gifts offered him by the Samnite
ambassadors. See Virgil, *Aen.* VI, 843-44; Valerius Maxi-
mus, *Fact. dict. memor.* I, viii, 6; II, ix, 4; IV, iv, 3; Augus-
tine, *De civ. Dei* V, xviii, 2; and Dante's remarks in *De mon.*
II, v, 11:

> Nonne Fabricius altum nobis dedit exemplum avaritie
> resistendi cum, pauper existens, pro fide qua rei publice
> tenebatur auri grande pondus oblatum derisit, ac deri-
> sum, verba sibi convenientia fundens, despexit et refu-
> tavit? Huius autem memoriam confirmavit Poeta noster
> in sexto cum caneret:

> > parvoque potentem
> > Fabricium.

> Did not Fabricius give us a lofty example of resisting
> greed when, in the fidelity that held him to the Com-
> monwealth, poor as he was, he scoffed at the great pile
> of gold offered to him, and having scoffed thereat and
> uttered words worthy of himself, contemned and refused
> it? His memory, too, our poet confirmed in the sixth,
> when he sang:—"And Fabricius, mighty on his little."

29. *contezza*: "Knowledge," "acquaintance." Cf. "conto"
in *Purg.* XIII, 105.

31–33. *la larghezza . . . giovinezza*: The third example of largess, the proper and laudable use of riches, as opposed to the ways of grasping avarice, is Nicholas, bishop of Myra in Lycia, Asia Minor, who is supposed to have lived in the fourth century under Constantine and to have been present at the Council of Nicaea (325). He is venerated as a saint by both the Greek and Roman Churches and is regarded as the patron saint of Russia and of virgins, sailors, travelers, merchants, thieves, and (as Santa Claus) of children. In the eleventh century his remains were transported to Bari, and he is hence sometimes known as Nicholas of Bari.

The allusion is to the tradition that Nicholas prevented an impoverished fellow citizen from prostituting his three daughters, by throwing purses of gold into their windows on three successive nights, thus furnishing each with a dowry. The incident is related in the *Legenda aurea* (III, 1) of Jacobus de Varagine, archbishop of Genoa from 1292 to 1298. Benvenuto tells the story as follows:

> Beatus Nicolaus mortuis parentibus volens sua bona pauperibus erogare, dum quidam nobilis tres filias adultas urgente inopia disponeret quaestum facere pro substentatione vitae, occulte de nocte proiecit per fenestram massam auri involutam pallio, ex quo primogenita maritata est; post tempus iterato, et tertio simile fecit, ex quo reliquae nupserunt; et invitus cognitus est a patre virginum.

> When the parents of the blessed Nicholas died, he wished to distribute his wealth among the poor. Learning that a certain nobleman, because of poverty, was prepared to make prostitutes of his three daughters in order to gain enough money to live, he one night wrapped a sum of gold in a cloak and threw it in the window, and by this the eldest was married; he did the same for the other two daughters and they got married. And it was against his will that the father of the girls discovered his identity.

34. *ben*: A noun here (as again in vs. 121) and the direct object of "favelle."   *favelle = favelli*.

36. *lode*: Plural of *loda*, in the sense of a deed worthy of praise (see "loda" in *Inf.* II, 103).   *rinovelle = rinovelli*.

37. *fia = sarà*.   *mercé*: Dante thus offers to pray for this soul or to have others pray for him.

38. *compiér*: The rhythm of the verse requires this accent on a verb which in modern Italian is always pronounced *còmpiere*.

39. *quella vita ch'al termine vola*: Cf. *Purg.* XXXIII, 54.

40–42. *Io ti dirò . . . morto*: Sapegno comments: "Credo che si possa . . . interpretare questo esordio come una formula di cortesia: ti risponderò, non in vista della mercede che mi promettesti, ma solo per ossequio alla luce della grazia divina che in te si rivela in un modo così straordinario." ("I think one can . . . interpret this exordium as a form of courtesy: 'I will answer you not because of the reward you promise me, but only out of respect for the light of Divine Grace that reveals itself in you in such an extraordinary way.'")

43–45. *Io fui radice . . . se ne schianta*: It should be borne in mind that genealogical "trees" in Dante's time were commonly drawn as trees, hence growing up, not turned down, as tables are today. The metaphor here draws on the image of a real tree, bearing the suggestion that it has now grown so tall that it casts its shade over all Christendom, a shade in which good fruit can rarely be produced. The speaker, as he then declares (vs. 49), is Hugh Capet, king of France from 987 to 996, the first king of the Capetian line. Porena comments:

Mettendo una condanna così grave a quella casa in bocca al suo capostipite, Dante vuol dare ad essa un carattere di assoluta verità e obiettività, come quando ha fatto condannare i Romagnoli da un Romagnolo, i Lombardi da un Lombardo, e farà condannare in Paradiso i Veneti da una Veneta e i papi da S. Pietro.

By putting such a grave condemnation of that house in the mouth of its founder, Dante means to give it the

quality of absolute truth, just as he did when he had the
Romagnoles condemned by a Romagnole, and the Lom-
bards by a Lombard; and in Paradise he will have the
Venetians condemned by a Venetian woman, and the
popes by St. Peter.

45. *rado* = *raramente.   se   ne   schianta*: "Is   picked
there," i.e., in the land that is overshadowed by this plant.

46. *Doagio, Lilla, Guanto e Bruggia*: Flanders is now indi-
cated by this mention of Douai, Lille, Ghent, and Bruges,
four of its principal cities. The reference here is to the events
which took place in Flanders between 1297 and 1304, in
which those towns played a conspicuous part.

In 1297, Guy of Dampierre, count of Flanders, having
by his alliance with Edward I of England excited the sus-
picions of Philip the Fair of France, was decoyed by the lat-
ter under a lying pretext to Corbeil, where he was kept pris-
oner until he had sworn to renounce all communication with
Edward. No sooner, however, did Guy regain his liberty than
he broke his oath. Philip thereupon proceeded to make war
upon him, and sent his brother, Charles of Valois, into
Flanders to subject the country. Guy, having been abandoned
by his ally, the king of England, who through the mediation
of Boniface VIII had made peace with Philip (March 1298),
was compelled to come to terms with Charles. It was agreed
that he should go to Paris with his two sons to sue for the
king's pardon, a safe-conduct for his return being promised
him in the event of peace not being concluded between them
within the year. Philip, however, declared that in offering
these terms Charles had exceeded his authority, and he
treacherously imprisoned Guy and his two sons. Treating
Flanders as a subject state, he visited the country in person
and was well received by a portion of the population. But
the cruelty and oppression of Châtillon, the French governor,
drove the lower classes to arms; they rose in every part of
the country, and with an army, which consisted mostly of
peasants and artisans, they totally defeated the French at
Courtrai (the Battle of the Spurs) on July 11, 1302. In this
battle, in which they lost the flower of their nobility, the

count of Artois among them, the French met with the venge-ance to which Dante alludes. After this defeat Philip made peace (in 1305) with Flanders, released his prisoners, and surrendered all the country north of the Lys to Robert de Béthune (eldest son of Guy, who had died in captivity), the southern portion being annexed to France.

47. *saria = sarebbe.*   *vendetta*: The "vengeance" came in 1302 at the disastrous defeat suffered by the French in the battle at Courtrai. See preceding note.

48. *cheggio = chiedo.*   *lui*: God.   *giuggia*: From the French *juge* (*juger*). The Gallicism is no doubt deliberate here.

49. *Ciappetta*: From the French Chapet, a form of the name that existed along with Capet in different French dialects.

49–60. *Chiamato fui . . . ossa*: The statements put by Dante into the mouth of Hugh Capet as to the origin of the Cape-tian dynasty are in several respects at variance with the his-torical facts and can be explained only on the supposition that Dante (as common tradition before him) has confused Hugh Capet with his father, Hugh the Great, some of the statements being applicable to the one, some to the other. The facts are as follows. Hugh the Great died in 956; Louis V, the last of the Carolingians, died in 987, in which year Hugh Capet became king (probably crowned at Noyon in July); on his death in 996, he was succeeded by his son Rob-ert, who had previously been crowned in December 987.

Dante makes Hugh Capet say, first, that he was the son of a butcher of Paris, whereas common tradition assigned this origin not to Hugh Capet, but to his father, Hugh the Great, and second that when the Carolingians came to an end he was so powerful that he was able to make his son king whereas on the failure of the Carolingian line Hugh Capet himself became king (987). Although it is urged in explana-tion of the expression "widowed crown" that he associated his son Robert with him in the government and had him

crowned in the same year (987) as his own accession, it is
not by any means likely that Dante was aware of these facts;
nor do they explain Hugh Capet's further statement (vss.
59-60) that with his son the Capetian line began, whereas
in fact it began with himself. On the other hand, this state-
ment could not apply to Hugh the Great, of whom Dante
seems to have been thinking, because he had already been
dead more than thirty years when the crown became vacant
by the death of Louis V and was seized by Hugh Capet.

The tradition that Hugh the Great, who in reality was de-
scended from the counts of Paris, was the son (or nephew)
of a butcher was commonly believed in the Middle Ages and
was, as Villani (IV, 4) records, accepted as true by most
people in Dante's time:

> Ugo Ciapetta . . . fallito il lignaggio di Carlo Magno,
> fu re di Francia nelli anni di Cristo 987. Questo Ugo
> fu duca d'Orliens (e per alcuno si scrive, che fur sempre
> i suoi antichi e duchi e di grande lignaggio) figliuolo
> d'Ugo il grande, e nato per madre della serocchia d'Otto
> primo della Magna; ma per li più si dice, che 'l padre
> fu uno grande e ricco borgese di Parigi stratto di nazione
> di buccieri, ovvero mercatante di bestie.

> When the line of Charlemagne died out, Hugh Capet
> became king of France, in the year 987. This Hugh was
> duke of Orleans. According to a few writers, his ances-
> tors had always been dukes of great lineage: his father
> was Hugh the Great, and his mother, a sister of Otto I
> of Germany. But most writers say his father was a very
> rich and powerful burgher of Paris, who had originally
> been a butcher or cattle merchant.

For the confusion of the two Hughs in the common tradition
and a discussion of the whole problem, with relevant bibli-
ography, see P. Rajna (1960).

50-51. *i Filippi e i Luigi . . . retta*: The kings of France
and of the Capetian line who bore the name of Philip and
Louis. From Hugh Capet down to the year 1300, the as-
sumed date of the journey, there were four kings of each

name in the Capetian line (dates in parentheses indicate dates of reign): Philip I (1060-1108), Philip Augustus (1180-1223), Philip III (1270-85), and Philip IV (1285-1314); Louis VI (1108-37), Louis VII (1137-80), Louis VIII (1223-26), and Louis IX (1226-70).

51. *per cui = dai quali.   novellamente*: "Of late." As noted above, the line begins with a Philip (Philip I) in 1060 and was continuing, in 1300, with a Philip (Philip IV).

52. *Figliuol fu' io d'un beccaio*: See n. to vss. 49-60. "Beccaio" counts as two syllables here. Cf. *Purg.* XIII, 22 and XIV, 66, where "migliaio" and "primaio" also count as two syllables.

53. *li regi antichi*: The Carolingians. Perhaps, owing to Dante's having confused the last of that line with the last of the Merovingians (see n. to vs. 54), it is the latter who are meant, the designation of ancient kings being more appropriately applied to them than to the comparatively recent Carolingians.

54. *fuor ch'un renduto*: Charles, duke of Lorraine, son of Louis IV, who was king of France from 936 to 954, and brother of Lothair, who reigned from 954 to 986. On the death, without issue, of Louis V (who reigned from 986 to 987), eldest son of Lothair, the rightful successor to the throne was his uncle, Charles, who was the last remaining representative of the Carolingian line; but because, as duke of Lorraine, he was a vassal of the German emperor, the French would not accept him as king. The throne was thereupon seized by Hugh Capet, who besieged Charles in Laon, took him prisoner, and kept him in captivity until his death in 992.

The difficulty here is that Charles of Lorraine, who is undoubtedly the person intended, did not become a monk. There can hardly be a question, however, that Dante has confused him, the last of the Carolingians, with Childeric III, the last of the Merovingians, who, after his deposition by Pépin le Bref in 752, was confined in the monastery of Saint-

Bertin, at Saint-Omer, where he died in 755. Villani (II, 12) writes: "[Stefano papa secondo] fece al detto Pipino molti brivilegi e grazie, e fecelo e confermò re di Francia, e dispuose Ilderigo re ch'era della prima schiatta, perocch'era uomo di niuno valore, e rendèsi monaco." ("[Pope Stephen II] bestowed many privileges and favors on Pépin; he had him made and confirmed king of France. And he deposed King Childeric, who was of the first line, for he was a man of no account; and Childeric became a monk.") *renduto*: A common term for a monk in early Italian; cf. the OFr *rendu*. See *rendersi* ("to join a religious order") as used in *Inf.* XXVII, 83.

55. *trova'mi = mi trovai.*

57. *e sì d'amici pieno*: "Pieno" here is an adjective modifying *mi* understood as direct object of "trova'" (the "mi" conjoined to this form in vs. 55 being an indirect object).

58–59. *la corona vedova . . . figlio*: The fact is that on the failure of the Carolingian line Hugh Capet himself became king. See n. to vss. 49-60.

60. *cominciar = cominciarono.   le sacrate ossa*: The kings of France were consecrated in the cathedral of Reims. In using the word "ossa," the poet is looking back over the line of kings as now entombed and duly monumentalized.

61. *Mentre che = fin che.* Cf. *Inf.* XIII, 18-19.   *la gran dota provenzale*: On the division of the Carolingian empire in 843, Provence fell to Lothair, who left it with the title of king to his son Charles (855). It afterwards became a part of the kingdom of Arles as a feudal fief and was reunited to the Empire in 1033 by Conrad II; but the union remained almost nominal, the counts of Provence claiming to be independent. In 1246, through the marriage of Charles of Anjou, brother of Louis IX of France, with Beatrice, heiress of Raymond Berenger IV of Provence, Provence became a dependency of the royal house of France, and it remained in the possession of the house of Anjou until 1486, when it was formally annexed to the French crown by Charles VIII.

62. *al sangue mio non tolse la vergogna*: I.e., until the desire for and the gaining of "the great dowry of Provence" had so inured my race to evil works that it rendered them incapable of feeling shame for their deeds.

64. *Lì*: In the taking of the rich dowry of Provence, which was not achieved without fraud and a certain violence, since Beatrice had been promised in marriage to Count Raymond of Toulouse in the first place, and not to Charles of Anjou.

65. *la sua rapina*: The object of "cominciò." *e poscia, per ammenda*: This is obviously said with bitter sarcasm, which increases through repetition, reaching a climax in its use, for the third time, in vs. 69.

66. *Pontì e Normandia prese e Guascogna*: Ponthieu, former district of France, consisting of a "county," and comprising part of the province of Picardy, is included in the modern department of Somme and was situated at the mouth of the river of that name, with Abbeville for its capital. It belonged to the English crown, having been ceded to Edward I by Philip III in 1279; the succession to it was, however, disputed in 1290 between Prince Edward (afterwards Edward II) and the count of Aumale, and it was held by the king of France until 1299, when Edward I recovered it as the dowry of his second wife, Margaret of France, daughter of Philip III. It was in respect of Ponthieu, Guyenne, and Gascony that Edward I was the vassal of the French king and was summoned by Philip the Fair to appear before him after the piratical warfare between the English and French in 1292-93, in which the latter suffered a disastrous defeat. Edward refused to obey the summons, but eventually, in virtue of an agreement made (in 1294) with Philip by his brother Edmund, earl of Lancaster, consented to allow the former to occupy the English provinces in France, on the secret understanding that they should be restored at the expiration of six weeks. When this period came to an end, however, Philip refused to carry out his engagement, and retained possession of the provinces, which were not restored until the treaty of Chartres in 1299.

Normandy, ancient duchy in the north of France, comprising the modern departments of Seine-Inférieure, Eure, Orne, Calvados, and Manche, was attached to the English crown from the Norman Conquest (1066) until 1204, when, together with Maine, Anjou, and Touraine, it was conquered by Philip Augustus. The English claim on Normandy, however, was not renounced until the end of the century, during the reign of Philip the Fair.

Gascony, a historical region in southwest France, for many years was held by the kings of England, the French crown claiming homage from them in consideration of their tenure of it. The incident alluded to by Hugh Capet is related by Villani (VIII, 4) as follows:

Nel detto anno 1293, avendo avuta battaglia e ruberia in mare tra' Guasconi che erano uomini del re d'Inghilterra, e' Normandi che sono sotto il re di Francia, della quale i Normandi ebbono il peggiore, e vegnendosi a dolere dell'ingiuria e dammaggio ricevuto da' Guasconi al loro re di Francia, lo re fece richiedere il re Adoardo d'Inghilterra (il quale per sorte tenea la Guascogna dovendone fare omaggio al re di Francia) che dovesse far fare l'ammenda alle sue genti, e venire personalmente a fare omaggio della detta Guascogna al re di Francia, e se ciò non facesse a certo termine a lui dato, il re di Francia col suo consiglio de' dodici peri il privava del ducato di Guascogna. Per la qual cosa il re Adoardo il quale era di grande cuore e prodezza, e per suo senno e valore fatte di grandi cose oltremare e di qua, isdegnò di non volere fare personalmente il detto omaggio, ma mandò in Francia messer Amondo suo fratello che facesse per lui, e soddisfacesse il dammaggio ricevuto per la gente del re di Francia. Ma per l'orgoglio e cuvidigia de' Franceschi, il re Filippo di Francia nol volle accettare, per avere cagione di torre al re d'Inghilterra la Guascogna, lungamente conceputa e desiderata. Per la qual cosa si cominciò dura e aspra guerra tra' Franceschi e gl'Inghilesi in terra e in mare, onde molta gente morirono, e furono presi e diserti dall'una parte e dall'altra. . . . E 'l seguente anno il re Filippo di Fran-

cia mandò in Guascogna messer Carlo di Valos suo fra-
tello con grande cavalleria, e prese Bordello e molte
terre e castella sopra il re d'Inghilterra, e in mare mise
grande navilio in corso sopra gl'Inghilesi.

In the year 1293 the Gascons, who were obedient to the
king of England, and the Normans, who are under the
king of France, engaged in a sea battle that ended in
piratical plundering. The Normans, who got the worst
of it, went to the king of France to complain of the in-
jury and the damage done them by the Gascons. The
king sent word to King Edward of England (who, as
lord of Gascony, had to do homage to the king
of France) that he was to have his men make restitu-
tion, and that he himself was to come to do homage for
Gascony to the king of France. If he did not come with-
in a set time, the king of France with his council of
twelve would deprive him of the duchy of Gascony.
King Edward, a brave man of great heart, whose good
sense and valor were responsible for great deeds both
here and beyond the sea, disdainfully refused to do that
homage personally. Instead, he sent to France his
brother Edmund to do it for him and to recompense the
king's men for the damage done them. But French pride
and cupidity caused King Philip of France not to ac-
cept, so that he might have an excuse to take away
Gascony from the king of England, which had long been
his wish and design. For these reasons, a long and bit-
ter war ensued between France and England, fought on
both land and on sea. Many men were killed on both
sides, many were captured, and many deserted. . . . The
following year King Philip of France had his brother
Messer Charles of Valois invade Gascony with a large
force of cavalry. He took Bordeaux as well as many
towns and castles from the king of England; and on the
sea, he sent forth a great fleet against the English.

Thus England was robbed by "force and fraud" of
these territories.

As Butler points out, there is some confusion of chronol-
ogy here, for Normandy had been taken from the English

by Philip Augustus in 1204, long before the union of Provence with France, which was brought about in 1246. The English, however, did not renounce their claim upon Normandy until some time later; Villani (XII, 63), in fact, represents Edward III as justifying himself to his barons for his projected invasion of France on the ground that the French king was in wrongful possession of the English provinces of Gascony, Ponthieu (which he says Edward II received as the dowry of his wife Isabella of France), and Normandy: "Nel detto anno 1346, avendo il re Adoardo raunato suo navilio . . . per passare nel reame di Francia . . . e comunicatosi co' suoi baroni, e a loro fatta una bella diceria, com'egli con giusta causa andava sopra il re di Francia che gli occupava la Guascogna a torto, e la contea di Pontì per la dote della sua madre, e per frode gli tenea la Normandia." ("In the year 1346, King Edward assembled his fleet . . . to invade the kingdom of France . . . and he called together his barons and held a great speech, in which he said that, in a just cause, he was attacking the king of France, who was wrongfully occupying Gascony and the county of Ponthieu, which were his mother's dowry, and was holding Normandy under fraudulent pretexts.")

67. *Carlo venne in Italia*: Charles of Anjou, having been invited by Urban IV to assume the crown of Naples and Sicily, in response to the entreaties of the new pope, Clement IV, came into Italy in 1265 and in little more than three years, by his defeat of Manfred at Benevento (February 26, 1266) and of Conradin at Tagliacozzo (August 23, 1268), completely and finally crushed the power of the Hohenstaufen in Italy. For additional details on Charles' entrance into Italy and the battle of Benevento, see n. to *Purg.* III, 112.

68. *vittima fé di Curradino*: Conradin, son of the Emperor Conrad IV, was the last legitimate representative of the Swabian line and the last scion of the Hohenstaufen line. On the sudden death of his father in 1254, Conradin, who was barely three years old, was the rightful claimant to the crown of Naples and Sicily. But his uncle, Manfred, assuming first

the regency in Conradin's name, on a report of his death
(which he himself is supposed to have originated), accepted
the crown at the invitation of the great nobles (1258). He
met the protests of Conradin's mother by saying it was not
in the interests of the realm that the kingdom should be ruled
by a woman and an infant. After Manfred's defeat and death
at Benevento (February 26, 1266), the kingdom, impatient
of the French yoke and the Ghibellines throughout Italy,
called upon Conradin to assert his hereditary rights. In re-
sponse to this appeal Conradin descended into Italy in the
next year with an army in order to wrest his kingdom from
Charles of Anjou (Villani, VII, 23). But the attempt resulted
in a disastrous failure. Conradin was defeated by Charles at
Tagliacozzo (August 23, 1268) and having been betrayed
into his hands was executed at Naples (October 29).   *fé*
= *fece.*

69. *ripinse al ciel Tommaso*: The Thomas referred to by
Dante here is Thomas Aquinas, the famous scholastic theo-
logian and philosopher, who was born in 1225 or 1226. In
January 1274, he was summoned by Gregory X to attend
the Council of Lyons, and, though ill at the time, he set out
on the journey but died, after lingering for some weeks at
the monastery of Fossanova, near Terracina, on March 7 of
that year. The belief that he had been poisoned at the in-
stance of Charles of Anjou was current in Dante's day (see
P. Toynbee, 1968, pp. 614-15) but seems to be completely
unfounded. See *Par.* X-XI.

70. *Tempo vegg' io*: At this point Hugh passes to prophecy.
     vegg' io: Hugh begins now to repeat *veggio* as he has
repeated *per ammenda.*   *ancoi*: The present day (Latin
hanc hodie). Cf. *Purg.* XIII, 52; XXXIII, 96.

71. *tragge*: "Tempo" is the subject of the verb.   *un altro
Carlo*: This other Charles is Charles of Valois, who was
born in 1270 and died in 1325, the third son of Philip III of
France (by his wife Isabella of Aragon). Charles was sum-
moned to Italy by Boniface VIII for the twofold purpose of
helping Charles II of Naples in his war against Frederick II

of Sicily in Sicily and of making peace between the contending factions of the Bianchi and Neri in Tuscany, the pope promising in return to secure his election as emperor. Charles arrived in Florence on All Saints' Day, 1301. On the events in Florence that resulted in Dante's exile, see nn. to *Inf.* VI, 65-66 and 67-68.

72. *per far conoscer meglio*: The irony continues.   *sé*: Not a true reflexive, since "tempo" is the subject of the verb.

73. *Sanz' arme*: Charles came with only a small force of cavalry, since, for the campaign in Sicily, he expected to have the army of Charles II and to have full support in arms and money from Pope Boniface.

73–74. *con la lancia . . . Giuda*: Judas' lance is one of deceit and treachery.

75. *fa scoppiar la pancia*: Benvenuto writes: "Eo tempore Florentia erat valde corpulenta, plena civibus, inflata superbia. Et iste Carolus scidit eam per ventrem, ita quod fecit inde exire intestina vitalia, scilicet, praecipuos cives, de quorum numero fuit iste praeclarus poeta." ("In that time Florence had grown fat, full of citizens and bursting with pride. And this Charles ripped her belly open so that he made her guts burst out, that is to say, her principal citizens, among whom was this famous poet.")

76. *non terra*: The words bear an allusion to Charles' nickname, "Sanzaterra." His countrymen remarked of him that he was "fils de roi, frère de roi, oncle de trois rois, père de roi, et jamais roi" ("son of a king, brother of a king, uncle of three kings, father of a king, but never a king"), he having unsuccessfully aspired to no less than four crowns, those of Aragon, of Sicily, of Constantinople (through his second wife, Catherine, daughter of Philip de Courtenay, titular emperor of Constantinople), and of the Empire. In November of 1302 Charles returned to France, the barren result of his expedition into Italy having earned him the nickname Carlo Sanzaterra (Lackland). Charles died at Nogent le Roi in 1325, leaving a son, Philip, who afterwards (in 1328) be-

came king of France as Philip VI, being the first of the Valois line.

77–78. *per sé tanto più grave . . . conta*: Charles will count as nothing the guilt and the shame he will incur and so will die unrepentant and will go to Hell.

79. *L'altro*: Yet another Charles. This one, Charles II, king of Naples, was born in 1248, the son of Charles of Anjou. After the Sicilian Vespers (in 1282) Charles, who was then prince of Salerno, set out from Provence to join his father in his attempt to recover the island of Sicily and was entrusted by him with the command of the fleet at Naples, but with strict injunctions not to engage the enemy. Incensed, however, by the taunts of the Sicilian admiral, Ruggiero di Loria, who was in command of the fleet of Pedro III of Aragon, Charles came out and attacked him, but was totally defeated (June 1284) and himself taken prisoner on board his ship and conveyed to Sicily.

80–81. *veggio vender sua figlia . . . schiave*: Beatrice, youngest daughter of Charles II of Naples, was married in 1305 to Azzo VIII, marquis of Este, in consideration, it was said, of a large sum of money. This transaction Dante compares to the selling of female slaves by corsairs. To add to the disgrace of the proceeding, it appears that Azzo was a great deal older than Beatrice.

81. *come fanno i corsar de l'altre schiave*: "Altre" is pleonastic here, and "l'altre schiave" should not be translated as "other slave women" but simply as "slave women." Such a redundant use of *altro*, in its various forms, is common in the Romance languages.

82. *farne = fare a noi*. Del Lungo comments: "Fare a noi uomini; quasi rifacendosi egli stesso uomo vivente in questo nostro mondo." ("Do to human beings; almost as if he were considering himself to be a living man again in our world.")

85–87. *Perché men paia . . . catto*: The irony begins to reach its climax here, quickening through the repetition of "veggio," as Hugh prophesies the infamous deeds of Philip the Fair. See *Purg.* VII, 109, where he is called the "mal di Francia," and the note to that verse. The reign of Philip is famous for his bitter quarrel with Boniface VIII, the origin of which was the taxation of the clergy by Philip, which led to the issue of the famous bull *Clericis laicos* (1296), in which Boniface declared the property of the Church to be severed from all secular obligations, and himself as pope to be the one exclusive trustee of all possessions held throughout Christendom by the clergy, on which no aid or subsidy could be raised without his consent. Philip replied that if the clergy might not be taxed for the exigencies of France, or be in any way tributary to the king, France would cease to be tributary to the pope; and he issued an edict prohibiting the export of gold, silver, and valuables from the kingdom, thus depriving the pope of all supplies from France. After a lull the quarrel culminated in the excommunication of the French king by Boniface. The bull of excommunication was ordered to be suspended in the porch of the cathedral of Anagni on September 8, 1303, but on the eve of that day Sciarra Colonna, whose house Boniface had so bitterly wronged, and William of Nogaret, the emissary of the king of France, suddenly appeared in Anagni with an armed force. They seized the person of the pope, after heaping every indignity on him, and held him prisoner for three days, while the soldiers plundered his palace. He was at last rescued by the people of Anagni, who expelled the soldiers and forced Sciarra and Nogaret to flee. Boniface was helped to Rome, where, a month after his rescue from prison, he died on October 12, 1303.

86. *Alagna*: Anagni, town in Latium, situated on a hill about forty miles southeast of Rome, was celebrated as the birthplace of Pope Boniface VIII and as the scene of his imprisonment by Philip the Fair of France.   *lo fiordaliso*: The fleur-de-lis, royal emblem of France.

87. *Cristo esser catto*: Notwithstanding his personal hatred for Boniface, Dante refuses in any way to condone the enor-

mity of the offense done in laying hands on the vicar of Christ and, through him, on Christ himself.   *catto*: "Seized"; from the Latin *captus*.

88. *Veggiolo = lo vedo.   un'altra volta esser deriso*: The mocking of Christ is recounted in Matt. 27:28-31:

> Et exuentes eum, chlamydem coccineam circumdederunt ei. Et plectentes coronam de spinis posuerunt super caput eius, et arundinem in dextera eius; et genu flexo ante eum illudebant ei, dicentes: Ave, rex Iudaeorum. Et expuentes in eum, acceperunt arundinem et percutiebant caput eius. Et postquam illuserunt ei, exuerunt eum chlamyde, et induerunt eum vestimentis eius; et duxerunt eum ut crucifigerent.

> And they stripped him and put on him a scarlet cloak; and plaiting a crown of thorns, they put it upon his head, and a reed into his right hand; and bending the knee before him they mocked him, saying, "Hail, King of the Jews!" And they spat on him, and took the reed and kept striking him on the head.

> And when they had mocked him, they took the cloak off him and put his own garments on him, and led him away to crucify him.

89. *veggio rinovellar l'aceto e 'l fiele*: See Matt. 27:34: "Et dederunt ei vinum bibere cum felle mistum; et cum gustasset, noluit bibere." ("And they gave him wine to drink mixed with gall; but when he had tasted it, he would not drink.")

90. *e tra vivi ladroni esser anciso*: See Matt. 27:38: "Tunc crucifixi sunt cum eo duo latrones, unus a dextris et unus a sinistris." ("Then two robbers were crucified with him, one on his right hand and one on his left.") The "vivi ladroni" are Sciarra Colonna and William of Nogaret (see n. to vs. 86). Boniface died as a result of their outrage upon him.   *anciso = ucciso.*

91. *il novo Pilato*: This name for Philip appears quite naturally, given the context, but Dante is not the only one to

apply it to him. Benedict XI, who succeeded Boniface, is reported to have spoken of the outrage of Anagni in similar terms (see P. Fedele, 1921, pp. 210-11).

92–93. *ma sanza decreto . . . vele*: In this curious mixed metaphor, the reference is to the persecution and destruction of the Knights Templars by Philip. The Knights Templars were one of the three great military orders founded in the twelfth century for the defense of the Latin kingdom of Jerusalem (the other two being the Knights Hospitalers or Knights of St. John, and the Teutonic Knights). The original founder of the order was a Burgundian knight, Hugues de Payens, by whom it was instituted, with the approval of Pope Honorius II, early in the twelfth century. The Templars derived their name from the circumstance that they were quartered in the palace of the Latin Kings on Mount Moriah, which was also known as Solomon's temple. After having existed as a powerful and wealthy order for nearly two centuries they were in 1307 accused by Philip the Fair of heresy, sacrilege, and other hideous offenses, in consequence of which he ordered their arrest and by means of diabolical tortures wrung from them confessions (for the most part undoubtedly false) of their alleged enormities. Five years later at Philip's instigation they were condemned by Clement V, and the order was suppressed by decree of the Council of Vienne (May 1312); in the following year the grand master, Jacques de Molay, was burned alive at Paris in the presence of the king. The French king's motive in aiming at the destruction of the Templars was, it can hardly be doubted, a desire to get possession of the immense wealth of the order (see G. Salvemini, 1901, pp. 123-24).

92. *decreto*: Papal decree.

93. *portar nel Tempio le cupide vele*: This metaphor is that of a pirate's ship entering a port to capture and pillage, the *in* of "nel" serving both its ordinary meaning in this respect (see "in Alagna intrar" in vs. 86) and the meaning "against" (Latin *in*).

94–96. *O Segnor mio . . . secreto?* Cf. Ps. 57:11[58:10]:
"Laetabitur iustus cum viderit vindictam." ("The just man
shall be glad when he sees vengeance.")

95. *a veder la vendetta*: Cf. *Inf.* XIV, 60.

96. *fa dolce l'ira tua*: Thomas Aquinas (*Summa theol.* III,
Suppl., q. 94, a. 3, ad 2) says: "Quamvis Deus non delecte-
tur in poenis, inquantum huiusmodi, delectatur tamen in eis,
inquantum sunt per suam iustitiam ordinatae." ("Although
God rejoices not in punishments as such, He rejoices in them
as being ordered by His justice.") Dino Compagni notes in
his *Cronica* (III, 37): "Molta pace dà a coloro nell'animo,
che le ingiurie da' potenti ricevono, quando veggiono che
Iddio se ne ricorda. E come si conoscono aperte le vendette
di Dio, quando egli à molto indugiato e sofferto! ma quando
lo indugia, è per maggior punizione." ("Those who have
been injured by the powerful receive great solace in their
hearts when they see that God has not forgotten. How well
they recognize the vengeance of God, even when He has put
it off and tolerated it for a long time. But when God puts it
off, it is only to make the punishment greater.") The "venge-
ance" came in 1302, when Philip's troops were defeated at
Bruges and Courtrai and the French driven from Flanders
(see n. to vs. 46).

97–123. *Ciò ch'io dica . . . persona*: Thus far Hugh has
given a rather lengthy answer to the question "chi fosti" (vs.
35). He now goes on to answer Dante's second question (vss.
35-36).

97–98. *quell' unica sposa de lo Spirito Santo*: The Virgin
Mary. See Matt. 1:20: "Quod enim in ea natum est, de
Spiritu Sancto est." ("For that which is begotten in her is
of the Holy Spirit.") Also see Luc. 1:35.

99. *chiosa*: Cf. *Inf.* XV, 89.

100. *risposto = risposta*. "Risposto" is a noun here; the
meaning *responsorium* has been suggested. M. Barbi (1934b,
p. 229) notes:

Il T[orraca] pensa qui al *responsorium* o *responsum*
delle ballate; ma perchè non al responsorio secondo il
rito ecclesiastico? Dopo le preci ricordano le anime
esempi di povertà e di larghezza, come, in coro, dopo le
lezioni si cantano quelle parole che si dicono re-
sponsorio.

Torraca thinks here of the *responsorium* or *responsum*
of ballads. But why not the "responsory" of the eccle-
siastical rite? After the prayers, the souls recall exam-
ples of poverty and generosity; and after the les-
sons, come those words sung in chorus and called
"responsory."

prece = preci. Prece is a feminine plural form common in
early Italian.

101. *el*: Impersonal, as in the English "when it grows dark."

102. *suon*: "Discourse." Cf. *Purg.* XIX, 136. *pren-
demo = prendiamo.*

103. *Pigmalion*: The examples of avarice, which begin with
Pygmalion, show the usual alternation of the non-biblical
with the biblical and proceed by pairs here. Pygmalion was
the son of Belus, king of Tyre, whom he succeeded, and
brother of Dido, whose husband, Sichaeus, he murdered
for the sake of his wealth. Dido, being made aware of the
murder by the appearance of Sichaeus to her in a dream,
secretly sailed from Tyre with the treasure and landed
in Africa, where she founded the city of Carthage.

104. *cui*: Direct object of "fece" in the next verse, of which
"la voglia sua . . . ghiotta" is the subject.   *paricida*:
Sichaeus was both the uncle and the brother-in-law of Pyg-
malion. The word *parricida* was used in Latin in this broader
sense to mean the murderer of a near relative.

106. *la miseria*: The miserable condition.   *Mida*: Midas,
a king of Phrygia, who, in return for his kindness to Silenus,
the companion and instructor of Bacchus, was allowed by
Bacchus to make a request of him, which the god promised

to grant. Midas, in his greed for wealth, desired that everything he touched should be turned to gold. Bacchus fulfilled his desire, but Midas, finding that even the food which he touched turned to gold, soon implored him to take his favor back. The god accordingly ordered him to bathe in the sources of the Pactolus near Mount Tmolus, the sands of which thenceforth became rich in gold, while Midas was relieved from his fatal gift. Afterwards, when Pan and Apollo were engaged in a musical contest on the flute and lyre, Midas was chosen to decide between them, and, on his deciding in favor of Pan, Apollo, to punish him for his bad taste, condemned him to wear the ears of an ass.

107. *che*: The antecedent is "miseria," i.e., the fact that his food and drink turned to gold.

108. *per la qual sempre convien che si rida*: This will always make men laugh when they think of it.

109–11. *Del folle Acàn . . . morda*: Achan, son of Carmi, of the tribe of Judah, who "tulit aliquid de anathemate" ("took goods that were under the ban"), according to Iosue 7:1, in appropriating part of the spoil of Jericho, contrary to the commands of Joshua. After the defeat of the Israelites in their attack on Ai, Achan confessed his guilt, and the booty was discovered. Thereupon he and his whole family were stoned to death by command of Joshua, and their remains and property were burned (Iosue 6:19; 7:1-26).

112. *accusiam col marito Saffira*: Ananias, a disciple at Jerusalem, and his wife Sapphira, having sold their goods for the benefit of the Church, kept back part of the price, bringing the remainder to the apostles, as if it had been the whole. Being rebuked by Peter for their hypocrisy, they both fell dead at his feet (Actus 5:1-11).

113. *i calci ch'ebbe Eliodoro*: Heliodorus, treasurer of Seleucus IV Philopator, king of Syria (187-175 B.C.), by whom he was commissioned to remove the treasures from the temple at Jerusalem. For an account of what then took place, see II Mach. 3:25-27:

Apparuit enim illis quidam equus terribilem habens sessorem, optimis operimentis adornatus; isque cum impetu Heliodoro priores calces elisit, qui autem ei sedebat videbatur arma habere aurea. Alii etiam apparuerunt duo iuvenes virtute decori, optimi gloria speciosique amictu, qui circumsteterunt eum et ex utraque parte flagellabant sine intermissione, multis plagis verberantes. Subito autem Heliodorus concidit in terram; eumque multa caligine circumfusum rapuerunt, atque in sella gestatoria positum eiecerunt.

For there appeared to them a horse with a terrible rider upon him, adorned with a very rich covering. And he ran fiercely and struck Heliodorus with his fore feet: and he that sat upon him seemed to have armour of gold.

Moreover there appeared two other young men, beautiful and strong, bright and glorious, and in comely apparel: who stood by him on either side and scourged him without ceasing with many stripes.

And Heliodorus suddenly fell to the ground: and they took him up covered with great darkness: and having put him into a litter they carried him out.

Seleucus was succeeded by his brother Antiochus IV Epiphanes, whose persecution of the Jews caused the revolt of the Maccabees.

115. *Polinestòr ch'ancise Polidoro*: Just before Troy fell into the hands of the Greeks, Priam entrusted his son Polydorus, with a large sum of money, to Polymestor, a Thracian king; but after the destruction of Troy, Polymestor killed his ward for the sake of the treasure and cast his body into the sea (see *Inf.* XXX, 18). The story is told by Ovid, who uses the term *avarus*. See *Metam.* XIII, 429-38:

Est, ubi Troia fuit, Phrygiae contraria tellus
Bistoniis habitata viris: Polymestoris illic
regia dives erat, cui te commisit alendum
clam, Polydore, pater Phrygiisque removit ab armis,
consilium sapiens, sceleris nisi praemia magnas
adiecisset opes, animi inritamen avari.

ut cecidit fortuna Phrygum, capit inpius ensem
rex Thracum iuguloque sui demisit alumni
et, tamquam tolli cum corpore crimina possent,
exanimem scopulo subiectas misit in undas.

Opposite to Phrygia where Troy stood, there lies a land
where dwelt the Bistones. There was the luxurious court
of Polymestor, to whom your father, Polydorus, secretly
commended you for care, sending you far from
Phrygia's strife; a prudent plan, if he had not sent with
you a great store of treasure, the prize of crime, a
temptation to a greedy soul. When the Phrygian for-
tunes waned, the impious Thracian king took his sword
and thrust it into his young charge's throat; and just as
if a murder could be disposed of with the victim's body,
he threw the corpse from a cliff into the waves below.

ancise = uccise. Cf. vs. 90.

116-17. *Crasso . . . l'oro?* Marcus Licinius Crassus, sur-
named Dives ("the wealthy"), was born *ca.* 112 B.C. and
was consul with Pompey in 70 B.C. and triumvir with Caesar
and Pompey in 60. His ruling passion was the love of money,
which he set himself to accumulate by every possible means.
Orosius, *Hist.* VI, xiii, 1, calls him "homo inexplebilis cupi-
ditatis" ("a man of insatiable cupidity"). With Pompey in
55 he was consul for the second time; in 54, he was governor
of the province of Syria, where he looked to increase greatly
his wealth, but in 53 he was defeated and killed by
the Parthians, who cut off his head and sent it, together with
his right hand, to the Parthian king, in token of their victory,
who then had his mouth filled with molten gold in mockery
of his passion for money. See R. Sabbadini (1915).

117. *dilci = dillo a noi.*

119. *ch'ad ir ci sprona*: Other editors have followed the
reading of other MSS and have "ch'a dir ci sprona." The
meaning is essentially the same in either case, "ir" being fig-
urative, of course.

494

121. *però = perciò.   al ben*: I.e., the examples of voluntary poverty and generosity. Cf. "ben," vs. 34.   *ci*: Here on this terrace.

125. *brigavam*: Compare the expression *darsi briga di*, "to go to the trouble to."   *soverchiar la strada*: Cf. the Latin *superare iter*.

126. *tanto quanto al poder n'era permesso*: Dante and Virgil have to continue with "short steps" (vs. 16) because of the many souls lying on the terrace.   *n' = ne (ci)*.

128. *mi prese un gelo*: Cf. *Purg.* IX, 42.

130–32. *Certo non si scoteo . . . cielo*: The island of Delos, smallest of the Cyclades, was said to have been raised from the deep by Neptune, but it was a floating island until, according to one version, Jupiter fixed it with adamantine chains to the bottom of the sea in order that Latona might have a refuge from the wrath of Juno. Here Latona gave birth to Apollo and Diana (hence their epithets Delius and Delia), her offspring by Jupiter. See Ovid's version of the story in *Metam.* VI, 186-91, where he says of Latona, "cui maxima quondam / exiguam sedem pariturae terra negavit" ("to whom the broad earth once refused a tiny spot for bringing forth her children"):

> nec caelo nec humo nec aquis dea vestra recepta est:
> exsul erat mundi, donec miserata vagantem
> "hospita tu terris erras, ego" dixit "in undis"
> instabilemque locum Delos dedit. . . .

Neither heaven nor earth nor sea was open for this goddess of yours; she was outlawed from the universe, until Delos, pitying the wanderer, said to her: "You are a vagrant on the land; I, on the sea," and gave her a place that stood never still.

See, also, Virgil, *Aen.* III, 73-77:

> Sacra mari colitur medio gratissima tellus
> Nereidum matri et Neptuno Aegaeo,
> quam pius Arquitenens oras et litora circum

errantem Mycono e celsa Gyaroque revinxit,
immotamque coli dedit et contemnere ventos.

In mid-sea lies a holy land, most dear to the mother of
the Nereids and Aegean Neptune, which, as it wandered
round coasts and shores, the grateful archer-god bound
fast to lofty Myconos and Gyaros, suffering it to lie un-
moved and slight the winds.

It should be noted that the simile is especially appropriate
for the trembling of the mountain of Purgatory because it,
too, is an island.

130. *si scoteo* = *si scosse*.

132. *li due occhi del cielo*: Apollo and Diana, the Sun and
the Moon.

134. *inverso me si feo*: Cf. *farsi verso qualcuno.*   *feo*
= *fece.*

135. *mentr'* = *mentre (fin che).*

136–37. *"Gloria in excelsis" tutti "Deo" dicean*: Cf. Luc.
2:13-14: "Et subito facta est cum angelo multitudo militiae
caelestis, laudantium Deum et dicentium: Gloria in altissimis
Deo, et in terra pax hominibus bonae voluntatis." ("And
suddenly there was with the angel a multitude of the heav-
enly host praising God and saying, 'Glory to God in the high-
est, and on earth peace among men of good will.' ")

138. *poteo* = *potè.*

139–40. *immobili e sospesi . . . canto*: Cf. Luc. 2:8-10:
"Et pastores erant in regione eadem, vigilantes et cus-
todientes vigilias noctis super gregem suum. Et ecce angelus
Domini stetit iuxta illos, et claritas Dei circumfulsit illos; et
timuerunt timore magno. Et dixit illis angelus: Nolite
timere." ("And there were shepherds in the same district
living in the fields and keeping watch over their flock by
night. And behold, an angel of the Lord stood by them and
the glory of God shone round about them, and they feared

exceedingly. And the angel said to them, 'Do not be afraid.'") Cf. vs. 135: "non dubbiar."

140. *udir = udirono.*

141. *'l tremar cessò ed el compiési*: On the conjunction "ed" here, Sapegno observes: "La congiunzione *ed* sottolinea la simultaneità dei due fatti: il cessare del terremoto e la fine del canto." ("The conjunction *ed* [and] underscores the simultaneity of the two facts: the end of the earthquake and the end of the song.")   *el*: The song.   *compiési = si compié.*

142. *cammin santo*: Cf. *Purg.* XII, 115.

145. *Nulla ignoranza mai con tanta guerra*: Cf. Sapien. 14:22: "sed et in magno viventes inscientiae bello" ("but even though they live in a great war of ignorance").

148. *pareami = mi pareva.*

149. *er' oso = osavo.* Cf. *Purg.* XI, 126.

150. *lì*: Either in what Dante could observe about him or in his own troubled thoughts.   *potea = potevo.*

151. *m'andava*: This is the distancing pleonastic reflexive. See n. to *Inf.* VII, 94 and *passim.*

CANTO XXI

1. *La sete natural*: See *Metaphys*. I, 1, 980ᵃ, where Aristotle states that all men naturally desire to know, a passage referred to by Dante in *Conv*. I, i, 1: "Sì come dice lo Filosofo nel principio de la Prima Filosofia, tutti li uomini naturalmente desiderano di sapere." ("As saith the Philosopher in the beginning of the First Philosophy, 'All men by nature desire to know.'")   *non sazia = non si sazia.*

2–3. *se non con l'acqua . . . grazia*: See Ioan. 4: 5-15:

Venit ergo in civitatem Samariae quae dicitur Sichar, iuxta praedium quod dedit Iacob Ioseph filio suo. Erat autem ibi fons Iacob.

Iesus ergo, fatigatus ex itinere, sedebat sic supra fontem.

Hora erat quasi sexta. Venit mulier de Samaria haurire aquam; dicit ei Iesus: Da mihi bibere. Discipuli enim eius abierant in civitatem, ut cibos emerent. Dicit ergo ei mulier illa samaritana: Quomodo tu, Iudaeus cum sis, bibere a me poscis, quae sum mulier samaritana? Non enim coutuntur Iudaei Samaritanis. Respondit Iesus, et dixit ei: Si scires donum Dei, et quis est qui dicit tibi: Da mihi bibere, tu forsitan petisses ab eo, et dedisset tibi aquam vivam. Dicit ei mulier: Do-

mine, neque in quo haurias habes, et puteus altus est;
unde ergo habes aquam vivam? Numquid tu maior es
patre nostro Iacob, qui dedit nobis puteum, et ipse ex
eo bibit et filii eius et pecora eius? Respondit Iesus et
dixit ei:

Omnis qui bibit ex aqua hac, sitiet iterum; qui autem
biberit ex aqua quam ego dabo ei, non sitiet in aeter-
num, sed aqua quam ego dabo ei fiet in eo fons aquae
salientis in vitam aeternam.

Dicit ad eum mulier: Domine, da mihi hanc aquam,
ut non sitiam, neque veniam huc haurire.

He came, accordingly, to a town of Samaria called
Sichar, near the field that Jacob gave to his son Joseph.
Now Jacob's well was there. Jesus therefore, wearied
as he was from the journey, was sitting at the well. It
was about the sixth hour. There came a Samaritan
woman to draw water.

Jesus said to her, "Give me to drink"; for his disciples
had gone away into the town to buy food. The Samari-
tan woman therefore said to him, "How is it that thou,
although thou art a Jew, dost ask drink of me, who am
a Samaritan woman?" For Jews do not associate with
Samaritans.

Jesus answered and said to her, "If thou didst know
the gift of God, and who it is who says to thee, 'Give
me to drink,' thou, perhaps, wouldst have asked of him,
and he would have given thee living water." The woman
said to him, "Sir, thou hast nothing to draw with, and the
well is deep. Whence then hast thou living water? Art
thou greater than our father Jacob who gave us the well,
and drank from it, himself, and his sons, and his
flocks?" In answer Jesus said to her, "Everyone who
drinks of this water will thirst again. He, however, who
drinks of the water that I will give him shall never thirst;
but the water that I will give him shall become in him
a fountain of water, springing up unto life everlasting."
The woman said to him, "Sir, give me this water that I
may not thirst, or come here to draw."

The woman asked to be given of the water, and that water was grace. Cf. *Par.* IV, 124-32.

2. *la femminetta*: The diminutive suffix (see *mulier* in the Latin) expresses the woman's lowly station and her simplicity.

4. *mi travagliava*: Cf. *Purg.* XX, 145-46. *pungeami* = *mi pungeva*. *la fretta*: Cf. *Purg.* XX, 149.

5. *per la 'mpacciata via*: See n. to *Purg.* XX, 126. *'mpacciata* = *impacciata (impedita)*. Cf. "luoghi spediti" in *Purg.* XX, 5.

6. *condoleami* = *mi condolevo*.

7. *Ed ecco*: And lo, all of a sudden. Cf. *Inf.* I, 31, and see a similar beginning in the passage quoted from Luke in the following note.   *ne = ci.*

7-9. *scrive Luca . . . buca*: See Luc. 24:13-16:

Et ecce duo ex illis ibant ipsa die in castellum, quod erat in spatio stadiorum sexaginta ab Ierusalem, nomine Emmaus. Et ipsi loquebantur ad invicem de his omnibus quae acciderant. Et factum est dum fabularentur et secum quaererent, et ipse Iesus appropinquans ibat cum illis. Oculi autem illorum tenebantur ne eum agnoscerent.

And behold, two of them were going that very day to a village named Emmaus, which is sixty stadia from Jerusalem. And they were talking to each other about all these things that had happened. And it came to pass, while they were conversing and arguing together, that Jesus himself also drew near and went along with them; but their eyes were held, that they should not recognize him.

9. *surto* = *risorto*.   *sepulcral buca*: Cf. Mar. 15:46: "quod erat excisum de petra" ("which had been hewn out of a rock").

10–13. *ci apparve un'ombra . . . pace*: There is an apparent contradiction, or, we might say, a violation of the point of view, in these verses. First we are told that the soul appears and comes along looking down at its feet, at the crowd lying there, in order to avoid stepping on the souls; then we are told that Dante and Virgil did not see the soul until it spoke to them, and presumably until they turned to it. How, then, does Dante know what the soul was doing before he and Virgil noticed it? Some commentators take the phrase "guardando la turba che giace" to refer to Dante and Virgil, but this does not help the matter much. It is barely possible that the good Dante nodded this once, and if so, this unique violation of the point of view can serve to remind us how strictly he respected it throughout his long narrative. It is also possible, of course, that Dante did not nod at all, but that we are to take the "ci apparve" and the "ci addemmo" as a single identical moment and the touch about looking down at the crowd that lay at his feet to be a sort of retrospective projection of what the soul must have been doing as it came along, since it—and indeed Dante and Virgil—presumably continue to do this, i.e., pick their way among the recumbent souls. Even so, a certain difficulty remains.

10. *venìa = veniva.*

12. *ci addemmo* (infinitive, *addarsi*) *= ci accorgemmo.* Note Fra Giordano's use of this word in *Prediche inedite* LXXXVIII: "Gli uomeni non pensano questo fatto e non ci si addanno. E però essi credono pur saziare corporalmente, e non si addanno che tutto quello desiderio e quella fame è pur dell'anima." ("Men do not think about this matter, and take no notice of it. And so they believe only in corporeal satisfaction, not noticing that all that desire and that hunger belong to the soul.")   *sì parlò pria*: For this construction, see *Inf.* XIX, 44; XXIX, 30.

13. *O frati miei*: The greeting is familiar and cordial. Cf. *Inf.* XXVI, 112.   *Dio vi dea pace*: Actually it was not to the two who were on the way to Emmaus that the resurrected Christ spoke this greeting, as Dante seems to imply

here, but to the disciples assembled in Jerusalem, when the two had returned to them and were telling them of His appearance to them. See Luc. 24:35-36: "Et ipsi narrabant quae gesta erant in via, et quomodo cognoverunt eum in fractione panis. Dum autem haec loquuntur, stetit Iesus in medio eorum, et dicit eis: Pax vobis." ("And they themselves began to relate what had happened on the journey, and how they recognized him in the breaking of the bread. Now while they were talking of these things, Jesus stood in their midst, and said to them, 'Peace to you!'") Jesus had already recommended such a greeting to his disciples (see Matt. 10:12), and it is part of the Gloria (Luc. 2:14): "et in terra pax hominibus bonae voluntatis" ("and on earth peace among men of good will"). Cf. vs. 136 of the preceding canto. *dea = dia.*

14. *Noi ci volgemmo*: This does not necessarily imply that Dante and Virgil actually *turn* around to look back. The soul overtakes them, and they look toward it when it is more or less abreast of them; then all three hurry on their way (vs. 19). *sùbiti*: Plural adjective with the force of an adverb, *subitamente.*

15. *rendéli = gli rese.* *'l cenno ch'a ciò si conface*: Just what this fitting sign is we are not told, but it is surely a gesture (a bow or sign with the hand) and not a verbal reply, for this Virgil then gives. *conface = confà.*

16–18. *Nel beato concilio . . . essilio*: This, then, is Virgil's reply.

16. *beato concilio*: The assembly of the blessed in Paradise. Cf. *Par.* XXIII, 138; XXVI, 120.

17. *verace corte*: The "court of Heaven" is a common epithet in the *Paradiso.* Here, however, it implies a tribunal that pronounces sentence of exile.

18. *rilega = relega.* *etterno essilio*: Cf. *Inf.* I, 125-26; XXIII, 126.

19. *parte*: Cf. *Inf.* XXIX, 16.   *forte*: In great haste.
Cf. *Inf.* XIII, 116; *Purg.* XXIV, 2.

20–21. *se voi siete ombre . . . scorte*: The soul speaks in
the plural and pays no attention to the fact that Virgil spoke
only of himself and his own condition; accordingly he takes
Dante for a spirit. It should be noted that Dante and Virgil
are now on the western side of the mountain and that it is
mid-morning (it will be said to be between 10:00 and 11:00
A.M. in the next circle, *Purg.* XXII, 118-19), so that they
move in the shadow of the mountain where Dante's body
would not cast a shadow.

21. *la sua scala*: The mountain of Purgatory is God's stair-
way: it leads to Him. Virgil, then, in his reply will speak only
of the upward way (vs. 29), not of the descent to Hell.
scorte: "Guided." The infinitive is *scorgere*.

22–23. *Se tu riguardi a' segni . . . profila*: These verses pre-
sent the question of whether the shades bear P's on their fore-
heads, a problem concerning which Torraca is the most artic-
ulate among modern commentators:

> Pare che l'ombra sappia già il significato de' "segni";
> ma, in tal caso, saprebbe anche chi è che li "profila,"
> e Virgilio le regalerebbe una notizia superflua. Il fatto
> è che nessuna delle ombre del Purgatorio, con le quali
> Dante parla, porta de' P in fronte, nemmeno questa,
> che lo accompagnerà fino al Paradiso terrestre. Questa,
> si potrebbe opporre, è già tutta monda, non deve patire
> altra pena; ma le altre? . . . Se, invece, le lettere sono
> incise sulla fronte del solo Dante, il quale, vivo, con
> tutto il corpo, deve percorrere le cornici del monte:
> l'ombra non ne può saper niente, ed è opportuna, utile
> l'avvertenza: *e che l'angel profila*.

It seems that the shade already knows the significance
of the "signs"; but in that case, it would also know who
it is that "traces" them, and Virgil's information to him
would be quite superfluous. The fact is that none of the
shades with whom Dante has spoken in Purgatory bears

any P on its forehead—not even this one, which will accompany him to the Earthly Paradise. Someone might reply by saying that this shade is already completely purged, and that it will not undergo any more punishment. But then what about the others? . . . If, instead, the letters are incised only on the forehead of Dante, who, as a living man, with his whole body, must traverse all the cornices of the mountain, then the shade cannot know anything about them, and this information is both useful and opportune, as is the information that the angel traces them.

Nor is it a sufficient rebuttal to this to observe, as Barbi (1934b, p. 229) does: "Dante, è vero, non fa notar mai i P sulla fronte degli spiriti che si purgano; gli basta che il lettore indovini che li hanno dal suo caso. E qui conferma la cosa indirettamente." ("Dante, it is true, never mentions the P's on the foreheads of the spirits being purged. He is content to have the reader guess that they have them, because he does. And this indirectly confirms it.") On the contrary, the fact that Dante nowhere explicitly states, or even implies, that the spirits have P's traced on their foreheads is in itself enough to assure us that, in his conception, they simply do not bear such marks; for we have only to consider how often the fact would have been observed of this or that spirit, e.g., that he has only so many P's left to be erased. For instance, Statius would now have no P's left on his forehead, since he is ready to climb straightway to the summit and proceeds to do so. We are, therefore, bound to think that Virgil points to the "segni" on Dante's brow as to something exceptional, as exceptional as his journey itself, and Statius must be told that the angel traced them there and also that Dante is still living (vss. 25-27). To be sure, the verb "profila" is in the present tense; but we know of no other instance of a living man's passing this way, or of any destined to pass this way in the future, and so we must understand it as applying only to Dante. To be sure, if another living man should journey this way again, the angel (if he admitted him at the gate) would presumably trace the P's on his forehead, too.

24. *ben vedrai che coi buon convien ch'e' regni*: There have been previous predictions that Dante will be saved and be among the elect in Heaven one day. Cf. *Inf.* III, 91-93 and *passim*. This is an expression of hope put in the mouth of souls beyond and, in strict doctrine, cannot rest on any certainty, of course. *Purg.* VIII, 60, suggests that Dante wins to his second and final journey to God by entering now on this one as a living man, and some such meaning seems to be conveyed by Virgil's words now. Thus the P's denote one who is making the first journey while yet alive. Obviously the allegory of the journey is here prominently to the fore.

   coi buon convien ch'e' regni: Cf. II Tim. 2:12: "Si sustinebimus, et conregnabimus." ("If we endure, we shall also reign with him.")   *ch'e' = che egli*.

25-27. *lei che dì e notte fila . . . compila*: The reference is to Lachesis, the second of the three Fates, on to whose distaff Clotho, the first of the Fates, was supposed to place a certain quantity of wool at the birth of every mortal, the length of time it took to spin being the duration of the individual's life.

26. *li = gli.*   *tratta*: "Spun out."   *la conocchia*: The full distaff prepared by Clotho.

27. *impone*: "Puts upon." But the verb suggests the fateful decree which this represents.   *compila*: "Arranges," "packs."

28-30. *l'anima sua . . . adocchia*: Virgil speaks of Dante's soul as making the journey, and he then refers to his own "school" (vs. 33) as guiding him as far as it can. The allegory of the poem is still to the fore, this being an itinerary of the mind (soul) to God, in which Virgil is the light of natural reason. And yet, in the literal journey, out of which such meaning arises, Dante moves here in the flesh and must see (*adocchiare*) with the eyes of the flesh, and not as spirits see, even though his "anima" is "sister" (created by the same God) to that of the souls of the dead.

31–32. *l'ampia gola d'inferno*: Limbo, which is the widest and uppermost of the circles and is the throat, as it were, to the rest of the cavity.

32. *mostrarli = mostrargli. Mostrare* here has the intransitive sense of "to guide."   *mosterrolli = gli mostrerò.* The form *mosterrò* was common in early Italian.

33. *mia scola*: Virgil's mention of his "school" and such verses as vs. 124 are important signals to allegory. See n. to vss. 28-30.

34–35. *perché tai crolli diè*: For *dare crollo*, see *Inf.* XXV, 9, and for *crollare* in much the same sense, see *Purg.* V, 14.

35. *diè = diede.*   *ad una*: Namely, *voce* or *volta.*

35–36. *perché tutto . . . gridare*: Petrocchi has chosen to make the mountain the subject. Other editors have "tutti ad una parver gridare," which makes the souls the subject, rather than the mountain.

36. *infino a' suoi piè molli*: Clear down to the base of the mountain, where its shores are bathed by the ocean.

37. *diè = diede.*

38. *pur con la speranza*: With only the expectation, i.e., of satisfaction.

39. *la mia sete men digiuna*: Cf. the Latin *ieiunia sitis.*

40–42. *Cosa non è che sanza ordine . . . montagna*: "Religione" here has several possible meanings, but the verb "senta" suggests some personal subject, such as "community." As we soon see, the expression denotes Purgatory proper and excludes the long slope of Antepurgatory with its many souls. We should remember that one soul (Sapia, in *Purg.* XIII, 94-95) of this region within the gate has observed that all here are citizens "of one true city." A sharp dividing line is thus drawn at the gate to Purgatory proper. Above that, as "religione" suggests, the souls form one community. This, in a sense, is already part of the heavenly city, although one may perhaps speak of different "convents," this of Purgatory and the heavenly one (see, in fact, vs. 62: "convento"). *Religione*, in early Italian, can mean "convent" or "monastery," but it can also mean *legge*, "law." A translator must choose, and I have chosen the latter meaning as that which is uppermost in the context.

43. *Libero è qui da ogne alterazione*: "Qui" is best construed as an adverb of place that functions as subject of the verb. Cf. *Purg.* X, 79, where the adverb "intorno" is used in the same way. Purgatory proper is (miraculously) free of all such changes in the elements and in the weather as are named in vss. 46-57.

44-45. *di quel che 'l ciel . . . cagion*: The reference is to the unchanging heavens (typically the singular is here used for the plural), which receive influences one from the other. Mount Purgatory above the gate undergoes only this kind of influence.

46-48. *Per che non pioggia . . . breve*: The gate to Purgatory proper, we are now told, is an even more remarkable dividing line than we had realized: above it ("la scaletta di tre gradi breve") there is no alteration of the elements and it is almost as if it were situated above the circle of the moon in this respect (but not literally). On the other hand apparently we are to conceive that below the gate it can rain, snow, hail, frost, and so on—in fact, there has been dew (*Purg.* I, 121). Poor souls of the negligent, if they must endure such inclement weather!

46. *grando = grandine*.

49. *paion = appariscono*.

50. *coruscar = corruscar*.

50-51. *figlia di Taumante . . . contrade*: The reference is to Iris, the daughter of Thaumas and Electra and the personification of the rainbow, which, since it is always opposite the sun, is seen in many different quarters of the sky. Ovid mentions her in *Metam.* XIV, 845.

52. *secco vapor*: Dry vapors within the earth were thought to be the cause of earthquakes. Ristoro d'Arezzo, in *Della comp*. VII, iv, 6 (p. 216), explains:

> Entrando lo calore del sole entro per lo corpo, lo quale ha a risolvere l'umidità in vapore, risolve l'umidità della terra e diventane vapore ventoso . . . e anche può essere mosso dalla virtù del cielo; onde, non potendovi istare, combatte colla terra per uscire fuori, e se truova la terra dura e soda, levala su e giù, e falla tremare.

> When the heat of the sun enters into the body [of the earth], which has to resolve the humidity into vapor, it dries the humidity of the earth, which then becomes a windy vapor . . . and it [the windy vapor] can also be moved by virtue of the heavens; whereupon, since it cannot remain still, it fights with the earth, to get out. If it finds the earth hard and solid, it moves it up and down and makes it tremble.

Cf. *Inf*. III, 133.

53-54. *al sommo d'i tre gradi . . . piante*: The topmost step, which is red as blood and symbolizes Christ's sacrifice. The angel (vicar of Peter, since it holds Peter's keys) rests its feet on this step and is seated on the threshold of diamond, symbol of the eternal and changeless. See *Purg*. IX, 93-105.

53. *ch'io parlai*: For this use of *parlare* with the accusative, cf. *Inf*. IV, 104; XXI, 1; and *passim*.

55. *Trema forse più giù poco o assai*: The "forse" introduces a note of uncertainty that will become more emphatic in vs. 57: "non so come."

56. *per vento che 'n terra si nasconda*: Cf. vs. 52.

57. *non so come*: The base of the mountain can quake and there can be rain there, but above the gate there are no such alterations ever, there is only "spiritual causation." It is all quite miraculous.

58. *Tremaci = trema qua su.*

59. *sentesi = si sente.*   *sì che surga*: So that a soul may rise if it is lying or seated, as some are on some terraces.
o che si mova: Or so that a soul, if it is already erect, may set out on its upward journey. The soul who speaks has done both, but knows, of course, that not all souls on other terraces would have to rise up.

60. *e tal grido seconda*: And such a shout follows upon that. This is the answer to Virgil's second question, concerning the shout that he and Dante had heard (*Purg.* XX, 133).

62. *tutto libero a mutar convento*: Since this soul, answering Virgil, is speaking of times when the mountain quakes and the Gloria is shouted, "convento" must mean Purgatory, on the one hand, and Paradise, on the other. Cf. "miglior soglia," vs. 69.

63. *l'alma sorprende*: Only then, and all of a sudden, does the soul know that it has served its full time in this second realm "dove l'umano spirito si purga / e di salire al ciel diventa degno" (*Purg.* I, 5-6).   *di voler le giova*: "Succors it" with willing, i.e., with the will power to rise and move up.

64. *Prima vuol ben*: Before that it does indeed wish to rise.

64-66. *ma non lascia il talento . . . tormento*: The "talento" is the desire which led to the sinful act and, in this context, might be termed the conditioned will, as distinguished from the absolute will, which corresponds to the natural appetite for the good (cf. *Purg.* XVII-XVIII) that cannot err, since in desiring happiness it desires God. Elective love can err and is in fact out of harmony with natural appetite when it is sinful and may be said to be "contra voglia," i.e., counter to natural desire. Now God's justice disposes that the purgatorial punishment operate on the familiar principle of *contrapasso*, so that the soul that undergoes punishment here is placed in a condition that matches that of the soul in the act of sin. Here the "talento" desires (inclines to) the punishment (as it did the sinful pleasure) and thus pulls against the absolute will which desires to know God. "Talento" is the subject of "lascia" and the antecedent of "che," which in turn is the object of "pone." Cf. *Inf.* V, 39: "che la ragion sommettono al talento."

67. *E io*: The soul is the Roman poet Statius, as it will soon declare. Publius Papinius Statius, who was born in Naples *ca.* A.D. 45 and died *ca.* A.D. 96, was the most eminent poet of the Silver Age of Latin literature. The greater part of his life was spent at Rome, where he had access to the court, his father, who was a grammarian, having been tutor and favorite of Domitian. He won the prize, probably in 89, at the annual festival instituted by Domitian at Alba. His chief work is the *Thebaid*, an epic poem in hexameters (in twelve books) on the expedition of the Seven against Thebes and the quarrel between Eteocles and Polynices, which was published *ca.* 92 as the result of twelve years' labor, with a dedication to Domitian. He then began another epic, the *Achilleid*, on the life of Achilles and the whole Trojan war, but only the first book and part of the second were completed; besides these he published at various times a collection of miscellaneous and occasional poems on different subjects (in five books) under the title of *Silvae*.

Dante, by an error common to medieval writers, describes Statius as a native of Toulouse (vs. 89), in which he is followed by Boccaccio, who in the *Amorosa visione* (V, 34) speaks of "Stazio di Tolosa," and Chaucer, who in the *House of Fame* (vs. 1460) speaks of "the Tholosan that highte Stace." This error arose apparently from a confusion of the poet Statius with a rhetorician of the same name, Lucius Statius, who was born at Toulouse at the beginning of Nero's reign (*ca.* A.D. 58). Statius himself indicates that he was a native of Naples in the *Silvae*, but the latter was not known in Dante's time, the manuscript from which all the existing manuscripts are derived not having been discovered until the beginning of the fifteenth century. The University of Toulouse (founded in 1215) claimed Statius as the first founder of its school, just as Naples claimed Virgil as the founder of its own.

Dante, by a poetical fiction for which there does not appear to be any historical foundation, in the next canto (*Purg.*

XXII, 88-91) will represent Statius as having secretly embraced Christianity before the completion of the *Thebaid*.

68. *cinquecent' anni e più*: From Statius we get some measure of the normal length of time required for purgation from sin in Purgatory. He has lain face down in this fifth circle for over five hundred years to purge the sin of prodigality; and, as he will tell us in *Purg.* XXII, 92, he spent over four hundred years on the fourth, purging sloth. Since he has been dead some 1,200 years, he must have spent the rest of the time in Antepurgatory or in other circles below.

   pur mo sentii: Statius was thus surprised by the free will to change his cloister.

69. *libera volontà di miglior soglia*: Cf. vss. 62-63.

70. *sentisti*: Statius speaks in the singular here, to Virgil, who asked the question. And yet he is speaking to both Virgil and Dante, of course, as "ne" in vs. 73 indicates.

72. *che tosto sù li 'nvii*: In expressing this wish for the souls who are not yet freed from torment, as it is, the liberated soul shows true charity.

73. *ne = ci.   però = perciò.   el*: Pleonastic impersonal pronoun (*egli*).

75. *quant' el mi fece prode*: "How much good he did me." Cf. *Purg.* XV, 42. Porena observes: "D'un cibo o d'una bevanda, *far pro* o *far prode* si dice anche nel senso che sono piaciuti e si sono gustati molto: onde qui l'espressione continua la metafora della sete e del bere." ("*Far pro* or *fare prode* is also said of food or drink, in the sense that they have been enjoyed or that they tasted very good. Here, then, the expression continues the metaphor of thirst and drink.")

   el = egli (Statius).

76-77. *la rete che qui vi 'mpiglia*: We may remember how the avaricious were said to be "legati e presi" (*Purg.* XIX, 124) in their torment, and now we understand this better in terms of the "talento," vs. 64.

77. *e come si scalappia*: I.e., how the *calappio*, the noose of a snare (*rete*), is untied. The verb is based on the positive form *accalappiare* (see E. G. Parodi, 1957, p. 267).

78. *ci*: I.e., here in Purgatory proper. *congaudete*: In the singing of the Gloria when a soul is liberated. See I Cor. 12:26: "Gloriatur unum membrum, congaudent omnia membra." ("If one member glories, all the members rejoice with it.")

79. *piacciati = ti piaccia.*

81. *ne le parole tue mi cappia*: The meaning may be either (1) let it (i.e., the two matters taken as one) be contained in your words for me, or (2) let it be contained in my understanding, through your words. *cappia*: Subjunctive form of *capere*. Cf. *Par*. III, 76.

82–84. *Nel tempo che 'l buon Tito . . . venduto*: Titus, son and successor of Vespasian, was Roman Emperor from A.D. 79 to A.D. 81. He served under his father in the Jewish wars, and when Vespasian was proclaimed emperor and returned to Italy in 70, he remained in Palestine in order to carry on the siege of Jerusalem, which he captured, after a siege of several months, in September of that year. In the following year he returned to Rome and celebrated the conquest of the Jews in a triumph with his father.

Titus is also mentioned by the Emperor Justinian in the heaven of Mercury (*Par*. VI, 92); in both passages reference is made to the destruction of Jerusalem by Titus, which Dante here says was the vengeance upon the Jews for the Crucifixion of Christ, whereby in its turn the sin of Adam was avenged. This theory that Titus, as the destroyer of Jerusalem, was the avenger of the death of Christ, was borrowed by Dante from Orosius, who, in recording the triumph of Titus after his victory, says (*Hist*. VII, iii, 8 and ix, 9):

> Capta eversaque urbe Hierosolymorum . . . extinctisque Iudaeis Titus, qui ad vindicandum Domini Iesu Christi sanguinem iudicio Dei fuerat ordinatus, victor triumphans cum Vespasiano patre Ianum clausit. . . . iure

enim idem honos ultioni passionis Domini inpensus est, qui etiam nativitati fuerat adtributus.

After the capture and overthrow of Jerusalem . . . and after the total destruction of the Jewish nation, Titus, who had been appointed by the decree of God to avenge the blood of the Lord Jesus Christ, celebrated with his father Vespasian his victory by a triumph and closed the Temple of Janus. . . . It was indeed right that the same honor should be paid to the avenging of the Lord's Passion as had been bestowed upon His Nativity.

83. *le fóra = i fori*, the wounds of Christ.

84. *per Giuda = da Giuda.*   *venduto*: Judas Iscariot sold Christ for thirty pieces of silver.

85. *col nome che più dura e più onora*: See Lucan, *Phars.* IX, 980-86:

> O sacer et magnus vatum labor! omnia fato
> Eripis et populis donas mortalibus aevum.
> Invidia sacrae, Caesar, ne tangere famae;
> Nam, si quid Latiis fas est promittere Musis,
> Quantum Zmyrnaei durabunt vatis honores,
> Venturi me teque legent; Pharsalia nostra
> Vivet, et a nullo tenebris damnabimur aevo.

How mighty, how sacred is the poet's task! He snatches all things from destruction and gives to mortal men immortality. Be not jealous, Caesar, of those whom fame has consecrated; for, if it is permissible for the Latin Muses to promise aught, then, as long as the fame of Smyrna's bard endures, posterity shall read my verse and your deeds; our Pharsalia shall live on, and no age will ever doom us to oblivion.

86. *di là*: In the world of the living.

88. *Tanto fu dolce*: See Juvenal (who in *Purg.* XXII, 14, will be remembered in connection with Statius), *Satires* VII, 82-86, where mention is made of Statius' "sweetness":

curritur ad vocem iucundam et carmen amicae
Thebaidos, laetam cum fecit Statius urbem
promisitque diem: tanta dulcedine captos
adficit ille animos tantaque libidine volgi
auditur . . .

When Statius has gladdened the city by promising a
day, people flock to hear his pleasing voice and his loved
Thebais; so charmed are their souls by his sweetness,
with such rapture does the multitude listen to him!

In *Conv.* IV, xxv, 6, Dante refers to "Stazio, lo dolce poeta"
("Statius, the sweet poet"). See E. Moore (1896), pp. 256-
57. *mio vocale spirto*: "My poetic voice."

89. *tolosano*: See n. to vs. 67.

90. *mertai = meritai*.

92-93. *cantai di Tebe . . . caddi in via*: See n. to vs. 67.

93. *la seconda soma*: The *Achilleid*.

94-96. *Al mio ardor . . . mille*: For this and the tribute to
Virgil which continues in these verses, see Statius' final apos-
trophe to his own poem in *Theb.* XII, 810-19:

Durabisne procul dominoque legere superstes,
o mihi bissenos multum vigilata per annos
Thebai? iam certe praesens tibi Fama benignum
stravit iter coepitque novam monstrare futuris.
iam te magnanimus dignatur noscere Caesar,
Itala iam studio discit memoratque iuventus.
vive, precor; nec tu divinam Aeneida tempta,
sed longe sequere et vestigia semper adora.
mox, tibi si quis adhuc praetendit nubila livor,
occidet, et meriti post me referentur honores.

Wilt thou endure in the time to come, O my *Thebaid*,
for twelve years object of my wakeful toil, wilt thou
survive thy master and be read? Of a truth already pres-
ent Fame hath paved thee a friendly road, and begun to
hold thee up, young as thou art, to future ages. Already

great-hearted Caesar deigns to know thee, and the youth
of Italy eagerly learns and recounts thy verse. O live,
I pray! nor rival the divine *Aeneid*, but follow afar and
ever venerate its footsteps. Soon, if any envy as yet
o'erclouds thee, it shall pass away, and, after I am gone,
thy well-won honours shall be duly paid.

94. *fuor = furono*, of which "faville" is the subject.

95. *scaldar = scaldarono.*

96. *sono = si sono.   allumati*: "Kindled" (rather than
"illuminated"). Cf. *Purg.* XXIV, 151.   *più di mille*: An
indefinite number meant to denote a multitude. Cf. *Inf.* VIII,
82, and *passim.*

98. *fummi = mi fu.   nutrice*: Cf. *Purg.* XXII, 102:
"lattar."

99. *sanz' essa non fermai peso di dramma*: See the quota-
tion from the *Thebaid* in n. to vss. 94-96. Benvenuto speaks
of Statius as "simia Virgilii." *Fermare peso* in this context
must mean "to set down something of some weight," i.e.,
importance, value.   *peso di dramma*: A dram's weight,
the eighth part of an ounce, i.e., practically nothing.

100–101. *E per esser vivuto ... Virgilio*: This aspiration repre-
sents great love on the part of one who has just been liberated
from Purgatory and can now proceed to eternal beatitude.

100. *vivuto = vissuto.*

101. *assentirei = consentirei.   un sole*: A year.

102. *deggio = devo.   al mio uscir di bando*: Which can
take place right now, of course.   *bando*: "Exile" or
"banishment" from Paradise, but quite different from Virgil's
"exile" therefrom. Cf. vs. 18.

103. *Volser*: Past absolute of *volgere*, here transitive, Vir-
gil being the object, "queste parole" the subject.

104. *viso*: "Expression" as well as "face," for the mouth is
silent.

105. *la virtù che vuole*: The will.

109. *Io pur sorrisi*: "I only smiled."   *ammicca*: *Ammiccare* means "to communicate silently," as by a wink of the eye.

110. *riguardommi = mi riguardò*.

111. *'l sembiante*: "Expression" of thoughts and feelings.

112. *Se tanto labore in bene assommi*: The familiar formula of adjuration.   *labore*: A Latinism, referring to the labor of this upward journey.   *assommi*: "Complete itself." Cf. *Par.* XXXI, 94.

113. *testeso = testè*. Its use is common in early Italian, in prose as well as verse.

114. *un lampeggiar di riso*: The verb *lampeggiare* is the equivalent of *corruscare* (cf. vs. 50). Note Dante's definition of laughter in *Conv.* III, viii, 11: "E che è ridere se non una corruscazione de la dilettazione de l'anima, cioè uno lume apparente di fuori secondo sta dentro?" ("And what is laughter save a coruscation of the delight of the soul, that is to say, a light appearing outwardly according as it exists within?")   *dimostrommi = mi dimostrò*.

115. *Or son io*: The passing to the vivid present is most effective.

121. *Forse che = forse*.

122. *fei = feci*.

123. *vo' = voglio*.

124. *Questi che guida in alto li occhi miei*: See n. to vs. 33. Here as elsewhere guidance by Virgil (or by Beatrice) stresses vision, that is, guidance of the *eyes*.

126. *forte*: Other editors have "forza" or "forze." But Petrocchi has "forte," as justified by the most authoritative manuscripts, taking it to be the adjective used as a noun, meaning "capacity," "ability."

128–29. *ed esser credi . . . dicesti*: I.e., "credi quelle parole, e non altro, esser cagione al mio ridere."

130–32. *Già s'inchinava . . . vedi*: The situation recalls Dante's kneeling before the recumbent pope in *Purg.* XIX, 127-32, and, in "frate, non far," bears the same echo of the verses from Apoc. 19:10. Note also the use of *frate* in *Purg.* XIX, 133, and Apoc. 19:10.

131. *el = egli.   li = gli.*

135. *dismento = dimentico.* Cf. *ammentarsi*, "to remember," in *Purg.* XIV, 56.

CANTO XXII

1. *Già era l'angel dietro a noi rimaso*: This is the only time that Dante tells in retrospect of the guardian angel at the foot of the stairs; this avoids interrupting the more interesting matter of the exchange between Virgil and Statius.

2. *n' = ne (ci).*   *vòlti*: "Turned."

3. *un colpo*: Literally, "a blow," i.e., one of the P's which the angel traced on Dante's forehead. See *Purg.* IX, 112-14.
  raso: Past participle of *radere*. Cf. *Purg.* XII, 123.

4-6. *e quei c'hanno a giustizia . . . forniro*: The angel recited part of the fourth beatitude (Matt. 5:6), "beati qui . . . sitiunt iustitiam" ("blessed are they who . . . thirst for justice"), which is appropriate for those who are liberated from the thirst for gold and earthly wealth. The beatitude, like the punishment, applies particularly to avarice, not to prodigality. Righteousness or justice is intended here as moderation, the opposite of avarice.

5. *n' = ne (ci).*

6. *sanz' altro*: The angel has recited "beati qui sitiunt iustitiam," without the rest of the beatitude, which speaks of

hunger and will be used in the next circle (*Purg.* XXIV, 151-54).   *forniro* = *fornirono*, "completed."

7. *più lieve che per l'altre foci*: This has happened before (see *Purg.* XII, 116), as Virgil had indicated it would (*Purg.* IV, 88-90). For "foci" in the sense of passageways between the circles, see *Purg.* XII, 112.

8. *m'andava*: Again the so-called pleonastic pronoun, in its distinguishing "distancing" function. Cf. vs. 127: "e io soletto."   *labore*: A Latinism, meaning "great effort" (cf. *Purg.* XXI, 112, and *Conv.* II, xv, 5).

10-12. *Amore, acceso di virtù . . . fore*: A variation on the law of love pronounced by Francesca in quite another context (*Inf.* V, 103), but with the same metaphor of "kindling." See Scartazzini-Vandelli for the following quotation from Fra Giordano:

> Bene è vero che talora l'uno amerà l'altro e non sarà amato egli da lui, però forse che nol saprà, chè 'l cuore non si può vedere; ma se interverrà che nullo segno d'amore si mostri per lo quale si ne possa avvedere, ovvero che gli sia detto per altrui: "La cotale persona t'ama e vuolti bene," di necessità conviene ch'ami lui.

> It is indeed true that sometimes one man will love another and will not be loved in return, perhaps because the person does not know he is being loved, for the heart cannot be seen. But if some sign of love is given by which he becomes aware of it, or if someone says to him, "that person loves you and wishes you well," then he must of necessity love him in return.

In his *Exp. Eth. Nicom.* VIII, lect. 1, n. 1538 Thomas Aquinas notes that "virtus est causa verae amicitiae." ("Virtue is the cause of true friendship.")

12. *fore* = *fuori*.

14. *Giovenale*: Juvenal (Decimus Junius Juvenalis), the great Roman satirist, was born probably (*ca.* A.D. 60) in the reign of Nero (A.D. 54-68) and died (*ca.* A.D. 140) in the

reign of Antoninus Pius (A.D. 138-61). His extant works consist of sixteen satires. Dante does not show any close acquaintance with Juvenal's satires, such quotations as he takes from them being apparently at second hand.

17. *strinse*: Cf. *Inf.* V, 128.   *di = per*. Cf. "de" in *Inf.* V, 101: "prese costui de la bella persona."

18. *mi parran corte queste scale*: I.e., because of my great desire to be with you and talk with you.

19–21. *e come amico . . . ragiona*: Cf. "frate" in the preceding canto, vs. 131, which was a form of address that already was inviting Statius to such a relationship. Now "amico" is repeated as the invitation becomes more urgent.

21. *omai*: Momigliano refers to this as "ultimo, delicato riflesso della scena del canto XXI. *Ora che ti ho messo à ton aise*, diremmo noi." ("A final, delicate reflection of the scene in Canto XXI. Now that I have put you at your ease, we would say.")

22–23. *come poté trovar . . . avarizia*: "Avarizia" is the subject of "trovar . . . loco."

23. *senno*: Statius, being a poet, is wise, of course.

24. *per tua cura*: Sapegno comments: "Virgilio vuol dire insomma 'la saggezza che avesti è tutta merito tuo'; respingendo in tal modo, discretamente, le umili espressioni di gratitudine del discepolo." ("Virgil, then, is saying: 'The wisdom you had is all your own merit,' thus discreetly rejecting the humble expressions of gratitude from his disciple.")

25. *fenno = fecero*.

26. *un poco a riso*: Cf. *Purg.* IV, 122.

27. *d'amor m'è caro cenno = m'è caro cenno d'amore*.

28–33. *Veramente più volte . . . era*: Statius is very gentle in setting Virgil right. He begins with a generalization and concludes with the delicate "forse."

31-32. *La tua dimanda . . . esser*: I.e., "la tua dimanda mi avvera che il tuo credere sia che . . ." As indicated by Porena, the construction echoes a possible Latin construction, *tuam opinionem esse*.

34-35. *avarizia fu partita . . . dismisura*: Statius speaks the language of Aristotle's ethics. On avarice and prodigality as excesses to one side and the other of the mean, see *Inf.* VII, 40-45. See Horace, *Epistles* I, xviii, 9: "Virtus est medium vitiorum et utrimque reductum." ("Virtue is a mean between vices, remote from both extremes.")

35. *dismisura*: Cf. *Inf.* VII, 42; XVI, 74.

36. *migliaia di lunari*: More than six thousand months, in fact. *Lunari* is the plural of *lunare*, "month."

37. *mia cura*: My endeavors.

38. *intesi*: "Paid attention to."   *chiame = chiami*.

39. *crucciato quasi*: "As one angered against."

40-41. *Per che non reggi tu . . . mortali?* The reference is to *Aen.* III, 56-57: "Quid non mortalia pectora cogis, / auri sacra fames!" ("To what dost thou not drive the hearts of men, O accursed hunger for gold!") These verses from the *Aeneid* concern the episode involving the tomb of Polydorus (already referred to by Dante in *Inf.* XIII, 46-48) where the cruel murder for gold of the youth by Polymestor is remembered (cf. *Purg.* XX, 114-15). Clearly, in such a context the words represent a vehement denunciation of avarice. But the sense in which Statius means he took those words, when he found in them an admonition which enlightened him as to his erring ways in prodigality, has been much debated. In general, two interpretations seem possible.

Statius (i.e., Dante the poet) chose to understand "sacra fames" as "holy hunger," i.e., "temperate," and "cogis," which he translated as "reggi," in the sense of "govern," "control." Thus Statius found in Virgil's verses the meaning: "Why, O blessed hunger for gold, do you not govern mortal appetite?" Among the early commentators Buti understands the verses in this way:

> O sacra fame Dell'oro; cioè o santo desiderio dell'oro:
> allora è santo lo desiderio dell'oro, quando sta nel
> mezzo e non passa ne l'estremi, Per che non reggi; nel
> mezzo, l'appetito dei mortali; sicchè non s'allarghi a
> volerne troppo, ch'è avarizia; e non si ristringa a non
> volerlo punto e gittarlo, che è prodigalità?

> O sacred hunger for gold, i.e., o holy desire for gold
> (because the desire for gold is holy if it stays moderate
> and does not pass the extremes), why do you not keep
> the appetites of mortals moderate, so that it does not
> grow and want too much, which is avarice, or so that
> it does not shrink and want none at all, and throws it
> away, which is prodigality?

Benvenuto takes quite a different view of the meaning: "Cupiditas auri compellit corda hominum ad omnia magna mala . . . hic Statius largius interpretatur istud dictum, et dicit quod Virgilius arguit intemperantiam divitiarum tam in dando quam in retinendo." ("The lust for gold drives the heart of man to all manner of evil . . . here Statius interprets the remark in its widest sense, and he says that Virgil censures the disorder of riches both in giving and receiving.") Statius, therefore, would have understood Virgil's verses in their proper sense, as an imprecation against human appetite for riches and explicitly against such cupidity as drove Polymestor to slay Polydorus, but implicitly as a denunciation of "want of measure" taken either way, as avarice or prodigality, and so would have seen the light respecting his own sinful ways in regard to the latter excess and would have "corrected" his ways.

Either view of the meaning is possible, but the second seems more plausible since it respects the meaning of Virgil's verses in their context, for it seems unlikely that Dante would impute to Statius such a misreading as would make "sacra fames" mean "holy hunger" instead of "accursed hunger," when the reference is to the "hunger" of Polymestor. It would seem better, in this case, then, as

Sapegno advocates, to adopt the reading "per che" instead
of "perchè," as some editors have done. Sapegno says: "Leg-
gendo 'per che,' o anche 'a che' (e non 'perchè,' come oggi
si preferisce), intenderemo dunque la parafrasi dantesca così:
'per quali opere, a quali malvagità, non trascini tu, o ese-
cranda fame dell'oro, l'appetito dei mortali?' " ("If we read
per che [for what] or *a che* [to what] instead of *perchè* [why],
which is the preferred reading today, we could understand
Dante's paraphrase in this manner: 'For what works, toward
what evil, are you not capable of luring the appetite of men,
o wicked hunger for gold?' ")

It may be noted that Virgil used the phrase elsewhere in
a most famous passage of the *Aeneid* (IV, 412): "Improbe
Amor, quid non mortalia pectora cogis!" ("O tyrant Love,
to what dost thou not drive the hearts of men!")

To see prodigality as a hunger for riches presents a cer-
tain difficulty, to be sure, since the prodigal is reckless and
wasteful of riches. But Statius sees the matter correctly, i.e.,
in terms of an appetite respecting riches that can exceed to
either side and therein be sinful, as he clearly goes on to say,
vss. 43-44. See A. Mancini (1928), p. 115:

> Quanto al primo punto, è naturale che il cruccio di Vir-
> gilio si manifesti in un'apostrofe contro un vizio e non
> contro una virtù, quale sarebbe in sostanza la modera-
> zione o temperanza, e penso anch'io che Dante abbia
> inteso il *sacra* a dovere, come richiedeva il contesto
> virgiliano, nè mi fa dubitare il fatto, osservato dal Pi-
> sani, che Dante nella *Commedia* adoperi la parola
> "sacro" sempre in buon senso. Ma la difficoltà è l'altra;
> e, poichè superarla bisogna, non pare si possa altrimenti
> se non intendendo che Stazio fu tratto a meditare sulla
> sua colpa dalla riprensione dell'opposta. In sostanza
> prodigalità ed avarizia, come colpe in "dritta opposi-
> zione," si purgano nello stesso luogo, e per esse si of-
> fende uno stesso principio, quello della liberalità (per
> la dottrina dell'Aquinate mi piace rimandare, pur dis-
> sentendo nelle conclusioni, al Pisani), la quale è mode-
> ratrice così del nostro dare come del nostro ricevere;

nè manca ai luoghi virgiliani del terzo e del quarto del-l'Eneide un principio etico comune che è anche per Virgilio quello dell'eccesso, *amor* che è *improbus* e quindi *sacer*. In conclusione Dante ha attribuito a Stazio quelle illazioni etiche che erano nella tradizione dottrinaria, facendo sì che egli cogliesse nelle parole di Virgilio la radice delle opposte colpe e argomentasse dalla condanna dell'avarizia la condanna, da motivarsi ugualmente, della prodigalità.

As for the first point, it is natural that Virgil's anger should manifest itself in an apostrophe against a vice, and not against a virtue, which is in fact what moderation and temperance are. I too think that Dante understood the word *sacra* properly and as the Virgilian context required. Nor am I made doubtful by the fact, noted by Pisani, that Dante always uses the word *sacro* in a good sense throughout the *Comedy*. The difficulty we must overcome is another, and overcome it we must; and it would seem that the only way to do it is by understanding that Statius was drawn to meditate on his fault by revulsion against the opposite fault. In substance, prodigality and avarice, as "directly opposed" faults, are purged in the same place and are offenses against the same principle, the principle of generosity (for Aquinas' doctrine, I should like to refer the reader to Pisani . . . though I disagree with the conclusions). Generosity moderates both our giving and our receiving. Nor do the Virgilian passages in the third and fourth books of the *Aeneid* lack a common ethical principle which, for Virgil too, is a principle of excess, *amor* (love) which is *improbus* (improper) and therefore *sacer* (wicked). In conclusion, Dante has attributed to Statius those ethical inferences which were in the doctrinal tradition, making him find in Virgil's words the root of the opposite faults and making him argue from the punishment of avarice to the punishment of prodigality, which punishments have the same rationale.

42. *voltando sentirei le giostre grame*: I.e., I should now

be among the prodigal of the fourth circle of Hell (*Inf.* VII) who roll great stones about and clash ("joust") with their opposites, the avaricious.

43. *aprir l'ali*: Cf. *Purg.* X, 25, where the metaphor of wings is used of the eyes.

44. *pente'mi = mi pentii*. Cf. "penter," vs. 48.

45. *di quel*: Of prodigality.

46. *risurgeran*: On the Judgment Day.   *coi crini scemi*: Cf. *Inf.* VII, 57.

47. *per ignoranza*: Not realizing that prodigality is a grave sin. They are, none the less, responsible. See Thomas Aquinas, *Summa theol.* I-II, q. 76, a. 2, resp.

48. *ne li stremi*: *In extremis*.

49. *rimbecca*: Literally, "strikes back." Landino comments: "Proprio rimbeccare è quando ripercotiamo indietro la palla, che ci viene incontro." ("*Rimbeccare* is when we hit back a ball that is coming toward us.") The clashing of the avaricious and prodigal in Hell expresses this same meaning.

50. *alcun peccato*: Although Statius generalizes with respect to the pairing of all sins, the pair avarice-prodigality is the only such combination found in *Inferno* or *Purgatorio*.

51. *suo verde secca*: See *maturare* used in *Purg.* XIX, 91 and compare references to the unripeness or "green" of pride and, by extension, of any sin in *Inf.* XIV, 48, and XXV, 18.

54. *incontrato = avvenuto*. Cf. *Inf.* IX, 20; XXII, 32.

55. *Or*: The word turns the reader's attention to another subject.

56. *la doppia trestizia di Giocasta*: "The twofold woe of Jocasta" is the principal subject of the *Thebaid* and is a way of saying "when you composed the *Thebaid* . . . " Jocasta, wife of Laius, king of Thebes, was the mother of Oedipus, whom she afterwards married without knowing his true iden-

tity and by whom she became the mother of Eteocles and Polynices (as well as of Antigone and Ismene, mentioned below). The fratricidal strife of Polynices and Eteocles, culminating in their killing each other in single combat during the war of the Seven against Thebes, was their mother's double sorrow. See n. to *Inf.* XXVI, 54.

57. *disse 'l cantor de' buccolici carmi*: Virgil is so named in anticipation of Statius' paraphrase in vss. 70-72 of verses from the fourth *Bucolic* (or *Eclogue*).

58. *Cliò*: Clio, the Muse of History, invoked by Statius as such in *Theb.* I, 41, and X, 630-31, and therefore as his muse in the telling of his history. It is a mistake to understand Virgil's meaning to be that since Statius invoked such a muse, he must have been a pagan. Virgil simply means "it does not appear from what you wrote under the inspiration of Clio, your muse, i.e., from what you say in your poem." Cf. *Purg.* I, 9-10, where much the same is said of Calliope as Dante's inspiration and accompanist.

60. *la fede, sanza qual ben far non basta*: See *Inf.* IV, 31-42. *qual = la qual*. *ben far*: The subject of "basta."

61. *qual sole o quai candele*: The pairing of these terms suggests that "sole" represents some light from above, some divine illumination, whereas "candele" denotes enlightenment from human sources. Virgil will then be said to have lighted the way of Statius with a lantern.

62. *ti stenebraron*: The time of paganism was commonly called a time of darkness, in Statius' day, an extension of the darkness that prevailed generally in the world before Christ came as a "sun." *Tenebrae* or "night" is the common metaphor for this (and in this way the *tenebre* of Limbo have their symbolic import; cf. *Inf.* IV, 69, and the note, as well as *Purg.* VII, 29). See "notte" in vs. 67.

63. *pescator*: Peter, first a fisherman, then a fisher of men (see Mar. 1:17 and *Par.* XVIII, 136). For the navigation figure, implied in the expression *drizzar le vele* (here the

more appropriate because of "pescator"), as a metaphor for the way of life, see *Inf*. XXVII, 80-81; *Purg*. XII, 5.

65. *verso Parnaso*: A term coordinate to "appresso Dio" in the following verse. As Statius will say in another way (vs. 73), Virgil first brought him to be a poet, then to be a Christian.   *Parnaso*: Parnassus (modern Liákoura), mountain of about 8,060 feet in Greece, north of the Gulf of Corinth and about 83 miles northwest of Athens; situated primarily in ancient Phocis. Its two peaks, whence Parnassus is frequently spoken of by classical authors as double-headed (Lucan, *Phars*. III, 173; V, 72; Ovid, *Metam*. I, 316; II, 221; Statius, *Theb*. VII, 346), are mentioned by Isidore of Seville (*Etym*. XIV, viii, 11). Mount Parnassus was sacred to Apollo and the Muses. Just above Delphi (at the foot of the mountain to the south) is the Castalian Spring, the water of which is referred to here.

66. *appresso Dio*: As a coordinate phrase, the meaning is "on the way of God," i.e., "in the true faith," by which Statius became a Christian.

67-69. *come quei che va di notte . . . dotte*: Note the figure in Augustine, *De symbolo: sermo ad catechumenos* IV, 4 (col. 664): "O Iudaei, ad hoc ferentes in manibus lucernam Legis, ut aliis viam demonstretis, et vobis tenebras ingeratis." ("O Jews, you carry in your hands the torch of the law, and while you light the way for others, you are yourselves enshrouded in darkness.") And E. Moore (1896, p. 294) points to a similar figure in lines of Ennius quoted by Cicero, *De officiis* I, xvi, 51:

> Homó, qui erranti cómiter monstrát viam,
> Quasi lúmen de suo lúmine accendát, facit.
> Nihiló minus ipsi lúcet, cum illi accénderit.

> Who kindly sets a wand'rer on his way
> Does e'en as if he lit another's lamp by his:
> No less shines his, when he his friend's hath lit.

69. *fa le persone dotte*: I.e., makes them wise (enlightens them) as to the true way.

70–72. *quando dicesti: "Secol si rinova . . . nova"*: Dante has translated, and slightly paraphrased, the famous "prophetic" verses of Virgil's fourth *Eclogue*. See *Eclog*. IV, 5-7:

> magnus ab integro saeclorum nascitur ordo.
> iam redit et Virgo, redeunt Saturnia regna;
> iam nova progenies caelo demittitur alto.

The great line of the centuries begins anew. Now the Virgin returns, the reign of Saturn returns; now a new progeny descends from heaven on high.

In *De mon*. I, xi, 1 Dante writes:

> Preterea, mundus optime dispositus est cum iustitia in eo potissima est. Unde Virgilius commendare volens illud seculum quod suo tempore surgere videbatur, in suis Bucolicis cantabat:

> Iam redit et Virgo, redeunt Saturnia regna.

> "Virgo" namque vocabatur Iustitia, quam etiam Astream vocabant; "Saturnia regna" dicebant optima tempora, que etiam "aurea" nuncupabant.

Moreover, the world is best disposed when justice is most potent therein; whence Virgil, in praise of that age which was visibly rising in his own day, sang in his *Bucolics:*

> "*Iam redit et Virgo, redeunt Saturnia regna.*"

By "Virgin" he meant Justice, who was also called Astraea. By "Saturnian kingdoms" he meant the best ages, which were also called the golden.

Thus Dante replaces "Virgo" with "giustizia" and "Saturnia regna" with "primo tempo umano" (see also *Inf*. XIV, 96, and *Epist*. VII, 6). And on the myth of Astraea in this connection and its application to the allegory of the poem, see C. S. Singleton (1958), pp. 184-203.

Who the child was whose birth is thus predicted by Virgil is not known, but the received opinion is that it was the infant son of Gaius Asinius Pollio, whose consulship, 40 B.C., occurred during the time the poem was written (between 42 and 37 B.C.).

74. *veggi = veda*, second person.   *mei = meglio.*

75. *a colorare*: "To color" the design he has traced thus far.

76-77. *tutto quanto pregno de la vera credenza*: Porena observes that the world, were it only the civilized world, was far from being wholly Christian in the time of Statius, but the glad tidings had circulated a little everywhere and were not limited to Palestine. See the quotation from Orosius in the n. to vs. 83.

78. *li messaggi de l'etterno regno*: The apostles, who were sowing the true faith at Rome in the time of Statius.

79. *la parola tua sopra toccata*: The verses of Virgil's fourth *Eclogue* spoken by Statius in vss. 70-72.

81. *usata = usanza.* E. G. Parodi (1957, p. 246) refers to two examples in prose of this unusual form.

82. *Vennermi . . . parendo = mi vennero parendo.* A progressive construction: "More and more they came to seem to me."

83. *Domizian*: Domitian (Titus Flavius Domitianus Augustus), third of the Flavian emperors of Rome, second son of Vespasian, and successor of his brother, Titus, was born at Rome in A.D. 51, became emperor in 81, and was murdered in 96. Among the many crimes imputed to him was a relentless persecution of the Christians, which is mentioned by Tertullian and Eusebius, but of which there is no other historical record. Dante's authority for Domitian's persecution of the Christians was doubtless Orosius (*Hist.* VII, x, 1), who says of Domitian: "Per annos XV ad hoc paulatim per omnes scelerum gradus crevit, ut confirmatissimam toto orbe Christi Ecclesiam datis ubique crudelissimae persecutionis edictis convellere auderet." ("For fifteen years this ruler progressed through every degree of wickedness. Finally he dared to issue edicts for a general and most cruel persecution to uproot the Christian Church, which was now very firmly established throughout the world.")

84. *fur = furono*, of which "pianti" is the subject.

85. *per me si stette*: For this construction, see *Inf*. I, 126; *Purg*. XVI, 118-19. The meaning is: "as long as I lived in the world yonder."

87. *fer = fecero.* *sette*: In *Conv.* IV, xxii, 15, Dante writes: "Per queste tre donne si possono intendere le tre sette de la vita attiva, cioè li Epicurei, li Stoici e li Peripatetici." ("By these three ladies may be understood the three schools of the active life, to wit, the Epicureans, the Stoics, and the Peripatetics.")

88-89. *E pria ch'io conducessi . . . poetando*: See Statius, *Theb.* VII, 424-25: "Iam ripas, Asope, tuas Boeotaque ventum / flumina." ("Already they were come to thy banks, Asopus, and the Boeotian streams.") Several of the early commentators take the reference to be precise and to mean "before I reached this point in my poem," but it is possible to understand it to mean simply "before I began to write the Thebaid." In *Purg*. XVIII, 91 Dante refers to two rivers of Thebes.

89. *ebb' io battesmo*: Cf. *Inf*. IV, 35-36: "battesmo, / ch'è porta de la fede che tu credi."

90. *chiuso cristian*: Cf. "occultus" as used of Joseph of Arimathea in Ioan. 19:38: "Post haec autem rogavit Pilatum Ioseph ab Arimathaea (eo quod esset discipulus Iesu, occultus autem propter metum Iudaeorum), ut tolleret corpus Iesu. Et permisit Pilatus. Venit ergo, et tulit corpus Iesu." ("Now after these things Joseph of Arimathea, because he was a disciple of Jesus [although for fear of the Jews a secret one], besought Pilate that he might take away the body of Jesus. And Pilate gave permission. He came, therefore, and took away the body of Jesus.") *fu'mi*: An excellent example of the so-called pleonastic reflexive in its function of setting off the subject. Cf. *Inf*. VII, 94, and *passim*.

92. *tepidezza*: Subject of "fé" (*fece*) in the following verse. *il quarto cerchio*: The fourth circle of Purgatory, where

the slothful run day and night. Statius had to speed about there for more than four centuries ("il quarto centesmo"), literally, until the fourth hundredth year had passed; cf. *Par.* IX, 40.

95. *quanto bene io dico*: "All the good I speak of," i.e., the true way of the Christian faith.

96. *mentre che del salire avem soverchio*: "While we have yet to climb," i.e., before we come to the end of the stairway we are now ascending. *avem = abbiamo.*

97. *dov' è Terrenzio nostro antico*: The theme of "ubi sunt" begins here with all the melancholy that can attach to it. *Terrenzio*: Terence (Publius Terentius Afer), celebrated Roman comic poet, was born at Carthage *ca.* 195 B.C. and died in Greece in 159 B.C. Dante shows no direct acquaintance with the works of Terence. For a quotation from his *Eunuchus*, undoubtedly taken at second hand from Cicero's *De amicitia*, see *Inf.* XVIII, 133-35.

98. *Cecilio*: Caecilius Statius, Roman comic poet, contemporary of Ennius and immediate predecessor of Terence. Dante may have got the name of Caecilius from Horace, by whom he is twice mentioned in his lists of Roman poets. See Horace, *Epistles* II, i, 57-59:

> dicitur . . .
> Plautus ad exemplar Siculi properare Epicharmi,
> vincere Caecilius gravitate, Terentius arte.

'Tis said . . . Plautus hurries along like his model, Epicharmus of Sicily. Caecilius wins the prize for dignity, Terence for art.

In *Ars poetica* (vss. 53-55) Horace writes:

> . . . quid autem
> Caecilio Plautoque dabit Romanus ademptum
> Vergilio Varioque? . . .

Why indeed shall Romans grant this licence to Caecilius and Plautus, and refuse it to Virgil and Varius?

Caecilius is also mentioned, together with Plautus and "Terentius vester," by Augustine in the *De civitate Dei* (II, 12), with which Dante was familiar.

Plauto: Plautus (Titus Maccius Plautus), the Roman comic playwright, was born at Sarsina in Umbria *ca.* 250 B.C. and died in 184 B.C. Dante does not appear to have had any direct acquaintance with his writings, but he might have known of him through various sources, as in the list of Roman poets given by Horace and the passage in the *De civitate Dei* of Augustine referred to above.

Varro: Lucius Varius Rufus, Roman poet of the Augustan age, intimate friend of both Virgil and Horace and one of the editors of the *Aeneid* after the death of the author. He wrote a tragedy on the story of Thyestes, which was acted at the games held to celebrate the victory of Actium (31 B.C.) and was highly praised by Quintilian as worthy of comparison with the Greek tragedies. Subsequently he wrote epics on the death of Julius Caesar and on the achievements of Agrippa, of the former of which a few fragments have been preserved; Virgil is said to have introduced lines from it into the *Aeneid*. Varius is mentioned by Horace four times, each time in conjunction with Virgil (*Satires* I, vi, 55; x, 44-45; *Epistles* II, i, 247; *Ars poetica*, vss. 54-55) and once also in conjunction with Caecilius and Plautus (*Ars poetica*, vss. 53-55). He is also mentioned by Virgil himself (*Eclog.* IX, 35). On the problem in general, see U. Bosco (1942), pp. 143-47. *Varro*, for *Varus* or *Varius*, is a popular form, with a doubling of the *r* comparable to that in *Terrenzio*.

99. *in qual vico*: "In what circle," what circle of Hell. *Vico* literally means "street" (cf. *Par.* X, 137).

100. *Persio*: Persius (Aulus Persius Flaccus), Roman satirist, lived from A.D. 34 to A.D. 62. Dante was apparently not familiar with his writings. Brunetto Latini twice quotes him in his *Tresor* (II, lxxiv, 5 and lxxxii, 4) but both times at second hand.

101-2. *quel Greco . . . mai*: Homer. See *Inf.* IV, 86-88, where Dante refers to Homer as "poeta sovrano."

102. *lattar* = *lattarono*. Cf. "nutrice," vs. 105.

103. *nel primo cinghio*: Limbo.   *carcere cieco*: Cf. *Inf.* X, 58-59, and *Aen.* VI, 734.

104. *del monte*: Parnassus, mentioned in vs. 65.

105. *le nutrice nostre*: The Muses.   *seco = con sè*.

106. *Euripide*: Euripides, Greek playwright, was probably born in 485 B.C.; he died in 406. Eighteen of his tragedies in more or less complete form and fragments of about sixty others are extant.   *Antifonte*: Antiphon, Greek tragic poet mentioned by Aristotle in *Rhet.* II, 2, 1379[b]; 6, 1385[a]; 23, 1399[b]. Plutarch includes him among the greatest of the tragic authors. Only fragments of three tragedies have been preserved.

107. *Simonide*: Simonides, Greek lyric poet who lived from *ca.* 556 B.C. to 467 B.C. Dante refers to him in *Conv.* IV, xiii, 8, as being cited by Aristotle, but this is in fact not the case; see E. Moore (1896), p. 105.   *Agatone*: Agathon, Greek tragic poet, was born *ca.* 448 B.C. and died *ca.* 402. None of his works has come down to us. Dante refers to him in *De mon.* III, vi, 7.

108. *lauro*: These poets were crowned with the laurel. Statius has spoken of his own crown (*Purg.* XXI, 90) as being of myrtle.   *ornar = ornarono*.

109. *si veggion = si vedono*.   *de le genti tue*: I.e., those who are characters in Statius' two poems. The first six mentioned are found in the *Thebaid*, the last two in the *Achilleid*. Obviously Dante takes them all to be real historical persons.

110. *Antigone*: Antigone, daughter of Oedipus and Jocasta.   *Deifile*: Pronounced *Deìfile*. Deipyle was the daughter of Adrastus, king of Argos, and sister of Argia.   *Argia*: Wife of Polynices of Thebes, from whom she received the fatal necklace of Harmonia, with which Eriphyle was bribed to betray the hiding-place of her husband, Amphiaraus (see *Purg.* XII, 50-51). She and her sister Deipyle are mentioned as examples of modesty in *Conv.* IV, xxv, 8, where Dante refers to Statius, *Theb.* I, 527-39.

111. *Ismene*: Ismene, daughter of Oedipus and Jocasta. She is here spoken of as being "sad still as she was" on account of the terrible tragedies she witnessed—the violent death of her betrothed, the blinding of her father, Oedipus, by his own hand, the suicide of her mother, Jocasta, the deaths at each other's hands of her brothers, Eteocles and Polynices, and the total ruin and downfall of her father's kingdom.

112. *Védeisi = vi si vede.   quella che mostrò Langia*: Hypsipyle, daughter of Thoas, king of Lemnos (she is mentioned in *Inf.* XVIII, 92). Langia was a fountain near Nemea in the Peloponnesus, to which Hypsipyle conducted Adrastus and his companions; during her absence on this errand her charge, Archemorus, son of Lycurgus, king of Nemea, whom she had laid on the grass, was attacked and slain by a serpent, whereupon Lycurgus determined to put her to death, but was prevented by the opportune arrival of her two sons.

113. *èvvi = vi è.   la figlia di Tiresia*: The only daughter of Tiresias who is mentioned in the *Thebaid*, Manto, was placed by Dante among the soothsayers in the fourth *bolgia* of the eighth circle of Hell, but by an oversight the poet here mentions her as being among those who are in Limbo. Many attempts have been made to exculpate Dante from this momentary nodding, which is unique in the entire poem, in fact, but none has proved persuasive.   *Teti*: Thetis, one of the Nereids, daughter of Nereus and Doris, was wedded to Peleus, by whom she became the mother of Achilles and as such is frequently mentioned in the *Achilleid*. Dante mentions her in *Purg.* IX, 37.

114. *e con le suore sue Deidamia*: Deidamia, mentioned by Dante in *Inf.* XXVI, 62, was the daughter of Lycomedes, king of Skyros, with whom Thetis left her son Achilles. Achilles remained hidden, dressed like a woman, among the several daughters of Lycomedes, until Ulysses persuaded him to accompany him to Troy.   *suore = sorelle.*

115. *Tacevansi ambedue già li poeti*: Recently (vs. 96) Statius seemed to indicate that their talk in this vein might last only as long as they were climbing the stairs.   *Tacevansi = si tacevano.*

116. *di novo*: "Now," i.e., they *begin* only now to look around them. For a somewhat different use of the phrase, see *Purg.* XVIII, 27, and n. to *Purg.* XVIII, 26-27. In the present context the phrase clearly signifies "now," "only now," and was so used in early Italian and in scholastic Latin. Also see Boccaccio, *Decam.* X, 8 (vol. II, p. 285, l. 36 - p. 286, l. 1), where *ora* is even used with *di novo*: "Non usa ora la fortuna di nuovo varie vie ed istrumenti nuovi a recare le cose agli effetti diterminati." ("Fortune is not now for the first time using different paths and new instruments to bring things to their determined effects.")

117. *da pareti*: For *parete* in the masculine, see *Purg.* XIX, 48.

118–19. *e già le quattro ancelle . . . dietro*: Cf. *Purg.* XII, 80-81, and see the note to those verses. "Le quattro ancelle" ("the four handmaids") here means "quattro delle ancelle" ("four of the handmaids"). On the use of the article with a numeral in such cases, cf. *Inf.* XXV, 33, and *Purg.* XV, 80.

119–20. *e la quinta . . . corno*: The fifth handmaid of the Sun's chariot is directing its course, that is, it is now between 10:00 and 11:00 A.M. The *temo* is the chariot pole, which in a morning hour points upward toward the meridian and is now quite "blazing."

121–23. *Io credo ch'a lo stremo . . . solemo*: Once again (here and through the following tercet) the point is made that the proper direction for circling the mountain is counterclockwise. Virgil should indeed know this by now!

121. *stremo*: The outer edge of the terrace. If they turn their right shoulders to this, they will be going round to the right.

122. *ne = ci.*

123. *solemo* = *sogliamo.*

125. *con men sospetto*: "With less hesitation" or doubt as to whether they were taking the right way.

126. *per l'assentir*: Because Statius has also turned to the right, and purged and liberated as he is, he can hardly fail to go in the proper direction.

129. *ch'a poetar mi davano intelletto*: The discourse of the two ancient poets inspires and instructs Dante in the art of poetry, gives him understanding of it. Cf. Ps. 118[119]:130: "Declaratio sermonum tuorum illuminat, et intellectum dat parvulis." ("The revelation of your words sheds light, giving understanding to the simple.")

131. *in mezza strada*: Porena notes that this is a Latinizing construction for "in the middle of the road." Cf. *Inf.* XIV, 94; *Purg.* XIX, 20.

132. *con pomi*: "With fruits." Cf. *Inf.* XIII, 6; XVI, 61.

133–34. *e come abete . . . ramo*: Strange as it is to imagine, the tree is, as it were, turned upside down. The symbolic meaning of this will become clear.

135. *perché persona sù non vada*: We are to conceive that the tree would be harder to climb for being so turned. This is perhaps not literally true, but the symbolic injunction "not to climb" is clear.

136. *Dal lato onde 'l cammin nostro era chiuso*: On the inner side, bounded by the wall of the terrace.   *chiuso*: "Closed."

137–38. *cadea de l'alta roccia . . . suso*: The "liquor" falls from the rock wall down over the leaves. The construction "per . . . suso" is essentially the same as *su per*, as in *Inf.* IX, 64; XIX, 29. See again in *Purg.* XXIII, 69: "che si distende su per sua verdura."

139. *s'appressaro* = *s'appressarono.*

140. *una voce*: The origin of this voice remains as mysterious as that of those other voices in the circle of envy (*Purg.* XIII, 28-36), even though Dante peers intently up into its branches to see who might be speaking thus (see *Purg.* XXIII, 1-3).

141. *caro = carestia*. The voice would say this, of course, to any spirit that must approach to pick the fruit.

142-44. *Più pensava Maria . . . bocca*: Since this will prove to be the circle of gluttony, Mary is here given as an example of temperance, the opposing virtue. Cf. Conrad of Saxony, *Speculum beatae Mariae Virginis* IV (p. 45): "Maria contra gulam *temperatissima* per sobrietatem." ("Mary by her austerity is most temperate against gluttony.")

143. *le nozze*: At the marriage feast of Cana. Cf. *Purg.* XIII, 29, where Dante also uses this example. There it shows the charity of Mary, here her temperance.

144. *ch'or per voi risponde*: Benvenuto comments: "Quae bucca nunc orat ad Deum pro nobis." ("And this mouth now prays to God for us.")

145-46. *E le Romane antiche . . . d'acqua*: Thomas Aquinas, *Summa theol.* II-II, q. 149, a. 4, resp., quoting Valerius Maximus, says: "Mulieres apud Romanos antiquitus non bibebant vinum." ("Among the ancient Romans women drank no wine.") Valerius Maximus (*Fact. dict. memor.* II, 1, 5) says: "Vini usus olim Romanis feminis ignotus fuit, ne scilicet in aliquod dedecus prolaberentur." ("At one time it was unheard of for a woman to drink wine among the Romans, lest by it she chance to do something undignified.") See Aulus Gellius, *Attic Nights* X, xxiii, 1-5.

146. *Daniello*: See Dan. 1:3-20, especially vs. 8: "Proposuit autem Daniel in corde suo ne pollueretur de mensa regis neque de vino potus eius, et rogavit eunuchorum praepositum ne contaminaretur." ("But Daniel purposed in his heart that he would not be defiled with the king's table nor with the wine which he drank: and he requested the master

of the eunuchs that he might not be defiled.") Also note vs. 17: "Pueris autem his dedit Deus scientiam et disciplinam in omni libro et sapientia, Danieli autem intelligentiam omnium visionum et somniorum." ("And to these children God gave knowledge and understanding in every book and wisdom: but to Daniel the understanding *also* of all visions and dreams.")

148–50. *Lo secol primo . . . ruscello*: The Golden Age, or age of Saturn (see vs. 71: "primo tempo umano"). Cf. Ovid, *Metam.* I, 89-112 and Boethius, *Consol. philos.* II, v, vss. 1-12:

> Felix nimium prior aetas
> Contenta fidelibus arvis
> Nec inerti perdita luxu,
> Facili quae sera solebat
> Ieiunia solvere glande.
> Non Bacchica munera norant
> Liquido confundere melle
> Nec lucida vellera Serum
> Tyrio miscere veneno.
> Somnos dabat herba salubres,
> Potum quoque lubricus amnis,
> Umbras altissima pinus.

> Too much the former age was blest,
> When fields their pleaséd owners failéd not,
>   Who, with no slothful lust opprest,
> Broke their long fasts with acorns eas'ly got.
>   No wine with honey mixéd was,
> Nor did they silk in purple colours steep;
>   They slept upon the wholesome grass,
> And their cool drink did fetch from rivers deep.
>   The pines did hide them with their shade . . .

148. *quant' oro fu bello* = *fu bello quanto oro* [*è bello*].

150. *nettare*: Pronounced *nèttare*. Cf. *Purg.* XXVIII, 144.
nettare con sete ogne ruscello: I.e., made every streamlet taste like nectar. Cf. "nettare" in *Purg.* XXVIII, 144.

151–52. *Mele e locuste furon le vivande . . . diserto*: Compare Matt. 3:4: "Ipse autem Ioannes habebat vestimentum de pilis camelorum et zonam pelliceam circa lumbos suos; esca autem eius erat locustae et mel sylvestre." ("But John himself had a garment of camel's hair and a leathern girdle about his loins, and his food was locusts and wild honey.")

152. *nodriro = nutrirono.*

153–54. *glorioso e tanto grande . . . aperto*: Cf. Matt. 11:11: "Amen dico vobis, non surrexit inter natos mulierum maior Ioanne Baptista." ("Amen I say to you, among those born of women there has not risen a greater than John the Baptist.") Cf. Luc. 1:15 or, even better, Luc. 7:28.

154. *per = da.*   *aperto*: "Revealed."

CANTO XXIII

2–3. *sì come far suole chi . . . perde*: The *Ottimo Commento* elaborates: "Siccome fanno coloro, che con loro arco o saeppolo vanno perdendo tempo a diletto dietro alli uccellini, che per ferirli li vanno agguatando tra foglie e foglie." ("As those do who go around with their bow or arrow losing time running after birds and peering in among the leaves, waiting for a chance to shoot them.") Dante's judgment on the hunting of birds—and perhaps by implication on all other sports—as a waste of time is evident enough. Bird-hunting was a popular sport of the aristocracy in the Middle Ages.

4. *lo più che padre*: Virgil.   *Figliuole*: From the Latin vocative *filiole*, "little son." For other examples of the use of this form, see E. G. Parodi (1957), p. 248.

5. *vienne*: The imperative *vieni* + the adverb *ne* ("on," "along").   *oramai*: I.e., now that our allotted time is running out, as he then goes on to say.   *'l tempo che n'è imposto*: Cf. a similar indication in *Inf.* XXIX, 10-12, that the journey through Hell must be completed within a definite time; also see *Par.* XXII, 124. These are all signals of the end and come in the next-to-last circle of each of the three realms.   *n' = ne (ci)*.

8. *savi*: The two ancient poets. Cf. *Inf.* IV, 110.   *sìe* = *così*. For the added *e* (as in "udìe" and "parturìe" in rhyme in vss. 10 and 12) see *Purg.* IV, 47.

11. *Labia mea, Domine*: These words are from the Miserere (Ps. 50[51]), which souls in Antepurgatory were singing (*Purg.* V, 24). Here, as in many other instances, Dante expects the reader to know the verse and recall it all and thus come, in this case, to the words that speak of praising God (Ps. 50:17[51:15]): "Domine, labia mea aperies; et os meum annuntiabit laudem tuam." ("O Lord, open my lips, and my mouth shall proclaim your praise.") The *contrapasso* aspect of the punishment that can already be glimpsed will later become evident.

12. *diletto e doglia*: The song gives pleasure, the weeping causes compassionate grief. Cf. vs. 10.

13. *che è quel ch'i' odo?* Dante and Virgil are facing ahead and so away from the crowd of souls who approach from behind; hence Dante does not see them yet.

14–15. *Ombre che vanno . . . nodo*: The "forse" should be understood as applying to the whole statement: "Forse ombre che . . ."

15. *nodo*: Cf. *Purg.* XVI, 24: "d'iracundia van solvendo il nodo."

16. *i peregrin pensosi*: Compare *Vita nuova* XL, 9, where Dante writes:

> Deh peregrini che pensosi andate,
> forse di cosa che non v'è presente,
> venite voi da sì lontana gente,
> com'a la vista voi ne dimostrate . . . ?

Ah ye pilgrims, that go lost in thought, perchance of a thing that is not present to you, come ye from folk so far away as by your aspect ye show forth?

In *Purg.* VIII, 4-6, Dante speaks of the "new pilgrim" whose thoughts turn homeward. These souls are "thoughtful" in a similar way, as they seek to purge themselves (to "loose the knot") that they may one day proceed to their heavenly home. Porena notes that "la similitudine è di quelle che vanno oltre i loro limiti puramente formali." ("The similarity [between the souls and pilgrims] is of the kind that goes beyond purely formal limits.") He continues: "Quelle anime ricordano i pellegrini anche perchè alternano canti e pause; e, come i pellegrini, anche nel silenzio delle pause meditano." ("Those souls also bring pilgrims to mind because they alternate songs with pauses and, like pilgrims, meditate even in the silence of the pauses.")

17. *giugnendo* = *raggiungendo*. For *giungere* in this sense, see *Inf.* VIII, 18.   *nota*: "Known."

18. *si volgono ad essa*: "Turn toward them." See n. to *Purg.* XXI, 14.   *restanno* = *ristanno*.

19. *di retro a noi*: Note the retrospective focus on Statius in *Purg.* XXI as he comes up behind Virgil and Dante before he is actually seen by them (see n. to *Purg.* XXI, 10-13).   *mota* = *mossa*, "moved," i.e., "moving," "walking."

20. *ci ammirava*: The souls, as we learn later (vss. 113-14), are marveling that Dante casts a shadow. The sun is now high enough for this, as apparently it was not earlier in the morning, when Statius first saw Dante (see *Purg.* XXI, 19-20). See M. A. Orr (1956), p. 259, who notes a special difficulty here.

21. *tacita*: See Porena's comment in the n. to vs. 16, on the custom of pilgrims in this regard.   *devota*: The souls remain lost in thought and praise God in their minds, even though they are not singing the verse now, and look with wonder toward Dante.

22-24. *Ne li occhi . . . s'informava*: Compare the description of Famine in the passage quoted from Ovid in the n. to vs. 26.

26. *Erisittone*: Erysichthon was the son of the Thessalian King Triopas. Having cut down trees in a grove sacred to

Ceres, he was afflicted by the goddess with a fearful hunger, which drove him finally to devour his own flesh. Dante probably got the story from Ovid, *Metam.* VIII, 738-878. In *Metam.* VIII, 799-806 Ovid affords the following description of Famine:

> quaesitamque Famem lapidoso vidit in agro
> unguibus et raras vellentem dentibus herbas.
> hirtus erat crinis, cava lumina, pallor in ore,
> labra incana situ, scabrae rubigine fauces,
> dura cutis, per quam spectari viscera possent;
> ossa sub incurvis exstabant arida lumbis,
> ventris erat pro ventre locus; pendere putares
> pectus et a spinae tantummodo crate teneri.

Seeking out Famine, she saw her in a stony field, plucking with nails and teeth at the scanty herbage. Her hair hung in matted locks, her eyes were sunken, her face ghastly pale; her lips were wan and foul, her throat rough with scurf; her skin was hard and dry so that the entrails could be seen through it; her skinny hip-bones bulged out beneath her hollow loins, and her belly was but a belly's place; her breast seemed to be hanging free and just to be held by the framework of the spine.

Ovid ends the tale of Erysichthon (*Metam.* VIII, 875-78):

> vis tamen illa mali postquam consumpserat omnem
> materiam dederatque gravi nova pabula morbo,
> ipse suos artus lacero divellere morsu
> coepit et infelix minuendo corpus alebat.

At last, when the strength of the plague had consumed all these provisions, and but added to his fatal malady, the wretched man began to tear his own flesh with his greedy teeth and, by consuming his own body, fed himself.

fatto secco: "Dried up."

28–30. *Ecco la gente . . . becco*: According to Flavius Josephus (*The Jewish War* VI, 201-13), during the siege of Jerusalem by Titus a certain Jewess named Mary was driven by famine to kill and eat her own infant son. The story is told

on the authority of Josephus by John of Salisbury in the
Policraticus (II, 6) and by Vincent of Beauvais in the *Speculum historiale* (X, 5). Benvenuto's account, which is evidently condensed from one of these, is as follows:

Mulier quaedam nobilis genere et divitiis nomine Maria
inventa est in alia multitudine quae confluxerat ad urbem
tempore obsidionis . . . cuius facultates tyranni
primo invaserant, deinde per momenta satellites latronum
reliquias rapiebant, propter quod mulier indignatione
et insania accensa saepe illos provocabat
maledictis ad interficiendum se; sed cum nullus vel ira
vel miseria mactaret illam, nec aliqua via posset quaerere
victum, fame et ira, pessimis consultoribus, instigante,
armatur contra iura naturae. Nam assumpto
infantulo quem lactabat dicere coepit: infelicis matris
infelicior fili: in bello, fame, rapina latronum cui te
reservabo? Nam si vita sperari possit, iugo romanae
servitutis servamur; sed iam nunc ipsam servitutem
fames praevenit, et praedones peiores fame et servitute
nos premunt. Veni ergo, mi fili, esto matri cibus, praedonibus
furor, saeculis fabula, quae sola deficiebat
miseriis iudaeorum. Et cum haec dixisset, simul filium
iugulavit, et medium assavit, et reliquum reservavit.
Et ecce praedones incitati odore carnis, mortem minantes
nisi cibum quem senserant daret. Tunc illa infuriata
dixit: certe partem optimam reservavi; et continuo detexit
membra infantis; sed illi quamvis crudeles territi
sunt nimis, nec potuerunt facere verbum, vincente
naturali pietate. Illa vero vultu crudeli ferocior latronibus,
dixit: filius meus est, meus partus, meum peccatum,
comedite; nam et ego prior comedi quae genui:
nolite fieri misericordiores matre, aut foemina molliores.
Illi trementes recesserunt, hunc solum miserae matri
relinquentes cibum.

Among the crowd that flocked to the city at the time of
the siege there was a certain noble and wealthy woman
named Mary . . . whose property the tyrants first attacked;
then gradually their underlings stole the rest of

her resources. As a result, the woman, flying into an indignant rage and driven almost mad, taunted them with curses to provoke them to kill her; yet when no one would, either through anger or hatred, lay a hand on her, and since she could not manage to live any other way, hunger and anger—poor advisers indeed—drove her to sin against nature itself. She took into her arms the child she was nursing and said: "You pitiful child of an unhappy mother, why should I preserve you for the toils of war and famine and the wicked hands of brigands to destroy you? If there were any hope of life for you, it would be no more than the yoke of Roman slavery; and now already hunger precedes slavery, and now brigands that are worse than hunger and slavery encompass you. So, my son, come, be food for your mother, bring furor to these bandits, become a legend for future ages, as suffering the only woe that was spared the Jews." And, when she had said this, she strangled the child and with her teeth bit into his body and put it aside. The soldiers, excited by the odor of meat, threatened her with death unless she gave them some of the food they had smelled. In a voice filled with madness she screamed at them: "Of course, I have kept the better part for myself," and she uncovered the body of the child before them. Depraved as they were, they were horrified at the sight, nor could they utter a word, silenced by natural pity. She, with a look on her face far crueler than any murderer, said to them: "He is my son, the fruit of my womb, my sin; come, eat some of him, for I have already eaten, I who gave birth to him. Surely you are not going to be more merciful than a mother, softer than a woman!" But they withdrew in horror, leaving the food solely for the unhappy mother.

In using Erysichthon and Mary as two examples of fearful hunger Dante has followed his familiar pattern of alternating classical and non-classical incidents.

30. *diè = diede.   diè di becco*: As if she were a vulture or some carrion-eating bird.

31. *Parean l'occhiaie anella sanza gemme*: See Shakespeare, *King Lear*, Act V, sc. 3, ll. 188-90:

> ... and in this habit
> Met I my father with his bleeding rings,
> Their precious stones new lost ....

32-33. *chi nel viso ... l'emme*: There was a belief popular in Dante's time that the word *omo* (i.e., *homo*, "man") could be seen in a human face, the eyes forming the two *o*'s, and the nose and outline of the eye sockets forming the *m*; it was also believed that *dei* could be seen there. (See Fig. 3.) This belief is witnessed by a reference to it in a sermon

Figure 3. A typical *m* in uncial script and the face of man

of a Brother Berthold, a Franciscan friar of Regensburg in the thirteenth century quoted by Longfellow as follows:

Now behold, ye blessed children of God, the Almighty has created you soul and body. And he has written it under your eyes and on your faces, that you are created in his likeness. He has written it upon your very faces with ornamented letters. With great diligence are they embellished and ornamented. This your learned men will understand, but the unlearned may not understand it. The two eyes are two *o*'s. The *h* is properly no letter; it only helps the others; so that *homo* with an *h* means Man. Likewise the brows arched above and the nose down between them are an *m*, beautiful with three strokes. So is the ear a *d*, beautifully rounded and ornamented. So are the nostrils beautifully formed like a Greek *ε*, beautifully rounded and ornamented. So is the mouth an *i*, beautifully adorned and ornamented. Now behold, ye good Christian people, how skilfully he has adorned you with these six letters, to show that ye

are his own, and that he has created you! Now read me
an *o* and an *m* and another *o* together; that spells *homo*.
Then read me a *d* and an *e* and an *i* together; that spells
dei. *Homo dei*, man of God, man of God!

33. *avria = avrebbe.*   *l'emme*: The image is precise only
if we think of an uncial *m*, with two *o*'s set in it for the eyes.

34-36. *Chi crederebbe . . . como*: The word order here
should be construed: "Chi, non sappiendo como, crede-
rebbe . . . ."

35. *governasse*: Cf. "governo" in *Inf*. XXVII, 47 and *Purg*.
V, 108, and see *Vita nuova* IV, 2, as well as IV, 3, where
the word is rephrased as *distrutto*.

36. *quel*: I.e., *odore.*   *sappiendo = sapendo.*   *como
= come.*

37. *era = ero.*   *che = che cosa.*

39. *squama*: The *scabbie* referred to in vss. 49 and 58, a
sign of extreme starvation.

40. *ed ecco*: See n. to *Inf*. XXI, 7.   *del = dal* (cf. *Inf*.
XXI, 47).

41. *fiso = fisamente.*

42. *Qual grazia m'è questa?* I.e., "qual grazia è questa per
me."

45. *conquiso*: Past participle of *conquidere*. Cf. *Rime*
LXXI, 5-11, where Dante writes of a lady who lies dead:

> Ben ha le sue sembianze sì cambiate,
> e la figura sua mi par sì spenta,
> ch'al mio parere ella non rappresenta
> quella che fa parer l'altre beate.
>
> Se nostra donna conoscer non poi,
> ch'è sì conquisa, non mi par gran fatto,
> però che quel medesmo avvenne a noi.

Truly hath she so changed a semblance, and to me her form appeareth so spent, that to my seeming she resembleth not her who maketh the others appear blest.

If thou canst not recognise our lady that is so stricken, 'tis no great marvel methinks, for that very same did hap to us.

46. *raccese* = *riaccese*.

47. *a la*: Respecting, with regard to.   *cangiata* = *cambiata*.   *labbia*: "Face" (see *Inf.* VII, 7; XIV, 67).

48. *Forese*: Forese Donati, who was nicknamed Bicci Novello, was a contemporary and friend of Dante. He died on July 28, 1296. His friendship with Dante is attested not only by references in the *Divine Comedy*, but also by the fact that they engaged in a poetical correspondence or *tenzone* (written probably between 1293 and 1296), consisting of six sonnets, *Rime* LXXIII-LXXVIII (three addressed by Dante to Forese, and three of his in reply), in which they both indulged in personalities, not always, apparently, good-naturedly.

In two of these sonnets Dante makes direct allusion to Forese's gluttonous propensities. One (*Rime* LXXVII) begins:

> Bicci novel, figliuol di non so cui,
> s'i' non ne domandasse monna Tessa,
> giù per la gola tanta roba hai messa,
> ch'a forza ti convien torre l'altrui.

Young Bicci, son of I don't know who (short of asking my lady Tessa), you've stuffed so much down your gorge that you're driven to take from others.

In another (*Rime* LXXIII) he commiserates with Forese's wife on account of her spouse's irregular habits:

> Chi udisse tossir la mal fatata
> moglie di Bicci vocato Forese,
> potrebbe dir ch'ell'ha forse vernata
> ove si fa 'l cristallo in quel paese.
> Di mezzo agosto la truovi infreddata;
> or sappi che de' far d'ogni altro mese!

E non le val perchè dorma calzata,
merzè del copertoio c'ha cortonese.
La tosse, 'l freddo e l'altra mala voglia
no l'addovien per omor ch'abbia vecchi
ma per difetto ch'ella sente al nido.
Piange la madre, c'ha più d'una doglia,
dicendo: "Lassa, che per fichi secchi
messa l'avre' 'n casa del conte Guido!"

Anyone who heard the coughing of the luckless wife of Bicci (called Forese) might say that maybe she'd passed the winter in the land where crystal is made. You'll find her frozen in mid-August—so guess how she must fare in any other month! And it's no use her keeping her stockings on—the cover is too short. . . .

The coughing and cold and other troubles—these don't come to her from ageing humours, but from the lack she feels in the nest. Her mother, who has more than one affliction, weeps saying: "Alas, for dried figs I could have married her to Count Guido!"

Forese retorted by making reflections upon Dante's father and implying, apparently, that the latter was a coward. On these sonnets, see M. Barbi (1956, 1932); see also the commentary in *Rime*, edited by G. Contini (1965), pp. 81-93.

The *Anonimo fiorentino*, quoting *Rime* LXXV, says of Forese:

Questa anima . . . si fu Forese fratello di messere Corso Donati da Firenze, il quale fu molto corrotto nel vizio della gola, et nella prima vita fu molto dimestico dell'Auttore, per la qual dimestichezza egli fece festa a Dante: et molti sonetti et cose in rima scrisse l'uno all'altro; et fra gli altri l'Auttore, riprendendolo di questo vizio della gola, gli scrisse uno Sonetto in questa forma:

Ben ti faranno il nodo Salomone,
Bicci novello, i petti delle starne,
Ma peggio fia la lonza del castrone,
Chè 'l cuojo farà vendetta della carne etc.

Questo Forese Donati fu chiamato per sopra nome Bicci.

This soul . . . was Forese, brother of Messer Corso Donati of Florence. Forese was steeped in the vice of gluttony. In the former life he and Dante had been very intimate, and that is the reason he greets Dante so warmly. They wrote many sonnets and rhymes to each other. In one of these sonnets, in which he reprimands him for his vice of gluttony, Dante writes: "Partridge breasts, young Bicci, will truss you in Solomon's knot all right! But loins of mutton will be still worse for you, for the skin will take revenge for the flesh!" This Forese Donati was called by the nickname Bicci.

Benvenuto says of him:

Iste fuit quidam concivis suus, nomine Foresius, natione florentinus, genere nobilis, frater famosi militis Cursii de Donatis, amicus et affinis nostri poetae, cum quo vixerat ad tempus familiariter. Et quia noverat eum multum laborasse vitio gulae, licet esset aliter vir bonus, ideo introducit eum hic ita maceratum.

This man was a fellow-citizen of his [Dante's] by the name of Forese, Florentine by birth and noble, brother of the famous soldier Corso Donati, and he was the familiar friend of our poet, with whom he lived in friendly relations for a time. And because he [Dante] knew him to be much given to the vice of gluttony, though otherwise a good man, he therefore introduces him here as being thus punished.

49. *contendere*: "Pay attention to," "attend to." See Scartazzini-Vandelli for the following quotation from Fra Giordano: "Le donne amministravano le necessitadi degli Apostoli, i quali non poteano contendere alle cose mondane." ("The women took care of the needs of the apostles, who could not attend to worldly matters.")

52. *il ver di te*: Your true story, i.e., how you have come here alive. Forese can see that Dante casts a shadow (see vss. 112-14).

54. *favelle* = *favelli*.

55. *La faccia tua*: Dante continues to gaze intently into Forese's face.   *ch'io lagrimai già morta*: Dante had wept over the face of his dead friend.

56. *non minor doglia*: Cf. *Inf.* XVI, 52.

57. *torta*: Literally, "twisted," i.e., disfigured by starvation.

58. *Però = perciò.   mi dì = dimmi.   che = che cosa.*
     sfoglia: "Peels off" (referring to the scab flaking off), or perhaps "strips," as of leaves.

61. *De l'etterno = da l'etterno.   consiglio*: God's will and counsel.

62–63. *ne la pianta rimasa dietro*: What is said of this tree applies to the other (or perhaps there is more than one other) on this terrace. See *Purg.* XXIV, 106-7.

63. *m'assottiglio*: "I grow thin."

64. *esta = questa.   piangendo canta*: Cf. vs. 10.

66. *si rifà santa*: "Make themselves holy again." They are but souls now and as such make themselves pure as God created them. See Dante, *Conv.* IV, xxviii, 2: "Ella ritorna a Dio, sì come a quello porto onde ella si partio quando venne ad intrare nel mare di questa vita." ("She [the noble soul] returns to God, as to that port whence she departed when she came to enter upon the sea of this life.")

67. *n'accende = ci accende.*

68. *del pomo*: From the fruit tree. Cf. *Purg.* XXIV, 104.
     sprazzo: Cf. *Purg.* XXII, 137-38.

69. *su per*: See n. to *Purg.* XXII, 137-38.

70. *spazzo*: "Floor." Cf. *Inf.* XIV, 13.

71. *si rinfresca*: "Renews itself." Each time the souls come to one of the trees (vs. 73) the torment is renewed.

72. *io dico pena, e dovria dir sollazzo*: Again the sweet-bitter motif that is first expressed in "piangere e cantar," vs.

10, and then repeated in vss. 64 and 86.   *dovria* = *dovrei*.

73. *quella voglia*: That same desire.   *a li alberi ci mena*: See *Purg.* XXIV, 106-11.

74. *che menò Cristo lieto a dire "Elì"*: Cf. Matt. 27:46: "Et circa horam nonam clamavit Iesus voce magna dicens: Eli, eli, lamma sabacthani? hoc est: Deus meus, Deus meus, ut quid dereliquisti me?" ("But about the ninth hour Jesus cried out with a loud voice, saying 'Eli, Eli, lema sabacthani,' that is, 'My God, my God, why hast thou forsaken me?'")

78. *cinqu' anni*: Less than four years have passed, in fact, since this is the spring of 1300 and Forese had died in July 1296. Five is merely a round number.

79-80. *la possa . . . di peccar più*: The power, the possibility, of sinning more. For *possa*, cf. *Purg.* V, 66.

80. *che*: Connects with "prima" of the preceding verse.

81. *del buon dolor ch'a Dio ne rimarita*: The wholesome grief of repentance that reconciles us with God. See *Purg.* V, 55-56.

82. *ancora*: Cf. *Inf.* XXXIII, 121.

83-84. *Io ti credea . . . ristora*: In Antepurgatory among the lethargic, who are destined to remain there for a period equal to that of their lives on earth (see *Purg.* IV, 130-34; XI, 127-32).

86. *lo dolce assenzo d'i martìri*: An effective restatement of the joy-in-suffering motif. See n. to vs. 72.

87. *Nella*: Possibly an abbreviation of Giovanella, diminutive of Giovanna. The early commentators tell us little about Nella beyond what may be gathered from Forese's own words. Benvenuto, who refers to Forese's wife as Anella, says:

> Sciendum [est] quod Foresius . . . habuit in vita unam uxorem suam, cui nomen fuit Anella, mulier quidem

sobria et pudica, quae temperanter vixit cum isto guloso, cui habebat semper praeparare delicata cibaria, in quo magis virtus eius enituit. Et sicut in vita numquam cessabat revocare eum ab errore suo, ita post mortem numquam cessavit orare pro eo.

It should be noted that Forese had a wife whose name was Anella, a quiet and chaste woman; she lived temperately with that glutton, for whom she had to prepare the most exquisite dishes, the more credit to her virtue. And, just as while he lived she sought to wean him from his vice, so after his death she prayed constantly for him.

con suo pianger dirotto: Her flood of tears.

88-89. *Con suoi prieghi . . . s'aspetta*: Nella's prayers on Forese's behalf have caused his stay in Antepurgatory to be shortened.

90. *li altri giri*: The lower circles of Purgatory proper.

92. *la vedovella mia*: The suffix *-ella* is one of endearment.

94. *la Barbagia*: A mountainous district in the central part of Sardinia (see C. S. Singleton, *Inferno Commentary*, Map 3, following p. 683), the inhabitants of which are said to have descended from a settlement of prisoners planted by the Vandals. They were proverbial in the Middle Ages, according to the early commentators, for the laxity of their morals and their loose living. Benvenuto says that the women were in the habit of exposing their breasts: "Pro calore et prava consuetudine vadunt indutae panno lineo albo, excollatae ita, ut ostendant pectus et ubera." ("Because of heat and indecent custom they go clothed in white linen dresses so low at the collar as to expose their breasts.") In Dante's time they formed a semi-savage independent tribe and refused to acknowledge the Pisan government. Benvenuto says they were a remnant left at the time when Sardinia was reconquered from the Saracens, which, from the mention of "saracine" (vs. 103), appears to have been Dante's view of their origin. See Fazio degli Uberti, *Dittamondo* III, xii, 55-63.

96. *la Barbagia dov' io la lasciai*: Florence.

97. *che vuo' tu ch'io dica?* Torraca notes that this form, which is still alive, is generally used to cut off a conversation in order to get to more important matters.

99. *cui*: Dative.

100. *in pergamo interdetto*: Torraca comments: "Quando il cardinale Latino vietò alle donne di portar vesti con la coda lunga, 'fece predicar questo per le chiese, e l'impose alle donne sotto precetto; e che nessun sacerdote le potesse assolvere se non obbedissero': Salimbene." ("When Cardinal Latino prohibited women from wearing dresses with a long train, 'he had this preached in the churches and had it imposed upon the women as an order, and no priest could absolve them if they disobeyed' [Salimbene].")

103. *fuor = furono*.

104. *cui*: Dative.

105. *o spiritali o altre discipline*: The *Ottimo Commento* notes: "E dice, che bisognerà non solamente il comandamento del Diocesano, ma ancora che il Comune faccia sua legge proibitiva." ("And he says that not only is the diocesan ruling necessary, but that the commune too must enact a prohibition.") Villani has several references (IX, 245; X, 11, 150) to sumptuary laws directed a few years later against what he calls (IX, 245) "i disordinati ornamenti delle donne di Firenze" ("the excessive adornments of the women of Florence"). In one of these (X, 150) the extravagant headdresses and girdles alluded to by Cacciaguida (*Par.* XV, 100-102) are specifically mentioned:

Nel detto anno [1330] . . . essendo le donne di Firenze molto trascorse in soperchi ornamenti di corone e ghirlande d'oro e d'argento, e di perle e pietre preziose, e reti e intrecciatoi di perle, e altri divisati ornamenti di testa di grande costo . . . fu sopra ciò provveduto . . . che niuna donna non potesse portare nulla corona nè ghirlanda nè d'oro nè d'ariento nè di perle nè di pietre nè di seta nè di niuna similitudine di corona nè di ghirlanda, eziandio di carta dipinta, nè rete nè trecciere di nulla spezie se non semplici . . . nè potere portare più di due anella in dito, nè nullo schaggiale nè cintura di più di dodici spranghe d'argento.

In that year [1330] . . . because the women of Florence had fallen into the habit of adorning themselves extravagantly with coronets and garlands of silver and gold, pearls and jewels, with nets and braids studded with pearls, and other very expensive ornaments devised for the head . . . it was ruled . . . that women could not wear a coronet or a garland of gold, silver, pearls, jewels, or silk, nor anything even resembling a coronet or garland, even of colored paper; nor could they wear nets or braids of any sort, unless they were very simple . . . nor could they wear more than two rings on their fingers, or any kind of belt or girdle that had more than twelve silver links.

106. *fosser certe = sapessero.*

107. *'l ciel*: The heavens in their turning. See *Purg.* XXIV, 88, where the turning of the heavens is the instrument of divine vengeance.   *veloce = velocemente.*   *loro*: Dative, "for them."   *ammanna*: Cf. *Purg.* XXIX, 49.

108. *già per urlare avrian le bocche aperte*: Porena comments: " 'Per urlare' è causale; quindi 'già urlerebbero con le bocche spalancate.' " (" 'Per urlare' is causal: 'they would already be yelling with their mouths wide open.' ") *avrian = avrebbero.*

109-11. *se l'antiveder . . . nanna*: In *Epist.* VI, 17, Dante writes:

Et si presaga mens mea non fallitur, sic signis veridicis sicut inexpugnabilibus argumentis instructa prenuntians, urbem diutino merore confectam in manus alienorum tradi finaliter, plurima vestri parte seu nece seu captivitate deperdita, perpessuri exilium pauci cum fletu cernetis.

And—if my presaging mind be not deceived, as it announceth that which it hath learned from truth-telling signs, and arguments that may not be gainsaid—your city, worn out with long-drawn sufferings, shall be given at last into the hands of the aliens, the greatest part of you scattered in death and captivity, while the few that are left to endure their exile shall look on and weep.

The letter was written in March 1311 to "the most infamous Florentines." Dante never saw the prophecy come true in either case, and just how the dire events to come were to fall upon the lascivious women of Florence in particular, as a just vengeance upon their loose ways, is not clear. Perhaps Forese was deceived in his "antiveder" after all. There is a distinct Old Testament flavor to the prophecy. Cf. Isa. 3:16-17:

Et dixit Dominus: Pro eo quod elevatae sunt filiae Sion, et ambulaverunt extento collo, et nutibus oculorum ibant et plaudebant, ambulabant pedibus suis et composito gradu incedebant; decalvabit Dominus verticem filiarum Sion, et Dominus crinem earum nudabit.

And the Lord said: Because the daughters of Sion are haughty, and have walked with stretched-out necks and wanton glances of their eyes, and made a noise as they walked with their feet, and moved in a set pace: The Lord will make bald the crown of the head of the daughters of Sion: and the Lord will discover their hair.

110-11. *prima fien triste . . . nanna*: Since the prophecy would seem to point to an event some fifteen years off, many commentators think the Guelph defeat at Montecatini on August 29, 1315, is intended, but it is not at all certain that the reference is to that.

110. *fien = saranno*.

111. *colui che*: "Colui che" is the subject of "impeli." The women will be sorrowful before he who is now (in 1300) consoled with a lullaby shall have hair on his cheeks, i.e., shall reach puberty.

112. *or*: I.e., now that I have satisfied you in your questions, be pleased to answer mine (vss. 52-53).

114. *là dove 'l sol veli*: The cause of their wonder when they first came up to Dante (vss. 20-21).

115. *a mente = a memoria.*

116. *qual fosti meco, e qual io teco fui*: I.e., the kind of life we two led together.

117. *fia = sarà.*

119. *l'altr' ier*: "The other day" in the sense of "a few days ago": five days, in fact.

119–20. *quando tonda . . . colui*: Cf. the reference to the full moon over the dark wood in *Inf.* XX, 127-29.

120. *vi*: The adverb "there."   *la suora di colui*: The sister of the Sun (Apollo) is the Moon (Diana). See *Purg.* XX, 130-32.

122. *d'i = dei.   veri morti*: The dead of Hell, who endure the "second death" (*Inf.* I, 117), are the "truly dead" in their spiritual death.

123. *che 'l seconda = che lo seconda.* Cf. *Purg.* XVI, 33.

125. *salendo e rigirando*: Climbing from terrace to terrace and going round part of a circle in each, hence the prefix *ri-*.

126. *che drizza voi che 'l mondo fece torti*: The mountain "straightens" their wills, which were made "crooked" in the world. See *Purg.* XXVII, 140, where Dante's own will is declared straight ("dritto") again.

127–29. *Tanto dice . . . rimagna*: Cf. *Inf.* I, 112-23; *Purg.* VI, 46-48. "Tanto" goes with the "che" in the following verse.

127. *compagna = compagnia* (cf. *Inf.* XXVI, 101; *Purg.* III, 4).

128. *fia = sarà.*

131. *addita'lo = lo additai.*

131–33. *e quest' altro . . . sgombra*: Thus Dante answers Forese's question concerning the two souls ahead (vss. 52-53), but, for all we are told, Forese feels no surprise at the presence of Virgil here, nor does Dante even bother to name Statius to him.

CANTO XXIV

1–2. *Né 'l dir . . . facea*: The first "dir" is the subject of "facea," and "andar" is the object; then "andar" becomes the subject and "lui" (i.e., *dir*) the object.

2–3. *andavam forte . . . vento*: Cf. *Purg.* IV, 88-93.

2. *forte*: "Rapidly." Cf. *Purg.* XXI, 19.

3. *pinta = spinta.*

4. *parean = parevano. cose rimorte*: Cf. Iudas 12: "arbores . . . bis mortuae" ("trees . . . twice dead").

5–6. *ammirazione traean = traevano ammirazione. Trarre* can mean either "to draw" or "to shoot." The latter meaning seems to fit the context better, the object being "ammirazione . . . di me." For *trarre* in this sense, cf. *Purg.* III, 69.

7. *continuando al mio sermone*: I.e., continuing the talk with Forese.

8–9. *Ella sen va . . . cagione*: The observation regarding Statius suggests that, liberated as he is from this realm, as the closing words of the preceding canto stated, he could move instantly—or at least very fast (the "forse" leaves this dark)—to the summit of the mountain, where, as we shall see, he must pass through the water of two streams before he may ascend to Paradise. Thus the fact that he delays this great moment in order to walk along with Virgil registers, in its own way, his great affection for him and his desire to be with him as long as possible. Cf. *Purg.* XXI, 100-102.

8. *Ella*: The shade of Statius. His reference to Statius in the third person registers very clearly the fact that Dante's words to Forese continue directly.   *sen = se ne.*   *tarda*: I.e., *lentamente*.

9. *per altrui cagione*: Because of Virgil, who, because of Dante, is also going more slowly than he would have to do otherwise. "Altrui" here is the possessive.

10. *Piccarda*: Dante will meet Piccarda, the sister of Forese, in the heaven of the moon (*Par.* III, 34-123), among those who failed to keep their religious vows. In their accounts of Piccarda the early commentators state that being devoutly disposed in her girlhood she entered a convent in Florence, but was forced thence by her brother Corso (see Dante's mention of him in vss. 82-87) in order that he might marry her to a Florentine named Rossellino della Tosa; they add that very shortly after her marriage she fell ill and died, in answer, it is presumed, to her prayer that she might be saved from violating her vow of virginity. Benvenuto points out that of the three—Corso, Forese, and Piccarda—Dante places one in Hell, one in Purgatory, and one in Paradise.

15. *ne l'alto Olimpo*: Cf. "o sommo Giove" in *Purg.* VI, 118.   *di sua corona*: See II Tim. 4:7-8: "Bonum certamen certavi, cursum consummavi, fidem servavi; in reliquo reposita est mihi corona iustitiae, quam reddet mihi Dominus in illa die, iustus iudex." ("I have fought the good fight, I have finished the course, I have kept the faith. For the rest, there is laid up for me a crown of justice, which the Lord, the just Judge, will give to me in that day.")

16–18. *Qui non si vieta . . . dieta*: Torraca comments: "Più che a Dante, fa l'osservazione a sè stesso, come per giustificarsi o scusarsi, e mostra la gentilezza dell'animo suo."

("He [Forese] is making this observation not so much to Dante as to himself, as if to justify or excuse himself; and he is showing the gentleness of his soul.")

17–18. *munta . . . via*: "Milked dry." Cf. *Inf.* XII, 133-36 and *Purg.* XIII, 57, and see "conquiso" in *Purg.* XXIII, 45.

18. *dieta = digiuno* (see vs. 23).

20. *Bonagiunta da Lucca*: Torraca observes that Bonagiunta was a fairly common name in Florence, hence the special need to specify "da Lucca." Bonagiunta Orbicciani degli Overardi, the son of Perfetto di Orbicciano of Lucca, was a notary and poet of the latter half of the thirteenth century. A considerable number of his poems have been preserved. See A. Parducci (1905), pp. xv-xxx, 3-64, and G. Contini (1960), vol. I, pp. 257-82. Benvenuto, in his gloss on vs. 34, says that Bonagiunta was more addicted to wine than to versifying, but was a facile writer and addressed some of his poems to Dante, who had been acquainted with him:

> Iste autem fuit Bonagiunta de Urbisanis, vir honorabilis, de civitate lucana, luculentus orator in lingua materna, et facilis inventor rhythmorum, sed facilior vinorum, qui noverat autorem in vita, et aliquando scripserat sibi. Ideo autor fingit eum ita familiariter loqui secum de ipso et de aliis inventoribus modernis.

> This was Bonagiunta Orbicciani, an honorable man, of the city of Lucca, a brilliant orator in the mother tongue, with a great facility in finding rhymes but more adept at [finding] wines. He knew the author while he was alive and sometimes wrote to him. Hence, the author portrays him as conversing with him in friendly fashion about himself and other modern poets.

20–24. *quella faccia . . . vernaccia*: This pope is not named, but is easily recognized as Martin IV (Simon de Brie or Brion), who was born *ca.* 1210 and was a native of Montpincé in Brie. He was treasurer of St. Martin of Tours and was appointed chancellor of France by Louis IX in 1260; in 1261 Urban IV made him a cardinal, and in 1264 he acted as legate in France for Urban and for his successors Clement IV and Gregory X and was entrusted with the negotiations as to the offer of the crown of Naples and Sicily to Charles of Anjou. Six months after the death of Nicholas III (August 22, 1280) he was elected pope at Viterbo, through the influence of Charles of Anjou, on February 22, 1281, and was crowned at Orvieto on March 23, the Romans having refused to admit him within their walls. In the first year of his pontificate, at the bidding of Charles, Martin IV excommunicated the Greek emperor, Michael VIII Palaeologus, thereby destroying the possibility of a union between the Eastern and Western Churches. After the Sicilian Vespers in 1282 and the loss of Sicily by the house of Anjou, he vainly endeavored to compel Pedro III of Aragon, who had taken possession of the island, to restore it to Charles. Among the cardinals created by him was Dante's bitter enemy, Benedetto Caetani, afterward Pope Boniface VIII. Martin IV died on March 28, 1285, after a reign of four years. The cause of his death is said to have been a surfeit of eels from Lake Bolsena, which, according to Francesco Pipino (*Chronicon* IV, 21), a contemporary of Dante, he used to keep in milk and then stew in wine.

23. *Torso*: Tours.

24. *Bolsena*: Lake Bolsena (the *lacus Volsiniensis* of the Romans), in Latium, a few miles north-northwest of Viterbo, is one of the largest lakes in central Italy. It was, and is, famous for its eels. *vernaccia*: Torraca comments: "*La vernaccia*: vino bianco, detto così da Vernaccio, ora Vernazza, a pochi chilometri da Spezia. 'Vicino a Chiavari . . . si fa molto vino di vernaccia, e il vino di quella terra è ottimo'; Salimbene." ("La Vernaccia: a white wine, so called because it came from Vernaccio, now Vernazza, a few kilometers from La Spezia. 'Near Chiavari . . . a great deal of Vernaccia wine is produced; and the wine from that land is excellent' [Salimbene].")

26. *del nomar parean tutti contenti*: All are pleased to be named, because then Dante can report to the living that they are here in Purgatory among the elect-to-be and so can ask that their speedier advance here be prayed for.

27. *però = per ciò*, "on that account."   *un atto bruno*: A scowl.

28. *per fame a vòto usar li denti*: Cf. Ovid's description of Erysichthon (*Metam.* VIII, 824-27):

> ... petit ille dapes sub imagine somni,
> oraque vana movet dentemque in dente fatigat,
> exercetque cibo delusum guttur inani
> proque epulis tenues nequiquam devorat auras.

And in his sleep he dreams of feasting, champs his jaws on nothing, wearies tooth upon tooth, cheats his gullet with fancied food; for his banquet is nothing but empty air.

29. *Ubaldin da la Pila*: Ubaldino degli Ubaldini dalla Pila (La Pila is a castle in the Mugello, or upper valley of the Sieve, a tributary of the Arno, north of Florence) was a member of the powerful Ghibelline family of the Ubaldini, to which belonged the famous Cardinal Ottaviano degli Ubaldini (mentioned in *Inf.* X, 120) and Ugolino d'Azzo (see *Purg.* XIV, 105). Ubaldino was the father of Archbishop Ruggieri degli Ubaldini of Pisa (see *Inf.* XXXIII, 14). It seems that he died in 1291. Benvenuto gives the following account of him:

> Iste fuit quidam nobilis miles de clara familia Ubaldinorum, de qua fuerunt multi valentes viri; et ipse fuit liberalis et civilis, frater cardinalis Octaviani magnifici, qui semel duxit papam cum tota curia in montes Florentiae ad domum et castellum istius Ubaldini, et ibi stetit pluribus mensibus. Modo poeta posuit cardinalem in inferno, tamquam epicureum, et istum posuit in purgatorio pro guloso. . . . Ubaldini fuerunt florentini, quibus datae sunt Alpes Florentiae sub gubernatione et defensione, sed ipsi sciverunt continuare posses-

sionem per longa tempora: et diebus istis sunt destructi per commune Florentiae. . . . [Iste Ubaldinus] fuit prodigi ingenii ad omnia irritamenta gulae. Ipse enim de more suo quotidie inquirebat ab expensore suo quid ordinasset pro prandio vel coena; et illo respondente hoc et illud, respondebat: facias etiam sic; nec umquam ille poterat tam varia ordinare, quin iste semper adderet aliquid.

This man was a noble soldier of the famous family of the Ubaldini, which produced a number of worthy men; he was generous and patriotic, and his brother was the eminent Cardinal Ottaviano who had once invited the pope and his curia to the home and castle of the Ubaldini in the hills near Florence where they stayed for several months. Here the poet places the cardinal in Hell as an epicurean and the brother in Purgatory as a glutton. . . . The Ubaldini were Florentines who were charged with the rule and defense of the Florentine Alps, and they were able to maintain control for a long time; however, in those days they were overthrown by the commune of Florence. . . . [Ubaldino] was of remarkable ingenuity in catering to his gluttony. Every day he would consult with his steward as to what was planned for dinner or supper; when he was told that such and such was on the menu, he would say: "Let us have thus and so, too." The steward was never able to plan a dinner to which his master would not always add some special dish.

Ubaldino forms the subject of one of Sacchetti's stories (*novella* CCV).

Bonifazio: A bishop who is identified by modern commentators with Bonifazio de' Fieschi of Genoa, archbishop of Ravenna from 1274 to 1295 and nephew of Innocent IV. He was appointed archbishop of Ravenna by Gregory X in 1274, during the second Council of Lyons, and was sent to France by Honorius IV in 1285 to help Edward I of England in his efforts to bring about a reconciliation between Alfonso III of Aragon and Philip the Fair and to negotiate for the release of Charles II of Naples. He died February 1, 1295. He is known to have been immensely wealthy and to have possessed a great collection of plate and rich embroideries. See E. Levi (1921), pp. 20-23, 78-89, and especially pp. 80-81 for the text of a letter from Bonifazio to the commune of Savignano dated October 29, 1281.

30. *che pasturò col rocco molte genti*: With reference to the term *rocco* used by Dante here of the pastoral staff, Lana says that Boniface "fu arcivescovo di Ravenna, lo quale non porta lo pastorale così ritorto come li altri arcivescovi, ma è fatto di sopra al modo di rocco delli scacchi." ("He was archbishop of Ravenna. The archbishop of Ravenna does not have his crosier as curved at the end as other archbishops; his is made at the top like the rook in a chess set.") The ancient pastoral staff of the archbishops of Ravenna, which is still preserved, bears at the top an ornament shaped like a chess rook, answering to the description given by Lana. See the illustrations given by C. Ricci (1921), p. 613.

The whole clause is probably ironically ambiguous, as Ricci points out (1891, p. 121): "Il verbo *pasturare* presenta in questo caso due tagli e con l'ambiguità determina l'epigramma fra il *pasturare* il gregge cristiano con la parola evangelica e la pietà, e il *pasturare* o sfamare il gregge dei cortigiani che gli si addensavano intorno." ("In this case, the verb *pasturare*—to pasture or feed—has a double meaning, and the ambiguity determines the epigram between feeding the Christian flock with the evangelical word and with piety and feeding the hungry flock of courtiers who crowded around him.")

31-33. *Vidi messer Marchese . . . sazio*: The reference to Messer Marchese here is to his having been an insatiable winebibber during his lifetime, in illustration of which Benvenuto relates a story of how one day he sent for his cellarer and asked him what people said of him in the city, to which the cellarer replied, "Master, everybody says that you do nothing but drink," whereupon Messer Marchese rejoined with a smile, "Why don't they say that I am always thirsty?"

Messer Marchese, who was *podestà* of Faenza in 1296, appears to have been a member of the Argogliosi family of Forlì.

31. *ebbe spazio*: There is clearly a touch of the same irony here as is felt in vs. 30.

33. *e sì fu tal*: Some editors place an accent on "sì" here. Although this is certainly a possible reading, it seems better to consider the "si" as the familiar pleonastic reflexive, in its specifying function.

34–35. *s'apprezza più d'un che d'altro*: The expression *apprezzarsi di* means "to take note of," "to pay attention to."

35. *fei = feci*.

36. *di me aver contezza*: To wish to know about me, my story. It is clear that Bonagiunta knows who Dante is.

37. *Gentucca*: Nothing certain is known of the meaning of the word here. According to the most probable interpretation, Gentucca is the name of a Lucchese lady who befriended Dante in exile. Curiously enough, however, several of the earlier commentators understand the word "Gentucca" to be not a proper name but a pejorative of *gente*. The *Ottimo Commento*, for example, says: "E dicea: *io non so che gente bassa* . . . cioè la Parte Bianca di Firenze." ("And he said: 'I know not what low people' . . . that is, the White party of Florence.") The *Anonimo fiorentino*'s interpretation is: "Ciò è, secondo il vulgare lucchese, dicea che gentucca, ciò è che genticella è questa?" ("That is, according to the Lucchese dialect, he was saying what little people, i.e., what small folk is this?") The first to take the word as the name of a lady, and to identify her with the "femmina" of the obscure prophecy that begins in vs. 43, appears to have been Buti:

> Finge l'autore ch'elli nol sapesse intendere, perchè secondo la sua fizione non era anco stato quello ch'elli predicea et annunziava; cioè ch'elli dovea essere confinato di Fiorensa a Lucca, e quive si dovea innamorare

d'una gentil donna che sarebbe nominata Gentucca, e
così era avvenuto innanti che l'autore scrivesse questa
parte che l'autore, essendo a Lucca non potendo stare
a Fiorensa, puose amore ad una gentil donna chiamata
madonna Gentucca, che era di Rossimpelo, per la virtù
grande et onestà che era in lei, non per altro amore.

The author pretends he does not understand, because,
according to the fiction he has created, the things pre-
dicted and announced here have not yet taken place,
i.e., that he would be banished from Florence to Lucca
and that he would fall in love there with a gentle lady
called Gentucca. This had happened before the author
wrote this part: the author, in Lucca because he was
unable to remain in Florence, fell in love with a gentle
lady called Madonna Gentucca, of the Rossimpelo
family. He loved her for the great virtue and honesty
that were in her, not with any other love.

The view adopted by the majority of modern commentators
is that an unidentified lady by this name in Lucca showed
kindness and hospitality to the exiled Dante, the exact time
of this sojourn unfortunately being undocumented. See F.
Novati (1908), pp. 198-202; E. Levi (1921), pp. 30-33,
99-105.

38. *là*: In the mouth.

38-39. *la piaga de la giustizia*: The fasting and the conse-
quent torment of hunger and the wasting away.

39. *li*: For this shift to a plural pronoun, see *Purg.* VII,
65-66. *pilucca*: "Plucks," as if it picked bits from them
all the while. Literally, *piluccare* denotes the plucking of
grapes, one by one, from a bunch of grapes. The image of
eating and consequently the *contrapasso* turn of phrase are
surely not unintentional. Cf. "sfoglia," *Purg.* XXIII, 58.

40. *vaga*: "Desirous."

41. *fa sì ch'io t'intenda*: "Speak so that I may understand
you."

42. *appaga*: Imperative, with a double object, "te" and "me."

43. *Femmina*: "Femmina" is used for *donna* here. The term in general does not necessarily have a pejorative sense and certainly does not in this case.　*e non porta ancor benda*: Del Lungo comments: "È ancora giovinetta nubile: la benda, copertura della testa con soggòlo, era di donna o maritata (la benda nera) o vedova (la benda bianca; cf. *Purg.* VIII, 74)." ("She is still young and single; the wimple, a head cover with a chinstrap, was for married women—a black wimple—or for widows—a white wimple; cf. *Purg.* VIII, 74.")

45. *come ch'om la riprenda*: Dante himself has already blamed Lucca in *Inf.* XXI, 41-42.

46. *con questo antivedere*: Cf. *Purg.* XXIII, 109.

47. *prendesti errore*: If you have misconstrued, conceived a mistaken idea.

48. *dichiareranti* = *ti dichiareranno.*　*ancor*: "Finally."
le cose vere: "The real events."

49-51. *Ma dì s'i' veggio . . . d'amore*: Bonagiunta has already recognized Dante. In his commentary (p. 233) Porena comments: "La sua domanda è dunque una di quelle che non esprimono se non una meraviglia gioconda di aver dinanzi proprio quella persona: come quando Dante aveva esclamato *Or sei tu quel Virgilio e quella fonte* ecc. ecc., senza menomamente dubitare che l'autore dell'Eneide sia Virgilio." ("His question, then, is one of those that express joyous amazement, at having precisely that person before him: just as Dante had exclaimed 'Are you that Virgil, that source, etc.' without having the slightest doubt that the author of the *Aeneid* is Virgil.")

49-50. *fore trasse*: Produced.

50. *nove* = *nuove.*　*rime*: The word here signifies a poem or poetry, as it often does in Dante's usage.

51. *Donne ch'avete intelletto d'amore*: The first verse of the
first *canzone* of the *Vita nuova*, a canzone which represents
a new beginning and new style in Dante's poem to and about
Beatrice. See *Vita nuova* XIX, 1-2:

> Avvenne poi che passando per uno cammino lungo lo
> quale sen gia uno rivo chiaro molto, a me giunse tanta
> volontade di dire, che io cominciai a pensare lo modo
> ch'io tenesse; e pensai che parlare di lei non si convenia
> che io facesse, se io non parlasse a donne in seconda
> persona, e non ad ogni donna, ma solamente a coloro
> che sono gentili e che non sono pure femmine. Allora
> dico che la mia lingua parlò quasi come per se stessa
> mossa, e disse: *Donne ch'avete intelletto d'amore.*

> It then befell, that passing by a way along which there
> coursed a river of most clear waters, so great a desire
> to speak possessed me, that I began to ponder on the
> style I should use, and I thought that it was not fitting
> to speak of her except I spake to ladies in the second
> person, and not to every lady but to such only as are
> gentle and not mere women. Then I say that my tongue
> spake as if moved by itself and said: *Ladies, that have
> intelligence of love.*

52-54. *I' mi son un che ... significando*: The pronoun "mi"
is a clear example of the so-called pleonastic reflexive, and
in this context it adds a touch that amounts to saying: "As for
myself, I am one who . . . ." Later it is evident from the use
of the plural "pens," vs. 58, that Bonagiunta thinks of Dante
as initiating a new style with this poem, one that was then
followed by other poets, and the "mi" here seems to register
Dante's awareness of this imputed honor and to serve as a
modest disclaimer to speak for anyone but himself in formu-
lating his *credo*. On the whole much-debated conception,
see C. S. Singleton (1949), pp. 92-94.

54. *ditta = detta.   vo = vado.   vo   significando*: A
progressive construction.

55. *O frate*: For the tone, see n. to *Purg.* IV, 127.   *issa*:
For the form *issa*, see *Inf.* XXIII, 7 and the note. E. G. Pa-

rodi (1957, p. 261) points out that some early commentators characterize the word as being specifically the speech of Lucca.   *il nodo*: "The impediment."

56. *'l Notaro*: Giacomo da Lentini, commonly called "the Notary," of Lentini, in Sicily. He belonged, in the first half of the thirteenth century, to the Sicilian school of poetry that flourished under the Emperor Frederick II (encountered in *Inf.* X, 119) and his son Manfred (see *Purg.* III, 112). There is reason to believe that he studied at Bologna and afterward lived in Tuscany, where his reputation was such that he was regarded as the chief of the lyric poets before Guittone d'Arezzo. A great many of his *canzoni* and sonnets, which exhibit marked traces of Provençal influence, have been preserved (see G. Contini, 1960, vol. I, pp. 49-90). The first line of his *canzone* beginning "Madonna, dir vo voglio" (see G. Contini, 1960, vol. I, p. 51) is quoted by Dante in *De vulg. eloqu.* I, xii, 8, as an example of polished diction, though the author's name is not given.

Guittone: Fra Guittone d'Arezzo, one of the early Italian poets, was born *ca.* 1230 at Santa Firmina, near Arezzo. Little is known of the details of his life, a great part of which was spent in Florence, where Dante may have known him. His father, Michele, held the position of chamberlain of the city of Arezzo, in which office he was assisted by his son. About the year 1266, or perhaps earlier, Guittone, who was married and had a family, entered the order of the Frati Gaudenti (which included married men and even women), his previous life having been more or less given up to worldly pleasures. In 1285 he was at Bologna on business connected with his order. In 1293 he helped to found the monastery of Santa Maria degli Angioli at Florence, in which city he appears to have died in the following year. See A. Pellizzari (1906); G. Contini (1960), vol. I, pp. 189-255. Dante mentions Guittone again in *Purg.* XXVI, 124.

57. *di qua dal dolce stil novo*: Literally, "this side of the sweet new style."   *dolce stil novo*: This is the origin of the phrase which has become a chapter heading in so many

histories of Italian literature.   *ch'i' odo*: Bonagiunta recognizes the definition of the style, the program of it, as it were.

58. *le vostre penne*: With this shift to the plural, imputing to several poets, who are not named, the program or creed that Dante the wayfarer has claimed for himself (see n. on vss. 52-54), Dante the poet bequeathed to literary history a problem that is still debated, namely, whether there actually was any such school of poetry.

59. *di retro al dittator sen vanno strette*: Following Love's dictation. Cf. vss. 52-54.   *sen = se ne.   sen vanno strette*: This extends to the plural what was said of Dante alone in vs. 54: "vo significando." "Sen vanno" represents the same progressive sense.   *strette = strettamente*, i.e., exactly according to his (Love's) dictation.

61. *e qual più a gradire oltre si mette = e qual si mette a gradire più oltre*. Petrocchi has ably defended the reading "gradire," according to the early MSS. *Gradire* would thus be a Latinism (based on *gradior*). Several examples of its use in early Italian are given by Petrocchi (see his long note on this). "E qual più a gradire oltre si metter" thus comes to mean, freely, "and whosoever would venture to go further."

61-62. *qual più . . . stilo*: Whoever seeks to go more deeply into the difference between the two schools beyond what I have just stated will see no better than I do now.

63. *quasi contentato*: "As one who is content."

64-68. *Come li augei . . . passo*: Compare Lucan, *Phars.* V, 711-16:

> Strymona sic gelidum bruma pellente relinquunt
> Poturae te, Nile, grues, primoque volatu
> Effingunt varias casu monstrante figuras;
> Mox, ubi percussit tensas Notus altior alas,
> Confusos temere inmixtae glomerantur in orbes,
> Et turbata perit dispersis littera pinnis.

Thus, when cranes are driven by winter from the frozen Strymon to drink the water of the Nile, at the beginning of their flight they describe various chance-taught figures; but later, when a loftier wind beats on their outspread wings, they combine at random and form disordered packs, until the letter is broken and disappears as the birds are scattered.

Cranes normally fly in single file (cf. *Inf.* V, 46-47). Thus the figure fits the situation here with respect to the souls who first altered the order of their movement along the terrace, making a band as they paused to wonder at the living Dante, and now hurry on and go in file, like cranes.

64. *augei = augelli (uccelli).   vernan = svernano.*

66. *in filo = in fila.* Cf. *Inf.* V, 47.

68. *volgendo 'l viso*: They face toward their path ahead.

69. *per voler*: The desire to hasten their purgation.

70. *trottare = correre.* In early Italian the verb was commonly used of a man's running. Cf. Boccaccio, *Decam.* II, 2 (vol. I, p. 80, l. 22).

71. *e si passeggia*: Some editors prefer to interpret the "si" here as "sì," the adverb, but it seems a clear instance of the pleonastic reflexive in its separating, distancing function. Porena so interprets it, calling it a pseudo-reflexive: " 'Passeggia (va di passo) per suo conto' lasciando che altri corra." ("He strolls along—he walks along—at his own pace, letting the others run.") But he admits that "sì" is possible. And Del Lungo observes: " 'Si,' pleonastico, di usuale proprietà presso gli antichi; ma che qui segna distacco fra lo aver corso ('trottare') e, ora, il passeggiare." ("The pleonastic *si*, as it was properly used by the ancient writers. Here, though, it indicates the change from having run (*trottare*) to walking now.") See n. to vs. 33.

72. *l'affollar*: The verb is based on the Latin *follis*, meaning "bellows," and refers to the heaving of the chest and panting of one who has been running. Cf. *Purg.* XV, 51. *casso*: Cf. *Inf.* XII, 122 and *passim*.

74. *sen veniva = se ne veniva*. Again the "se" (*si*) has something of the same distancing function as in vs. 71.

75. *fia = sarà.*   *riveggia = riveda.*

76. *lui = a lui.*   *mi viva*: Again the pleonastic reflexive. Cf. vs. 52. It is most common after *non sapere*.

77. *il tornar mio*: The subject of "fia" (*sarà*).

78. *ch'io non sia col voler prima a la riva*: No matter how soon Dante may return here after death, it will not be soon enough. Some interpreters would understand "riva" to mean either the shore near Ostia whence the souls depart for Purgatory (see *Purg.* II, 100-102) or that of Purgatory where they arrive. Either of these interpretations is possible, but this is more probably only a metaphor, as in *Purg.* XXV, 54, and *Par.* XXVI, 63. In any case Dante once again expresses his belief that he is to be among the elect, even as Charon had predicted (*Inf.* III, 91-92), and so will pass through Purgatory after death. But will Forese still be here?

79. *però che = perciò che.*   *'l loco u' fui a viver posto*: Florence.   *'u = ove.*   *a viver posto*: Almost despite himself, as Porena notes.

80. *si spolpa*: The verb belongs to the semantic field of the *contrapasso*, as do *sfogliare* and *piluccare*.

81. *ruina*: Cf. *Purg.* XII, 55; XVII, 39.   *disposto*: "Inclined to," "on the point of." Porena comments:

> Questo è uno dei pochissimi luoghi del poema in cui il Dante scrittore si sostituisce al Dante personaggio del poema stesso: giacchè non è verosimile che il Dante della primavera del '300, ancora in piena attività nella vita politica della sua patria, fosse già così distaccato dalle cose terrene, nutrisse già un simile sconforto, un simile desiderio di morte.

> This is one of the very few places in the poem where Dante the writer substitutes himself for Dante the character in the poem itself. For it is hardly likely that in the

spring of 1300, Dante, still fully active in the political
life of his city, would already be so detached from earth-
ly things, or that he would be nourishing such anguish,
or such a desire for death.

82. *Or va*: Cf. *Purg.* VIII, 133, where the expression also
serves to introduce a prophecy. Porena suggests the mean-
ing "sta tranquillo."   *quei che più n'ha colpa*: Corso Do-
nati, Forese's and Piccarda's brother, who became the leader
of the Neri faction in Florence. In the summer of 1300 the
priors of Florence, of whom Dante was one, in order to put
an end to the disturbances occasioned by the Bianchi and
Neri feud, decided to exile the heads of both parties. Corso,
counting on the sympathies of Boniface VIII, repaired to
Rome and urged the pope to send Charles of Valois to Flor-
ence to pacify the city in his name. Villani (VIII, 43) writes:

> Informato papa Bonifazio del male stato e dubitoso
> della città di Firenze . . . con loro procaccio e studio, e
> di messer Corso Donati che seguiva la corte, sì prese
> per consiglio il detto papa Bonifazio, di mandare per
> messer Carlo di Valos fratello del re di Francia . . . [e]
> gli diè titolo di paciario in Toscana, per recare colla
> sua forza la città di Firenze al suo intendimento.

> Pope Boniface was informed of the evil and dubious
> condition of the city of Florence . . . as a result of their
> urging and their scheming, as well as that of Messer
> Corso Donati, who was following the court, the said
> Pope Boniface took counsel to send for Messer Charles
> of Valois, brother of the king of France . . . [and] he
> gave him the title of pacifier of Tuscany, so that he
> might use his forces to get the city of Florence to do his
> bidding.

Charles entered Florence on November 1, 1301, and was
followed not long after by Corso Donati and a band of exiled
Neri, who forced their way into the city, broke open the pris-
ons, and at the head of the rabble attacked the houses of the
Bianchi, pillaging, burning, and murdering for five days and
nights, without any attempt being made by Charles to check

them. After the departure of the latter, the Neri were left
in possession of Florence, and Corso now attempted to get
the supreme power into his own hands. But his pretensions
soon rendered him an object of detestation and suspicion,
and at length he was formally charged by the priors with con-
spiring against the liberties of the commonwealth in concert
with his father-in-law, the Ghibelline captain Uguccione della
Faggiuola, and was summoned to appear before the *podestà*.
On his refusal to comply he was condemned to death as a
traitor. Villani (VIII, 96) gives the following account:

> Nel detto anno 1308, essendo nella città di Firenze
> cresciuto scandolo tra' nobili e potenti popolani di parte
> nera che guidavano la città, per invidia di stato e di
> signoria . . . erano partiti in setta; e dell'una era capo
> messer Corso de' Donati con seguito d'alquanti nobili
> e di certi popolani . . . e dell'altra parte erano capo
> messer Rosso della Tosa . . . [con] più altri casati
> grandi e popolani, e la maggiore parte della buona gente
> della cittade, i quali aveano gli ufici e 'l governamento
> della terra e del popolo. Messer Corso e' suoi seguaci
> parendo loro esser male trattati degli onori e ofici a loro
> guisa parendogli essere più degni, perocch'erano stati
> i principali ricoveratori dello stato de' neri, e cacciatori
> della parte bianca; ma per l'altra parte si disse, che mes-
> ser Corso volea essere signore della cittade e non com-
> pagnone; quale che si fosse il vero o la cagione, i detti,
> e quegli che reggeano il popolo l'aveano in odio e a
> grande sospetto, dappoi s'era imparentato con Uguc-
> cione della Faggiuola, ghibellino e nimico de' Fiorentini;
> e ancora il temeano per lo suo grande animo e podere
> e seguito . . . e massimamente perchè trovarono
> [ch'avea] fatta lega e giura col detto Uguccione della
> Faggiuola suo suocero, e mandato per lui e per suo
> aiuto. Per la qual cosa, e per grande gelosia, subita-
> mente si levò la cittade a romore, e . . . fu data una in-
> quisizione ovvero accusa alla podestà . . . incontro al
> detto messer Corso, opponendogli come dovea e volea
> tradire il popolo, sommettere lo stato della cittade, fac-

cendo venire Uguccione da Faggiuola co' ghibellini e
nimici del comune. E la richesta gli fu fatta, e poi il
bando, e poi la condannagione.

In that year, 1308, hostility arose in the city of Florence
between the nobles and the powerful commoners, both
of the Black party, which was in control of the city. Be-
cause they were envious of each other's power and
dominion . . . they had formed factions: the one was
headed by Messer Corso Donati, whose following in-
cluded a good many noblemen and certain commoners
. . . and the head of the other was Messer Rosso della
Tosa . . . with some families of noblemen and common-
ers behind him, as well as the majority of the good peo-
ple of the city—men who held offices and were re-
sponsible for the administration of the city and its
population. Messer Corso and his followers believed
they were not getting enough honors and offices in the
city. Indeed, they believed they were more deserving
than those other men, because they had been mainly
responsible for putting the Blacks back in power and
for having expelled the Whites. But the other side said
that Messer Corso wanted to become lord of the city,
and not merely to be an equal. Whatever the truth or
the reasons may have been, these people [Messer Ros-
so's faction] and those who controlled the government
hated him and were very suspicious of him, especially
since he had become related by marriage to Uguccione
della Faggiuola, who was a Ghibelline and an enemy
of Florence. Moreover, Messer Corso was feared be-
cause of his great bravery, power, and following . . . and
especially because it was discovered that he had made
an alliance and covenant with this Uguccione della Fag-
giuola, his father-in-law, and that he had sent for him
and his men. For this reason, and because of the great
rivalry, the city was soon in an uproar, and . . . the
podestà was ordered to make an investigation, or rather
an accusation . . . against Messer Corso, charging him
with wanting to betray the people and to destroy the

city by calling in Uguccione della Faggiuola and the
Ghibellines and enemies of the commune. He was or-
dered to appear; then the proclamation against him was
issued, and then he was condemned.

Besieged in his own house, Corso was eventually slain while
attempting to escape, October 6, 1308. Villani (VIII, 96)
tells of his capture and death:

Messer Corso tutto solo andandosene, fu giunto e preso
sopra a Rovezzano da certi Catalani a cavallo, e
menandolne preso a Firenze, come fu di costa a san
Salvi, pregando quegli che 'l menavano, e promettendo
loro molta moneta se lo scampassono, i detti volendolo
pure menare a Firenze, siccom'era loro imposto da' si-
gnori, messer Corso per paura di venire alle mani de'
suoi nemici e d'essere giustiziato dal popolo, essendo
compreso forte di gotte nelle mani e ne' piedi, si lasciò
cadere da cavallo. I detti Catalani veggendolo in terra,
l'uno di loro gli diede d'una lancia per la gola d'uno
colpo mortale, e lasciaronlo per morto.

Messer Corso, who had fled alone, was overtaken and
captured at Rovezzano by certain Catalan horsemen.
They were taking him prisoner to Florence and were
near San Salvi, when he begged them to let him go,
promising large sums of money in return. But those men
were determined to take him back to Florence, as they
had been ordered to do by the priors. Because he was
so afraid of falling into the hands of his enemies and be-
ing executed by the people, Messer Corso, being badly
afflicted with gout in his hands and feet, let himself fall
from his horse. Seeing him on the ground, one of the
Catalans thrust a lance through his throat, dealing him
a mortal blow; and they left him for dead.

83–84. *vegg' io a coda d'una bestia . . . scolpa*: I.e., dragged
at the tail of a beast toward the valley of Hell. Some, taking
the words literally, think Dante means that Corso was
dragged to death at his horse's heels. This, however, does
not agree with the account of his death given by Villani

(quoted in n. to vs. 82), who states that Corso, having been overtaken in his flight from Florence by some Catalan mercenaries, threw himself from his horse, and while on the ground was speared in the throat by one of his captors. As Villani was on the spot and must have known the facts, we must assume either (with Scartazzini-Vandelli) that a distorted account of the incident reached Dante in exile, or (with Butler) that Forese's language is metaphorical, the *bestia* being "the popular party, of which Corso once thought himself the head, while he was really being dragged on by them, and by which he was ultimately destroyed." Benvenuto, who wrote with Villani's description before him, takes Dante's words literally and tries to reconcile the two accounts:

> Et fugiens solus, cum non posset flectere precibus vel promissis milites catalanos persequentes eum . . . permisit sponte se cadere ab equo, vel casu cecidit, ut aliqui volunt. Et cum equus traheret eum retento pede in stapite, percussus est lethaliter in gutture ab uno milite.

> Fleeing alone, and not being able to ward off, either by entreaties or by promises, the Catalan soldiers who were pursuing him . . . he intentionally allowed himself to fall from his horse, or he fell accidentally, as some would have it. While the horse was dragging him by one foot still in the stirrup, he was mortally wounded in the throat by a soldier.

The version in Dino Compagni's *Cronica* (III, 21), which agrees in the main with that of Villani, is as follows:

> Messer Corso, infermo per le gotti, fuggia verso la badia di San Salvi, dove già molti mali avea fatti e fatti fare. Gli sgarigli il presono, e reconobberlo: e volendolne menare, si difendeva con belle parole, sì come savio cavaliere. Intanto sopravenne uno giovane cognato del mariscalco. Stimolato da altri d'ucciderlo, nol volle fare; e ritornandosi indietro, vi fu rimandato: il quale la seconda volta li diè d'una lancia catelanesca nella gola, e uno altro colpo nel fianco; e cadde in terra. Alcuni

monaci ne 'l portorono alla badia; e quivi morì . . . e fu sepulto.

Messer Corso, who was afflicted with gout, was fleeing toward the abbey of San Salvi, where he himself had committed many misdeeds and had caused others to commit them as well. The Catalan soldiers took him and recognized him. They wanted to take him back, but he defended himself with fine words, as befits a wise knight. Then a young brother-in-law of the stable master arrived. The others tried to incite him to kill Messer Corso, but he refused. He went back, but they made him return. This second time, he put a Catalan lance through Messer Corso's throat and gave him another blow in the side, so that he fell to the ground. Several monks carried him back to the abbey, where he died . . . and was buried.

Grandgent observes that Dante appears to have recast the literal event into the story of a death-ride on a Hell-horse and refers to E. Levi (1921, pp. 50-51), who calls attention to a twelfth-century carving on the church of San Zeno in Verona, in which Theodoric in a wild hunt is precipitated into Hell by a horse. It seems important to note also that traitors and murderers were sometimes condemned to be tied to the tail of a horse and dragged to the place of execution. Cf. M. Barbi (1934b), p. 250: "Dante trasforma il particolare della caduta di Corso da cavallo in un vero trascinamento alla coda d'una bestia, per assegnargli la pena dei traditori e dei micidiali." ("Dante transforms the detail about Corso's fall from the horse into a true dragging at the tail of an animal, in order to mete out to him the punishment assigned to traitors and murderers.") Barbi cites examples of this punishment.

86. *il percuote = lo percuote*. This implies that he was either kicked by the horse or knocked against some object in the road.

88. *Non hanno molto a volger quelle ruote*: I.e., the heavenly spheres will not have turned many years.

89-90. *che ti fia chiaro . . . puote*: The events referred to by Forese will be clear in eight years, in fact, since Corso was to meet his death on October 6, 1308.

90. *puote = può*.

91. *Tu*: Emphatic use of a subject pronoun. *ti rimani = rimanti*, imperative.

94-97. *Qual esce . . . valchi*: Forese's departure recalls that of Brunetto Latini (*Inf.* XV, 121-24).

94-99. *Qual esce . . . marescalchi*: The use of this military figure, which finally ends in referring to Virgil and Statius as "marshalls," is very curious.

94. *gualoppo = galoppo*.

95. *di schiera che cavalchi*: Del Lungo comments: "Intendi, in faccia al nemico: e propriamente, schiera di cosiddetti 'feditori,' che erano avanguardia di cavalleria, cioè in condizione di 'ferire' i primi colpi, 'farsi onor del primo intoppo,' del primo scontro col nemico." ("Read: confronting the enemy. Properly, a company of so-called *feditori* [those who deal the blows], who were the avant-garde of the cavalry; that is, they were in a position to 'deal' the first blows, 'to have the honor of overcoming the first obstacle,' the honor of the first encounter with the enemy.")

97. *con maggior valchi*: Buti comments: "cioè con maggiori passi che non andavamo noi" ("that is to say, with greater steps than we were taking"). *valchi = valichi*.

98. *con esso i due*: Virgil and Statius. For this emphatic use of *esso*, cf. *Purg.* IV, 27.

99. *fuor = furono*. *marescalchi*: Leaders. The term continues the military figure.

100. *E quando innanzi a noi intrato fue*: *Tanto* is understood, either before "innanzi" or after "fue." For the expression *intrare innanzi,* see Boccaccio, *Decam.* V, 7 (vol. I, p. 384, ll. 18, 21-22): "Pietro, che giovane era, e la fanciulla

. . . essendo già tanto entrati innanzi alla donna ed agli altri, che appena si vedevano" ("Pietro, who was young, and a girl . . . having gone on ahead of the lady and the others, who were almost out of sight"). *fue = fu.*

101–2. *li occhi miei . . . sue*: I.e., my eyes could no longer follow his person any more than my mind could follow the obscure words of his prophecy. Since Forese apparently soon disappears from sight—perhaps around a sharp bend in the terrace, Dante must not be able to follow him with his eyes for very long.

101. *fero = fecero.*

103. *parvermi = mi parvero.*

103–4. *i rami gravidi e vivaci d'un altro pomo*: Compare the chorus' description of the torment of Tantalus in Seneca's *Thyestes*, vss. 152-57:

> Stat lassus vacuo gutture Tantalus;
> impendet capiti plurima noxio
> Phineis avibus praeda fugacior;
> hinc illinc gravidis frondibus incubat
> et curvata suis fetibus ac tremens
> alludit patulis arbor hiatibus.

Weary, with empty throat, stands Tantalus; above his guilty head hangs food in plenty, than Phineus' birds more elusive; on either side, with laden boughs, a tree leans over him and, bending and trembling 'neath its weight of fruit, makes sport with his wide-straining jaws.

No more than two trees are described as being on this terrace (for the first, see *Purg.* XXII, 130-35). But any symmetrical spacing would require that there be others, since the wayfarers have turned only a comparatively short distance around the circle. Moreover, what is said of the first tree is surely to be understood of this second one, i.e., that it is turned upside down and that the tempting liquid falls over its leaves from the terrace wall. The "vivaci" may refer to the bright green color of the leaves or to the vigorousness of the branches.

105. *per esser pur allora vòlto in laci*: Some interpreters take this to mean not that Dante has come into sight of the tree by rounding a rather sharp bend at this point, turning in the direction of the tree in that sense, but that he has held his eyes so fixed on the figure of Forese that he has not noticed the tree and becomes aware of it only now. Either meaning seems possible. See n. to vss. 101-2.   *laci = là*. Cf. "lici" for *lì* in *Inf*. XIV, 84, and *Purg*. VII, 64. Such forms were used in early Italian prose. See E. G. Parodi (1957), p. 261.

106-8. *Vidi gente . . . vani*: Cf. Seneca's verses, continuing the description of the torment of Tantalus (*Thyestes*, vss. 162-68):

> sed tunc divitias omne nemus suas
> demittit propius pomaque desuper
> insultant foliis mitia languidis
> accenduntque famem, quae iubet irritas
> exercere manus. has ubi protulit
> et falli libuit, totus in arduum
> autumnus rapitur silvaque mobilis.

But then the whole grove lets its riches down nearer still, and the mellow fruits above his head mock him with drooping boughs and whet again the hunger, which bids him ply his hands in vain. When he has stretched these forth and gladly has been baffled, the whole ripe harvest of the bending woods is snatched far out of reach.

108. *vani*: "Fond," implying that they do this over and over again and always in vain.

109-11. *e 'l pregato non risponde . . . nasconde*: The image suggested by the simile is of an adult person who dangles some fruit before a child, but holds it well out of its reach. Cf. *Purg*. XXVII, 45.

111. *disio*: The object of desire, the fruit.

112. *ricreduta*: This, too, happens over and over again.

116. *legno*: I.e., *albero*.

118. *non so chi diceva*: Again the source of the voice is a mystery. Cf. *Purg*. XXII, 140.

119. *ristretti*: Pressing in close to the inner wall of the terrace to keep as far away from the tree as possible.

121. *Ricordivi = vi ricordi*, the impersonal use of the verb in the subjunctive. Cf. *Purg*. V, 133: "ricorditi di me."

121-23. *d'i maladetti . . . petti*: Centaurs, a mythical race of creatures, half horse and half man. With the exception of Chiron, they are said to have been the offspring of Ixion, king of the Lapithae, and Nephele, a cloud-born woman—hence Dante refers to them as "formed in the clouds." The reference to their gluttony and the "miseri guadagni" ("wretched gains") thereof (vs. 129) concerns their fight with the Lapithae and Theseus at the wedding of Pirithoüs, their half-brother, and Hippodamia. Dante got the story from Ovid, who tells how during the wedding feast the centaur Eurytus, inflamed with wine, attempts to carry off the bride, while his companions seize the other women; see *Metam*. XII, 210-12, 215-25:

> Duxerat Hippodamen audaci Ixione natus
> nubigenasque feros positis ex ordine mensis
> arboribus tecto discumbere iusserat antro.
>
> .   .   .   .
>
> ecce canunt Hymenaeon, et ignibus atria fumant,
> cinctaque adest virgo matrum nuruumque caterva,
> praesignis facie; felicem diximus illa
> coniuge Pirithoum, quod paene fefellimus omen.
> nam tibi, saevorum saevissime Centaurorum,
> Euryte, quam vino pectus, tam virgine visa
> ardet, et ebrietas geminata libidine regnat.
> protinus eversae turbant convivia mensae,
> raptaturque comis per vim nova nupta prehensis.
> Eurytus Hippodamen, alii, quam quisque probabant
> aut poterant, rapiunt, captaeque erat urbis imago.

Bold Ixion's son had wed Hippodame and had invited the cloud-born centaurs to recline at the tables, set in

order in a well-shaded grotto. . . . Behold, they were
singing the nuptial song, the great hall smoked with the
fires, and in came the maiden escorted by a throng of
matrons and young wives, herself of surpassing beauty.
We congratulated Pirithoüs upon his bride, an act which
all but undid the good omen of the wedding. For your
heart, Eurytus, wildest of the wild centaurs, was in-
flamed as well by the sight of the maiden as with wine,
and it was swayed by drunken passion redoubled by
lust. Straightway the tables were overturned and the
banquet in an uproar, and the bride was caught by her
hair and dragged violently away. Eurytus caught up
Hippodame, and others, each took one for himself ac-
cording as he fancied or as he could, and the scene
looked like the sacking of a town.

Theseus rescues Hippodamia, and the fight becomes general.
Ovid (*Metam.* XII, 227-31) writes:

. . . primus "quae te vecordia," Theseus
"Euryte, pulsat," ait, "qui me vivente lacessas
Pirithoum violesque duos ignarus in uno?"
[neve ea magnanimus frustra memoraverit ore,
submovet instantes raptamque furentibus aufert.]

Theseus first cried out: "What madness, Eurytus, drives
you to this, that while I still live you dare provoke Pi-
rithoüs and, not knowing what you do, attack two men
in one?" The great-souled hero, that he might justify
his threat, thrust aside the opposing centaurs and res-
cued the ravished maid from their mad hands.

123. *combatter* = *combatterono*.

124-26. *li Ebrei ch'al ber . . . colli*: The Hebrews of
Gideon's army who, not being able to restrain their desire for
water, "showed themselves weak at the drinking," i.e., bowed
down on their knees to drink. See Iudic. 7:4-8:

Dixitque Dominus ad Gedeon: Adhuc populus multus
est; duc eos ad aquas et ibi probabo illos, et de quo
dixero tibi ut tecum vadat, ipse pergat; quem ire pro-
hibuero, revertatur. Cumque descendisset populus ad

aquas, dixit Dominus ad Gedeon: Qui lingua lambuerint
aquas sicut solent canes lambere, separabis eos seorsum;
qui autem curvatis genibus biberint, in altera parte
erunt. Fuit itaque numerus eorum qui manu ad os pro-
iiciente lambuerant aquas, trecenti viri; omnis autem
reliqua multitudo flexo poplite biberat. Et ait Dominus
ad Gedeon: In trecentis viris qui lambuerunt aquas
liberabo vos, et tradam in manu tua Madian; omnis
autem reliqua multitudo revertatur in locum suum.
Sumptis itaque pro numero cibariis et tubis, omnem
reliquam multitudinem abire praecepit ad tabernacula
sua; et ipse cum trecentis viris se certamini dedit. Castra
autem Madian erant subter in valle.

The Lord said to Gedeon, "There are still too many
soldiers. Lead them down to the water and I will test
them for you there. If I tell you that a certain man is to
go with you, he must go with you. But no one is to go
if I tell you he must not." When Gedeon led the soldiers
down to the water, the Lord said to him, "You shall set
to one side everyone who laps up the water as a dog
does with its tongue; to the other, everyone who kneels
down to drink." Those who lapped up the water raised
to their mouths by hand numbered three hundred, but
all the rest of the soldiers knelt down to drink the water.
The Lord said to Gedeon, "By means of the three hun-
dred who lapped up the water I will save you and will
deliver Madian into your power. So let all the other sol-
diers go home." Their horns, and such supplies as the
soldiers had with them, were taken up, and Gedeon
ordered the rest of the Israelites to their tents, but kept
the three hundred men. Now the camp of Madian was
beneath him in the valley.

124. *mostrar = mostrarono.*

125. *Gedeon*: Gideon, one of the judges of Israel who de-
livered the Jews from the Midianites. The passage quoted in
the n. to vss. 124-26 continues (Iudic. 7:9): "Eadem nocte
dixit Dominus ad eum: Surge et descende in castra, quia

tradidi eos in manu tua." ("That night the Lord said to Gedeon, 'Go, descend on the camp, for I have delivered it up to you.' ")

126. *Madian*: Midian, ancient region of northwest Arabia, east of the Gulf of Aqaba, here used for the Midianites themselves, who were descended from Midian, the son of Abraham and Keturah (see Gen. 25:1-2).

127. *a l'un d'i due vivagni*: The inner margin. For "vivagno" in the sense of "edge," see *Inf*. XXIII, 49.

129. *guadagni*: "Wages," in the sense the English has in "the wages of sin is death." The adjective "miseri" turns the meaning "gain" to "punishment," retribution.

130. *rallargati*: "Spread out" again, with Dante following behind the two ancient poets.   *sola*: No souls and no trees in sight. Cf. vs. 133.

131. *mille passi*: The subject of "portar."   *portar = portarono*.

132. *contemplando ciascun*: An absolute construction, "ciascun" being the subject of the participle.

133. *voi sol tre = voi tre soli*. For this kind of rhyme (made up of two words), cf. *Inf*. VII, 28; XXX, 87; and *passim*. The three are alone in the sense that they do not come, as do the souls of this terrace, in a larger group.

135. *poltre*: The adjective may mean either "sluggish" or "coltish" (cf. *puledre* and OFr *poultre*), but the term is probably intended to signify Dante's being aroused from the inner quiet of contemplation (see vs. 132), which, in the case of the beast in simile, would mean one that was going along peacefully and a bit drowsily. Del Lungo conceives of the "sùbita voce" as part of the simile, this being, in the case of the beast, the voice of the driver.

136. *fossi = fosse*.

137–39. *non si videro ... vidi un*: Cf. Apoc. 1:14-16:

> Caput autem eius et capilli erant candidi tamquam lana
> alba et tamquam nix, et oculi eius tamquam flamma
> ignis, et pedes eius similes aurichalco, sicut in camino
> ardenti, et vox illius tamquam vox aquarum multarum.
> Et habebat in dextera sua stellas septem, et de ore eius
> gladius utraque parte acutus exibat, et facies eius sicut
> sol lucet in virtute sua.

> But his head and his hair were white as white wool, and
> as snow, and his eyes were as a flame of fire; his feet
> were like fine brass, as in a glowing furnace, and his
> voice like the voice of many waters. And he had in his
> right hand seven stars. And out of his mouth came forth
> a sharp two-edged sword; and his countenance was like
> the sun shining in its power.

140. *dar volta = svoltarsi*. In this instance, as before, the
turn into the passageway is to the left.

141. *quinci = di qui.   per pace*: "For peace" as the
goal. See *Purg.* V, 61. Peace is especially significant as such
a term here, since the sins of concupiscence are without
peace. Cf. *Inf.* I, 58, and V, 99, and see n. to *Inf.* V, 99.

143. *mi volsi dietro a' miei dottori*: Dante turns toward the
place from where the angel's voice comes, and although he
cannot see Virgil and Statius, he knows that they must have
responded to the invitation and turned toward the stairs.

145–47. *E quale . . . fiori*: The *Anonimo fiorentino* com-
ments: "Vuole dire che, innanzi che si lievi l'alba, comincia
a trarre uno venticello, che si chiama aura, et questa aura,
ciò è questo venticello, che si lieva da' fiori et dall'erbe odo-
rifere, rende odore et soavità." ("It means that, before the sun
rises, a little wind begins to blow, and it is called *aura*. This
aura, that is, this little wind, which rises from the odoriferous
flowers and grass, brings fragrance and mildness.") Cf. *Purg.*
XXVIII, 7.

146. *movesi = si move.   olezza*: "Wafts fragrance."

148. *dar*: "Strike."

148–49. *per mezza la fronte* = *in mezzo alla fronte.*

150. *d'ambrosia l'orezza*: The "breath" or "fragrance" of ambrosia. Cf. Virgil, *Aen.* I, 402-4:

> Dixit et avertens rosea cervice refulsit,
> ambrosiaeque comae divinum vertice odorem
> spiravere . . .

She spake, and as she turned away, her roseate neck flashed bright. From her head her ambrosial tresses breathed celestial fragrance.

See also Virgil, *Georg.* IV, 415: "Haec ait et liquidum ambrosiae diffundit odorem." ("She spake, and shed abroad ambrosia's fragrant stream.")

151–54. *Beati cui alluma . . . giusto*: Cf. Matt. 5:6: "Beati qui esuriunt et sitiunt iustitiam, quoniam ipsi saturabuntur." ("Blessed are they who hunger and thirst for justice, for they shall be satisfied.") Already at the exit of the preceding circle of the avaricious this beatitude had served in part; see *Purg.* XXII, 6: "con '*sitiunt*,' sanz' altro." Now "sitiunt" is omitted and "esuriunt" is cited in the paraphrase, this applying more appropriately to gluttony, even as thirst to desire for riches.

151. *cui*: I.e., *coloro i quali.* *alluma* = *illumina.* "Tanto di grazia" is the subject. Cf. "allumati" in *Purg.* XXI, 96.

152. *amor del gusto*: Love of the palate, i.e., of that which pleases the palate.

153. *non fuma*: "Amor del gusto" is the subject and "troppo disir" the object of "fuma."

154. *esuriendo sempre quanto è giusto*: This is perhaps deliberately ambiguous and is the richer in meaning for being so. It can mean either hungering as much as is right (observing temperance in eating) or hungering after all that is just, i.e., after justice, as the beatitude has it.

CANTO XXV

1. *Ora era onde 'l salir non volea storpio*: Virgil has already stated that the time allotted for the journey through Purgatory must be apportioned (*Purg.* XXIII, 5-6), and the opening statement of this canto echoes a note of that urgency, which is the "stimolo" implied in vs. 6. *non volea storpio*: Freely, "could do without impediment." The passageway is narrow, the climb steep, and time presses, for the sun has already passed the meridian. For *storpio* in the sense of "obstacle," see the examples given by E. G. Parodi (1957), p. 284; also see M. Barbi (1934b), p. 231.

2-3. *ché 'l sole . . . Scorpio*: E. Moore (1887, p. 108) explains: "The Sun being now rather backward in Aries, the time when Taurus is on the Meridian of Noon, and the opposite sign of Scorpio on that of midnight as here described, would be generally understood to be about 2 P.M. though, as each constellation covers many degrees of space, the indication is only an approximate one." (See Fig. 4, p. 590.) As so often through Purgatory, the reader is reminded of the antipodal position of Jerusalem with respect to this mountain, and of the hour there. The wayfarers have spent almost four hours on the terrace of the gluttons (see *Purg.* XXII, 118-20).

589

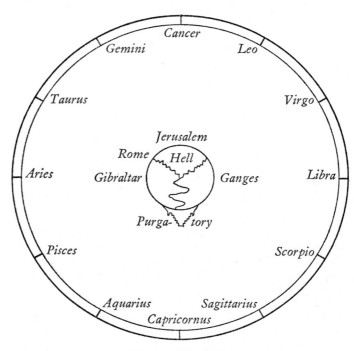

Figure 4. The Zodiac

2. *merigge*: From the Latin *meridies*. Cf. *Purg.* XXXIII, 104.

4. *non s'affigge*: Cf. *Inf.* XII, 115 and *passim*; *Purg.* XI, 135.

5. *vassi = si va*. The reflexive serves to "distance" the subject and to reflect his determination to continue on his way.
   che che: I.e., *qualsiasi cosa.*   *li = gli.*   *appaia = apparisca.*

6. *se di bisogno stimolo*: The more usual word order would be "se stimolo di bisogno."   *trafigge*: "Pierces," "goads."

7. *callaia*: Elsewhere such a narrow passageway is termed a *calla*: *Purg.* IV, 22; IX, 123. See E. G. Parodi (1957), p. 245.

8. *uno innanzi altro*: The three proceed in single file, Virgil first, Statius second, and Dante last. And the reader is to conceive of them as so positioned all during Statius' fairly lengthy disquisition.

9. *artezza*: "Narrowness." Cf. "arte" in *Purg.* XXVII, 130.
   dispaia: "Unmates," i.e., forcing them to proceed in single file.

13. *accesa e spenta*: I.e., now kindled and now extinguished, even as the storkling's wing was raised, then lowered.

14–15. *infino a l'atto . . . s'argomenta*: Even to the point of opening his mouth.

15. *dicer = dire.*   *s'argomenta*: "Makes ready."

16–17. *Non lasciò . . . ma disse*: I.e., "non lasciò di parlare, ma disse."

16. *per l'andar che fosse ratto*: Though our pace was fast.

17–18. *Scocca l'arco . . . tratto*: The metaphor is that of an arrow in a bow drawn back so far that the head, the iron, touches the bow itself. The image of the bow and arrow implied in the verb *scoccare* was commonly used to express intention, purpose; here it refers to Dante's pressing question. Cf. *Inf.* XXV, 96; *Purg.* VI, 130-31.

20. *Come si può far magro*: Porena comments: "Dovrebbe dire 'come si può farsi magro?' ma l'uno dei due *si*, il riflessivo, è soppresso, assorbito dal *si* soggetto impersonale." ("He should say 'how can one make oneself lean?' but one of these two *si*'s, the reflexive, disappears, absorbed by the *si* which is the impersonal subject.")

21. *là dove l'uopo di nodrir non tocca*: Porena paraphrases this as follows: "dove non si è toccati dal bisogno di nutrirsi"

("where the need to nourish oneself is not felt"). Since these are shades and hence do not have real bodies, Dante wonders how it is possible for them to become lean.

22. *t'ammentassi* = *ti rammentassi*. Cf. *Purg.* XIV, 56.

22-23. *come Meleagro . . . stizzo*: Meleager, son of Oeneus, king of Calydon in Aetolia, took part in the expedition of the Argonauts under Jason and afterwards was leader of the heroes who slew the Calydonian boar. He gave the skin of the boar to Atalanta, whom he loved, but his mother's brothers, the sons of Thestius, took it from her, whereupon Meleager in fury slew them. He thus unwittingly brought about his own death. When he was seven days old the Fates had declared that his life would last as long as the piece of wood which was burning on the hearth should remain unconsumed. His mother, Althaea, hearing this, extinguished the firebrand and kept it carefully concealed; but now, to avenge the death of her brothers, she threw it into the fire and it was consumed, whereupon Meleager expired. Althaea then, in despair at what she had done, put an end to herself. In *Metam.* VIII, 445-532, Ovid tells of Meleager's end. See especially vss. 513-25:

> aut dedit aut visus gemitus est ipse dedisse
> stipes, ut invitis conreptus ab ignibus arsit.
>   Inscius atque absens flamma Meleagros ab illa
> uritur et caecis torreri viscera sentit
> ignibus ac magnos superat virtute dolores.
> quod tamen ignavo cadat et sine sanguine leto,
> maeret et Ancaei felicia vulnera dicit
> grandaevumque patrem fratresque piasque sorores
> cum gemitu sociamque tori vocat ore supremo,
> forsitan et matrem. crescunt ignisque dolorque
> languescuntque iterum; simul est exstinctus uterque,
> inque leves abiit paulatim spiritus auras
> paulatim cana prunam velante favilla.

The brand either gave or seemed to give a groan as it was caught and consumed by the unwilling fire.

Unconscious, far away, Meleager burns with those

flames; he feels his vitals scorching with hidden fire, and o'ercomes the great pain with fortitude. But yet he grieves that he must die a cowardly and bloodless death, and he calls Ancaeus happy for the wounds he suffered. With groans of pain he calls with his dying breath on his aged father, his brothers and loving sisters and his wife, perchance also upon his mother. The fire and his pains increase, and then die down. Both fire and pain go out together; his spirit gradually slips away into the thin air as white ashes gradually overspread the glowing coals.

In an attempt to help Dante understand how the souls, which are incorporeal, can become lean, Virgil asks him to compare this situation with that in which there is no visible bond between the wasting away of Meleager and the consuming of a firebrand.

23. *stizzo*: Cf. *Inf.* XIII, 40.

24. *fora = sarebbe.*   *agro*: "Harsh-tasting." Cf. "duro," vs. 27.

25. *al vostro guizzo*: The shift to the second person plural (continued in "vostra image" in the following verse) obviously generalizes the experience. *Guizzo* and *guizzare* suggest the least—the slightest—movement, any movement whatsoever.

27. *vizzo*: "Soft" and, more literally, "easy to chew." Cf. *avvizzito*.

28. *Ma perché dentro a tuo voler t'adage*: Here "voler" (as "disio" in *Purg.* XXIV, 111, and elsewhere in the poem) denotes the object of the will, i.e., "in order that you may rest in the truth you desire to know."   *adage*: Subjunctive.

29. *ecco qui Stazio*: We must bear in mind that the three are proceeding in single file, with Virgil in the lead and Statius second. The words, therefore, do not point out Statius so much as they say: "Here we have Statius."   *chiamo e prego*: "I call upon him and I entreat him."

30. *de le tue piage*: Though we may conceive of ignorance as a wound, it is hard to feel that the poet's hand has not been a little forced by the rhyme at this point. *piage = piaghe*. See *Inf*. XXV, 31, where "biece" is used for *bieche*.

31. *la veduta etterna*: A view exceeding Virgil's understanding in some respects, since it involves a divine mystery which only the Christian Statius has some knowledge of, namely, the "breathing in" of the individual and immortal soul by God (vss. 70-72). *dislego*: Literally, "untie." Cf. the Latin *explicare*.

32. *là dove tu sie*: Literally, "there where you are." *sie = sia*.

33. *discolpi me*: The whole phrase "non potert' io far nego" serves as subject of the verb, which is in the subjunctive: "Let my inability to deny you excuse me."

36. *fiero = saranno*. "Parole mie" (vs. 34) is the subject.
  al come che tu die: "Concerning the 'how' which you say," i.e., about which you ask. *die = di' (dici)*.

37-44. *Sangue perfetto . . . dire*: B. Nardi (1960, pp. 46-47) notes: "Secondo appunto la ben nota definizione dello Stagirita, lo sperma è un *excrementum alimenti sanguinei, quod ultimum in membra digeritur*; e secondo quella non meno nota di Avicenna, *sperma est superfluitas digestionis quartae, resudans a venis, tertia digestione iam expleta*." ("According to the well-known definition of the Stagyrite, the sperm is an 'excretion of the sanguineous nourishment that is digested in the members last'; and according to the equally well-known definition of Avicenna, 'sperm is the superfluity of the fourth digestion, which comes forth from the veins after the third digestion is over.'") See Aristotle, *De gener. animal.* I, 17-19, especially 726^a-726^b; II, 3, 737^a; and the reference to Avicenna's *Canon* cited by Nardi (p. 47, n. 2). Nardi continues (p. 47):

Secondo il concetto aristotelico, l'alimento non si converte nella sostanza del corpo nutrito se non dopo una serie di trasformazioni o *digestioni*, attraverso le quali cessa di essere *dissimile* ed è reso perfettamente *assimilabile*. Queste digestioni per le quali il cibo passa, secondo Avicenna, sono quattro: la prima si compie nello stomaco e nel ventre; la seconda nel fegato, ove il chilo comincia a trasformarsi in sangue; la terza nelle vene, ove il sangue grezzo e imperfetto, uscito dal fegato, vien depurato dalle superfluità acquose e si converte in sangue perfetto che si raccoglie nel lago del cuore; finalmente la quarta digestione avviene nelle singole membra, delle quali l'alimento sanguigno ristora le perdite e produce lo sviluppo.

According to the Aristotelian concept, food converts itself into the substance of the body it nourishes only after a series of transformations, or *digestions*, through which it ceases to be dissimilar and becomes perfectly *assimilable*. According to Avicenna, food must pass through four of these digestions: the first is accomplished in the stomach and in the belly; the second is in the liver, where the chyle begins to be transformed into blood; the third is in the veins, where the crude and imperfect blood sent forth by the liver is purified of its watery superfluities and converted into perfect blood, which gathers in the lake of the heart; finally, the fourth digestion takes place in the individual members, where the sanguineous nourishment replaces losses and produces development.

See Aristotle, *De anima* II, 4, 416[b], and the references afforded by Nardi (p. 47, n. 5) to Avicenna's *De animalibus* and *Canon*. Nardi (p. 48) goes on to say:

Sotto la guida della virtù *informativa*, derivata dal cuore, il sangue vien recato, per le vene, al convito delle membra, ove si celebra, come dice Alberto, la quarta digestione. E la parte più sottile dell'alimento sanguigno, la più eletta e quindi suscettibile di migliore virtù, va a nutrire i *membra radicalia,* cioè quelle parti che sono la radice e il fondamento di tutto l'organismo, come il cuore e il cervello. Ma non tutto quello che è stato loro imbandito si beve dalle assetate vene e si fa membra; anzi una parte rimane, come superfluo, *quasi alimento che di mensa leve*. Di questo *superfluo*, anzi, secondo Alberto, del superfluo dell'alimento di cui si son cibati i *membra radicalia*, si genera appunto lo sperma. Per questo appunto Avicenna dice che "sperma fit ex sanguine bono et decocto decoctione bona et completa," e che esso è una *superfluitas* dell'ultima digestione.

Under the guidance of the formative virtue, which derives from the heart, the blood is taken through the veins to the banquet in the members, where, as Albertus says, the fourth digestion is celebrated. The most subtle part of the sanguineous nourishment, the most select and therefore susceptible of the highest virtue, goes to nourish the fundamental members, that is to say, those parts that are the basis and the foundation of the whole organism, like the heart and the brain. But not all of that which has been served to them is drunk by the thirsty veins, to become members; in fact, a portion remains, as though superfluous, "quasi alimento che di mensa leve." From this superfluity—in fact, according to Albertus, from the superfluity of the nourishment taken by the fundamental members—precisely the sperm is generated. That is why Avicenna says: "Sperm is made of good blood and distilled from a good and complete digestion"; and it is a superfluity of the final digestion.

See Albertus Magnus, *De animalibus* III, ii, 8, and Nardi's reference (p. 48, n. 5) to Avicenna's *De animalibus*. Nardi (pp. 48-49) explains:

Ma il residuo dell'ultima digestione non è ancora sperma atto alla generazione, ed ha bisogno di una nuova digestione per diventarlo. Questa nuova digestione avviene nei condotti, pei quali il sangue perfetto, residuo dell'ultima digestione, discende dall'aorta e dai reni ai testicoli, e quindi nei vasi seminali *ad basem virgae, ov'è più bello tacer che dire,* come si esprime

Dante parafrasando Aristotele. Nei vasi seminali avviene la così detta *digestio spermatica*, nella quale il sangue, residuo della quarta digestione, perde il color rosso e si fa bianco e disposto alla generazione di un nuovo organismo.

But the residue of the final digestion is not yet sperm that can generate; to become that, it must go through another digestion. This new digestion takes place in the veins through which perfect blood, the residue of the final digestion, descends from the aorta and the kidneys to the testicles, and thence to the seminal vessels at the base of the penis, "of which it is better to be silent than to speak," as Dante says, paraphrasing Aristotle. In the seminal vessels, the so-called digestion of the sperm takes place, in which the blood, residue of the fourth digestion, loses its red color and becomes white and capable of generating a new organism.

See Aristotle, *Hist. animal.* III, 1, 510^{a}; *De gener. animal.* I, 13, 720^{a}.

39. *leve = levi*, "you remove," i.e., one removes.

40-41. *prende nel core . . . informativa*: On the informative virtue, or formative virtue, as it was also called, Nardi (1949, pp. 262-63) writes:

In particolare, non è ben chiaro che cosa sia, per Aristotele, la virtù o natura posseduta dal seme maschile, e quale ne sia la funzione nella formazione e nello sviluppo dell'embrione. In un altro luogo del *De gener. animal.*, III, c. 11, egli dice che "gli animali e le piante son generate dalla terra e dall'umore, perchè nella terra è l'umore, nell'umore lo spirito, e il calore animale è da per tutto, di guisa che in certo modo tutte le cose son piene di anima." Riferendosi appunto a questo concetto, egli afferma (II, c. 3), che quello che rende fecondi i semi è "il così detto calore," che non è fuoco ma spirito e natura analoga dell'elemento degli astri. Questa virtù del seme è quella che Galeno chiamò *for-*

mativa, perchè presiede alla formazione dell'embrione e del feto. . . .

. . . Poichè dunque il seme paterno è considerato come l'agente strumentale della generazione, gli Scolastici ne conclusero ch'esso dovesse possedere una virtù attiva derivata dall'anima dell'agente principale, il padre. A questa virtù che dà impulso e presiede allo sviluppo del nuovo organismo vivente, fu da essi riservato il nome di *virtù formativa* o *informativa*.

In particular, it is not very clear what virtue or nature the male seed possesses, according to Aristotle, or what its function is in the formation and development of the embryo. In another place in *De gener. animal.* III, 11 [762^a], he says that "animals and plants are generated by the earth and by humors; for the humor is in the earth, the spirit is in the humor, and animal heat is everywhere, so that in a certain sense all things are full of soul (*anima*)." Referring precisely to this concept, he affirms (II, 3 [736^b]) that what renders the seed fertile is "the so-called heat," which is not fire, but spirit and nature analogous to the element of the stars. This virtue in the seed is the one Galen called "formative," because it presides over the formation of the embryo and the fetus. . . .

. . . Therefore, since the paternal seed is considered the instrumental agent of generation, the Scholastics concluded that it must possess an active virtue derived from the soul of the principal agent, the father. For this virtue, which gives the impulse to and presides over the development of the new living organism, they reserved the name of formative, or informative, virtue.

In the *Convivio* (IV, xxi, 4) Dante terms it "la vertù de l'anima generativa" and "la vertù formativa."

The phrase "a tutte membra umane virtute informativa" should be construed "virtute informativa a tutte membra umane," i.e., as B. Nardi observes (1960, p. 49), directed toward creating the members of a new organism.

41–42. *come quello . . . vane*: See n. to vss. 37-44. Under the direction of the formative virtue the perfect blood which collects in the lake of the heart flows forth therefrom into the veins, where the "third digestion" takes place, and then into the individual members where nourishment replaces losses and produces development. That which becomes the male sperm retains this virtue. As Nardi observes (1960, p. 49): "La stessa *virtù informativa* che aveva il sangue per la sua assimilazione nelle membra, diventa, nel seme, *virtù informativa* diretta a creare le membra di un nuovo organismo." ("The same formative virtue which the blood possessed in order to become assimilated in the members becomes, in the sperm, the formative virtue directed toward creating the members of a new organism.")

42. *vane = va* with the addition of *ne*, often made when the verb form ends in an accented vowel. For other instances, see *Inf.* XI, 31 ("pòne"), *Inf.* XVIII, 87 ("féne"), and *Purg.* IV, 22 ("salìne"). See E. G. Parodi (1957), p. 243.

43–44. *Ancor digesto . . . dire*: See nn. to vss. 37-44 and 41-42.

44–45. *e quindi poscia geme . . . vasello*: And thence, from the testicles, the perfect blood, now having become the sperm through another "digestion," issues forth and drips (see "geme" in *Inf.* XIII, 41) over the blood of the female in a natural vessel, the uterus. B. Nardi (1960, p. 49) explains: "Il seme mascolino, così elaborato, *geme sovr'altrui sangue in natural vasello*, cioè sul *sanguis menstruus* fornito dalla madre." ("Thus elaborated, the masculine seed 'drips over the blood of the other, in a natural vessel'; that is to say, over the menstrual blood furnished by the mother.") Nardi continues: "Anche il sangue femmineo è un *superfluo* della quarta digestione, come il seme paterno; ma al primo manca quell'ulteriore digestione complementare, che è propria invece del secondo." ("The female blood is also a superfluity of the fourth digestion, like the paternal seed; but the former lacks that final complementary digestion, which is proper to the latter.") In *Conv.* IV, xxi, 4, Dante says: "E però dico che quando l'umano seme cade nel suo recettaculo, cioè ne

la matrice, esso porta seco la vertù de l'anima generativa."
("And therefore I say that when the human seed falls into
its receptacle, that is, into the matrix, it bears with it the vir-
tue of the generative soul.")

46. *Ivi s'accoglie l'uno e l'altro insieme*: There is mingled
the one blood with the other.

47. *l'un disposto a patire e l'altro a fare*: Nardi (1960,
p. 49) comments: "Il *sanguis menstruus* è un principio es-
senzialmente passivo. L'uno, afferma Dante con Aristotele,
è disposto a patire, l'altro a fare; l'uno fornisce la materia
del processo genetico, l'altro la forma." ("The menstrual
blood is an essentially passive principle. Dante, following
Aristotle, affirms that the one is disposed to undergo, and the
other to do. The one furnishes the matter of the genetic proc-
ess, the other furnishes the form.") See Aristotle, *De gener.
animal.* I, 2, 716^a; I, 19, 727^a; II, 4, 738^b. Cf. Thomas
Aquinas, *Summa theol.* I, q. 118, a. 1, ad 4: "In animalibus
perfectis, quae generantur ex coitu, virtus activa est in semine
maris, secundum Philosophum in lib. 1 de Generat. animal.,
cap. 2 et 20; materia autem foetus est illud quod ministratur
a femina." ("In perfect animals, generated by coition, the
active force is in the semen of the male, as the Philosopher
says, *De Gener. Animal.* ii, 3 [737^a]; but the foetal matter
is provided by the female.")

48. *perfetto loco*: The heart, where the blood, through di-
gestion, is made perfect and whence it flows, is pumped,
through the aorta to become the sperm.

49–50. *e, giunto lui . . . prima*: B. Nardi (1960, pp. 49-50)
says: "Tosto che il seme ha raggiunto nella matrice il prin-
cipio passivo, comincia ad agire su questo, ed anzi tutto lo
coagula. . . . Aristotele infatti compara l'azione del seme ma-
scolino sul sangue femmineo all'azione del caglio sul latte.
E l'idea, ripresa e sviluppata da Avicenna, era divenuta
comune nell'embriologia medievale." ("As soon as the semen
has reached the passive principle in the womb, it begins to
act on it, and in fact it coagulates it completely. . . . In fact,

Aristotle compares the action of the male semen on the female blood to the action of curd on milk. And this idea, taken up and developed by Avicenna, had become common in medieval embryology.") See Aristotle, *De gener. animal.* II, 4, 739ᵇ, and the references afforded by Nardi (p. 50, n. 4) to Avicenna's *Canon* and *De animalibus.* Cf. Iob 10:10; Sapien. 7:2. The *Anonimo fiorentino*, commenting on vs. 43, states: "come il presame fa il latte" ("just as rennet does in milk").

50. *e poi avviva*: "And then vivifies," gives life to. The *virtù informativa* is thus a *virtù vivificans*, effecting a vegetative soul, first of all. On this point, see the interesting observations by B. Nardi (1960, pp. 50-51) regarding the difference at this point between the doctrine adopted by Dante and that of Albertus Magnus.

51. *ciò che per sua matera fé constare*: That which the male sperm, the perfect blood that took on the informing virtue in the heart, has now caused to coagulate and become consistent, to serve as its material, i.e., the female menstrual blood.

52-54. *Anima fatta . . . riva*: B. Nardi (1960, p. 52) elaborates:

> Allo stesso modo che nel *Convivio*, l'*anima in vita*, cioè l'anima sensitiva in atto, era tirata dalla potenza attiva del seme, per virtù del cielo, così qui la virtù attiva del seme si fa anzi tutto anima vegetativa simile a quella delle piante. Con questa differenza, tuttavia, che l'anima delle piante è *a riva*, cioè ha compiuto tutto il suo sviluppo e non è capace di ulteriore perfezione; invece, la virtù attiva del seme umano, divenuta anima vegetativa, è *in via* a diventare anima sensitiva; poichè l'anima del generante, da cui deriva, tende a trasfondere nel generato la propria forma, secondo il motto scolastico: *agens agit sibi simile.* E perciò l'anima vegetativa, nell'animale e nell'uomo, non si limita ad attuare nell'embrione le funzioni puramente vegetative, ma *ipsae virtutes vegetabilis non vegetant nisi ad formam sensus, eo quod in sensitivo complentur.*

Just as in the *Convivio*, the live soul, that is to say, the sensitive soul in act, was drawn by the active potency of the seed, by virtue of the heavens, so here the active virtue of the semen becomes first of all a vegetative soul, similar to that of plants. But with this difference: that the soul of plants is at the shore [i.e., at its destination], that is to say, it has accomplished its entire development and is not capable of any further perfection. Instead, the active virtue of the human semen, which has become a vegetative soul, is *in via* [on the way] to becoming a sensitive soul. For the soul of the generator from whom it derives tends to transfuse its own form into that which it generates, according to the Scholastic formulation: "The acts of any agent are similar to the agent." And so in men and animals, the vegetative soul does not limit itself to actuating the purely vegetative functions in the embryo; rather, "these vegetative virtues vegetate only in the direction of the sensitive form, because they find their completion in the sensitive."

For the quotation that closes this passage from Nardi, see Albertus Magnus, *De nat. et orig. animae* I, 4.

For the three *potentiae* or "souls"—vegetative, sensitive, and intellective—see *Conv.* III, ii, 11-14:

Dico adunque che lo Filosofo nel secondo de l'Anima, partendo le potenze di quella, dice che l'anima principalmente hae tre potenze, cioè vivere, sentire e ragionare: e dice anche muovere; ma questa si può col sentire fare una, però che ogni anima che sente, o con tutti i sensi o con alcuno solo, si muove; sì che muovere è una potenza congiunta col sentire. E secondo che esso dice, è manifestissimo che queste potenze sono intra sè per modo che l'una è fondamento de l'altra; e quella che è fondamento puote per sè essere partita, ma l'altra, che si fonda sopra essa, non può da quella essere partita. Onde la potenza vegetativa, per la quale si vive, è fondamento sopra 'l quale si sente, cioè vede, ode, gusta, odora e tocca; e questa vegetativa potenza per sè puote essere anima, sì come vedemo ne le piante tutte. La

sensitiva sanza quella essere non puote, e non si truova
in alcuna cosa che non viva; e questa sensitiva potenza
è fondamento de la intellettiva, cioè de la ragione: e
però ne le cose animate mortali la ragionativa potenza
sanza la sensitiva non si truova, ma la sensitiva si truova
sanza questa, sì come ne le bestie, ne li uccelli, ne' pesci
e in ogni animale bruto vedemo. E quella anima che
tutte queste potenze comprende, e perfettissima di tutte
l'altre, è l'anima umana, la quale con la nobilitade de
la potenza ultima, cioè ragione, participa de la divina
natura a guisa di sempiterna intelligenzia; però che
l'anima è tanto in quella sovrana potenza nobilitata e
dinudata da materia, che la divina luce, come in angelo,
raggia in quella: e però è l'uomo divino animale da li
filosofi chiamato.

I say then that the Philosopher in the second *Of the Soul*
[see Aristotle, *De anima* II, 2, 413^b] when analysing
its powers, says that the soul has in the main three pow-
ers, to wit, life, sense and reason; and he also mentions
motion, but this may be united with sense, for every
soul that has sense (either with all the senses or some
one of them only), has motion also; so that motion is
a power inseparable from sense. And, as he says, it is
quite plain that these powers are so related to each
other that one is the foundation of the other. And that
which is the foundation may exist by itself apart; but
the other, which is founded upon it, may not exist apart
from it. Wherefore the vegetative power, whereby things
live, is the foundation upon which rests the sensitive
life, to wit, sight, hearing, taste, smell and touch; and
this vegetative power may constitute a soul in itself, as
we see in all the plants. The sensitive power cannot exist
without this; there is nothing that feels, without being
alive. And this sensitive power is the foundation of the
intellectual power, to wit the reason; and therefore,
amongst mortal things that have life, the rational power
without the sensitive is not to be found; but the sensi-
tive power is to be found without the other, as we see

in the beasts and in the birds and in the fishes and in
every brute animal. And that soul which embraces all
these powers is the most perfect of all the rest. And the
human soul, which is associated with the nobility of the
highest power, to wit reason, participates in the divine
nature after the fashion of an eternal intelligence; be-
cause the soul is so ennobled, and stripped of material,
in this sovran power, that the divine light shines in it as
in an angel; and therefore man has been called by the
philosophers the "divine animal."

55–56. *tanto ovra poi . . . marino*: Nardi (1960, p. 52)
explains:

Onde la stessa virtù attiva del seme, che s'era fatta
anima vegetativa, diventa ora anima sensitiva che *si
move e sente*, in quanto il suo atto *si prende nel disposto
paziente*, cioè nel corpo che dall'anima acquista la capa-
cità di muoversi e di sentire.

Si move e sente, non però ancora alla maniera degli
organismi perfetti la cui sensibilità è differenziata nella
varietà dei loro organi; ma piuttosto come gli animali
più imperfetti, come fungo marino, cioè come la spugna,
che, secondo la zoologia aristotelica e medievale, oc-
cupa il posto infimo nella scala degli animali e si trova
sul confine del regno animale e di quello vegetale.

Whereupon the same active virtue of the semen, which
had become a vegetative soul, now becomes a sensitive
soul that "moves and feels," inasmuch as it "takes its
act in the predisposed subject" [*Conv.* II, ix, 7], that is
to say, in the body which gets its ability to move and
feel from the soul.

"It moves and feels," but not yet like a perfect organ-
ism, whose sensibility is differentiated in the variety
of its organs. Rather, it moves and feels like more im-
perfect animals, like a sea fungus, that is to say, like a
sponge, which according to Aristotelian and medieval
zoology occupies the lowest place in the scale of animals
and is on the border between the animal and vegetable
worlds.

See Aristotle, *Hist. animal.* VIII, 1, 588ᵇ; V, 16, 548ᵇ; Albertus Magnus, *De animalibus* XXI, i, 6; XXI, ii. Also see E. Moore (1896), p. 137.

57. *ad organar le posse ond' è semente*: Referring to Aristotle, *De anima* II, 4, 415ᵇ, Nardi notes (1960, pp. 52-53):

Come quelli della spugna anche i primi movimenti dell'embrione si riducono alla semplice costrizione. E la sua prima sensibilità, indifferenziata e confusa, si determina man mano che l'anima vien costruendo gli organi nei quali attua le sue *posse*, cioè le sue potenze e capacità: giacchè, secondo il profondo concetto di Aristotele, l'anima non solo è atto, ma altresì causa e principio del corpo vivente.

Also like those of the sponge, the first movements of the embryo amount to simple constriction. Its first sensibility, undifferentiated and confused, is gradually determined as the soul builds the organs in which it will actuate its powers, that is to say, its potencies and capacities. For, according to the profound concept of Aristotle, the soul is not only act, but also the cause and principle of the living body.

58-60. *Or si spiega . . . intende*: See Nardi (1960), p. 53: "E tosto che la virtù attiva proveniente dal cuor del generante, 'dove natura a tutte membra intende,' ha preso ad avvivare la materia fornita dalla madre, nutrendosi di quella, comincia a fabbricare l'organismo, dispiegando le sue latenti capacità, e distendendosi nelle membra da sè create." ("And as soon as the active virtue that comes from the heart of the generator, 'where nature makes provision for all the members,' has begun to enliven the matter furnished by the mother, while it nourishes itself thereupon, it begins to form the organism, unfolding its latent potentialities and extending itself into the members that it has created.")

61. *Ma come d'animal divegna fante*: Nature has now carried her handiwork as far as she can: the fetus has all its organs and the animal stage as such is complete. But how the animal becomes a human being, how it acquires a soul,

is the difficult point, "forte ad intendere," as Dante, referring to Rom. 11:33, says in the *Convivio* (IV, xxi, 6):

> Non si maravigli alcuno, s'io parlo sì che par forte ad intendere; chè a me medesimo pare maraviglia, come cotale produzione si può pur conchiudere e con lo intelletto vedere. Non è cosa da manifestare a lingua, lingua, dico veramente, volgare. Per che io voglio dire come l'Apostolo: "O altezza de le divizie de la sapienza di Dio, come sono incomprensibili li tuoi giudicii e investigabili le tue vie!"

> Let no man marvel if I speak in such wise as seems hard to understand; for to me myself it seems a marvel how such a producing can be arrived at by argument and perceived by the intellect; and it is not a thing to expound in language—I mean in any language truly vernacular. Wherefore I would say like the apostle: "Oh, height of the wealth of the wisdom of God, how incomprehensible are thy judgments, and thy ways past finding out!"

fante: A human being (cf. *Purg.* XI, 66). *Fante* is from the Latin *fari*, "to speak," the capacity that distinguishes man from other animals. See Dante, *De vulg. eloqu.* I, ii-iii, especially I, ii, 1: "Nam eorum que sunt omnium soli homini datum est loqui, cum solum sibi necessarium fuerit." ("For to man alone of all existing beings was speech given, because for him alone was it necessary.") This ability signifies the rational soul that is specifically human. Thus, in a passage in the *Convivio* in which Dante speculates on the subtraction of the rational faculty from man, he observes (*Conv.* IV, vii, 15): "Come levando l'ultimo canto del pentangulo rimane quadrangulo e non più pentangulo, così levando l'ultima potenza de l'anima, cioè la ragione, non rimane più uomo, ma cosa con anima sensitiva solamente, cioè animale bruto." ("Just as if you withdraw the last side of a pentagon you have a quadrangle left, but no longer a pentagon, so if you withdraw the last power of the soul, that is the reason, the man is no longer left, but something with a sensitive soul only; that is, a brute animal.")

62–66. *quest' è tal punto . . . assunto*: This wiser one is Averroës, who, as Dante says in *Inf*. IV, 144, "made the great commentary" of Aristotle. B. Nardi (1960, p. 54) notes: "Per il commentatore arabo di Aristotele, l'*intelletto possibile* è una sostanza separata da materia e disgiunta dall'anima sensitiva che è forma e atto del corpo, alla quale si unisce solo nell'operazione dell'intendere." ("For the Arab commentator on Aristotle, the possible intellect is a substance separate from matter and unconnected with the sensitive soul, which is the form and act of the body, and with which it is united only in the operation of understanding.") See Averroës, *Comm. De anima* III, comm. 5. As Dante will indicate (vss. 72-75), this is an erroneous interpretation.

67–72. *Apri a la verità . . . repleto*: How the embryo acquires a rational soul is the point where Statius' knowledge exceeds Virgil's ken—i.e., the light of natural reason—and partakes of the "eternal view," of a revealed supernatural order of knowledge. Aristotle, to be sure, also held that the rational soul comes from without, but he left the mystery at that. Statius, the Christian, knows more, at least as much as is revealed to us in the Bible. See Gen. 1:27: "Et creavit Deus hominem ad imaginem suam; ad imaginem Dei creavit illum, masculum et feminam creavit eos." ("God created man in his image. In the image of God he created him. Male and female he created them.") Also see Sapien. 15:10-11: "Cinis est enim cor eius, et terra supervacua spes illius, et luto vilior vita eius; quoniam ignoravit qui se finxit, et qui inspiravit illi animam quae operatur, et qui insufflavit ei spiritum vitalem." ("Ashes his heart is! more worthless than earth is his hope, and more ignoble than clay his life; because he knew not the one who fashioned him, and breathed into him a quickening soul, and infused a vital spirit.") But Statius, it must be admitted, also knows a good deal of specifically *scholastic* theology!

In good Christian doctrine the intellective soul which God now breathes into the completed handiwork of Nature must indeed come from Him and cannot have a natural origin, i.e., cannot come from the seed of the parent. Thus Thomas

Aquinas (*Summa theol.* I, q. 118, a. 2, resp.) says on the *anima intellectiva*:

> Et cum sit immaterialis substantia, non potest causari per generationem, sed solum per creationem a Deo. Ponere ergo animam intellectivam a generante causari, nihil est aliud quam ponere eam non subsistentem, et per consequens corrumpi eam cum corpore. Et ideo haereticum est dicere, quod anima intellectiva traducatur cum semine.

> Moreover, since it is an immaterial substance it cannot be caused through generation, but only through creation by God. Therefore to hold that the intellectual soul is caused by the begetter, is nothing else than to hold the soul to be non-subsistent, and consequently to perish with the body. It is therefore heretical to say that the intellectual soul is transmitted with the semen.

Marco Lombardo, claiming that he was a "vera spia" of the truth, expounded this orthodox Christian doctrine in *Purg.* XVI, 85-86, where he stated that the soul "esce di mano a lui che la vagheggia / prima che sia, a guisa di fanciulla."

69. *l'articular del cerebro*: The finishing touch of Nature's handiwork.

70. *lo motor primo a lui si volge*: For the action of the First Mover (the term is Aristotelian) in giving the intellective soul to be the body's form, see Thomas Aquinas, *Summa theol.* I, q. 105, a. 2, resp.:

> Nam omnis motus corporis cuiuscumque vel consequitur formam aliquam, sicut motus localis gravium et levium consequitur formam quae datur a generante, ratione cuius generans dicitur movens; vel est via ad formam aliquam, sicut calefactio est via ad formam ignis. Eiusdem autem est imprimere formam, et disponere ad formam, et dare motum consequentem ad formam. Ignis enim non solum generat alium ignem, sed etiam calefacit, et sursum movet. Cum igitur Deus possit immediate formam materiae imprimere, consequens est

*ut possit secundum quemcumque motum corpus quod-
cumque movere.*

For every movement of any body whatever, either re-
sults from a form, as the movements of things heavy
and light result from the form which they have from
their generating cause, for which reason the generator
is called the mover; or else tends to a form, as heating
tends to the form of heat. Now it belongs to the same
cause, to imprint a form, to dispose to that form, and
to give the movement which results from that form; for
fire not only generates fire, but it also heats and moves
things upwards. Therefore, as God can imprint form
immediately in matter, it follows that he can move any
body whatever in respect of any movement whatever.

The choice of the term *motor primo* thus suggests the mov-
ing, the launching into life of the intellective soul, the "spirito
novo" of vs. 72.   *a lui*: To the fetus, now fully formed.
    lieto: Cf. *Purg.* XVI, 89: "lieto fattore."

71. *sovra tant' arte di natura*: As if God admired Nature's
handiwork! By this turn of phrase the line between Na-
ture's province and God's is stressed.   *e spira*: As in the
Bible (see quotations in n. to vss. 67-72). There is nothing
of this, needless to say, in Aristotle's philosophy.

72. *spirito novo, di vertù repleto*: The intellective soul, the
immortal part of the human creature and form of the body.
This rational soul, though its two powers are the intellect
and the will, takes its name from that of intellect—see Thom-
as Aquinas, *Summa theol.* I, q. 79, a. 1, ad. 1: "Denomi-
natur enim anima sensitiva nomine principalioris suae po-
tentiae, quae est sensus; et similiter anima intellectiva
quandoque nomine intellectus, quasi a principaliori sua vir-
tute." ("For the sensitive soul takes its name from its chief
power, which is sense. And in like manner the intellectual
soul is sometimes called intellect, as from its chief power.")
Similarly, the rational soul is sometimes denoted by the more
specific term of *intellectus possibilis*. See Dante, *Conv.* III,
ii, 14.

73. *ciò che trova attivo quivi*: The powers of the vegetative and sensitive souls.

73–74. *tira in sua sustanzia*: On this particular point, when the new spirit draws into its substance that which it finds active already in the souls of the fetus, see B. Nardi (1960), p. 55:

> Tosto che l'anima sensitiva ha finito di *organar le posse ond'è semente,* e *l'articular del cerebro è perfetto,* il Primo Motore, cioè Dio, si volge all'embrione così organizzato, e, compiacendosi *di tant'arte di natura,* la reca a compimento spirando uno *spirito nuovo* che assorbe in sè e *tira in sua sustanzia* quello *che trova attivo quivi.* Lo *spirito nuovo,* creato direttamente da Dio, è *l'intelletto possibile* del *Convivio*; ed è ripieno di virtù, in quanto "potenzialmente in sè adduce tutte le forme universali, secondo che sono nel suo produttore," e non nel senso che esso rechi con sè, nell'embrione, una nuova virtù vegetativa e sensitiva. Che questa venga creata da Dio non ve n'è bisogno, poichè lo *spirito nuovo* la trova già attiva nell'embrione, e non fa che tirarla *in sua sustanzia,* per formare con essa *un'alma sola,* dotata di vita vegetativa, di senso e del potere di riflessione, cioè di pensiero.

As soon as the sensitive soul has finished developing the organs for the powers whereof it is the germ, and the articulation of the brain is perfected, the First Mover, that is, God, turns to the embryo thus organized and rejoicing over such handiwork of nature, completes its formation by breathing a new spirit which absorbs into itself and draws into its own substance that which it finds active there. This new spirit, created directly by God, is the possible intellect of the *Convivio*, and it is full of power, in that it "potentially absorbs into itself all the universal forms, according as they are in its producer," and not in the sense that it brings with it, into the embryo, a new vegetative and sensitive power. That this [power] should be created by God is not needful, since the new spirit finds it already active in the embryo and only draws it into its own substance to form with it a single soul, endowed with vegetative life, with senses, and with the power of reflection, that is, of thought.

74–75. *e fassi un'alma sola . . . rigira*: Cf. *Purg.* IV, 5-6. On the unity of the soul, see Thomas Aquinas, *Summa theol.* I, q. 76, a. 3, resp.:

Si igitur homo ab alia forma haberet quod sit vivum, scilicet ab anima vegetabili, et ab alia forma quod sit animal, scilicet ab anima sensibili, et ab alia quod sit homo, scilicet ab anima rationali; sequeretur quod homo non esset unum simpliciter, sicut et Aristoteles argumentatur contra Platonem, in 3 Metaph. (text. 20), quod si alia esset idea animalis, et alia bipedis, non esset unum simpliciter animal bipes. Et propter hoc, in 1 de Anima (text. 90), contra ponentes diversas animas in corpore inquirit, quid contineat illas, id est quid faciat ex eis unum. Et non potest dici, quod uniantur per corporis unitatem; quia magis anima continet corpus, et facit ipsum esse unum, quam e converso. . . .

Sic ergo dicendum quod eadem numero est anima in homine, sensitiva et intellectiva et nutritiva.

Quomodo autem hoc contingat, de facili considerari potest, si quis differentias specierum et formarum attendat. Inveniuntur enim rerum species et formae differre ab invicem secundum perfectius et minus perfectum; sicut in rerum ordine animata perfectiora sunt inanimatis, et animalia plantis, et homines animalibus brutis: et in singulis horum generum sunt gradus diversi. Et ideo Aristoteles, in 8 Metaph. (text. 10), assimilat species rerum numeris, qui differunt specie secundum additionem vel subtractionem unitatis; et in 2 de Anima (text. 30 et 31), comparat diversas animas speciebus figurarum, quarum una continet aliam, sicut pentagonum continet tetragonum, et excedit. Sic igitur anima intellectiva continet in sua virtute quidquid habet anima sensitiva brutorum, et nutritiva plantarum. Sicut ergo superficies quae habet figuram pentagonam non per aliam figuram est tetragona, et per aliam pentagona, quia superflueret figura tetragona, ex quo in pentagona continetur; ita nec per aliam animam Socrates est homo, et per aliam animal, sed per unam et eamdem.

If, therefore, man were *living* by one form, the vegetative soul, and *animal* by another form, the sensitive soul, and *man* by another form, the intellectual soul, it would follow that man is not absolutely one. Thus Aristotle argues, *Metaph.* viii. [6, 1045^a] (Did. vii. 6), against Plato, that if the idea of an animal is distinct from the idea of a biped, then a biped animal is not absolutely one. For this reason, against those who hold that there are several souls in the body, he asks (*De Anima* i. 5 [411^b]), *what contains them?*—that is, what makes them one? It cannot be said that they are united by the one body; because rather does the soul contain the body and make it one, than the reverse. . . .

We must therefore conclude that in man the sensitive soul, the intellectual soul, and the nutritive soul are numerically one soul. This can easily be explained, if we consider the differences of species and forms. For we observe that the species and forms of things differ from one another, as the perfect and the imperfect; as in the order of things, the animate are more perfect than the inanimate, and animals more perfect than plants, and man than brute animals; and in each of these genera there are various degrees. For this reason Aristotle, *Metaph.* viii. [3, 1043^b-1044^a] (Did. vii. 3), compares the species of things to numbers, which differ in species by the addition or subtraction of unity. And (*De Anima* ii. 3 [414^b]) he compares the various souls to the species of figures, one of which contains another; as a pentagon contains and exceeds a tetragon. Thus the intellectual soul contains virtually whatever belongs to the sensitive soul of brute animals, and to the nutritive soul of plants. Therefore, as a surface which is of a pentagonal shape, is not tetragonal by one shape, and pentagonal by another—since a tetragonal shape would

be superfluous as contained in the pentagonal—so
neither is Socrates a man by one soul, and animal by
another; but by one and the same soul he is both animal
and man.

Dante, in *Conv.* IV, vii, 15, makes use of this passage from
Aristotle's *De anima* comparing souls to figures (see quota-
tion in n. to vs. 61); see also *Conv.* IV, xix, 6.

Aquinas goes on (*Summa theol.* I, q. 76, a. 3, ad 1) to
point out that the sensitive soul becomes incorruptible when
it is united with the rational soul:

Anima sensitiva non habet incorruptibilitatem ex hoc
quod est sensitiva; sed ex hoc quod est intellectiva, ei
incorruptibilitas debetur. Quando ergo anima est sensi-
tiva tantum, corruptibilis est, quando vero cum sensitivo
intellectivum habet, est incorruptibilis; licet enim sensi-
tivum incorruptionem non det, tamen incorruptionem
intellectivo auferre non potest.

The sensitive soul is incorruptible, not by reason of its
being sensitive, but by reason of its being intellectual.
When, therefore, a soul is sensitive only, it is corrupti-
ble; but when with sensibility it has also intellectuality,
it is incorruptible. For although sensibility does not give
incorruptibility, yet it cannot deprive intellectuality of
its incorruptibility.

This is a point that counts for a good deal in the argument
here as it proceeds, since the soul, when separated from the
body at death, is said to bear with it, *in virtute*, the sensitive
soul, now one with the intellective and incorruptible, because
the intellective soul has drawn the sensitive and the nutritive
souls "into its substance."

74. *fassi = si fa.* The subject is "spirito novo" (vs. 72).
This transformation, brought about by the spirit, bears wit-
ness to its new power, its virtue.

75. *vive e sente e sé in sé rigira*: The verbs denote the ac-
tivities of the vegetative, the sensitive, and the rational
"souls," now better termed *potentiae*, respectively. See n. to

vss. 52-54. For "sé in sé rigira" to denote intellection, see *Conv*. IV, ii, 18: "Però che essa filosofia, che è . . . amoroso uso di sapienza, se medesima riguarda . . . che altro non è a dire, se non che l'anima filosofante non solamente contempla essa veritate, ma ancora contempla lo suo contemplare medesimo." ("Because philosophy, which . . . is 'the loving exercise of wisdom,' contemplates herself . . . what else is this but to say that the philosophising soul not only contemplates the truth, but also contemplates its own contemplation.")

76. *la parola*: My words.

77–78. *guarda il calor* . . . *cola*: See B. Nardi (1960), p. 56, n. 3: "Materialmente l'immagine dantesca è suggerita da Cicerone, *De sen.*, XV, 53, ma idealmente essa deriva dall'immagine consimile dell'unione della luce solare e di quella del fuoco nell'aria." ("Materially, the Dantesque image is suggested by Cicero, *De senectute* XV, 53; but ideally, it derives from the similar image of the union of the light of the sun and the light of fire in the air.") Note Nardi's reference on this point. Thus, analogously, the new spirit, joined to the fetus, Nature's handiwork, results in a new substance, which is both human, i.e., natural (juice of the vine), and divine (the sun).

78. *giunto a*: "Blended with." *l'omor che de la vite cola*: The grape, of course, after it has been gathered from the vine, is pressed to make wine. The process of fermentation was not understood at the time.

79. *Quando Làchesis non ha più del lino*: At the moment of death. See *Purg.* XXI, 25.

80. *solvesi = si solve*. The subject is the *anima* or "alma" of vs. 74. B. Nardi (1960, p. 58) says: "Al separarsi dal corpo, trae seco *e l'umano e 'l divino*, cioè appunto l'anima vegetativo-sensitiva, venuta per generazione dalla virtù del generante, e l'intelletto possibile, che è lo spirito nuovo creato da Dio." ("Upon separating itself from the body, it

[the human soul] takes with it both the human and the divine, that is to say, precisely the vegetative-sensitive soul, which came by way of generation by virtue of the generator, and the possible intellect, which is the new spirit created by God.")

80–81. *e in virtute . . . divino*: The "divine" is, of course, the intellective soul created by God, the "human" part is what was called nature's handiwork, the vegetative and sensitive powers. It is these that are "in virtute," since the divine part is now said to be more acute than before. B. Nardi (1960, p. 58) explains:

> Le facoltà vegetative e sensitive . . . per esser prive dello strumento necessario, cessano dal loro atto secondo, e perdurano solo nel loro atto primo, in quanto son congiunte all'intelletto. In altre parole, la parte vegetativa e sensitiva dell'anima, non potendo più spiegarsi e distendersi nelle membra del corpo, che è disciolto, torna a vivere di quella vita latente ch'era propria del seme umano, ossia ritorna ad essere pura *virtù informativa*.

> The vegetative and sensitive faculties . . . being deprived of the necessary instrument, discontinue their second act and perdure only in their first act, inasmuch as they are conjoined with the intellect. In other words, because the vegetative and sensitive part of the soul is no longer able to unfold and extend itself into the members of the body, which is dissolved, it goes back to live that latent life which was proper to the human semen; that is, it goes back to being pure formative virtue.

This would seem to be the meaning of "in virtute."

Thomas Aquinas uses *virtute* in a way similar to that of "in virtute." See *Summa theol.* I, q. 77, a. 8, resp.:

> Quaedam vero potentiae sunt in coniuncto sicut in subiecto, sicut omnes potentiae sensitivae partis et nutritivae. Destructo autem subiecto, non potest accidens remanere. Unde corrupto coniuncto, non manent huiusmodi potentiae actu, sed virtute tantum manent in anima sicut in principio vel radice.

But other powers are subjected in the composite; as all the powers of the sensitive and nutritive parts. Now accidents cannot remain after the destruction of the subject. Wherefore, the composite being destroyed, such powers do not remain actually; but they remain virtually in the soul, as in their principle or root.

Also see *Summa theol.* I, q. 76, a. 4, resp.:

Unde dicendum est, quod nulla alia forma substantialis est in homine nisi sola anima intellectiva, et quod ipsa sicut virtute continet animam sensitivam et nutritivam, ita virtute continet omnes inferiores formas, et facit ipsa sola quidquid imperfectiores formae in aliis faciunt.

Whence we must conclude, that there is no other substantial form in man besides the intellectual soul; and that the soul, as it virtually contains the sensitive and nutritive souls, so does it virtually contain all inferior forms, and itself alone does whatever the imperfect forms do in other things.

82. *l'altre potenze tutte quante mute*: "Altre" anticipates the naming of the three powers in the next verse; and since the three yet to be named are powers of the intellective soul, these "mute" powers must be those of the vegetative and sensitive souls.

83. *memoria, intelligenza e volontade*: B. Nardi (1960, p. 58) writes: "Le tre facoltà della psicologia agostiniana, nelle quali risplende l'immagine della Trinità, cioè la memoria, l'intelligenza e la volontà, libere ormai dal corpo di cui non hanno bisogno per la loro operazione, sono più attive di quando erano legate alla materia." ("The three faculties of Augustinian psychology, in which there shines forth the image of the Trinity, that is, the memory, the intelligence, and the will, liberated now from the body, which they no longer need for their operation, are more active than they were when bound to matter.") See Augustine, *De Trinitate* IX and X. In *De Trinitate* X, xi, 18, Augustine states: "Memoria, intelligentia, voluntas [sunt] una mens." ("The memory, the intelligence and the will constitute one mind.")

85. *Sanza restarsi*: The *anima* is the subject.

85–86. *per sé stessa . . . rive*: The soul falls either to the shore of Acheron (*Inf*. III, 122-23) or to the shore near the mouth of the Tiber (*Purg*. II, 100-102).

86. *mirabilmente*: Mysteriously and by divine decree.

87. *quivi conosce prima le sue strade*: Only when it finds itself on the one shore or the other does the soul know what its eternal destiny is.

88. *Tosto che loco lì la circunscrive*: Strictly speaking, the soul, without the body, may not be said to be circumscribed by space; but the soul, in this case, is going to take on at least the semblance of a body, and the locating of it in space anticipates the fact. Compare Thomas Aquinas, *Summa theol*. I, q. 52, a. 2, resp.:

> Sic igitur patet quod diversimode esse in loco convenit corpori, et Angelo, et Deo. Nam corpus est in loco circumscriptive, quia commensuratur loco: Angelus autem non circumscriptive, cum non commensuretur loco, sed definitive; quia ita est in uno loco quod non in alio; Deus autem neque circumscriptive, neque definitive, quia est ubique.

> So, then, it is evident that to be in a place appertains quite differently to a body, to an angel, and to God. For a body is in a place in a circumscribed fashion, since it is measured by the place. An angel, however, is not there in a circumscribed fashion, since he is not measured by the place, but definitively, because he is in one place in such a manner that he is not in another. But God is neither circumscriptively nor definitively there, because He is everywhere.

89–90. *la virtù formativa . . . vive*: Writes B. Nardi (1960), p. 58: "La stessa *virtù informativa* che aveva organizzato il corpo terreno nel seno materno, raggia intorno nell'aere vicino e imprende a organizzare un corpo più sottile e leggiero, nel quale riacquista l'atto di anima vegetativa e sensitiva con tutti i cinque sensi." ("The same formative virtue that had organized the earthly body in the maternal womb now radiates into the nearby air and begins to organize a lighter, more subtle body in which it re-acquires the act of the vegetative and the sensitive soul with all five senses.") The air, as will now be explained, serves in lieu of the material body ("membra vive").

91. *piorno* = *piovorno*, "full of moisture," as of rain (*piova*).

92. *l'altrui raggio*: The ray of the sun. "Altrui" here is possessive.

93. *di diversi color diventa addorno*: The rainbow. Thus, the comparison suggests, souls in the afterlife have, as it were, "rainbow bodies."

95. *in lui*: "In it," i.e., the air.   *suggella*: The subject is "l'alma che ristette" in the following verse.

96. *virtualmente*: See n. to vss. 80-81 for the use of the Latin *virtute*.   *l'alma che ristette*: The soul that has found its place on the one shore or the other. See n. to vss. 85-86.

97-98. *e simigliante . . . il foco*: According to this conception, the fire is the invisible element, the flame its visible manifestation, i.e., that which it forms in the air.

99. *sua forma novella*: The subject of "segue."

100. *Però che* = *per ciò che*.   *quindi*: "Thereby," i.e., by way of the aerial body.   *sua paruta*: "Its visibility."

101. *è chiamata ombra*: Because it is unsubstantial but visible.   *organa* = *organizza*.

101-2. *organa poi . . . veduta*: Thus all the senses are organized, that is, the activities of the sensitive soul, which is brought with it *in virtute*.

103. *Quindi*: By virtue of the aerial body. Cf. Virgil, *Aen.* VI, 733: "hinc metuunt cupiuntque, dolent gaudentque" ("hence their fears and desires, their griefs and joys").

106. *ci affliggono*: "Affect us." Cf. the Latin *nos afficiunt*.

107. *l'ombra si figura*: [The shade takes on this or that appearance—of extreme emaciation in the present case, from a desire to eat. Their apparently wasted bodies are thus the expression of a desire, not the result of actual starvation, which is not possible here.]

108. *quest' è la cagion di che tu miri*: This was the cause of Dante's wonder and brought up the whole question.

109–10. *E già venuto . . . s'era per noi*: Cf. the Latin *ventum erat a nobis*. See *Inf.* I, 126 ("per me si vegna") and *Purg.* XXII, 85 ("per me si stette").

109. *l'ultima tortura*: This confirms what the knowledgeable reader would expect—namely, that the seventh terrace, which Statius, Virgil, and Dante now come to, is the last and contains the last purgatorial "torture."

110. *e vòlto*: I.e., "e si era volto per noi."

112–14. *Quivi la ripa . . . sequestra*: From the upright inner wall a horizontal flame shoots forth as far as the outer edge of the terrace, but there a vertical blast of air by deflecting the flame upward "sequesters a path" along the outside edge of the terrace.

112. *balestra*: "Sweeps," suggesting a powerful sweep of fire.

113. *e la cornice*: The outer edge of the terrace.

114. *che la reflette*: Which turns it, blows it back.   *da lei*: I.e., from the fire.

115. *ne = ci.*   *convenia = conveniva.*

117. *quinci*: I.e., on the left side.   *quindi*: I.e., on the right side, which is "free."

120. *però ch' = perciò che.*   *potrebbesi = si potrebbe.*

121. *Summae Deus clementiae*: See E. Moore (1899), pp. 260-61:

Here arises a curious point well worthy of our attention. A hymn beginning with these precise words is used on one of the Festivals of the Blessed Virgin ("Septem Dolorum"); but there is another hymn beginning, "Summae *Parens* clementiae," which occurs in the regular office for Matins on Saturday. Now the contents of this latter hymn are most appropriate for the purpose to which Dante applies it, while those of the other hymn, "Summae *Deus* clementiae," are not at all so. It has sometimes therefore been supposed that Dante intended to refer to this Matins Hymn, though he has not quite accurately quoted it. The true explanation is curiously different from this. The Matins hymn originally, and in Dante's time, was in fact in the form "Summae *Deus* clementiae," not *Parens*, exactly as Dante quotes it, though it is no longer so in the present Breviary. The alteration in this line (as well as several others coming afterwards in the same hymn) was introduced in the year 1631, at the revision of Urban VIII, by whom many of the ancient hymns were somewhat modernized, harsh or rugged expressions being softened down, and other adaptations or supposed improvements introduced. If any one will refer to this Saturday Matins hymn in some of the ancient uses (such e.g. as Sarum, Hereford, York), it will be found in the form quoted by Dante. Indeed, he could no more be expected to quote it in any other, than Milton could be expected to recognize the version of Brady and Tate. Thus we see in all these cases that Dante drew upon very familiar and well-known parts of the Offices of the Church, in prescribing prayers or meditations for the discipline of the several classes of penitents.

M. Britt (1955, pp. 45-46) affords the following text and translation of the Saturday Matins hymn:

> Summæ Parens clementiæ,
> Mundi regis qui machinam,
> Unius et substantiæ,
> Trinusque personis Deus:

Nostros pius cum canticis
Fletus benigne suscipe:
Ut corde puro sordium
Te perfruamur largius.

Lumbos, iecurque morbidum
Flammis adure congruis,
Accincti ut artus excubent,
Luxu remoto pessimo.

Quicumque ut horas noctium
Nunc concinendo rumpimus,
Ditemur omnes affatim
Donis beatæ patriæ.

Præsta, Pater piissime,
Patrique compar Unice,
Cum Spiritu Paraclito
Regnans per omne sæculum.

Great God of boundless mercy hear;
Thou Ruler of this earthly sphere;
In substance one, in Persons three,
Dread Trinity in Unity!

Do Thou in love accept our lays
Of mingled penitence and praise;
And set our hearts from error free,
More fully to rejoice in Thee.

Our reins and hearts in pity heal,
And with Thy chastening fires anneal;
Gird Thou our loins, each passion quell,
And every harmful lust expel.

Now as our anthems, upward borne,
Awake the silence of the morn,
Enrich us with Thy gifts of grace,
From heaven, Thy blissful dwelling place!

Hear Thou our prayer, Almighty King;
Hear Thou our praises, while we sing,
Adoring with the heavenly host
The Father, Son, and Holy Ghost.

123. *che di volger mi fé caler non meno*: Which made me no less concerned to attend to the singing, no less concerned, that is, than I was to watch my step also, because of the danger of falling over. Cf. vss. 125-26.

126. *compartendo la vista a quando a quando*: Dividing my gaze between the souls in the fire and my steps.

127. *Appresso il fine ch'a quell' inno fassi*: The poet makes a special point of the fact that the spirits sing the hymn in its entirety, thus suggesting that the reader recall it all—especially its third stanza. *fassi = si fa*.

128. *gridavano*: The past descriptive tense (instead of a narrative *gridarono*) suggests repetition. Cf. "ricominciavan" in the following verse and the other verbs that follow here.
  Virum non cognosco: Cf. Luc. 1:34: "Dixit autem Maria ad angelum: Quomodo fiet istud, quoniam virum non cognosco?") ("But Mary said to the angel, 'How shall this happen, since I do not know man?'")

129. *bassi*: The spirits shout aloud the examples, then lower their voices as they sing the hymn.

130. *anco*: "Once more."

130–32. *Al bosco si tenne Diana . . . tòsco*: Helice or Callisto, daughter of Lycaon, king of Arcadia, was one of Diana's nymphs, but was dismissed when Diana discovered that she had been seduced by Jupiter, by whom she became the mother of Arcas. The story is told by Ovid, *Metam.* II, 401-530.

131. *caccionne = ne cacciò*. Cf. *Metam.* II, 465: "deque suo iussit secedere coetu" ("and so expelled her from her company").

134. *fuor = furono*.

135. *imponne = ci impone*, singular verb with dual subject.

136. *questo modo*: The constant alternation of the hymn and the recitation of examples of chastity.   *lor*: Dative.

138–39. *cura . . . pasti . . . piaga*: The terms bear a medical connotation that is confirmed in the final "si ricuscia." The cure is the fire (and the third stanza of the hymn should be remembered); the diet is the hymn and the examples recited.

139. *da sezzo*: "At last." Cf. *Inf.* VII, 130.

CANTO XXVI

1. *Mentre che sì per l'orlo, uno innanzi altro*: The three travelers walk on, in single file, along the outer edge of the terrace, where an upward blast of air "sequesters a path" from the flames shooting out from the bank (see *Purg.* XXV, 114). This is a typical "continuing" opening for a canto, carrying on with the action that closed the preceding canto. Compare the close of *Inf.* IX and the beginning of *Inf.* X.

3. *diceami* = *mi diceva.*   *giovi*: "Let it profit you."
ti scaltro: Buti comments: "Ti scorgo la via e faccioti pratico et accorto." ("I will point out the way to you and make you expert and alert.")

4. *feriami* = *mi feriva.*

4–6. *il sole . . . cilestro*: Dante, facing south-southwest, has the sun on his right in the later afternoon. It is now about 4:00 or 5:00 P.M., since the sun strikes Dante from the side, which means that it is fairly low in the sky; the azure of the western sky is turned pale by the light. The travelers have thus taken a good long while to climb up from the sixth circle, since it was only 2:00 P.M. when they began the ascent (see *Purg.* XXV, 1-3).

6. *di cilestro*: From the azure aspect it had when the sun was higher.

7–8. *io facea con l'ombra . . . fiamma*: Dante's shadow falls on the flames, to his left, which are made pale by the sunlight, but take on their natural color in the shade cast by Dante's living body.

8. *pur a tanto indizio*: "At this mere sign," i.e., that Dante is here in the flesh.

9. *poner = porre.*

10–11. *diede inizio loro*: "Prompted them."

11–12. *cominciarsi a dir = cominciarono a dir. Tra loro* is understood here ("cominciarono a dir tra loro").

12. *corpo fittizio*: The aerial, "unreal" body as explained in the preceding canto (see *Purg.* XXV, 88-108); literally, "fictitious body."

13. *verso me . . . farsi*: This is one of the familiar idioms (cf. *Purg.* VIII, 52) meaning "to approach someone" (*farsi verso qualcuno*) or "to step forward," "to advance" (*farsi avanti*). It is used, in varying forms, twice again in this canto, vss. 31, 136.

14. *certi*: "Some."   *si fero = si fecero.*

14–15. *sempre con riguardo . . . arsi*: Vernon observes:
They would not for one single instant interrupt their penance. It must be noticed that in Purgatory the spirits not only submit willingly to the chastisement imposed upon them, but they actually love it. In *Purg.* XI, 73, Oderisi begs Dante to walk stooping beside him; in XIV, 124, Guido del Duca begs him to depart as he is more desirous of weeping than of talking; in XVI, 142, Marco Lombardo will not listen any more to him for fear of leaving the pitchy smoke; in XVIII, 115, the penitents beg him not to ascribe it to any discourtesy if they leave him, but only to their wish to move on; in

XIX, 139, Pope Adrian begs Dante to pass on and not retard his penitent weeping; in XXIV, 91, Forese leaves him because he says that in that kingdom the time is too precious; and here the penitents take heed to keep within the flames.

16. *O tu che vai, non per esser più tardo*: The manner of address is very courteous. The words constitute a kind of *captatio benevolentiae*, implying as they do that there is visibly no lack of zeal on Dante's part in going on his way toward the summit.

17. *a li altri dopo = dietro a li altri.*

18. *'n sete*: "In [real] thirst," which, in this case, as in the comparison that follows (vss. 20-21), is also thirst to know.

e 'n foco ardo: One can almost hear Guido da Montefeltro's similar plea (*Inf.* XXVII, 23-24).

19. *è uopo*: *Abbisogna*. Cf. "l'uopo," *Purg.* XXV, 21.

20-21. *ché tutti questi . . . Etiopo*: Peoples of torrid climates, where cold water is scarce.

22. *Dinne = dicci.*   *parete*: Obstacle.

23. *pur come*: "Quite as if."

24. *di morte . . . rete*: Benvenuto comments: "Mors enim piscatur in magno mari mortalium, et omnia genera animantium capit." ("Death goes fishing in the vast sea of mortal men and catches all kinds of living things.")

25-26. *mi fora già manifesto = mi sarei già manifestato.*

26. *non fossi atteso = non avessi atteso. Attendere*, in the sense of "attend to," commonly takes *essere* as auxiliary; cf. *Inf.* XIII, 109.

27. *altra novità*: On this use of a redundant *altro*, see *Purg.* XX, 81.

29. *col viso incontro a questa*: Facing the people whom Dante had encountered first and therefore proceeding in the

opposite direction. The fact is striking and should cause surprise, since this means that these new people are proceeding around to the left or clockwise, an unusual direction for Purgatory. When later we learn the sin for which these souls are being punished here, the point takes on special significance.

30. *sospeso*: "Wondering," "pondering." Cf. *Purg.* XII, 78.

31. *Lì*: "There," at the meeting of the two groups.   *farsi presta*: "Come quickly forward."

32–33. *e basciarsi una con una . . . festa*: Clearly this presents an aspect of *contrapasso*, for now these souls, who will prove to be the lustful, exchange in place of their former lascivious kisses the holy kiss as commended by the apostle Paul in Rom. 16:16: "Salutate invicem in osculo sancto." ("Greet one another with a holy kiss.")

33. *sanza restar = senza fermarsi*. The touch, indeed, signifies a holy kiss, not a lingering voluptuous one.   *festa*: "Salutation." See "accoglienza" (vs. 37) in much the same meaning. Cf. the expression *fare festa ad uno*, "to welcome someone warmly."

34–36. *così per entro . . . fortuna*: See Virgil's simile of the ants in *Aen.* IV, 404-7 and their *nigrum agmen*, of which Dante's "schiera bruna" may well be an echo. Note also Ovid, *Metam.* VII, 624-26, although there is no special touch there that Dante might have imitated. Compare Pliny, *Nat. hist.* XI, xxxvi, 109-10:

> iam in opere qui labor, quae sedulitas! et quoniam ex diverso convehunt altera alterius ignarae certi dies ad recognitionem mutuam nundinis dantur. quae tunc earum concursatio, quam diligens cum obviis quaedam conlocutio atque percontatio!

> Again what industry and what diligence is displayed in their work! and since they bring their burdens together from opposite directions, and are unknown to one another, certain days are assigned for market so that they may become acquainted. How they flock together on

these occasions! How busily they converse, so to speak, with those they meet and press them with questions!

As in so many other instances, however, it is certainly not necessary to assume that Dante had a literary source in this case. Many of his similes must be drawn from direct observation.

36. *spiar*: "Inquire." Cf. M. Barbi (1934b), p. 250; G. Vidossich (1906), p. 143; and F. Torraca (1921), p. 226.

37. *parton*: Literally, "divide."

38. *prima che 'l primo passo lì trascorra*: Before the first step is taken by any beyond this point. For *trascorrere* in this sense, see *Inf.* XXV, 34.

39. *sopragridar*: "To outcry." Each tries to shout louder than the other.

40. *la nova gente*: Those who had come up more recently and move in the clockwise direction. *Soddoma e Gomorra*: Biblical cities destroyed by fire from heaven because of the wickedness of their inhabitants (see Gen. 19:1-28). Cf. *Inf.* XI, 50, where Sodom is also mentioned, and *Inf.* XIV-XVI, where a rain of fire is the punishment.

41. *l'altra*: The other people, those who go in the same direction as the three travelers.

41-42. *Ne la vacca entra Pasife . . . corra*: Pasiphaë became the mother of the monstrous Minotaur through intercourse with a bull, by concealing herself within a wooden cow made for her by Daedalus. See *Inf.* XII, 12-13. Her story, which Dante may have got from Virgil (*Eclog.* VI, 45-60; *Aen.* VI, 24-26, 447) or Ovid (*Metam.* VIII, 131-37; *Ars amat.* I, 289-326), is thus told by the *Anonimo fiorentino*:

> In questo mezzo ch'egli stette a oste, la reina Pasife, moglie del re Minos, avea uno prato di rietro al suo palagio, nel quale fra gli altri armenti v'era uno bellissimo toro, del quale la Reina s'accese di disusitata lussuria; et però che non sapea da sè trovare il modo, ebbe con-

siglio con uno ingegnoso maestro chiamato Dedalo, il
quale fe una vacca di legno, et copersela d'uno cuojo
di vacca et missevi dentro la Reina; onde il toro, cre-
dendo questa essere vacca, la montò; onde Pasife, in-
gravidata, partorì uno il quale era bue dalla cintola in
giù, e da indi in su uomo ferocissimo, et fu chiamato
Minutauro.

At this time he [Minos] was away at war; Queen
Pasiphaë, the wife of King Minos, had a field behind her
palace, in which, among other animals, there was a very
beautiful bull. The queen became inflamed with an un-
natural lust for that bull. Since she herself could not
think of any way, she took counsel with an ingenious
craftsman named Daedalus. He had a wooden cow
made, covered it with cowhide, and put the queen in-
side. Whereupon the bull, thinking it was a cow,
mounted it. Pasiphaë got pregnant and gave birth to
something that was a bull from the waist down and from
the waist up was a most ferocious man. And he was
called Minotaur.

43–45. *come grue . . . schife*: The only other simile of
cranes used in the poem is that of *Inf.* V, 46-47, which is
employed to describe the lustful of Hell. It will be noted that
Dante's improbable figure of the birds flying in opposite di-
rections in migration is purely hypothetical, as is indicated
by the verb "volassero" (subjunctive). Dante was perhaps
thinking of Lucan, *Phars.* V, 711-16, or VII, 832-34.

43. *montagne Rife*: The Riphaean Mountains (Greek
Ῥῖπαι, Latin *Rhipaei* or *Rhiphaei*; see Servius on Virgil,
Georg. III, 382) were supposed by the ancient Greeks to be
a lofty range at the extreme north of the world. The exact
location was never agreed on, but, with the expansion of the
known world, the supposed location of the range extended
farther and farther north. The name was applied by classical
writers to the range in the most northern part of Scythia. See
Aristotle, *Meteor.* I, 13, 350b; Virgil, *Georg.* I, 240-41, and
IV, 517-19; and Lucan, *Phars.* III, 272-76. Early geographi-

cal writers placed the range northeast of Mount Alaunus on the frontiers of Asiatic Sarmatia, and some gave it as the source of the river Tanais (pronounced Tanaïs), the modern Don; according to this account, it could be regarded as a western branch of the Ural Mountains. The Riphaean Mountains did not disappear from maps until the Renaissance.

Orosius (*Hist.* I, ii, 4) says: "Europa incipit . . . sub plaga septentrionis, a flumine Tanai, qua Riphaei montes Sarmatico aversi oceano Tanaim fluvium fundunt." ("Europe begins . . . in the north at the Tanaïs River, where the Riphaean Mountains, standing back from the Sarmatian Sea, pour forth the Tanaïs flood.") Brunetto Latini (*Tresor* I, cxxiii, 18) remarks that "a l'entree d'orient est la terre d'Escite. Desouz est mont Rifet, et l'Iparborei." ("At the gateway to the Orient is the land of the Scythians. Below it is the Riphaean Mountain, and the Hyperborean.") And Benvenuto explains Dante's reference: "Hoc est dicere versus septentrionem; montes enim riphei sunt in partibus aquilonis sub nostro polo." ("This means toward the north; the Riphaean Mountains are to the north under our pole.")   *Rife*: Here used in rhyme for *Rifee*, from *Rifeo*.

44. *l'arene*: The sands of the Libyan desert.

46. *l'una gente sen va*: "L'una gente" are the Sodomites, who sinned against nature and proceed in the clockwise direction.   *l'altra sen vene*: "L'altra" are those who sinned against what Dante in vs. 83 calls "human law" and who go in a counterclockwise direction, thus coming along with the three poets.   *sen = se ne.*

47. *a' primi canti = ai canti di prima*, i.e., the hymn "Summae Deus clementiae."

48. *al gridar*: To the shouting of the examples of lust or the opposing virtue (*Purg.* XXV, 128-35).   *che più lor si convene*: The examples, in either case, which "most befit them."

49. *raccostansi = si raccostano.   come davanti = come prima* (see vss. 13-15).

50. *essi medesmi = essi stessi.*

52. *due volte*: Before the meeting of the two groups and now, as the one approaches a second time.   *lor grato*: What they desired to know, as indicated by the request of vss. 22-24.

54. *quando che sia*: See *Purg.* XXI, 58-66.   *di pace stato*: It will be recalled how emphatically in the case of Francesca and Paolo and the other lustful of Hell it was brought out that peace was forever denied such sinners.

55-56. *non son rimase . . . là*: I.e., my soul is here with my body, I have not died either young or old. Benvenuto observes that this means that Dante is not only alive, but of middle age. See "acerbo" in the sense of "green," "unripe," in *Inf.* XXV, 18.

57. *col sangue suo e con le sue giunture*: The features of blood and joints are those which are most conspicuously absent from the fictitious bodies of these souls.

58. *Quinci*: "By this way."   *vo = vado.*   *per non esser più cieco*: Cf. *Purg.* XXI, 124.

59. *donna è di sopra che m'acquista grazia*: Beatrice. Some interpreters understand the lady to be the Virgin Mary, although this arose more from the reading "n'acquista," in place of "m'acquista."

60. *'l mortal*: The mortal part of me. Cf. "quel d'Adamo" in *Purg.* IX, 10.   *per vostro mondo*: The world of the dead.

61–63. *Ma se la vostra maggior . . . spazia*: The familiar hortative "if" clause.

61. *maggior voglia*: The greatest desire of these souls is to complete their purgation and rise to the bliss of Paradise.

61–62. *sazia tosto divegna = tosto divenga sazia.*

62. *'l ciel*: The Empyrean. Beatrice descended from it to Limbo. See *Inf.* II, 84, where it is referred to as an "ampio loco."

63. *e più ampio si spazia*: The Empyrean is the tenth and outermost of the heavens, hence it has the largest circumference. In *Conv.* II, iii, 11, Dante writes: "Questo è lo soprano edificio del mondo, nel quale tutto lo mondo s'inchiude, e di fuori dal quale nulla è." ("This is the sovran edifice of the world, wherein all the world is included, and outside of which there is nought.")

64. *acciò ch'ancor carte ne verghi*: Literally, "that I may yet rule pages about it." The verb *vergare* refers to the drawing of lines to guide the writing in manuscripts; here, of course, it signifies the writing itself, the report the wayfarer will make of his journey through the afterlife. This turn of phrase anticipates the fact that the verses are now to turn precisely on the subject of writing poetry.

66. *di retro a' vostri terghi*: I.e., in a direction opposite to yours.

67. *stupido = stupito*. Cf. *Purg.* IV, 59.   *si turba*: "Becomes confused."

68–69. *lo montanaro . . . s'inurba*: The man from the hills or mountains, when he comes to the city. For *inurbarsi,* see E. G. Parodi (1957), p. 267.

70. *paruta*: Cf. *Purg.* XXV, 100.

71. *scarche = scariche*, "disburdened."

72. *lo qual ne li alti cuor tosto s'attuta*: This observation is not only intended to have general validity, but is calculated to dispose the reader well toward the soul who will now speak, who is by implication an *alto cuor*. He happens to be the poet who wrote a famous poem about the *cuor gentile*.
    tosto s'attuta = presto s'attutisce, "is soon abated."

73. *le nostre marche*: Cf. *Purg.* XIX, 45.

74. *colei*: The feminine demonstrative is used here because it refers to *anima*.   *che pria m'inchiese = che prima mi aveva interrogato*. For such a use of the past absolute (somewhat determined by the rhyme), cf. *Inf*. XIX, 126 ("discese") and *passim*.

75. *per morir meglio*: The moment of death and true repentance at death is the decisive one.   *esperienza imbarche*: "You take on, as cargo, experience" of our regions. The figure draws on that of the navigation of this life, for which cf. *Inf*. XXVII, 81; *Purg*. XII, 6.

E. H. Wilkins (1917, p. 30) points out that in a sonnet ("[O] caro padre meo, de vostra laude," in G. Contini, 1960, vol. II, p. 484) which Guido Guinizzelli wrote to Guittone d'Arezzo (who is mentioned in vs. 124) there is a rhyme series employing the words *embarchi, archi, Marchi, sovralarchi*, and that Guittone replied with these same rhymes. Dante's use of "imbarche" here may well be, therefore, a case similar to that noted in the n. to *Inf*. X, 69, and thus part of the striking feature of anticipation and imitation which Dante as poet enters into when he is dealing with other poets. See nn. to vss. 92 and 137-38.

76. *La gente che non vien con noi*: Those who go in the opposite direction around the terrace (vs. 66).   *offese*: "Sinned."

77-78. *di ciò per che già Cesar . . . s'intese*: Sodomy. The reference is to an incident which is said to have taken place during one of Caesar's triumphs, when he was greeted by the crowd with shouts of "Regina," in allusion to the common belief that while in Bithynia he had committed sodomy with King Nicomedes. The *Anonimo fiorentino* says:

> Poi che Cesare ebbe vinta l'ultima battaglia contro a' figliuoli di Pompeo appresso a Monda . . . tornò a Roma, dove gli furon fatti cinque triunfi; et però che lecito era a ciascuno di rimproverare al triunfatore ogni suo vizio . . . uno gridò contro a Cesare: *O regina di Bitinia, come se'oggi onorato!* rimproverandogli il vizio di sodomita, il quale avea usato in lui il re di Bitinia.

After Caesar had won the last battle against the sons of
Pompey, at Munda . . . he returned to Rome, where his
arrival was celebrated with five triumphs. Because any-
one was allowed to rebuke the triumphant for any vice
he had . . . one person cried out to Caesar: "Oh queen
of Bithynia, how you are honored today!" reproaching
him for the vice of sodomy, which the king of Bithynia
indulged in with him.

Suetonius, in his life of Caesar, gives the following account
(*De vita Caesarum* I, xlix, 1-4):

Pudicitiae eius famam nihil quidem praeter Nicomedis
contubernium laesit, gravi tamen et perenni obprobrio
et ad omnium convicia exposito. Omitto Calvi Licini
notissimos versus:

> Bithynia quicquid
> et pedicator Caesaris umquam habuit.

Praetereo actiones Dolabellae et Curionis patris, in qui-
bus eum Dolabella "paelicem reginae, spondam interio-
rem regiae lecticae," at Curio "stabulum Nicomedis et
Bithynicum fornicem" dicunt. Missa etiam facio edicta
Bibuli, quibus proscripsit: collegam suum Bithynicam
reginam, eique antea regem fuisse cordi, nunc esse reg-
num. Quo tempore, ut Marcus Brutus refert, Octavius
etiam quidam valitudine mentis liberius dicax conventu
maximo, cum Pompeium regem appellasset, ipsum regi-
nam salutavit. Sed C. Memmius etiam ad cyathum et
vinum Nicomedi stetisse obicit, cum reliquis exoletis,
pleno convivio, accubantibus nonnullis urbicis negotia-
toribus, quorum refert nomina. Cicero vero non con-
tentus in quibusdam epistulis scripsisse a satellitibus
eum in cubiculum regium eductum in aureo lecto veste
purpurea decubuisse floremque aetatis a Venere orti
in Bithynia contaminatum, quondam etiam in senatu
defendenti ei Nysae causam, filiae Nicomedis, bene-
ficiaque regis in se commemoranti: "Remove," inquit,
"istaec, oro te, quando notum est, et quid ille tibi et
quid illi tute dederis." Gallico denique triumpho milites

eius inter cetera carmina, qualia currum prosequentes ioculariter canunt, etiam illud vulgatissimum pronuntia-verunt:

> Gallias Caesar subegit, Nicomedes Caesarem:
> Ecce Caesar nunc triumphat qui subegit Gallias,
> Nicomedes non triumphat qui subegit Caesarem.

There was no stain on his reputation for chastity except his intimacy with King Nicomedes, but that was a deep and lasting reproach, which laid him open to insults from every quarter. I say nothing of the notorious lines of Licinius Calvus:

> Whate'er Bithynia had, and Caesar's paramour.

I pass over, too, the invectives of Dolabella and the elder Curio, in which Dolabella calls him "the queen's rival, the inner partner of the royal couch," and Curio, "the brothel of Nicomedes and the stew of Bithynia." I take no account of the edicts of Bibulus, in which he posted his colleague as "the queen of Bithynia," saying that "of yore he was enamoured of a king, but now of a king's estate." At this same time, so Marcus Brutus declares, one Octavius, a man whose disordered mind made him somewhat free with his tongue, after salut-ing Pompey as "king" in a crowded assembly, greeted Caesar as "queen." But Gaius Memmius makes the di-rect charge that he acted as cup-bearer to Nicomedes with the rest of his wantons at a large dinner-party, and that among the guests were some merchants from Rome, whose names Memmius gives. Cicero, indeed, is not content with having written in sundry letters that Caesar was led by the king's attendants to the royal apartments, that he lay on a golden couch arrayed in purple, and that the virginity of this son of Venus was lost in Bithynia; but when Caesar was once addressing the senate in defence of Nysa, daughter of Nicomedes, and was enumerating his obligations to the king, Cicero cried: "No more of that, pray, for it is well known what he gave you, and what you gave him in turn." Finally,

in his Gallic triumph his soldiers, among the bantering
songs which are usually sung by those who follow the
chariot, shouted these lines, which became a by-word:

> All the Gauls did Caesar vanquish, Nicomedes
> vanquished him;
> Lo! now Caesar rides in triumph, victor over all
> the Gauls,
> Nicomedes does not triumph, who subdued the
> conqueror.

The commentators suppose that Dante, who speaks of
Caesar's having been greeted as "Regina" during a triumph,
confused the two incidents referred to by Suetonius—his
being saluted as "Regina" in a public assembly and his be-
ing mocked by his soldiers during a triumph on account of
his supposed unnatural intercourse with Nicomedes. Dante's
authority, however, was probably not Suetonius but the
Magnae derivationes of Uguccione da Pisa, whose version
of the incident, given under the word *triumphus*, exactly
agrees with that of Dante; for the following quotation from
the *Magnae derivationes*, see P. Toynbee (1902), p. 113:

> In illa die licebat cuilibet dicere in personam trium-
> phantis quicquid vellet, unde Cesari triumphanti fer-
> tur quidam dixisse, cum deberet induci in civitatem:
> *Aperite portas regi calvo et regine Bitinie,* volens sig-
> nificare quod calvus erat, et quod succuba extiterat regis
> Bitinie; et alius de eodem vitio: *Ave rex et regina!*

> On such a day anyone could say anything he wished to
> the person who was having a triumph. Thus the story
> is told that when Caesar was being led into the city in
> triumph, someone said: "Open the gates for King Baldy
> and the Queen of Bithynia!" This referred to the fact
> that he was bald and that he had lain with the King of
> Bithynia. Another, with the same vice in mind, said:
> "Hail, King and Queen!"

Dante was well acquainted with this work of Uguccione, of
which he made considerable use and which he quotes by
name in *Conv.* IV, vi, 5. See P. Toynbee (1902), pp.
97-114.

79. *però = per ciò.   si parton*: "They depart from us."

81. *e aiutan l'arsura vergognando*: "And with their shame they aid the burning."

82. *ermafrodito*: Heterosexual, and therefore natural. Hermaphroditus was the son of Mercury (Hermes) and Venus (Aphrodite), as his name witnesses. Having inherited the beauty of both his parents, he excited the love of the nymph of the fountain of Salmacis, near Halicarnassus, who tried in vain to win his affections. One day as he was bathing in the fountain she embraced him and prayed to the gods that she might be united with him forever. The gods granted the request, and the bodies of the two became united together, but retained the characteristics of both sexes. The story is told by Ovid, *Metam.* IV, 285-388.

Thomas Aquinas says on this point (*Summa theol.* II-II, q. 154, a. 12, ad 4): "Gravissimum autem est peccatum *bestialitatis*, quia non servatur debita species. . . . Post hoc autem est *vitium Sodomiticum*, cum ibi non servetur debitus sexus. Post hoc autem est peccatum ex eo quod non servatur debitus modus concumbendi." ("While the most grievous is the sin of bestiality, because use of the due species is not observed. . . . After this comes the sin of sodomy, because use of the right sex is not observed. Lastly comes the sin of not observing the right manner of copulation.")

83. *ma*: The conjunction clearly implies that "ermafrodito" might also be used of a love that is not sinful.   *servammo = osservammo.   umana legge*: Right reason. Compare the lustful of *Inf.* V, of whom it is said that they "la ragion sommettono al talento" (*Inf.* V, 39).

84. *seguendo come bestie l'appetito*: Not observing the law of reason, which is what distinguishes man from beast. Cf. *Conv.* II, vii, 3-4:

È da sapere che le cose deono essere denominate da l'ultima nobilitade de la loro forma; sì come l'uomo da la ragione, e non dal senso nè d'altro che sia meno nobile. Onde, quando si dice l'uomo vivere, si dee in-

tendere l'uomo usare la ragione, che è sua speziale vita
e atto de la sua più nobile parte. E però chi da la ra-
gione si parte, e usa pur la parte sensitiva, non vive
uomo, ma vive bestia.

Be it known that things should be named from the dis-
tinguishing nobility of their form; as man from reason,
and not from sense nor from aught else that is less no-
ble. Hence when we say that a man is living, it should
be understood that the man hath the use of his reason,
which is his special life, and is the actualising of his most
noble part. And therefore he who severs himself from
reason, and hath only use of his sensitive part, doth not
live as a man, but liveth as a beast.

85. *per noi = da noi.*   *si legge:* It is said by us. For a
similar use of *leggere*, see *Inf.* X, 65.

86. *partinci = ci partiamo.* Cf. vs. 79: "si parton." This is
the same moment of separation, when they break off the
salutation.   *colei:* Pasiphaë (vss. 41-42).

87. *che s'imbestiò ne le 'mbestiate schegge:* This is one of
the great verses of the poem. The "bestialized planks" are,
of course, the planks of which the wooden cow was fashioned
by Daedalus. See n. to vss. 41-42.

88. *nostri atti:* I.e., what we do here, in our purgation.

89. *a nome:* Dante has asked these souls who they are
(vs. 65).   *semo = siamo.*

90. *tempo non è di dire:* I.e., it would take too long to tell
(the name of each).   *e non saprei:* "Nor should I know"
(i.e., know how to name them all, they are so many).

91. *Farotti = ti farò.*   *ben di me volere scemo:* I will
gladly reduce your desire to know who I am.

92. *Guido Guinizzelli:* Guido Guinizzelli (or Guinizelli—
the spelling with double *zz* is now the more commonly ac-
cepted) was the most illustrious of the Italian poets prior to
Dante. For all his fame, the facts of Guido's life and indeed

of his precise identification are scant and disputed by scholars. Some hold that he died probably before November of 1276. See A. Bongioanni (1897); G. Contini (1960), vol. II, pp. 447-49.

Guido Guinizzelli, who at first was a great admirer of Guittone d'Arezzo, but afterwards condemned him (see vss. 124-26), became the center of a school of Bolognese poets, and from him sprang subsequently the illustrious school of the *dolce stil novo* (see *Purg.* XXIV, 57), the school of Dante himself, who acknowledges Guido as his father. The extant poems of Guido Guinizzelli, several of which are quoted by Dante, consist of *canzoni* and sonnets, dealing for the most part with love, some being of a satiric turn. See G. Contini (1960), vol. II, pp. 450-85; E. Monaci (1955), pp. 345-50. Dante mentions Guido in his works several times, among them being *Conv.* IV, xx, 7; *De vulg. eloqu.* I, xv, 6; *Vita nuova* XX, 3; and *Purg.* XI, 97; see also *Purg.* XXIV, 58-60. For the famous *canzone* of Guido Guinizzelli to which Dante so often refers ("Al cor gentil rempaira sempre amore"), see G. Contini (1960), vol. II, pp. 460-64.

e già mi purgo: We do not know exactly when Guido died, but his time in Purgatory in any case has been remarkably brief since he is already on the last terrace.

93. *per ben dolermi prima ch'a lo stremo*: Because of my deep repentance before the end of life. Compare the references to repentance in *Purg.* XIII, 124-25, and XXIII, 81.

94-95. *Quali ne la tristizia . . . madre*: The simile is effective, for one thing, in withholding report of Dante's reaction to the name of Guido Guinizzelli.

94. *tristizia*: This, given the context, is wrath as well as grief, in which regard we may recall that the wrathful of Styx referred to themselves as "tristi" (*Inf.* VII, 121). The passage in Statius' *Thebaid* which is surely Dante's source in this case stresses the *insana ira* and the *furor* (see *Theb.* V, 654-55, 663) of Lycurgus as well as his great grief.   *Licurgo*: Lycurgus, king of Nemea, whose son Archemorus, while under the charge of Hypsipyle, was killed by a snake. One

day, as Hypsipyle was seated in a wood near Nemea with the child, the seven heroes who were warring against Thebes passed by and, being thirsty, asked her to show them a fountain. Hypsipyle thereupon put down the child upon the grass and led the warriors to the fountain of Langia (*Purg.* XXII, 112). When she returned, she found Archemorus dead from the bite of a serpent. Enraged at the death of his child, Lycurgus determined to put Hypsipyle to death and was proceeding to put his resolve into execution when Thoas and Euneus, Hypsipyle's two sons, opportunely arrived and saved her. Dante got the story from Statius, *Theb.* V, 499-730.

95. *si fer = si fecero.*

96. *ma non a tanto insurgo*: But I do not rise to such heights of boldness as to rush in to embrace Guido, now to be called "father," as the two sons did their mother. See *Theb.* V, 720-22:

> . . . per tela manusque
> inruerant, matremque avidis complexibus ambo
> diripiunt flentes alternaque pectora mutant . . .

> Straight had they rushed through weapons and troops of men, and both with tears snatch their mother to their greedy embrace and in turn press her to their bosoms.

No doubt, had he braved the fire, Dante would have embraced his new-found "father" by clasping him about the ankles, as Statius would have done to Virgil (*Purg.* XXI, 130). E. Moore (1896, p. 247) observes that this touch in the simile is especially interesting "because in the merely allusive character of the reference Dante appears to assume familiarity with the passage on the part of his readers also: otherwise the statement 'ma non a tanto insurgo' lacks its explanation." Moore continues: "The meaning is . . . that Dante did not go so far as they did in the expression of his emotions, inasmuch as he did not actually run and embrace Guido Guinicelli. But only familiarity with the passage referred to could supply this necessary gloss."

97. *nomar = nominare.*

98. *li altri miei miglior*: Just which poets Dante would have considered to be his betters in the art of poetry we are nowhere told.

99. *usar = usarono*, "practiced."

100–101. *e sanza udire . . . lui*: Dante was quite young when Guido died and thus he is seeing him for the first time.

101. *lunga fiata = lungo tempo.*   *rimirando*: Gazing with wonder (cf. "rimirando," vs. 68) and feasting his eyes on him (cf. "pasciuto," vs. 103).

102. *in là*: I.e., *verso di lui.*

105. *con l'affermar che fa credere altrui*: Dante affirmed with an oath, as vs. 109 makes clear. "Altrui" is the subject of "credere."

106. *tal vestigio*: Such an impression.

107. *per quel ch'i' odo*: Because of what I hear of you, i.e., that you are here in the flesh and will return to the world of the living, where you have offered to do me a favor.

108. *che Letè nol può tòrre*: The traditional river of oblivion (which Dante has conceived as being situated at the summit of the mountain and through which all souls must pass, as Guido apparently knows) cannot take that impression from my memory.   *né far bigio*: "Nor make gray."

109. *Ma se le tue parole or ver giuraro*: Guido is not really questioning this, of course. It is simply a way of adjuring Dante to tell what Guido now asks.   *giuraro = giurarono.*

110. *che è cagion per che = qual è la cagione per cui.*

112. *dolci detti*: Poems, sweet in style, significant in doctrine. In *Vita nuova* XX, 3, where Guido is called "il saggio" and is remembered for the *detto* of the opening line of his famous sonnet, Dante writes: "Amore e 'l cor gentil sono una cosa, / sì come il saggio in suo dittare pone." ("Love and a gentle heart are one same thing, even as the poet teacheth in his rhymes.") Cf. Petrarch, *Rime* XXVI, 10-11:

"Al buon testor degli amorosi detti / rendete onor." ("Do honor to the good weaver of amorous songs.")   *vostri*: It should be noted that Dante addresses "father" Guido in the respectful second person plural as he did the father of Guido Cavalcanti (*Inf.* X, 63), Brunetto Latini (*Inf.* XV, 30), and a pope, Adrian V (*Purg.* XIX, 131), and as he will his great-great-grandfather in Paradise (*Par.* XVI, 10).

113. *l'uso moderno*: The practice of writing poetry in the vernacular, on which Dante wrote his treatise *De vulgari eloquentia*.

114. *faranno cari ancora i loro incostri*: Will ever make precious the ink they are written in.

115. *O frate*: For the tone of this, compare *Purg.* IV, 127; XI, 82; XXIII, 97.   *questi ch'io ti cerno*: The spirit pointed out by Guido is Arnaut Daniel, who flourished as a poet between 1180 and *ca.* 1210 and belonged to a noble family of Ribérac in Périgord (in the modern department of Dordogne). Little is known of his life. He appears to have been a personal friend of the famous Bertran de Born. He spent much of his time at the court of Richard Coeur de Lion. Arnaut is said to have been the originator of the *sestina*, a form of composition which Dante imitated from him, and he is pre-eminent as a poet in the purposely obscure style known as *trobar clus*, with the result that his poems are not easy to understand. See U. A. Canello (1883).

117. *miglior fabbro del parlar materno*: Guido, as he has already indicated, had to spend little time in the other circles of Purgatory. He is purged of whatever pride in the excellence of his own art he may have had and seems to be more humble than Oderisi (cf. *Purg.* XI, 82-84), whom his words now recall to the reader. Since Arnaut wrote in Provençal, and Guido in Italian, this is a comparison not unlike that of *Purg.* VII, 16-17, where Sordello (who wrote in Provençal) addresses Virgil (who wrote in Latin) as the "gloria di Latin" and credits him with showing what "our tongue" (considering Latin and its Romance derivatives as one lan-

guage) could do, although here Guido speaks in terms of the "mother tongue," by which Dante meant the language learned from one's mother as opposed to that learned from books, a meaning that excludes Latin. See L. Spitzer (1948), pp. 15-65.

118–19. *Versi d'amore . . . tutti*: If Arnaut was a better craftsman in the mother tongue, this would mean that Guido considers Arnaut to have surpassed him, though Guido wrote in Italian and Arnaut in Provençal. Now Guido's encomium goes on to include all who wrote poetry in Provençal—*langue d'oc*—and those who wrote prose in French—*langue d'oïl* (having regard to Dante's statement in *De vulg. eloqu.* I, x, 2, that everything in vernacular prose, whether translated or original, was in French). This has been misunderstood by some as meaning that Arnaut was pre-eminent as a writer of both love verse and prose romances. There is no evidence, however, that Arnaut wrote any romances, in prose or verse, and there is little doubt that the real meaning of Dante's phrase, suggested by the comment of Buti, is that Arnaut surpassed all writers of love verse and prose romance, that is to say, that Arnaut was superior to all who wrote either in Provençal or in French. For a fuller statement of these views, see P. Toynbee (1902), pp. 262-65. The construction here appears somewhat elliptical, the notion of "fabbro del parlar materno" being carried over and understood now in the plural: "he surpassed all craftsmen in the mother tongue, whether writers of love verses (Italian and Provençal) or writers of prose."

120. *quel di Lemosì*: The reference is to the troubadour Giraud de Borneil, who came from the vicinity of Excideuil near Limoges. Born about the middle of the twelfth century, he died *ca.* 1220. According to his old Provençal biography he was born of humble parents, but was remarkable for his learning and intelligence and so greatly excelled in his art that he was called by his contemporaries "the master of the troubadours." In the *De vulgari eloquentia* Dante refers to him as Gerardus de Brunel (I, ix, 3) and as Gerardus de

Bornello (II, ii, 9). He is pointed out as the singer of recti-
tude, as Arnaut Daniel is of love and Bertran de Born of
arms, in *De vulg. eloqu.* II, ii, 9, where he is quoted as such.
Dante notes that he wrote *canzoni* in the most illustrious
style, the first line of one of them being quoted in *De vulg.
eloqu.* II, vi, 6. A number of his poems have been preserved.
See H. J. Chaytor (1902), pp. 29-46; A. Jeanroy (1934);
A. Kolsen (1910); F. Diez (1882), pp. 110-24.

121. *voce*: "Report," mere popular opinion.   *drizzan li
volti*: I.e., give heed to.

122. *sua = loro*.   *oppinione = opinione*.

123. *arte*: The rules of art.   *per lor s'ascolti*: See vs.
85: "per noi si legge."

124-26. *Così fer molti . . . persone*: See *Purg.* XI, 97-98,
where a similar surpassing of one poet by another—and, by
implication, one school of poets by another school—is set
forth.

124. *fer = fecero*.

125. *grido*: I.e., *voce* (see vs. 121).   *lui = a lui*.
pregio: Praise. In *Conv.* I, xi, 4, Dante notes: "E sì come
colui che è cieco de li occhi sensibili va sempre secondo che
li altri giudicando lo male e lo bene, così colui che è cieco
del lume de la discrezione sempre va nel suo giudicio secondo
il grido, o diritto o falso." ("And like as he who is blind with
the eyes of sense must ever judge of evil or good according
to others, so he who is blind of the light of discernment must
ever follow in his judgment after mere report, true or false.")
He continues (*Conv.* I, xi, 5-6): "E li ciechi . . . che sono
quasi infiniti, con la mano in su la spalla a questi mentitori,
sono caduti ne la fossa de la falsa oppinione, de la quale
uscire non sanno. De l'abito di questa luce discretiva mas-
simamente le populari persone sono orbate." ("The blind
ones . . . who are almost without number, with their hands
upon the shoulders of these liars, have fallen into the ditch
of the false opinion from which they know not how to escape.

To the habit of this light of discernment the populace are specially blinded.") Compare Eccles. 1:15: "Stultorum infinitus est numerus." ("The number of the foolish is infinite.")

126. *fin che l'ha vinto il ver con più persone*: Until the truth (the true estimate of his worth) prevailed with many people, counterbalancing "the many of old" who held the wrong opinion. Other interpreters prefer to understand this to mean, as Sapegno does, "grazie alla fama assodata di molti poeti a lui superiori" ("thanks to the well-established fame of many poets superior to him"); or they concur with Porena, who interprets it as follows: "Il vero merito ha vinto Guittone, in persona di parecchi poeti: oggi parecchi poeti sono giustamente pregiati più di Guittone." ("The true merit of many other poets has defeated Guittone: today many poets are rightly esteemed more highly than Guittone.")

127. *Or*: This signals a change of subject, meaning, as Torraca observes, "basti di ciò; pensiamo a cose maggiori." ("Enough of that; let us think of more important things.")

se: The meaning is "since" rather than "if," for Guido does not doubt the fact, of course. Cf. vs. 109. *privilegio*: In the context the term means "grace," but it has something of its common legal meaning, i.e., the grant of a special right or immunity to some person or class of persons. Buti comments: "Li privilegi sono certezza e prova de le grazie e de le autoritadi concedute da' signori ai loro minori, e però si può ponere lo privilegio per la grazia." ("Privileges are the certification and proof of the good grace and of the authority conceded by lords to their inferiors. Therefore, privilege can be substituted for grace.")

128–29. *al chiostro nel quale . . . collegio*: Buti comments: "In paradiso lo quale è chiusura de' beati, come lo chiostro è de' religiosi . . . come l'abbate è padre e signore dei monaci; così Cristo via maggiormente è padre e signore de' beati." ("In Paradise, which is the enclosure of the blessed, just as the cloister is for the religious . . . and as the abbot is father and lord of the monks, so Christ in an even greater way is father and lord of the blessed.")

130. *falli per me un dir d'un paternostro*: Literally, "cause there the saying for me of a Paternoster," i.e., say an "Our Father" there for me. Some editors have "fagli" in place of "falli," taking the *li* of "falli" to represent *gli*, that is, to Christ. But a Paternoster addressed specifically to the Son and not the Father would not be particularly appropriate, and this *li* is surely the equivalent of the modern *vi* or *ci*, the adverb that indicates a place already mentioned—in this case, the "chiostro" where Christ is abbot.

131. *quanto bisogna a noi di questo mondo*: That is, without the verse (Matt. 6:13) "ne nos inducas in tentationem, sed libera nos a malo" ("lead us not into temptation, but deliver us from evil"), since this no longer applies to those who are in Purgatory proper, for the reason given in the next verse. The proud of the first circle included this verse, but added that it was said for those who were left behind (*Purg.* XI, 22-24).

133-34. *per dar luogo . . . avea*: "Altrui" seems clearly dative, but the syntax and meaning of "secondo" are uncertain. There appear to be at least two possible meanings. "Secondo" may be an adjective modifying "luogo" and meaning "suited," indicating a place suited to another, whom he had near, i.e., who was near or just behind him. In this case there should be a comma after "secondo," so that the reading would be "per dar luogo altrui secondo, / che presso avea." Or "secondo" may be an adjective modifying "altrui," meaning "to give place to another after [himself] whom he had near," in which case the comma after "secondo" might be omitted. The second meaning seems preferable.

135. *come per l'acqua il pesce andando al fondo*: For a similar image, see *Par.* V, 100-102.

136. *Io mi fei . . . innanzi*: Cf. vss. 13-14.

137–38. *e dissi ch'al suo nome . . . loco*: The phrasing is *précieux* and is but another instance of Dante's anticipation of the style of a poet whom he encounters in the afterlife. See n. to vs. 115.

139. *liberamente*: "Willingly." Cf. *Purg.* XI, 134.

140–47. *Tan m'abellis . . . dolor*: Arnaut speaks in his native tongue, Provençal. The text of these verses is somewhat uncertain, but the variants are not many or very significant. See R. Renier (1895), pp. 315-18. The following is the translation with comment given by Scartazzini-Vandelli, by which anyone who reads Italian will be able to recognize cognate words and constructions:

Tradotti letteralmente questi versi provenzali suonano: "Tanto m'abbella (= mi piace; *Par.* XXVI, 132) la vostra cortese domanda, che io non mi posso nè voglio a voi coprire (nascondere). Io sono Arnaldo, che piango e vo cantando [l'inno *Summae Deus clementiae*]; pensoso veggo la passata follia, e veggo giubilante la gioia che spero, dinanzi [a me, nel futuro]. Ora vi prego per quel valore [Dio] che vi guida al sommo della scala [del Purg.], sovvengavi a tempo del mio dolore!" Su la lez. di questi vv., guasti da amanuensi ed editori ignari del provenzale, cfr. *R. Renier* in *Giorn. stor. d. lett. ital.*, XXV, 315 sg.: la lez. del Renier s'è qui modificata sul fondam. de' mss.—*plor . . . denan*: Senso: "piango lacrime di penitenza; ma se mi contrista il ricordo di mie colpe, mi conforta il pensiero della gioia eterna che m'attende."

Translated literally, these Provençal verses mean: "Your courteous request so pleases me ('mi piace'; *Par.* XXVI, 132), that I neither can nor will conceal myself from you. I am Arnaut, who weep and sing [the hymn 'Summae Deus clementiae']; thoughtfully, I look back on my past folly, and jubilantly I see before me [in the future] the joy I hope for. Now I pray you, by that goodness [God] that guides you to the summit of the ladder [of Purgatory], take thought betimes of my pain." For the reading of these verses, which have been mutilated by amanuenses and editors ignorant of Provençal, cf. R. Renier, in *Giornale storico della letteratura italiana* XXV, 315ff. Renier's reading has been modified here, on the basis of the MSS.—*plor . . . denan*: The sense: I weep tears of penitence; but if I am saddened by the memory of my faults, I am gladdened by the thought of the eternal joy that awaits me.

148. *nel foco che li affina*: In the fire that "refines" Arnaut and all the lustful of this last terrace. "Affina" keeps the connotation of "refine" as used of smelting, as of metals when they are purified. Cf. *Purg.* XXIV, 137-38.

CANTO XXVII

1–5. *Sì come quando . . . sole*: This is a kind of pseudo-simile since the actual position of the sun is as Dante describes it, seen in the familiar global view which brings in the four cardinal points on the earth by which the sun's course is measured. (See C. S. Singleton, *Inferno Commentary*, Fig. 7, p. 640.) When it is sunrise in Jerusalem (vss. 1-2), it is midnight in Spain (vs. 3), noon on the Ganges (vs. 4), and sunset in Purgatory. For similar statements, see *Purg.* II, 1-9; III, 25-27; IV, 137-39; IX, 7-9.

1. *vibra*: "Sole," vs. 5, is the subject.

2. *il suo fattor*: God, triune Creator of all things. The second person of the triune God, Christ, became flesh and shed His blood for us. On medieval maps of the world the figure of Christ on the Cross often indicates Jerusalem, at the center of the inhabited hemisphere of land.

3–4. *cadendo Ibero . . . riarse*: These two verses represent a type of ablative absolute construction.

3. *Ibero*: The river Ebro (the ancient Iberus) in Spain. Dante uses the form "Ebro" in *Par.* IX, 89.   *sotto l'alta Libra*: The river Ebro is said to fall under the Scales, the

constellation opposite Aries. It is midnight at the Strait of Gibraltar.

4. *nona*: For this use of *nona* (literally, the ninth hour of the day, or 3:00 P.M.) to mean "noon," i.e., when the sun is on the meridian, cf. G. Villani (XI, 100), "essendo il sole al meriggio, che noi volgarmente diciamo ora di nona" ("the sun being at the meridian, which we call in common parlance the hour of Nones"), and *Conv.* IV, xxiii, 15-16. Grandgent notes that "the sun, in Aries, is over eastern Asia, so that the waters of the river Ganges are 'scorched by noon.'"
riarse: *Riarse* is the past participle of *riardere*, the prefix *ri-* serving to intensify; *essendo* is understood as the auxiliary.

6. *come = quando.   l'angel di Dio*: As in the other circles, an angel stands at this exit.

7. *Fuor de la fiamma stava in su la riva*: The angel stands in the path which is "sequestered" from the flame, along the edge of the terrace.

8. *Beati mundo corde*: See Matt. 5:8: "Beati mundo corde, quoniam ipsi Deum videbunt." ("Blessed are the clean of heart, for they shall see God.") The sixth beatitude is especially appropriate here, with its blessing on those who are clean of heart, who have purged themselves of all lustful inclinations, which arise as bad love in the heart, and its promise of heavenly beatitude in the vision of God which souls who are now leaving this, the last of the purgatorial terraces, are soon to enjoy.

9. *che la nostra*: Than our human voice.

10-12. *Più non si va . . . sorde*: These are words which the angel addresses to all souls who, like Statius, come to this last exit, which explains the impersonal construction and the form of address "holy souls," which, strictly speaking, would apply neither to Virgil nor to Dante at this point. Here again the presence of Statius serves to indicate what each and every purged and liberated soul does as it proceeds to the summit of the mountain.

12. *al cantar di là*: See vss. 55-56.   *di là = dal di là*, i.e., from the other side of the fire.

13. *li = gli*.

14. *per ch'io*: I.e., "per la qual cosa io."

15. *qual è colui che ne la fossa è messo*: Some interpret this to mean "as one who is laid in the grave," i.e., pale as a corpse; but it seems more appropriate to understand "fossa" as "pit" rather than "grave," the reference being to the punishment known as *propagginazione*, by which criminals were buried alive head downward (see *Inf.* XIX, 50-51). Compare Dante's cold fright of *Purg.* XX, 128-29.

16. *In su le man commesse mi protesi*: M. Barbi (1934b, p. 231) quite rightly objects to Torraca's interpretation (still followed by other commentators) of "in su" as meaning *in alto*, as if Dante reached up with clasped hands in horror. Instead, Dante must have his hands clasped and pressed back against his garments to keep them from the fire, and this accounts for his posture.

18. *umani corpi già veduti accesi*: Burning at the stake was not an uncommon punishment in Dante's day. The poet himself was condemned to it, in his exile, if he were to be taken in Florentine territory.

19. *Volsersi = si volsero.   le buone scorte*: Note that Statius is again referred to as a guide.

21. *qui*: I.e., in this fire.

22. *Ricorditi = ti ricordi*, impersonal imperative with the verb in the subjunctive. Cf. *Inf.* XXVIII, 73; *Purg.* V, 133.

23. *sovresso Gerion*: "On very Geryon." The reader will recall what a frightening experience the ride down on the back of that monster was for Dante (see *Inf.* XVII, 85-136).

25-30. *Credi per certo . . . panni*: The concept of fire having the supernatural power of burning spiritually without burning materially connects with the flaming sword of the

Cherubim placed to guard the way to the tree of life in Eden (Gen. 3:24) after Adam and Eve had been expelled. Hugh of St. Victor, *Adnotationes elucidatoriae in Pentateuchon,* on Gen. 3 (col. 43), notes:

> Cherubim ut repellat diabolum, ignis ut hominem. Et notandum, Deum speciem ignis facere aut fecisse, ut in vita sancti Nicolai legitur, cuius natura dicitur esse ut si quis manum adhibuerit, ardorem quidem sentit, sed nullam patitur adustionem, et est ignis ille talis naturae quod comburit spiritum, nec eget materia quam consumat, sicut nec ille qui est in sphaera solis. Iste autem noster ignis et eget materia, et solum corpus urit.

> Just as the Cherubim repel the devil, so fire will man. It is to be noted that God makes and has made fire, as we read in the life of St. Nicholas, to be of such a nature that, if one puts his hand near it, he will feel heat but not be burned. Also, this fire is of such a nature that it can burn a spirit, and it does not need matter to consume, even as that which is in the sun, whereas our fire must have matter and burns only our bodies.

25. *dentro a l'alvo*: "In the midst of." *Alvo* is from the Latin *alvus,* "belly."

27. *d'un capel calvo*: Cf. Luc. 21:18: "Et capillus de capite vestro non peribit." ("Yet not a hair of your head shall perish.") Also see Actus 27:34.

29. *fatti ver' lei*: For *farsi verso qualcuno,* cf. *Purg.* XXVI, 13. *lei = essa* (i.e., "la fiamma").

29–30. *fatti far credenza . . . panni*: A touch which suggests that Dante was in fact holding back his garment from the flame (see vs. 16) and that now he might cause his garments to touch the fire. On "fatti far credenza" Buti comments: "cioè esperienzia la quale fa credere" ("that is, an experience that makes you believe"). The expression *far credenza* derives from the custom of a prince's having someone else taste his food to guard against poison (a *credenza* being the side table on which the food was placed for tasting). Boc-

caccio, referring to a gift of chicken or some other food se-
cretly filled with poison, uses the expression in *Il Filocolo*
II (p. 99): "Come il presente davanti a voi sarà posato . . .
fate che in alcun modo o cane o altra bestia faccia la cre-
denza, acciò che altra persona non ne morisse." ("When the
gift is put before you . . . in some way have a dog or some
other animal try it [*faccia la credenza*], so that no person will
die from it.")

30. *al lembo* = *dal lembo*.

32. *volgiti in qua e vieni*: *entra sicuro*: Dante's eyes are
fixed on the fire in terror. Virgil commands him to look to-
ward him and to come to him and so free himself from his
paralyzing fear.

33. *E io pur fermo e contra coscienza*: The verse is the
more effective for having no verb.   *contra coscienza*:
Dante knows that he should obey his trusty guide.

34. *duro*: Compare Thomas Aquinas, *Summa theol.* III,
Suppl., q. 1, a. 1, resp.: "Ille autem qui in suo sensu perse-
verat, rigidus, et durus per similitudinem vocatur." ("Now
he that persists in his own judgment, is metaphorically called
rigid and hard.") Cf. *Inf.* XXVII, 56 and vs. 40 of this canto,
"durezza."

35. *turbato*: "Vexed," "annoyed."

37-39. *Come al nome di Tisbe . . . vermiglio*: The two lov-
ers Pyramus and Thisbe dwelt in adjoining houses at
Babylon and used to converse together secretly through a
hole in the wall, since their parents would not sanction their
marriage. On one occasion they agreed to meet at the tomb
of Ninus, and when Thisbe, who arrived first, was waiting
for Pyramus, she perceived a lioness which had just torn in
pieces an ox. In terror she fled, in her flight dropping her gar-
ment, which the lioness soiled with blood. In the meantime
Pyramus came to the tomb and, finding Thisbe's garment
covered with blood, supposed that she had been killed. In
despair he stabbed himself at the foot of a mulberry tree,

the fruit of which, from being white, thenceforth became crimson like blood. When Thisbe returned and discovered her lover, who was just able to recognize her before he died, she slew herself at his side. The story is told by Ovid, *Metam.* IV, 55-166. Dante's reference is particularly to Ovid's account of how Thisbe called upon her dying lover (*Metam.* IV, 142-46):

> "Pyrame," clamavit, "quis te mihi casus ademit?
> Pyrame, responde! tua te carissima Thisbe
> nominat; exaudi vultusque attolle iacentes!"
> ad nomen Thisbes oculos a morte gravatos
> Pyramus erexit visaque recondidit illa.

She wailed: "O my Pyramus, what mischance has reft you from me? Pyramus! answer me. 'Tis your dearest Thisbe calling you. Oh, listen, and lift your drooping head!" At the name of Thisbe, Pyramus lifted his eyes, now heavy with death, and having looked upon her face, closed them again.

40. *la mia durezza fatta solla*: A kind of ablative absolute. For "durezza," cf. "duro," vs. 34.   *solla*: "Soft." Cf. *Inf.* XVI, 28; *Purg.* V, 18.

41. *mi volsi al savio duca*: Dante obeys Virgil's command (vs. 32).

42. *rampolla*: "Springs up," as water in a spring.

43. *crollò la fronte*: Cf. Inf. XXII, 107: "crollando 'l capo." The gesture expresses surprise or amazement, feigned, of course, in this instance, since Virgil knows that the mention of Beatrice has already had its calculated effect.

44. *volenci = vogliamoci*. The reflexive *ci* depends on "star" (*starsi*), "to stay."

45. *come al fanciul si fa ch'è vinto al pome*: Cf. *Purg.* XXIV, 108-11.   *pome = pomo. Pome* is an archaic form common in early Italian prose as well as verse. See E. G. Parodi (1957), p. 245.

48. *divise*: "Had separated us." They had come along in single file with Virgil in the lead and Statius next, followed by Dante, as in the long climb from the sixth terrace (*Purg.* XXV, 7-9).

49. *Sì com'*: See "com'" in *Inf.* XXVI, 12; *Purg.* XI, 92.
   un bogliente vetro: "Boiling glass." Benvenuto comments: "quod est summe calidum" ("which is very hot").

54. *parmi = mi pare.*

55. *Guidavaci = ci guidava.*

56. *di là*: On the other side of the fire (cf. vs. 12).   *a lei*: "To it," the voice.

57. *fuor*: Out of the fire.

58. *Venite, benedicti Patris mei*: The words that Christ will speak to the just souls on His right hand at the Last Judgment. See Matt. 25:34: "Tunc dicet Rex his qui a dextris eius erunt: Venite, benedicti Patris mei, possidete paratum vobis regnum a constitutione mundi." ("Then the king will say to those on his right hand, 'Come, blessed of my Father, take possession of the kingdom prepared for you from the foundation of the world.' ")The words are most appropriate here, as addressed to all "holy souls" (vs. 11) who come forth from the cleansing fire and have completed their purgation. Dante expected the reader to continue the words actually spoken by the angel and thus come to the meaningful "possidete . . . regnum." E. H. Wilkins (1927, p. 5) calls attention to a mosaic in the Baptistery of Florence (a mosaic that was there in Dante's time) which shows a gate guarded by an angel who is welcoming a newly arrived soul and to the right of this another angel who is leading a group of the blessed toward the gate and who bears a banner inscribed: "Venite beneditti Patris mei possidete preparatum." ("Come, ye blessed of my father, possess [the kingdom] prepared.")

59. *dentro a un lume*: The angel, like the others before, is dazzlingly bright.

61–63. *"Lo sol sen va,"* . . . *annera*: Cf. Ioan. 12:35: "Ambulate dum lucem habetis, ut non vos tenebrae comprehendant." ("Walk while you have the light, that darkness may not overtake you.") The three are urged to hurry for the good reason that was first explained by Sordello in *Purg.* VII, 44-60.

64–66. *Dritta salia* . . . *basso*: The stairway goes from west to east, straight up through the rock, so that Dante, having the setting sun at his back, casts a shadow before him.

67. *E di pochi scaglion levammo i saggi*: Literally, "and we took samples of only a few steps." Porena comments:

> *Saggio* sostantivo, dal latino *exagium*, significò prima esperimento, prova. Si chiamò anche così quel pezzetto di minerale che si toglieva da una massa maggiore per riconoscere la natura di questa, fare quello che oggi si direbbe l'analisi: onde l'espressione *togliere* o *levare il saggio* nel senso di saggiare, sperimentare.

> *Saggio*, substantive, from the Latin *exagium*, first signified experiment, trial. It was also the name for that little piece of some mineral that was taken from a larger mass in order to understand its nature, to make what today would be called an analysis. And thus we have the expression *togliere* or *levare il saggio* (to take a sample), in the sense of *saggiare* (to test), *sperimentare* (to experiment).

See *Antiche rime volgari DCCLXXXI*, 3-4, where, as Torraca indicates, the phrase is used: "Però del meo saver levate sagio / E laove bisongnasse fate giunta." ("And so test [*levate sagio*] my knowledge / and, where necessary, add to it.") Regarding the rhyme *saggi/saggi*, see a similar situation in *Inf.* XXII, 73 and 75.

67–69. *E di pochi* . . . *saggi*: Dante's body casts a long shadow, which can be seen by Virgil and Statius, who are in front of him. It fades out now as the sun sets.

68. *che = quando.*   *corcar = coricarsi.* Cf. *Purg.* XVII, 9.

71. *orizzonte*: The subject of "fosse . . . fatto."

72. *e notte avesse tutte sue dispense*: "Notte" is the subject of "avesse." The literal meaning of "dispense" in this context is uncertain, but "privileges" in the sense of "the parts which she is privileged to occupy" seems the probable meaning, hence "before night had occupied all her domains," i.e., claimed the entire horizon.

73. *ciascun di noi d'un grado fece letto*: Apparently the reader is to imagine that Virgil and Statius (two spirits who, strictly speaking, should have no need of rest!) both lie down, as Dante does, each on a step of the stair, for the night.

74. *la natura del monte*: Cf. "la natura del loco" in *Inf.* XVI, 17.

74–75. *ci affranse . . . diletto*: Even as Sordello first explained would occur when night fell (*Purg.* VII, 53-57).

76. *manse = mansuete.*

76–85. *Quali si stanno . . . allotta*: The feature of the herdsman standing (vs. 81) has nothing to correspond to it in the scene it would illustrate in this case, since Virgil and Statius are lying down, each on a step of the stair. This, Torraca thinks, may be what prompted the poet to proceed to a second simile of the herdsman (vss. 82-84). Torraca comments:

> Ma l'imagine di questo pastore, che non s'adagia, che, appoggiato al lungo bastone, custodisce le capre di pieno giorno, non si adattava interamente a Virgilio e a Stazio, distesi su gli scaglioni mentre calava la notte; e Dante le sostituisce quella del *mandriano*, che passa la notte in campagna, coricato accanto alla sua mandra.

> But the image of this herdsman who is not lying down and who, leaning on his long staff, watches over his goats in broad daylight was not entirely fitting for Virgil and Statius, stretched out on the steps as night falls. And so Dante replaces it with the image of the herdsman who spends the night in the open, lying near his herd.

77. *rapide*: "Swift." However, the adjective may mean "voracious" and is so interpreted by Buti, who comments: "cioè rapaci, quando si pascevano" ("that is, rapacious when they were eating"). *proterve*: "Frisky." Cf. Virgil, *Georg.* IV, 10: "haedique petulci" ("or sportive kids").

78. *pranse*: From the Latin *pransus*, from *prandere*, "to eat." It may be construed either as a past participle or an adjective here.

81. *e lor di posa serve*: And watches over their rest.

82. *fori*: "Out in the open."

83. *lungo il pecuglio suo queto pernotta*: "Queto" may be taken as modifying either "pecuglio" or the "mandrian." *pernotta*: "Reclines through the night," "rests through the night," but ever alert and watchful. Virgil and Statius, who lie and do not sleep, correspond to this figure.

85. *allotta* = *allora*.

87. *fasciati*: Literally, "swathed," "bound," by the walls of the narrow passageway through the rock.

88. *parer* = *apparire*.   *del di fori*: "Of the outside," i.e., anything outside the passageway. In fact, Dante can see only a little of the sky.

91. *ruminando*: The verb catches the full import of the two similes of the flocks at rest, chewing the cud, and the mood of quiet contemplation that prevails.

92–93. *il sonno che sovente . . . novelle*: This clearly suggests that the dream now to be recounted is prophetic. Sleep, somewhat personified, is said to "have news" of the event before it happens. The indication in vss. 94-95 that this third dream comes in the early hours just before dawn further underscores this point and suggests its similarity to the other two dreams (*Purg.* IX, 13-18, and XIX, 1-6).

94. *credo*: The little touch of uncertainty was missing in the account of the hour at which the other two dreams came

and (though the reader probably thought nothing of it in those two cases) might have been introduced there as well, especially in the case of the second dream, for how, we may ask, did the sleeping Dante know at what hour it came to him?

95. *Citerea*: Cytherea, epithet of Venus, who was so called from Cythera (now Cerigo), an island off the southeast coast of the Peloponnesus, near which she is said to have risen from the foam of the sea. Dante here applies the name to the planet Venus, the time indicated being the early morning before dawn. Cf. *Purg.* I, 19-21, where Venus is also described as shining bright just before dawn. On the auspicious connotation of this, see n. to *Purg.* I, 19.

98. *landa*: A level clearing surrounded by trees, as in *Inf.* XIV (except so very different from that barren place!).

100–108. *Sappia qualunque . . . appaga*: In three highly condensed tercets the prophetic (and clearly allegorical) dream is recounted. Laban's daughters Leah and Rachel, of the Old Testament, were long established allegorical figures of the active and contemplative life respectively. Leah was the first wife of Jacob; Rachel was his second wife. Cf. *Inf.* IV, 60, where Jacob's years of service for Rachel are referred to.

100. *qualunque = chiunque*.

101. *i' mi son Lia*: The reflexive is the familiar pleonastic pronoun common in statements of identification. Cf. *Purg.* XXIV, 52.

101–2. *vo movendo intorno le belle mani*: Signifying the active life and its works, which are as fair as the hands that perform them. Leah will then see with delight, in her mirror, that this is so.

103. *Per piacermi a lo specchio*: Buti comments: "per avere complacenzia di me quando io mi specchierò; cioè quando io esaminerò e considererò ne la coscienzia, che è lo specchio d'ogni uno, quali siano l'opere mie" ("in order

to be satisfied with myself when I look in the mirror; that is, when I shall examine and consider what my works are in [my] conscience, which is the mirror for each of us").

104–5. *mai non si smaga dal suo miraglio*: "Never turns away from her mirror." Note "smaghi" in *Purg.* X, 106, and "dismago" in *Purg.* XIX, 20, and compare "volsi" in *Purg.* XIX, 22.

105. *siede tutto giorno*: Benvenuto observes: "Idest, quiescit in speculatione." ("That is, she rests in speculation.") *tutto giorno*: Constantly.

106. *Ell' è d'i suoi belli occhi veder vaga*: Rachel's eyes are beautiful, even as Leah's hands are said to be. The object of contemplation is truth, but philosophy, as Dante says in the *Convivio*, not only contemplates truth, but contemplates the contemplation itself, here signified by Rachel's constant desire to see her own eyes. See *Conv.* IV, ii, 18:

> Filosofia, che è . . . amoroso uso di sapienza, se medesima riguarda, quando apparisce la bellezza de li occhi suoi a lei; che altro non è a dire, se non che l'anima filosofante non solamente contempla essa veritate, ma ancora contempla lo suo contemplare medesimo e la bellezza di quello, rivolgendosi sovra se stessa e di se stessa innamorando per la bellezza del suo primo guardare.

> Philosophy, which . . . is "the loving exercise of wisdom," contemplates herself when the beauty of her eyes is revealed to herself. And what else is this but to say that the philosophising soul not only contemplates the truth, but also contemplates its own contemplation and the beauty thereof, turning upon itself and enamouring itself of itself by reason of the beauty of its direct contemplation?

109. *splendori antelucani*: As Dante states in the *Convivio* (III, xiv, 5), *splendore* denotes reflected light:

> Dico che l'usanza de' filosofi è di chiamare "luce" lo lume, in quanto esso è nel suo fontale principio; di

chiamare "raggio," in quanto esso è per lo mezzo, dal
principio al primo corpo dove si termina; di chiamare
"splendore," in quanto esso è in altra parte alluminata
ripercosso.

I say that it is the custom of the philosophers to call
the luminous principle *light*, in so far as it exists in the
source from which it springs, and to call it a *ray* in so
far as it exists in the medium (between its source and
the first body whereby it is arrested), and to call it
splendour in so far as it is thrown back upon some other
illuminated part.

See "antelucani" in Sapien. 11:23: "tamquam gutta roris
antelucani quae descendit in terram" ("or a drop of morn-
ing dew come down upon the earth").

110–11. *che tanto a' pellegrin . . . lontani*: The nearer pil-
grims come to home ("tornando") with each day of their re-
turn journey, the more eager they become to reach journey's
end and so welcome the coming of day when they can be on
their way. For the pilgrim homesick even after the first day
of the outbound journey, see *Purg.* VIII, 4-6. Clearly the
touch signals the fact that, for Dante the pilgrim, "home" is,
in some sense, near now.

113. *leva'mi = mi levai*.

115. *Quel dolce pome*: Happiness.   *che per tanti rami*:
Mortals seek happiness on many different boughs, i.e., seek
it in many ways according to differing notions of what con-
stitutes happiness. See the quotation from Boethius in the
following note.

116. *la cura de' mortali*: "Cura" (subject of "cercando")
means "endeavor" or "pursuit." See Boethius, *Consol. philos.*
III, 2, ll. 2-5: "Omnis mortalium cura quam multiplicium
studiorum labor exercet, diverso quidem calle procedit, sed
ad unum tamen beatitudinis finem nititur pervenire." ("All
men's thoughts, which are turmoiled with manifold cares,
take indeed divers courses, but yet endeavour to attain the
same end of happiness.") Boethius goes on to review the

various conceptions men have of happiness. Cf. *Inf.* XVI,
61, where Dante also alludes to the "dolci pomi," the good
which every man perceives dimly as his ultimate desire and
goal and which each strives to reach (see *Purg.* XVII, 127-
29). Cf., for another pointer to the fact that the goal thus
promised is happiness, *Purg.* XXX, 75.

117. *oggi porrà in pace le tue fami*: If Dante's hunger for
this sweet fruit is to be satisfied today, then the reader should
be alert to see just how this will happen. It is thus a promise
which, like the promise of the dream, is to be carried along
now with a certain suspense as to how it will be realized. To
attain peace is to reach a goal, which should mean to reach
home, in some sense, according to the suggestion made by
the pilgrim image. For the notion of peace as sweet fruit and
fruition, see Thomas Aquinas, *Summa theol.* I-II, q. 11, a.
3, resp.:

> Ad rationem fructus duo pertinent, scilicet quod sit ulti-
> mum, et quod appetitum quietet quadam dulcedine vel
> delectatione. Ultimum autem est simpliciter et secun-
> dum quid; simpliciter quidem quod ad aliud non refer-
> tur; sed secundum quid, quod est aliquorum ultimum.
>
> Quod ergo est simpliciter ultimum, in quo aliquis
> delectatur sicut in ultimo fine, hoc proprie dicitur fruc-
> tus, et eo proprie dicitur aliquis frui.

> The notion of fruit implies two things: first that it
> should come last; second, that it should calm the appe-
> tite with a certain sweetness and delight. Now a thing
> is last either simply or relatively; simply, if it be referred
> to nothing else; relatively, if it is the last in a particular
> series. Therefore that which is last simply, and in which
> one delights as in the last end, is properly called fruit;
> and this it is that one is properly said to enjoy.

118–19. *queste cotali parole*: Words so meaningful.

119. *furo* = *furono*. *strenne*: Auspicious gifts, gifts
auguring happiness. Cf. M. Barbi (1934b), pp. 283-84.

120. *queste*: I.e., "parole." *iguali* = *uguali*.

123. *sentia = sentivo.   crescer le penne*: The climb is easy now, even as Virgil predicted it would be (*Purg.* IV, 91-94; XII, 121-26). The last P has been removed from Dante's forehead (though no explicit mention of the fact was made), and he is much lighter and fairly flies to the promised goal.

127. *Il temporal foco*: The fire of Purgatory, i.e., all the purgatorial punishments (see *Inf.* I, 118-20) which will not endure eternally as will the fire of Hell, but only until the Judgment Day.   *e l'etterno*: The fire of Hell. Cf. Thomas Aquinas, *Summa theol.* Suppl., append., "Articuli duo de Purgatorio," a. 2, obj. 1: "Poena damnatorum est aeterna, ut dicitur Matth. 25, 46: *Ibunt hi in ignem aeternum.* Sed purgatorius ignis est temporalis." ("The punishment of the damned is eternal, according to Matth. XXV. 46, *These shall go into everlasting punishment* [Vulg.,—*fire*]. But the fire of Purgatory is temporary.")

130. *ingegno*: "Devising."   *arte*: Wit put to work.

131. *per duce*: In place of Virgil, who has been guide to this point. Henceforth Dante's own pleasure shall be his guide.

132. *arte*: Cf. Matt. 7:14: "Quam angusta porta et arcta via est quae ducit ad vitam, et pauci sunt qui inveniunt eam!" ("How narrow the gate and close the way that leads to life! And few there are who find it.") Cf. *Purg.* X, 16.

133. *Vedi lo sol che 'n fronte ti riluce*: We are again reminded that Dante faces east and the dawn as he moves into the garden, and we should recall that he was facing west when he began the climb up the mountain (*Purg.* III, 16-18). Hence he has finally circled halfway round the mountain in the ascent.

135. *che qui la terra sol da sé produce*: A point explained in the next canto, *Purg.* XXVIII, 118-20.

136–37. *li occhi belli . . . lagrimando*: Cf. *Inf.* II, 116. Virgil declared at the outset (*Inf.* I, 123) that he would leave Dante with Beatrice at this point.

137. *fenno = fecero.*

138. *seder ti puoi*: Like Rachel, in contemplation. See vs. 105. *e puoi andar tra elli*: Like Leah, among the flowers and shrubs.

139. *Non aspettar mio dir più*: The words of vss. 139-42 are, in fact, the last that Virgil speaks to Dante.

140. *libero, dritto e sano è tuo arbitrio*: Free will, the central subject of the *Purgatorio* (*Purg.* XVI-XVIII), is finally in the central focus at the end. Dante, who was said by Virgil at the beginning (*Purg.* I, 71) to be seeking liberty, has now attained it. His will is free, straight (straightened), and whole again, like man's will before original sin (he having now returned to Eden, as we soon learn). For the notion of "straightening" the will in Purgatory, see *Purg.* XXIII, 126. And for the word *sano* in this sense, see *Conv.* IV, xv, 11, where Dante writes: "Onde è da sapere che lo nostro intelletto si può dir sano e infermo: e dico intelletto per la nobile parte de l'anima nostra, che con uno vocabulo 'mente' si può chiamare. Sano dire si può, quando per malizia d'animo o di corpo impedito non è ne la sua operazione." ("Wherefore be it known that our intellect may be spoken of as sound or sick; and I mean by 'intellect' the noble part of our soul which may be indicated by the common term 'mind.' Sound it may be called when not impeded in its activity by ill either of mind or of body.")

141. *fora = sarebbe. a suo senno*: "Discernment." Free will involves rational discernment. See Dante's comment in *De mon.* I, xii, 3: "Et ideo dico quod iudicium medium est apprehensionis et appetitus: nam primo res apprehenditur, deinde apprehensa bona vel mala iudicatur; et ultimo iudicans prosequitur sive fugit." ("Therefore I say that judgment is the link between apprehension and appetite. For first a thing is apprehended, then when apprehended it is judged

to be good or bad, and finally he who has so judged it pursues or shuns it.") Cf. *Purg.* XVI, 75-76. And it is evident that the notion of reason sitting in supreme rule over the lower faculties derives from Aristotle and brings with it the notion of rule by a king (hence the "crowning" of Dante). See Thomas Aquinas, *Summa theol.* I-II, q. 9, a. 2, ad 3:

> Sicut Philosophus dicit in 1 Polit. (cap. 3, post med.), ratio, in qua est voluntas, movet suo imperio irascibilem et concupiscibilem; non quidem despotico principatu, sicut movetur servus a domino; sed principatu regali seu politico, sicut liberi homines reguntur a gubernante, qui tamen possunt contra movere.

> As the Philosopher says (*Polit.* i. 2), the reason, in which resides the will, moves, by its command, the irascible and concupiscible powers, not, indeed, *by a despotic sovereignty*, as a slave is moved by his master, but by a *royal and politic sovereignty*, as free men are ruled by their governor, and can nevertheless act counter to his commands.

On Aquinas' reference to Aristotle, see *Polit.* I, 2, 1254^b.

142. *te sovra te corono e mitrio*: Virgil's words "crowning" and "mitering" Dante over himself complete his declaration to his charge that he has been brought to justice, inner justice. On the justice to which Virgil can lead, corresponding in the individual to what was called *iustitia civilis* in a social sense (the kind to which the Romans led the world), see C. S. Singleton (1958), pp. 64-69. The fact that this is *that* kind of justice, and not *iustitia infusa* (which Dante will attain only when he attains to Beatrice), requires that the crown and miter (implied in the corresponding verbs) be the crown and miter which were used in the crowning of an emperor, and it should not be construed as pointing to *two* powers, empire and church respectively. On the use of the miter in the crowning of a temporal ruler, see E. H. Kantorowicz (1957), pp. 491-92.

CANTO XXVIII

Special Note: For the full meaning of Virgil's words of dismissal to Dante, which close the preceding canto (*Purg.* XXVII, 127-42) and end Virgil's guidance, the reader is urged to see C. S. Singleton (1958), *passim*, but especially pp. 257-67, where the broad pattern of justification is scrutinized. Then, after a thoughtful reading of the present canto, he may find some clarification of the several major patterns of meaning which are now emerging in clearer outline (here as Dante leaves Virgil's guidance and proceeds into the Garden of Eden to meet the lady who will eventually be called Matelda) if he will read chaps. xi-xiii of that work, which apply to the whole event at the summit of the mountain in its successive stages. What may be termed a fulfillment of patterns, visible and comprehensible in retrospect, is now taking place, a process which is followed out in the comprehensive presentation of Singleton's work.

1. *già*: "Already," i.e., "without waiting longer" (vs. 4), Dante is eager to move forward, letting his own pleasure be his guide now.   *cercar*: "To explore."

2. *la divina foresta*: Before this the reader did not know that there was a forest here at the summit, much less a "divine" one, and the adjective serves to create a little suspense

until the reason for its existence is disclosed. Dante now, at
the end of his climb with Virgil, moves into a forest bright
with morning light, even as he came forth from a dark wood
at the beginning of his journey.   *viva*: "Verdant,"
"luxuriant."

3. *temperava il novo giorno*: The early morning sun was
shining in Dante's eyes a moment before (see *Purg*. XXVII,
133).

4. *sanza più aspettar*: In willing obedience to Virgil (*Purg*.
XXVII, 139). We are reminded that Dante now for the first
time moves forward alone, without looking to Virgil for
guidance.   *la riva*: The outer edge of the level at the
summit, now to be called a "campagna."

5. *lento lento*: This too is something unusual, after all the
haste of the journey to reach this place.

6. *su per*: "Across," not up and across, since Dante walks
on the level here.   *auliva*: "Gave forth fragrance." This
is a Latinism that belongs to the poetic language of the day
and contributes to the pastoral atmosphere of the whole de-
scription, as do words such as "aura" (vs. 7) and "augel-
letti" (vs. 14).

8. *feria = feriva*.

9. *più*: I.e., *maggiore*.

10. *pronte*: Quick to respond, in their trembling, to the soft
breeze.

11–12. *a la parte . . . monte*: Toward the west, the direction
in which the mountain casts its shade in early morning.

12. *u' = ove*.

13. *dal loro esser dritto*: From the upright state they would
have been in had there been no breeze.   *sparte*: "De-
flected." *Sparte* is the past participle of *spargere*.

14. *li augelletti*: A form which, modified as it is by senti-

ment in its diminutive suffix -*etti*, belongs to the poetic language, particularly to that of the pastoral tradition.

15. *lasciasser*: "Left off." *ogne lor arte*: I.e., flitting among the branches and singing and perhaps also building nests, since, as we now learn, it is eternal spring here.

16. *l'ore prime*: The first hours of the day. This cannot be *óre*, "breezes," as some interpreters would have it, since the breeze here is always the same and does not rise at dawn. See Boccaccio, *Decam.* V, introd. (vol. I, p. 343, ll. 2-4): "da' dolci canti degli uccelli li quali la prima ora del giorno su per gli albuscelli tutti lieti cantavano" ("from the sweet songs of the birds, which were all greeting with their songs the first hour of the day").

17. *ricevieno = ricevevano*.

18. *bordone a le sue rime*: In musical terminology, the burden is the drone of an instrument (as of a bagpipe) or other background accompaniment. The term thus suggests that this is a morning concert in which the branches of the trees keep up an accompaniment to the singing ("rime") of the birds. *sue = loro*.

19. *tal qual*: Such an accompaniment as. *di ramo in ramo si raccoglie*: Gathers into a single sound from the many boughs.

20. *la pineta in su 'l lito di Chiassi*: The famous pine forest that extended (as it still does) along the shore of the Adriatic for several miles near Ravenna. The Roman Classis, the ancient harbor of Ravenna, under Augustus was an important naval station and at one time a large town. The name is still preserved in that of the beautiful church of Sant'Apollinare in Classe, which stands on the site of part of the old town.

21. *quand' Eolo scilocco fuor discioglie*: Aeolus, god of the winds, which he was supposed to keep shut up in a mountain and release at will. He is here said to let out the sirocco, the southeast wind that blows across to Italy from the African coast.

22. *Già m'avean trasportato i lenti passi*: The going is now entirely without effort, after the long hard climb; it is as if Dante's steps carried him along.

23. *la selva antica*: Cf. Virgil, *Aen.* VI, 179: "Itur in antiquam silvam." ("They pass into the forest primeval.") We are soon to learn why the wood is called "ancient."

24. *non potea rivedere ond' io mi 'ntrassi*: For a similar backward glance over the way, see *Inf.* XV, 13-15.

25. *ed ecco più andar mi tolse un rio*: "Più andar" is the object of "tolse," and "rio" is the subject.

26–27. *che 'nver' sinistra . . . uscìo*: The stream flows north at this point, and Dante is on the left bank. For a possible Virgilian echo, cf. *Georg.* IV, 19: "tenuis fugiens per gramina rivus" ("and a tiny brook stealing through the grass").

27. *uscìo*: *Usciva*, a descriptive tense, would be expected here, and the use of the past absolute is somewhat forced by the rhyme.

28. *di qua*: In the northern, inhabited hemisphere.

29. *parrieno = parrebbero.*

30. *verso di*: Cf. *Purg.* III, 51.

32–33. *sotto l'ombra perpetua . . . luna*: This touch concerning a cool perpetual shade is a common feature of ideal paradises for poets who live under the hot Mediterranean sun. Compare Ovid's description of the scene from which Proserpina was taken, particularly *Metam.* V, 388-89: "Silva coronat aquas cingens latus omne suisque / frondibus ut velo Phoebeos submovet ictus." ("A wood crowns the heights around its waters on every side, and with its foliage as with an awning keeps off the sun's hot rays.") And see Ps. 120[121]:6: "Per diem sol non uret te, neque luna per noctem." ("The sun shall not harm you by day, nor the moon by night.")

36. *mai*: Plural of *maio*, the flowered May branch that was used in the celebration of May Day, like the modern May basket. From this meaning the word came to be used of any flowered branch.

37. *elli appare*: "There appears." "Elli" is a pleonastic subject.

40. *una donna soletta*: The maiden going about alone is a traditional feature of the *pastorella*. See, for instance, Guido Cavalcanti's *pastorella* "In un boschetto trova' pasturella" (in G. Contini, 1960, vol. II, pp. 555-56). *che si gia*: The reflexive pronoun "si" has the familiar distancing function of the so-called pleonastic reflexive. See *Inf.* VII, 94, and *Vita nuova* XXVI, 6: "Ella si va, sentendosi laudare." ("She goeth her way, hearing her praises.") Rossi-Frascino, terming it an ethical dative, comments: "Quel 'si' etico aggiunge raccoglimento ed intimità all'azione." ("That ethical dative 'si' adds inwardness and intimacy to the action.")

41. *scegliendo fior da fiore*: This touch will remind the reader of Leah in the dream (*Purg.* XXVII, 99). This lady also weaves a garland, as vs. 68 suggests.

42. *pinta = dipinta.*

43. *a' raggi d'amore*: The shining of Cytherea at the hour of the dream (*Purg.* XXVII, 95-96) has already introduced this touch, and soon Venus herself, burning with love, will be mentioned (vss. 64-66). The corresponding figure in the *pastorella*, the shepherdess or maiden, is commonly seen to be in love, and there is a continuing stress on the fact that this lady is enamored (see *Purg.* XXIX, 1).

44. *vo' = voglio.*

44-45. *a' sembianti . . . core*: In *Vita nuova* XV, 5, Dante writes in a similar vein: "Lo viso mostra lo color del core." ("My countenance sheweth the hue of my heart.") In *Vita nuova* XXI, 2, he says: "Ne li occhi porta la mia donna Amore." ("In her eyes my lady beareth Love.")

46. *vegnati = ti vegna.*   *vegnati in voglia*: A very polite and gracious phrasing of a request.

48. *che tu canti*: *Cosa* is understood ("che cosa tu canti").

50–51. *Proserpina . . . primavera*: Proserpina, daughter of Jupiter and Ceres, was gathering flowers in a meadow near Enna in Sicily, when Pluto suddenly appeared and carried her off to be the queen of the lower world. The story is told by Ovid, *Metam.* V, 385-408, and it is evident that Dante has taken a number of details from his verses in his own description of the lady who appears in the forest. See *Metam.* V, 385-96:

> Haud procul Hennaeis lacus est a moenibus altae,
> nomine Pergus, aquae: non illo plura Caystros
> carmina cycnorum labentibus audit in undis.
> silva coronat aquas cingens latus omne suisque
> frondibus ut velo Phoebeos submovet ictus;
> frigora dant rami, tyrios humus umida flores:
> perpetuum ver est. quo dum Proserpina loco
> ludit et aut violas aut candida lilia carpit,
> dumque puellari studio calathosque sinumque
> inplet et aequales certat superare legendo,
> paene simul visa est dilectaque raptaque Diti:
> usque adeo est properatus amor. . . .

Not far from Henna's walls there is a deep pool of water, Pergus by name. Not Caÿster on its gliding waters hears more songs of swans than does this pool. A wood crowns the heights around its waters on every side, and with its foliage as with an awning keeps off the sun's hot rays. The branches afford a pleasing coolness, and the well-watered ground bears bright-coloured flowers. There spring is everlasting. Within this grove Proserpina was playing, and gathering violets or white lilies. And while with girlish eagerness she was filling her basket and her bosom, and striving to surpass her mates in gathering, almost in one act did Pluto see and love and carry her away: so precipitate was his love.

51. *primavera*: Not merely the flowers which Proserpina had plucked but the whole flowering grove about her, corresponding in the implied simile to that in which this lady walks about. Buti explains: "lo prato e la verdura ne la quale ella era a colliere fiori" ("the fields and meadow, where she was plucking flowers").

52–54. *Come si volge . . . mette*: Apparently this for Dante represents a most beautiful manner of dancing, modest and becoming to a maiden. The feet are barely lifted from the ground and are kept close together. And if the turning is as in a dance, it is in this case highly stylized and almost ritualistic. Added to this is the modest lowering of the eyes.

55. *volsesi = si volse.*

57. *avvalli*: Cf. *Purg.* XIII, 63. Here the verb is in the hypothetical subjunctive.

60. *co' suoi intendimenti*: Dante not only hears the song but makes out its words and their meaning. What these are he does not tell us.

61–62. *dove l'erbe . . . fiume*: At just the point ("già") where the grass is bathed by the water, i.e., on the very edge of the bank.

61. *sono = suono.*

64–66. *Non credo . . . costume*: While Venus was kissing her son Cupid, she was unintentionally wounded by him and fell madly in love with Adonis. The incident is recounted by Ovid, *Metam.* X, 525-32:

> namque pharetratus dum dat puer oscula matri,
> inscius exstanti destrinxit harundine pectus;
> laesa manu natum dea reppulit: altius actum
> vulnus erat specie primoque fefellerat ipsam.
> capta viri forma non iam Cythereia curat
> litora, non alto repetit Paphon aequore cinctam
> piscosamque Cnidon gravidamve Amathunta metallis:
> abstinet et caelo: caelo praefertur Adonis.

For while the goddess' son, with quiver on shoulder, was kissing his mother, he chanced unwittingly to graze her breast with a projecting arrow. The wounded goddess pushed her son away with her hand; but the scratch had gone deeper than she thought, and she herself was at first deceived. Now, smitten with the beauty of a mortal, she cares no more for the borders of Cythera, nor does she seek Paphos, girt by the deep sea, nor fish-haunted Cnidos, nor Amathus, rich in precious ores. She stays away even from the skies; Adonis is preferred to heaven.

Again Dante uses a simile of profane love, and the reference to Venus connects now with the touch about Cytherea (i.e., Venus), the morning star, which was shining in the hour in which the dream of Leah came (*Purg.* XXVII, 94-96), as well as at the hour in which Dante first arrived in Purgatory (*Purg.* I, 19-20). Thus love is most emphatically the dominant theme.

66. *fuor di tutto suo costume*: Quite contrary to Cupid's custom, which was to aim his arrows intentionally. This wounding of his mother was unintentional. See Ovid's "inscius," *Metam.* X, 526.

67. *dritta*: "Standing." Cf. *Inf.* IV, 5.

68. *trattando*: "Weaving," i.e., a garland. This seems the likely meaning, since the lady was seen to cull flowers (vs. 41), presumably for such a purpose. And the touch recalls Leah, of course, who was making herself a wreath (*Purg.* XXVII, 102). Some editors prefer "traendo" ("trailing").
  più color: Flowers of many colors. "Più color" is understood as the antecedent of "che," in the following verse, which is in turn the object of "gitta."

69. *che l'alta terra sanza seme gitta*: A matter that is touched on in *Purg.* XXVII, 134-35, and that will be explained in vss. 109-20. So it was in the Golden Age (referred to in vs. 140) as Ovid tells in verses which Dante undoubtedly has in mind as he describes this forest. See *Metam.* I, 107-10:

> ver erat aeternum, placidique tepentibus auris
> mulcebant zephyri natos sine semine flores;
> mox etiam fruges tellus inarata ferebat,
> nec renovatus ager gravidis canebat aristis . . .

Then spring was everlasting, and gentle zephyrs with warm breath played with the flowers that sprang unplanted. Anon the earth, untilled, brought forth her stores of grain, and the fields, though unfallowed, grew white with the heavy, bearded wheat.

gitta = getta.

70. *Tre passi ci facea il fiume lontani*: The stream is certainly not very wide, but Dante somehow knows that he must not attempt to cross it yet.

71. *Elesponto, là 've passò Serse*: Xerxes, son of Darius, was king of Persia from 486 B.C. to 465 B.C. In the spring of 480 B.C. he set out from Sardis at the head of a countless host on his memorable expedition against Greece, crossed the Hellespont, and marched on Athens. But he was defeated, and his fleet was dispersed at the battle of Salamis, and he was obliged to retreat. In his *Hist.* II, ix, 2, and II, x, 8-10, Orosius describes the size of Xerxes' forces and goes on to moralize on the humiliation of Xerxes' defeat, which according to vs. 72 should serve as a bridle to all human pride:

> Xerxes septingenta milia armatorum de regno et trecenta de auxiliis, rostratas etiam naves mille ducentas, onerarias autem tria milia numero habuisse narratur; ut merito inopinato exercitu inmensaeque classi vix ad potum flumina, vix terras ad ingressum, vix maria ad cursum suffecisse memoratum sit. . . .
>
> Rex Abydum, ubi pontem veluti victor maris conserverat, cum paucis proficiscitur. sed cum pontem hibernis tempestatibus dissolutum offendisset, piscatoria scapha trepidus transiit. erat sane quod spectare humanum genus et dolere debuerit mutationes rerum hac vel maxime varietate permetiens: exiguo contentum latere navigio, sub quo ipsum pelagus ante latuisset et

iugum captivitatis suae iuncto ponte portasset; vilissimo
unius servuli egere ministerio, cuius potentiae, dum
montes exciduntur, valles replentur, amnes exhauriun-
tur, ipsa etiam rerum natura cessisset.

Xerxes' forces are said to have numbered seven hundred
thousand soldiers from his own kingdom and three hun-
dred thousand from allied states; he also had one thou-
sand and two hundred beaked ships and three thousand
transports. Thus it has been recorded, and not without
reason, that there were scarcely enough rivers to drink
from, scarcely enough lands to invade, and scarcely
enough seas to traverse for an army so unprecedented
in size and for a fleet so huge. . . .

The king set out with a few men for Abydos, where,
as though he were conqueror of the sea, he had built a
bridge. But when he found that the bridge had been
shattered by winter storms, he crossed over in a fishing
skiff in fear and trembling. What a sight for men to look
upon and grieve over as they measured the fickleness
of fate by this great reversal of fortune! He before whom
the very sea had lain concealed and had borne as the
yoke of its captivity the bridge that joined its shores
was content to hide in a tiny boat; he to whose power
nature herself had yielded as he leveled mountains, filled
valleys, and emptied rivers, lacked even the humble
service of a single slave.

See *De mon.* II, viii, 7, where Dante speaks of Xerxes
as "miserabiliter ab incepto repulsus" ("miserably repelled
from his attempt") and where he recalls Lucan's verses
(*Phars.* II, 672-73). See also Valerius Maximus, *Fact. dict.
memor.* IX, v, ext. 2.

72. *freno*: "Bridle." The term refers to the daring crossing
itself and the humiliation it led to, as an example for
all prideful men.

73-74. *più odio da Leandro . . . Abido*: Leander, a youth
of Abydos, used to swim across the Hellespont every night
to visit Hero, the priestess of Venus at Sestos. Dante may

have had the story from Ovid, *Heroides* XVIII-XIX. Hero, appealing to Neptune to smooth the passage for her lover, says (*Heroides* XIX, 139-46):

> Cur igitur, totiens vires expertus amoris,
> adsuetum nobis turbine claudis iter?
> parce, ferox, latoque mari tua proelia misce!
> seducit terras haec brevis unda duas.
> te decet aut magnas magnum iactare carinas,
> aut etiam totis classibus esse trucem;
> turpe deo pelagi iuvenem terrere natantem,
> gloriaque est stagno quolibet ista minor.

Why, then, dost thou, who hast felt so many times the power of love, close up with whirling storm the way we have learned to know? Spare us, impetuous one, and mingle thy battles out upon the open deep! These waters, that separate two lands, are scant. It befits thee, who art mighty, either to toss about the mighty keel, or to be fierce even with entire fleets; 'tis shame for the god of the great sea to terrify a swimming youth—that glory is less than should come from troubling any pond.

74. *per mareggiare*: Because of the turbulent waves.
intra Sesto e Abido: Abydos, in Asia Minor, on the narrowest part of the Hellespont, is opposite Sestos in Thrace.

75. *quel*: The stream blocking his way ("fiume," vs. 70).
perch' allor non s'aperse: Again it is evident (though not explained) that Dante feels somehow that he must not attempt to cross the narrow stream, much as he desires to do so. It is as if he would cross over only if the water should be opened for him, as the Red Sea was to the Israelites (see *Purg.* XVIII, 134).

76. *Voi siete nuovi*: The lady addresses Virgil and Statius as well as Dante, and the reader may feel a little surprised that the two ancient poets who bring up the rear have not already disappeared from the scene.

76-79. *e forse perch' io rido . . . sospetto*: There is no reason why Dante or the two poets should marvel that this lady

smiles and rejoices in such a beautiful spot. The poet is call-
ing particular attention to that fact, which is all-important
in the understanding of the allegory, and to do so is again to
make special use of the little word *forse* (see *Purg.* VIII, 99,
and *Inf.* X, 63, as well as vs. 141 below).

77–78. *in questo luogo . . . nido*: We begin to understand
now why the forest was termed "divina" at the beginning of
the canto, for this place "chosen for the human race as its
nest" must be the Garden of Eden, chosen by God as man's
first abode. Moreover, Adam's sin had dire consequences for
human nature, hence the choice of this particular way of re-
ferring to our first parents and the long line of their descend-
ants, all of whom would have lived in this Paradise for their
allotted time on earth. "Nido" strongly suggests as much, ex-
cept that, had there been no sin, no one was to fly this nest
except at the *end* of his life on earth. It was to have been our
natural place of abode, our "home."

79. *tienvi = vi tiene.   sospetto*: "Sospetto" ("wonder-
ment") is the subject of *tiene*.

80. *ma luce rende il salmo Delectasti*: The reference here
is to Ps. 91:5-6[92:4-5]. See C. S. Singleton (1958),
pp. 206-7:

> The psalm referred to is the ninety-first of the Vulgate
> Bible, as perhaps Virgil, at least, could not be expected
> to know. But we, as readers, are also new to this place
> and we too, it is assumed, will wonder at Matelda's joy;
> and thus, upon her suggestion, we recall this particular
> psalm for the light it can bring. If we turn to the psalm
> we see that certain specific verses are intended to be
> called to mind, for "delectasti" is not the first word of
> the psalm, nor is the verse containing that word the first
> verse. The point of the reference is thereby the more
> evident; and the verses intended must be these:
>
>> Quia delectasti me, Domine, in factura tua;
>> et in operibus manuum tuarum exsultabo.
>> Quam magnificata sunt opera tua, Domine.

Because Thou didst delight me, Lord, in Thy work;
and in the works of Thy hands I will rejoice.
How praiseworthy are Thy works, O Lord.

It may be of more than mere erudite interest to note that over a century before Dante wrote this canto of his poem, Peter Abelard had found that this particular psalm, and indeed the same verses referred to by Matelda, were relevant to the matter of the original condition of man in Eden. In his treatise on the work of the Creation, *Hexaemeron*, when he enters into the "moral" interpretation of the events in Genesis, Abelard writes a commentary on those delights which man, even now in his fallen condition, may experience in the created universe, in all the creatures which have been made for him:

> The things and creatures of the universe can hold out a varied pleasure to man, according to the diversity of man's senses: as with song they caress his ear, or with the beauty of their form they delight his eye, or with sweet odor refresh his sense of smell; or by whatsoever manner through their divers natures studiously known by man they may otherwise inspire in us love and praise of the Creator, even as the Psalmist says, addressing Him: "Delectasti me, Domine, in factura tua et in operibus manuum tuarum exsultabo."

The meaning of Matelda's reference to the psalm would be evident, even without testimony of this kind from Abelard. But his mention of the verses in precisely this context is of special interest, since he singles out the same verses as Matelda does to explain her own joy. Moreover, by what Abelard here observes respecting the delights which man may have from God's work now, after the Fall, we are prompted to think how much greater those delights must have been in Eden. Abelard specifically refers to the beauties of nature that meet our eyes, to the songs of birds and the fragrance of flowers in particular. And we may note that as Dante first enters

the divine forest at the summit of the mountain, these
are severally the specific delights which he experiences.
Still more important, in guiding us to the whole mean-
ing of the reference to this particular psalm, is Abe-
lard's qualification of it as a song in praise and love of
the Creator. This, too, must be the essential point of
Matelda's alluding to it, this must be the light which,
as she says, should derive from it. We are not to under-
stand merely that Matelda feels delight and joy in these
wonders of God's handiwork, even as Adam must have
felt them here. Matelda, by her allusion to the psalm,
is telling us that the joy she experiences is the joy of
love, and that her song (the words of which we do not
hear) is a love song in praise of the Lord who made
these things. Thus it is evident at once to Dante, at his
first glimpse of this maiden, that Matelda is in love. It
is presumed that we should wonder: in love how? What
is the cause and object of her love, alone as she is in
Eden? Now, it is in answer to this question that the
psalm *Delectasti* should "uncloud our minds": Matelda
rejoices, even as the Psalmist, in the works of God, and
her song is a song in praise of Him.

For the reference to Abelard, see *Expositio in Hexaemeron*
(col. 762D).

81. *puote = può.   disnebbiar*: Cf. "nebbia" in vs. 90.
  vostro intelletto: The lady's address to all three poets ends
here, and she now proceeds to single out Dante, with the "tu"
of the next verse.

83-84. *presta ad ogne tua question*: Ready to oblige you
by answering your every question.

84. *tanto che basti*: Until it is sufficient, until you are
satisfied.

85-87. *"L'acqua" . . . questa*: According to the explanation
that was given by Statius (*Purg.* XXI, 43-72), the area of
Purgatory proper, from the gate up, is exempt from all
changes or alteration except for spiritual causes, such as the

trembling of the mountain that occurred when Statius com-
pleted his purgation. This point Dante now remembers, term-
ing it his "recent faith," and wonders that there can be any
wind here at the summit or any running water, phenomena
which seem contrary to what Statius affirmed. Could it be
that rain falls here, to provide the water? Apparently this
lady is able to read Dante's mind, for she understands at once
what the "belief" he has had from Statius is.

89. *per sua cagion*: By its own (special) cause.   *face =*
fa.

90. *la nebbia*: See "disnebbiar" in vs. 81 above.   *fiede*
= *fedisce,* "strikes," i.e., besets.

91. *Lo sommo Ben*: God.   *che solo esso a sé piace*:
Only in Himself, in His own perfection, can God find com-
plete satisfaction. He created other beings that they in turn
might love Him even as He loves Himself.

92. *fé l'uom buono*: Cf. Eccles. 7:30[29], "fecerit Deus
hominem rectum" ("God made mankind straight"), a verse
quoted time and again by theologians in their discussion of
original rectitude or original justice. See C. S. Singleton
(1958), pp. 222-53. We should also recall that when the
Lord looked upon all His creation, He found it very good
(Gen. 1:31).   *a bene*: God established man in original
justice, that he might live and act according to perfect virtue.
See C. S. Singleton (1958), p. 210, and *passim*.

92-93. *e questo loco . . . pace*: Men were to live in the ter-
restrial paradise (it is now abundantly clear that this must
be Eden), each his appointed time, and then were to be
transported directly to the Paradise above and to eternal bliss
and peace, there in the vision of God. The peace of
the earthly Paradise was an anticipation, a token of eternal
peace. As for there being a token peace here, the reader will
recall Virgil's promise to Dante, that he is to attain to peace
this very day (*Purg.* XXVII, 117).

94. *Per sua difalta*: Man's default, of course, was his orig-
inal sin, which caused him to be driven from Eden.   *qui
dimorò poco*: Later, in Paradise, we are to learn from none
other than Adam himself how he and Eve dwelt in the gar-
den about six hours only! See *Par.* XXVI, 139-42.

95. *in pianto e in affanno*: Cf. Gen. 3:17-19:

> Adae vero dixit: Quia audisti vocem uxoris tuae, et co-
> medisti de ligno ex quo praeceperam tibi ne comederes,
> maledicta terra in opere tuo; in laboribus comedes ex
> ea cunctis diebus vitae tuae. Spinas et tribulos germi-
> nabit tibi et comedes herbam terrae in sudore vultus
> tui vesceris pane, donec revertaris in terram de qua
> sumptus es; quia pulvis es, et in pulverem reverteris.

> And to Adam he said, "Because you have listened to
> your wife, and have eaten of the tree of which I com-
> manded you not to eat: Cursed be the ground because
> of you; in toil shall you eat of it all the days of your life;
> thorns and thistles shall it bring forth to you, and you
> shall eat the plants of the field. In the sweat of your
> brow you shall eat bread, till you return to the ground,
> since out of it you were taken; for dust you are and unto
> dust you shall return."

96. *onesto riso e dolce gioco*: Such joy and sweet sport as
the lady across the stream from Dante showed her life in
Eden to be; for such was that of Adam and Eve, in their short
time there, and such would life have been for all mankind.

97. *sotto da sé*: "Beneath it," i.e., below the upper reaches
of the mountain. The phrase anticipates "questo monte salìo"
of vs. 101.

98. *l'essalazion*: Plural, as seen by the verb "vanno" in the
next verse. The "exhalations" of water and earth (moist
earth, in this case) are the "vapors" that produce rain. Cf.
Purg. V, 110-11. Dry vapor (mentioned by Statius in *Purg.*
XXI, 52-53, as rising no farther than the three steps of the
gate of Purgatory proper) is wind.

99. *dietro al calor*: Humid vapors are drawn up by the heat of the sun and rise toward that body as far as they can, until they are converted into rain by the air in its cold sphere above (cf. vs. 122), i.e., in what, following Aristotle, was termed the middle zone of the atmosphere. B. Nardi (1930, p. 364) calls attention to Albertus Magnus, who states in his *Commentarii in secundum librum Sententiarum* (VI, a. 5, ad q. 3): "Media autem inter has frigida est vehementer . . . et ideo tempestuosa, et generantur ibi tempestates, et nives, et grandines." ("The middle zone is exceedingly cold . . . and so it is stormy, and storms and snow and hail are generated there.")

101. *salio = salì*.

102. *libero n'è d'indi ove si serra*: It is free of such exhalations of earth and water, up from the place where "it is locked" ("si serra"), i.e., from the gate of Purgatory. Hence, as Statius explained (*Purg.* XXI, 46-48), no rain falls here, and there are no storms above the gate.

103. *Or*: "Or" (*ora*) serves to indicate that the exposition takes a new turn at this stage. Up to this point the lady has simply confirmed what Statius had previously affirmed. Now, to answer Dante's question, she must explain how it is that there is wind and running water at this summit that is above atmospheric change.

103-4. *in circuito . . . volta*: The "primal revolution" is that of the Primum Mobile, which in its diurnal revolution sweeps the other spheres or heavens with it around the earth and at the same time causes the atmosphere (the sphere of air, which is beneath that of fire and above that of earth— see C. S. Singleton, *Inferno Commentary*, Fig. 1, p. 34, and Fig. 2, p. 35) to circle the earth with it. In *Meteor.* I, 3, 341[a], Aristotle states that the air flows in a circuit since it is carried along in the total circulation, and Thomas Aquinas (*Exp. Meteor.* I, lect. 5), commenting on Aristotle, notes: "Et sic ille aer, qui excedit omnem altitudinem montium, in circuitu fluit; aer autem qui continetur infra montium al-

titudinem, impeditur ab hoc fluxu ex partibus terrae im-
mobilibus." ("And accordingly that air, which exceeds the
altitude of all the mountains, flows in a circuit; but the air
which is contained in the midst of high mountains is im-
peded in its flow by the immobile parts of the earth.")

105. *se non li è rotto il cerchio d'alcun canto*: Of course,
on or near the surface of the earth "exhalations" can cause
wind to blow in another direction, or the circling air can meet
with some obstruction, such as mountains and trees, which
can alter its course ("break the circuit at some point"). Ap-
parently the circling air does not cause a breeze to blow on
the terraces above the gate, but only at the summit.   *li =
gli*, referring to "aere."   *d'alcun canto*: "Somewhere,"
"in some part."

106-8. *in questa altezza . . . folta*: The air that is swept
about the earth from east to west by the Primum Mobile
strikes the summit of this mountain, which rises so high that
it is "free in the pure air," and causes in the dense wood the
sound which has been compared to that of the "pine wood
on the shore of Chiassi." In fact, it has already been noted
(vss. 11-12) that the breeze blows from the east.

109-11. *e la percossa pianta . . . scuote*: The lady at this
point begins to offer more, by way of explanation, than is
strictly called for by Dante's question. As she now explains,
the circling air carries the seeds and generative virtues of
plants in this forest to the hemisphere inhabited by man. For,
according to Genesis (1:11-12), here in the Paradise were
created all the kinds of plants:

> Et ait: Germinet terra herbam virentem et facientem
> semen, et lignum pomiferum faciens fructum iuxta
> genus suum, cuius semen in semetipso sit super terram.
> Et factum est ita. Et protulit terra herbam virentem et
> facientem semen iuxta genus suum, lignumque faciens
> fructum et habens unumquodque sementem secundum
> speciem suam. Et vidit Deus quod esset bonum.

> Then God said, "Let the earth bring forth vegetation:
> seed-bearing plants and all kinds of fruit trees that bear

fruit containing their seed." And so it was. The earth brought forth vegetation, every kind of seed-bearing plant and all kinds of trees that bear fruit containing their seed. God saw that it was good.

Also see Gen. 1:29: "Ecce dedi vobis omnem herbam afferentem semen super terram, et universa ligna quae habent in semetipsis sementem generis sui." ("See, I give you every seed-bearing plant on the earth and every tree which has seed-bearing fruit.") But the problem is, how were the seeds of plants carried to the other hemisphere? This the lady is explaining.

109. *pianta*: Singular for plural *piante*, the grasses and shrubs and trees of the forest (see *Purg.* XXVII, 134).
tanto puote: "Has such power."

110. *virtute*: Seed (visible or invisible: see vs. 117) or generative power, conceivably not in the form of seed. Diverse plants are generated of "diverse virtues" (vs. 114).

111. *quella*: The "aura," subject of "scuote."   *scuote*: The breeze "shakes" or "scatters" abroad the virtues with which it is impregnated. The object of "scuote" is not expressed, but it is understood to be the "virtute."

112. *l'altra terra*: The other hemisphere of land, inhabited by man after the Fall.

112–13. *secondo ch'è degna . . . ciel*: According as it is worthy, i.e., fitted, to receive the virtue of a given plant, worthy, that is, in itself or in its climate and situation ("ciel").

114. *legna*: Plural of *legno*, "plant." Cf. "lignum" in the passage quoted from Genesis in n. to vss. 109-11; see also *Inf.* XIII, 73 and *passim*.

115. *di là*: In the other—the inhabited—hemisphere, where plants seem to spring up ("take root," vs. 117) without visi-

ble seed. These come from the virtue of some plant in Eden, carried to our part of the earth by the circling breeze.

116. *udito questo*: If this were heard (and understood).

117. *vi*: I.e., *di là*.

118. *dei = devi.*   *campagna santa*: The plain at the summit is "holy" for the same reason that the forest is divine (vs. 2).

119. *d'ogne semenza è piena*: This according to Genesis (see n. to vss. 109-11) and as specifically affirmed of the Paradise itself in Gen. 2:9: "Produxitque Dominus Deus de humo omne lignum pulchrum visu et ad vescendum suave, lignum etiam vitae in medio paradisi, lignumque scientiae boni et mali." ("The Lord God made to grow out of the ground all kinds of trees pleasant to the sight and good for food, the tree of life also in the midst of the garden, and the tree of the knowledge of good and evil.")

120. *e frutto ha in sé che di là non si schianta*: And certain fruits grow on the holy plain which are not picked "yonder," i.e., in our hemisphere. This need not mean simply the fruit of the two very special trees referred to in the passage quoted in the n. to vs. 119. The Paradise must be more perfect than the region of the earth where man lives after the Fall and so must have varieties of fruit that are not known to us here. A principle of plenitude would require this to be so.

121–26. *L'acqua che vedi . . . aperta*: The lady now returns to Dante's wonder about the presence of running water at this summit, water which suggests that it may rain here. But this water, it is now explained, does not come from rainfall. It comes from a "vein" (and is, therefore, spring water) that is ever replenished, not naturally but supernaturally, i.e., directly by the will of God.

122. *che ristori vapor*: "Vapor" is the subject, "che" the object, "ristori" being in the hypothetical subjunctive, as is "converta," which follows.   *che gel converta*: See n. to vs. 99.

123. *come fiume ch'acquista e perde lena*: Rivers naturally vary in volume according to the amount of rainfall that feeds them.

124. *ma esce di fontana*: Thus we learn that the source of the stream is a spring, a "fountain," which every reader of Genesis might expect to be the case here, to irrigate the plain in place of rain, for in Gen. 2:6 it is said: "Sed fons ascendebat e terra irrigans universam superficiem terrae." ("But a mist rose from the earth and watered all the surface of the ground.") And, following on this, Gen. 2:10 tells of a river: "Et fluvius egrediebatur de loco voluptatis ad irrigandum paradisum." ("A river rose in Eden watering the garden.")

126. *quant' ella versa da due parti aperta*: Dante will come to the fountain later (*Purg.* XXXIII, 112-14) and will observe the font at first hand.   *aperta = apertamente*.

127. *Da questa parte*: On the side where we now are.

128. *altrui*: Dative, depending on the verb *togliere*, which takes the preposition *a*.

130. *Letè*: From the Greek λήθη, "oblivion." While in Hell Dante asked about the location of this river and was told (*Inf.* XIV, 136-38) that he would see it in Purgatory where the souls bathe when their guilt is removed. How this happens we are soon to see, but meanwhile it is clear that Dante the poet has chosen to place here, on the summit of Mount Purgatory, a stream that the classical poets placed in the nether regions, which explains why Dante the wayfarer asked about it in Hell. The river was also mentioned previously by Guido Guinizzelli, who referred to its power to cause forgetfulness (*Purg.* XXVI, 108).

130-31. *Eunoè*: From the Greek εὔνους, "well-minded," a name coined by Dante on the model of Protonoe (see *Conv.* II, iii, 11), which he found in Uguccione da Pisa, *Magnae derivationes* (see P. Toynbee, 1902, p. 104): "*nois* idest mens . . . *hec protonoe*, id est prima nois, id est divina mens" ("*nois*, that is mind . . . *hec protonoe*, that is, the first mind, that is, the divine mind"). It is said to restore the memory of good deeds (just as Lethe, which must be drunk first, takes away the memory of sinful deeds), and a draught from it will be said to be surpassingly sweet (*Purg.* XXXIII, 138).

131–32. *si chiama . . . gustato*: "L'acqua" of vs. 121 continues to be understood as the subject: the source is one, the water is one, and it does not produce its full effect unless it (i.e., the water in both streams) is tasted, first in the one ("quinci," in Lethe) and then in the other ("quindi," in Eunoe). Some commentators have argued against such an interpretation, although not persuasively, holding that the effect of Eunoe is the main point here. For a review of the several opinions, see Petrocchi's note on vss. 130-32. To be sure, Lethe does produce its effect before Dante tastes of Eunoe; but the subject of the statement is the "acqua" which runs in *both* streams.

133. *esto = questo*, i.e., *sapore*, the savor of the water in the one stream and the other. Nothing is actually said of the sweetness of Lethe, but this is understood; as for the savor of Eunoe, see *Purg.* XXXIII, 138.

134. *assai*: Cf. the French *assez*.

136. *darotti = ti darò.   un corollario*: The first meaning of *corollarium* in Latin is "gift," "present," "gratuity"; in philosophical and mathematical writings it took on the meaning that we commonly ascribe to the word in modern languages. See Boethius, *Consol. philos.* III, x, ll. 80-83, where Lady Philosophy speaks: "Super haec . . . igitur veluti geometrae solent demonstratis propositis aliquid inferre quae porismata ipsi vocant, ita ego quoque tibi veluti corollarium dabo." ("Upon this then . . . as the geometricians are wont, out of their propositions which they have demonstrated, to infer something which they call *porismata* (deductions) so will I give thee as it were a *corollarium*.") There, as here, discourse concerns blessedness.   *ancor per grazia*: As an added gift.

138. *se oltre promession*: The promise of vss. 88-90, which has now been fulfilled. *teco = con te.* *si spazia*: "Extends."

139. *Quelli ch'anticamente poetaro*: The ancient poets, and especially Ovid. *poetaro = poetarono*, "poetized."

140. *l'età de l'oro e suo stato felice*: Though many ancient poets sang of the Golden Age, the most famous description of man's happy condition in that first time is Ovid's *Metam.* I, 89-112:

> Aurea prima sata est aetas, quae vindice nullo,
> sponte sua, sine lege fidem rectumque colebat.
> poena metusque aberant, nec verba minantia fixo
> aere legebantur, nec supplex turba timebat
> iudicis ora sui, sed erant sine iudice tuti.
> nondum caesa suis, peregrinum ut viseret orbem,
> montibus in liquidas pinus descenderat undas,
> nullaque mortales praeter sua litora norant;
> nondum praecipites cingebant oppida fossae;
> non tuba directi, non aeris cornua flexi,
> non galeae, non ensis erant: sine militis usu
> mollia securae peragebant otia gentes.
> ipsa quoque inmunis rastroque intacta nec ullis
> saucia vomeribus per se dabat omnia tellus,
> contentique cibis nullo cogente creatis
> arbuteos fetus montanaque fraga legebant
> cornaque et in duris haerentia mora rubetis
> et quae deciderant patula Iovis arbore glandes.
> ver erat aeternum, placidique tepentibus auris
> mulcebant zephyri natos sine semine flores;
> mox etiam fruges tellus inarata ferebat,
> nec renovatus ager gravidis canebat aristis;
> flumina iam lactis, iam flumina nectaris ibant,
> flavaque de viridi stillabant ilice mella.

Golden was that first age, which, with no one to compel, without a law, of its own will, kept faith and did the right. There was no fear of punishment, no threat-

ening words were to be read on brazen tablets; no sup-
pliant throng gazed fearfully upon its judge's face; but
without judges lived secure. Not yet had the pine-tree,
felled on its native mountains, descended thence into
the watery plain to visit other lands; men knew no
shores except their own. Not yet were cities begirt with
steep moats; there were no trumpets of straight, no
horns of curving brass, no swords or helmets. There
was no need at all of armed men, for nations, secure
from war's alarms, passed the years in gentle ease. The
earth herself, without compulsion, untouched by hoe or
plowshare, of herself gave all things needful. And men,
content with food which came with no one's seeking,
gathered the arbute fruit, strawberries from the moun-
tain-sides, cornel-cherries, berries hanging thick upon
the prickly bramble, and acorns fallen from the spread-
ing tree of Jove. Then spring was everlasting, and gentle
zephyrs with warm breath played with the flowers that
sprang unplanted. Anon the earth, untilled, brought
forth her stores of grain, and the fields, though unfal-
lowed, grew white with the heavy, bearded wheat.
Streams of milk and streams of sweet nectar flowed,
and yellow honey was distilled from the verdant oak.

See C. S. Singleton (1958), pp. 191-94.

141. *forse*: On the use of this word to suggest allegory (here
a concordance between two views of man's first condition),
see vs. 76.   *in Parnaso*: I.e., in poetic vision. The moun-
tain of Parnassus was sacred to Apollo and the Muses, and
was celebrated as an inspiring source of poetry and song.
When poets poetize, it is as if they were "in (i.e., on) Par-
nassus."   *sognaro = sognarono*. Thus the ancient poets
in their vision of man's first condition, as they wrote of the
Golden Age, had a dim glimpse of the truth. The true ac-
count of man's condition in that first time is given in Genesis.
For further connections with myth and with Astraea, see
C. S. Singleton (1958), pp. 194-201. The corollary points
to a concordance between the "scriptura paganorum"
("scripture of the pagans"), as Dante terms the writings of

the ancient poets in his *Letter to Can Grande* (*Epist.* XIII, 63), and the Holy Scriptures.

142. *l'umana radice*: The "prima gente" (*Purg.* I, 24), Adam and Eve. Cf. *Purg.* XX, 43, where Hugh Capet speaks of himself as the "radice" of the Capetian line.

143. *qui primavera sempre*: Compare Ovid, *Metam.* I, 107, "ver erat aeternum" ("then spring was everlasting"), and Virgil, *Georg.* II, 149, "hic ver adsiduum." ("Here is eternal spring.")

144. *nettare è questo di che ciascun dice*: Again it is chiefly Ovid who tells of this feature (*Metam.* I, 111): "Iam flumina nectaris ibant." ("Streams of sweet nectar flowed.") "Nettare" is pronounced *nèttare*.

145. *Io mi rivolsi 'n dietro allora tutto*: Benvenuto comments: "Quasi dicens tacite: istud tangit vos antiquos poetas." ("As if tacitly saying: 'This touches you ancient poets.'")

146. *con riso*: With a smile of recognition and acknowledgment of the truth spoken by the lady.

147. *l'ultimo costrutto*: The corollary about the Golden Age.

CANTO XXIX

Special Note: For a clearer understanding of the advent and triumph of Beatrice, which is the central event of *Purg.* XXIX, XXX, and XXXI, the reader is invited to read C. S. Singleton (1954), pp. 45-60. The event unfolding through these three cantos bears a complex burden of symbolic meanings and takes place in and through a subtle succession of scenes which together make up the whole play of these cantos. It is no accident, for instance, that there are precisely three cantos involved here and that the central canto of this trio, in which Beatrice finally appears on the chariot, is numbered thirty (XXX). Even the verses of the tercet in which she emerges to view, vss. 31-33, bear the number three, and "donna m'apparve" falls central to this trio, in *Purg.* XXX, 32.

It is most important for the reader to understand that in broadest outline Beatrice's advent and Dante's attaining to her complete a pattern of justification so broad as to reach back, in its beginning, to the start of this journey (*Inf.* I); and this pattern, in its several lines of meaning, is the main object of study in C. S. Singleton (1958).

1. *Cantando come donna innamorata*: This opening verse serves to focus again on the lady in the role in which she was

first seen, thus bringing over into this canto a major theme of the preceding one, a theme concerning love, the pastoral, and the lady encountered alone. The continuing presence of the *pastorella* theme is made the more evident by the fact that the opening verse here clearly echoes Guido Cavalcanti's "cantava come fosse 'namorata" ("singing as though she were in love"), vs. 7 of "In un boschetto trova' pasturella," in G. Contini (1960), vol. II, p. 555. But this theme of profane love is fused here with that of charity, love of a higher order.

3. *Beati quorum tecta sunt peccata*: Although the lady sings these words immediately after ending her words of *Purg*. XXVIII, 144, this "beatitude," dealing as it does with the removal of sin, represents an abrupt change in outlook, for it concerns not ancient poets or their dreams of a Golden Age, but the "covering of sins" as through Christ that became possible. The words look, therefore, to what is now to come. We may take the blessing to apply to both Dante and Statius, but primarily to the living man, since what comes now comes for him alone, although Statius, like Dante, must cross through Lethe, which perhaps we are to understand as "covering his sins." Insofar as the words of the psalm do also apply to Statius, i.e., to his drinking of Lethe, they connect with the end of the lady's words in *Purg*. XXVIII, 144, which speak of the streams flowing with nectar in the Golden Age.

For the source of Dante's words, see Ps. 31[32]:1: "Beati quorum remissae sunt iniquitates, et quorum tecta sunt peccata." ("Happy is he whose fault is taken away, whose sin is covered.") By shortening the "beatitude" Dante has made it more like those of the Sermon on the Mount that were heard through the ascent of Purgatory. This psalm, it should be noted, is one in praise of justice and of the righteous of heart, its closing verse (which Dante would have expected his reader to remember) being: "Laetamini in Domino et exultate iusti, et gloriamini omnes recti corde." ("Be glad in the Lord and rejoice, you just; exult, all you upright of heart.") Paul saw its main theme as justice, as is evident from Rom. 4:3-8:

Credidit Abraham Deo, et reputatum est illi ad iusti-
tiam. Ei autem qui operatur, merces non imputatur se-
cundum gratiam, sed secundum debitum; ei vero qui
non operatur, credenti autem in eum qui iustificat im-
pium, reputatur fides eius ad iustitiam secundum propo-
situm gratiae Dei. Sicut et David dicit beatitudinem
hominis, cui Deus accepto fert iustitiam sine operibus:
Beati quorum remissae sunt iniquitates, et quorum tecta
sunt peccata; beatus vir cui non imputavit Dominus
peccatum.

"Abraham believed God and it was credited to him as
justice." Now to him who works, the reward is not cred-
ited as a favor but as something due. But to him who
does not work, but believes in him who justifies the im-
pious, his faith is credited to him as justice according
to the plan of God's grace. Thus David declares the
blessedness of the man to whom God credits justice
without works: "Blessed are they whose iniquities are
forgiven, and whose sins are covered; blessed is the man
to whom the Lord will not credit sin."

Now since the attainment of justice and justification is pre-
cisely the guiding theme of the allegory here, this "beatitude"
is especially appropriate in its present context.

4-6. *E come ninfe . . . sole*: The simile may seem inappro-
priate at first, until we see that its function is to bring over
into this canto something of the focus of the lady's last words
of the preceding canto, which touched on ancient poets and
their myths, *their* pastoral themes corresponding to those of
modern poets. The lady, "singing like an enamored lady"
(with the echo of Cavalcanti pointed out in n. to vs. 1), is
like a figure in some modern *pastorella*, while the simile sug-
gests a correspondence between the modern and that which
the ancient poets dreamed of in Parnassus.

4. *si givan sole*: The pleonastic reflexive is used here in its
isolating function. In *Purg.* XXVIII, 40, the lady is first seen
to wander alone, and we recall Cavalcanti's "sola sola per lo
bosco gia" ("she was walking through the wood, all alone"),

vs. 12 of "In un boschetto trova' pasturella," in G. Contini (1960), vol. II, p. 555.

6. *qual di veder, qual di fuggir lo sole*: The verse evokes the vastness of the forest (cf. vs. 17) with its patchwork of sun and shade, "wild" shade, as it is called.

7. *contra 'l fiume, andando*: Upstream, against the current, which means, at this point, toward the south, since Lethe here flows north.

8–9. *e io pari di lei . . . seguitando*: Dante walks opposite the lady, on his side of the stream, keeping pace with her dainty steps.

10. *Non eran cento tra ' suoi passi e ' miei*: Not only is "cento" a good round number, but to reckon the distance in terms of how far both have gone is to keep the two figures, Dante and the lady, in the picture and so keep the two banks in view.

11–12. *le ripe igualmente . . . rendei*: The stream turns a right angle without changing in width. This is presented as simply a physical feature of the stream, but the symbolic necessity of having the stream run from east to west is clearly what determines the bend. Dante and the lady (and Virgil and Statius, for that matter, lest they be forgotten!) will now be facing east as they follow along the banks of Lethe.

11. *igualmente = ugualmente.* *dier = diedero*. For *dar volta*, cf., for example, *Purg.* V, 41; XXIV, 140.

12. *per modo ch'a levante mi rendei*: The direction is explicitly indicated, that we may realize its symbolic import. The faithful Christian faces east when he prays facing the altar in most "oriented" churches, because, according to *Il libro di Sidrach* CCCXLI, "the grace of God comes from there" (cf. *Purg.* IV, 53-54). In fact, God's grace is soon to come here as a rising sun, as a sun of justice. See *Purg.* VIII, 11, on which Benvenuto comments: "Orantes convertunt se ad orientem . . . ut sol iustitiae oriatur super eos." ("Those who pray turn to the east . . . that the sun of justice

may shine upon them.") The Advent of Christ at the Last Judgment will also become part of the meaning of the whole event here at the summit, and accordingly the coming of the procession out of the east will take on yet another dimension of meaning. See the quotations from *Il libro di Sidrach* and Bonaventura in n. to *Purg.* VIII, 11, as well as the notes to Bonaventura's *Comm. Sapien.* XVI, 28, in which the editors quote John of Damascus.

Thus the right-angle turn of the stream is the first of many signs which serve to change the scene, to set the stage, as it were, for another act. Momigliano appropriately terms it a kind of curtain. And there will be other such curtains raised and lowered in the action, the total enactment, here at the summit.

13. *così*: In the new direction, eastward.

14. *si torse* = *si volse*. Cf. *Purg.* XXVIII, 145.

15. *Frate mio*: This manner of address registers a change of tone, dropping it to a more familiar, intimate level. Beatrice will do something of the same (*Purg.* XXXIII, 23) when the procession, with the frame of meaning which it provides, is dissolved. In short, the change of tone also signals a change of acts.

16. *lustro*: Glowing light. Cf. *Par.* XIV, 68.   *sùbito* = *subitaneo*.

18. *di balenar mi mise in forse*: Left me in doubt as to whether it was lightning or not. Cf. *Inf.* VIII, 110. On the symbolic significance of lightning in the present context, see the quotation from Bonaventura in n. to vs. 12.

19. *come vien, resta*: Ceases almost as soon as it comes, instantaneously. For *restare* in this sense, cf. *Inf.* XXV, 135.

20. *quel*: The "lustro" of vs. 16.

23–24. *buon zelo . . . Eva*: For righteous zeal, cf. *Purg.* VIII, 83. In his thoughts Dante reproves "Eve's daring," that is, the act of pride that was her sin, and then Adam's, and brought about their expulsion from Eden.

25. *là dove ubidia la terra e 'l cielo*: "Terra" and "cielo" form the dual subject. "Cielo" in this case must mean primarily the angels (since at the time that Eve was in Eden Satan and his rebellious band had fallen), and "terra" denotes especially the creatures of the Garden of Eden, as well as the things and forces of nature generally.   *ubidia* = *ubbidiva*.

26. *femmina, sola*: One sole woman.   *pur testé formata*: Formed only a short while before. Eve had been "formed" very recently indeed, if she and Adam were expelled from Eden after being there only some six hours (see n. to *Purg.* XXVIII, 94). It should be noted moreover that Eve was judged to be more to blame than Adam for their sin. See I Tim. 2:14: "Et Adam non est seductus, mulier autem seducta in praevaricatione fuit." ("And Adam was not deceived, but the woman was deceived and was in sin.") Thomas Aquinas, quoting Augustine's *De Genesi ad litteram* (XI, xlii, 59), writes in *Summa theol.* II-II, q. 163, a. 4, resp.:

> Sed quantum ad speciem superbiae gravius peccavit mulier, triplici ratione. Primo quidem quia maior elatio fuit mulieris quam viri; mulier enim credidit verum esse quod serpens suasit, scilicet quod Deus prohibuerit ligni esum, ne ad eius similitudinem pervenirent; et ita dum per esum ligni vetiti Dei similitudinem consequi voluit, superbia eius ad hoc se erexit quod contra Dei voluntatem aliquid voluit obtinere. Sed vir non credidit hoc esse verum: unde non voluit consequi divinam similitudinem contra Dei voluntatem; sed in hoc superbivit, quod voluit eam consequi per seipsum. Secundo, quia mulier non solum ipsa peccavit, sed etiam viro peccatum suggessit: unde peccavit et in Deum et in proximum. Tertio, in hoc quod peccatum viri diminutum est ex hoc quod in *peccatum consensit amicabili quadam benevolentia, qua plerumque fit ut offendatur Deus, ne homo ex amico fiat inimicus, quod eum facere*

non debuisse divinae sententiae iustus exitus indicavit,
ut Augustinus dicit, 11 super Gen. ad litt. (cap. ult. a
med.). Et sic patet quod peccatum mulieris fuit gravius
quam peccatum viri.

But as regards the species of pride, the woman sinned
more grievously, for three reasons. First, because she
was more puffed up than the man. For the woman be-
lieved in the serpent's persuasive words, namely that
God had forbidden them to eat of the tree, lest they
should become like to Him; so that in wishing to attain
to God's likeness by eating of the forbidden fruit, her
pride rose to the height of desiring to obtain something
against God's will. On the other hand, the man did not
believe this to be true; wherefore he did not wish to at-
tain to God's likeness against God's will: but his pride
consisted in wishing to attain thereto by his own pow-
er.—Secondly, the woman not only herself sinned, but
suggested sin to the man; wherefore she sinned against
both God and her neighbor.—Thirdly, the man's sin was
diminished by the fact that, as Augustine says (*Gen.
ad lit.* xi. 42), *he consented to the sin out of a certain
friendly good-will, on account of which a man some-
times will offend God rather than make an enemy of
his friend. That he ought not to have done so is shown
by the just issue of the Divine sentence.*

   It is therefore evident that the woman's sin was more
grievous than the man's.

testé: See the longer form "testeso" in *Purg.* XXI, 113.

27. *non sofferse di star sotto alcun velo*: Cf. the serpent's
promise to Eve if she would eat of the fruit of the forbidden
tree (Gen. 3:5): "Scit enim Deus quod in quocumque die
comederitis ex eo, aperientur oculi vestri, et eritis sicut dii
scientes bonum et malum." ("For God knows that when you
eat of it, your eyes will be opened and you will be like God,
knowing good and evil.") Thus Eve's veil was the veil of
ignorance, its removal through sin the equivalent of opening
the eyes.

28. *divota*: Obedient to God's command.

29–30. *avrei quelle ineffabili delizie . . . fiata*: Adam and
Eve, before sin, were endowed with original justice, which
gave them immortality, and we, their progeny, were each to
receive such a gift at birth. We were to enjoy life in the Gar-
den of Eden until such time as God should uplift each to his
eternal reward in Heaven, of which the delights of Eden were
an anticipation; see "arr'" (*arra*) in *Purg.* XXVIII, 93, and
"primizie" in vs. 31, below. Augustine draws the following
picture of what our life in Eden would have been if we had
not been exiled from that delightful place through the sin of
our first parents (*De civ. Dei* XIV, 26):

> Vivebat itaque homo in paradiso sicut volebat, quam-
> diu hoc volebat quod Deus iusserat: *vivebat fruens Deo,*
> ex quo bono erat bonus: vivebat sine ulla egestate, ita
> semper vivere habens in potestate. Cibus aderat, ne
> esuriret; potus, ne sitiret; lignum vitae, ne illum senecta
> dissolveret. Nihil corruptionis in corpore vel ex corpore
> ullas molestias ullis eius sensibus ingerebat. Nullus in-
> trinsecus morbus, nullus ictus metuebatur extrinsecus.
> Summa in carne sanitas, in anima tota tranquillitas. Si-
> cut in paradiso nullus aestus aut frigus, ita in eius ha-
> bitatore nulla ex cupiditate vel timore accedebat bonae
> voluntatis offensio. Nihil omnino triste, nihil erat ina-
> niter laetum: *guadium verum perpetuabatur ex Deo,*
> *in quem flagrabat charitas de corde puro et conscientia*
> *bona et fide non ficta* (I *Tim.* I, 5). (Italics added.)

This passage is translated as follows in the Loeb Classical
Library:

> Accordingly, man lived in paradise just as he chose for
> as long a time as his choice coincided with God's com-
> mand. He lived in the enjoyment of God, whose good-
> ness ensured his goodness. He lived without any want
> and had it in his power always to live such a life. He
> had food at hand against hunger, drink against thirst
> and the tree of life against the decay of old age. There
> was no deterioration in the body or arising from it to

cause any discomfort to any of his senses. There was no
fear of disease from within or of injury from without.
He had perfect health in his flesh and complete tran-
quility in his soul.

Just as in paradise it was neither too hot nor too cold,
so in its occupant there was no interference from desire
or fear to thwart his good will. There was no depress-
ing gloom at all, no unreal gaiety. True joy emanated
continuously from God, for whom there glowed "love
from a pure heart and a good conscience and sincere
faith."

Dante's thought, therefore, in reproving Eve (see the lament
over the loss of the four stars, *Purg.* I, 26-27) is that, but
for her sin, he would have been born in Eden (in 1265 one
wonders?) and would have lived a long life here, before ris-
ing to eternal blessedness.

30. *fiata*: I.e., *tempo*.

31. *m'andava*: The familiar isolating reflexive again. See
n. to vs. 4.

31–32. *primizie de l'etterno piacer*: Cf. *arra d'etterna pace*
in *Purg.* XXVIII, 93. The "eternal happiness" will consist
in seeing God face to face and in loving and praising Him
forever. Concerning "primizie," i.e., first tastes, see Thomas
Aquinas, *De veritate* q. 18, a. 1, ad 1:

> Homo igitur in statu post peccatum indiget ad cogno-
> scendum Deum medio, quod est quasi speculum, in quo
> resultat ipsius Dei similitudo; oportet enim ut per ea
> quae facta sunt, in invisibilia eius veniamus, ut dicitur
> Rom. 1. Hoc autem medio non indigebat homo in statu
> innocentiae; indigebat autem medio quod est quasi
> species rei visae; quia per aliquod spirituale lumen
> menti hominis influxum divinitus, quod erat quasi simi-
> litudo expressa lucis increatae, Deum videbat. Sed hoc
> medio non indigebit in patria, quia ipsam Dei essentiam
> per se ipsam videbit, non per aliquam eius similitudinem
> vel intelligibilem vel sensibilem, cum nulla creata simi-

litudo adeo possit perfecte Deum repraesentare, ut per eam videns ipsam Dei essentiam cognoscere aliquis possit. Indigebit autem lumine gloriae in patria, quod erit quasi medium sub quo videtur, secundum illud Psalm. 35, 10: *In lumine tuo videbimus lumen,* eo quod ista visio nulli creaturae est naturalis, sed soli Deo; unde nulla creatura in eam ex sua natura potest pertingere; sed ad eam consequendam oportet quod illustretur lumine divinitus emisso. Secunda autem visio, quae est per medium, quod est species, est naturalis Angelo, sed est supra naturam hominis. Unde ad eam indiget lumine gratiae.

Therefore, to know God, man, as he is after the fall, needs a medium which is like a mirror, in which there arises a likeness of God himself. For we must reach "the invisible things of him . . . by the things that are made," according to Romans (1:20). Man in the state of innocence, however, did not need this medium, but he did need a medium which is somewhat like the species of the thing seen, because he saw God through a spiritual light which was given to the human mind by God, and which was a kind of expressed likeness of the uncreated light.

But he will not need this medium in heaven, because he will see the essence of God in itself and not through any intelligible or sensible likeness of it, since no created likeness can so perfectly represent God that one who sees through it can know the essence of God. Yet, he will need the light of glory [in heaven], which will be a kind of medium under which God is seen, according to Psalms (35:10[36:9]): "In thy light we shall see light." The reason for this is that this sight is not natural to any creature, but only to God. As a result, no creature can reach it by his own natural power, but to acquire it one must be enlightened by a divinely given light.

The second sight, through a medium which is an intentional likeness, is natural to the angels, but above

human nature. Accordingly, for it man needs the light of grace.
See C. S. Singleton (1958), pp. 18-19.

32. *tutto sospeso*: In greatest suspense and amazement.

33. *e disioso ancora a più letizie*: Among which anticipated delights must be the expectation that he is to see Beatrice at any moment now, for her coming here has been promised him.

34. *dinanzi a noi*: I.e., in the east. The fact that Dante is facing east should not be forgotten, for much of the symbolism of what comes now is framed by this fact.   *un foco acceso*: What seemed like lightning before now grows so bright as to seem a blazing fire; and the color of fire or flame or lightning is the color of love or charity.

35. *ci = a noi.*

36. *e 'l dolce suon per canti era già inteso*: And what was first heard simply as a melody is now made out to be chanting. The gradual disclosure of what comes is thus begun and will continue throughout the canto.

37–42. *O sacrosante Vergini . . . versi*: A strategy of gradual disclosure involves withholding, quite as much as showing, and thereby suspense is generated. These two tercets do serve to withhold and at the same time to stress the awesomeness of what is to come. Such minor invocations (they are frequent in classical poetry) serve a different purpose from that served by the principal ones at the beginning of *cantiche*, as in *Inf.* II, 7-9; *Purg.* I, 7-12; *Par.* I, 13-36. Compare *Inf.* XXXII, 10-11, and *Par.* XVIII, 82-87.

37–38. *fami, freddi o vigilie mai*: See *Par.* XXV, 1-3, and II Cor. 11:27: "in labore et aerumna, in vigiliis multis, in fame et siti, in ieiuniis multis, in frigore et nuditate" ("in labor and hardships, in many sleepless nights, in hunger and thirst, in fastings often, in cold and nakedness").

39. *ch'io mercé vi chiami*: "That I call upon you for my reward," the "premio dell'amore portato" ("the reward for the love I bore you"), as Buti glosses it.

40. *Elicona*: Helicon, famous mountain range of Boeotia believed sacred to Apollo and the Muses. The fountains of the Muses, Aganippe and Hippocrene, were located there. See Virgil, *Aen.* VII, 641, "pandite nunc Helicona, deae, cantusque movete" ("now fling wide Helicon, ye goddesses, and wake your song"), a good example of the lesser kind of invocation to the Muses that is common to Virgil and classical style, which Dante is doubtless imitating in this case. See n. to vss. 37-42. It is possible, of course, that Dante misunderstood these verses in the *Aeneid* and took Helicon to be a fountain, but it is not necessary to assume this. Clearly Helicon is called upon to pour forth the water of its fountains, that the poet may drink of them.

41. *Uranìe*: Muse of Astronomy. At the beginning of the *Purgatorio* it is Calliope, the Muse of Epic Poetry, who is singled out as chief among the nine Muses, following an episode from Ovid (see n. to *Purg.* I, 9-12). Now the *cantica* is coming to a close, and this special invocation of Urania signifies the advent of high things of supranatural origin. For the form *Uranie*, instead of *Urania*, see Petrocchi's justification.

42. *forti cose a pensar*: Things hard for the poet to rethink (in memory), and for others to conceive through his words. Certainly the meaning is not that these things are hard "to think" in the sense of "to invent," in poetizing, for Dante will never undermine the basic fiction of his poem, which is that it is not a fiction.   *mettere in versi*: Depends on "m'aiuti."

43. *Poco più oltre*: I.e., when I had gone forward a little farther.

43-45. *sette alberi d'oro . . . loro*: The intervening space makes what will soon appear to be candlesticks seem to be golden tree trunks. The candlesticks are massive, as is clearly suggested by these verses, and, as will be evident later, they are borne by no visible hands but come forward of themselves, which fact, along with many another feature, clearly signifies the supranatural character of what now appears. "Il lungo tratto del mezzo ch'era ancor tra noi e loro" is the subject of "falsava," the object of this verb being "sette alberi d'oro." The falseness of the appearance is evident to Dante moments later, and the judgment made here is made from that later awareness.

46. *ma quand' i' fui sì presso di lor fatto*: Cf. the expression *farsi verso qualcosa* in *Purg.* XXVII, 29 ("fatti ver' lei").

47. *l'obietto comun*: The *sensibile commune* of scholastic philosophy, an object of perception that is not the proper object of any one sense but common to several or all. The conception and terminology derive primarily from Aristotle; see *De anima* II, 6, 418[a]:

> Dico autem proprium quidem, quod non contingit altero sensu sentiri, et circa quod non contingit errare, ut visus coloris, et auditus soni, et gustus saporis. Tactus autem plures habet differentias. Sed unusquisque sensus iudicat de his, et non decipitur, neque visus, quoniam color, neque auditus, quoniam sonus sit; sed quid est coloratum, aut ubi, aut quid sonans. Huiusmodi igitur dicuntur propria uniuscuiusque sensus obiecta.
>
> Communia autem sunt motus, quies, numerus, figura, magnitudo: huiusmodi enim nullius sensus sunt propria, sed communia omnibus. Tactu enim motus aliquis sensibilis, et visu: per se igitur sunt sensibilia haec.
>
> Now I call that the *proper* object of each sense which does not fall within the ambit of another sense, and about which there can be no mistake,—as sight is of colour, and hearing of sound, and taste of savour; while touch has several different objects. Each particular sense can discern these proper objects without deception; thus sight errs not as to colour, nor hearing as to sound; though it might err about *what* is coloured, or *where*

it is, or about what is giving forth a sound. This, then, is what is meant by the proper objects of particular senses.

Now the sense-objects *in common* are movement, rest, number, shape, dimension. Qualities of this kind are proper to no one sense, but are common to all; thus a movement is perceptible both by touch and by sight. These, then, are the essential objects of sensation.

This quotation from the *De anima* may be found in Thomas Aquinas, *Opera omnia*, vol. XX, p. 69, or in A. M. Pirotta (1936), p. 134. That this passage was well known to Dante is witnessed by *Conv.* III, ix, 6. Thus Dante's "obietto comun" is the *sensibile commune*. In the present instance it is plainly shape, movement, and perhaps dimension, as applied to the candlesticks, which at a distance appear to be tree trunks.   *che 'l senso inganna*: Thomas Aquinas (*De anima expositio* II, lect. 13, n. 385) comments on the above-cited passage from Aristotle: "Sed circa sensibilia per accidens vels communia, decipiuntur sensus." ("But the senses *can* be deceived both about objects only incidentally sensible and about objects common to several senses.") The sense that is deceived in this case is sight.

48. *non perdea per distanza alcun suo atto*: Every feature of the "obietto comun" can now be made out, and Dante sees that the seven things are in motion (and so can hardly be tree trunks). "Atto" is used to include the motion which is now perceived, but it can refer to other features as well. Cf. *Purg.* XIII, 55-56.

49. *la virtù ch'a ragion discorso ammanna*: This faculty is known in scholastic philosophy as the *vis estimativa* or *vis cogitativa*. It is also termed *ratio particularis*, a faculty capable of sorting out and distinguishing individual objects as perceived by the senses (as in the present instance), but it is not the *ratio intellectiva* which deals with such objects as universal "intentions." See Thomas Aquinas, *Summa theol.* I, q. 78, a. 4, resp.:

Considerandum est autem quod quantum ad formas sensibiles non est differentia inter hominem et alia ani-

malia; similiter enim immutantur a sensibibus exteriori-
bus; sed quantum ad intentiones praedictas, differentia
est. Nam alia animalia percipiunt huiusmodi intentiones
solum naturali quodam instinctu, homo autem per
quamdam collationem. Et ideo quae in aliis animalibus
dicitur *aestimativa naturalis*, in homine dicitur *cogita-
tiva*, quae per collationem quamdam huiusmodi inten-
tiones adinvenit. Unde etiam dicitur *ratio particularis*,
cui medici assignant determinatum organum, scilicet
mediam partem capitis. Est enim collativa intentionum
individualium, sicut *ratio intellectiva* est collativa in-
tentionum universalium.

Now, we must observe that as to sensible forms there
is no difference between man and other animals; for
they are similarly immuted by the extrinsic sensible.
But there is a difference as to the above intentions: for
other animals perceive these intentions only by some
natural instinct, while man perceives them by means of
collation of ideas. Therefore the power which in other
animals is called the natural estimative, in man is called
the *cogitative*, which by some sort of collation discov-
ers these intentions. Wherefore it is also called the *par-
ticular reason*, to which medical men assign a certain
particular organ, namely, the middle part of the head:
for it compares individual intentions, just as the intel-
lectual reason compares universal intentions.

For the faculty of perception, which presents the impression
to the reason, see *Purg.* XVIII, 22-23. The verb "apprese"
(vs. 50) bears the suggestion of this function here.   *am-
manna*: "Prepares" (by way of the collation referred to
above). Dante uses the verb in *Purg.* XXIII, 107, to mean
"prepare," "make ready."

50. *sì com' elli eran candelabri apprese*: Candlesticks, in-
stead of tree trunks, make a considerable symbolic differ-
ence, being distinctly reminiscent of the prophetic vision of
John in the Apocalypse, in the strikingly similar context of
seven spirits. Compare Apoc. 1:4 and *passim*, but particu-
larly 1:12-13: "Et conversus vidi septem candelabra aurea,

et in medio septem candelabrorum aureorum similem filio hominis." ("And having turned, I saw seven golden lamp-stands; and in the midst of the seven lamp-stands One like to a son of man.") Thus, for a reader who begins now to sense the symbolic value of the seven golden candlesticks, their coming here amounts to a prophetic signal of an advent, even as in the Apocalypse.   *sì com'*: "That." *apprese*: "Ascertained."

51. *e ne le voci del cantare "Osanna"*: "Apprese" is again understood as the verb, i.e., "apprese 'Osanna' ne le voci del cantar." "Hosanna," of course, makes another clear suggestion of a coming, being the cry with which the crowds welcomed Jesus in His entry into Jerusalem (Matt. 21:9). A reader familiar with the *Vita nuova* will recall that when Beatrice is seen (in a vision) to depart this life and rise to heaven just such a cry attends the event (XXIII, 7 and 25). Can it be that Beatrice will now *return* to the call of "hosanna," and that it is for her, and not for the Son of Man?

52. *Di sopra fiammeggiava il bello arnese*: The seven candlesticks each bear a light at the top, where the lighted candle would normally be placed.   *fiammeggiava*: Again flame and the color of flame are stressed. Cf. n. to vs. 34.
 arnese: The term, making a unit of the seven candlesticks, views them as one object, one ensemble. This proves to be significant, symbolically, when the seven lights are seen to represent the seven spirits of God as well as the seven-fold Spirit of God; cf. Isa. 11:2: "Et requiescet super eum spiritus Domini." ("And the spirit of the Lord shall rest upon him.") See Apoc. 4:5, "et septem lampades ardentes ante thronum, qui sunt septem spiritus Dei" ("and there are seven lamps burning before the throne, which are the seven spirits of God"), where the plural is so used in a context rich with other features which surround these lamps here. It becomes clear later that the seven candlesticks are actually seven and separate, not joined in any visible way (hence we are not to think of them as forming a kind of seven-branched menorah), yet they are, by this touch, viewed as being *one*

spirit. The comparison with the brightness of the moon (vs. 53) reinforces the conception of them as a single luminous body.

53–54. *per sereno ... mese*: When the moon is brightest.

55. *ammirazion*: "Amazement" (cf. "stupor," vs. 57).

56. *al buon Virgilio*: This is not the first time this adjective has been used of Virgil (cf. *Purg.* XIX, 34), but it is far more commonly used when he is called *maestro* or *duca*. Virgil, however, is no longer master, guide, or teacher, but is now only the *good* Virgil.

57. *carca di stupor non meno = carca di stupore non inferiore al mio.* Virgil is quite as amazed as Dante at this supernatural spectacle.   *stupor*: See *Conv.* IV, xxv, 5, where Dante defines *stupore*: "Lo stupore è uno stordimento d'animo, per grandi e maravigliose cose vedere o udire o per alcuno modo sentire." ("Bemazement is bewilderment of mind on seeing or hearing, or in any wise perceiving, great and wonderful things.")

58. *rendei l'aspetto*: "I turned back my gaze."   *l'alte cose*: The candlesticks, which are carried by no one but come forward of themselves, are wonderfully ablaze "di sopra," i.e., *in alto*. Cf. the "vive luci" (vs. 62).

"Alte cose" should not be taken to include other features of the procession, for these are not yet admitted to view, even though it is scarcely possible that they are not already within Dante's field of vision. It will be noted that the poet has thus begun to focus on the various elements or units of the procession in the strict order of their coming, one after another. We see only the first group or part of the procession as Dante gazes at it to the exclusion of all else, turning to Virgil and then back to it, so that the lady chides him for this, urging him to look at that which comes after. The poet's strategy in this is quite clear, and the final effect of such a gradual disclosure will be that of a *revelation*.

59. *movieno = movevano.*   *tardi = tardamente.*

60. *foran = sarebbero state.* *da novelle spose*: The bride on her way to the bridegroom's house must walk slowly as in a solemn procession. See Federigo Frezzi, *Quadriregio* I, xvi, 64-65: "e, come va per via sposa novella / a passi rari e porta gli occhi bassi" ("just as the bride walks with slow steps and eyes downcast").

61-62. *Perché pur ardi . . . luci*: "Why are you so ardent only [pur] at the sight of the living lights?" Given the present context of flames and fire and love, the verb *ardere* is especially appropriate.

64-65. *Genti vid' io allor . . . bianco*: As he looks at the people following after the candlesticks, Dante again sees only one single unit of the procession at a time. The gradual disclosure proceeds thus in strict order.

64. *come a lor duci*: The seven-fold Spirit of God, or (now in the plural) the seven spirits, are guiding the people, who follow after.

65. *vestite di bianco*: In the pattern of the whole procession, color will be seen to be significant, of course, and when these people turn out to be twenty-four elders, the allusion to the Apocalypse (Apoc. 4:4) is clear.

66. *e tal candor di qua già mai non fuci*: Cf. Mar. 9:2[3], describing Jesus' transfiguration: "Et vestimenta eius facta sunt splendentia et candida nimis velut nix, qualia fullo non potest super terram candida facere." ("And his garments became shining, exceedingly white as snow, as no fuller on earth can whiten.")   *di qua*: In our part of the world, among the living.   *fuci = ci fu.* For the single consonant (*c* in this case), where a doubling of the consonant would be expected, see "parlòmi," *Purg.* XIV, 76 and *passim*, and E. G. Parodi (1957), p. 236.

67-69. *L'acqua imprendea . . . anco*: Dante has the stream on his left, and it is gleaming with reflected light, now that the seven lights are so near, approaching downstream on the opposite bank. On the reading "imprendea" as justified by the early MSS, see Petrocchi.

68. *rendea*: "Reflected."   *me = a me*.

70. *posta*: "Posta" suggests a post of observation, from which to await the coming of something (cf. "posta" in *Inf.* XIII, 113, and the verb *appostare*), and the place where Dante halts proves to be just that, for he will see the procession now, as each unit passes before him on the opposite side of the stream, which he now faces. This is plainly another strategical procedure to insure that the procession is watched as a gradual disclosure (see C. S. Singleton, 1954, pp. 48-49), for the reader sees only what Dante sees, of course, and in the order in which he sees it.

71. *solo il fiume mi facea distante*: A very short distance indeed, since the river is only three paces wide (see *Purg.* XXVIII, 70).

73. *andar davante*: Advance past Dante on the other bank.

74. *lasciando dietro a sé l'aere dipinto*: The candlesticks are termed "sublime things" in vs. 58. We should imagine them as being high enough to leave the air above the procession painted as described. This "sky" is then called a "bel ciel" in vs. 82.

75. *e di tratti pennelli avean sembiante*: The image is precise. The flame at the top of each candlestick and the candlestick itself are aptly compared to a painter's brush, the flame corresponding to the tuft of bristles and the candlestick to the shaft or handle. Then, since the candlesticks are moving forward leaving the air above "painted" with bands of color, they can be compared to brushes which, after being dipped into the paint, are moving or being drawn across a surface (here, as it were, a ceiling), each leaving a strip or band of color behind it. And the flame is bent back, as it is drawn through the air, as a brush pressed against the surface of a ceiling would be.

The fact that these lights leave behind them such streamers, which continue to hang back over the procession like a canopy, is symbolic. Such a figure, once we recognize that the seven lights represent the seven-fold Spirit of the Lord (see n. to vs. 52), should call to mind the familiar passage in Isaiah (11:1-2) where the prophet foresees that the "virga de radice Iesse" ("rod out of the root of Jesse"), the Christ who is to come, shall blossom and the seven-fold Spirit of the Lord shall rest upon him. Here, then, is yet another prophetic signal of an advent. Cf. n. to vs. 51.

76. *lì sopra*: The adverbial phrase serves as a kind of subject of the verb "rimanea," indicating the space above, the ceiling or "sky," as it is then called (vs. 82). For the construction, cf. *Purg.* X, 79.   *distinto*: "Marked."

77–78. *tutte in quei colori . . . Sole*: The seven bands taken together contain all the colors of the rainbow, the bow the sun makes. This may also be an image drawn from the Apocalypse. Cf. Apoc. 4:3: "Iris erat in circuitu sedis." ("There was a rainbow round about the throne.")

78. *Delia*: Surname of Diana, goddess of the Moon, who was born on the island of Delos; hence the moon. *il cinto*: The lunar halo.

79. *ostendali*: The image of the bands of color stretching out behind and the lights on candlesticks as paint brushes now changes to that of banners or standards, and these, of course, would head a procession, possibly of some king or other royal personage. The chariot soon to be named makes this clearly a triumphal procession, and the changed image of banners anticipates this. Benvenuto, commenting on "in dietro," explains: "Ostendalia enim appellantur in mundo signa imperatoris, quae ostenduntur quando vadit in expeditionem, et ista sunt signa summi imperatoris qui veniebat cum suo exercitu." ("For, in the world, the standards of an emperor are termed banners, which are displayed when he goes off on a campaign, and these are the standards of the highest Emperor, who was coming with his army.")

79–80. *in dietro . . . vista*: These banners are much longer than banners ever were, for they stretch back farther than the eye can see.

81. *diece passi distavan quei di fori*: The outer bands of this rainbow are ten paces apart, i.e., the width of the group of seven bands is ten steps. The symbolism of the perfect number ten, in this case, is uncertain. Inevitably, many interpreters think of the Ten Commandments.

82. *Sotto così bel ciel*: The streaks of color, or the rainbow-colored standards, are now termed a "sky" which covers the procession. This image should be kept in mind for a proper understanding of *Purg.* XXXI, 144, where a harmonizing heaven will be referred to.   *diviso*: "Recount." Cf. the French *deviser*.

83. *ventiquattro seniori*: A clear echo of Apoc. 4:4: "Et in circuitu sedis sedilia viginti quattuor, et super thronos viginti quattuor seniores sedentes circumamicti vestimentis albis." ("And round about the throne are twenty-four seats; and upon the seats twenty-four elders sitting, clothed in white garments.")   *a due a due*: The elders walk two by two and close enough together, surely, to be beneath the "canopy," which is ten paces wide.

84. *coronati venien di fiordaliso*: As will be clear, the color of the crowns in each unit of the procession is a very important feature. Here that color is white, these being crowns of the fleur-de-lis, or lily (cf. "gigli," vs. 146). The lily is, of course, a significant symbol in itself in this case, being a token of the faith in the Redeemer who is to come, and these elders prove to be the twenty-four books of the Old Testament, as Jerome, in his preface to the Latin translation of the Bible, reckons them, comparing them precisely to the twenty-four elders of the Apocalypse. Jerome divides the books of the Old Testament into three groups—the first comprises the five books of Moses; the second comprises eight prophetical books; and the third comprises nine hagiographical books, to which he adds Ruth and Lamentations, making twenty-

four in all. P. Toynbee (1968, p. 100) provides the following quotation from Jerome:

Primus liber, quem nos Genesim dicimus; secundus, qui Exodus appellatur; tertius, Leviticus; quartus, quem Numeros vocamus; quintus, qui Deuteronomium praenotatur. Hi sunt quinque libri Moysi, quos proprie תורה Thora is est. Secundum, prophetarum ordinem faciunt: et incipiunt ab Iesu filio Nave; deinde subtexunt Iudicum librum et in eum compingunt Ruth: quia in diebus Iudicum facta narratur historia; tertius sequitur Samuel, quem nos Regum primum et secundum dicimus; quartus Regum, qui tertio et quarto Regum volumine continetur; . . . quintus Isaias; sextus, Ieremias; septimus, Ezechiel; octavus, liber duodecim Prophetarum. Tertius ordo, Hagiographa possidet: et primus liber incipit a Iob; secundus a David; tertius est Salomon, tres libros habens Proverbia; quartus, Ecclesiasten; quintus, Canticum Canticorum; sextus est Daniel; septimus, . . . qui liber apud nos Paralipomenon primus et secundus inscribitur; octavus, Esdras; nonus, Esther. Atque ita fiunt pariter veteris legis libri viginti duo: id est, Moysi quinque, prophetarum octo, Hagiographorum novem. Quamquam nonnulli Ruth et Cinoth (i.e., Lamentationes) inter Hagiographa scriptitent, et hos libros in suo putent numero supputandos, ac per hoc esse priscae legis libros viginti quatuor: quos sub numero viginti quatuor seniorum Apocalypsis Ioannis inducit adorantes Agnum.

The first book is the one we call Genesis; the second, Exodus; the third, Leviticus; the fourth, Numbers; and the fifth, Deuteronomy. These are the five books of Moses which the Hebrews call the Law. Next, the prophets follow in order: they begin with the book of Jesus, son of Nave [Joshua, son of Nun]; they work in the book of Judges, and to it they add Ruth, which together with Judges forms the history; third follows Samuel, which we call I and II Kings; fourth they place Kings, which we call III and IV Kings . . . Isaiah is fifth;

Jeremiah, sixth; Ezekiel, seventh; and the eighth is the
book of the twelve [minor] prophets. The third group
contains the hagiographies: of these the book of Job
comes first; followed by David; Solomon, third, contain-
ing three books of Proverbs; Ecclesiastes is fourth;
Canticle of Canticles, fifth; the sixth, Daniel; the seventh
. . . the book we call Paralipomenon I and II [I and II
Chronicles]; Esdras is eighth; and Esther, ninth. Hence,
in the Old Law there are twenty-two books, that is, five
books of Moses, eight of prophets, and nine of the hagi-
ographies. Some would place the books of Ruth and
Qinoth (i.e., Lamentations) among the hagiographies
and add them to their count; thus, for them, the Old
Law had twenty-four books; and it is the number of
twenty-four elders that John, in the Apocalypse, men-
tions as adoring the Lamb.

85–86. *Tutti cantavan: "Benedicta tue . . . d'Adamo"*: The
words of Gabriel to Mary are clearly echoed here. See Luc.
1:28: "Et ingressus angelus ad eam dixit: Ave, gratia plena,
Dominus tecum, benedicta tu in mulieribus." ("And when
the angel had come to her, he said, 'Hail, full of grace, the
Lord is with thee. Blessed art thou among women.'")
Dante has changed "in mulieribus" to "ne le figlie d'Adamo,"
not inappropriately, since this now is the Garden of Eden,
where Adam was first placed. See also Elisabeth's words to
Mary in Luc. 1:42.

85. *Benedicta*: The Latin form renders the biblical echo
very distinctly.   *tue = tu.*

86–87. *e benedette sieno . . . tue*: This additional blessing
goes quite beyond the words addressed to Mary; and since
we are expecting Beatrice to come, could these words not be
a welcoming salutation to her? Again the poet is guiding his
reader into a deliberate ambiguity (see C. S. Singleton, 1954,
pp. 50-52). The salutation to Mary which is heard in the
chant of the elders, who are the books of the Old Testament,
amounts to a prophetic call, not for Beatrice's appearance
here, but for the Advent of the Son of Man (see the signal

in the seven-fold Spirit of God that was to rest upon Him who was to come, and the signal of hosanna above); but these latter words now seem to herald some lady for her beauty.

88. *l'altre fresche erbette*: "Altre" here is probably another instance of the redundant use of this adjective. Cf. *Purg.* XX, 81.

90. *fuor = furono.*

91. *come luce luce in ciel seconda*: The image is that of one constellation (made up of several stars) replacing another in the sky, as the sphere of the stars turns about the earth. Thus, in the space directly in front of Dante across the stream, a second group replaces the first, and the focus of attention is held strictly on this spot. Benvenuto comments: "Et est propria comparatio, quia sicut in coelo una stella oritur post aliam ad illuminandum mundum tempore noctis, ita primo libri antiqui luxerunt in mundo in tempore tenebrarum; postea venerunt maiores luces in tempore gratiae, scilicet libri evangelistarum." ("And the comparison is proper, since just as in the heavens one star rises after another to illumine the world at night, so first the ancient books shed light upon the world in the hour of darkness; afterwards, there came greater lights in the era of grace, that is, the books of the Evangelists.")

92. *quattro animali*: See the description in Ezech. 10:4-14:

Et elevata est gloria Domini desuper cherub ad limen domus, et repleta est domus nube, et atrium repletum est splendore gloriae Domini. Et sonitus alarum cherubim audiebatur usque ad atrium exterius, quasi vox Dei omnipotentis loquentis.

Cumque praecepisset viro qui indutus erat lineis, dicens: Sume ignem de medio rotarum quae sunt inter cherubim, ingressus ille stetit iuxta rotam; et extendit cherub manum de medio cherubim ad ignem qui erat inter cherubim, et sumpsit, et dedit in manus eius qui indutus erat lineis; qui accipiens egressus est. Et apparuit in cherubim similitudo manus hominis subtus

pennas eorum, et vidi, et ecce quattuor rotae iuxta che-
rubim; rota una iuxta cherub unum, et rota alia iuxta
cherub unum, species autem rotarum erat quasi visio
lapidis chrysolithi, et aspectus earum similitudo una
quattuor, quasi sit rota in medio rotae. Cumque am-
bularent in quattuor partes, gradiebantur et non rever-
tebantur ambulantes, sed ad locum ad quem ire declina-
bat quae prima erat, sequebantur et ceterae nec con-
vertebantur. Et omne corpus earum et colla et manus
et pennae et circuli plena erant oculis in circuitu quat-
tuor rotarum; et rotas istas vocavit volubiles audiente
me. Quattuor autem facies habebat unum: facies una
facies cherub, et facies secunda facies hominis, et in
tertio facies leonis, et in quarto facies aquilae.

And the glory of the Lord was lifted up from above the
cherub to the threshold of the house: and the house
was filled with the cloud, and the court was filled with
the brightness of the glory of the Lord.

And the sound of the wings of the cherubims was
heard even to the outward court as the voice of God
Almighty speaking.

And when he had commanded the man that was
clothed with linen, saying: Take fire from the midst of
the wheels that are between the cherubims: he went in
and stood beside the wheel.

And one cherub stretched out his arm from the midst
of the cherubims to the fire that was between the cheru-
bims: and he took and put it into the hands of him that
was clothed with linen. Who took it and went forth.

And there appeared in the cherubims the likeness
of a man's hand under their wings.

And I saw, and behold *there were* four wheels by the
cherubims: one wheel by one cherub, and another wheel
by another cherub: and the appearance of the wheels
was to the sight like the chrysolite stone.

And as to their appearance, all four were alike: as
if a wheel were in the midst of a wheel.

And when they went, they went by four ways: and
they turned not when they went: but to the place

whither they first turned the rest also followed and did not turn back.

And their whole body and their necks and their hands and their wings and the circles were full of eyes, round about the four wheels.

And these wheels he called Voluble, in my hearing.

And every one had four faces: one face *was* the face of a cherub: and the second face, the face of a man: and in the third was the face of a lion: and in the fourth the face of an eagle.

All details here are clearly relevant, and Dante's procession owes much to this passage, as his reference to it (vs. 100) clearly indicates. See also Apoc. 4:6-8:

> Et in conspectu sedis tamquam mare vitreum simile crystallo, et in medio sedis et in circuitu sedis quattuor animalia plena oculis ante et retro; et animal primum simile leoni, et secundum animal simile vitulo, et tertium animal habens faciem quasi hominis, et quartum animal simile aquilae volanti. Et quattuor animalia singula eorum habebant alas senas, et in circuitu et intus plena sunt oculis, et requiem non habebant die ac nocte dicentia: Sanctus, sanctus, sanctus Dominus Deus omnipotens, qui erat et qui est et qui venturus est.

> And before the throne there is, as it were, a sea of glass like to crystal, and in the midst of the throne, and round the throne, are four living creatures, full of eyes before and behind. And the first living creature is like a lion and the second like a calf, and the third has the face, as it were, of a man, and the fourth is like an eagle flying. And the four living creatures have each of them six wings; round about and within they are full of eyes. And they do not rest day and night, saying, "Holy, holy, holy, the Lord God almighty, who was, and who is, and who is coming."

According to a long and well-founded tradition the four animals symbolize the Evangelists, which means that in the procession they are the corresponding Four Gospels.

93. *coronati ciascun di verde fronda*: Again it is the color of the crown which is significant. The elders of the first group are crowned in white, the color of faith. These animals of the second and central group (called a "nodo," "knot," in vs. 133) are crowned in green, the color of hope as especially connected with Christ, our hope (I Tim. 1:1). The color green will be re-affirmed in the crown Beatrice will wear when she appears at the center of this central group.

94. *Ognuno era pennuto di sei ali*: This is the point on which the accounts in Ezekiel and the Apocalypse differ (see vss. 104-5), that of the latter agreeing with Dante's experience.

95. *le penne piene d'occhi*: As both Ezekiel and the Apocalypse have it (see n. to vs. 92).   *Argo*: Argus, surnamed Panoptes ("all-seeing") because he had a hundred eyes, was, according to one account, the son of Arestor. Juno, jealous of Jupiter's love for Io, set Argus to watch over her after she had been metamorphosed into a cow, but Jupiter commanded Mercury to slay him. Mercury therefore descended to earth in the guise of a shepherd and, having beguiled Argus to sleep with stories and songs, cut off his head. Juno thereupon transplanted his eyes into the tail of her favorite bird, the peacock. See Ovid, *Metam*. I, 622-723.

96. *se fosser vivi*: This touch makes it clear that the eyes in the wings are not as they are in the peacock's tail, but are living as the eyes of Argus were when he was alive.

97–98. *più non spargo rime*: "I do not expend [literally, scatter] more rhymes [i.e., verses]." In "spargo" there is the suggestion of waste or lavishness, which is reinforced by the opposing phrase "non posso esser largo" of vs. 99.

100. *ma leggi Ezechiel*: Ezekiel has already been cited in vss. 92 and 95.

102. *con vento e con nube e con igne*: See the quotation from Ezekiel in n. to vs. 92.

103. *i = li.*

717

105. *Giovanni è meco e da lui si diparte*: Cf. the quotation from the Apocalypse in the n. to vs. 92. Ezekiel is far more detailed in the description of the four animals.

106. *contenne*: Another instance of a past definite tense in a rhyme position where the imperfect (*conteneva*) would be normal. The requirement of the rhyme has forced the poet's hand. Cf. "pose" in *Inf.* XXXII, 128.

107. *un carro, in su due rote, triunfale*: The kind of two-wheeled chariot used by the ancient Romans in war and in triumphal processions. As will become evident in the symbolism of the procession, this chariot represents the Church. But it is also, in this instance, a triumphal chariot, and as such it is strangely empty! Whose triumph is this?

108. *al collo d'un grifon*: The griffin symbolizes Christ in His two natures, human and divine (see *Purg.* XXXI, 80-81, and XXXII, 96). Isidore of Seville (*Etym.* XII, ii, 17) describes the animal, half eagle and half lion, and (VII, ii, 43-44) compares Christ both to a lion and to an eagle.
   tirato venne: With the symbols of the Church and Christ, Dante has now begun to draw upon the Song of Solomon, Canticle of Canticles, traditionally interpreted as a dialogue between the two. See Cant. 1:3[4]: "Trahe me, post te curremus." (" 'Draw me!' Chorus: 'We will follow you.' ") He also refers to this biblical passage in *De mon.* III, iii, 12: "Hoc enim est quod dicit Ecclesia loquens ad sponsum: 'Trahe me post te.' " ("For this is what the church means when she says to the Bridegroom, 'Draw me after thee.' ")

109. *ale*: This is an archaic singular form of *ala*.

110. *tra la mezzana e le tre e tre liste*: The image is quite precise. The wings of the griffin, upstretched, pass on either side of the middle band of light and thus have on either side three bands, symbol of the Trinity. If to either of these groups the middle band be added, the result is four, the symbol of humanity, and the numbers so divided equal 3 + 1 + 3.

111. *sì ch'a nulla, fendendo, facea male*: The wings in no way disturb the bands in this 3 + 1 + 3 arrangement, which would seem to signify that the two natures of Christ represented by the wings are in harmony with the divine and the human as represented by the streamers of light arranged in combinations of three and four.

112. *Tanto salivan che non eran viste*: This no doubt symbolizes the resurrected Christ, who rose to Heaven, beyond our sight. See n. to vs. 108 for a passage from Isidore of Seville in which Christ is compared to an eagle.

113. *le membra d'oro avea*: Cf. Cant. 5:11: "Caput eius aurum optimum." ("His head is pure gold.")   *quant' era uccello*: I.e., the head, neck, and wings, this being the divine part, as it were.

114. *e bianche l'altre, di vermiglio miste*: The rest of the body of the strange animal is that of a lion, symbolizing the human part, which is white because pure and is mingled with crimson, to symbolize Christ's Passion. Thus Benvenuto comments: "Ideo bene dicit: et ille gryphus, *le membra d'oro avea, quant'era uccello*, quantum ad divinitatem, quae est incorruptibilis, immortalis, *e bianche l'altre*, quantum ad carnem humanam puram. Et dicit: *di vermiglio miste*, quia sanguine rubricata in ipsa passione." ("Therefore he well says: that griffin 'had his members of gold in so far as he was bird,' in respect to his divinity, which is incorruptible and immortal, 'and the others white,' in regard to his purely human flesh. And he says: 'mixed with red' because colored by the blood of His Passion.") Here Dante is again drawing on the Canticle of Canticles. Cf. Cant. 5:10: "Dilectus meus candidus et rubicundus." ("My lover is radiant and ruddy.")

115-16. *Non che Roma . . . rallegrasse*: A second *non* might have been expected after "bello," and one such is understood. The chariot, as noted in vs. 107, is the two-wheeled type used in wars and triumphs by the ancient Romans.

116. *Affricano*: Publius Cornelius Scipio Aemilianus Africanus Numantinus, known as Scipio the Younger, was born

ca. 185 B.C. and died in 129 B.C. He was the adopted son of Publius Cornelius Scipio, the son of Scipio Africanus the Elder, the conqueror of Hannibal. He took and burned Carthage, for which he was honored with a triumph at Rome and with the surname Africanus, which he had already inherited, by adoption, from the conqueror of Hannibal.

o vero = ovvero. *Augusto*: Augustus, the first Roman Emperor. See n. to *Purg.* VII, 6. Augustus' triumphs are mentioned by Virgil, *Aen.* VIII, 714-15, "at Caesar, triplici invectus Romana triumpho / moenia" ("but Caesar, entering the walls of Rome in triple triumph"), and by Suetonius, *De vita Caesarum* II, xxii, 1: "Curulis triumphos tris egit, Delmaticum, Actiacum, Alexandrinum." ("He celebrated three regular triumphs for his victories in Dalmatia, at Actium, and at Alexandria.")

117. *quel del Sol*: The chariot of the Sun is described by Ovid, *Metam.* II, 107-10:

> aureus axis erat, temo aureus, aurea summae
> curvatura rotae, radiorum argenteus ordo;
> per iuga chrysolithi positaeque ex ordine gemmae
> clara repercusso reddebant lumina Phoebo.

> Its axle was of gold, the pole of gold; its wheels had golden tyres and a ring of silver spokes. Along the yoke chrysolites and jewels set in fair array gave back their bright glow to the reflected rays of Phoebus.

saria = sarebbe. *pover con ello*: "Poor compared with it."

118-20. *quel del Sol . . . giusto*: The story of Phaëthon's ill-fated driving of the chariot of the Sun has been referred to already in *Inf.* XVII, 106-8, and *Purg.* IV, 71-72 (see n. to *Inf.* XVII, 107). Because Phaëthon was too weak to hold the horses, they rushed out of their usual track and approached so near the Earth that they almost set her on fire. Jupiter, thereupon, in answer to the prayer of Earth, killed Phaëthon with a thunderbolt.

119. *per l'orazion de la Terra devota*: See Ovid's version

of Earth's plea in *Metam*. II, 272-300. Earth is indeed "devout," for she speaks to Jove in complete submission to his will. See *Metam*. II, 279-81:

> si placet hoc meruique, quid o tua fulmina cessant,
> summe deum? liceat periturae viribus ignis
> igne perire tuo clademque auctore levare!

> If this is thy will, and I have deserved all this, why, O
> king of all the gods, are thy lightnings idle? If I must die
> by fire, oh, let me perish by thy fire and lighten my suf-
> fering by thought of him who sent it.

120. *quando fu Giove arcanamente giusto*: In his letter to the Italian cardinals (*Epist*. XI, 5) Dante alludes to the incident in connection with their neglect of the Church: "Vos equidem, Ecclesie militantis veluti primi prepositi pili, per manifestam orbitam Crucifixi currum Sponse regere negligentes, non aliter quam falsus auriga Pheton exorbitastis." ("But ye, as it were the officers of the first rank of church militant, neglecting to guide the chariot of the spouse along the manifest track of the Crucified, have gone astray no otherwise than the false driver Phaeton.") No doubt this concordance of pagan mythology, the "scriptura paganorum" ("scripture of the pagans") of *Epist*. XIII, 63, and events connected with the Church underlies the notion here that Jove was mysteriously just when he struck down Phaëthon. The mystery lies precisely in that sense of concordance.

121. *Tre donne*: The three theological virtues. *da la destra rota*: "At the right wheel" is a position of higher dignity than at the left, where the lower order of the cardinal virtues will be seen dancing.

121-22. *in giro ... danzando*: The three dance a round ("in giro").

122-23. *l'una tanto rossa . . . nota*: Charity, named first because she is the highest virtue of the three and the leader of the others. Fire and the color of fire further point up the fact that this is charity or love.

123. *fora = sarebbe stata.*

124–25. *l'altr' era come se . . . fatte*: Hope, symbolized by her emerald color. Green was the established color for that virtue, as already noted in regard to the crowns of the four animals. Cf. *Purg.* VIII, 28, 106. For *smeraldo*, see *Purg.* VII, 75, and XXXI, 116, where it is used for Beatrice's eyes. It is not that this maiden is simply robed in green, but she is green to the bone, green through and through.

126. *la terza parea neve*: Faith, who is pure white. The white crowns of the twenty-four elders have already symbolized this virtue.   *testé mossa*: "Newly fallen" ("moved" from above).

127–28. *e or parean . . . rossa*: Now faith leads the other two in the dance, and now charity. For the point of doctrine symbolized in this, see Thomas Aquinas, *Summa theol.* II-II, q. 17, a. 7, where we read that faith precedes (hence "leads") hope.

128–29. *e dal canto di questa . . . ratte*: Charity leads the other two in setting the tempo of the dance, by which is denoted the superiority of charity among the three virtues. On this point theological doctrine agrees with Paul (I Cor. 13:2, 13). Cf. Thomas Aquinas, *Summa theol.* II-II, q. 23, a. 6, resp.: "Et ideo charitas est excellentior fide et spe, et per consequens omnibus aliis virtutibus; sicut etiam prudentia, quae attingit rationem secundum se, est excellentior quam aliae virtutes morales quae attingunt rationem secundum quod ex ea medium constituitur in operationibus, vel passionibus humanis." ("Hence charity is more excellent than faith or hope, and, consequently, than all the other virtues, just as prudence, which by itself attains reason, is more excellent than the other moral virtues, which attain reason in so far as it appoints the mean in human operations or passions.") For prudence in this role, see vs. 132.

129. *toglien = toglievano.*   *e tarde e ratte*: Dancing now more slowly and now faster.

130. *Da la sinistra*: The lesser side; see n. to vs. 121.

quattro facean festa: The four moral or cardinal virtues, prudence, temperance, justice, and fortitude, also known as the virtues of the active life. See C. S. Singleton (1958), pp. 160-64.

131. *in porpore vestite*: A most significant touch, as E. Moore (1903, pp. 184-86) points out, for in the Middle Ages the term "purple" was actually used for deep red, and Dante's use of that color here symbolizes the fact that these are the cardinal virtues that partake of charity, hence are the *infused* cardinal virtues, as distinguished from the *acquired* cardinal virtues, which bear the same names and were known and accessible to the pagans. Infused cardinal virtues, according to Thomas Aquinas (*Summa theol.* I-II, q. 65, a. 2), cannot be without charity. See C. S. Singleton (1958), pp. 160-61.

131–32. *dietro al modo . . . testa*: This is prudence, acknowledged to be the chief of the moral virtues (see n. to vs. 130 and cf. Aristotle, *Eth. Nicom.* VI, 13, 1144^b). The rather grotesque feature of three eyes set in her head symbolizes her vision of past, present, and future. In *Conv.* IV, xxvii, 5, Dante writes: "Conviensi adunque essere prudente, cioè savio: e a ciò essere si richiede buona memoria de le vedute cose, buona conoscenza de le presenti e buona provedenza de le future." ("It is fitting, then, to be prudent, that is wise; and to be so demands a good memory of things formerly seen, and good knowledge of things present, and good foresight of things to come.") See Cicero, *De inventione* II, liii, 160; Thomas Aquinas, *Summa theol.* I-II, q. 57, a. 6, ad 4.

133. *il pertrattato nodo*: See "pertratta" in *Inf.* XI, 80. The second group (and the central one, as it turns out) is wider than the rest of the procession, which consists of a line of figures walking two by two. White, green, and red, all the colors of the whole line (except the rainbow colors of the canopy), are present in the virtues in this central knot, and these will be Beatrice's colors, when she appears there on the

chariot. But the principal color of the middle group, as an element of the whole, is the green of the crowns of the four animals.

134. *due vecchi in abito dispari*: The two old men are unlike in dress, as vss. 136-41 indicate.

135. *ma pari in atto*: "But alike in mien."   *sodo*: "Staid."

136-37. *L'un si mostrava . . . Ipocràte*: Wearing the robes of a physician, one of the men shows himself to be a follower of Hippocrates. He is the Acts of the Apostles and resembles their author, Luke, the beloved physician (Col. 4:14), and when we see that the figure who walks beside him is the Epistles of Paul, we understand that those who follow the central knot and constitute the third group are, in fact, the remaining books of the New Testament.

137. *Ipocràte*: The most famous physician of antiquity, already named as being among the virtuous pagans of Limbo (see *Inf.* IV, 143).

137-38. *che natura . . . cari*: Nature holds man dearest among the animals, since he is the most noble. We recall God's delight at Nature's work in forming the human creature as an animal (*Purg.* XXV, 70-71). And Aristotle agrees with Nature, as Dante reminds us in the *Convivio* (II, viii, 10): "Ciascuno è certo che la natura umana è perfettissima di tutte l'altre nature di qua giù; e questo nullo niega, e Aristotile l'afferma, quando dice . . . che l'uomo è perfettissimo di tutti li animali." ("Everyone is assured that human nature is the most perfect of all other natures here below; and this is denied of none; and Aristotle averreth it when he saith . . . that man is the most perfect of all the animals.")

139-40. *mostrava l'altro . . . aguta*: The concern contrary to that of the physician, which is to heal, is to wound; hence this old man bears a bright, sharp sword. The figure represents the Epistles of Paul and (as in the case of Luke for Acts) resembles the author himself, who is often represented

in art with a sword, i.e., the sword of the word of God. See
Isa. 49:2; Heb. 4:12; and Eph. 6:17: "gladium spiritus,
quod est verbum Dei" ("the sword of the spirit, that is, the
word of God"). The sword is also, iconographically, the sym-
bol of Paul's martyrdom.

142. *quattro in umile paruta*: These four of humble mien
are the minor or canonical Epistles of James, Peter, John,
and Jude. For "paruta" in this sense, cf. *Purg.* XXV, 100.

143. *un vecchio solo*: The old man who brings up the rear
and walks alone is the last book of the Scriptures, the
Apocalypse, the vision of John while he was "in spiritu" ("in
the spirit"), Apoc. 1:10. Grandgent comments: "In art John
is often depicted asleep. It was commonly believed that he
was sleeping in Ephesus, not to wake until the Judgment
Day."

145–48. *E questi sette . . . vermigli*: Their crowns of red
distinguish these seven as the third group. Thus the colors
of the three groups prove to be white, green, and red, in that
order, which are the colors of the three theological virtues,
faith, hope, and charity; or, in "chronological" order, faith
precedes Christ, the Gospels follow and, crowned in green,
are our hope; and charity follows His coming.

147. *brolo*: "Garland." Originally the word meant a "closed
wood" or "garden" and is probably of French origin. See
E. G. Parodi (1957), p. 278.

149. *avria = avrebbe.   poco lontano aspetto*: "A gaze
[spectator] from not far off." This is the subject of "avria."

150. *che tutti ardesser*: Again the color of charity is given
as that of fire, here at the end of the procession as at the be-
ginning (cf. vss. 34-35).   *di sopra da' cigli*: I.e., around
the head, where garlands are worn.

151. *quando il carro a me fu a rimpetto*: Dante has chosen
an excellent post (cf. vs. 70) from which to view the whole
spectacle, since its center stops directly opposite him on the

other bank of the stream. But this is quite understandable, since, as we are to see, the procession comes for him alone.

152. *un tuon*: Obviously a signal of supernatural origin here.

153. *più*: I.e., *oltre*.

154. *fermandosi ivi con le prime insegne*: The seven lights and candlesticks, called standards in vs. 79, are now termed ensigns. They are also styled "duci" or guides in simile in vs. 64, and the phrasing here suggests that they do indeed bring the whole procession to a halt in halting themselves. In this way our attention is brought back to them, at the head of the whole array, where we should see them miraculously suspended in midair, their streamers hanging back over the whole procession like a "fair sky" (vs. 82), which means, back over a triumphal chariot at the center—but the chariot is still empty!

CANTO XXX

1. *il settentrion del primo cielo*: The seven candlesticks representing the seven-fold Spirit of God (see n. to *Purg.* XXIX, 52) are metaphorically termed the Septentrion (from the Latin *septem triones,* "seven ploughing oxen"). In *De mon.* II, viii, 13, Dante cites verses of Boethius (*Consol. philos.* II, vi, vs. 10) in which reference is made to the "septem gelidi triones" ("the seven chill oxen"). The Empyrean, in which the seven-fold Spirit of God eternally abides, is the last heaven if the heavenly spheres are counted out from center (see C. S. Singleton, *Inferno Commentary*, Fig. 1, p. 34), but is here called the first, beginning with the outermost, or tenth. The constellation used as a paragon by Dante here is probably that of Ursa Minor, i.e., the Little Dipper, which contains the North Star. The metaphor is to develop into a simile, the first term of which is the "Septentrion of the first heaven."

2. *che né occaso mai seppe né orto*: M. A. Orr (1956, p. 193) observes: "Like the seven stars, also, the heavenly Septentrion is said figuratively to know neither setting nor rising."

3. *né d'altra nebbia che di colpa velo*: Although clouds can obscure the stars of the constellations, only sin can veil "il

727

settentrion del primo cielo." See Augustine, *Conf.* II, 3: "Et in omnibus erat caligo intercludens mihi, deus meus, serenitatem veritatis tuae, et prodiebat tamquam ex adipe iniquitas mea." ("And in all these, there was a mist depriving my sight, O my God, of the brightness of thy truth; and mine iniquity came from me, as if swelling from a fatness.") Also see Isa. 59:2, "sed iniquitates vestrae diviserunt inter vos et Deum vestrum, et peccata vestra absconderunt faciem eius a vobis" ("but your iniquities have divided between you and your God: and your sins have hid his face from you"), a verse which is cited by Thomas Aquinas in *Summa theol.* I, q. 48, a. 4, resp.: "Quae quidem peccata sunt quasi obstacula interposita inter nos et Deum, secundum illud Isa. 59, 2." ("And these sins, indeed, are like obstacles interposed between us and God, according to Isa. lix. 2.") Thus the opening figure of the canto is already relevant to the penance which Dante will undergo before Beatrice, and since it was here in Eden that man first sinned, causing the mists to separate him from the Spirit of God, the figure is especially significant.

4. *lì*: In the procession.

4–5. *ciascuno accorto di suo dover*: The seven candlesticks lead the procession and now cause it to halt.

5. *'l più basso*: The Septentrion below. M. A. Orr (1956, p. 193), preferring to understand the reference to be to Ursa Major, rather than to Ursa Minor, remarks:

> Because it is spoken of as guiding mariners, some commentators have taken the above to refer rather to Septentrio Minor (Ursa Minor), which also has seven chief stars, and is a better guide because nearer the Pole, as Thales taught; but the comparatively faint stars of the Little Bear would not be so apt a comparison with the celestial lights.

She goes on, however, to remind us that in *Par.* II, 9, both Ursa Major and Ursa Minor are referred to as guides at sea, and that in *Purg.* IV, 65, they are spoken of together to indicate the northern part of the sky. But surely the fact that Ursa Minor contains the North Star leads us to understand it as the constellation intended.   *face = fa.*

6. *qual*: "Him who," i.e., the helmsman.   *a porto*: As to a haven of rest. This finds a corresponding term in the turning of the elders to the chariot "as to their peace" (vs. 9). Thus the divine Septentrion not only brings the procession to a halt but prompts the elders of the first group to turn and face the chariot.

7. *s'affisse*: The verb is emphatic, reinforced as it is by "fermo." Cf. *Inf.* XII, 115; *Purg.* XI, 135.

7–8. *la gente verace . . . esso*: The twenty-four elders, as the books of the Old Testament (*Purg.* XXIX, 83-84), are not only veridical, but are truly prophetic of the Advent of Christ. And now one of them will announce an "advent."

9. *al carro volse sé*: Since those who came in the third group followed the chariot and hence are already facing it, this turning about of those who preceded it means that now all eyes are upon the chariot at the center, a triumphal chariot with no one in triumph upon it yet.   *come a sua pace*: The books of the Old Testament look to the chariot now, awaiting thereon the appearance of the one expected, even as in the unfolding line of history they looked to the Advent of the Christ who would come as our peace. Cf. Eph. 2:14: "Ipse enim est pax nostra." ("For he himself [Christ] is our peace.") See also Rom. 5:1-2: "Iustificati ergo ex fide, pacem habeamus ad Deum per Dominum nostrum Iesum Christum, per quem et habemus accessum per fidem in gratiam istam, in qua stamus, et gloriamur in spe gloriae filiorum Dei." ("Having been justified therefore by faith, let us have peace with God through our Lord Jesus Christ, through whom we also have access by faith unto that grace in which we stand, and exult in the hope of the glory of the sons of God.") Both justification and filiation with God are relevant to the context here in its symbolic dimensions and the analogy Beatrice-Christ. See C. S. Singleton (1958), pp. 72-85.

10. *un di loro*: The elder who represents the Solomonic books, but here especially the Song of Solomon, Canticle of Canticles. *quasi da ciel messo = quasi messo da ciel.* "Messo" may be understood as the past participle of *mettere* or as a noun, i.e., "messenger" (cf. *Inf.* IX, 85). This touch makes the words spoken by this "book" a kind of annunciation.

11–12. *"Veni, sponsa, de Libano"* . . . *tre volte*: Cf. Cant. 4:8: "Veni de Libano, sponsa mea, veni de Libano, veni, coronaberis." ("Come from Lebanon, my bride, come from Lebanon, come and you shall be crowned.") Thus not only is the call "veni" uttered thrice in the verses of the Canticle of Canticles, as echoed here, but that call is followed there by the promise of a crowning, and this in turn enters appropriately into the figure of a triumph in which someone yet to appear is to be exalted (cf. *Purg.* XXIV, 14-15). Our guiding expectation that Beatrice is the one who is to come is now further heightened by this call for a "sponsa," in the feminine. Moreover the "sponsa" who is to come cannot be the Church (as the *sponsa* was commonly understood in the orthodox interpretation), for the Church is here already in the procession, being represented by the chariot itself. But the *sponsa* of the Canticle of Canticles was also understood to be Sapientia, the wisdom of God, and since Sapientia in fact proves to be one of the names Beatrice bears in the allegory of the poem, the call for her advent that this proves to be is highly significant.

12. *e tutti li altri appresso*: The other books of the Old Testament all join in the prophetic and welcoming cry.

13–18. *Quali i beati . . . etterna*: Even as those who are to stand on Christ's right at the Last Judgment shall rise forth from the grave, so these who appear now arise. The simile is striking especially in that its main function is to bring into the context of the action that Advent of Christ which is to be at the end of time. (On the figure of the three comings of Christ and the allegorical dimensions arising out of such a conception, see C. S. Singleton, 1958, pp. 72-85.) The guid-

ing intention of the poet is all the more evident here by vir-
tue of its being based, actually, on very slight similarity. The
saints will stand forth from their tombs; but in the other term
of the comparison these are the angels (see vs. 83) who sud-
denly appear on the chariot and who certainly do not rise up
out of anything resembling tombs (for how would any such
be on this chariot, a vehicle that has been compared to an
ancient Roman triumphal chariot?). Moreover these angels
must descend from Heaven in order to appear upon the
chariot and so do not rise up at all.

13. *novissimo*: The last of all. Cf. the Latin *novissime*,
"lastly," "last of all," "finally."   *bando*: A public procla-
mation, usually made after a trumpet is sounded—here, the
angel's trumpet at the Last Judgment (the "gran sentenza"
of *Inf.* VI, 104).

14. *surgeran presti*: Torraca observes that the accent of the
verse falls strongly on "presti." The soul will return to its
body and be more perfect for being "reclothed" in its flesh
and so will rise forth from the tomb quickly, eager (since
these are saints) to assemble when Christ comes to judge all.

15. *la revestita voce alleluiando*: An absolute construction
in which "voce" is the subject of the verb *alleluiare*. The al-
ternate reading, which has "carne" instead of "voce," is
found only in three late MSS (see Petrocchi's vol. I, *Intro-
duzione*, pp. 218-20). The reclad voice is the voice of the
resurrected body. Benvenuto comments: "*La voce rivestita*,
scilicet, a corpore, quasi dicat, resumptis organis corporali-
bus, ita quod tunc erit perfectior." ("*La voce rivestita*, that
is, from the body, as if to say, after they have regained their
bodily organs, so that then it would be more perfect.")
Souls have voices before the voice of the body is regained,
of course, as every reader of the *Inferno* and *Purgatorio*
knows; but after regaining their bodies, they will be able to
shout hallelujah with their bodily voices.

16. *basterna*: "Covered vehicle." The suggestion of a veiled
effect in the connotation of this particular term is important,

731

clearly, in the context. Pietro di Dante glosses: "idest curru, delicatis pannis cooperto et decorato" ("that is, a chariot covered and decorated with fine cloth"). Benvenuto observes:

> Est enim basterna vehiculum itineris, sic dicta, quasi vesterna, quia vestibus mollibus sternitur, et a duobus animalibus trahitur, in qua mulieres nobiles deferuntur: et sic vide quantum metaphora sit propria, quia ista biga ducitur in via quae peregrinatur in ista vita, et trahitur ab animali duarum naturarum, et est multipliciter adornata, in qua defertur nobilissima domina, scilicet Beatrix.

> For a *basterna* is a vehicle for travel, so to speak, as if *vesterna*, because it is lined with soft robes and is drawn by two animals, in which noble ladies were transported. Notice how appropriate the metaphor is, because that carriage moves along the road which the pilgrimage of life follows, and it is drawn by an animal of two natures and is wonderfully adorned, in which the most noble lady, that is, Beatrice, is carried.

17. *si levar = si levarono. cento*: An indeterminate number, as elsewhere in the poem (cf. *Inf.* XXVIII, 52; *Purg.* II, 45). See Dan. 7:10: "Millia millium ministrabant ei et decies millies centena millia assistebant ei." ("Thousands of thousands ministered to him, and ten thousand times a hundred thousand stood before him.") On this biblical passage Thomas Aquinas (*Summa theol.* I, q. 112, a. 4, ad 2) remarks: "Et sic ministrantium numerus ponitur indefinitus, ad significandum excessum." ("Thus the number of those who minister is indefinite, and signifies excess.") *ad vocem tanti senis*: "At the voice of so great an elder." Besides providing the needed rhyme (with "venis," vs. 19), the Latin serves to elevate and solemnize. Cf. *Purg.* XIX, 99.

18. *ministri e messaggier di vita etterna*: As angels now come to herald the advent of Beatrice, who comes to judge, Christ will come with His mighty angels (II Thess. 1:7). On angels as ministers and messengers, see Thomas Aquinas,

Summa theol. I, q. 112, "De missione angelorum," and *De veritate* q. 18, a. 5, ad 3: "Adam habuit cognitionem Angelorum, inquantum erant propter ipsum facti. Scivit enim eos esse consortes suae beatitudinis, et ministros suae salutis in via." ("Adam had knowledge of the angels in so far as they were made for his sake. For he knew that they would be companions of his beatitude and helpers for his salvation in this life.")

19. *Tutti dicean: "Benedictus qui venis!"* The welcoming cry in the masculine is remarkable in view of the fact that it is Beatrice who comes. It serves, in fact, to guide the reader yet farther along the line of a deliberate ambiguity. Is it Christ who comes now? But Christ is already on the scene, in the figure of the griffin. Is it Beatrice who comes as the bride from Lebanon? Then why not "benedicta quae venis"? The cry, in any event, brings immediately to mind Christ's entry into Jerusalem on Palm Sunday and the strewing of fronds, matched in the scene here by the tossing of flowers. Cf. Matt. 21:4-9:

> Hoc autem totum factum est, ut adimpleretur quod dictum est per prophetam dicentem: Dicite filiae Sion: Ecce rex tuus venit tibi mansuetus, sedens super asinam et pullum filium subiugalis. Euntes autem discipuli fecerunt sicut praecepit illis Iesus; et adduxerunt asinam et pullum, et imposuerunt super eos vestimenta sua, et eum desuper sedere fecerunt. Plurima autem turba straverunt vestimenta sua in via; alii autem caedebant ramos de arboribus, et sternebant in via. Turbae autem quae praecedebant et quae sequebantur clamabant dicentes: Hosanna filio David! Benedictus qui venit in nomine Domini: hosanna in altissimis!

> Now this was done that what was spoken through the prophet might be fulfilled, "Tell the daughter of Sion: Behold, thy king comes to thee, meek and seated upon an ass, and upon a colt, the foal of a beast of burden."

> So the disciples went and did as Jesus had directed them. And they brought the ass and the colt, laid their cloaks on them, and made him sit thereon. And most

of the crowd spread their cloaks upon the road, while others were cutting branches from the trees, and strewing them on the road. And the crowds that went before him, and those that followed, kept crying out, saying, "Hosanna to the Son of David! Blessed is he who comes in the name of the Lord! Hosanna in the highest!"

Dante's verse is designed to call vividly to the reader's mind this whole scene of Christ's entry into Jerusalem, a scene already evoked by the cry of hosanna in *Purg.* XXIX, 51. "Venis," in place of "venit," is more direct and immediate.

Moreover, since the figure of the blessed at the resurrection of the body has come into the context, it should perhaps be recalled here, as Grandgent notes, that "benedictus qui venit" are the last words sung by the assistants before the Canon of the Mass, expressing the expectation of the bodily coming of Christ. The words of welcome are from Ps. 117[118]:26, "benedictus qui venit in nomine Domini" ("blessed is he who comes in the name of the Lord"), and thus belong to the Old Testament as well as to the New. J.S.P. Tatlock (1934-35, p. 122) observes that the words were also used as "a cry of ceremonial welcome to great personages on earth; as to a Lombard king coming for his coronation at Milan, by the Canterbury monks to Archbishop Thomas Becket returning from exile in 1171, and to Pope Innocent IV in Genoa in 1244."

20. *e fior gittando e di sopra e dintorno*: As if this were another Palm Sunday. But the flowers form what is called a "cloud" (vs. 28), a touch which is also important in the symbolism. See n. to vs. 25.

21. *Manibus, oh, date lilia plenis*: This most remarkable farewell verse, taken from *Aen.* VI, 883, is turned toward Virgil, though it serves in the literal meaning as an utterance of the welcoming angels, who, as will be seen, toss flowers for Beatrice. It bears the haunting sadness of its context in the *Aeneid* and functions as a climax to the whole strain of pathos that has attached to the figure of the "sweet father," as he will now be called when suddenly he is no longer by

Dante's side. See *Aen.* VI, 867-86 (the last spoken words
of the sixth book of the *Aeneid*) for Anchises' prophecy of
the early death of the youth Marcellus:

> Tum pater Anchises lacrimis ingressus obortis:
> "o gnate, ingentem luctum ne quaere tuorum.
> ostendent terris hunc tantum fata, nec ultra
> esse sinent. nimium vobis Romana propago
> visa potens, superi, propria haec si dona fuissent.
> quantos ille virum magnam Mavortis ad urbem
> campus aget gemitus! vel quae, Tiberine, videbis
> funera, cum tumulum praeterlabere recentem!
> nec puer Iliaca quisquam de gente Latinos
> in tantum spe tollet avos, nec Romula quondam
> ullo se tantum tellus iactabit alumno.
> heu pietas, heu prisca fides, invictaque bello
> dextera! non illi se quisquam impune tulisset
> obvius armato, seu cum pedes iret in hostem,
> seu spumantis equi foderet calcaribus armos.
> heu! miserande puer, si qua fata aspera rumpas,
> tu Marcellus eris! manibus date lilia plenis,
> purpureos spargam flores animamque nepotis
> his saltem accumulem donis et fungar inani
> munere." . . .

Then father Anchises with upwelling tears began: "O
my son, ask not of the vast sorrow of thy people. Him
the fates shall but show to earth, nor longer suffer him
to stay. Too mighty, O gods, ye deemed the Roman
stock would be, were these gifts lasting. What wailing
of men shall that famous Field waft to Mavors' mighty
city! What funeral-state, O Tiber, shalt thou see, as thou
glidest past the new-built tomb! No youth of Ilian stock
shall exalt so greatly with his promise his Latin fore-
fathers, nor shall the land of Romulus ever take such
pride in any of her sons. Alas for goodness! alas for old-
world honour, and the hand invincible in war! Against
him in arms would none have advanced unscathed,
whether on foot he met the foe, or dug his spurs into the
flanks of his foaming horse. Ah! child of pity, if haply

thou couldst burst the harsh bonds of fate, thou shalt
be Marcellus! Give me lilies with full hand: let me scat-
ter purple flowers; let me heap o'er my offspring's shade
at least these gifts and fulfil an unavailing service."

22–32. *Io vidi già . . . m'apparve*: This remarkable simile
is rich in symbolic significance. Since a rising sun is the estab-
lished image for the coming of Christ, Beatrice's advent in
such a figure clearly sustains the analogy that is continued in
a deliberate ambiguity all through this canto, as it has been
in the preceding one. Dante is not facing east at the moment,
but the procession and the chariot were first seen to come
out of the east, where a dawning sun might be expected to
appear (see n. to *Purg.* XXIX, 12). Actually, when Beatrice
appears on the chariot, it must be that she comes from above,
since her abode is in Heaven, as every reader knows. She
comes from on high, which, in a verse in Luke spoken by
Zacharias, the father of John the Baptist, when he regained
his power of speech, may also mean out of the east. See Luc.
1:78-79: "per viscera misericordiae Dei nostri, in quibus
visitavit nos oriens ex alto; illuminare his qui in tenebris et
in umbra mortis sedent, ad dirigendos pedes nostros in viam
pacis" ("because of the loving-kindness of our God, where-
with the Orient from on high has visited us, To shine on
those who sit in darkness and in the shadow of death, to
guide our feet into the way of peace"). Beatrice comes in the
figure of a sun rising (by implication) from on high; yet the
procession has brought her empty chariot out of the east.

The poet is also showing responsibility to another aspect
of doctrine, as reflected in a sermon of Bernard of Clairvaux
on Advent, which joins the notion of a dawn from on high
with that of Christ's splendor, which is too bright for our
mortal eyes. Hence the "dawn" in which Beatrice comes as
a sun is attended by tempering vapors so that the eye can
endure it for a long time. Even as the words "benedictus qui
venit" announce the expectation of Christ's bodily presence
in the Mass (see n. to vs. 19), so this figure suggests the Ad-
vent of Christ in the Incarnation. In his *Sermones de tempore*
(*In adventu Domini* I, 8) Bernard writes:

Propterea benignissimus Salvator et medicus animarum
descendit ab altitudine sua, et claritatem suam infirmis
occulis temperavit. Induit se laterna quadam, illo utique
glorioso et ab omni labe purissimo corpore quod susce-
pit. Haec est enim illa levissima plane et praefulgida
nubes, supra quam ascensurum eum propheta praedixe-
rat, ut descenderet Aegyptum (*Isa.* xix, 1).

Therefore the kindly Saviour and Physician of souls
comes down from the heights, and he tempers the bril-
liance of his light for tender eyes. He carries with Him
a lantern, in the glorified body, free of the slightest
stain, that He has assumed. This indeed is that light-
some and gleaming cloud, which the prophet had said
He was to ascend upon, that he might descend into
Egypt (Isa. 19:1).

The luminous cloud, in the analogy, is matched by the "cloud
of flowers" in which Beatrice finally appears, so that the eye
can endure her advent thus.

24. *l'altro ciel*: The rest of the sky.

25. *e la faccia del sol nascere ombrata*: This is matched, in
the second term of the simile, by the cloud of flowers and
also by Beatrice's veiled face. It should be remembered that
in His ascension Christ rose in a cloud. See Actus 1:9: "Et
cum haec dixisset, videntibus illis, elevatus est; et nubes
suscepit eum ab oculis eorum." ("And when he had said this,
he was lifted up before their eyes, and a cloud took him out
of their sight.") Beatrice, too, in a vision of her death in the
Vita nuova (XXIII, 25), is seen to ascend as a little cloud,
to the cry of hosanna. Christ is to return "cum nubibus, et
videbit eum omnis oculus" ("with the clouds, and every eye
shall see him"), as stated in Apoc. 1:7, and so now does Bea-
trice. The analogy Beatrice-Christ continues to be the con-
trolling pattern of the imagery.

29. *le mani angeliche*: The ministers and messengers of
eternal life toss the flowers as they shout: "Benedictus qui
venis!" (vs. 19). See vs. 21: *"Manibus, oh, date lilia plenis!"*

30. *dentro e di fori*: The flowers fall back, into the chariot and outside of it.

31–33. *sovra candido vel . . . viva*: It is no accident that Beatrice appears, finally, in verses bearing these significant numbers, and it will be noted that "donna," subject of the verb "apparve," is the first word of the central verse of this tercet. Beatrice (we are not actually told yet that it is she, but who else would it be, so long awaited as she is?) is dressed in the three dominant colors of the procession, which are those of faith (her veil), hope (her mantle and crown), and charity (the color of her robe beneath the mantle). She appears in the central group of the four beasts crowned in green (*Purg.* XXIX, 92-93), and she herself is crowned in green (her eyes are also green—see *Purg.* XXXI, 116), in keeping with the color of the middle group. Yet the third verse of the tercet is given over to the color of charity or love, the color of flame, which is that of the crowns of the third group, the remaining books of the New Testament. (It should be recalled that in the *Vita nuova* Beatrice is, in her first appearance, dressed in crimson—see *Vita nuova* II, 3.)

Thus, finally, at the center of the procession and on the triumphal chariot itself, toward which all were looking and upon which the hundred angels appeared with their welcoming cry, Beatrice comes. It is one of the great moments of the poem. And before she comes, as we soon learn, Virgil is gone from the scene. See C. S. Singleton (1954), pp. 52-53.

31. *cinta d'uliva*: Since the olive is the tree of Minerva, the goddess of wisdom, olive green may be said to be her color. Thus, when it becomes clear in the allegory that one of Beatrice's names is Sapienzia, or Wisdom, the symbolism of her crown will be evident. The olive frond, moreover, is the symbol of peace, and we recall that the elders faced the chariot where she was to appear as "their peace." Buti sees these several meanings here in the crown of olive: "Si significa la pace, la quale è nell'animo quando s'è adornato di fede, e la vittoria . . . e significa la sapienzia: imperò che l'ulivo è consecrato a Pallade che è la Dia de la sapienzia, la quale è co-

rona de la santa Teologia." ("It can mean peace, which is in the soul that has adorned itself with faith; and victory . . . and wisdom, for the olive is sacred to Pallas, who is the goddess of wisdom; and wisdom is the crown of sacred theology.")

34–36. *cotanto tempo . . . affranto*: Since Beatrice died in June 1290 and it is now the spring of 1300, it has been ten years (cf. "la decenne sete," *Purg.* XXXII, 2) since Dante felt faint in her presence, as he so often did when he encountered her while she was still alive.

36. *di stupor, tremando, affranto*: Cf. *Vita nuova* II, 4; XI, 3; XIV, 4-5; XXIV, 1; and *passim*. Dante, in the *Vita nuova*, reaches such a point in this regard that certain ladies question him about it in one of the most charming and significant episodes of that early work. See C. S. Singleton (1949), pp. 82-84.

37. *sanza de li occhi aver più conoscenza*: Dante cannot actually see that this is Beatrice, concealed as she is by the white veil in the cloud of flowers.   *de li occhi = da li occhi*.

38. *per occulta virtù che da lei mosse*: Recognition by "occult virtue" is common enough in medieval narrative. Cf. Boccaccio, *Decam.* II, 6 (vol. I, p. 119, ll. 12-13). *mosse = si mosse*.

39. *d'antico amor*: Cf. vs. 48: "l'antica fiamma." Everywhere the reappearance of Beatrice connects with Dante's experience as recounted in the *Vita nuova*. According to *Vita nuova* II, 2, Dante first became enamored of Beatrice when he was almost nine and she herself was eight years old.

40–42. *Tosto che ne la vista . . . fosse*: Much here is reminiscent of Boethius. Cf. *Consol. philos.* I, iii, ll. 3-6: "Itaque ubi in eam deduxi oculos intuitumque defixi, respicio nutricem meam cuius ab adulescentia laribus obversatus fueram Philosophiam." ("Wherefore casting mine eyes upon her somewhat stedfastly, I beheld my nurse Philosophy, in whose house I had remained from my youth.")

42. *prima ch'io fuor di puerizia fosse*: Cf. *Vita nuova* II, 2, "io la vidi quasi da la fine del mio nono" ("I beheld her almost at the end of my ninth"), and XII, 7, "come tu fosti suo tostamente da la tua puerizia" ("how thou wast hers, right from thy very boyhood"). In *Rime* CXI, 1-2, Dante writes: "Io sono stato con Amore insieme / da la circulazion del sol mia nona." ("I have been with Love together since my ninth revolution of the sun.")

43–46. *volsimi a la sinistra . . . Virgilio*: Dante is facing the stream, and since Virgil has been following behind, with Statius, he would now be standing on Dante's left.

43. *volsimi = mi volsi.*   *respitto*: Grandgent points out that this is a noun which derives from the old verb *ri-* or *respittare*, "to expect." Del Lungo comments: "con la sospensione d'animo, con l'affannosa incertezza" ("with the spirit in suspense, with anxious uncertainty"). Cf. the Provençal *respieit*, "trust," "hopeful expectation."

44. *corre a la mamma*: Virgil, who has so often been referred to as a father, now in this figure becomes a mother, and Beatrice, so stern at the moment, will often figure as mother from now on (see vs. 79 and *Par.* I, 102). The term presents another glimpse of the transition from the first guide to the second which is evident in vs. 21, a verse that is both a farewell to Virgil and a welcome to Beatrice. Virgil is called father, "dolcissimo patre," for the last time in vs. 50.

46. *Virgilio*: Virgil is simply Virgil now, not the "good master" or "guide." His name is shorn of all epithets, except that of "dolcissimo patre" in vs. 50.   *dramma*: "Dram," the minutest quantity. Cf. *Purg.* XXI, 99.

47. *di sangue m'è rimaso che non tremi*: In the physiology of the time the blood was thought to register emotion. See *Inf.* I, 90, *Purg.* XI, 138, and, for the blood as the seat of the soul, *Purg.* V, 74.

48. *conosco i segni de l'antica fiamma*: Again, as in vs. 21, one of Virgil's own verses becomes a verse of this farewell

to him. See *Aen.* IV, 23, where Dido says to Anna: "Adgnosco veteris vestigia flammae." ("I recognize the traces of the olden flame.") On the antiquity of Dante's "flame," see n. to vs. 39.

49–51. *Ma Virgilio . . . die'mi*: It is also by deliberate design that Virgil is named once in vs. 46, then thrice in a single tercet observing that he is gone (vss. 49-51), then finally once in vs. 55 by Beatrice, following the unique naming of Dante himself: $1 + 3 + 1$.

Commentators (see E. Moore, 1896, pp. 20-21) have noted in the triune farewell to Virgil of this tercet an echo of other verses of his, *Georg.* IV, 525-27:

> . . . Eurydicen vox ipsa et frigida lingua,
> a miseram Eurydicen! anima fugiente vocabat,
> Eurydicen toto referebant flumine ripae.

> The bare voice and death-cold tongue, with fleeting breath, called Eurydice—ah, hapless Eurydice! "Eurydice" the banks re-echoed, all adown the stream.

This passage from the *Georgics* follows close upon Orpheus' loss of Eurydice when he looked back at her and she vanished and returned to deepest Hades. The echo, thus, because of this context, is most appropriate.

49. *n'avea lasciati = ci aveva lasciati.* "Us" must include Statius, of course (even though we had almost forgotten about him), but it includes Beatrice, too, and is part of the strategy of transition already noted in the n. to vs. 44.

51. *Virgilio a cui per mia salute die'mi*: This naming of Virgil looks back down the line of his long guidance almost to the very beginning of the action, *Inf.* I, 63.   *die'mi = mi diedi.*

52. *né quantunque perdeo l'antica matre*: Cf. *Purg.* XXIX, 23-30. Again there comes, here in Eden, the thought of loss of Eden in consequence of the sin of Eve, who was more to blame than Adam (see n. to *Purg.* XXIX, 26).   *perdeo = perdè* (cf. "appario," vs. 64).   *l'antica matre*: Both "patre" and "matre," instead of *padre* and *madre*, may be

regarded as somewhat dictated by the rhyme with "atre" (vs. 54), yet in the farewell to Virgil the word "patre," clearly much closer to the Latin *pater*, seems most fitting, and "matre" has a more ancient sound itself.

53. *valse*: The subject is the whole phrase "quantunque perdeo l'antica matre." *le guance nette di rugiada*: A touch which looks back to the beginning of the *Purgatorio* and the successful ascent of the mountain (cf. *Purg.* I, 121-29) even as vs. 51 looks back to the beginning of the *Inferno* and the unsuccessful attempt. *nette = nettate*.

54. *tornasser atre*: I.e., as his cheeks had been when he came forth from Hell (see *Purg.* I, 95-96). Compare "atre" with the Latin *ater*, "black," "dark," and see *Inf.* VI, 16.

55. *Dante*: The first word Beatrice addresses to Dante is his own name. This is the more striking in that it is the only place in the poem (and, for that matter, in all Dante's works, except in certain letters and in titles of works) where his name appears, and vs. 63 seems to apologize even for this unique occurrence, appealing to the necessity for it. See n. to vs. 63. The name, spoken by Beatrice in the context of her severity and the figure of a mother (vs. 79) in which she is cast (see n. to vs. 44), establishes at once the tone and manner of Beatrice's dealing with Dante now, a manner which may come to the reader as a surprise, since Virgil said that Beatrice would come with smiling eyes (*Purg.* XXVII, 136). Instead she is a *madre superba* (vs. 79).

56-57. *non pianger . . . pianger*: Matching the three mentions of Virgil's name in the farewell tercet, *piangere* is used thrice in the first tercet spoken by Beatrice.

56. *anco = ancora*, "yet."

57. *per altra spada*: For the metaphor of cutting words, see n. to *Purg.* XXIX, 139-40.

58-60. *Quasi ammiraglio . . . l'incora*: The main purpose of the simile is to convey the regal and haughty bearing of Beatrice (cf. vs. 70: "regalmente," "proterva"), as that of

a great personage, such as an admiral or king, standing now
upon a chariot which is her triumphal chariot, in command
of the whole "fleet." There is a certain lack of correspond-
ence between the first term of the simile and the second.
Beatrice does not really command the procession any more
than the personage in a triumph commands; nor are there
"other ships" ("altri legni") here or others under her com-
mand ("gente che ministra") who need to be urged to a good
performance of their duties; nor, finally, is the figure of the
admiral who moves about the ship ("in poppa e in prora")
matched by that of Beatrice, for we can only imagine her as
standing "pur ferma," as in vs. 100, on the left side of the
chariot, facing Dante.

59–60. *ministra per li altri legni*: Cf. Virgil, *Aen.* VI, 302:
"Ipse ratem conto subigit velisque ministrat." ("Unaided,
he poles the boat, tends the sails.")

61. *in su la sponda del carro sinistra*: Beatrice stands as
near to the edge of the chariot as she can. The word *sponda*
might be used either of the side of a vehicle in this sense or
the side of a vessel.

62. *al suon del nome mio*: See n. to vs. 55.

63. *che di necessità qui si registra*: In a literal sense the ne-
cessity of recording the name here is simply that Beatrice
uttered it, for this account is given as a true report of what
took place. But this is so obvious a fact that we look for a
deeper meaning and find it in the allegorical dimension.
Dante's journey is not only his, in a literal sense; it is the
journey of Everyman, in allegory. Everyman is so aided by
the grace of God that he may return to Eden in the allegorical
sense here intended. But if Everyman does this, will he meet
there a Beatrice who will upbraid him as she does Dante for
backslidings and forgetfulness? Beatrice, we recall, *does* have
meaning for mankind generally and not only for Dante alone
(*Inf.* II, 76-78). Clearly this is not the meaning. Dante's con-
fession to Beatrice, mainly made indirectly through her
charges in this canto and the next, is a *personal* confession.

We are not to seek to read it as Everyman's. And this unique naming of Dante as the protagonist declares as much: such is its necessity. In *Conv.* I, ii, 3, Dante writes: "Non si concede per li retorici alcuno di se medesimo sanza necessaria cagione parlare." ("Rhetoricians forbid a man to speak of himself, except on needful occasion.")

64-65. *pria m'appario velata*: Beatrice is no longer veiled by the cloud of flowers, as she was when she first appeared (vss. 28-32).

64. *appario = apparì (apparve)*. Cf. "perdeo," vs. 52.

65. *l'angelica festa*: The flowers tossed by the angels. "Festa" here bears something of the meaning it has in the expression *fare festa a qualcuno*, "to give glad welcome to someone."

66. *drizzar li occhi*: This depends on "vidi la donna," vs. 64. *ver' = verso*. *di qua dal rio*: On the side of the stream where Dante is standing.

68. *cerchiato de le fronde di Minerva*: Crowned with the olive (vs. 31). The olive was sacred to Minerva, the Greek goddess Athena (see n. to *Purg.* XV, 98), who was known as the goddess of wisdom. Dante also mentions Minerva in *Conv.* II, iv, 6, "sì come a Pallade o vero Minerva, la quale dissero dea di sapienza" ("for Pallas or Minerva, whom they called goddess of wisdom"), and *Par.* II, 8.

69. *parer = apparire*. *manifesta*: Wholly visible. The veil still covers Beatrice's face even though the cloud of flowers does not hide her now.

71. *continuò come colui che dice*: Cf. *Inf.* V, 126, "dirò come colui che piange e dice," words spoken by Francesca.

73. *Guardaci*: Commentators differ in their interpretation of *ci* here. It could be the pronoun, in which case Beatrice, in her regal manner, would be using the plural of majesty, speaking as a monarch would, in the first person plural. This

reading is often accompanied by "ben sem, ben sem" in the rest of the verse, continuing such a plural (*sem = siamo*). Or *ci* might be construed as the adverb *qui*, in which case the rest of the verse is usually given in the reading here adopted.

Ben son, ben son: The cutting sarcasm of the repetition is clear: "Look well, I am indeed Beatrice." The words suggest a Dante who is gazing as intently as he can to make out Beatrice's face through the veil.   *Beatrice*: Finally the lady is named or, rather, names herself, and she has thus pronounced the names of Dante, Virgil, and Beatrice—in that order.

74. *Come degnasti d'accedere al monte?* "How is it that you deigned to climb the mountain?" The sharp sarcasm continues and leads into the following verse. Regarding *accedere al monte* in the sense of "climb the mountain," see *Purg.* II, 60, where the souls newly arrived on the shore of Purgatory, with the mountain rising before them, say to Virgil and Dante, "mostratene la via di gire al monte," which clearly means the way by which the ascent is possible. Beatrice here speaks of Dante's coming to the summit, as the meaning "qui" in the following verse demands. The bitter cut of "degnasti" in such a context is evident, for Beatrice knows that Dante was told by Virgil that it was her descent to Limbo that made it possible for him to give himself to Virgil for his own salvation (vs. 51); he might never have climbed to this summit without her coming thus to the rescue.   *degnasti = ti degnasti*.

75. *non sapei tu che qui è l'uom felice?* "Qui" is in an emphatic position in the verse and means specifically the summit of the mountain where Dante now stands. On happiness as the goal at the summit, see n. to *Inf.* I, 77-78, and Virgil's promise of the "sweet fruit," *Purg.* XXVII, 115-17. Before coming here Dante did not know that the Garden of Eden was situated at the summit of the mountain, where our first parents had known the happiness which Matelda has been seen to enjoy, but now this knowledge also can enter into the meaning of Beatrice's words.   *sapei = sapevi*.

76. *fonte*: The clear stream of Lethe, which flows from a "fontana" (*Purg.* XXVIII, 124).

77. *i = li.   trassi a l'erba*: Dante cannot bear to see his own image reflected in the clear water of the stream and turns his eyes to the grass of the bank.

79. *Così la madre*: Cf. vs. 44.   *superba*: "Haughty."

80–81. *perché d'amaro sente il sapor de la pietade acerba* = *perché il sapor de la pietade acerba sa di amaro.*

81. *pietade acerba*: The pity of the mother is "acerba" ("unripe"), that is, it is not yet the moment for her to reveal it, though the child knows it is there and will finally manifest itself. On *acerbo* in the sense of "unripe" (and in rhyme with *superbo*), see *Inf.* XXV, 18; *Par.* XIX, 48.

82. *li angeli*: The hundred ministers and messengers of eternal life who appeared on the chariot tossing the cloud of flowers. They now serve as a kind of chorus, as in ancient Greek drama.   *cantaro = cantarono.*

83. *di sùbito*: This touch stresses the angels' prompt compassion and ready appeal to Beatrice to show her pity, which is still unripe.

83–84. *"In te, Domine, speravi"* . . . *passaro*: The angels, in chorus, praying to God for Dante, but also, by indirection, for Beatrice's mercy, sing the first part of the thirtieth psalm. See Ps. 30:2-9[31:1-8]:

> In te, Domine, speravi, non confundar in aeternum; in iustitia tua libera me. Inclina ad me aurem tuam, accelera ut eruas me. Esto mihi in Deum protectorem et in domum refugii, ut salvum me facias. Quoniam fortitudo mea et refugium meum es tu, et propter nomen tuum deduces me et enutries me. Educes me de laqueo hoc quem absconderunt mihi, quoniam tu es protector meus. In manus tuas commendo spiritum meum; redemisti me, Domine, Deus veritatis. Odisti observantes vanitates supervacue, ego autem in Domino speravi.

Exultabo et laetabor in misericordia tua, quoniam respexisti humilitatem meam, salvasti de necessitatibus animam meam, nec conclusisti me in manibus inimici: statuisti in loco spatioso pedes meos.

In you, O Lord, I take refuge; let me never be put to shame. In your justice rescue me, incline your ear to me, make haste to deliver me! Be my rock of refuge, a stronghold to give me safety. You are my rock and my fortress; for your name's sake you will lead and guide me. You will free me from the snare they set for me, for you are my refuge. Into your hands I commend my spirit; you will redeem me, O Lord, O faithful God. You hate those who worship vain idols, but my trust is in the Lord. I will rejoice and be glad of your kindness, when you have seen my affliction and watched over me in my distress, not shutting me up in the grip of the enemy but enabling me to stand in a spacious place.

For the appropriateness of the words "in iustitia tua libera me" at the beginning of the psalm (appropriate because in allegory the goal here at the summit is justification, which is also *libertà*), see C. S. Singleton (1958), pp. 101-21. The words of the last verse sung by the angels are also relevant, since through God's mercy and Beatrice's descent at the beginning of the journey Dante is now privileged to stand in this spacious place at the summit. And it may be noted that the psalm itself bears the not insignificant number of thirty.

84. *passaro = passarono.*

85-99. *Sì come neve . . . petto*: For the whole figure here, compare Augustine's account of the long gathering up of his own misery before his conversion and the mighty storm and shower of tears that arose within him (*Conf.* VIII, 12): "Ubi vero a fundo arcano alta consideratio traxit et congessit totam miseriam meam in conspectu cordis mei, oborta est procella ingens, ferens ingentem imbrem lacrimarum." ("So soon therefore as a deep consideration even from the secret bottom of my soul, had drawn together and laid all my misery upon one heap before the eyes of my heart; there rose up a mighty storm, bringing as mighty a shower of tears with it.")

85. *le vive travi*: The living trees which will serve as beams when cut. Cf. Ovid, *Metam.* VIII, 329: "Silva frequens trabibus." ("There was a forest thick with trees.") The metaphor is common in the Latin poets.

86. *lo dosso d'Italia*: The ridge of the Apennines.

87. *venti schiavi*: Northeast winds blowing from Slavonia (*Schiavonia*).

88. *in sé stessa trapela*: The snow, melting first on the surface, where it is exposed to the sun, seeps down through its mass.

89. *la terra che perde ombra*: The hot regions of Africa, in which the sun is vertically overhead at times, and no shadow is cast by any object. See Lucan, *Phars.* IX, 528-32, 538-39:

> Hic quoque nil obstat Phoebo, cum cardine summo
> Stat librata dies; truncum vix protegit arbor:
> Tam brevis in medium radiis conpellitur umbra.
> Deprensum est hunc esse locum, qua circulus alti
> Solstitii medium signorum percutit orbem.
> At tibi, quaecumque es Libyco gens igne dirempta,
> In Noton umbra cadit, quae nobis exit in Arcton.

But even here the sun finds no hindrance, when the orb of day stands poised in the zenith: the trees can scarce shelter their own trunks—so small is the compass of the shadow thrown by his rays. It has been ascertained that this is the spot where the circle of the upper solstice strikes the Zodiac, equidistant from the poles. But the shadow of people (if such there be) who are separated from us by the heats of Libya falls to the South, whereas ours falls northwards.

spiri: "Breathes forth" its hot winds. The subjunctive is required by "pur che" ("if only").

92. *anzi 'l cantar*: "Before the singing."   *di quei*: Of the angels.   *notan*: Cf. *Purg.* XXXII, 33. Buti comments:

"Notare è nel canto seguitare le note; cioè li segni del canto."
("In singing, *notare* means to follow the notes, which are
the signs of the song.") Landino explains: "Come il buon
musico cantando segue le note descritte nel libro, così gli
Angeli riguardando l'influentie, e gli effetti, che procedono
da' perpetui movimenti de' cieli, cantano quello, che veggono
segnato nell'ordine fatale della divina providentia." ("Just
as a good musician, when singing, follows the notes in the
book, so the angels, looking at the influences and effects that
proceed from the perpetual movements of the heavens, sing
what they see indicated in the inevitable order of Divine
Providence.") Cf. vss. 103-5.

94. *tempre*: "Modulations." Cf. *Par.* X, 146.

95. *lor = essi*. "Lor" is the subject of "compartire."   *par
che = come se*.

96. *stempre = stempri*.

97–99. *lo gel che m'era intorno . . . petto*: This continues
the figure of vss. 85-89.

98. *fessi = si fece*.

100. *pur ferma*: Beatrice is unrelenting and stands unmoved.
coscia: The *sponda sinistra* (vs. 61).

101. *le sustanze pie*: See *Conv.* II, iv, 2, where Dante re-
fers to "sustanze separate da materia, cioè intelligenze, le
quali la volgare gente chiamano Angeli" ("substances sejunct
from matter, to wit, Intelligences, which are vulgarly called
Angels").

103–5. *Voi vigilate ne l'etterno die . . . vie*: The angels keep
perpetual vigil in the Empyrean, gazing into God's light, in
which they see all things. The "everlasting day" is the eternal
present of the Empyrean, which is outside of time. Ristoro
d'Arezzo writes in *Della comp.* VII, ii, 1 (pp. 183-84): "Le
virtudi del cielo colle sue intelligenze, le quali non dormono
e vegghiano sempre sopra l'operazione del mondo." ("The
virtues of the heavens with their Intelligences do not sleep;

they are constantly watching over the functioning of the world.") Cf. *Par*. XXIX, 76-78. In *Conv*. III, vi, 4-5, Dante explains: "Ciascuno Intelletto di sopra . . . conosce quello che è sopra sè e quello che è sotto sè. Conosce adunque Iddio sì come sua cagione, conosce quello che è sotto sè sì come suo effetto." ("Every supernal intellect . . . hath knowledge of that which is above itself, and of that which is below itself. It hath knowledge, then, of God, as its cause; it hath knowledge, then, of that which is beneath it as its effect.")

103. *die* = *dì*.

104. *non fura*: Literally, "does not rob." Cf. *Inf*. XXV, 29.

105. *passo che faccia il secol per sue vie*: "Any step that the world below takes along its way," i.e., in time.

106. *è con più cura*: "Is more concerned."

107. *colui che di là piagne*: The words are clearly disdainful.

108. *d'una misura*: I.e., *della medesima misura*.

109–14. *Non pur per ovra . . . vicine*: The first of these two tercets speaks of Nature's part in generation, the second of God's, in terms of His grace. See Thomas Aquinas, *De virtutibus cardinalibus* a. 2, ad 1: "Propter inclinationem quae est ex natura, vel ex aliquo dono gratiae, quam habet aliquis magis ad opus unius virtutis quam alterius, contingit quod aliquis promptior est ad actum unius virtutis quam alterius." ("Because of the inclination which is from nature, or from some gift of grace, which some man has more power to produce its effect than does another, it comes about that one is more readily responsive to some act of virtue than is another.") Compare *Inf*. XV, 55-56, and *Par*. XXII, 112-20, as well as *Conv*. IV, xxi, 7, where Dante says:

E però che la complessione del seme puote essere migliore e men buona, e la disposizione del seminante puote essere migliore e men buona, e la disposizione del Cielo

a questo effetto puote essere buona, migliore e ottima
(la quale si varia per le constellazioni, che continua-
mente si transmutano), incontra che de l'umano seme
e di queste vertudi più pura [e men pura] anima si pro-
duce; e, secondo la sua puritade, discende in essa la
vertude intellettuale possibile che detta è, e come
detto è.

And because the complexion of the seed may be more
or less good, and the disposition of the sower may be
more or less good, and the disposition of the heaven
for the effect may be good, better or best (since it varies
by reason of the constellations which are continually
changing), it comes to pass that from the human seed,
and from these virtues, the soul is produced more or
less pure. And according to its purity there descends
into it the possible intellectual virtue, which has been
spoken of, and in the way spoken of.

112. *larghezza di grazie divine*: In *Conv*. IV, xxi, 11, Dante
writes:

Per via teologica si può dire che, poi che la somma dei-
tade, cioè Dio, vede apparecchiata la sua creatura a
ricevere del suo beneficio, tanto largamente in quella ne
mette quanto apparecchiata è a riceverne. E però che
da ineffabile caritate vegnono questi doni, e la divina
caritate sia appropriata a lo Spirito Santo, quindi è che
chiamati sono Doni di Spirito Santo.

By way of theological science it may be said that when
the supreme Deity, that is God, sees his creature pre-
pared to receive of his benefaction, he commits to it as
largely thereof as it is prepared to receive. And because
these gifts come from ineffable love, and the divine love
is appropriated to the Holy Spirit, they are thence called
gifts of the Holy Spirit.

113. *sì alti vapori*: "Such lofty mists" or "clouds," i.e.,
source and origin, in divine causality.   *piova = pioggia*.
Cf. *Par*. XIV, 27: "l'etterna ploia."

114. *nostre viste*: Beatrice speaks as one of the blessed, and she speaks to angels, who share in the vigil of the eternal day (vs. 103), and yet even they cannot see clearly the source of God's grace.

115. *ne la sua vita nova*: In his youth.

116. *virtualmente*: Cf. *Purg.* XXV, 96. *ogne abito destro*: "Every good disposition."

119. *col mal seme e non cólto = seminato con mal seme e non coltivato.*

121-23. *Alcun tempo . . . vòlto*: This tercet contains in miniature the story of the *Vita nuova,* and, though spoken here by Beatrice, it holds to the lyrical focus of that early work and sees Beatrice not as she would have seen herself, but as Dante saw her.

123. *in dritta parte vòlto*: I.e., turned toward God. Cf. *Inf.* I, 3: "la diritta via."

124-25. *Sì tosto come . . . etade*: The first age is adolescence, the second *gioventute*, as Dante explains in *Conv.* IV, xxiv, 1: "Dico che la umana vita si parte per quattro etadi. La prima si chiama Adolescenzia, cioè 'accrescimento di vita'; la seconda si chiama Gioventute, cioè 'etade che puote giovare.'" ("I say that human life is divided into four ages. The first is called adolescence, that is, the 'increasing' of life. The second is called 'manhood,' that is to say, the age of achievement.") In *Conv.* IV, xxiv, 2, Dante notes: "De la prima nullo dubita, ma ciascuno savio s'accorda ch'ella dura in fino al venticinquesimo anno." ("As to the first, no one hesitates, but every sage agrees that it lasts up to the twenty-fifth year.")

125. *e mutai vita*: According to the account in the *Vita nuova* (XXIX, 1), Beatrice died and passed to eternal glory in 1290, i.e., on the verge of her "Gioventute," or second age, being twenty-four at the time.

126. *questi si tolse a me, e diessi altrui*: The pronoun "altrui" is personal (dative), and to every reader of the *Vita*

nuova (XXXV-XXXVIII) it will recall the episode of the "gentile donna giovane e bella molto" to whom, according to the story, Dante felt strongly attracted after the death of Beatrice. But by that account this infatuation did not last long, and his love for Beatrice finally won out. Beatrice's charge is therefore not clear in its import, nor will it become any clearer for being repeated in the next canto, vss. 59-60. Perhaps the personal pronoun represents a kind of personification of the "deceptive images of good" (vs. 131 below), and it is in those terms that the same charge is repeated in *Purg.* XXXI.   *diessi = si diede.*

130. *per via non vera*: Cf. *Inf.* I, 3: "ché la diritta via era smarrita."

131. *imagini di ben seguendo false*: Compare the dream of the *antica strega, Purg.* XIX, 7-24.

132. *che nulla promession rendono intera*: Such, in fact, was the significance of all the physical defects of the woman in the dream of *Purg.* XIX. Boethius writes in a similar vein in *Consol. philos.* III, viii, ll. 1-3, 31-35:

> Nihil igitur dubium est quin hae ad beatitudinem viae devia quaedam sint nec perducere quemquam eo valeant ad quod se perducturas esse promittunt. . . . Ex quibus omnibus illud redigere in summam licet, quod haec quae nec praestare quae pollicentur bona possunt nec omnium bonorum congregatione perfecta sunt, ea nec ad beatitudinem quasi quidam calles ferunt nec beatos ipsa perficiunt.

> Wherefore there is no doubt but that these ways to happiness are only certain by-paths, which can never bring any man thither whither they promise to lead him. . . . Out of which we may briefly collect this sum; that these goods, which can neither perform that they promise, nor are perfect by having all that is good, do neither, as so many paths, lead men to happiness, nor make men happy of themselves.

In *Conv.* IV, xii, 2-4, Dante states: "E qui si vuole sapere che le cose defettive possono aver li loro difetti per modo che ne la prima faccia non paiono, ma sotto pretesto di perfezione la imperfezione si nasconde." ("And here be it known that defective things may harbour their defects in such fashion that they appear not at first sight, the imperfection hiding under a pretext of perfection.") He notes: "E quelle cose che prima non mostrano li loro difetti sono più pericolose, però che di loro molte fiate prendere guardia non si può. . . . Promettono le false traditrici sempre . . . rendere lo raunatore pieno d'ogni appagamento; e con questa promissione conducono l'umana volontade in vizio d'avarizia." ("And those things which at first conceal their defects are the most dangerous; because, in many cases, we cannot be on our guard against them. . . . The false traitoresses ever promise to make him who gathers them full of satisfaction . . . and with this promise they lead the human will to the vice of avarice.")

133. *Né l'impetrare ispirazion mi valse*: Nor did it avail me to implore and gain inspirations of God for him. One such inspiration is recounted in the *Vita nuova* (XXXIX, 1): "Contra questo avversario de la ragione si levoe un die, quasi ne l'ora de la nona, una forte imaginazione in me, che mi parve vedere questa gloriosa Beatrice con quelle vestimenta sanguigne co le quali apparve prima a li occhi miei; e pareami giovane in simile etade in quale io prima la vidi." ("Against this adversary of reason there arose one day a mighty vision within me, almost at the hour of noon; for methought I beheld this glorious Beatrice, in those crimson garments wherein she first appeared to mine eyes, and she seemed to me youthful and of an age like to that in which I first beheld her.") And, in *Vita nuova* XLII, 1, Dante tells of yet another inspiration, a "mirabile visione" ("wondrous vision") that appeared to him.

134. *in sogno e altrimenti*: Neither of the above-recounted inspirations came to Dante in a dream. According to Beatrice there were yet others sent to him in his sleep.

135. *lo rivocai*: I.e., to the true way. *sì poco a lui ne calse*: So little did it matter to him. *calse*: Past absolute form of *calere*.

136–37. *Tanto giù cadde . . . corti*: In his shameful life with Forese, for one thing. See *Purg.* XXIII, 115-17.

136. *argomenti*: "Measures." Cf. "s'argomentin," *Inf.* XXII, 21.

137. *corti*: "Insufficient."

138. *fuor che mostrarli le perdute genti*: The journey through Hell, therefore, was a necessity. Virgil implied as much when he said to Cato (*Purg.* I, 62-63) that "non li era altra via / che questa per la quale i' mi son messo." *mostrarli = mostrargli*.

139. *Per questo visitai l'uscio d'i morti*: Once again the reader is carried by such a memory back to the beginning of the poem and to *Inf.* II in particular. The phrase "uscio d'i morti," as Porena observes, renders the scriptural *portae inferi*, which in ecclesiastical usage came to stand for Hell. Beatrice descended only to Limbo, it will be recalled.

140. *colui*: Virgil.

141. *piangendo*: Once again Beatrice's tears are remembered. Cf. *Inf.* II, 116, and *Purg.* XXVII, 137.

142. *fato di Dio*: Decree of God, which is what the pagan concept of fate became in Christian doctrine. See Augustine, *De civ. Dei* V, i-ix, 4; Boethius, *Consol. philos.* IV, vi, ll. 1-86; Thomas Aquinas, *Summa theol.* I, q. 116, a. 2 and a. 4.

143. *vivanda*: The taste of the living waters of Lethe.

144. *scotto*: "Scot," i.e., payment for goods or entertainment. "Scotto di pentimento" means contrition for the backsliding with which Beatrice has charged Dante. Dante may not obtain forgetfulness of sin without first showing contrition of the heart and confession by the mouth, normally two essentials of the sacrament of penance.

CANTO XXXI

1. *fiume sacro*: The adjective signals the act of a sacrament which Dante is now undergoing, the act of penance.

2-3. *volgendo suo parlare . . . acro*: The reader will recall that Beatrice, whose speech is here compared to a sword (cf. *Purg.* XXX, 57), began her encounter with Dante by addressing him directly, calling him by his first name (*Purg.* XXX, 55), and then passed to indirect address, speaking to the angels (*Purg.* XXX, 103-45), i.e., "with the edge" of her speech. Here she returns to direct address, speaking to Dante himself "with the point" of her speech. Her accusation now is to be taken as applying only to Dante, whose name has been given "of necessity" (*Purg.* XXX, 63), and this is the necessity of that naming. Beatrice's charges are charges of backsliding and aversion of which the individual Dante, and he alone, is guilty. The Beatrice who is known to readers of the *Vita nuova* now comes prominently to the fore—a Beatrice who in that early work is *not* an allegorical figure. (See C. S. Singleton, 1954, pp. 45-60, 90-94.) However, when Dante's personal penance here before Beatrice is completed, and he is drawn across the river and led up to Beatrice by the virtues, Beatrice, by a new pose, her eyes fixed on the griffin (vss. 120-23), takes on symbolical meaning which exceeds that which she represents while she exacts penance of Dante. These are subtle changes in the framing.

3. *acro*: "Keen." Cf. *Purg.* IX, 136.

4. *cunta*: From the root of the Latin *cunctari*, "to delay."

5. *questo*: All the foregoing accusation (*Purg.* XXX, 109-38).

6. *tua confession*: The term is clear and points to the act of confession by the lips, *confessio oris*, which is the second act of penance, following contrition of the heart, *contritio cordis* (see *Purg.* XXX, 85-99), and without which remission of sins is normally not possible in the Church.

9. *li organi suoi*: The throat and the mouth.

10. *Poco sofferse*: Beatrice waits, i.e., endures this, for only a moment. "Poco" here has its negative meaning, i.e., "but little."

11. *Rispondi a me*: The sternness of Beatrice's tone continues in the use of the disjunctive "me" with its emphasis. *Rispondimi*, as Torraca observes, would have quite another meaning.

12. *acqua*: The water of Lethe.   *offense*: "Made dim," "canceled," or, more literally, "impaired."

14. *sì*: Dante's "sì" is the beginning of his actual confession admitting to the truth of Beatrice's charges. The rest of the confession is contained in the single tercet of vss. 34-36.

15. *al quale intender fuor mestier le viste*: Only by seeing the movement of his lips could one understand his faint "sì" as such.   *fuor mestier = furono mestiere*.

16–17. *Come balestro frange . . . l'arco*: "Corda" and "arco" are objects of "frange." Porena notes that the crossbow could be cranked up mechanically to a tension far greater than that possible with the ordinary hand-drawn bow. The simile is one that finds its allusive relevance in being precisely one of a "breaking," the literal meaning of *contritio*, so that contrition of the heart is here continued into the act of confession. On the literal meaning of *contritio*, see Thomas Aquinas, *Summa theol.* III, Suppl., q. 1, a. 1, resp.:

Respondeo dicendum, quod ut dicitur Eccli. 10, 15, *Initium omnis peccati est superbia,* per quam homo sensui suo inhaerens, a mandatis divinis recedit. Et ideo oportet quod illud quod destruit peccatum, hominem a proprio sensu discedere faciat; ille autem qui in suo sensu perseverat, rigidus, et durus per similitudinem vocatur; sicut durum in materialibus dicitur quod non cedit tactui: unde et frangi dicitur aliquis quando a suo sensu divellitur. Sed inter fractionem, et comminutionem, sive contritionem in rebus materialibus unde haec nomina ad spiritualia transferuntur hoc interest, ut dicitur in 4 Meteor. (cap. 7 et 9), quod frangi dicuntur aliqua quando in magnas partes dividuntur, sed comminui, vel conteri, quando ad partes minimas reducitur hoc quod in se solidum erat. Et quia ad dimissionem peccati requiritur quod affectum peccati homo totaliter dimittat, quem per quamdam continuitatem et soliditatem in sensu suo habebat; ideo actus ille quo peccatum dimittitur, contritio dicitur per similitudinem. . . . Alia autem definitio invenitur Isidori, lib. 2, de sum. Bono, cap. 12 quae talis est: *Contritio est compunctio et humilitas mentis cum lacrymis veniens de recordatione peccati et timore iudicii.* Et haec quidem tangit rationem nominis in hoc quod dicit *humilitas mentis:* quia sicut per superbiam aliquis in suo sensu redditur rigidus, ita per hoc quod a suo sensu contritus recedit, humiliatur. Tangit etiam modum exteriorem in hoc quod dicit *cum lacrymis*; et principium contritionis in hoc quod dicit; *veniens de recordatione peccati* etc. Alia sumitur ex verbis Augustini (implic. sup. psalm. 46, ante med.), quae tangit effectum contritionis, quae est: *Contritio est dolor remittens peccatum.*

I answer that, As stated in Ecclus. x. 15, *pride is the beginning of all sin,* because thereby man clings to his

own judgment, and strays from the Divine command-
ments. Consequently that which destroys sin must needs
make man give up his own judgment. Now he that per-
sists in his own judgment, is called metaphorically rigid
and hard even as what in material things is called hard
is that which does not yield to the touch: wherefore
anyone is said to be broken when he is torn from his
own judgment. But, in material things, whence these ex-
pressions are transferred to spiritual things, there is a dif-
ference between breaking and crushing or contrition, as
stated in *Meteor.* iv, in that we speak of breaking when
a thing is sundered into large parts, but of crushing
or contrition when that which was in itself solid is re-
duced to minute particles [see Aristotle, *Meteor.* iv, 9,
386ᵃ]. And since, for the remission of sin, it is neces-
sary that man should put aside entirely his attachment
to sin, which implies a certain state of continuity and
solidity in his mind, therefore it is that the act through
which sin is cast aside is called contrition meta-
phorically. . . . Another definition is given by Isidore
(*De Sum. Bono*, ii. 12) as follows: *Contrition is a tear-
ful sorrow and humility of mind, arising from remem-
brance of sin and fear of the Judgment.* Here we have
an allusion to the derivation of the word, when it is said
that it is *humility of the mind*, because just as pride
makes the mind rigid, so is a man humbled, when con-
trition leads him to give up his mind. Also the external
manner is indicated by the word *tearful*, and the origin
of contrition, by the words, *arising from remembrance
of sin*, etc.—Another definition is taken from the words
of Augustine (implicitly, on Ps. xlvi[xlvii]), and indi-
cates the effect of contrition. It runs thus: *Contrition is
the sorrow which takes away sin.*

One may perhaps see more clearly, looking back, that the
simile of melting snow in *Purg.* XXX, 85-90, also alludes to
the literal sense of *contritio* as Thomas Aquinas represents
it. A "breaking up" of ice there, a "breaking" of a crossbow
here, and, in a third simile, an "uprooting" (vss. 70-72) all

reflect the sense intended by Thomas Aquinas. The first few questions of the treatise on penance of the *Summa theologica* were written by Thomas Aquinas just before his death, and the *Summa* was then continued probably by Fra Rainaldo da Piperno and was based on Aquinas' earlier commentary on the fourth book of the *Sentences* of Peter Lombard; this section, from which the above quotation is taken, is commonly termed the *Supplementum* to the *Summa theologica*.

16. *balestro = balestra*. Cf. *Inf.* XXXI, 83.

17. *da troppa tesa*: From excessive tension or strain.

19. *sottesso*: This might be written *sott'esso*. *Esso* (from the Latin *ipsum*) intensifies the meaning: "under that very charge."

21. *e la voce allentò per lo suo varco*: Cf. Virgil, *Aen.* XI, 151: "Et via vix tandem voci laxata dolore est." ("And scarce from sorrow at the last does his speech find open way.")   *allentò*: Here used intransitively.

22. *i mie' disiri*: "Desires for me." For this use of the possessive, see vs. 54: "suo disio."

23–24. *che ti menavano . . . s'aspiri*: This "bene" is, by definition, God, since only in Him can our desires and our love find rest and so have no need to aspire further. Vss. 22-24 hark back to Beatrice's role in Dante's life as recounted in the *Vita nuova* and seem to sum up that narrative in three verses.

25. *quai fossi attraversati o quai catene*: Grandgent comments that the reference is to the obstacles used to prevent the passage of a hostile army or fleet. Beatrice's charge is that such obstacles caused Dante to despair of his further advance toward God. The barring of the gates of the city of Dis, in Inferno (*Inf.* VIII, 82–IX, 105), represents in allegory the danger of despair caused by such obstacles.   *fossi attraversati*: "Cross-ditches." For the word *attraversato* used in this sense, see *Inf.* XXIII, 118.   *catene*: Chains such as barred the gates of cities.

27. *dovessiti = ti dovessi.*

28. *quali agevolezze o quali avanzi*: Porena notes that the two terms are the opposites of "fossi attraversati" and "catene" (vs. 25). As Torraca (followed by others) observes, the terms *agevolezza* and *avanzo* may belong to the language of merchants and merchandising, but as used here they take on somewhat different meanings better understood respectively as *agi* ("comforts") and *miglioramenti* ("gains"). Torraca quotes the following passage from Fra Giordano in which "agevolezza" appears. See Fra Giordano, *Prediche inedite* XX (p. 113): "Se Iddio ti trae di tribulazione od angoscia, e ponti in istato di riposo od agevolezza" ("if God takes you from tribulation or suffering, and puts you in the condition of rest or ease"). Boccaccio uses "avanzi" in the sense here intended in *Decam.* X, 9 (vol. II, p. 291, l. 4).

29. *ne la fronte de li altri*: *Beni* is understood ("ne la fronte de li altri beni"), "goods" other than the supreme good named in vss. 23-24. In "fronte" (literally, "forehead") a personification is suggested, which anticipates the "serene" (Sirens) of vs. 45, and is carried further here by the phrase "lor passeggiare anzi" in vs. 30.

30. *per che = per cui.   dovessi lor passeggiare anzi*: This should be construed as "dovessi passeggiare davanti a loro." The personification of the "other" goods continues. It was Bernardino Daniello (in his commentary of 1568) who first proposed that the phrase "passeggiare anzi" should be understood in the sense of "to court," i.e., by passing frequently back and forth before the house of the lady love, a standard custom, certainly, of lovers in Dante's time as later. M. Barbi (1934b, p. 284) has championed this meaning, with many references to support it.

31. *tratta*: Noun derived from *trarre*, here in the sense of "to heave."

34. *Le presenti cose*: "Present things" refer to things that were before Dante's eyes and his mind's eye after Beatrice's death, as her face no longer was. "Presenti" is thus opposed

to Beatrice's *absent* beauty, which once led toward God (vss. 23-24).

35. *col falso lor piacer*: "With their false pleasure," but perhaps also their false beauty. *Piacere* in Dante's usage lends itself to this ambiguity (cf. *Inf.* V, 104; *Purg.* XVIII, 21 and 27). The "piacer" of present things anticipates and opposes Beatrice's "piacer" (vs. 50), where again the ambiguity of the term continues.   *volser miei passi*: "Turned my steps aside" from the straight way and, perhaps, into the dark wood of *Inf.* I, 1-3.

36. *vostro viso*: It is clear from these first words in direct address to Beatrice that Dante will use the respectful second person plural, *voi*, in speaking to her, whereas she has already addressed him with the familiar *tu*. In the early Italian love lyric and in Dante's early poems it is customary for the poet-lover to address *madonna* with the respectful *voi*. Dante continues now to observe such usage and will do so until the very last words of address to Beatrice, in *Par.* XXXI, 79-90. Readers of the present translation, in which the English *thou* has not been used, should bear Dante's usage in mind, confirming it in the Italian text.

38. *fora = sarebbe.*

39. *da tal giudice*: By God, who sees all things and through whom the blessed in the heavenly court can see and know many things, as will be made abundantly clear in the *Paradiso*.

40. *gota*: Grandgent proposes that "the use of *gota*, 'cheek,' instead of 'lips,' was perhaps suggested, not only by the rime, but also by the idea of the blush of shame that accompanies the words."

41. *in nostra corte*: In the heavenly court, where Beatrice and the angels abide.

42. *rivolge sé contra 'l taglio la rota*: Grandgent comments: "The sword of justice is blunted, i.e., tempered with mercy."

43. *mo*: "Now."   *porte* = [*tu*] *porti* (subjunctive).

45. *le serene*: The allurements of the world and of the flesh, as they offer a pleasure that is false in its promise. Cf. the dream of the self-declared Siren in *Purg.* XIX, 19-24, and see Dante's *Epist.* V, 13: "Nec seducat alludens cupiditas, more Sirenum nescio qua dulcedine vigiliam rationis mortificans." ("Nor let illusive greed seduce you, siren-like, doing to death, by some charm, the vigil of reason.") On this reference to the Sirens Grandgent observes:

> On the completion of Dante's confession Beatrice rebukes him once more, "that he may be stronger another time when he hears the sirens" (ll. 44-5). It will be remembered that in Dante's second dream a siren (XIX, 19) represented the sins of the flesh. On the other hand, in [Boethius] *Consolatio Philosophiae*, I, Pr. i [ll. 39-41], in a situation somewhat analogous to the one under discussion, Philosophy, finding the exiled and imprisoned author in the company of the muses of poetry, drives them away, saying: "Sed abite potius, *Sirenes* usque in exitium dulces, meisque eum Musis curandum [sanandumque] relinquite" ["rather get you gone, you Sirens pleasant even to destruction, and leave him to my Muses to be cured and healed"]—the sirens of poetry must yield the place to the muses of philosophy. Beatrice's "sirens," then, can be used on either side of the argument.

46. *il seme del piangere*: Grandgent notes that this odd phrase is evidently due to a reminiscence of Ps. 125[126]:5, "qui seminant in lacrimis, in exultatione metent" ("those that sow in tears shall reap rejoicing"), and he points out that P. Rajna (1928), p. 306, cites the first line of a riddle, perhaps of the eighth century, of Anglo-Saxon provenience: "candida virgo suas lacrimas dum seminat atras" ("while the fair virgin sows her bitter tears").

48. *mover dovieti*: I.e., "ti avrebbe dovuto muovere." *dovieti* = *ti doveva*.

50. *piacer*: A "beauty" or perhaps (see n. to vs. 35) a "delight," but the meaning "beauty" seems predominant, as Beatrice's "piacer" is said to surpass any created by nature or by art. "Piacer," two verses later, continues with the meaning "beauty" as the predominant sense.

51. *so' 'n = sono in.* *'n terra sparte*: Cf. Gen. 3:19: "in pulverem reverteris" ("unto dust you shall return").

52. *'l sommo piacer*: Beatrice's surpassing beauty. *fallio = fallì.* The verb means "failed," but it anticipates the adjective "fallaci," meaning "deceitful," in vs. 56: even Beatrice's beauty could prove to be fallacious, like all mortal things.

54. *nel suo disio*: "Into desire of it." For this use of the possessive, cf. vs. 22.

55–56. *lo primo strale de le cose fallaci*: The first arrow is clearly the failure of Beatrice's supreme beauty, which proved, through her death, to be a fallacious mortal thing. Cf. Virgil, *Aen.* IV, 17: "postquam primus amor deceptam morte fefellit" ("since my first love, turning traitor, cheated me by death").

57. *tale*: I.e., deceptive, as mortal things prove to be. Beatrice speaks as the immortal soul that she now is, divested by death of her mortal body that was once so beautiful.

58. *dovea gravar*: The subjects of "dovea gravar" are "pargoletta" and "altra novità" of vss. 59 and 60.

59. *pargoletta*: The lady of Dante's *Rime* LXXXVII and LXXXIX is called *pargoletta*, as is the lady of one of his *rime petrose* (so called because they were written about a lady who was hard as *pietra*, "stone"), *Rime* C. See *Rime* LXXXVII, 1; LXXXIX, 2; C, 72. Momigliano observes that this term seems to be the specification of the "altrui" of *Purg.* XXX, 126, but adds that it is a specification that continues to remain in the nature of allusion and that the poet could not have gone beyond such a term, a kind of *senhal*, without lowering this scene of high rebuke to one of a worldly jealousy.

60. *novità*: Many MSS, followed by modern editors, have
"vanità," but Petrocchi argues persuasively for the reading
"novità." Both terms in the context of Beatrice's reproaches
are more or less synonymous.   *breve uso*: "Brief dura-
tion," i.e., in the pleasure it can offer.

61. *Novo*: "Young."   *augelletto*: I.e., *uccelletto*. The
diminutive suffix adds to the "youth" of the bird.   *due o
tre aspetta*: It takes at least two or three shots (see vs. 59)
to teach the fledgling to be cautious.

62–63. *ma dinanzi . . . saetta*: Cf. Prov. 1:17: "Frustra
autem iacitur rete ante oculos pennatorum." ("It is in vain
that a net is spread before the eyes of any bird.") Also see
Eccles. 7:27[26].

62. *dinanzi da = dinanzi a.*   *pennuti*: "Full-fledged,"
i.e., experienced.

64–67. *Quali fanciulli . . . io*: Through this metaphor
Dante's bearing before Beatrice continues to be that of a
child toward his mother, as in *Purg.* XXX, 79.

65. *stannosi = si stanno.* The reflexive here is the familiar
pleonastic *si* in its distancing function, continued in the "mi"
of vs. 67.

66. *sé riconoscendo*: "Recognizing their fault." *Riconos-
cersi* in early Italian is frequently used in this meaning.

67. *Quando*: "Since."

68. *barba*: Grandgent notes that Dante is apparently play-
ing on the double sense of "beard" and "chin" that *barba*
had in many regions in the Middle Ages, and he cites
A. Sepulcri (1910), pp. 191-94, concerning this.

70–73. *Con men di resistenza . . . il mento*: This is the third
simile which draws on the literal meaning of *contritio* as a
"breaking up" or "uprooting" (see n. to vss. 16-17) and
therefore conveys the meaning that contrition of the heart,
which is often termed the first stage of the sacrament of pen-

ance, continues here through confession (and beyond—see vss. 86-89). The construction "con men di resistenza . . . ch'io non levai al suo comando il mento" is elliptical and in full statement would be "con men di resistenza di quella con cui io levai al suo comando il mento."

71. *nostral*: "Native," coming from our pole, i.e., from the north, as opposed to the south wind, from Africa.

72. *Iarba*: Iarbas, or Hiarbas, was king of the Gaetulians in North Africa at the time Dido founded Carthage; he was among those who sued in vain for her hand (Virgil, *Aen.* IV, 36, 196, 326; Ovid, *Fasti* III, 552-54).

75. *il velen de l'argomento*: The "venom of her speech" consists in the implication that the beard, the plumage of the full-fledged (cf. *Purg.* I, 42), is inconsistent with Dante's childish posture, as in vss. 64-66.

76-81. *E come la mia faccia . . . nature*: There is a notable change of scene at this point, signaled by the angels' ceasing to strew flowers and, even more strikingly, by Beatrice's new pose, as she turns away from Dante (signifying that contrition and confession are now finished) to gaze fixedly upon the griffin. Such a manner of changing scene in these cantos of the procession has been noted before (see n. to *Purg.* XXX, 9) and will continue.

77-78. *posarsi quelle prime creature . . . comprese*: The angels are "primal creatures" because they were created first among creatures by God. Cf. *Inf.* VII, 95.

79. *le mie luci*: My eyes.   *poco sicure*: Tearful still and timid for shame.

80. *volta in su la fiera*: Referring to the griffin.

81. *una persona in due nature*: Cf. *Purg.* XXIX, 113-14, where the two natures of the "twofold animal" (vs. 122) are first indicated, it being, literally, part eagle and part lion. Now, of course, the animal is seen in its symbolic meaning as Christ, who is one person in two natures.

83. *pariemi* = *mi pareva*.

84. *vincer che l'altre qui*: "Than she surpassed all other women." "Vincer" is insistently repeated.

85–89. *Di penter . . . vinto*: The act of penance clearly continues still in this climax of contrition, Dante's falling here carrying out the simile of the robust oak's uprooting and consequent fall. Grandgent observes that "this swoon evidently represents *satisfaction*, the last stage of the sacrament of penance." But this is quite possibly not so, since this particular act of penance here before Beatrice can have as its third stage that of absolution, that of being taken through the stream of Lethe to the blessed shore and then led to Beatrice by the two groups of virtues.

85. *penter* (pronounced *pentèr*) = *pentere*, from the Latin *poenitere*. *Pentere* was often used in early Italian instead of *pentire*. Cf. *Inf.* XXVII, 119.   *ivi*: Though commonly spatial in meaning, the adverb also bears a temporal meaning here.

86. *qual mi torse*: "Whatsoever one had drawn me."

87. *nel suo amor*: "In love of it." For this use of the possessive, see vss. 22 and 54.

88. *riconoscenza*: "Recognition" of sin or guilt.

89. *femmi* = *mi fei*, i.e., *mi feci*.

90. *salsi* = *se lo sa*. Cf. *Purg.* V, 135.

91. *virtù di fuor*: "My outward faculties," my sense of outward things. It was believed that when a person fainted, the blood flowed back to the heart from all the other organs, suspending their activity. Cf. n. to *Inf.* I, 20 and *Rime* CIII, 45-47:

> e 'l sangue, ch'è per le vene disperso,
> fuggendo corre verso
> lo cor, che 'l chiama; ond'io rimango bianco.

And the blood, all scattered through the veins, flees running towards the heart that summons it, and I am left all blanched.

rendemmi = mi rendè.

92. *la donna ch'io avea trovata sola*: This lady, whom Dante first met alone (*Purg.* XXVIII, 40), has been on the scene for some time now, but still has not been named, and she is not to be named until quite near the end of this *cantica* (*Purg.* XXXIII, 119). Her name, Matelda, leaves serious problems of interpretation, as will be noted. For the moment, it appears that it is Matelda's function to administer the water of the two streams Lethe and Eunoe to all souls reaching this summit as well as to Dante in this most exceptional case of a living man's presence here. (See *Purg.* XXXIII, 134-35, where Statius is invited by Matelda to drink of the second stream.)

Statius was last seen (*Purg.* XXVIII, 146) before Virgil departed the scene (see *Purg.* XXX, 49), and as Dante's encounter with Beatrice became a personal encounter (as the reader well understands by now), no further mention of Statius' presence on the scene has been made. His crossing of Lethe is not mentioned, but we learn that all souls reaching this summit must drink of both the streams (*Purg.* XXVIII, 131-32). He must therefore *drink* of Lethe, but just how he *crosses* that stream is not told. There will be no question of crossing Eunoe, but only of drinking of it.

Statius' presence throughout all this part of the poem is a most valuable exegetical guide, for we know from what he does, and does not do, just what every soul that reaches the summit must do. In addition to this, we know that it is Matelda's function to administer the water of the two streams to *all* souls who reach this summit. But since Beatrice pays no attention to Statius and he is left out of view in the whole episode of the three cantos of Beatrice's triumph (*Purg.* XXIX-XXXI), we also know that Beatrice's coming is for the living man Dante *only* and is not for each and every soul reaching the summit—in fact, it is never repeated for them. This is extremely valuable in guiding us to the right focus on

Beatrice's advent in its total significance and the *limits* of its import.

93. *sopra me*: As will be seen from the following verse, Dante and Matelda have begun to cross the river. Matelda walks on the surface of the water, and Dante is immersed. She is above him in this sense.   *Tiemmi* = *tienimi*, imperative.

96. *sovresso l'acqua*: Over the very surface of the water, *esso* (Latin *ipsum*) added to *sovra* serving to stress this.
scola: "Shuttle," as used in weaving, which is indeed very light and passes back and forth on the very surface of the fabric being woven. Some texts have "spola," the more usual form for "shuttle," but the word *scola* also existed in this meaning (as it still does in Tuscan speech) and has been accepted by Petrocchi (see his note).

97. *beata riva*: A shore called "blessed" clearly points to this far shore as a blessed goal in the journey, so that crossing over to it can seem to be a crossing to some promised land or to Eden proper (see C. S. Singleton, 1958, pp. 254-87). The reader will recall that the stream itself is called a "fiume sacro" in the opening verse of this present canto. This crossing over and the attainment of the far shore and Beatrice complete a total pattern of justification, as the reader may now see in retrospect. See C. S. Singleton (1958), pp. 57-121.

98. *"Asperges me" sì dolcemente udissi*: See Ps. 50:9 [51:7]: "Asperges me hyssopo, et mundabor; lavabis me, et super nivem dealbabor." ("Cleanse me of sin with hyssop, that I may be purified; wash me, and I shall be whiter than snow.") The angels presumably sing this. The *Ottimo Commento* has an enlightening comment here: "Questo *Asperges* . . . si dice quando per lo prete si gitta l'acqua benedetta sopra il confesso peccatore, il quale elli assolve." ("This 'Asperges' . . . is pronounced when the priest sprinkles the holy water on the sinner who has confessed himself, thus absolving him.")

Dante's crossing of Lethe, immersed therein, is therefore the absolution which completes the act of penance as well as the pattern of justification. Dante is now absolved of his sins, has confessed to Beatrice, and may be led up to her by her handmaids, the seven virtues. His drinking of Lethe, which Matelda will force him to do (vss. 101-2), is not part of this pattern, but is that which he and Statius and every soul that reaches this summit must do. The reader will do well to distinguish this drinking and its significance from the immersion, as in a kind of baptism (but not an actual baptism, for the sacrament of baptism is not to be repeated). Baptism absolves from the guilt of original sin, penance from that of personal sin, and it is personal sin for which Dante has felt contrition and to which he has confessed. It should be remembered that the whole act of penance now completed was announced by Matelda (see her words of *Purg.* XXIX, 3: "Beati quorum tecta sunt peccata"). When Dante comes forth from the water of Lethe, his sins will be "covered," forgiven and remitted.

In this connection it is illuminating to consider more of the fiftieth psalm than simply the verse cited. It is a prayer of repentance, in which David asks the Lord for mercy and forgiveness of his sins. See Ps. 50:1-20[51:1-18]:

> In finem. Psalmus David, cum venit ad eum Nathan propheta, quando intravit ad Bethsabee. Miserere mei, Deus, secundum magnam misericordiam tuam; et secundum multitudinem miserationum tuarum dele iniquitatem meam. Amplius lava me ab iniquitate mea, et a peccato meo munda me. Quoniam iniquitatem meam ego cognosco, et peccatum meum contra me est semper. Tibi soli peccavi, et malum coram te feci, ut iustificeris in sermonibus tuis, et vincas cum iudicaris. Ecce enim in iniquitatibus conceptus sum, et in peccatis concepit me mater mea. Ecce enim veritatem dilexisti, incerta et occulta sapientiae tuae manifestasti mihi. Asperges me hyssopo, et mundabor; lavabis me, et super nivem dealbabor. Auditui meo dabis gaudium et laetitiam, et exultabunt ossa humiliata. Averte faciem tuam a pecca-

tis meis, et omnes iniquitates meas dele. Cor mundum crea in me, Deus; et spiritum rectum innova in visceribus meis. Ne proiicias me a facie tua, et spiritum sanctum tuum ne auferas a me. Redde mihi laetitiam salutaris tui, et spiritu principali confirma me. Docebo iniquos vias tuas, et impii ad te convertentur. Libera me de sanguinibus, Deus, Deus salutis meae, et exultabit lingua mea iustitiam tuam. Domine, labia mea aperies; et os meum annuntiabit laudem tuam. Quoniam si voluisses sacrificium, dedissem utique; holocaustis non delectaberis. Sacrificium Deo spiritus contribulatus; cor contritum et humiliatum, Deus, non despicies. Benigne fac, Domine, in bona voluntate tua Sion, ut aedificentur muri Ierusalem.

For the leader. A psalm of David, when Nathan the prophet came to him after his sin with Bethsabee.

Have mercy on me, O God, in your goodness; in the greatness of your compassion wipe out my offense. Thoroughly wash me from my guilt and of my sin cleanse me.

For I acknowledge my offense, and my sin is before me always: "Against you only have I sinned, and done what is evil in your sight"—that you may be justified in your sentence, vindicated when you condemn. Indeed, in guilt was I born, and in sin my mother conceived me; behold, you are pleased with sincerity of heart, and in my inmost being you teach me wisdom.

Cleanse me of sin with hyssop, that I may be purified; wash me, and I shall be whiter than snow. Let me hear the sounds of joy and gladness; the bones you have crushed shall rejoice. Turn away your face from my sins, and blot out all my guilt.

A clean heart create for me, O God, and a steadfast spirit renew within me. Cast me not out from your presence, and your holy spirit take not from me. Give me back the joy of your salvation, and a willing spirit sustain in me.

I will teach transgressors your ways, and sinners shall

return to you. Free me from blood guilt, O God, my saving God: then my tongue shall revel in your justice. O Lord, open my lips, and my mouth shall proclaim your praise. For you are not pleased with sacrifices; should I offer a holocaust, you would not accept it. My sacrifice, O God, is a contrite spirit; a heart contrite and humbled, O God, you will not spurn.

Be bountiful, O Lord, to Sion in your kindness by rebuilding the walls of Jerusalem.

99. *non ch'io lo scriva*: "Far less write it," i.e., far less would I know how to describe such beauty.

100. *aprissi = si aprì.*

101. *abbracciommi = mi abbracciò.*

101-2. *mi sommerse . . . inghiottissi*: For this drinking of Lethe, as distinguishable in its meaning from the bathing in that river, see n. to vs. 98. Drinking of the water of Lethe takes away the memory of sin, even as drinking of the river Eunoe restores the memory of every good deed (*Purg.* XXVIII, 127-29).

103. *Indi*: The adverb here bears a temporal rather than a spatial meaning ("then," rather than "thence").

103-4. *bagnato m'offerse . . . belle*: "Bathed" stresses the line of meaning that has to do with purification and the remission of sins, as the wayfarer is now led to Beatrice's handmaids, the virtues who came at the left wheel of her chariot, which is the wheel nearest the stream (Beatrice, it will be recalled, came to the left side of the chariot to speak to Dante across the stream: *Purg.* XXX, 61).

104. *le quattro belle*: These are the infused cardinal virtues, as their purple color declares (see n. to *Purg.* XXIX, 131). In attaining to them, Dante is completing the process of "justification of the ungodly" (on this pattern of meaning, see C. S. Singleton, 1958, pp. 162-67, and *passim*).

105. *e ciascuna del braccio mi coperse*: The four maidens have Dante at the center of their dance now, and each reaches her arm over him, all presumably clasping hands over his head as they dance around him, forming as it were a sort of crown over him, so that he can be seen to receive the four infused cardinal virtues as a crown. The crown which Virgil offered was that of the acquired cardinal virtues (though this was not explicitly stated). See C. S. Singleton (1958), pp. 65-69, and *passim*.

106. *nel ciel siamo stelle*: Now, for the first time since these four stars were first seen and were left obscure in their meaning (*Purg.* I, 23-24), we are given an insight into their significance. On this declared identification of the four maidens here with the four stars there mentioned and the entire pattern of meaning which emerges in consequence, see C. S. Singleton (1958), pp. 159-83.

107-8. *pria che Beatrice . . . ancelle*: These four infused virtues were assigned to Beatrice as her handmaids before she "descended to the world." The same statement might, of course, be made by the three theological virtues who dance at the other wheel, for as a group of seven in all, they clearly bring out one of Beatrice's meanings or names in this pageant, namely, Sapientia, or Wisdom. The Biblical seven pillars of Wisdom have become seven handmaids. On this whole pattern of meaning, see C. S. Singleton (1958), pp. 122-38, and *passim*.

The scriptural figure of Sapientia is presented chiefly in the books of Wisdom, Ecclesiasticus, and Proverbs, called therefore the sapiential books of the Bible. It is in Prov. 9:1 that we read: "Sapientia aedificavit sibi domum, excidit columnas septem." ("Wisdom has built her house, she has set up her seven columns.") Just before this (Prov. 8:22-23) we read the words which Wisdom speaks of herself: "Dominus possedit me in initio viarum suarum antequam quidquam faceret a principio; ab aeterno ordinata sum, et ex antiquis antequam terra fieret." ("The Lord begot me, the first-born of his ways, the forerunner of his prodigies of long ago; from of old I was poured forth, at the first, before the earth.")

The figure of Sapientia, in the Bible, is indeed a mysterious and somewhat puzzling one for Christian theologians, and Beatrice, in assuming the name of Wisdom (among her other names), takes on some of that mystery, as in these verses of the *Purgatorio*. Her descent to the world, as Wisdom, was after the world was made! And her handmaids were appointed to attend her in her descent to the world. On the other hand, Beatrice here is always the Beatrice of the *Vita nuova* as well, in which she does not take on the name of Sapientia by any implication but in which (in *Vita nuova* X, 2) she is declared to be the "regina de le vertudi" ("queen of the virtues") and (in *Vita nuova* XXVI, 6) "una cosa venuta / da cielo in terra a miracol mostrare" ("a thing come from heaven to earth, to show forth a miracle"). Dante worked with the figure of Wisdom in the *Convivio* and then fused that figure with Beatrice as she is in the *Divine Comedy*. On the complexities of meaning involved, see C. S. Singleton (1954), pp. 92-94.

109. *Merrenti* = *ti meneremo*.

110. *dentro*: In Beatrice's eyes.

111. *le tre di là, che miran più profondo*: "The three on the other side" are those who came dancing at the right wheel of the chariot (see *Purg.* XXIX, 121-29 and nn. to these verses) and are the theological virtues, as distinguished from the four cardinal virtues. The theological virtues, as stars in the sky visible at night in Purgatory (*Purg.* VIII, 85-93), are contemplative virtues, whereas the cardinal virtues are active virtues. The three therefore see more deeply than do the four. In terms of rising to Heaven, as Dante states the matter in the *Convivio* (III, xiv, 15), the three theological virtues are the means or way by which we rise: "per le quali tre virtudi si sale a filosofare a quelle Atene celestiali" ("by which three virtues we rise to philosophise in that celestial Athens"). See C. S. Singleton (1958), pp. 163-67, and *passim*.

112. *cominciaro* = *cominciarono*.

113. *al petto del grifon seco menarmi*: Dante is led to a position facing the griffin and accordingly is now in front of the chariot. This represents a marked change of scene in this pageant, with Beatrice now striking a new pose. The virtues lead Dante to a position from which Beatrice will be seen as Revelation. *seco menarmi = mi menarono con sé.*

114. *ove Beatrice stava volta a noi*: Beatrice originally was standing on the left side of the chariot (*Purg.* XXX, 61), but she now has come to the front of it and faces toward Dante, though her eyes, as is then clear, are actually fixed on the griffin. Such is the new pose and new frame of symbolic meaning.

116. *li smeraldi*: The eyes of Beatrice are called emeralds in a symbolic sense only, and yet vs. 117 brings in the Beatrice of the *Vita nuova*. The two verses thus serve as a good example of the fusion of the Beatrice of the *Vita nuova* with the figure of Lady Philosophy of the *Convivio* (see C. S. Singleton, 1954, pp. 92-94; 1958, pp. 122-38).

119. *strinsermi = mi strinsero.*

120. *che pur sopra 'l grifone stavan saldi*: Beatrice, with her eyes fixed on the griffin, is now "acting out" her meaning as Revelation, her eyes being fixed upon Christ alone, as represented by the griffin in its dual nature, eagle and lion.

121-23. *Come in lo specchio . . . reggimenti*: Beatrice's eyes, through the simile, become a mirror through which we may "see" one of the deepest—perhaps *the* deepest—mysteries of the Christian faith: Christ as God and Christ as man, two natures in one person. For this *kind* of vision in this life, Paul's words are fundamental (I Cor. 13:12): "Videmus nunc per speculum in aenigmate." ("We see now through a mirror in an obscure manner.") It should be noted also, since Sapientia remains (along with Revelation) one of the names of Beatrice, that in Sapien. 7:26 Sapientia is termed a mirror of the majesty of God.

122. *la doppia fiera*: The griffin, which literally is part eagle and part lion (see *Purg.* XXIX, 108, 113-14) and which symbolically is Christ in His two natures.

123. *or con altri, or con altri reggimenti*: Through the mirror of Revelation Christ's two natures can be glimpsed, not *together* in one person, but alternately, now one, now the other. The mystery of their oneness remains, a mystery which will prove to be the last gazed upon in the poem, in *Par.* XXXIII, 127-45, where the seeing is face to face and recalls more of the words of Paul (I Cor. 13:12): "Videmus nunc per speculum in aenigmate, tunc autem facie ad faciem." ("We see now through a mirror in an obscure manner, but then face to face.") It is also relevant to remember that these words of Paul come in a context of love (charity), indeed are followed immediately (I Cor. 13:12-13) by: "Nunc cognosco ex parte, tunc autem cognoscam sicut et cognitus sum. Nunc autem manent fides, spes, caritas, tria haec; maior autem horum est caritas." ("Now I know in part, but then I shall know even as I have been known. So there abide faith, hope and charity, these three; but the greatest of these is charity.")

"Altri . . . altri," as a construction, is modeled on the Latin *alteri . . . alteri*, rather than on *uni . . . alteri*. "Reggimenti" is somewhat mysterious in its meaning here: "mode," "actions," and "conduct" are all possible translations. But the term clearly suggests that the glimpse through Revelation of now one and now the other is a glimpse of something in action, not simply a static vision of now one nature and now the other. This is borne out by the verb "si trasmutava" in vs. 126.

125. *la cosa in sé star queta*: "The thing in itself" is, of course, the griffin, which remains unchanged and motionless as Dante looks across it as he gazes into Beatrice's eyes.

126. *ne l'idolo suo*: In the image of the griffin, mirrored in Beatrice's eyes, which does reveal itself now in the one mode, now in the other.

128-29. *di quel cibo . . . asseta*: The phrasing here clearly echoes what Sapientia says of herself in Ecclus. 24:29: "Qui edunt me adhuc esurient, et qui bibunt me adhuc sitient." ("He who eats of me will hunger still, he who drinks of me will thirst for more.") This echo brings out even more clearly the fact that one of the names of Beatrice is indeed Sapientia. See C. S. Singleton (1958), pp. 122-38.

130. *tribo*: From the Latin *tribus*. This is a noun that is masculine in early Italian, but feminine in modern Italian: *la tribù*.

131. *fero = fecero*.

132. *caribo*: A kind of dance music, not the dance itself. Cf. the Provençal *garip*.

134. *sua = loro*.   *al tuo fedele*: Dante is called Beatrice's "faithful" one now, as one whose sins of backsliding have been forgiven. He was termed a faithful one at the beginning of the poem (*Inf.* II, 97-99) by Mary.

135. *che, per vederti, ha mossi passi tanti*: This points to Beatrice as the goal of the journey so far. The phrase "passi tanti" indicates the entire journey through Inferno and the long hard climb up from the center of the earth to Purgatory.

136. *noi = a noi*.   *disvele = diveli* (subjunctive).

138. *la seconda bellezza*: Grandgent notes that the first beauty is the eyes and the second is the mouth, and he calls attention to Dante's words in *Conv.* III, xv, 2-3:

> E qui si conviene sapere che li occhi de la Sapienza sono le sue demonstrazioni, con le quali si vede la veritade certissimamente; e lo suo riso sono le sue persuasioni, ne le quali si dimostra la luce interiore de la Sapienza sotto alcuno velamento: e in queste due cose si sente quel piacere altissimo di beatitudine, lo quale è massimo bene in Paradiso. Questo piacere in altra cosa di qua giù essere non può, se non nel guardare in questi occhi e in questo riso.

And here it is right to know that the eyes of wisdom are
her demonstrations, whereby the truth is seen most cer-
tainly, and her smile is her persuasions, whereby the
inner light of wisdom is revealed behind a certain veil;
and in these two is felt that loftiest joy of blessedness
which is the supreme good in Paradise. This pleasure
may not be in ought else here below save in looking
upon these eyes and this smile.

139. *O isplendor di viva luce etterna*: For Beatrice as a mir-
ror or reflection of God's light, see n. to vss. 121-23. Her
name Revelation and her name Sapientia are emphasized
here, for *revelatio* means an "unveiling."

140. *chi*: "Whoever," i.e., whichever poet, in his dedication
to his art and inspiration.   *palido = pallido*.

141. *sua cisterna*: Castalia, the spring of Parnassus. Cf.
Purg. XXII, 65. These verses amount to a minor invocation,
indirectly turned to the Muses, preceding the final disclosure
or unveiling of Beatrice.

143. *paresti = apparisti*.

144-45. *là dove armonizzando . . . ti solvesti*: "Ciel" quali-
fied by "armonizzando" here appears to refer to the seven
streamers of light which hang over the whole procession and
symbolize the seven-fold Spirit of the Lord. This canopy is
in fact termed a *cielo* ("heaven") in *Purg.* XXIX, 82—in-
deed, it is called a "bel ciel," and its harmonizing is stressed
by comparing it to the rainbow (*Purg.* XXIX, 77-78). In this
final unveiling of Beatrice the reader is thus reminded that
one feature of this scene is constant: the seven-fold Spirit
of the Lord which hangs over the whole like a canopy or
heaven, that spirit which the prophet Isaiah had foreseen
would come to rest over the Christ who was to come—see
Isa. 11:2: "Et requiescat super eum spiritus Domini." ("And
the spirit of the Lord shall rest upon him.") In just such a
way Beatrice now, in her analogy to Christ, which is con-
stantly brought out in this procession, is overshadowed by
such a heaven, although in a figurative sense only, for there

is no shadow here, where the "splendor of living light eternal" is finally unveiled.

145. *aperto*: In the context the adjective is ambiguous. It would seem to modify "aere," but those commentators who protest that "open air" would be almost meaningless for being so obvious seem to be right. "Aperto" in the masculine could modify "isplendor" (vs. 139) as the subject of the proposition, in which case it would be an adjective used as an adverb (common in Italian) and thus mean *apertamente*, serving together with "solvesti" to mean "openly disclose yourself," or, in the context, "wholly" or even "finally disclose yourself."

CANTO XXXII

Special Note: Beatrice's triumph and the splendid climax of her unveiling are complete; the journey to Beatrice is terminated. The scene changes radically now, and the action centers around a tree in Eden. This commentary can follow in some detail the shifts in scene and in the context of meaning, but I wish to urge that the reader find time for the fundamental essays of E. Moore, "The Apocalyptic Vision" and "The DXV Prophecy," in the third series of his *Studies in Dante* (1903), pp. 178-220, 253-83. Though originally published in 1903, Moore's interpretation of *Purg.* XXXII-XXXIII seems to me to be still the most persuasive, even though the material written about these cantos has grown enormously since (see the bibliography under the entry "Cinquecento diece e cinque" in the *Enciclopedia dantesca*). Accordingly, in the following notes, I draw extensively on Moore's interpretation and refer to it constantly. But I have inevitably fragmentized his total argument by scattering quotations from it through these notes, and for that reason I hope that the reader will find it possible to read his essays, which are now also available in an edition reprinted in 1968.

2. *la decenne sete*: As recounted in the *Vita nuova* (XXIX, 1), Beatrice died in 1290; the fictional date of this journey and of the present encounter is 1300.

3. *li altri sensi m'eran tutti spenti*: See *Purg*. IV, 1-12, and the note to these verses.

4. *essi*: The eyes.

5. *non caler*: Indifference. "Caler" is the infinitive, here used with "non" as a substantive.

6. *traéli = li traeva.   l'antica rete*: Cf. *Purg*. XXX, 39; XXXI, 116-17.

8. *ver' la sinistra mia da quelle dee*: The divinities to which this reference is made are the three theological virtues (see *Purg*. XXIX, 121-22, and n. to *Purg*. XXIX, 121). Dante is still standing before the griffin and is facing the chariot and Beatrice. These three virtues have left their own position at the right wheel of the chariot to join him here and are accordingly on his left.

9. *Troppo fiso*: The verb of this injunction is understood: "You are looking too fixedly." In the context it should be noted that Dante is gazing now on a Beatrice who is the Beatrice of the *Vita nuova* in all her beauty, and in this focus for the moment she is not seen as Revelation or as the bearer of any other symbolic name. The virtues would seem to be indicating that Dante can look too intently on *that* Beatrice.

10–11. *la disposizion . . . percossi*: Such sight is nil, of course. As vs. 12 makes evident, Dante is momentarily blinded by the splendor of Beatrice, which equals that of the sun.

10. *èe = è*. Cf. *Inf*. XXIV, 90. So, in rhyme in vs. 12, "fée" *= fé (fece)*.

13–15. *al poco . . . rimossi*: Even the splendor of the procession is not to be compared with the dazzling brightness of Beatrice! These be strong words, calling the whole procession "poco" in comparison!

13. *il viso*: "My sight."   *riformossi = si riformò*.

14–15. *al molto sensibile*: The splendor of Beatrice. The terminology is Aristotelian, "sensibile" meaning the object offered to the senses and perceptible by them, by the sight in this instance. Cf. *Purg.* XV, 15: "soverchio visibile."

15. *a forza*: "Forcibly," by the injunction of the three virtues.

16–18. *vidi 'n sul braccio . . . volto*: The return now of the procession toward the east whence it came represents a radical change of scene and context of significance. Beatrice is still upon the chariot, of course, but will soon descend. Her triumph, as such, is over. The first unfolding or gradual coming of the procession (*Purg.* XXIX) bore the suggestion of a temporal process which, chronologically, represented in one aspect, as E. Moore (1903, p. 189) states it, "the growth and constitution of the Church from the dawn of Revelation to the close of the Canon of Scripture," with the Christ-event at its center. The military figure and the terms "essercito" (vs. 17) and "milizia" (vs. 22) serve to bring out even more emphatically the aspect of Church Militant, which is prominent in the total context of meaning from this point on.

16. *'n sul braccio destro*: The procession came out of the east, along the far side of Lethe toward Dante, and now, in returning, can wheel only to the right, for the stream is immediately on its left.

18. *col sole e con le sette fiamme al volto*: It is still morning in Eden, and the sun is in the east and "in the face" of the procession. The seven lights, as the banner of this militia of the heavenly kingdom, of its vanguard, still lead the twenty-four elders (*Purg.* XXIX, 82-84).

19–21. *Come sotto li scudi . . . mutarsi*: The figure is that of a troop of soldiers retreating, with their shields held over their heads.

20. *volgesi = si volge.*

23. *procedeva = precedeva.   trapassonne = ne trapassò*, the *ne* meaning *ci*, "us," i.e., Dante, who stands with the chariot, and the central group. This clearly indicates a very sharp backward turning of the procession.

24. *pria che piegasse il carro il primo legno*: "Before the chariot bent its first wood," i.e., its pole, which is the Cross.

25. *Indi a le rote si tornar le donne*: The virtues (*Purg.* XXIX, 121, 130) now return to the two wheels, though they are not said to dance beside them any longer as they did in the advent of Beatrice, when the procession was her triumph.
   si tornar = *si tornarono.*

26. *il benedetto carco*: The chariot which the griffin pulls.

27. *sì, che però nulla penna crollonne*: Christ sets the Church in motion again, by means of the Cross, without disturbing in any way His divine (eagle) part.   *però* = *per ciò.*   *crollonne* = *ne crollò.* The verb is here intransitive, "penna" being the subject.

28. *La bella donna che mi trasse al varco*: It will be noted that this lady, repeatedly termed "beautiful," is as yet unnamed in the poem; her name will prove to be Matelda (*Purg.* XXXIII, 119). The qualifying reference is to the events described in *Purg.* XXXI, 91-104.

29. *Stazio*: Statius has been on the scene all the while, but his presence has been completely overlooked since the disappearance of Virgil (the last explicit notice taken of him being in *Purg.* XXVIII, 146).

29–30. *la rota . . . arco*: The wheel that makes its turn with the smaller arc is the right wheel, since the whole procession has turned to the right. Dante and Statius, with Matelda, join the theological virtues at that wheel, which is the better side, the theological virtues being of a higher order than the virtues at the left wheel (see *Purg.* XXXI, 130).

31–32. *l'alta selva vòta . . . crese*: The Garden of Eden would still be inhabited by the human race, were it not for the sin of our first parents. Again, as in *Purg.* VIII, 99, and XXIX, 23-30, it is Eve who is blamed for this; yet, in vs. 37, it will be Adam who is remembered reproachfully, for only through *his* sin, not Eve's, did we all sin (cf. *Purg.* XXXIII, 61-63). See nn. to vss. 37-39 and to *Purg.* XXIX, 29-30.

32. *colpa*: Here used like the Latin ablative *culpa*, "through the fault." *crese = credette*.

33. *nota*: Song—but we are not told who sings.

34-35. *Forse in tre voli . . . saetta*: Cf. Ovid, *Metam*. VIII, 695-96; Statius, *Theb*. VI, 354.

34. *in tre voli*: Shot three times, i.e., the distance of three shots. *prese*: This is termed the "iterative" use of the preterite and might have been rendered by the present *prende*.

35. *disfrenata*: "Loosed from the bowcord." *eramo* (pronounced *eràmo*) = *eravamo*. It is a Latinism.

36. *Beatrice scese*: Clearly this act on the part of Beatrice radically changes the whole stage set, and a new play or act in the play can begin.

37-39. *Io senti' mormorare . . . ramo*: The mention of Adam and the tree stripped of its leaves and fruits brings us straightway to the center of meaning in this new enactment. And the tree will remain at the center. Clearly, in one of its meanings, it is literally the tree of the knowledge of good and evil of Gen. 2:15-17: "Tulit ergo Dominus Deus hominem, et posuit eum in paradiso voluptatis ut operaretur et custo-diret illum; praecepitque ei dicens: Ex omni ligno paradisi comede, de ligno autem scientiae boni et mali ne comedas, in quocumque enim die comederis ex eo morte morieris." ("The Lord God took the man and placed him in the garden of Eden to till it and to keep it. And the Lord God com-manded the man thus, 'From every tree of the garden you may eat; but from the tree of the knowledge of good and evil you must not eat; for the day you eat of it, you must die.' ") In *Purg.* XXXIII, 71-72, Beatrice declares that this tree sig-nifies morally the justice of God, "in the interdict," that is, in God's order to Adam *not* to eat of it. And this *interdict* aspect of meaning remains with the tree throughout the elaborate enactment in and around it. The Lord said, "Thou shalt not," and His justice as figured by the tree bears with it this original ban (see *Purg.* XXXIII, 61-63) even though the action that will be seen around it will extend, in chronological signification, from Adam all the way down to the early years of the fourteenth century.

Insofar as the tree symbolizes *ius* (law) or *iustitia* (justice), it extends and completes the pattern of justice which has been fulfilled in the individual Dante (justice as the goal of justification). But the tree stands for *ius* and *iustitia* in a far broader, social sense, involving mankind, Church, and Empire. It should not be construed as *meaning* Empire, however—a line of interpretation that has distorted much commentary on these cantos for a long time. Empire as such will come into the enactment in the familiar form of an eagle, even as the Church will be represented in this scene by the chariot, in the meaning already established for it; and the griffin will continue to represent Christ.

That this tree is stripped of all its leaves, its flowers, and its fruits clearly registers the consequences of Adam's sin in human nature generally and symbolizes the wounds that are now borne by mankind in consequence of our first father's sin. And the reproachful murmur by all the host here should bring to mind not only the verses of Genesis cited above, but such passages in the Scriptures as Rom. 5:12: "Propterea sicut per unum hominem peccatum in hunc mundum intravit, et per peccatum mors, et ita in omnes homines mors pertransiit, in quo omnes peccaverunt." ("Therefore as through one man sin entered into the world and through sin death, and thus death has passed unto all men because all have sinned.") Also see the apocryphal IV Esdrae 7:48: "O tu, quid fecisti, Adam? Si enim tu peccasti, non est factus solius tuus casus, sed et noster qui ex te advenimus." ("O thou Adam, what hast thou done? For though it was thou that sinned, thou art not fallen alone, but we all that come of thee.")

37. *a tutti = da tutti.*

38. *cerchiaro = cerchiarono.*

39. *e d'altra fronda*: Chimenz rightly observes that this is to be understood in the broader meaning of "flowers and fruits," i.e., all that which, besides the leaves, such a tree would produce before it was stripped.

40–41. *La coma sua . . . sù*: See *Purg.* XXXIII, 64-66, on the allegorical significance. Regarding the peculiar shape of the tree, the reader will recall that the two trees on the terrace of gluttony are said to derive from this tree and do in fact have precisely the shape of the parent tree (*Purg.* XXII, 131-34; XXIV, 106-11), and there it is suggested that these trees are so shaped that none should climb them (*Purg.* XXII, 135). It is the very shape of interdict, therefore, the shape of "thou shalt not," and brings out that aspect of this, the original tree of Eden, most graphically.

40. *coma*: "Tresses," i.e., branches.

41–42. *fora da l'Indi . . . ammirata*: India was famous for high trees; see Virgil, *Georg.* II, 122-24. For a symbolical tree of great height, cf. Dan. 4:8-24[11-17]; see n. to vs. 46.

43. *discindi*: "Tear off." Cf. Dante, *De mon.* III, x, 5: "Sed contra officium deputatum Imperatori est scindere Imperium." ("But it is counter to the office deputed to the emperor to rend the empire.") See *De mon.* II, xi, 1-10; xii, 1-8; Matt. 22:21.

44. *esto = questo.*   *legno*: See the biblical *lignum*, which is here echoed, in Gen. 2:16-17: "Ex omni ligno paradisi comede, de ligno autem scientiae boni et mali ne comedas." ("From every tree of the garden you may eat; but from the tree of the knowledge of good and evil you must not eat.") Here the term "pluck," rather than "eat," is applied to the tree, since there is no fruit on it to suggest eating.

45. *poscia che = poi che.*   *mal si torce il ventre quindi*: "For the belly is sadly racked afterwards."

46. *l'albero robusto*: This would seem to echo Dan. 4:17[20]: "arborem quam vidisti sublimem atque robustam" ("the tree which thou sawest which was high and strong").

47. *binato*: "Dual," of two natures, eagle and lion, divine and human respectively.

48. *Sì si conserva il seme d'ogne giusto*: The words of the griffin, his only utterance, clearly echo Jesus' words to John the Baptist (Matt. 3:15): "Sic enim decet nos implere omnem iustitiam." ("For so it becomes us to fulfill all justice.") See Rom. 5:19: "Sicut enim per inobedientiam unius hominis, peccatores constituti sunt multi, ita et per unius obeditionem, iusti constituentur multi." ("For just as by the disobedience of the one man the many were constituted sinners, so also by the obedience of the one the many will be constituted just.")

The tree is *ius*, law, and law in this conception is identical with God's will and providential plan. God's will requires man's obedience and Christ's obedience in atonement and redemption. As indicated in the n. to vss. 37-39, *Purg.* XXXIII, 71-72, brings out the meaning of the tree to be morally the justice of God. And justification of man, through Christ's obedient submission to the will of God, remains uppermost in the meaning here. Cf. Rom. 5:18: "Igitur, sicut per unius delictum in omnes homines in condemnationem, sic et per unius iustitiam in omnes homines in iustificationem vitae." ("Therefore as from the offense of the one man the result was unto condemnation to all men, so from the justice of the one the result is unto justification of life to all men.") Christ was obedient unto death, even death on the Cross— and immediately the Cross comes into the verses here, in symbol. See Phil. 2:5-8:

> Hoc enim sentite in vobis, quod et in Christo Iesu, qui, cum in forma Dei esset, non rapinam arbitratus est esse se aequalem Deo, sed semetipsum exinanivit, formam servi accipiens, in similitudinem hominum factus et habitu inventus ut homo. Humiliavit semetipsum factus obediens usque ad mortem, mortem autem crucis.

Have this mind in you which was also in Christ Jesus, who though he was by nature God, did not consider being equal to God a thing to be clung to, but emptied himself, taking the nature of a slave and being made like unto men. And appearing in the form of man, he humbled himself, becoming obedient to death, even to death on a cross.

Thus Thomas Aquinas (*Summa contra Gentiles* IV, 69) writes: "Dominus autem, quamdiu fuit in mundo, legem servaverit" ("since our Lord as long as He was in the world kept the Law").

49–51. *E vòlto al temo . . . legato*: The griffin draws out the pole from the chariot and binds it to the tree, from the wood of which it originally came. See E. Moore (1903), pp. 219-20, on the legend of the wood of the Cross:

The legend that the Cross was made from the wood of the Forbidden Tree in the Garden of Eden seems clearly recognized by allusion in *Purg.* xxxii. 51:—"E quel di lei a lei lasciò legato."

It is difficult, if not impossible, to find any other satisfactory explanation for these words. If it be accepted, it establishes beyond doubt that the pole of the car with the Crossbar symbolizes the Cross.

There is an elaborate monograph by Mussafia, *Sulla leggenda della Croce*, to which I owe some of the following references. It was a legend very widely spread, and is found in France, Spain, Italy, Germany, &c.

Thus the tradition, in one form or another, was so generally familiar that Dante would be safe in referring to it in this passing and allusive manner. The following strange medley is derived from the *Aurea Legenda*, c. lxviii. Seth is said to have planted an offshoot from the Tree of Knowledge on Adam's grave. By the time of Solomon it had grown to a very large tree. This he cut down, and employed either for one of his palaces, or as a bridge to cross a pool. The Queen of Sheba, to whom it was miraculously revealed that the Saviour of the world should one day hang upon this wood, refused to set foot on it, and warned Solomon of the revelation she had received. Solomon, hoping to avert such an evil prophecy (just as often in Greek mythology the oracular predictions were sought to be evaded), caused the beam to be buried at a great depth in the earth. At the spot was afterwards dug the Pool of Bethesda whose healing properties were due to the presence of this wood. Shortly before the Passion, the wood came to the surface, and was employed to form the Cross!

The *motif* of all this is obvious. It was deemed appropriate that the instrument of death should also be that of redemption. Compare a similar thought, as recognized in a sober form, by S. Paul in *Rom.* v. 19 and I *Cor.* xv. 21. Also we may note the curious comment of Pietro di Dante in *Par.* xxxii. 4, where Mary is described as having healed the wound which Eve inflicted. Hence, says Pietro, she is greeted with "Ave," which is "Eva" reversed.

Symbolically, the reuniting of the wood of the Cross to the tree from which it came signifies our redemption through Christ's sacrifice, his obedience even to death on the Cross. Hence the imagery of newness of life, of renewed life, which now follows in vss. 52-60.

49. *temo* = *timone*, "pole," i.e., the Cross. Cf. *Purg.* XXII, 119.

52. *le nostre piante*: Trees and plants in our northern hemisphere, in the world of the living.

52-54. *quando casca . . . lasca*: Grandgent explains that "when the sun's light descends 'mingled with that' of Aries, —the constellation which follows Pisces, the 'heavenly Carp,'—it is spring." Here "lasca" is used for fish in general, to indicate the constellation Pisces.

55. *turgide fansi*: Cf. Num. 17:8, where the flowering of the rod of Aaron is described: "Sequenti die regressus invenit germinasse virgam Aaron in domo Levi; et turgentibus gemmis eruperant flores." ("The next day, when Moses en-

tered the Tent, Aaron's staff, representing the house of Levi, had sprouted and put forth not only shoots, but blossoms as well.") See also Virgil, *Eclog.* VII, 48: "Iam laeto turgent in palmite gemmae." ("Now the buds swell on the gladsome tendril.")

56–57. *pria che 'l sole . . . altra stella*: The next constellation to which the sun "hitches his steeds" is Taurus, which follows Aries; thus, the meaning is "before a month has passed." See Virgil, *Aen.* I, 568; Ovid, *Metam.* II, 118.

58. *men che di rose e più che di viole*: The color between red and violet is purple and signifies Christ's sacrifice. The plant is symbolically colored with His blood and is renewed through His crucifixion. This signal now establishes this cardinal point of reference in time for the chronological sequence of events that follow. See a similar color symbolism in the third step at the gate of Purgatory (*Purg.* IX, 100-102, and n. to *Purg.* IX, 102). It will also be recalled that the cardinal virtues are wearing purple, to signify that they are the infused cardinal virtues, accessible to individuals in their justification, after Christ's great act of love, death on the Cross.

59–60. *s'innovò la pianta . . . sole*: The renewal of the tree is deliberately stressed by the verb, thereby emphasizing the newness of life made possible through Christ's blood and His great act of atonement for Adam's sin, which left the tree so bare.

60. *ramora = rami*, "branches." Such plurals are common in older Italian, e.g., *tempora, campora. sole*: "Stripped."

61. *qui*: "Here," in the world of the living.

63. *né la nota soffersi*: "Nor did I hear out the music." Dante falls asleep, perhaps overcome by the sweetness of the song. This sweet sleep may symbolize the peace and happiness that is possible after the atonement by Christ's sacrifice and reconciliation with God.

64–66. *come assonnaro . . . caro*: Grandgent explains: "The hundred eyes of Argus, the guardian of Io (cf. XXIX, 95), were put to sleep by Mercury's song of the nymph Syrinx, loved by Pan; Mercury then slew the over-vigilant guardian: *Met.*, I, 568-747."

69. *ma qual vuol sia che l'assonnar ben finga*: "But let him who will make a good counterfeit presentation of the act of falling asleep!" As Porena observes, this amounts to a considerable challenge, since no one can really represent in painting the *act* of falling to sleep.   *qual vuol sia*: Grandgent paraphrases this as follows: "Let it be he who wishes."

70. *Però = per ciò*.

71. *un splendor*: The cause of this brightness is mysterious.

72. *un chiamar*: It is the lady who is later to be named Matelda that calls thus (see vss. 82-84).

73. *Quali*: "Quali" is correlative with "tal" in vs. 82.
a veder: This is to be connected both with "condotti," vs. 76, and with "vinti," vs. 77.   *fioretti*: The foretaste of Christ's glory.   *melo*: Christ. Cf. Cant. 2:3: "Sicut malus inter ligna silvarum, sic dilectus meus inter filios." ("As an apple tree among the trees of the woods, so is my lover among men.")

73–90. *Quali a veder . . . profonda*: Grandgent (p. 624 of his commentary) comments on the scene of the Transfiguration as follows:

> When the sleeper comes to himself, he finds that the scene has been transformed. Christ and the Scriptures have left the earth and returned to Heaven, whence they came. They have left below, as their representative, the Church, with Revelation for its guide, and the seven-fold Spirit of God in the keeping of the seven Virtues. A change as wonderful as this was experienced once before, when the three disciples who had witnessed the Transfiguration recovered from their fright.

Grandgent goes on to quote Matt. 17:1-8:

791

Et post dies sex assumit Iesus Petrum et Iacobum et Ioannem fratrem eius; et ducit illos in montem excelsum seorsum. Et transfiguratus est ante eos; et resplenduit facies eius sicut sol, vestimenta autem eius facta sunt alba sicut nix. Et ecce apparuerunt illis Moyses et Elias cum eo loquentes. Respondens autem Petrus dixit ad Iesum: Domine, bonum est nos hic esse; si vis, faciamus hic tria tabernacula, tibi unum, Moysi unum, et Eliae unum. Adhuc eo loquente, ecce nubes lucida obumbravit eos, et ecce vox de nube dicens: Hic est Filius meus dilectus, in quo mihi bene complacui; ipsum audite. Et audientes discipuli ceciderunt in faciem suam, et timuerunt valde. Et accessit Iesus, et tetigit eos, dixitque eis: Surgite, et nolite timere. Levantes autem oculos suos, neminem viderunt, nisi solum Iesum.

Now after six days Jesus took Peter, James and his brother John, and led them up a high mountain by themselves, and was transfigured before them. And his face shone as the sun, and his garments became white as snow. And behold, there appeared to them Moses and Elias talking together with him. Then Peter addressed Jesus, saying, "Lord, it is good for us to be here. If thou wilt, let us set up three tents here, one for thee, one for Moses, and one for Elias." As he was still speaking, behold, a bright cloud overshadowed them, and behold, a voice out of the cloud said, "This is my beloved Son, in whom I am well pleased; hear him." And on hearing it the disciples fell on their faces and were exceedingly afraid. And Jesus came near and touched them, and said to them, "Arise, and do not be afraid." But lifting up their eyes, they saw no one but Jesus only.

As Grandgent notes in his discussion, Dante discusses the moral sense of this episode in *Conv.* II, i, 5, and refers to its allegorical significance in *De mon.* III, ix, 11.

74. *pome*: The full glory of Christ risen to Heaven. Cf. Apoc. 18:14: "et poma desiderii animae tuae" ("and the fruit which was the desire of thy soul").

75. *perpetue nozze*: See Apoc. 19:9: "Beati qui ad cenam nuptiarum Agni vocati sunt." ("Blessed are they who are called to the marriage supper of the Lamb.") Cf. *Par.* XXX, 135.

76–81. *Pietro e Giovanni . . . stola*: Cf. Matt. 17:1-8. In the *Paradiso* Peter, James, and John, as representatives of the three theological virtues faith, hope, and charity, conduct Dante's examination in these virtues in Heaven (*Par.* XXIV-XXVI).

78. *maggior sonni*: The sleep of death. See Luc. 7:14-15; Ioan. 11:43-44.

79. *scuola*: "Company," as in *Inf.* IV, 94.

80. *così di Moisè come d'Elia*: "Both by Moses and by Elias." Cf. Matt. 17:3.

81. *e al maestro suo cangiata stola*: Literally, "and [saw] their Master's raiment changed," but "stola" means "aspect" in a broader sense and implies the transfigured aspect of glory.

82–90. *tal torna' io . . . profonda*: This amounts to the second term of the simile, so complex and rich in its allusive meaning. Central to the whole, of course, is the figure of Beatrice in her analogy with Christ (see C. S. Singleton, 1954, pp. 45-60; 1958, pp. 72-85 and *passim*). To be sure, Beatrice has already descended from the chariot. But now, when Dante wakes up, he sees her very much changed in raiment, so to speak, seated on the bare ground—changed, that is, from the aspect she had in her triumph in *Purg.* XXX and XXXI. But we learn of an even greater event now: the whole scene is changed, for the griffin, symbolizing Christ, and all the figures in the procession (except the virtues and the chariot itself) have risen to Heaven or are in that moment rising. This, in the chronological sequence, signifies the Ascension of Christ, and Beatrice is now left behind as Revelation and as Wisdom (Sapientia with her seven handmaids,

the virtues). Thus the simile has brought about a transfigura-
tion in the whole scene and in the stage set of meaning. And
the time signal is of paramount importance: Beatrice now
appears as *Sapientia creata*, as Sapientia exists on earth
among men after Christ has risen to Heaven, where He
abides as *Sapientia increata*. For the analogy in these terms,
see C. S. Singleton (1958), pp. 130-34.

By way of this remarkable transformational simile, so rich
in meaning, the stage itself undergoes a subtle symbolic
change: the place there, literally, the Garden of Eden, be-
comes in some sense the earthly city of the saints or the jus-
tified (for Dante the wayfarer is justified now), and the canto
enters into the duality made famous by Augustine in his *De
civitate Dei* (as will be suggested with regard to vss. 100-
105). See n. to vss. 100-102.

Part of the complexity of the whole simile, in its second
term, has to do with the extended and dispersed nature of
that second term: Dante awakens to find Matelda standing
over him, but there is nothing in the simile as such to pro-
vide for the presence of Matelda at all. And it is not Christ
who is seen changed in his raiment, but Beatrice changed in
hers.

82-84. *quella pia . . . pria*: Again the specific name of Ma-
telda is avoided, and the lady, fair and kind, is indicated by
circumlocution.

85. *tutto in dubbio*: Dante is afraid Beatrice may no longer
be there.

86-87. *Vedi lei sotto la fronda . . . radice*: Beatrice sits
upon the roots of the renewed tree, and as we learn from vs.
94, she sits all alone, save for the seven virtues that attend
her as handmaids. Sitting "on the root" she sits at the point
of juncture between the pole of the chariot and the trunk of
the tree: the very reunion which transformed the tree.

88. *compagnia*: The seven virtues who have remained with
Beatrice (see vss. 97-99), being ordained to her as her hand-
maids (*Purg.* XXXI, 107-8), and who thus bring out her

meaning as Sapientia, the only figure known to us who did indeed have seven handmaids.

89. *li altri*: The thirty-five books of the Scriptures, the angels, who are being led by the griffin (Christ) upward to Heaven.   *dopo = dietro.   sen vanno suso*: The figure of ascension here is most important in establishing a chronological point of reference.

93. *quella*: Beatrice.   *intender*: "Attention," "concern."

94. *Sola sedeasi = si sedeva sola*, but the particular order of the words gives more meaning to the reflexive *si* in its distancing function, so often noted heretofore.

94–96. *Sola sedeasi . . . fera*: There is Beatrice, all alone, and Christ has risen. She sits on the earth, she *is* on the earth, left here by the risen Christ. See n. to vss. 86-87. Here, where Beatrice now sits, is not only Eden, but is here below *in the world* after Christ's Ascension. It is in the world, but only in the world of the justified, the righteous earthly city. See Beatrice's words in vss. 100-105.

99. *Aquilone*: The north wind.   *Austro*: The south wind. These two winds are mentioned together here as being typically boisterous.

100–102. *Qui sarai . . . romano*: Through failure to take note of the subtle changes of symbolic location, which the notes above have sought to observe, commentators have misunderstood Beatrice's words here. Some would have the meaning of her words be: "Here, when you return as a soul to Purgatory and reach this forest at the summit, you will remain but little while, etc." But this is completely banal, for we know from the presence of Statius, and from what happens to him here, that all souls will remain here at the summit only long enough to drink of the two streams. To contrast this brief and obvious time span with the eternity of Heaven makes little sense. Instead, as already noted, location has, symbolically, undergone a change, and Augustine's earthly and heavenly cities have emerged as central to the meaning. His heavenly city could not be more clearly indicated than by the famous vs. 102; his earthly city is ambiguous or equivocal, even as in the famous *De civitate Dei*, for there are two earthly cities, one made up of the righteous, those who are justified, and one made up of the wicked, those who live in sin. And in such a context the Apocalypse speaks of a tree of life (Apoc. 22:2) and of admission to it and of the wicked who remain without, even as the poet does here, with "qui" (Beatrice is seated at the root of the tree of life) distinguished from the "mondo che mal vive" (vs. 103) to which Dante is to return, to report what he sees here. See Apoc. 22:14-15:

Beati qui lavant stolas suas in sanguine Agni, ut sit potestas eorum in ligno vitae, et per portas intrent in civitatem: foris canes et venefici, et impudici et homicidae, et idolis servientes, et omnis qui amat et facit mendacium.

Blessed are they who wash their robes in the blood of the Lamb that they may have the right to the tree of life, and that by the gates they may enter into the city. Outside are the dogs, and the sorcerers, and the fornicators, and the murderers, and the idolators, and everyone who loves and practises falsehood.

This latter group, those excluded by wickedness, is the "mondo che mal vive" of the unrighteous, to which Dante must return. But allegorically, of course, he *is* living in the midst of that world, as all the righteous and the justified must do who make up the good earthly city which must exist with the bad earthly city.

100. *poco tempo*: This must not be understood as a prediction that Dante is not to live a long time yet in the world. This little time is little as compared with eternity, eternal life in the heavenly city, where Christ is. Nor is this the first time that the poet has predicted his own salvation.

101-2. *e sarai . . . romano*: I.e., "then you shall dwell forever in Heaven." Cf. Eph. 2:19: "Ergo iam non estis hospites et advenae, sed estis cives sanctorum et domestici Dei."

("Therefore, you are now no longer strangers and foreigners, but you are citizens with the saints and members of God's household.")

103. *Però = perciò.   in pro*: "For the benefit."   *del mondo che mal vive*: For the ambiguity of earthly and heavenly cities, and their subtle location as symbolically conveyed, see n. to vss. 100-102. Some additional texts seem worthy of note in this regard; see, for example, Ioan. 17:11, "et iam non sum in mundo, et hi in mundo sunt, et ego ad te venio" ("and I am no longer in the world, but these are in the world, and I am coming to thee") and Ioan. 17:14-16: "Ego dedi eis sermonem tuum, et mundus eos odio habuit, quia non sunt de mundo, sicut et ego non sum de mundo. Non rogo ut tollas eos de mundo, sed ut serves eos a malo. De mundo non sunt, sicut et ego non sum de mundo." ("I have given them thy word; and the world has hated them, because they are not of the world, even as I am not of the world. I do not pray that thou take them out of the world, but that thou keep them from evil. They are not of the world, even as I am not of the world.") It is this very ambiguity around which Augustine conceived his earthly city. As to literal location here, Beatrice and Dante are in the earthly Paradise, and Dante is to return to the evil world and report, for its benefit, that which he is now to witness.

105. *fa che tu scrive*: This is an imperative construction, corresponding to the Latin *fac ut scribas.   scrive = scriva*. Cf. Apoc. 1:11: "Quod vides, scribe in libro." ("What thou seest write in a book.")

109. *Non scese mai con sì veloce moto*: Here begins the dumb show or series of tableaux enacted around the tree of justice (see n. to vss. 37-39) which prove to represent seven principal calamities that have successively befallen the Church and are an offense to God's justice as represented by the tree. Such calamities, affecting the tree and the Church which is reunited to it, are termed "blasphemies of act" in *Purg.* XXXIII, 58-59. Of these calamities and the fact that they are precisely seven, E. Moore (1903, p. 201) observes:

I have never seen it noticed how Dante, with his usual love of symmetry, has distinguished the seven incidents by devoting precisely two *terzine* to each of them, excepting that the last, the concluding and contemporary catastrophe, has a few more lines than the others at the end of the Canto. Here is the list:—(1) ll. 112-117; (2) ll. 118-123; (3) ll. 124-129; (4) ll. 130-135; (5) ll. 136-141; (6) ll. 142-147; (7) ll. 148 to end.

Moore's interpretation of these tableaux can hardly be improved upon, and I venture to quote extensively from him.

The reader is not to forget that the ascension of the griffin and the rest of the procession (see vss. 88-90) has established a chronological frame for the events now symbolized around the tree and the chariot, making them all events occurring after Christ's Ascension and affecting His Church as established by Peter in Rome.

109-17. *Non scese mai . . . orza*: Some commentators suggest that ten persecutions of the Christian Church, instigated by the emperors from Nero (emperor, A.D. 54-68) to Diocletian (emperor, A.D. 284-305), are here signified. See, for instance, E. Moore (1903), p. 201:

The first of these calamities is the series of persecutions under the early Emperors, such as Nero, Domitian, &c. It is thus indicated. An eagle, the Imperial Eagle, swoops down through the branches of the Tree, rending its trunk and scattering its leaves and new-grown flowers. It then smites the Chariot with all its force, so that it reels like a storm-tossed ship.

For the eagle, cf. Virgil, *Aen.* I, 394; Ezech. 17:3; *Purg.* IX, 20; and *Par.* XVIII-XX, especially for the bird as the emblem of the Roman Empire. These emperors offend God's tree (blasphemy of act—see n. to vs. 109) by way of doing violence to the Church. It should not be forgotten that *now* this tree has purple flowers in its restored state, through Christ's atonement, and therefore the offense is even more blasphemous.

110. *piove*: "It falls." Cf. Ovid, *Metam.* VIII, 339: "ut ex-

cussis elisi nubibus ignes" ("like lightning struck out from the clashing clouds").

111. *quel confine che più va remoto*: From the highest regions of the air which have for confine the sphere of fire (see C. S. Singleton, *Inferno Commentary*, Fig. 2, p. 35).

113-14. *rompendo de la scorza . . . nove*: "De la" and "de le" are clearly partitive in meaning, but so also is "d'i" (*dei*), i.e., "some of."

114. *non che*: "As well as."

116. *come nave*: The simile is prompted by the ship as the traditional symbol of the Church. See the reference to Peter's ship in *Par.* XI, 119-20.   *fortuna*: "Storm."

117. *or da poggia, or da orza*: *Poggia* is the rope that attaches to the mast on the right, or starboard, side of a ship, just as *orza* is the corresponding rope on the left, or larboard, side.

118-23. *Poscia vidi . . . polpe*: On this second episode, E. Moore (1903, p. 202) observes:

> Next, the Car is invaded by a lean and hungry fox. But Beatrice herself speedily drives it away. This clearly refers to the early heresies, which were overcome and suppressed by the authority of the Church herself, and so she purged herself of them.
>
> In contrast with the assaults of persecution by open enemies from without, the mischief of heresy is aptly represented by the fox, for the operations of heretics "non furon leonine, ma di volpe" [*Inf.* XXVII, 75]. They claimed not only to be within the Church, but to represent the truest aspect of her teaching. "Of your own selves shall men arise, speaking perverse things." Note that it is precisely in reference to such false teachers that Ezekiel says, "Thy prophets are like the foxes in the desert" (xiii. 4). Also, to judge from chronological order, coming, as this does, *after* the early persecutions and *before* the Donation of Constantine (which will be

found denoted as the third calamity), the heresy principally indicated is probably Gnosticism, as Scartazzini suggests. He further points out that as the fox dashed into the very body of the Car from outside, so Gnosticism had its origin in the heathen philosophy, which claimed to expound by its own principles Christian revelation, and to possess the key of knowledge for the lack of which both the Old and New Testaments had been so far entirely misunderstood.

Moore also cites Augustine (*Enar. in Ps.* LXXX, 14), who says: "Vulpes insidiosos, maximeque haereticos significant; dolosos, fraudulentos." ("Insidious foxes, more than anything else, signify heretics; treacherous, fraudulent.")

118. *cuna*: "Cradle," i.e., the body of the chariot. Chimenz observes that the term is appropriate in suggesting that the fox seeks to make its den there, in the body of the chariot.

120. *d'ogne pasto buon parea digiuna*: Metaphorically the meaning is that the heretics were without sound doctrines.

122. *la donna mia*: Beatrice enters into the action (as Dante himself will at a later point), perhaps signifying that heresy is refuted by knowledge of divine things, as held by the Church, of which Beatrice is the type, in one of her meanings. *futa = fuga. Futa* is an archaic form which survives in popular speech. See E. G. Parodi (1957), p. 281.

124-29. *Poscia per indi . . . carca*: E. Moore (1903, p. 203) comments:

The third great calamity is the acquisition of temporal possessions through the "Donation of Constantine." The eagle descends once more, and leaves the Car covered with *its own feathers*. Note the expression, "di sè pennuta." This exactly describes the position maintained by Dante in the *De Mon.* It is of the very "form" or essence of the Church that she should have no such possessions. They are of the plumage of the eagle. They belong of right to the Emperor alone; he had no power or right to alienate them; nor had the Church any power or right to receive them. They were as wholly out of place as the feathers and plumage upon the triumphal Car. A bitter cry was heard from heaven upon the consummation of this disastrous event (ll. 127-129).

Moore and others note that possibly Dante had in mind a legend, mentioned by Pietro di Dante and others, that at the time when the Donation of Constantine was made a voice was heard from Heaven, which said (Moore, 1903, p. 203): "Hodie diffusum est venenum in Ecclesia Dei." ("Today poison is poured into the Church of God.") On the Donation and its disastrous effects, see *Inf.* XIX, 115-17; *Par.* XX, 55-60; *De mon.* III, x, 4-6.

124. *per indi ond' era pria venuta*: That is, down along the trunk (cf. vs. 113).

125. *l'arca*: The "ark," like the "cradle" above (vs. 118), means the body of the chariot, but perhaps, as Chimenz observes, the poet has used the word to suggest a chest or coffer that would contain money, riches, a meaning which would be most appropriate here.

127. *rammarca* = *rammarica*.

128-29. *tal voce . . . carca*: Perhaps the voice from Heaven is St. Peter's, in which case he uses (with a modification of sentiment) the accepted metaphor of a ship for the Church which he founded in Rome. Cf. vs. 116.

130-35. *Poi parve a me . . . vago*: Again E. Moore's interpretation seems correct. He observes (1903, pp. 204-5):

This fourth calamity or tribulation is more difficult to identify.

From the earth between the wheels of the Car issues a dragon. He fixes his envenomed tail through its floor, and drags away a part of it, and so goes his way.

The imagery is clearly derived from the Apocalypse, ch. xii. The dragon that comes from beneath is probably the devil, "the old serpent" (*Rev.* xii. 9), who inflicts this injury upon the Church (observe that the word

"Serpent" is the word used for the "dragon" of this passage when this disaster is again referred to in xxxiii. 34).
The carrying away of a part of the floor of the Car (an incident imitated from *Rev.* xii. 4, where the dragon's "tail drew the third part of the stars of heaven, and did cast them to the earth") seems beyond doubt to represent some great schism by which the Church was rent. Several of the early commentators think the reference is to Mohammedanism at the beginning of the seventh century. This is the view, I believe, most commonly held, and is, in my opinion, almost certainly the true one. It may perhaps be objected that this interpretation treats Mohammedanism as a kind of heresy, and one effecting a schism in the Church itself, rather than as an erroneous and rival system external to it. To this I would reply that, however we may now regard it, such a view would be quite in accordance with the position assigned to Mohammed in the *Inferno*, where he figures as the most conspicuous and typical example of the *Schismatics* in the ninth Bolgia of the eighth Circle in the *Inferno* (see Canto xxviii). It should also be remembered that Mohammed professed a deep reverence for Christ; he held Him to be the greatest of the prophets; he believed in His birth being miraculous; and also in His return to earth hereafter to establish peace and to reconcile Islam and Christianity, by restoring the latter from its corruptions (which were already gross enough even in Mohammed's day) to the ideal originally intended by Christ.

Thus then I would certainly explain the fourth great calamity of the Church.

132. *fisse = confisse, conficcò*. Cf. the Latin *fixit*.

135. *trasse del fondo*: "Pulled out some of the bottom." "Del" is partitive. Cf. vss. 113-14.   *gissen = se ne gì.*
    vago vago: The meaning of the adjective repeated is uncertain. "All satisfied" seems the most probable of the several proposed by the commentators. However, the meaning

might be "gloatingly," i.e., intent on doing more damage in the future.

136–41. *Quel che rimase . . . aperta*: E. Moore (1903, pp. 205-6) observes:

> The fifth vicissitude is a further accession of temporal possessions represented in the additional plumage (*v. supra*, l. 126) by which the whole Car is now entirely smothered and overgrown, wheels and pole and all. This no doubt refers to the Donations of Pepin (A.D. 755), and Charles the Great (A.D. 775), and other similar and rapidly growing accessions of wealth and endowments to the Church. Dante graphically says the change was effected before his eyes in less time than the mouth remains open in uttering a sigh (l. 141). These possessions had now become so vast as to alter the whole aspect of the Church, and to bring about a complete transformation of its original character (l. 142). Certainly nothing strikes us more in the whole of mediaeval history in every country of Europe than the keen and perpetual struggle in every grade of the Church to acquire more and more wealth. The constant quarrels of the Popes with the Emperors, and with our own English Kings, were almost invariably due to the exorbitant rapacity of Papal claims for money.

136. *gramigna*: A grass which grows very thick on the soil where it sprouts, especially if that soil is fertile ("vivace," vs. 137).

137. *da la piuma*: Goes with "si ricoperse" in vs. 139.

138. *forse con intenzion sana e benigna*: Cf. *Par.* XX, 55-57, where it is more clearly granted that Constantine made his Donation with "good intention."

142–47. *Trasformato così . . . fue*: E. Moore (1903, pp. 206-7) continues:

> Next follow still further and more hideous distortions of the outward form of the Church. It put forth seven

heads, three on its pole and one at each of its corners. The three first had two horns, and each of the others one. Again we recognize the source of this imagery in the Apocalypse, and we remember how Dante has employed it before, though differently, in *Inf.* xix. 109, 110. The interpretation of Dante's meaning here is extremely difficult. The number of heads and horns is no doubt dictated to him by the passage in the Apocalypse. Further, if with his habit of exact description he went on to specify how the ten horns were placed on the seven heads, they could hardly be otherwise distributed, i.e. three of the heads must have two horns apiece. But I can scarcely doubt that Dante intended some definite mystical meaning besides. The earliest, and still most common, explanation is that he refers to the seven capital or deadly sins, all of which now disfigured the hopelessly corrupted Church. The various attempts to explain why some of these have one horn and some two are not very convincing. If we are to take the reference to the seven deadly sins at all (which, however, I do not accept), it seems to me most natural to suggest that Pride, Envy, and Anger (the three worst sins) have two horns, because they involve sin against one's neighbour as well as against God; whereas the other four do not necessarily do so. This idea would accord well with Dante's well-known analysis and classification of the seven sins in *Purg.* xvii, especially ll. 112-114, and indeed as far as l. 126, in which these first three sins have special guilt in that they imply positive love of evil, and that evil must be not for oneself but for one's neighbour. But I cannot think this common explanation at all satisfactory.

Here I would venture to disagree with Moore and find the meaning represented by him as the most common explanation to be still the most satisfactory. For his own differing opinion, see E. Moore (1903), pp. 207-8.

142. *dificio*: The chariot. Cf. *Inf.* XXXIV, 7.

143. *teste per le parti sue*: Cf. Dante, *De mon.* I, xvi, 4: "genus humanum . . . bellua multorum capitum factum" ("race of men . . . transformed into a beast of many heads").

144. *tre sovra 'l temo e una in ciascun canto*: See Apoc. 12:3: "Et ecce draco magnus rufus, habens capita septem et cornua decem." ("And behold, a great red dragon having seven heads and ten horns.")   *temo*: Cf. vs. 49.

148–60. *Sicura, quasi rocca . . . belva*: On this seventh vicissitude E. Moore (1903, p. 208) observes: "This brings the panorama of the Church's history comparatively near to Dante's own time. Henceforth we have depicted contemporary troubles, and notably the Avignon captivity from 1305 onwards. These form the seventh and last of the tribulations here figured." Moore, referring to vs. 147, notes that "the Church has now become utterly corrupted and distorted beyond all recognition." He continues (1903, pp. 208-9):

> The seat in the Car itself is occupied no longer by Beatrice, or the ideal Papacy, but by a wanton and shameless harlot. Dante applies the same metaphor elsewhere to the corruption of the Roman Court, e.g. *Inf.* xix. 4 and *Par.* ix. 142. This imagery once more is borrowed obviously from the Apocalypse. The giant in this passage (xxxii. 152) carries on the metaphor of the kings of the earth who committed fornication with the great whore of the Book of Revelation. This giant figures no doubt chiefly Philip the Fair, but also other earlier representatives of the detested royal house of France. (For this see further *Purg.* xx.) Their friendly intrigues from time to time with different occupants of the Papal throne (e.g. Urban IV, Clement IV, Martin IV, Nicholas IV), which are here described as mutual caresses of the giant and the harlot ("baciavansi insieme," l. 153), were now replaced by the violent hostility between Philip and Boniface VIII. The gross outrage upon Boniface perpetrated by the myrmidons of Philip, Nogaret and Sciarra, at Anagni (for which see *Purg.* xx. 85 *seqq.*), may well be pointed at in the scourging of the harlot

by the giant, her former paramour, in ll. 155, 6. Then, full of jealousy and fury, the giant unbinds the chariot from the tree, and carries it away with the harlot out of sight. This quite evidently represents the removal of the Papal Seat from Rome to Avignon under Clement V in 1305.

Thus, chronologically, the show has passed into prophecy, with respect to the fictional date of the journey, which is 1300.

148–50. *Sicura, quasi rocca . . . m'apparve*: Cf. Apoc. 18:7, where the woman on the scarlet beast says in her heart: "Sedeo regina." ("I sit a queen.") This is the Roman curia in the time of Boniface VIII and Clement V, feeling very strong in temporal possessions.

149. *sciolta*: Probably with reference to her robe, which is "loose," suggesting profligacy, shamelessness.

150. *con le ciglia intorno pronte*: See Ecclus. 26:12: "Fornicatio mulieris in extollentia oculorum et in palpebris illius agnoscetur." ("By her eyelids and her haughty stare an unchaste wife can be recognized.") She is thus acting the part of the whore.

151. *li = gli*.

152. *di costa a lei dritto*: "Standing beside her." *un gigante*: See the quotation from E. Moore in n. to vss. 148-60. The house of France may be intended by the figure, not merely Philip the Fair. It should be noted that Dante refers to Philip as Goliath in his *Epist*. VII, 29.

153. *e basciavansi insieme*: The figure is truly that of a giant, since he must be standing on the ground and yet his head is level with that of the whore seated on the chariot. Cf. Apoc. 18:2-3: "Cecidit, cecidit Babylon magna . . . et reges terrae cum illa fornicati sunt." ("She has fallen, she has fallen, Babylon the great . . . and the kings of the earth have committed fornication with her.")

155. *a me rivolse*: That Dante should be made part of the scene, with this glance from the whore, makes for considerable difficulty in interpretation, but may be compared, in its way, to the intervention of Beatrice herself in the show (vs. 122). With these two exceptions the whole enactment is, as it were, self-contained. Yet Dante the poet has not hesitated to allow Dante the character to become, for a moment, part of the action. Is he then simply the typical Christian, and by extension, the Christian people? Or is he more specifically the *Italian* Christian people? Interpretations vary, nor is a precise determination of meaning possible, in this most curious involvement of Dante the character, who is supposed to be purely a spectator of the whole show (vss. 104-5).

158. *disciolse il mostro*: Since it was the griffin who bound the pole of the chariot to the tree (and the griffin represents Christ), the act of disjoining that which He united is awesome and fraught with evil meaning.   *trassel = lo trasse.*

per la selva: As suggested by E. Moore (see quotation in n. to vss. 148-60) and by most commentators, the dragging of the chariot, transformed into a monster, through the wood, so far as to hide it from Dante (presumably located in Italy) may be taken to signify the certain removal of the seat of the papacy to Avignon in 1309.

160. *a la puttana e a la nova belva*: This canto, having this many verses, is the longest canto in the poem. The shortest cantos have 115 verses (*Inf.* VI and XI).

CANTO XXXIII

1. *Deus, venerunt gentes*: These are the opening words of Ps. 78[79]. We are not told how much of this psalm the seven virtues, handmaids of Beatrice, actually sing, but since their recitation of it at this point has reference to the spectacle of the corruption of the Church just witnessed, which closes the preceding canto, the reader would do well to remember the first eight verses of the psalm.

Deus, venerunt gentes in hereditatem tuam, polluerunt templum sanctum tuum, posuerunt Ierusalem in pomorum custodiam. Posuerunt morticina servorum tuorum escas volatilibus caeli; carnes sanctorum tuorum bestiis terrae; effuderunt sanguinem eorum tamquam aquam in circuitu Ierusalem, et non erat qui sepeliret. Facti sumus opprobrium vicinis nostris, subsannatio et illusio his qui in circuitu nostro sunt. Usquequo, Domine? Irasceris in finem? Accendetur velut ignis zelus tuus? Effunde iram tuam in gentes quae te non noverunt, et in regna quae nomen tuum non invocaverunt. Quia comederunt Iacob, et locum eius desolaverunt. Ne memineris iniquitatum nostrarum antiquarum; cito anticipent nos misericordiae tuae, quia pauperes facti sumus nimis.

O God, the nations have come into your inheritance; they have defiled your holy temple, they have laid Jerusalem in ruins. They have given the corpses of your servants as food to the birds of heaven, the flesh of your faithful ones to the beasts of the earth. They have poured out their blood like water round about Jerusalem, and there is no one to bury them. We have become the reproach of our neighbors, the scorn and derision of those around us.

O Lord, how long? Will you be angry forever? Will your jealousy burn like fire? Pour out your wrath upon the nations that acknowledge you not, upon the kingdoms that call not upon your name; for they have devoured Jacob and laid waste his dwelling. Remember not against us the iniquities of the past; may your compassion quickly come to us, for we are brought very low.

alternando: The theological and the cardinal virtues sing the verses alternately, as the following verse makes evident.

3. *incominciaro = incominciarono.*

5. *sì fatta*: With such a look.

5–6. *che poco più . . . Maria*: Mary at the foot of the Cross was hardly more overcome by grief than Beatrice.

7. *dier = diedero.*

8. *in pè = in piede.*

10–12. *Modicum, et non . . . videbitis me*: With these words Beatrice joins her handmaids as if part of a chorus, as in Greek tragedy, commenting on the spectacle of the corrupted Church and particularly on the final scene, in which the giant dragged the chariot (the Church) off through the woods until it could no longer be seen (see n. to *Purg.* XXXII, 158). Thus, as in such choral utterances, Beatrice can speak in the first person, and she uses the prophetic words uttered by Christ to his disciples in Ioan. 16:16 and by such projection speaks for the Church, without identifying herself with it. Her prophecy, in such a focus, means that the corrupt Church will return and be saved from its corruption some day in the not too distant future.

The disciples were themselves puzzled by Christ's words, particularly by the "modicum" (see Ioan. 16:17-18 and Christ's answer in Ioan. 16:19-28).

11. *sorelle*: Beatrice's address to her handmaids as "sisters" is affectionate and familiar, even as it will soon be to Dante, addressing him as "brother" (vs. 23). The reader, remembering Beatrice's triumph and exalted station in the preceding cantos, will thus not fail to note a considerable change in her from her former elevation, a kind of stepping down.

13. *Poi le si mise innanzi tutte e sette*: Beatrice now wishes her seven handmaids, the virtues, to precede her (another token of her changed status). It should be remembered that Beatrice with her seven maidens in attendance is seen now primarily as Sapientia or Wisdom, and the explanation she is now to offer Dante in declaring the meaning of the dumb show depends greatly on Sapientia as her predominant name in this final canto.

14. *solo accennando*: Saying nothing, but merely with a gesture, beckoning.

15. *la donna*: Matelda. *'l savio che ristette*: Statius, called a "savio" because he is a poet, is still on the scene, though again the reader will realize that he has been practically forgotten. As noted, the advent of Beatrice has no real meaning for Statius. But, as we shall see, Matelda still has an office to discharge here, respecting the ancient poet as a soul liberated from Purgatory.

17. *lo decimo suo passo*: Grandgent observes that "the 9 to 10 steps probably represent a period of over 9 years, between 1305, when Clement V was induced by Philip the Fair to make Avignon the seat of the Papacy, and 1314, when both Clement and Philip died. After their death the world was in a better condition to expect a redeemer." See E. Gorra

(1907). E. Moore (1903, p. 263) offers a different explanation. Though it is possible that such symbolism is intended here, it seems highly improbable. "Ten steps" can mean merely "a few steps."

22. *seco*: "Seco" here means "with her," as "meco" in rhyme means "with me."

23. *Frate*: As already noted, this term of address serves to drop the level of discourse to the familiar. It is quite striking coming from Beatrice, but witnesses her change of position.   *t'attenti*: The phrasing "venture to" registers awareness on Beatrice's part that Dante would not have made so bold before, as his own words in the verses immediately following acknowledge in their tone and in the simile that introduces them.

29–30. *Madonna, mia bisogna . . . buono*: It will be noted that, for all Beatrice's invitation to enter into a more familiar relationship, Dante continues to address her as "Madonna" and to use the respectful *voi* in addressing her, as he will until almost the end of the poem.

32. *disviluppe = disviluppa*.

34. *'l vaso*: The chariot.   *'l serpente*: The dragon of *Purg.* XXXII, 131. Beatrice begins thus to declare the meaning of the show Dante has witnessed (see the preceding canto).

35. *fu e non è*: Cf. Apoc. 17:8: "Bestia quam vidisti fuit et non est." ("The beast that thou sawest was, and is not.") Thus the words return us to the vision, in the Apocalypse, of the woman on the scarlet beast, the great harlot (see n. to *Purg.* XXXII, 148-50), to the equivalent point in that scriptural context where the angel begins to declare the mystery of what has been witnessed there. See Apoc. 17:7-9.

> Et dixit mihi angelus: Quare miraris? Ego dicam tibi sacramentum mulieris et bestiae quae portat eam, quae habet capita septem et cornua decem. Bestia quam vidisti fuit et non est, et ascensura est de abysso et in in-

teritum ibit, et mirabuntur inhabitantes terram (quorum non sunt scripta nomina in libro vitae a constitutione mundi) videntes bestiam quae erat et non est. Et hic est sensus, qui habet sapientiam.

And the angel said to me, "Wherefore dost thou wonder? I will tell thee the mystery of the woman, and of the beast that carries her which has the seven heads and the ten horns. The beast that thou sawest was, and is not, and is about to come up from the abyss, and will go to destruction. And the inhabitants of the earth— whose names have not been written in the book of life from the foundation of the world—will wonder when they see the beast which was, and is not. And here is the meaning for him who has wisdom."

The meaning, as applied to the transformed chariot, the Church, in the spectacle of the preceding canto, is that the material Church has ceased to exist by becoming thus corrupt and by being dragged out of sight.   *chi n'ha colpa*: Those who are chiefly to blame are Pope Clement and Philip the Fair. See n. to vs. 17.

36. *che vendetta di Dio non teme suppe*: The term "suppe" here is most obscure in its meaning and has led to much discussion. The early commentators are puzzled, and many are the modern theories concerning the word, with no single interpretation winning a general consensus (see the *Enciclopedia dantesca*, under the entry "suppe"). However, in context, the meaning seems clear enough: "God's vengeance fears no impediment."

37–38. *Non sarà . . . carro*: In *Conv.* IV, iii, 6, Dante calls Frederick II, who died in 1250, the last Roman Emperor: "ultimo dico per rispetto al tempo presente, non ostante che Ridolfo e Andolfo e Alberto poi eletti siano, appresso la sua morte e de li suoi discendenti" ("I say the last up to the present time, notwithstanding that Rudolf and Adolf and Albert have been elected since his death and that of his descendants"). Grandgent notes that Dante says this because these three never came to Italy. See *Purg.* VI, 97; VII, 94.

37. *reda*: Grandgent calls attention to the rhymes in *-eda* in the prophetic vss. 13 and 15 of *Purg.* XX.

41. *a darne tempo già stelle propinque*: The obscure prophecy now to be made is clear in this part of itself: the one who is to come will come by way of propitious stellar influence, which in itself suggests that he will be a temporal ruler. Compare the prophecy of the "veltro" in *Inf.* I, 105, which (also most obscurely, to be sure) seems to speak of the birth of such a one as being in the sign of Gemini, the Twins, and thus to relate his coming to the stars.

43-44. *un cinquecento diece e cinque, messo di Dio*: The one who is to come will be God-sent and, as has been suggested, will be a temporal monarch. But the problem of the DXV (to put the five hundred, ten, and five into Roman numerals, as is commonly done) remains one of the most debated in Dante studies. The reader will find the latest summary of the many different attempts at a solution in the *Enciclopedia dantesca*, under the entry "Cinquecento diece e cinque." Perhaps the conclusion of this article (by P. Mazzamuto) may be quoted here in full as the most comprehensive statement of the most accepted general understanding of this riddle:

> Tutto, comunque, fa credere che, giusta l'autorevole opinione e le valide motivazioni del Parodi, il DXV sia Enrico VII, cioè l'erede dell'aquila, la stessa *sublimis Aquila* dell'epistola ai principi (V 11); e che, nel renderne la profezia, D. abbia seguito la tecnica criptografica usata da s. Giovanni nell'*Apocalisse* (XIII, 18), dove nel numero 666 si indica Nerone, e rimessa in vigore dalla simbolica medievale; e abbia così celebrato la felice coincidenza tra l'auspicato prossimo trionfo di Enrico VII e l'avvento della sesta epoca di Cristo (il 1315) vaticinato dai testi sacri dell'età di mezzo. E tutto fa pure pensare che D. tale coincidenza l'abbia concepita e immaginata, affidandosi non soltanto al gusto medievale della criptografia profetica, ma anche a un gusto letterario-scenografico, quasi da miniatura in-

castonata in un più ampio contesto figurativo: il *carro,* il *gigante,* la *fuia,* la cornice del Paradiso terrestre, un paesaggio reale e allegorico insieme e nel mezzo, con una sua luce particolare, in singolare corrispondenza col paesaggio celeste delle *stelle propinque,* il fatidico monogramma, che peraltro sembra dare consistenza e suggello alle attese del poeta così costantemente e intensamente vissute lungo l'esilio e ricreate lungo il poema.

Everything, however, leads us to believe that according to the authoritative opinion and the valid arguments of Parodi, the DXV is Henry VII, that is, the heir of the eagle, the same "sublime eagle" of the letter to the princes (V, 11); and that in making the prophecy, Dante has followed the cryptographic method used by St. John in the Apocalypse (13:18), where in the number 666 Nero is indicated, and the method was reinstated by medieval symbolism; and that he thus celebrated the happy coincidence between the hoped-for triumph of Henry VII in the near future and the advent of the sixth epoch of Christ (1315) prophesied by the sacred texts of the Middle Ages. Moreover, everything makes us think that Dante conceived and imagined such a coincidence, adopting not only the medieval taste for prophetic cryptography, but also a literary-scenographic taste, almost in the manner of a miniature set into a broader figurative context: the chariot, the giant, the harlot, the frame of the earthly Paradise, a scene both real and allegorical, and in the midst of this, with a particular light, in striking correspondence with the celestial focus on *stelle propinque* (stars which are near), the prophetic monogram, which moreover seems to give consistency and confirmation to the hopes of the poet so constantly and intensely held throughout his exile and recreated throughout his poem.

On the popularity of such prophesying by numbers, Grandgent (p. 635 of his commentary) observes:

The 13th and 14th centuries witnessed a considerable vogue of prophetic literature and mystic interpretation.

Aside from the Kabbalistic method,—which assigned numerical values to the letters, and explained one word by another whose letters added up to the same sum,— the transposition of letters was used, and the attribution of special significances to letters and numbers. Lucian, in *Alexander or the False Prophet*, gives the name of the pretender as "one, thirty, five, and twenty more"— which, substituting Greek letters for their numerical equivalents, reads ᾽Αλεξ. Speculation as to the secret meaning of numbers, which is so curiously illustrated in the *Vita Nuova*, Ch. XXX [XXIX], was common enough among scholars and theologians. A standing problem was the "number of the beast," in Rev. xiii, 18: "Here is wisdom. Let him that hath understanding count the number of the beast; for it is the number of a man; and his number is Six hundred threescore and six." Joachim and St. Thomas discuss the possible values of the letters and the numbers that make up DCLXVI, and point out (as Victorinus had done in the fourth century) that with a shift of its last two members the combination reads DIC LVX, the not very relevant Latin phrase, *dic, lux.*

The reader who has time for lengthy arguments toward the solution of this enigmatic prophecy will find those of E. Moore (1903, pp. 253-83) of special interest. Moore holds that the prediction applies specifically to Henry VII, who became emperor in 1308.

44. *anciderà = ucciderà.   la fuia*: The harlot who has stolen or usurped the place of rightful authority (see *Purg.* XXXII, 148-60). "Fuia" is from *fura.*

47. *Temi*: Themis was a daughter of Heaven (Uranus) and Earth (Gaea). She was regarded as a prophetic divinity and was supposed to have been Apollo's predecessor at Delphi. When Deucalion and Pyrrha asked how they were to repeople the earth after the deluge, Themis told them to cast their mother's bones behind them, the meaning being that they were to throw stones behind their backs (Ovid, *Metam.* I,

379-94). An account is given by Ovid of how, after the riddle of the Sphinx had been solved by Oedipus, Themis in anger sent a monster to ravage the flocks and fields of the Thebans. See *Metam.* VII, 762-65:

> protinus Aoniis inmittitur altera Thebis
> (scilicet alma Themis non talia linquit inulta!)
> pestis, et exitio multi pecorumque suoque
> rurigenae pavere feram . . .

Straightway a second monster was sent against Aonian Thebes (and surely kind Themis does not let such things go unpunished!) and many country dwellers were in terror of the fierce creature, fearing both for their own and their flocks' destruction.

Sfinge: The Sphinx was a she-monster who appeared in the neighborhood of Thebes and, seated on a rock, put a riddle to every Theban who passed by, slaying all those who could not supply the answer. The riddle—a creature with four feet has two feet and three feet and only one voice, but its feet vary, and when it has most, it is weakest—was solved by Oedipus, who replied that the creature was a man: in infancy he crawls upon all fours, in manhood he stands erect upon two feet, and in old age he supports his tottering steps with a staff. The Sphinx, on hearing the solution of the riddle, flung herself down from the rock and was killed. See Ovid, *Metam.* VII, 759-60; Statius, *Theb.* I, 66-67.

48. *attuia*: Probably from *attuiare*, a form of *atturare*, which could derive from the Provençal *aturar* in the sense of "impede." The form is unique with Dante. See the *Enciclopedia dantesca*, under the entry "attuiare."

49-51. *ma tosto fier . . . biade*: Grandgent (p. 636 of his commentary) observes:

> To emphasize the mysteriousness of his prediction, Dante compares it to the utterances of the goddess Themis, whose obscure oracle is recorded in *Met.*, I, 377-94, and to the riddle of the bloodthirsty Theban Sphinx, finally guessed by Oedipus (*Met.*, VII, 759-61; *Thebaid*, I, 66-7). Dark though his words may be,—

he adds,—the events shall ere long solve the problem—
even as Oedipus, the son of Laius, unraveled the
Sphinx's puzzle. Ovid, in *Met.*, VII, 759-60, relates that
this son of Laius had cleared up the riddles which had
never been understood before:

> "Carmina Laïades non intellecta priorum
> Solverat ingeniis."

["Oedipus, the son of Laïus, had solved the riddle which
had been inscrutable to the understanding of all be-
fore."] Dante, however, evidently read the passage in a
faulty text, which substituted *Naiades* for *Laiades* and
solvunt for *solverat*, and was thus led to believe that
Naiads, or water-nymphs, were the successful guessers.
Therefore, instead of saying "the events shall be the
Oedipus (or Laiades) that shall explain the mystery,"
he puts it: "The facts shall soon be the Naiads that shall
solve this hard enigma."

49. *fier = saranno.*

52. *porte = portate*, "uttered."

54. *del viver ch'è un correre a la morte*: See Augustine, *De
civ. Dei* XIII, 10:

> Ex quo enim quisque in isto corpore morituro esse
> coeperit, nunquam in eo non agitur ut mors veniat. Hoc
> enim agit eius mutabilitas toto tempore vitae huius (si
> tamen vita dicenda est), ut veniatur in mortem. Nemo
> quippe est qui non ei post annum sit, quam ante annum
> fuit, et cras quam hodie, et hodie quam heri, et paulo
> post quam nunc, et nunc quam paulo ante propinquior.
> Quoniam quidquid temporis vivitur, de spatio vivendi
> demitur; et quotidie fit minus minusque quod restat:
> ut omnino nihil sit aliud tempus vitae huius, quam
> cursus ad mortem . . .

> From the first moment that life begins in a mortal body
> every movement made hastens the approach of death,
> for the simple reason that, in the whole course of life
> —if it can be called life—the changes in the body make

up a march toward death. There is no one who will not be nearer to death next year than last, tomorrow than today, today than yesterday, a moment from now than now, and nearer now than a moment ago. For, every moment that is lived subtracts from the length of life, and day after day less and less remains. Thus, the course of life is nothing but a race toward death . . .

55. *aggi = abbi.*

57. *ch'è or due volte dirubata quivi*: The tree of law or God's justice has been despoiled by Adam and by the vicissitudes enacted in *Purg.* XXXII, 109-60, especially the culminating outrage done by the giant in detaching the chariot from the tree, for the binding of its pole to that plant had caused it to be restored from the despoilment resulting from Adam's disobedience.

58. *schianta*: Referring particularly to the eagle's violence to the tree (*Purg.* XXXII, 112-14).

61. *Per*: "Because of."

61–63. *Per morder quella . . . punio*: On the reference here to Adam, Grandgent comments: "Adam longed for redemption by Christ,—who took upon himself the punishment for Adam's sin,—during more than 5000 years, i.e., 930 on earth (Gen. v, 5) and 4302 in Limbus (*Par.* XXVI, 118-20). According to the chronology of Eusebius, Christ was born in the year 5200 after the creation."

65–66. *per singular cagione . . . cima*: See *Purg.* XXXII, 40-42.

67. *Elsa*: The Elsa is a river of Tuscany which rises in the hills to the west of Siena and, flowing northwest, joins the Arno a few miles west of Empoli. In certain parts of the river, especially in the neighborhood of Colle di Val d'Elsa, its water has the property of "petrifying" objects immersed in it, being charged with carbonic acid and subcarbonate of lime.

69. *'l piacer loro*: The pleasure they gave you.   *Piramo*: For the story of Pyramus and Thisbe, see n. to *Purg.* XXVII, 37-39. In mentioning Pyramus here, the poet is referring to the change of color in the mulberry, which is said to have turned from white to crimson when Pyramus stabbed himself at the foot of a mulberry tree. Beatrice is saying that Dante's vain thoughts have stained his mind even as the blood of Pyramus stained the mulberry.

70. *tante circostanze*: The vicissitudes enacted around the tree in *Purg.* XXXII.

71-72. *la giustizia di Dio . . . l'arbor*: As Grandgent observes (p. 623 of his commentary): "Law naturally takes the form, 'thou shalt not'; and the tree of knowledge of good and evil, the subject of God's first prohibition to man (Gen. ii, 17), is a fit symbol of divine Law." Divine law is now stated in terms of God's justice and of such prohibition. The reader will recall that, beginning with Virgil's words to Dante at the end of *Purg.* XXVII, justice, in one sense or another, has been the keynote of these final cantos of the *Purgatorio.* One also recalls that the very shape of the tree expresses interdiction.

72. *moralmente*: In the moral sense. The tree and the events around it are real, or they are the re-enactment symbolically of real vicissitudes. But they yield a moral meaning, as events in the poem often do in allegory. See C. S. Singleton (1954), pp. 84-90.

77. *'l = il*. This clearly refers to "all that you have been shown here."   *per quello*: "For the same reason."

78. *che si reca il bordon di palma cinto*: It was customary for a pilgrim to bring back his staff "wreathed with palm" from the Holy Land, to show where he had been and what he had seen.

85. *conoschi = conosca.   scuola*: Beatrice, who is *Sapientia desursum descendens* (Wisdom descending from above), judges in these words Dante's purely philosophical

studies, studies which are in part represented by his *Convivio*, highly imbued with the cult of Aristotle and with such philosophy as that ancient philosopher propounded without supernatural aid. The charge here can thus be seen as *one* aspect of Beatrice's charges against Dante as stated in *Purg.* XXX, 130-35. It should be noted that vs. 88 shifts to the plural "vostra," thus indicating that our human way, when purely human and unaided by the kind of Wisdom from above that Beatrice represents in the allegory, is far from the divine way. Beatrice, in the *Paradiso*, will amply demonstrate this truth. See Thomas Aquinas, *Summa theol.* I, q. 1, a. 6, ad 1: "Sacra doctrina non supponit sua principia ab aliqua scientia humana, sed a scientia divina, a qua, sicut a summa sapientia, omnis nostra cognitio ordinatur." ("Sacred doctrine derives its principles not from any human knowledge, but from the divine knowledge, through which, as through the highest wisdom, all our knowledge is set in order.")

86. *veggi = veda.*

87. *come*: "How," but meaning, in the context, "how poorly."

90. *il ciel che più alto festina*: The Primum Mobile is the ninth and outermost of the nine revolving heavens, the material heaven most distant from the earth. Cf. Isa. 55:8: "Non enim cogitationes meae cogitationes vestrae, neque viae vestrae viae meae, dicit Dominus." ("For my thoughts are not your thoughts: nor are your ways my ways, saith the Lord.")

93. *honne = ne ho.*

94-96. *E se tu ricordar . . . ancoi*: Lethe was the traditional river of the lower world from which the shades drank and thereby were granted forgetfulness of the past. (See n. to *Purg.* XXVIII, 130.) See Servius on *Aen.* VI, 703, 705, and 714; he says (705): "*Lethaeum* autem ἀπὸ τῆς λήθης constat, i.e. oblivione, esse dictum." ("But corresponding to ἀπὸ τῆς λήθης it is called *Lethaeum*, that is, oblivion.")

96. *ancoi*: "This day." Cf. *Purg.* XIII, 52; XX, 70.

99. *colpa ne la tua voglia altrove attenta*: Grandgent translates this: "That there was guilt in the turning of thy desire to another quarter." He comments: "Inasmuch as Lethe removes only the memory of *sin*, the fact that he has now forgotten his recreancy to Beatrice—which he remembered just before drinking of the stream (XXXI, 34-6)—proves that this estrangement was sinful."

101. *converrassi* = *si converrà*.

103–4. *E più corusco . . . merigge*: It is now noon, and when the sun is in that position, it appears to move slower than when it is near the horizon. Cf. *Par.* XXIII, 11-12.

105. *che qua e là, come li aspetti, fassi*: According to the point of view, explains Grandgent, the noonday circle or meridian shifts to one side and the other; it is not a fixed line, like the equator.   *fassi* = *si fa*.

106. *s'affisser* = *s'affissero*, "stopped."

107. *iscorta* = *scorta*.

108. *vestigge*: Plural of the older feminine singular *vestigia*.

110. *nigri* = *negri*.

111. *l'alpe*: Singular for plural, "mountains."

112. *Eufratès*: River of southwest Asia, which rises in Turkey and flows across Syria and Iraq into the Persian Gulf, after being joined by the Tigris. Of the four rivers mentioned in Genesis as being in the earthly Paradise, it is the last named (Gen. 2:10): "Et fluvius egrediebatur de loco voluptatis ad irrigandum paradisum, qui inde dividitur in quattuor capita." ("A river rose in Eden watering the garden; and from there, it separated into four branches.") Of these four, in Gen. 2:14, the third is named Tigris and the fourth Euphrates.   *Tigri*: River of southwest Asia which rises in Kurdistan in Turkey and flows through Iraq into the Persian Gulf, after being joined by the Euphrates.

113. *uscir d'una fontana*: The statement, found in several medieval authors, that the Tigris and Euphrates spring from the same source is contested by Roger Bacon, who discusses the question in Part IV of the *Opus maius*; he says (PP. 333-34):

> Varius autem est ortus eorum. . . . Quod autem Boetius quinto de consolatione et Sallustius dicunt, quod Tigris et Euphrates uno se fonte resolvunt, potest intelligi de fonte Paradisi; nam hoc verum est secundum Scripturam, quam Boetius saltem bene scivit, et Sallustius ex revolutione historiae Scripturae credere potuit; aut hoc verum est de ortu eorum in Armenia, quoniam uterque ibi oritur secundum Plinium; aut intelligi poterit de ortu eorum citra Taurum montem, nam occursu eius absorbentur in terram, et ex altera sui parte erumpunt.

> Their source is variously given. . . . The statement of Boetius in the fifth book on Consolation and that of Sallust that the Tigris and the Euphrates flow from the same source can be understood of their source in paradise; for this is a fact according to Scripture, with which Boetius at least was well acquainted, and Sallust might have believed from a study of the history in the Scriptures. This is also true as regards their origin in Armenia, since both rivers have their source there, according to Pliny [see *Nat. hist.* VI, ix, 25]; or it can be understood of their source this side of the Taurus range, for when they meet it they sink into the ground, and burst forth on the other side.

The assertion here attributed to Sallust is not to be found in any of his extant works. Dante may have had in mind the following passage from Boethius (*Consol. philos.* V, i, vss. 3-4):

> Tigris et Euphrates uno se fonte resolvunt
> Et mox abiunctis dissociantur aquis.

> Tigris from the same head doth with Euphrates rise,
> And forthwith they themselves divide in several parts.

On the matter of Dante's conception of two rivers only in the earthly Paradise, in place of the four named in Genesis (a

striking departure from scriptural authority in itself), see
C. S. Singleton (1958), pp. 159-83.

119. *Matelda*: This is the only mention of Matelda's name,
but it has left us with what has proved to be an insoluble
problem. We understand perhaps what the "fair lady" (as she
has been termed up to now) represents in symbol and al-
legory, i.e., natural justice (see C. S. Singleton, 1958,
pp. 204-53). But what historical personage is intended by
the name? Beatrice and Virgil were, first of all, historical,
they actually existed as individuals with such names. But
Matelda? Many have been the historical candidates pro-
posed, but it must be admitted that none is completely plausi-
ble. The historical Matelda (if Dante intended one) remains
shrouded in mystery. For a review of the many and various
theories that have been advanced, see the entry "Matelda"
in the *Enciclopedia dantesca*.

   Of course, it could be argued that the poet intended *no*
historical person here at all, remembering that with the pro-
cession here at the top of the mountain we have entered into
a radically different kind of allegory, in the sense that the fig-
ures that walk in the procession are books of the Bible, not
their historical authors. But then why name the lady at all?
Many a Dante scholar must have wished, in his perplexity,
that Matelda had remained without a name! In any case, the
puzzle remains.

125. *la memoria priva*: Grandgent comments: "Remorse
for his sin had made Dante forget the promise of good
(XXVIII, 127-33); now the recollection of sin has been re-
moved by Lethe, and the memory of the good that is his due
must be revived by Eunoe."

127. *Eunoè*: See n. to *Purg.* XXVIII, 130-31.

134. *mossesi = si mosse.   Stazio*: As noted before, Sta-
tius' presence here is a precious guide to the reader, since
what Statius does at the summit of the mountain is a sure
indication of what all souls must do when liberated from Pur-
gatory. Thus, though it is not explicitly stated, Statius must

have passed through Lethe, even as Dante did, and must have drunk of its water, for in *Purg.* XXVIII, 130-32, it is specifically stated that the one river and the other must be tasted, else their effective function is not realized. And now we see indeed that Statius must pass through and taste of Eunoe to become, like Dante, pure and ready to ascend to his reward. We hear no more of him. Presumably, he, like every soul who is thus liberated from Purgatory, rises directly to the Empyrean and to his eternal beatitude, there being a seat reserved for him in the great amphitheater of the elect which we are to see at the end.

But the fact that Matelda (now specifically named) has the office of drawing each and every soul that reaches the summit through the two streams of Lethe and Eunoe only compounds the mystery of her full meaning and of her (possible) historical identity! The phrasing of vs. 128 leaves no doubt about this: "come tu se' usa." But for all the mystery surrounding her, one thing is clear: Matelda performs this office for all souls, like Statius, that are liberated from Purgatory. Beatrice's advent had meaning for Dante, the living man, and no meaning whatever for Statius. Beatrice does not come to any soul who completes his progression through this second realm. But Matelda, apparently, takes each of the souls who reach this summit through the two rivers of Lethe and Eunoe.

136-41. *S'io avessi, lettor . . . l'arte*: The poet ends his second *cantica* with an address to the reader, claiming a certain limit of art, as though only so many pages and no more could be allotted to this *cantica*. "Ordite" (vs. 140) draws on the metaphor of weaving—the pattern pre-established, the design is such. Art requires it. Actually, the length of cantos throughout the poem varies, from 115 (the shortest) to 160 (the longest), as does the length of the *cantiche* (*Inferno* containing 4,720 verses; *Purgatorio,* 4,755 verses; and *Paradiso,* 4,758 verses). Thus the *cantiche* themselves are remarkably close to being equal in length. Such, finally, was the "curb of his art."

138. *non m'avria sazio = non mi avrebbe saziato.*

142–45. *Io ritornai . . . stelle*: The final theme of the *Purgatorio* matches its initial theme, essentially renewal, rebirth. See n. to *Purg.* I, 7.

145. *puro e disposto a salire a le stelle*: Thus the second *cantica*, like the first and the third, ends with the word *stelle*. See n. to *Inf.* XXXIV, 139.

List of Works Cited
and of Abbreviations

ABBREVIATIONS

a.　articulus

Aen.　*Aeneid* (Virgil)

Anonimo fiorentino　*Commento alla Divina Commedia d'anonimo fiorentino del secolo XIV*

Ars amat.　*Ars amatoria* (Ovid)

Comm. De anima　*Commentarium magnum in Aristotelis De anima libros* (Averroës)

Comm. in somn. Scip.　*Commentariorum in somnium Scipionis* (Macrobius)

Comm. Sapien.　*Commentarius in librum Sapientiae* (Bonaventura)

Comm. Sent. Petri Lombardi II　*Commentaria in quatuor libros Sententiarum magistri Petri Lombardi: In secundum librum Sententiarum* (Bonaventura)

Comm. Sent. Petri Lombardi IV　*Commentaria in quatuor libros Sententiarum magistri Petri Lombardi: In quartum librum Sententiarum* (Bonaventura)

Conf.　*Confessiones* (Augustine)

Consol. philos.　*Consolatio philosophiae* (Boethius)

Conv.　*Convivio* (Dante Alighieri)

De apprehen.　*Liber de apprehensione* (Albertus Magnus)

Decam.　*Il Decameron* (Giovanni Boccaccio)

De civ. Dei   *Ad Marcellinum De civitate Dei contra paganos* (Augustine)

De div. nat.   *De divisione naturae* (Johannes Scotus)

De doct. Chris.   *De doctrina Christiana* (Augustine)

De fin.   *De finibus bonorum et malorum* (Cicero)

De gener. animal.   *De generatione animalium* (Aristotle)

Della comp.   *Della composizione del mondo* (Ristoro d'Arezzo)

De mon.   *De monarchia* (Dante Alighieri)

De nat. et orig. animae   *Liber de natura et origine animae* (Albertus Magnus)

De vulg. eloqu.   *De vulgari eloquentia* (Dante Alighieri)

Eclog.   *Eclogues* (Virgil)

Enar. in Ps.   *Enarrationes in Psalmos* (Augustine)

Epist.   *Epistolae* (Dante Alighieri)

Eth. Nicom.   *Ethica Nicomachea* (Aristotle)

Etym.   *Etymologiarum sive Originum libri viginti* (Isidore of Seville)

Exp. Eth. Nicom.   *In decem libros Ethicorum ad Nicomachum expositio* (Thomas Aquinas)

Exp. Meteor.   *In quatuor libros Meteorologicorum expositio* (Thomas Aquinas)

Exp. Phys.   *In octo libros Physicorum expositio* (Thomas Aquinas)

Fact. dict. memor.   *Factorum et dictorum memorabilium libri novem* (Valerius Maximus)

Georg.   *Georgics* (Virgil)

Hist.   *Historiarum adversum paganos libri septem* (Orosius)

Hist. animal.   *De animalibus historia* (Aristotle)

Homil.   *Quadraginta homiliarum in Evangelia libri duo* (Gregory I)

Inf.   *Inferno* (Dante Alighieri)

In Ioan.   *In Ioannis evangelium tractatus CXXIV* (Augustine)

LCL   Loeb Classical Library

lect.   lectio

Metam.   *Metamorphoses* (Ovid)

Metaphys.   *Metaphysica* (Aristotle)

Meteor.   *Meteorologica* (Aristotle)

MLN   *Modern Language Notes*

Moral.   *Moralium libri, sive Expositio in librum b. Iob* (Gregory I)

Nat. hist.   *Naturalis historia* (Pliny)

obj.   objectio

OFr   Old French

Par.   *Paradiso* (Dante Alighieri)

Phars.   *Pharsalia* (Lucan)

P.L.   *Patrologiae cursus completus: Series Latina*, ed. J.-P. Migne. Paris, 1844-64 (with later printings).

PMLA   *Publications of the Modern Language Association of America*

Polit.   *Politica* (Aristotle)

Purg.   *Purgatorio* (Dante Alighieri)

q.   quaestio

resp.   respondeo

Rhet.   *Rhetorica* (Aristotle)

RIS   *Rerum Italicarum scriptores ab anno aerae Christianae quingentesimo ad millesimum quingentesimum*, ed. L. A. Muratori. Milan, 1723-51. New edn.: *Rerum Italicarum scriptores; Raccolta degli storici italiani dal cinquecento al millecinquecento,* rev. under the direction of G. Carducci, V. Fiorini, P. Fedele. Città di Castello, Bologna, 1900— (in progress).

Sent.   *Sententiarum libri quatuor* (Peter Lombard)

Summa theol.   *Summa theologica* (Thomas Aquinas)

Suppl.   Supplementum

Theb.   *Thebaid* (Statius)

LIST OF WORKS CITED

Unless specifically and otherwise stated, all classical Greek and Latin texts cited in the *Commentary* to the *Purgatorio* are those of the Loeb Classical Library, to which the reader should refer.

Abelard, Peter. *Expositio in Hexaemeron.* In Migne, *P.L.* CLXXVIII.

Aesop. *Favole d'Esopo volgarizzate per uno da Siena.* Florence, 1864.

Ageno, Franca. "Per l'interpretazione di quattro passi danteschi (*Inf.*, XXVI, 91 e 126; *Purg.*, XIII, 128; *Par.*, XVII, 66)." *Studi danteschi* XXXIV (1957): 205-15.

Agnelli, Giovanni. "Il verso 123 del canto XIII del *Purgatorio* nella favola, nei costumi e nelle tradizioni lombarde." *Giornale dantesco* II (1895): 87-102.

Agnolo di Tura. *Cronaca senese attribuita ad Agnolo di Tura del Grasso detta la Cronaca maggiore,* ed. Alessandro Lisini and Fabio Iacometti. In *RIS* XV, pt. 6, pp. 253-564. New edn.

Albertus Magnus. *Opera omnia,* ed. Auguste and Émile Borgnet. Paris, 1890-99:
    Commentarii in secundum librum Sententiarum, vol. XXVII

De animalibus, vols. XI-XII
De coelo et mundo, vol. IV
Liber de apprehensione, vol. V
Liber de natura et origine animae, vol. IX

Alighieri, Dante. *La Commedia secondo l'antica vulgata,* ed. Giorgio Petrocchi. Vol. I: *Introduzione*; vol. III: *Purgatorio*. Milan, 1966, 1967.

————. *Le opere di Dante: Testo critico della Società Dantesca Italiana*. 2d edn. Florence, 1960:

> *Convivio*, ed. Ernesto Giacomo Parodi and Flaminio Pellegrini, pp. 143-293.
>
> *De vulgari eloquentia*, ed. Pio Rajna, pp. 295-327.
>
> *La Divina Commedia*, ed. Giuseppe Vandelli, pp. 443-798.
>
> *Epistole*, ed. Ermenegildo Pistelli, pp. 383-415.
>
> *Monarchia*, ed. Enrico Rostagno, pp. 329-81.
>
> *Questio de aqua et terra*, ed. Ermenegildo Pistelli, pp. 429-42.
>
> *Rime; Rime dubbie*, ed. Michele Barbi, pp. 51-142.
>
> *Vita nuova*, ed. Michele Barbi, pp. 1-49.

————. *Rime,* ed. Gianfranco Contini, pp. 81-93. Turin, 1965.

————. TRANSLATIONS

The Convivio of Dante Alighieri, trans. Philip H. Wicksteed. The Temple Classics. London, 1903.

Dante's Lyric Poetry, trans. K. Foster and P. Boyde. Vol. I, pp. 149-55. Oxford, 1967.

A Translation of the Latin Works of Dante Alighieri. The Temple Classics. London, 1940:

> *The De monarchia*, trans. Philip H. Wicksteed, pp. 125-280.
>
> *The De vulgari eloquentia*, trans. A. G. Ferrers Howell, pp. 1-115.
>
> *Epistolae*, trans. Philip H. Wicksteed, pp. 293-368.
>
> *The Quaestio de aqua et terra*, trans. Philip H. Wicksteed, pp. 387-423.

The Vita Nuova and Canzoniere of Dante Alighieri, ed. and trans. Thomas Okey and Philip H. Wicksteed. The Temple Classics. London, 1906.

Amari, Michele. *La guerra del Vespro Siciliano*. 9th edn. Vol. III. Milan, 1886.

Ancona, Alessandro d'. *Lectura Dantis*: *Il canto VII del Purgatorio letto da Alessandro d'Ancona nella Sala di Dante in Orsanmichele*. Florence, 1901.

Ancona, Paolo d'. *La miniature italienne du Xᵉ au XVIᵉ siècle*, trans. M. P. Poirier. Paris, 1925.

Andreas Capellanus. *De amore*, ed. E. Trojel. Copenhagen, 1892.

———. *The Art of Courtly Love*, trans. John Jay Parry. New York, 1941.

Angelitti, F. Review of Alfraganus, *Il Libro dell'aggregazione delle stelle* (*Dante, Convivio, II, VI-134*) *secondo il codice mediceo-laurenziano, pl. 29, cod. 9 contemporaneo a Dante*, ed. Romeo Campani, 1910. In *Bullettino della Società Dantesca Italiana* N.S. XVIII (1911): 22-47.

Le antiche rime volgari, ed. A. D'Ancona and D. Comparetti. Vol. V. Bologna, 1888.

Aquarone, Bartolomeo. *Dante in Siena ovvero accenni nella Divina Commedia a cose sanesi*. Città di Castello, 1889.

Aquinas, Thomas. *Opera omnia*. Parma, 1852-73. Photolithographic reimpression, with Introduction by Vernon J. Bourke, New York, 1948-50:

> *De malo*, vol. VIII
> *De veritate,* vol. IX
> *De veritate Catholicae fidei contra Gentiles seu Summa philosophica*, vol. V
> *De virtutibus cardinalibus*, vol. VIII
> *In X libros Ethicorum ad Nicomachum expositio,* vol. XXI
> *In VIII libros Physicorum expositio*, vol. XVIII
> *In IV libros Meteorologicorum expositio*, vol. XIX
> *In III libros De anima expositio*, vol. XX
> *Summa theologica*, vols. I-IV.

———. MARIETTI PUBLICATIONS

In Aristotelis librum De anima commentarium, ed. Angelo M. Pirotta, O.P. 2d edn. Turin, 1936.

In decem libros Ethicorum Aristotelis ad Nicomachum

expositio, ed. Raimondo M. Spiazzi, O.P. 3rd edn. Turin, 1964.

In octo libros Physicorum Aristotelis expositio, ed. P. M. Maggiòlo, O.P. Turin, 1954.

————. TRANSLATIONS

Aristotle's de Anima, trans. Kenelm Foster, O.P. and Silvester Humphries, O.P. New Haven, 1951.

Commentary on Aristotle's Physics, trans. Richard J. Blackwell, Richard J. Spath, and W. Edmund Thirlkel. New Haven, 1963.

Commentary on the Nicomachean Ethics, trans. C. I. Litzinger, O.P. Vol. II. Chicago, 1964.

On the Truth of the Catholic Faith, Summa contra Gentiles. Book I: God, trans. Anton C. Pegis, F.R.S.C. Garden City, N.Y., 1955. *Book II: Creation*, trans. James F. Anderson. 1962. *Book III: Providence*, trans. Vernon J. Bourke. 2 vols. 1956. *Book IV: Salvation*, trans. Charles J. O'Neil. 1957.

Summa theologica, trans. Fathers of the English Dominican Province. 3 vols. New York, 1947-48.

Truth, trans. James V. McGlynn, S.J., Robert W. Mulligan, S.J., and Robert W. Schmidt, S.J. 3 vols. Chicago, 1952, 1953, 1954.

Aristotle. "Antiqua Translatio" in Thomas Aquinas, *Opera omnia*, Parma, 1852-73. Photolithographic reimpression, with Introduction by Vernon J. Bourke, New York, 1948-50:

> *De anima*, vol. XX
> *Ethica Nicomachea*, vol. XXI
> *Metaphysica*, vol. XX
> *Meteorologica*, vol. XIX
> *Physica*, vol. XVIII
> *Politica*, vol. XXI

————. *De animalibus historia,* ed. Leonhard Dittmeyer. Leipzig, 1907.

————. MARIETTI PUBLICATIONS

De anima. In Thomas Aquinas, *In Aristotelis librum De anima commentarium*, ed. Angelo M. Pirotta, O.P. 2d edn. Turin, 1936.

Ethica Nicomachea. In Thomas Aquinas, *In decem libros Ethicorum Aristotelis ad Nicomachum expositio,* ed. Raimondo M. Spiazzi, O.P. 3rd edn. Turin, 1964.

Metaphysica. In Thomas Aquinas, *In duodecim libros Metaphysicorum Aristotelis expositio,* ed. Raimondo M. Spiazzi, O.P. Turin, 1964.

Politica. In Thomas Aquinas, *In libros Politicorum Aristotelis expositio,* ed. Raimondo M. Spiazzi, O.P. Turin, 1951.

————. TRANSLATIONS

De anima. In *Aristotle's de Anima,* trans. Kenelm Foster, O.P. and Silvester Humphries, O.P. New Haven, 1951.

Metaphysics. In Thomas Aquinas, *Commentary on the Metaphysics of Aristotle,* trans. John P. Rowan. Vol. 1. Chicago, 1961.

Nicomachean Ethics. In Thomas Aquinas, *Commentary on the Nicomachean Ethics,* trans. C. I. Litzinger, O.P. 2 vols. Chicago, 1964.

Auerbach, Erich. "Saul's Pride (*Purg.* XII. 40-42)." *MLN* LXIV (1949): 267-69.

Augustine. *Ad Marcellinum De civitate Dei contra paganos.* In Migne, *P.L.* XLI.

————. *The City of God. Books VIII-XVI,* trans. Gerald G. Walsh, S.J. and Grace Monahan, O.S.U. *Books XVII-XXII,* trans. Gerald G. Walsh, S.J. and Daniel J. Honan. New York, 1952, 1954.

————. *De doctrina Christiana.* In Migne, *P.L.* XXXIV.

————. *Christian Instruction,* trans. John J. Gavigan, O.S.A. In *Christian Instruction; Admonition and Grace; The Christian Combat; Faith, Hope and Charity,* pp. 1-235. 2d edn. New York, 1950.

————. *De Genesi ad litteram.* In Migne, *P.L.* XXXIV.

————. *De sermone Domini in monte secundum Matthaeum.* In Migne, *P.L.* XXXIV.

————. *Commentary on the Lord's Sermon on the Mount with Seventeen Related Sermons,* trans. Denis J. Kavanagh, O.S.A. New York, 1951.

————. *De symbolo*: *sermo ad catechumenos*. In Migne, *P.L.* XL.

————. *De Trinitate*. In Migne, *P.L.* XLII.

————. *Enarrationes in Psalmos*. In Migne, *P.L.* XXXVII.

————. *Enchiridion ad Laurentium sive De fide, spe et charitate*. In Migne, *P.L.* XL.

————. *Faith, Hope and Charity*, trans. Bernard M. Peebles. In *Christian Instruction; Admonition and Grace; The Christian Combat; Faith, Hope and Charity*, pp. 355-472. 2d edn. New York, 1950.

————. *In Ioannis evangelium tractatus CXXIV*. In Migne, *P.L.* XXXV.

————. *St. Augustine's Confessions*, trans. William Watts 1631), preface by W.H.D. Rouse. Vol. I. LCL, 1912.

————. *Sermones ad populum*. In Migne, *P.L.* XXXIX.

Austin, H.D. "Dante Notes." *MLN* XXXVII (1922): 36-39.

————. "Di alcune metafore controverse nell'opera di Dante." *Giornale dantesco* XXXIII (1932): 91-142.

Averroës. *Commentarium magnum in Aristotelis De anima libros*, ed. F. Stuart Crawford. Cambridge, Mass., 1953.

Bacon, Roger. *The "Opus Maius" of Roger Bacon*, ed. John Henry Bridges. Vol. I. London, 1900.

————. *The Opus Maius of Roger Bacon*, trans. Robert Belle Burke. Vol. I. Philadelphia, 1928.

Banchi, L. Letter printed in *Giornale storico della letteratura italiana* I (1883): 523-24.

Barbi, Michele. Review of A. Lisini, *Nuovo documento della Pia de' Tolomei figlia di Buonincontro Guastelloni*, 1893; Pio Spagnotti, *La Pia de' Tolomei*: *saggio storico-critico*, 1893. In *Bullettino della Società Dantesca Italiana* N.S. I (1894): 60-64.

————. " 'Non esser duro più ch'altri sia stato,' *Inf.* XXVII, 56." *Studi danteschi* I (1920a): 137-42.

————. "Per un passo dell'epistola all'amico fiorentino." *Studi danteschi* II (1920b): 115-48.

————. " 'Sotto la guardia de la grave mora' (*Purg.*, III, 129)." *Studi danteschi* IV (1921a): 134-35.

Barbi, Michele. "La luna 'fatta com'un secchion che tutto arda' (*Purg.*, XVIII, 78)." *Studi danteschi* IV (1921b): 136-37.

———. "Ancora della tenzone di Dante con Forese." *Studi danteschi* XVI (1932): 69-103.

———. "Ancora sul testo della *Divina Commedia*." *Studi danteschi* XVIII (1934a): 5-57.

———. *Problemi di critica dantesca: Prima serie (1893-1918)*. Florence, 1934b.

———. "Tenzone con Forese Donati." In *Rime della Vita nuova e della giovinezza*, ed. M. Barbi and F. Maggini, pp. 275-373. Florence, 1956.

Barozzi, Niccolò. "Accenni a cose venete nel poem di Dante." In *Dante e il suo secolo*, ed. Mariano Cellini and Gaetano Ghivizzani, pp. 793-812. Florence, 1865.

Beck, J.-B. *Die Melodien der Troubadours*. Strasbourg, 1908.

Bernard of Clairvaux. *Sermones de tempore*. In Migne, *P.L.* CLXXXIII.

Biscaro, Gerolamo. "Dante e il buon Gherardo." *Studi medievali* N.S. 1 (1928): 74-113.

Boccaccio, Giovanni. *Amorosa visione*, ed. Vittore Branca. Florence, 1944.

———. *Il Decameron*, ed. Charles S. Singleton. 2 vols. Bari, 1955.

———. *Il Filocolo*, ed. Salvatore Battaglia. Bari, 1938.

Boethius. *The Theological Tractates; The Consolation of Philosophy* (trans. "I.T.," 1609). Ed. and trans. H. F. Stewart and E. K. Rand. LCL, 1962:

>*The Consolation of Philosophy*, pp. 128-411.

>*Quomodo substantiae in eo quod sint bonae sint cum non sint substantialia bona*, pp. 38-51.

Bonagiunta Orbicciani. See Contini, Gianfranco (1960).

Bonaventura. *Opera omnia*, ed. PP. Collegii a S. Bonaventura. Quaracchi, 1882-1902:

>*Collationes de septem donis Spiritus Sancti*, vol. V

>*Commentaria in quatuor libros Sententiarum magistri Petri Lombardi: In quartum librum Sententiarum*, vol. IV

>*Commentaria in quatuor libros Sententiarum*

magistri Petri Lombardi: In secundum librum Sententiarum, vol. II

Commentarius in librum Sapientiae, vol. VI

Sermones de Sanctis, vol. IX

Sermones de tempore, vol. IX

———. *See also* Conrad of Saxony.

Bonaventura, Arnaldo. *Dante e la musica*. Livorno, 1904.

Bongioanni, A. "Guido Guinizelli e la sua riforma poetica." *Giornale dantesco* IV (1897): 161-72, 248-83.

Bosco, Umberto. "Particolari danteschi." *Annali della R. Scuola Normale Superiore di Pisa, Lettere, storia e filosofia* ser. 2, XI (1942): 131-47.

Britt (O.S.B.), Matthew (ed.). *The Hymns of the Breviary and Missal*. Rev. edn. New York, 1955.

Busetto, Natale. "Il sonno, i sogni e le visioni." *Giornale dantesco* XIII (1905): 143-55.

Camilli, Amerindo. "La bolla giubilare di Bonifacio VIII e le indulgenze per i defunti e il ritardo di Casella." *Studi danteschi* XXX (1951): 207-9.

Canello, U. A. *La vita e le opere del trovatore Arnaldo Daniello*. Halle, 1883.

Casini, Tommaso. "Dante e la Romagna." *Giornale dantesco* I (1894): 19-27.

———. "Dante e la Romagna." *Giornale dantesco* IV (1897): 43-57.

Cavalcanti, Guido. *See* Contini, Gianfranco (1960).

Chaucer, Geoffrey. *The Works of Geoffrey Chaucer,* ed. F. N. Robinson. 2d edn. London, 1957.

Chaytor, H. J. *The Troubadours of Dante*. Oxford, 1902.

Ciacci, Gaspero. *Gli Aldobrandeschi nella storia e nella Divina Commedia*. Vol. I. Rome, 1935.

Cicchitto (O.F.M. Conv.), Leone. "Postille francescano-dantesche." *Miscellanea francescana* XXXV (1935): 107-17.

Cipolla, Francesco. "Noterelle dantesche." *Atti del R. Istituto Veneto di Scienze, Lettere ed Arti* ser. 7, VI (1894-95): 639-47.

Cipolla di Vallecorsa, C. "Perchè Dante prese in considerazione Traiano." *Giornale dantesco* xiv (1906): 199.

Compagni, Dino. *La cronica di Dino Compagni delle cose occorrenti ne' tempi suoi*, ed. Isidoro Del Lungo. In *RIS* ix, pt. 2. New edn.

Conrad of Saxony. *Speculum beatae Mariae Virginis.* Quaracchi, 1904.

Contini, Gianfranco (ed.). *Poeti del Duecento* (2 vols.; Milan, 1960):

      Bonagiunta Orbicciani, vol. i, pp. 257-82.

      Cavalcanti, Guido, vol. ii, pp. 487-567.

      Giacomo da Lentini, vol. i, pp. 49-90.

      Guinizzelli, Guido, vol. ii, pp. 447-85.

      Guittone d'Arezzo, vol. i, pp. 189-255.

————. *See* Alighieri, Dante.

Cook, Mabel Priscilla. "Indico legno." *PMLA* xviii (1903): 356-62.

Corpus chronicorum Bononiensium, ed. Albano Sorbelli. In *RIS* xviii, pt. i, vol. 3. New edn.

Crocioni, Giovanni. "Inanellare." *Lingua nostra* xiv (1953): 61-63.

Curtius, Ernst Robert. *European Literature and the Latin Middle Ages*, trans. from the German by Willard R. Trask. New York, 1953.

Davidsohn, Robert. *Firenze ai tempi di Dante*, trans. from the German by Eugenio Duprè Theseider. Florence, 1929.

Debenedetti, Santorre. "Documenti su Belacqua." *Bullettino della Società Dantesca Italiana* N.S. xiii (1906): 222-33.

Del Lungo, Isidoro. *Dino Compagni e la sua Cronica.* Vol. i, pt. 2. Florence, 1880.

————. *Dante ne' tempi di Dante.* Bologna, 1888.

Diez, Friedrich. *Leben und Werke der Troubadours.* 2d edn., ed. Karl Bartsch. Leipzig, 1882.

E.G.P. Review of Stefano Massa, *Così a sè e a noi buona ramogna quell'ombre orando*, 1897. In *Bullettino della Società Dantesca Italiana* N.S. vi (1899): 198-99.

Enciclopedia dantesca, ed. Umberto Bosco. 5 vols. Rome, 1970–(in progress).

Ercole, Francesco. Review of Mario Chiaudano, *Dante e il diritto romano*, 1912, extracted from *Giornale dantesco* xx (1912): 37-56, 94-119. In *Bullettino della Società Dantesca Italiana* N.S. xx (1913): 161-78.

Fatini, Giuseppe. " 'Dietro a le poste de le care piante' nella regione amiatina." *Giornale dantesco* xxv (1922): 38-47.

Fazio degli Uberti. *Il Dittamondo e le Rime*, ed. Giuseppe Corsi. Vol. 1: *Il Dittamondo*. Bari, 1952.

Fedele, Pietro. "Per la storia dell'attentato di Anagni." *Bullettino dell'Istituto Storico Italiano* xli (1921): 195-232.

Fiore di filosofi e di molti savi attribuito a Brunetto Latini, ed. Antonio Cappelli. Bologna, 1865.

Frezzi, Federigo. *Il Quadriregio*, ed. Enrico Filippini. Bari, 1914.

Gardner, Edmund G. *Dante and the Mystics*. London and New York, 1913.

Ghisalberti, Fausto. "Monticoli e Capelleti." *Giornale dantesco* xxxvi (1935): 27-69.

Giacomo da Lentini. *See* Contini, Gianfranco (1960).

Gihr, Nicholas. *The Holy Sacrifice of the Mass*, trans. from the German. St. Louis, 1949.

Gilby (O.P.), Thomas. *Barbara Celarent. A Description of Scholastic Dialectic*. London, 1949.

Giordano da Rivalto. *Prediche inedite del b. Giordano da Rivalto dell'ordine de' Predicatori*, ed. Enrico Narducci. Bologna, 1867.

Gorra, E. "I 'nove passi' di Beatrice." *Romanische Forschungen* xxiii (1907): 585-90.

Graf, Arturo. *Roma nella memoria e nelle immaginazioni del Medio Evo*. Turin, 1923.

Grandgent, Charles H. *"Quid ploras?" Annual Reports of the Dante Society* xlii-xliv (1926): 8-18.

Gregory I. *In librum primum Regum, qui et Samuelis dicitur, variarum expositionum*. In Migne, *P.L.* lxxix.

Gregory I. *Moralium libri, sive Expositio in librum b. Iob.*
In Migne, *P.L.* LXXV-LXXVI.

———. *Morals on the Book of Job,* trans. members of the
English Church. Vol. I; vol. III, pt. I. Oxford, 1844, 1847.

———. *XL Homiliarum in Evangelia libri duo.* In Migne,
P.L. LXXVI.

Guinizzelli, Guido. *See* Contini, Gianfranco (1960); Monaci,
Ernesto (1955).

Guittone d'Arezzo. *See* Contini, Gianfranco (1960).

Hamilton, George L. "The Pedigree of a Phrase in Dante
(*Purg.* VII, 107-8)." *The Romanic Review* XII (1921):
84-89.

Hatzantonis, Emmanuel S. "La Circe della *Divina Com-
media.*" *Romance Philology* XIII (1959-60): 390-400.

Hugh of St. Victor. *Adnotationes elucidatoriae in Penta-
teuchon.* In Migne, *P.L.* CLXXV.

Isidore of Seville. *Etymologiarum sive Originum libri XX,*
ed. W. M. Lindsay. Vol. II. Oxford, 1911.

Jacobus de Varagine. *Legenda aurea vulgo historia lom-
bardica dicta,* ed. T. Grässe. 2d edn. Leipzig, 1850.

Jeanroy, Alfred. *La Poésie lyrique des Troubadours.* 2 vols.
Toulouse and Paris, 1934.

Johannes Scotus. *De divisione naturae.* In Migne, *P.L.* CXXII.

John of Salisbury. *Policratici sive De nugis curialium et
vestigiis philosophorum libri VIII,* ed. Clemens C. I.
Webb. 2 vols. Oxford, 1909.

John the Deacon. *Sancti Gregorii Magni vita.* In Migne, *P.L.*
LXXV.

Julian, John. *A Dictionary of Hymnology.* New York, 1892.

Kantorowicz, Ernst H. "Dante's 'Two Suns.'" *University
of California Publications in Semitic Philology* XI (1951):
217-31.

———. *The King's Two Bodies. A Study in Mediaeval Po-
litical Theology.* Princeton, N.J., 1957.

Kolsen, Adolf. *Sämtliche Lieder des Trobadors Giraut de Bornelh.* Halle, 1910.

Latini, Brunetto. *Li livres dou tresor de Brunetto Latini,* ed. Francis J. Carmody. Berkeley, 1948.

Levi, Ezio. *Piccarda e Gentucca: Studi e ricerche dantesche.* Bologna, 1921.

Il libro di Sidrach, ed. Adolfo Bartoli. Vol. 1. Bologna, 1868.

Lisini, A. "A proposito di una recente pubblicazione su la 'Sapìa Dantesca.'" *Bullettino senese di storia patria* XXVII (1920): 61-89.

Litany of the Saints. In *The New Roman Missal,* ed. F. X. Lasance and Francis Augustine Walsh, O.S.B., pp. 1536-40. New York, 1945.

Loria, Cesare. *L'Italia nella Divina Commedia.* 2d edn. 2 vols. in 1. Florence, 1872.

Lubac, Henri de. *Surnaturel. Études historiques.* Paris, 1946.

Macrobius. *Commentariorum in somnium Scipionis.* In *Macrobius,* ed. Franz Eyssenhardt, pp. 465-641. Leipzig, 1868.

Maggini, F. Review of R. Davidsohn, *Forschungen zur älteren Geschichte von Florenz* (4 vols.), 1896-1908. In *Bullettino della Società Dantesca Italiana* N.S. XVII (1910): 120-30.

——. Review of Francesco Filippini, *Il Marco Lombardo dantesco,* 1924. In *Studi danteschi* X (1925): 146-47.

——. Review of Giovanni Colasanti, *La sepoltura di Manfredi lungo il Liri,* 1924, extracted from *Archivio della R. Società Romana di Storia Patria* XLVII (1924): 45-116; R. Pettazzoni, *La "grave mora" (Dante, Purgat. 3. 127 sg.): Studio su alcune forme e sopravvivenze della sacralità primitiva,* 1925, extracted from *Studi e materiali di storia delle religioni* I (1925): 1-65. In *Studi danteschi* XII (1927): 157-59.

Mancini, Augusto. Review of Enrico Cocchia, "Un preteso errore di Dante nell'interpretazione dell'*Eneide*." *Atti della*

R. *Accademia di Archeologia, Lettere e Belle Arti* [*di Napoli*], N.S. IX (1926): 485-98. In *Studi danteschi* XIII (1928): 113-15.

Mazzamuto, Pietro. "Cinquecento diece e cinque." In *Enciclopedia dantesca*, ed. Umberto Bosco. Vol. II, pp. 10-14. Rome, 1970.

Mercer, William. "The Pia of Dante." *The Academy* XXIX (1886): 434-35.

Monaci, Ernesto (ed.). "Rime di Guido Guinizelli." In *Crestomazia italiana dei primi secoli*, pp. 345-50. New edn., revised by Felice Arese. Rome, 1955.

Moore, Edward. *The Time-References in the Divina Commedia*. London, 1887.

————. *Studies in Dante. First Series: Scripture and Classical Authors in Dante*. Oxford, 1896 (reprinted 1969). *Second Series: Miscellaneous Essays*, 1899 (reprinted 1968). *Third Series: Miscellaneous Essays*, 1903 (reprinted 1968).

Nardi, Bruno. "Nuovi raffronti danteschi." *Giornale storico della letteratura italiana* LXXXV (1925): 94-97.

————. *Saggi di filosofia dantesca*. Milan, 1930.

————. *Dante e la cultura medievale: Nuovi saggi di filosofia dantesca*. 2d edn. Bari, 1949.

————. *Lectura Dantis: Il canto XV del Purgatorio*. Rome, 1953.

————. *Studi di filosofia medievale*. Rome, 1960.

Novati, Francesco. *Tre postille dantesche*. Milan, 1898.

————. *Indagini e postille dantesche*. Bologna, 1899.

————. *Freschi e minii del Dugento*. Milan, 1908.

Le novelle antiche, ed. Guido Biagi. Florence, 1880.

Il Novellino, ossia Libro di bel parlar gentile; I fatti di Enea di Frate Guido da Pisa; Il governo della famiglia di Agnolo Pandolfini, ed. Francesco Costèro. Milan, 1879.

Orosius. *Historiarum adversum paganos libri VII*, ed. Karl Zangemeister. Leipzig, 1889.

————. *Seven Books of History against the Pagans: The*

Apology of Paulus Orosius, trans. Irving Woodworth Raymond. New York, 1936.

Orr, M. A. *Dante and the Early Astronomers*. Rev. edn. London, 1956.

Ovidio, Francesco d'. *Nuovi studii danteschi: il Purgatorio e il suo preludio*. Milan, 1906.

——. *Nuovi studii danteschi: Ugolino, Pier della Vigna, i simoniaci, e discussioni varie*. Milan, 1907.

——. "Chioserelle a un passo del *Purgatorio*." *Studi danteschi* II (1920): 89-104.

Parducci, Amos. *I rimatori lucchesi del secolo XIII*. Bergamo, 1905.

Paris, Gaston. "La Légende de Trajan." *Bibliothèque de l'École des Hautes Études, Section des sciences philologiques et historiques* XXXV (Paris, 1878): 261-98.

Parodi, E. G. Review of Edward Moore, *Studies in Dante. Second Series: Miscellaneous Essays*, 1899. In *Bullettino della Società Dantesca Italiana* N.S. VIII (1901): 41-52.

——. " 'Più muover non mi può, per quella legge che fatta fu quand'io me n'uscì fuora' (*Purg.*, I, 89-90)." *Bullettino della Società Dantesca Italiana* N.S. XIX (1912): 225-26.

——. Review of Pasquale Villari, *Lectura Dantis: Dante e l'Italia*, 1914; *et al*. In *Bullettino della Società Dantesca Italiana* N.S. XXIV (1917): 1-57.

——. *Poesia e storia nella Divina Commedia*. Naples, 1920.

——. *Lingua e letteratura: Studi di teoria linguistica e di storia dell'italiano antico*, ed. Gianfranco Folena, pt. 2. Venice, 1957.

Passavanti, Iacopo. *Lo specchio della vera penitenza di Iacopo Passavanti*, ed. F.-L. Polidori. Florence, 1856.

Pelaez, Mario (ed.). *Rime antiche italiane secondo la lezione del codice vaticano 3214 e del codice casanatense d. v. 5*. Bologna, 1895.

Pellizzari, Achille. *La vita e le opere di Guittone d'Arezzo*. Pisa, 1906.

Peter Chrysologus. *Sermones.* In Migne, *P.L.* LII.

Peter Lombard. *Sententiarum libri quatuor.* In Migne, *P.L.* CXCII.

Petrarca, Francesco. *Rime, trionfi e poesie latine,* ed. F. Neri, G. Martellotti, E. Bianchi, N. Sapegno. Milan, 1951.

Pipino, Francesco. *Chronicon fratris Francisci Pipini Ordinis Praedicatorum.* In *RIS* IX, 587-752.

Pirotta (O.P.), Angelo M. (ed.). *See* Aquinas, Thomas (Marietti publications); Aristotle (Marietti publications).

Porena, M. "La parola più misteriosa della *Divina Commedia.*" *Atti della Accademia Nazionale dei Lincei, Classe di scienze morali, storiche e filologiche, rendiconti* ser. 8, 1 (1946-47): 387-95.

Preface to the Canon of the Mass. In *The New Roman Missal,* ed. F. X. Lasance and Francis Augustine Walsh, O.S.B., pp. 773-74. New York, 1945.

Prudentius. *Psychomachia.* In *Prudentius,* ed. and trans. H. J. Thomson. Vol. I, pp. 274-343. LCL, 1962.

Rajna, Pio. "Un indovinello volgare scritto alla fine del secolo VIII o al principio del IX." *Speculum* III (1928): 291-313.

————. " 'Ugo Ciappetta' nella *Divina Commedia* ('Purgatorio,' canto XX)." *Studi danteschi* XXXVII (1960): 5-20.

Renier, Rodolfo. "Sui brani in lingua d'oc del *Dittamondo* e della *Leandreide.*" *Giornale storico della letteratura italiana* XXV (1895): 311-37.

Ricci, Corrado. *L'ultimo rifugio di Dante Alighieri.* Milan, 1891.

———— (ed.). *La Divina Commedia illustrata nei luoghi e nelle persone.* Milan, 1921.

Ristoro d'Arezzo. *Della composizione del mondo di Ristoro d'Arezzo,* ed. Enrico Narducci. Milan, 1864.

Sabbadini, R. "*Purg.* XX, 117." *Bullettino della Società Dantesca Italiana* N.S. XXII (1915): 62-63.

Sacchetti, Franco. *Il Trecentonovelle,* ed. Vincenzo Pernicone. Florence, 1946.

Salvemini, G. *Studi storici*. Florence, 1901.

Sanesi, Ireneo. "Sapìa." *Studi danteschi* VI (1923): 99-111.

Sarolli, Gian Roberto. "Noterella biblica sui sette P." *Studi danteschi* XXXIV (1957): 217-22.

Sepulcri, Alessandro. "Noterelle di filologia dantesca." *Zeitschrift für romanische Philologie* XXXIV (1910): 191-95.

Servius. *Commentarii in Virgilium Serviani; sive Commentarii in Virgilium, qui Mauro Servio Honorato tribuuntur*, ed. H. Albrecht Lion. 2 vols. Göttingen, 1826.

Shakespeare, William. *The Complete Works of Shakespeare*, ed. George Lyman Kittredge. Boston, 1936.

Silverstein, Theodore. " 'Il giusto Mardoceo' (*Purg.* XVII, 29)." *MLN* LIII (1938): 188-90.

Singleton, Charles S. *An Essay on the Vita Nuova*. Cambridge, Mass., 1949.

———. *Dante Studies 1: Commedia, Elements of Structure*. Cambridge, Mass., 1954.

———. *Dante Studies 2: Journey to Beatrice*. Cambridge, Mass., 1958.

———. "In Exitu Israel de Aegypto." In *Dante: A Collection of Critical Essays*, ed. John Freccero, pp. 102-21. Englewood Cliffs, N.J., 1965.

Speroni, Charles. "Dante's Prophetic Morning-Dreams." *Studies in Philology* XLV (1948): 50-59.

Spiazzi, Raimondo M. (ed.). *See* Aquinas, Thomas (Marietti publications); Aristotle (Marietti publications).

Spitzer, Leo. *Essays in Historical Semantics*. New York, 1948.

Studi danteschi IV (1921): 153.

Tamassia, Nino. "Una nota dantesca." *Giornale storico della letteratura italiana* XXI (1893): 456-57.

Tatlock, J.S.P. "The Last Cantos of the *Purgatorio*." *Modern Philology* XXXII (1934-35): 113-23.

Tempesti, Folco. "Provenzan Salvani." *Bullettino senese di storia patria* N.S. VII (1936): 3-56.

Tertullian. *De anima*, ed. J. H. Waszink. Amsterdam, 1947.

Thorndike, Lynn. *A History of Magic and Experimental*

Science During the First Thirteen Centuries of our Era. Vol. II. New York, 1923.

Toesca, P. *Storia dell'arte italiana.* Turin, 1927.

Torraca, Francesco. Review of Gregorio Lajolo, *Sotto il velo della canzone "Tre donne intorno al cor mi son venute" di Dante Alighieri,* 1911. In *Bullettino della Società Dantesca Italiana* N.S. XIX (1912): 183-206.

————. *Nuovi studi danteschi nel VI centenario della morte di Dante.* Naples, 1921.

Toynbee, Paget. *Dante Studies and Researches.* London, 1902.

————. *A Dictionary of Proper Names and Notable Matters in the Works of Dante,* revised by Charles S. Singleton. Oxford, 1968.

Valerius Maximus. *Factorum et dictorum memorabilium libri novem,* ed. Karl Halm. Leipzig, 1865.

Vasari, Giorgio. *Le opere di Giorgio Vasari: Le vite de' più eccellenti pittori scultori ed architettori scritte da Giorgio Vasari pittore aretino,* ed. Gaetano Milanesi. Vol. I. Florence, 1906.

Vidossich, G. "La lingua del Tristano veneto." *Studj romanzi* IV (1906): 67-148.

Villani, Giovanni. *Cronica di Giovanni Villani,* ed. F. Gherardi Dragomanni. 4 vols. Florence, 1844-45.

Vincent of Beauvais. *Bibliotheca mundi seu Speculi maioris Vincentii Burgundi.* Vol. IV: *Speculum historiale.* Douai, 1624.

Vital, Adolfo. "Per le scalee che si fero ad etade Ch'era sicuro il quaderno . . . *Purgatorio,* XII, 104-105." In *Raccolta di studi di storia e critica letteraria dedicata a Francesco Flamini da' suoi discepoli,* pp. 391-401. Pisa, 1918.

Waszink, J. H. (ed.). *See* Tertullian.

Wilkins, Ernest Hatch. "Three Dante Notes." *Annual Report of the Dante Society* XXXIV (1917): 29-36.

————. "Dante and the Mosaics of his *Bel San Giovanni.*" *Speculum* II (1927): 1-10.

Zaccagnini, Guido. "Personaggi danteschi." *Giornale dantesco* XXVI (1923): 8-14.

Zdekauer, Lud. "Il giuoco in Italia nei secoli XIII e XIV e specialmente in Firenze." *Archivio storico italiano* ser. 4, XVIII (1886): 20-74.

EARLY COMMENTATORS

Anonimo fiorentino. Commento alla Divina Commedia d'anonimo fiorentino del secolo XIV, ed. Pietro Fanfani. Vol. II. Bologna, 1868.

Benvenuto da Imola. *Comentum super Dantis Aldigherij Comoediam*, ed. Giacomo Filippo Lacaita. Vols. III, IV. Florence, 1887.

Boccaccio, Giovanni. *Il comento alla Divina Commedia e gli altri scritti intorno a Dante*, ed. Domenico Guerri. Vol. II. Bari, 1918.

Buti, Francesco da. *Commento di Francesco da Buti sopra la Divina Comedia di Dante Allighieri*, ed. Crescentino Giannini. Vol. II. Pisa, 1860.

Daniello, Bernardino. *Dante con l'espositione di M. Bernardino Daniello da Lucca, sopra la sua Comedia dell'Inferno, del Purgatorio, & del Paradiso*. Venice, 1568.

Lana, Jacopo della. *Comedia di Dante degli Allagherii col commento di Jacopo della Lana bolognese*, ed. Luciano Scarabelli. Vol. II. Bologna, 1866.

Landino, Cristoforo. *Dante con l'espositioni di Christoforo Landino et d'Alessandro Vellutello. Sopra la sua Comedia dell'Inferno, del Purgatorio, e del Paradiso*. Venice, 1596.

L'Ottimo Commento della Divina Commedia, ed. Alessandro Torri. Vol. II. Pisa, 1828.

Pietro di Dante. *Super Dantis ipsius genitoris Comoediam commentarium*, ed. Vincenzio Nannucci. Florence, 1845.

MODERN COMMENTATORS

Butler, Arthur John. *The Purgatory of Dante Alighieri.* 2d edn. London, 1892.

Casella, Mario. *La Divina Commedia.* Bologna, 1964.

Casini, Tommaso and Barbi, S. A. *La Divina Commedia di Dante Alighieri,* comm. Tommaso Casini. 6th edn. revised by S. A. Barbi. Florence, 1926.

Chimenz, Siro A. *La Divina Commedia di Dante Alighieri.* Turin, 1962.

Del Lungo, Isidoro. *La Divina Commedia.* Florence, 1944.

Gmelin, Hermann. *Die göttliche Komödie.* Vol. ii: *Der Läuterungsberg.* Stuttgart, 1955.

Grandgent, C. H. *La Divina Commedia di Dante Alighieri.* Rev. edn. Boston, 1933.

Longfellow, Henry Wadsworth. *The Divine Comedy of Dante Alighieri.* Boston, 1895.

Momigliano, Attilio. *La Divina Commedia di Dante Alighieri.* Vol. ii: *Purgatorio.* Florence, 1953.

Norton, Charles Eliot. *The Divine Comedy of Dante Alighieri.* Rev. edn. Vol. ii: *Purgatory.* Boston, 1902.

Petrocchi, Giorgio. *La Commedia secondo l'antica vulgata.* Vol. i: *Introduzione.* Vol. iii: *Purgatorio.* Milan, 1966, 1967.

Porena, Manfredi. *La Divina Commedia di Dante Alighieri.* Vol. ii: *Purgatorio.* Bologna, 1947.

Rossi, Vittorio and Frascino, S. *La Divina Commedia di Dante Alighieri.* Vol. ii: *Il Purgatorio.* Rome, 1941.

Sapegno, Natalino. *La Divina Commedia.* Milan, 1957.

Scartazzini, G. A. *La Divina Commedia di Dante Alighieri.* Vol. ii: *Il Purgatorio.* Leipzig, 1875.

—— and Vandelli, Giuseppe. *La Divina Commedia: Testo critico della Società Dantesca Italiana,* comm. G. A. Scartazzini. 17th edn. revised by Giuseppe Vandelli. Milan, 1958.

Singleton, Charles S. *The Divine Comedy.* Vol. i: *Inferno,* pt. 2: *Commentary.* Princeton, N.J., 1970.

The Temple Classics. *The Purgatorio of Dante Alighieri,* ed. H. Oelsner, trans. Thomas Okey, with contributions by Philip H. Wicksteed. London, 1964.

Tommaseo, Niccolò. *Commedia di Dante Allighieri.* Vol. ii: *Il Purgatorio.* Milan, 1869.

Torraca, Francesco. *La Divina Commedia.* 12th edn. Vol. ii: *Purgatorio.* Rome, 1952.

Vandelli, Giuseppe. *La Divina Commedia.* In *Le opere di Dante: Testo critico della Società Dantesca Italiana,* ed. M. Barbi, E. G. Parodi, F. Pellegrini, E. Pistelli, P. Rajna, E. Rostagno, G. Vandelli, pp. 443-798. 2d edn. Florence, 1960.

Vernon, William Warren. *Readings on the Purgatorio of Dante.* Vol. II. London, 1889.